MOON HANDBOOKS

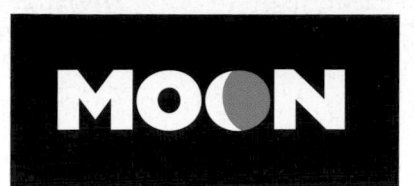

COLORADO

STEVE KNOPPER

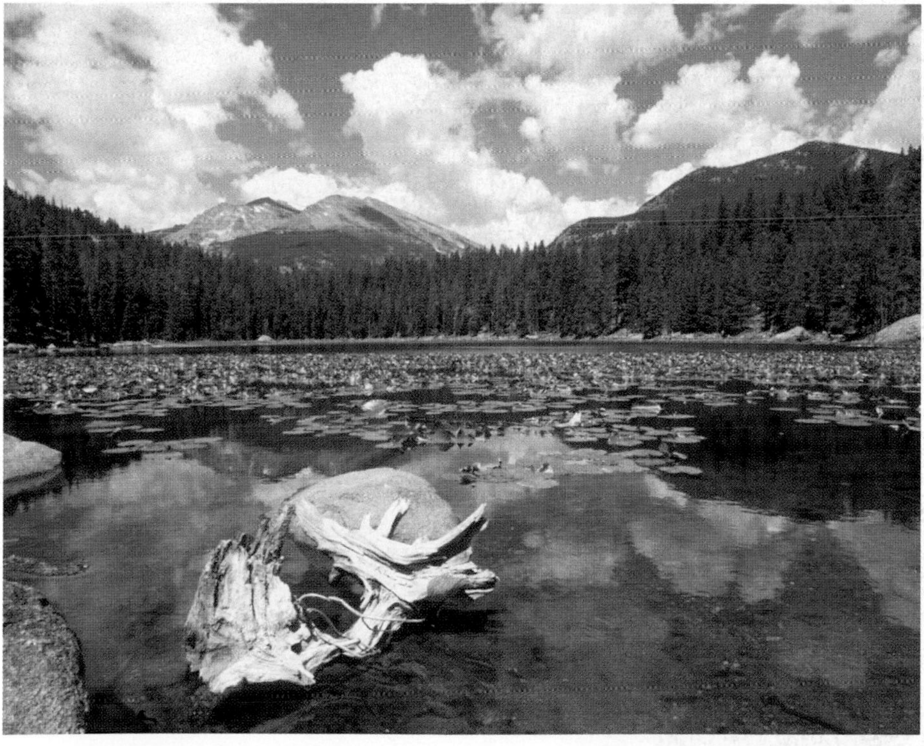

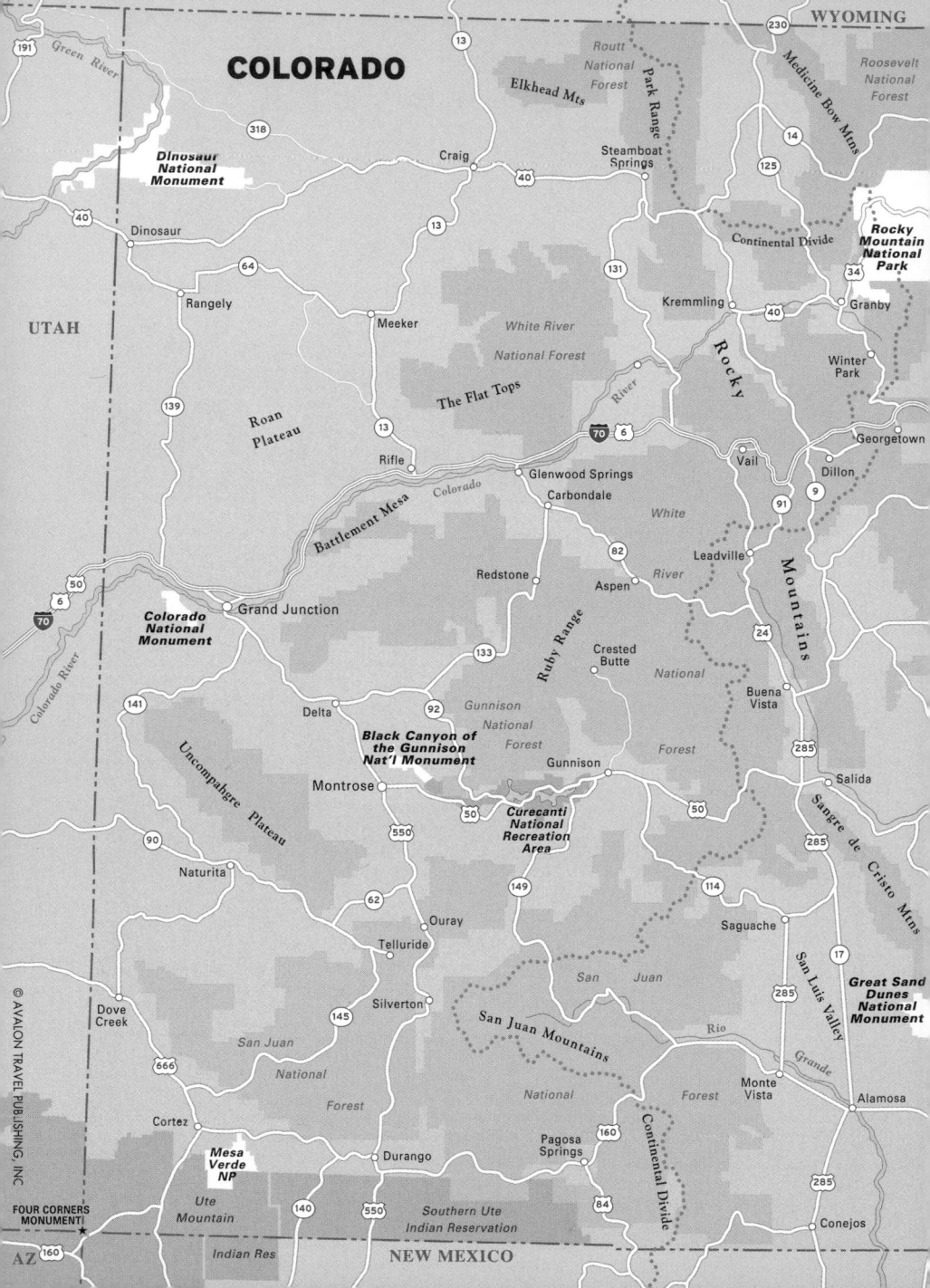

DISCOVER COLORADO

The mountains are everything in Colorado.

Looming over cities and towns, parks and forests, fields and stadiums, at elevations of 11,000 to 14,000 feet, they make themselves known even when hidden from view. From the Rockies in the north to the San Juans in the southwest, the mountains have spawned multibillion-dollar tourism industries, including internationally renowned ski resorts such as Aspen and Vail and the more recent outdoor phenomena of snowboarding and ice climbing. The mountains have also messed with Coors Field baseball pitchers, who've given up hundreds of home runs in the mile-high altitude and thin air. They've attracted endless visitors to the state, many of whom have landed in a place like Boulder or Telluride, glanced at the backdrop, and decided to buy houses immediately. And they've challenged countless adventurers with ski-season avalanches

winter in Rocky Mountain National Park

and impenetrable rock-climbing nooks. But the main reason I like living in Colorado is the mountains' presence; as I type this, houses and buildings block the mountains from my home's west-facing window, but I know they're there, kind of like the tide always knows the moon is there. Every now and then I'll be lost in thought, contemplating the terrible rush-hour traffic on Denver's highways, and look west to see the Rockies peeking through the skyline. During these moments I know why I always return to Colorado, no matter where else I've been.

"If it's winter, skiing is mandatory," opines the *AAA TourBook to Colorado,* and 11.6 million visitors a year believe this to be true. The state's 25 resorts offer a thrilling way to experience the Rockies, with runs like Telluride's sharp-dropping Little Rose and Aspen's bumpy Deception providing mountain air, valley views, and a workout all in the same 30-minute experience. The

Rocky Mountain National Park

snowcapped Rocky Mountains are Colorado's biggest draw, and tourism officials know it.

But while the University of Colorado at Boulder is filled with students who'd rather hit the slopes than crack the books, Colorado is far more than a framework for ski bums. The key is knowing where else to look. The high Rockies, along I-70 in the north-central part of the state, are just as fun to explore on foot (or snowboard or snowshoe or four-wheel-drive vehicle) as they are on skis. Rocky Mountain National Park, outside Estes Park, has 359 miles of trails, and hikers in all seasons can find themselves face to face with an unexpected waterfall or a rare bird. Boulder is practically a country unto itself — an aggressively liberal, environmentalist one — with smoke-free restaurants catering to all ethnicities and tastes grouped around the downtown, red-brick Pearl Street Mall. Denver continues its downtown renaissance, offering Major League Baseball and the Elitch Gardens amusement park at the heart of the city, plus zoos, parks, and trails on the outskirts.

on the trails at Chautauqua Park

Those are the basics. Travelers wanting a deeper look should proceed immediately down U.S. 285 from Denver to the San Juan Mountains in the southwest. Skiers (and bluegrass fans who attend a gigantic festival every June) may know Telluride for its scenic waterfalls and friendly hippie bars, but just as inviting is the Durango & Silverton Narrow Gauge Railroad. And who knew that in the northwest corner, Colorado and Utah share the sprawling Dinosaur National Monument (complete with giant skeletons)? Or that the south-central region, north of Alamosa, is home to the Colorado Gators, an alligator farm with 80 sharp-toothed creatures? Even the eastern third of the state, which is flat and dull and occasionally mocked by drivers from Nebraska and Kansas, contains historical charms such as the Summit Springs Battlefield, which marks an 1869 epic battle between Cheyennes, Arapahos, and pioneers.

I lived in Chicago for seven years, and there is nothing like riding a bicycle down the Magnificent Mile at 2 A.M. with the

Cliff Palace at Mesa Verde National Park

skyscrapers overhead. But the problem with Chicago is that any proper outdoors experience is at least a half-hour drive away. This is happily not the case in Colorado; upon researching *Moon Colorado*, I learned that almost anywhere you live or visit is within a few miles of some kind of beatific mountain peak, mesa, wilderness, valley, river or ancient Native American cliff dwelling. Just be careful not to try to see too much too quickly; upon researching *Moon Colorado*, I also received one speeding ticket and two warnings. Next time, I'll snowshoe.

Redstone, along the Crystal River

Contents

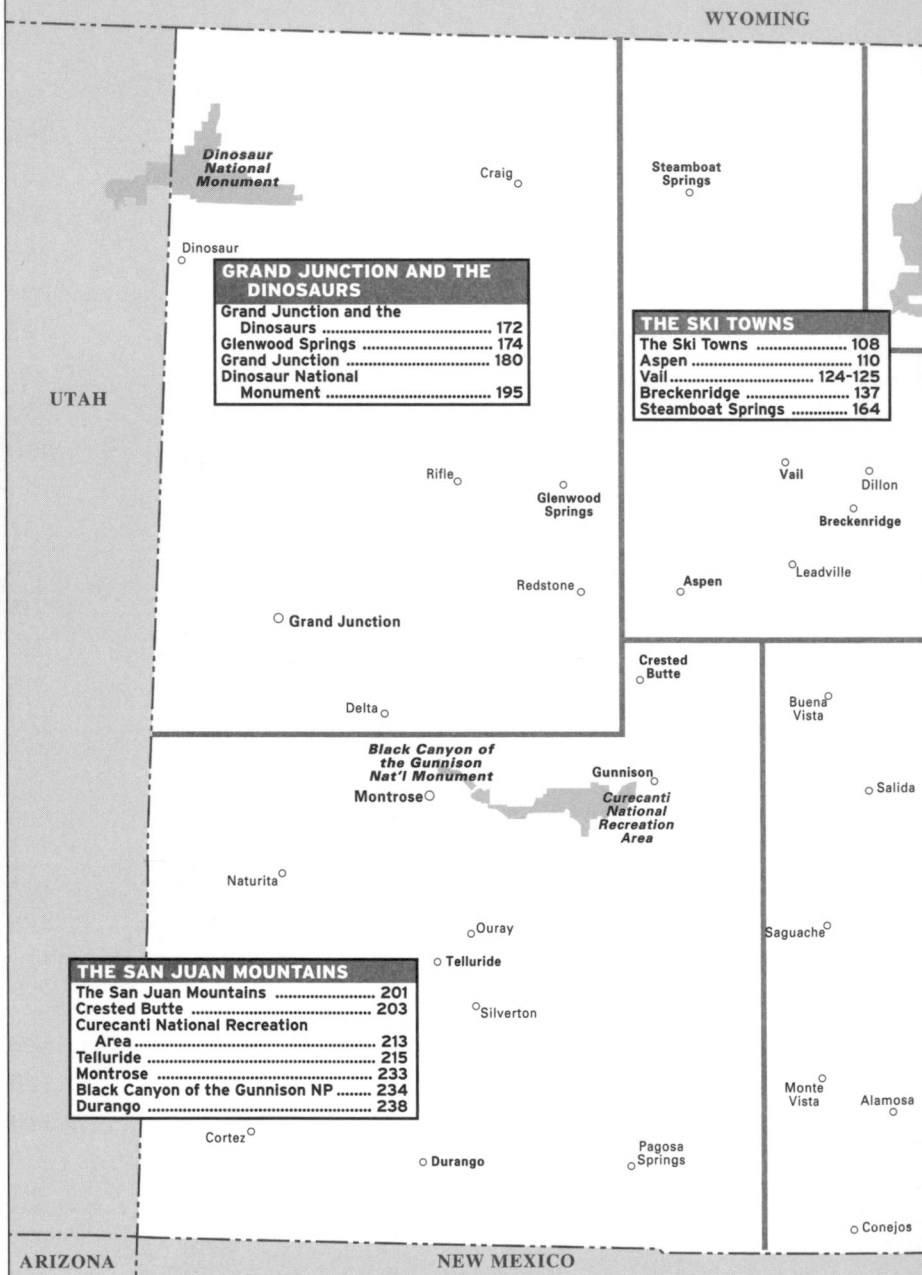

WYOMING

Dinosaur
National
Monument

Craig

Steamboat
Springs

Dinosaur

GRAND JUNCTION AND THE DINOSAURS

THE SKI TOWNS

UTAH

Rifle

Glenwood
Springs

Vail

Dillon

Breckenridge

Leadville

Redstone

Aspen

Grand Junction

Crested
Butte

Buena
Vista

Delta

Black Canyon of
the Gunnison
Nat'l Monument

Montrose

Gunnison

Curecanti
National
Recreation
Area

Salida

Naturita

Ouray

Saguache

THE SAN JUAN MOUNTAINS

Telluride

Silverton

Monte
Vista

Alamosa

Cortez

Durango

Pagosa
Springs

Conejos

ARIZONA

NEW MEXICO

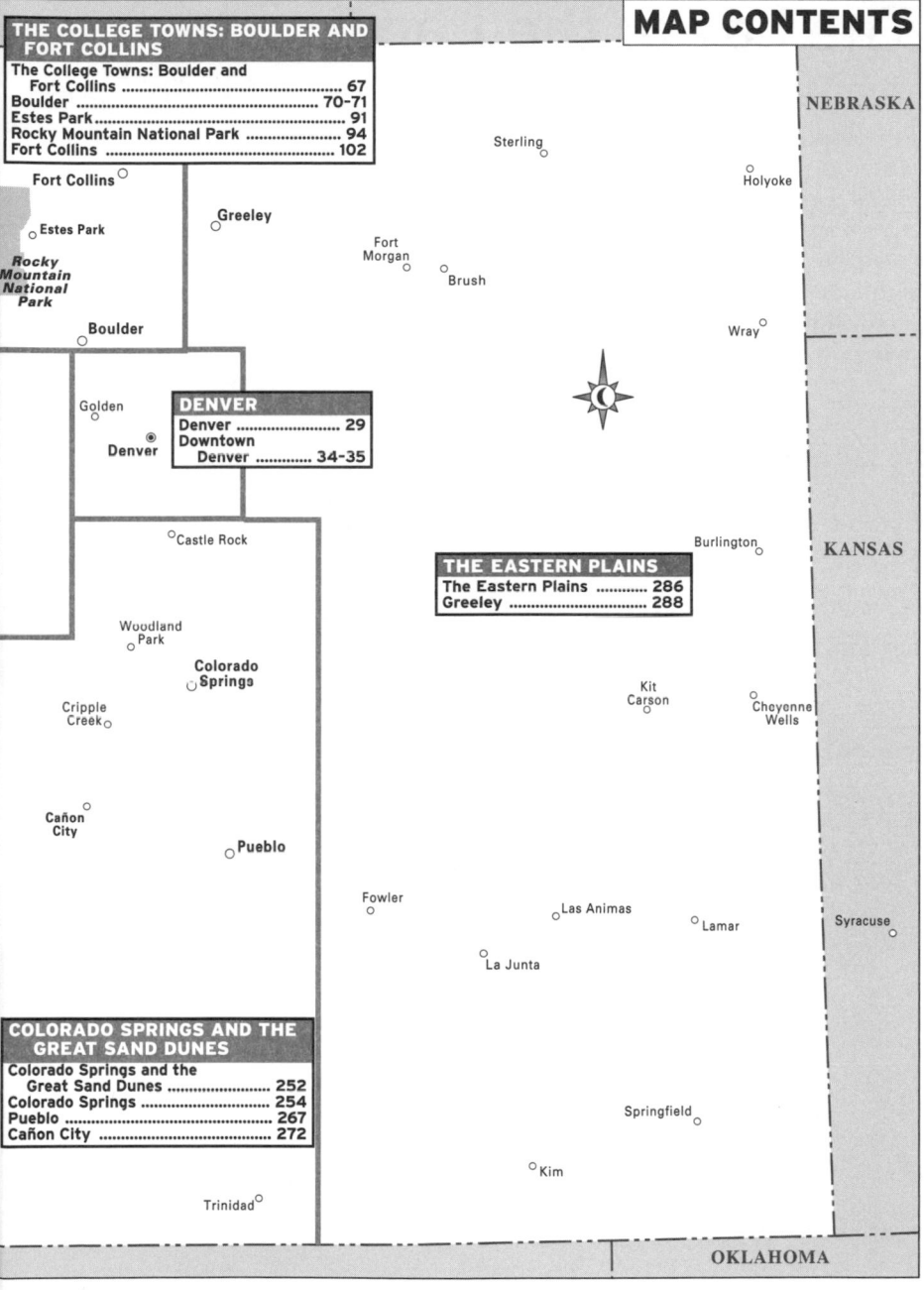

NEBRASKA

Fort Collins ○

○ Estes Park

Greeley ○

*Rocky
Mountain
National
Park*

Sterling ○

Holyoke ○

Fort
Morgan ○

○ Brush

Wray ○

Boulder ●

Golden ○

Denver ◉

○ Castle Rock

Burlington ○

KANSAS

Woodland
○ Park

Colorado
○ Springs

Cripple
Creek ○

Kit
Carson ○

Cheyenne
Wells ○

Cañon
City ○

○ Pueblo

Fowler
○

○ Las Animas

○ Lamar

Syracuse ○

○
La Junta

Springfield ○

○ Kim

Trinidad ○

OKLAHOMA

The Lay of the Land

In Colorado, people's attitudes change with the geography—many of the mountain towns, like Boulder, Aspen, Telluride, and Steamboat Springs, are filled with liberal, bohemian-leaning people who've escaped big jobs in big cities to live in the wilderness. Ranches and farms fill the Eastern Plains and other flat areas of Colorado, and that's where cowboys and farmers, who tend to be more conservative, have lived for years. In the middle is Colorado Springs, home of incredible mountain scenery as well as the U.S. Air Force Academy and the religious, very politically influential, conservative group Focus on the Family.

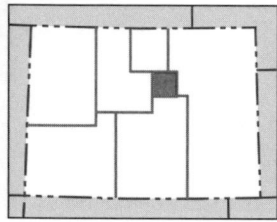

DENVER

Although many travelers still consider Denver a mere gateway to ski resorts or the Rocky Mountains, the city has jumped several notches on the sophistication scale in recent years. In the 1990s, it built a successful new airport and brought Major League Baseball to a resurgent part of downtown known as LoDo. Since then, gourmet restaurants and hipster clubs have joined the renaissance, invigorating the shopping districts **Larimer Square** and **16th Street Mall.** Prices aren't bad, sightseeing is plentiful, and hotels are available at all levels of luxury. The **Museum of Natural History,** with its world-class space exhibits and mountain views, is especially recommended, and the **Denver Botanic Gardens** display 32,000 kinds of plants throughout 23 acres.

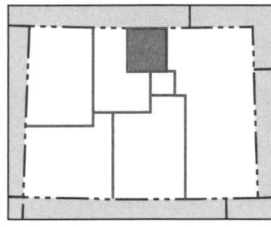

THE COLLEGE TOWNS: BOULDER AND FORT COLLINS

For decades, travelers have perceived Boulder, home of the **University of Colorado,** as some kind of Utopia—it's in a bowl directly beneath the Rocky Mountain foothills and the scenery is astounding. And while the city has grown more expensive and yuppie-centric over the years—and much of red-state Colorado disparages it as "The People's Republic of Boulder"—it's a wonderful place to visit: The restaurants are diverse and affordable, the pedestrian **Pearl Street Mall** is charmingly filled with guitarists and acrobats, and the options for live music, shopping, and sightseeing are as plentiful as ever. A smaller version of Boulder, just an hour's drive to the northeast, is Fort Collins, with **Colorado State University,** the historic shopping district **Old Town Square,** and trails and National Parks within easy driving distance.

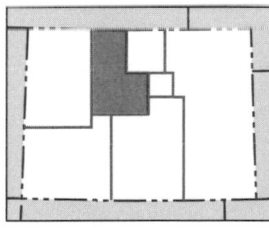

THE SKI TOWNS

Colorado's top ski resorts—**Aspen, Vail, Breckenridge, Winter Park, Arapahoe Basin, Copper Mountain,** and others—are bunched up along I-70 in the spectacular High Rockies, about two to three hours west of Denver. Every ski area has its own personality, in terms of moguls, prices, and general feel of the surrounding town, so regulars tend to pick their favorites and stick with them. Aspen and Vail, for example, emphasize shopping and general ritziness, while Winter Park and Breckenridge are less pretentious and snag more townies than tourists. Deals are plentiful during the off-season, and nonskiers are advised to plan trips in March and October, when the resorts turn into ghost towns, the hiking and cycling trails are blissfully uncrowded, and the food and accommodations, even in Aspen, are affordable.

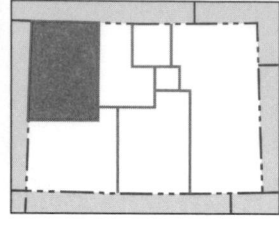

GRAND JUNCTION AND THE DINOSAURS

In the middle of nowhere, west of the Rockies, Grand Junction is the only major town (population 30,000) between Salt Lake City and Denver. It's part of the Grand Valley, at the Colorado and Gunnison Rivers, and nearby are such sights as the **Little Bookcliffs** (flat, steep mountains that extend for miles horizontally), the **Grand Mesa National Forest,** and the **Colorado National Monument.** Northwestern Colorado's cycling, cross-country skiing, and horseback-riding opportunities are surprisingly fertile—and surprisingly dinosaur-heavy, given the Jurassic-era bones at **Dinosaur National Monument,** overlapping the Colorado–Utah border.

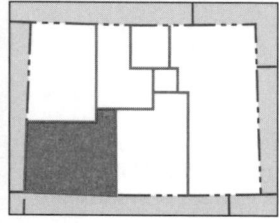

THE SAN JUAN MOUNTAINS

Underneath the towering San Juan Mountains, beatific Telluride is filled with tall waterfalls, breathtaking mountain views, few crowds, plentiful hiking and biking trails, summer festivals such as **Telluride Bluegrass,** hot springs, and a well-regarded ski area. Given the five-hour drive from Denver in the best of weather conditions, the region is hard to reach, but isolation only adds to its appeal. Other magnificent sights in southwestern Colorado: dramatically steep **Black Canyon of the Gunnison National Park;** one-mountain ski town **Crested Butte;** historic miner towns **Ouray** and **Silverton,** home of the **Durango & Silverton Narrow Gauge Railroad;** and the Native American–populated **Four Corners** region, where you can literally touch four different states simultaneously.

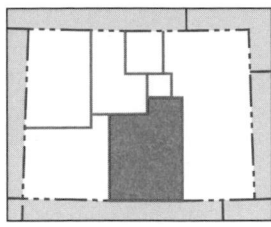

COLORADO SPRINGS AND THE GREAT SAND DUNES

Colorado Springs is famous these days for two basic reasons—the majestic **Pikes Peak** and a conservative, religious, and politically influential group called **Focus on the Family,** which has battled gay marriage and put Republicans into office. Some people of certain political persuasions plan trips around the Focus offices; others prefer less controversial but prettier attractions such as **Cave of the Winds** and **Garden of the Gods.** The city's lodging centerpiece is **The Broadmoor,** a former university complex that includes hiking trails, a small lake, and frilly pillows on four-corner beds. To the south, **Pueblo** is a big city with interesting historic sites and museums, while **Great Sand Dunes National Monument,** outside **Alamosa,** has 900-foot hills for climbing and "sand skiing."

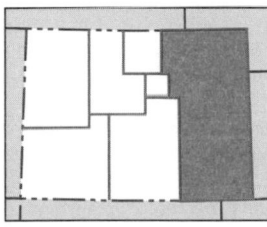

THE EASTERN PLAINS

While the drive from endless Nebraska (or Kansas) through eastern Colorado is flat and uneventful, especially compared to the vibrant Rocky Mountain regions that await in the rest of the state, the farm-and-ranch-filled plains are not without regional charms. You'll feel the car begin to climb around Sterling (home of the Native American **Overland Trail Museum**) and might consider a stop in Crook (including the 7,000-acre **Tamarack Ranch State Wildlife Area**) or Fort Morgan (which includes the big-rock-among-the-plains **Pawnee National Grassland**). Southeastern highlights include Lamar (the "Goose Hunting Capital of the World") and Las Animas (whose **Kit Carson Museum** is a tourist monument of the kitschy persuasion, up there with the World's Largest Badger).

Planning Your Trip

With a total land area of 104,100 square miles, Colorado is a challenge for travelers who want to "see everything"—even concentrated attractions like the north-central ski-resort towns bunched up along I-70 are spread out along miles and miles of highway. And once you hit the mountains, there's so much hiking, skiing, biking, and white-water rafting that even a thorough month-long trip is unlikely to cover more than just the basics.

That said, it's possible to sample a lot of Colorado by breaking the state into sections. Travelers can experience the aforementioned ski towns, from Aspen to Steamboat Springs, in a solid two-week trip; they can get the gist of Denver and Boulder (and a few interesting satellite towns, like Fort Collins, Golden, Central City, and Black Hawk) in about a week; the southwestern San Juan Mountains, including Telluride and Durango, require a week, depending on the weather; Colorado Springs is a long weekend, with maybe a few extra days if you add Pueblo and the nearby Great Sand Dunes Park; and the flat, spread-out Eastern Plains require tons of driving, but the traveling attractions aren't quite as rich.

WHEN TO GO

Winter is prime tourist season in Colorado, and from as early as October to as late as April, ski resorts fill up with out-of-towners—and good luck finding a reasonable hotel rate in Aspen, Vail, or Steamboat Springs. The summer can be crowded, too, especially if you're heading to a particular event, like the Telluride Bluegrass Festival in late June or the Greeley Independence Stampede on July Fourth weekend. Traffic along the main mountain highways, particularly I-70, which leads west from Denver through the Eisenhower Memorial Tunnel to Copper Mountain, Vail, and beyond, can be maddening at these times.

To avoid crowds and arrive more speedily at secluded mountain hamlets like Redstone, Westcliffe, and Pagosa Springs, it's best to plan a trip during the off-season. Even at the biggest ski resorts, hotels and restaurants are surprisingly cheap, mountain towns are blissfully under-populated, and deals and packages are common during early October or early May.

In many parts of Colorado, of course, the ski season is irrelevant. The Eastern Plains are likely to be quiet most of the year, and south-central attractions such as The Broadmoor in Colorado Springs, Rocky Mountain National Park near Estes Park and Boulder, and Mesa Verde National Park near the Four Corners are roomy and quiet during the winter.

WHAT TO TAKE

Designing a wardrobe for a trip to Colorado, especially when several different altitudes are involved, can be a nightmare of multiple suitcases. But the extra packing is usually necessary: Temperatures drop sharply the higher you go up in the mountains, and what seems adequate in, say, Denver or Boulder may not even be close by the time you hit Dillon or Silverthorne. (See-and-be-seen resort destinations such as Vail, Aspen, and Telluride complicate the packing process as well.) And that's true in the summer as well as the winter. It's smart to keep extra jackets, boots, and gloves in the car.

Water and sunscreen are crucial, as sunlight gets intense in high elevations. Bug spray helps on hikes through any forest or wilderness area.

When hiking, biking, cross-country skiing, or rock climbing through the mountains, be prepared for any weather extremity. You can be walking in Rocky Mountain National Park on a sunny spring day when an avalanche hits, so bring a backpack with as many emergency supplies as you can carry—energy bars, water, bandages, extra socks, and so forth.

The northwestern part of Colorado is usually mild, the Eastern Plains are usually hot, and central cities such as Denver, Boulder, Colorado Springs, and Pueblo usually approximate metropolitan areas all over the United States—with more sunshine throughout the year, that is.

Explore Colorado

14-DAY BEST OF COLORADO

Colorado's top tourist attractions—the ski resorts—bunch up along the High Rockies in the north-central part of the state. So most travelers get a skewed vision of what the square, land-locked state is all about. For ambitious visitors, here's a (literally!) up-and-down itinerary that begins in the big city and spirals through not only the **Summit County ski areas** but also the southwestern **San Juan Mountains** and the **Black Canyon of the Gunnison National Park.** Unless you're inclined to make the endless drive through Kansas, Nebraska, Utah, Wyoming, or Texas, plan to book a flight into **Denver International Airport** (DIA) and rent a car.

DAY 1

Fly into DIA, rent a car, and drive down I-70 and I-25 to downtown Denver. Spend two nights at the **Brown Palace,** the **Hotel Monaco,** the **Adam's Mark,** or any of the city's centrally located hotels.

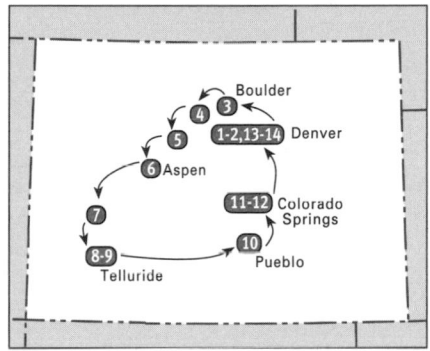

DAY 2

Explore Denver, beginning with the **Denver Museum of Nature & Science** in City Park, about a 10-minute trip by car on Colorado Boulevard south of I-70. The third floor offers the city's best view of the Rocky Mountains.

Return to downtown and hop on one of the free **16th Street Mall** buses for an afternoon of shopping. Later, depending on the time of year, catch a Colorado Rockies game at **Coors Field,** the Denver Broncos at **Invesco Stadium at Mile High,** or the Denver Nuggets or Colorado Avalanche at the **Pepsi Center.** For dinner, try one of the city's gourmet restaurants – **Mizuna, Rioja,** or **Tamayo.** Budget-conscious travelers should consider a Fat Tire beer and a buffalo burger at **My Brother's Bar.** Late-nighters might venture into **El Chapultepec** for live jazz and atmosphere.

DAY 3

Drive half an hour down U.S. 36 to Boulder and stay in the **Hotel Boulderado,** just in the shadow of the foothills. Tour the **University of Colorado** campus (off Broadway, south of downtown) and shop at the **Pearl Street Mall.**

DAY 4

Take I-70 west directly through the Rocky Mountains to begin a tour of select ski-resort towns. Go through the **Eisenhower Memorial Tunnel** and watch for the scenic **Continental Divide.** First stop: Winter Park, home of many cycling and hiking trails. And, of course, skiing. During the off-season, look for the abundant hotel and restaurant deals.

DAY 5

Next stop (farther west along I-70, about an

hour west of the Eisenhower Tunnel): Vail, home of beautifully coifed ski rats, pricey shopping, and some of the best mountain scenery in the High Rockies. Slopes are crowded in the winter, so I recommend dropping by in the summer for rock climbing or hiking in the backcountry. Try **Paragon Guides** for a tour.

DAY 6

Drive another hour down I-70, then head south at Glenwood Springs on Highway 82 to Aspen. Spend the night at the **Little Nell,** luxurious mountain home to the stars. Ski one of the four mountain runs, hike and bike, or just shop at one of the many high-end boutiques.

DAY 7

Return east to U.S. 24, drive to U.S. 285, turn west on U.S. 50, and make the five-hour drive southwest to the **San Juan Mountains.** Spend a luxurious few hours driving and hiking around **Black Canyon of the Gunnison National Park.** (Pack a picnic lunch as restaurants are few.)

DAYS 8-9

Take U.S. 50 west to U.S. 550, then turn south toward breathtaking Telluride and Silverton. These picturesque mountain hamlets have skiing options – not to mention excellent hotels – and the hiking trails outside Ouray allow ice-climbing in the winter. Explore the restaurants and gift shops on the main streets of Telluride, Silverton, and Ouray.

DAY 10

Head back toward Denver via U.S. 160 and I-25, spending the night in Pueblo for a break.

DAYS 11-12

Explore Colorado Springs (an hour north of Pueblo on I-25), specifically **Garden of the Gods,** and be sure to stay at the tony **Broadmoor Hotel.** Ambitious hikers may want to tackle **Pikes Peak,** which offers numerous trails. Also consider driving the three-hours-up-and-down **Pikes Peak Highway,** a twisty road straight uphill to the **Summit House** restaurant and gift shop.

DAY 13

Drive back to Denver (about an hour and a half north of Colorado Springs on I-25) and spend the last night checking out the hipster bars and live-music nightclubs of LoDo. Pick another downtown hotel for the last night.

DAY 14

Return home via DIA.

OUTDOOR ADVENTURE

Colorado is built for adventure, whether you're skiing or snowboarding in Vail or Snowmass, training for a cycling race in Boulder, or hiking **Pikes Peak** in Colorado Springs. Pretty much every outdoor sport—with the possible exception of water-skiing—is huge here. And there are outlets all over the state for hiking, mountain biking, rock climbing, kayaking, ice climbing, cycling, snowboarding, snowshoeing, and, of course, skiing. I've mapped out one possible cross-section of the state that hits several varieties of these sports, but many others are available. Just be sure to reserve bicycles, cars, and hotels on your itinerary before showing up; even in laid-back Colorado, it's possible to lose your place.

DAY 1
Take the bumpy flight into **Telluride Regional Airport.** Bring a bicycle if you can.

DAYS 2-3
Upon arrival, tour the area via glider using **Telluride Soaring.** Stay at the **New Sheridan Hotel** in downtown Telluride, and walk leisurely along Colorado Avenue straight into the mountains. Afterward, hit the Excelsior Café downtown for a glass of wine and some local atmosphere, eat a fancy meal at **221 South Oak Bistro,** and take the 13-minute gondola ride to the Mountain Village – the views on the way back down are incredible.

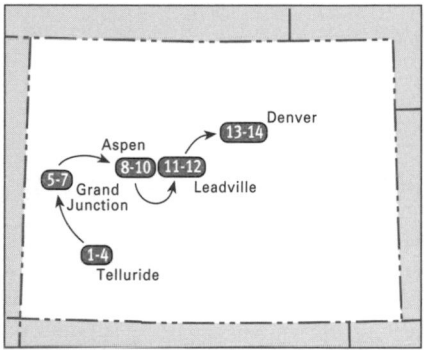

DAY 4
Hike the **Sneffels High Line Trail** or **Bridal Veil Falls,** both about 10 miles each way, through steep, rough terrain. Plan to stay in Telluride, as both trails are a short drive (or long bike ride) from town.

DAYS 5-6
Rent a car and drive north through Grand Junction. Bring your bicycle if you have it. If not, rent one in Grand Junction and ride the 23-mile path up 2,000-foot **Rim Rock Drive** in **Colorado National Monument.** After this strenuous ride, take a day of rest, checking out the wineries in Grand Junction and nearby Palisade, just east on I-70. Plan to stay at one of the nice but nondescript Grand Junction hotels, such as the Doubletree.

DAY 7
Using **Colorado Whitewater Rafting,** spend the day lurching down the Colorado River. Stay another night in Grand Junction; for dinner, try **Dolce Vita** or another one of the underrated restaurants along Main Street.

DAY 8
Drive northeast along I-70 to Aspen, stopping at Glenwood Springs for a steamy break at the **Yampah Spa & Salon: The Hot Spring Vapor Caves.** Consider spending the night at Glenwood Springs' historic **Hotel Colorado** if you don't want to make it all the way to Aspen.

DAY 9
After spending the night in an Aspen hotel, take a white-water rafting trip in the Aspen area through **Blazing Adventures.**

DAY 10

Return the rental car in Aspen. Spend the day window-shopping at fancy boutiques to prepare for the next day's bike trip. (Rent another bicycle in Aspen if you didn't bring your own.)

DAYS 11-12

Cycle 12,000-foot **Independence Pass** from Aspen to Leadville, a difficult, 32-mile route but worth it for the exhilarating mountain views. Spend a night or two in Leadville, checking out some historic buildings and nice restaurants, just to decompress after the intense ride.

DAY 13

Rent a car in Leadville. Drive back to Denver, north on U.S. 24 then east on I-70, about three hours total.

Stay at the **Hotel Monaco** downtown. If you get back to town early enough, rent a kayak at the **REI Store** in northwest Denver and take it along the **North Platte River,** beginning just behind REI. Don't forget to return the bike (but be sure to make arrangements in advance about returning an Aspen-rented bike in Denver).

DAY 14

Fly home from DIA.

MUSIC LOVER'S TOUR

One of Colorado's great secrets is the diversity of its live music scene. Most fans of pop and rock music know the state is famous for jam bands such as Big Head Todd and the Monsters, Leftover Salmon, and the Samples. But there are rich pockets for every type of music lover, and the many summer music festivals tend to reflect this eclecticism. The **Telluride Bluegrass Festival,** for example, attracts country and bluegrass acts, but it branches out so far that you may find yourself wondering about the title. Note that times, dates, and artist lineups of the festivals change yearly, so check out the Colorado Music Association's website (http://coloradomusic.org/festival.html) for updates.

Anchor your trip on one of the many summer music festivals: late July's **Music in the Mountains,** in Durango, is far from Denver but worth it for a variety of classical and chamber-music orchestras; the **Rocky Mountain Folks Festival,** in Lyons during late August, draws the rock 'n' rollier side of folk music, including Todd Snider and the Subdudes; and I recommend a trip to late June's **Telluride Bluegrass Festival,** combining traditionalists like Alison Krauss and Union Station with weirdo jammers Bela Fleck and the Flecktones and occasional hard-rockers.

Build in one "recovery day" in case your music festival of choice has been too festive (if you know what I mean). Then drive back to the Denver airport for the return flight.

DENVER

Red Rocks Amphitheatre, in Morrison about a half hour west of the city along I-70, is one of the best and most beautiful outdoor concert venues in the United States, and big-time acts from Coldplay to the White Stripes to the Dave Matthews Band to Norah Jones continue to play there regularly. Back in town, check out the **Fillmore Auditorium,** a medium-sized club with superb acoustics and a nice ambience underneath a large chandelier.

Catch a concert at the **Lion's Lair** for rugged rock 'n' roll, **Dazzle** for jazz, or the Fillmore Auditorium or the **Ogden Theatre** for larger shows. All are within walking distance. For old-fashioned country music, not to mention line-dancing lessons and boot shopping, drive to the **Grizzly Rose,** along I-25.

BOULDER

The **Fox Theatre** always has something going on, whether it's a top national act like the Rev. Horton Heat or a rising local band such as Rose Hill Drive. Other top live-music spots include the **Boulder Theater** and numerous venues on the University of Colorado campus (including **Macky Auditorium**). Boulder is also the home of superb record stores, including **Albums on the Hill.**

GOLDEN

Drive west to Golden for a nighttime stop at the **Buffalo Rose,** a homey mountain club that plays host to national blues, country, and rock acts (such as Hot Tuna) and jamming locals. The mountain-town scene has several notable clubs, many specializing in Grateful Dead-style rock and blues: Nederland's **Acoustic Café,** the **Mishawaka Amphitheatre** near Rocky Mountain National Park and Fort Collins, the **Fly Me to the Moon Saloon** in Telluride, **The Eldo** in Crested Butte, and many others.

TELLURIDE

The tiny mountain town in southwest Colorado is home to numerous major music festivals, beginning with the **Telluride Bluegrass Festival** in late June. Also noteworthy is the **Telluride Blues and Brews Festival** in mid-October. Check various town websites for information on other summer festivals, such as the **Breckenridge Music Festival** (mostly classical), **Rockygrass** in Lyons, and the **Bravo! Vail Valley Music Festival** (also classical).

14-DAY HISTORY TOUR

Colorado was largely founded in the late 1800s, when fortune-seekers around the United States cried, "Pikes Peak or bust!" and uprooted their lives and families to move here. Some of them got lucky, most didn't, but almost all of them wound up stuck in Colorado trying to figure out how to make money. Most cities, big and small, have some kind of museum or historical marker recalling these days—and many go even farther back, to the Utes and Arapahos who wandered the mountains and valleys before white people showed up.

DAY 1

Fly into the **Durango-La Plata County Airport** in southwest Colorado, take the 25-minute shuttle to the Victorian-furniture-decorated, 1887 **Strater Hotel,** and spend the late afternoon exploring the historic miners' buildings downtown.

DAYS 2-3

The hotel will tell you how to get to the **Du-** rango & Silverton Narrow Gauge Railroad,** a 45-mile line through the mountains that transported miners and their families as early as 1882. Once in Silverton, wander the early-1900s jail, hotel, and other buildings in the National Historic District downtown. Stay a night at Silverton's 1882 **Grand Imperial Hotel.** The next day, arrange for a shuttle at **Mountain Limo** (888/376-9770) to drive the 14 or so miles over steep mountain curves to Telluride. Arrange to rent a car there.

DAYS 4-5

In Telluride, stay at the **New Sheridan Hotel,** built in 1895, and spend a day looking at the downtown historic district. Miners settled here in the late 1800s, and according to legend, the word "Telluride" comes from skeptics who told their prospector friends, "To Hell you ride!"

DAYS 6-7

Drive north (take Highway 145 to Highway 62, then turn north on U.S. 550, about 45 minutes) to Ouray, another old mining town that maintains its Old West feel, and spend the night at the 1887 **Beaumont Hotel,** where Teddy Roosevelt and other luminaries stayed. The next morning, drive north on U.S. 550 to Montrose (about half an hour) and visit the **Ute Indian Museum** (just off the highway). Spend the night at a functional hotel in Montrose.

DAYS 8-9

Drive an hour east on U.S. 50 to Gunnison, then another hour north on Highway 135 to Crested Butte, where miners discovered gold in nearby Washington Gulch in the 1860s. Crested Butte is beautiful and funky, with several skier-oriented hotels. Try the **Grand Lodge Resort & Suites,** in the mountain village area a couple miles from town.

DAY 10

Drive north on the bumpy dirt Road 12 west from Crested Butte, then catch Highway 133 north to Redstone, about 45 minutes from Crested Butte. (Note that Kebler Pass is closed during the winter, so you'd need to take an alternate route.) Redstone is a history tourist's dream, with the old **Redstone Castle,** the historic **Redstone Inn,** and remnants of the **Coke Ovens,** all recalling the life of John C. Osgood, the railroad magnate who developed this area.

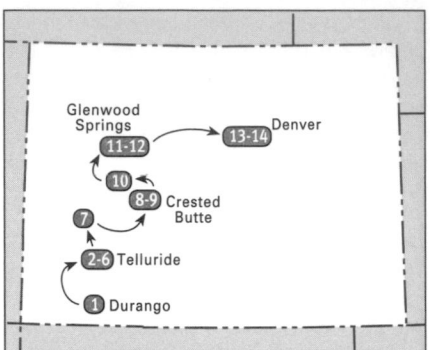

DAYS 11-12

Continue north on Highway 133, another half an hour, to I-70, and stay at Glenwood Springs' **Hotel Colorado,** which when it was built in 1893 was known as Colorado's "grande dame," drawing guests from Al Capone to Teddy Roosevelt (their pictures hang on the lobby walls).

DAY 13

Drive east on I-70 and, depending on how much time you have, stop in ski towns like Vail or Breckenridge, both of which were once mining towns that in the mid-20th century shifted to tourism. Just before Denver, make the small history museums off the highway in Georgetown and Idaho Springs a priority – these small, quiet, scenic regions were boomtowns for miners in the late 1800s, and many of the buildings have been carefully preserved. It takes about three hours to get from Glenwood Springs to Denver in optimum traffic conditions.

(If you have an extra day or two, just before Vail, take U.S. 24 south from I-70, about an hour each way, and stop in Leadville, former home of the tragic mining-era couple Horace and Baby Doe Tabor; numerous historic sites mark their time here, including the well-preserved **Augusta Tabor Home.**)

DAY 14

On your last day, check out some of Denver's

history museums, including the **Molly Brown House Museum** and, on the 16th Street Mall, the **Daniels and Fisher Tower.** For decades in the late 1800s, Colorado represented affluence and opportunity, and miners traveled to Denver from the western Rockies while presidents and kings came here from all over the world. Fly out from DIA.

10-DAY SKI BUM'S TOUR

Many travelers to Colorado have this vision of the state: an airport, a highway through the Rocky Mountains, and dozens of white, bumpy hills containing people with slats strapped to their feet. For these people, Colorado is a utopian escape from jobs and cities, and some of them pick colleges or houses here specifically because of the great skiing. And it *is* great—moguls of all sizes, for all skill levels, with crisp mountain air and forest scenes that look amazing from the den of a ski lodge. If that's your ultimate vacation, follow these instructions.

DAY 1
Fly into Denver International Airport, rent a car, and drive west on I-70 to **Winter Park** (on the way, eat lunch or dinner at BeauJo's pizza place in Idaho Springs).

DAYS 2-3
Ski two days in Winter Park, eat dinner at the high-end Dining Room at Sunspot, and breakfast at Deno's Mountain Bistro. Stay at **Zephyr Mountain Lodge,** a short walk from the express lift (but be sure to make reservations long in advance, especially for peak season).

DAYS 4-5
Drive to Vail, spend two days there for both skiing and shopping. (Also explore Beaver Creek.)

DAYS 6-8
Head southeast to Aspen, spend three days there to explore at least three of the four mountain runs. Stay at Hotel Jerome or Sky Hotel (or both), eat at Cache Cache (and, if you have the money, the Century Room in Hotel Jerome) and take in some live jazz at the **Main Street Bakery.**

DAYS 9-10
Drive back to Denver on I-70, staying at the Alpine Hideaway in Georgetown (and eating at the Red Ram Restaurant) to break up the highway trip.

10 DAYS IN THE ROCKIES (WITHOUT SKIING)

Those of us forever doomed to answer "no" to the questions "You're from Colorado? Do you ski?" have learned to make the best of our surroundings. Sometimes, we defensively inform our interrogators, there is no snow in the foothills and we have to find other things to do—hiking, cycling, catching a Rockies game at Coors Field, sunbathing in our backyards, that kind of thing. Besides, avoiding skiers in Colorado means a steady diet of sparse crowds and off-season deals. For visitors not bound to the November–April tourism season, or who just want to do something different in the winter, here's one way to enjoy the outdoors.

DAYS 1-2

Fly into Denver International Airport, rent a car, and head into the mountains to Estes Park. Stay at the **Stanley Hotel,** visit the knickknack shops downtown, and spend the second day hiking the trails and taking in the dramatic mountain-and-meadow scenery of **Rocky Mountain National Park.**

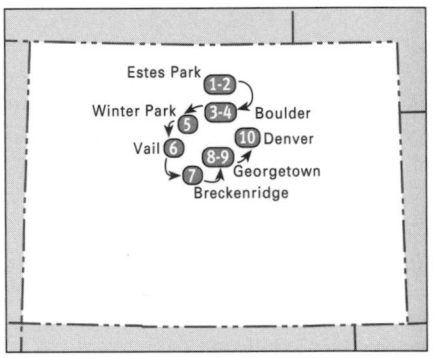

DAYS 3-4

Take Highway 7 south through Boulder and spend the night at the **Hotel Boulderado.** Explore the trails of **Chautauqua Park** and one or two of the foothills, such as **Sunshine Canyon** or **Flagstaff Mountain.**

DAY 5

Drive south on Highway 72 through Golden, Nederland, and Idaho Springs (stopping for pizza at **BeauJo's**), turn right on I-70, and wind up at Winter Park. Spend the night there.

DAY 6

Hike the trails in Winter Park or move on to the many hiking trails of Vail. (Bicycle rental is available, too.) Spend the day and night in Vail.

DAY 7

Backtrack on I-70 to Breckenridge and com-plete the trifecta of ski-resort towns directly off I-70 in the High Rockies. Again, there are excellent hiking and mountain-climbing trails here.

DAYS 8-9

After staying at a Breckenridge hotel, return east on I-70 toward Denver. Stop in the Dillon/Silverthorne area to explore the 9,000-foot-high **Lake Dillon.** Rent a boat at the chilly-blue reservoir. The **Alpine Hideaway,** farther down I-70 in Georgetown, is an excellent place to stay a night or two.

DAY 10

Drive back along I-70, east, to DIA.

DENVER

The blizzards in Denver are memorable, exhilarating, legendary—and all the better because within a week or two, the snow disappears, the temperatures rise, and suddenly it's spring again for the rest of the month. In a little more than a century, this onetime Old West outpost has boomed into a 500,000-population metropolis with a young, vibrant downtown core. Why? First, the weather—the snow is dramatic, and if you've ever lived in Chicago or Seattle, you won't miss the rain. Second, the altitude—5,280 feet, which explains the "Mile High City" nickname and attitude. And finally, the air—the city has cleaned up its "Brown Cloud" and major pollution problems of the 1970s and 1980s, and locals can breathe clearly again.

After the recession of the early 1990s, visionary leaders such as then-mayor Federico Peña revitalized several key parts of the city—Denver International Airport became one of the world's top transportation hubs; the Colorado Rockies brought Major League Baseball and built the old-school, purple-and-brown Coors Field as the heart of Lower Downtown (LoDo); and the classic amusement park Elitch Gardens moved from the outskirts to the center of town.

Over the next decade, the NFL's Denver Broncos built a new stadium and the NBA's Denver Nuggets built a new arena. With a popular young mayor (John Hickenlooper, who made his name as owner of the LoDo fixture Wynkoop Brewery) and a decent economy, Denver has transformed even troubled neighborhoods such as the northwest's venerable

HIGHLIGHTS

◖ Denver Botanic Gardens: If 32,000 plants from all over the world, arranged along calm walking paths, isn't enough, the Botanic Gardens has one of the best outdoor concert stages in the city (page 33).

◖ Six Flags Elitch Gardens: If rides like the Mind Eraser haven't torn apart your stomach *and* your mind, enjoy the prime central-Denver location of this classic amusement park (page 37).

◖ State Capitol: The gold-leaf dome has been a Denver classic since 1886, and it's one of the city's most distinctive and stately buildings (page 37).

◖ City Park: A 314-acre park in the northeast part of town, City Park is home to the Denver Zoo and the Denver Museum of Nature & Science—and it's a great place to walk a dog, kick a soccer ball, roll around on the grass, or fly a kite (page 37).

◖ Coors Field: The Colorado Rockies haven't been much to see in recent years, but their modern-and-retro, purple-and-black Major League Baseball park was an instant classic as soon as it went up in 1995 (page 39).

◖ Larimer Square: The shops, restaurants, and bars at the heart of LoDo are almost always jammed, and, thankfully, Mayor John Hickenlooper made the parking meters far more reasonable as soon as he took office (page 47).

◖ Tattered Cover: The Cherry Creek outlet of this two-bookstore chain is the best—every book you could want, attentive clerks, a huge magazine collection, a strong children's section, and a comfortable atmosphere with cushy chairs and coffee (page 48).

◖ Denver Flagship REI: With a mountain-bike track, a climbing wall, a kayaking haven out back, and tents and hiking equipment everywhere, the REI store is a place for outdoors types to get lost for hours at a time (page 48).

◖ A Concert at Red Rocks Amphitheatre: Whether Van Morrison, R.E.M., Norah Jones, or Alan Jackson (to name a few recent performers) is your thing, Red Rocks is perhaps the most spectacular venue to see a concert in the entire United States. It helped out a little-known band called U2 in 1983, anyhow (page 59).

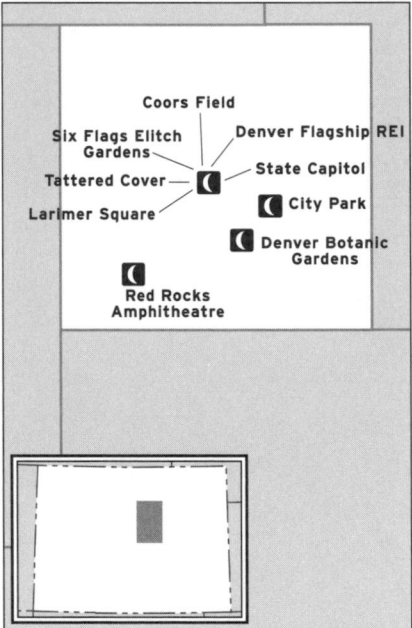

LOOK FOR ◖ TO FIND RECOMMENDED SIGHTS, ACTIVITIES, DINING, AND LODGING.

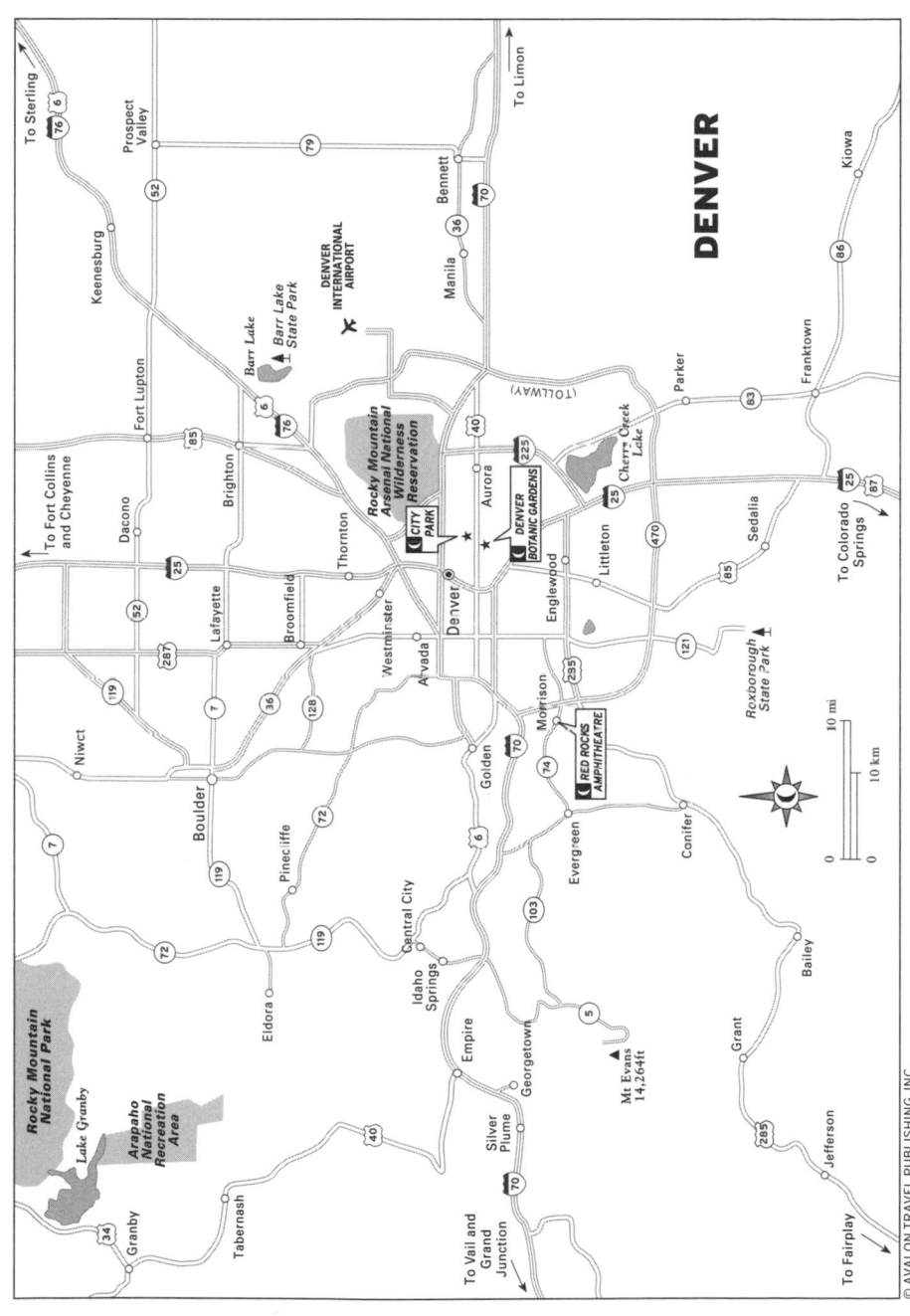

DENVER

To Sterling
Prospect Valley
To Limon
Keensburg
Fort Lupton
Barr Lake
Barr Lake State Park
DENVER INTERNATIONAL AIRPORT
Bennett
Manila
Brighton
Rocky Mountain Arsenal National Wilderness Reservation
(TOLLWAY)
Parker
Franktown
Kiowa
To Fort Collins and Cheyenne
Dacono
Thornton
Aurora
DENVER BOTANIC GARDENS
Cherry Creek Lake
Sedalia
To Colorado Springs
Lafayette
Broomfield
Westminster
CITY PARK
Denver
Englewood
Littleton
Niwot
Arvada
Boulder
Pinecliffe
Golden
Morrison
RED ROCKS AMPHITHEATRE
Roxborough State Park
Central City
Evergreen
Conifer
Bailey
Idaho Springs
Eldora
Empire
Georgetown
Grant
Mt Evans 14,264ft
Rocky Mountain National Park
Lake Granby
Arapaho National Recreation Area
Silver Plume
Granby
Tabernash
To Vail and Grand Junction
Jefferson
To Fairplay
285

10 mi
10 km
0
0

Highlands into yuppie havens filled with hipster restaurants and townie bars.

Although the recession of the early 2000s hit Denver hard, especially among the many high-tech workers who'd relocated here through the 1990s, further expansion seems inevitable. In 2004, voters passed the multibillion FasTracks initiative, which will bring an elaborate light-rail system to Denver and its surrounding suburbs (two million total population). And the city's Hispanic population, already at 31.7 percent, is growing at a rapid rate, and its cultural influence is spreading everywhere, from the *romantica* concerts by Los Temerarios and others at the Denver Coliseum to the many ramshackle Hatch, New Mexico, chile pepper stands that line Federal Boulevard on the north side of town.

PLANNING YOUR TIME

As with many big U.S. cities, it's possible to get a good feel for Denver in just a weekend—hit the LoDo bars and restaurants, stay in a nice hotel like the Brown Palace or the Adam's Mark, maybe take in a Rockies game or a trip to the mountains. But to truly capture the local flavor, spend a week. Fly into Denver International Airport, book a few nights at a few different hotels, and check out the less-publicized riches of the Denver Museum of Nature & Science or people-watch for hours on the 16th Street Mall. Day trips are nice—Central City and Black Hawk may well be the most charming gambling towns in the U.S., and Golden has the Coors Brewery tours, in addition to a nice old historic gold-mining district—but leave at least a few nights to get to the bottom of LoDo and the many diverse theaters and jazz-and-rock clubs.

HISTORY

When gold prospectors pushed to Colorado in the 1850s, they shouted, "Pikes Peak or bust!"—but they first discovered gold at the intersection of Cherry Creek and the South Platte River, about 100 miles to the north. The discovery, on November 22, 1858, kicked off the gold rush, beginning a migration of

the Colorado History Museum in downtown Denver

100,000 people to Colorado; the U.S. government established the state in 1861, and founders named the town for James W. Denver, governor of the Kansas territory (which, at the time, included eastern Colorado).

Civilization spread quickly after that—to the detriment of fur trappers, traders, and particularly Cheyennes and Arapahos, whose reservations had been on this land for decades. At first, Native Americans helped western settlers traverse Kansas and Colorado—they had traded with Anglo settlers for decades—but they were starting to get frustrated over unfavorable U.S. government treaties that forced them to surrender land and deplete their resources. As the Colorado gold rush turned into a boom, bands of tribes attacked the new settlers, infamously massacring the Hungate family on its ranch 30 miles from Denver in 1864 and marauding against wagon trains and miner camps.

The settlers fought back, and John Chivington, a Methodist preacher and colonel of the Third Regiment of Colorado Volunteer Cavalry, said, according to *Colorado: A History of the Centennial State* (1994): "I am fully satisfied that to kill them is the only way to have peace and quiet." Massacres ensued, particularly a November 29, 1864, ambush of a Cheyenne camp in southeastern Colorado, in which American soldiers killed more than 100 Cheyennes and, according to history books, raped and mutilated their women and shot their children. This led to a flurry of treaty negotiations, but skirmishes continued throughout the state until the natives were thoroughly displaced.

Having rid themselves of the "native problem," Americans in Denver built railroads, banks, breweries (including Coors), and meatpacking plants, turning the city into a major agricultural hub. From 1870 to 1890, Denver grew from 4,800 to 107,000 people, making it the second-biggest city in the West, after San Francisco. Although the 1893 depression and the U.S. government's decision to de-monetize silver ended this massive growth, Denver businessmen turned to farming, from wheat

and sugar beets to cows—thus the "Cowtown" label.

In the early 1900s, ambitious but sickly businessman Robert W. Speer came from Pennsylvania to Denver, declared the city "the Paris of America" and, in 1904, became mayor until he died of influenza in office 14 years later. During that time, Speer landscaped Civic Center, added zoological gardens to City Park, encouraged local philanthropists to build the Colorado Museum of Natural History (now the Denver Museum of Nature & Science) and other attractions, planted 110,000 trees, built parks, and generally turned Denver into what he called a "city beautiful." These innovations have defined Denver's character ever since.

Denver has since endured several busts (notably the Great Depression) and booms (the city took particular advantage of Franklin D. Roosevelt's New Deal, allowing his Civilian Conservation Corps to build Red Rocks Amphitheatre, in nearby Morrison, in the 1930s). Beginning in the 1960s, given nearby skiing tourism, the oil-and-gas industry, and an influx of federal employees at the U.S. Mint and other offices, Denver has grown into a stable western metropolis, able to withstand trauma such as the 1980s oil bust and the bursting of the Internet bubble in the early 21st century.

In 1995, thanks to the efforts of mayors Federico Peña and Wellington Webb, the city opened the $5 billion Denver International Airport, leading to a new boom and a resurgence of the downtown area. The old Mile High Stadium, home of the Denver Broncos, gave way to the flashy Invesco Field at Mile High, Major League Baseball planted the Colorado Rockies in a beautiful retro stadium downtown, the LoDo bar-and-shopping district flourished with fancy restaurants and a free downtown bus, and the metro area population hit 2.1 million in 2000 (including fast-growing suburbs like Thornton and Douglas County).

For a more elaborate version of Denver's history, go to www.denvergov.org/AboutDenver/history.asp, an excellent resource.

ORIENTATION

Downtown Denver is about an hour's drive from Denver International Airport off I-70. The main highways are the east–west I-70 and the north–south I-25, both of which provide access to the city's many suburbs—Westminster, Thornton, and Arvada to the north; Littleton, Englewood, and Lakewood to the south; and Aurora to the east. The mountains are due west on I-70, while Boulder is northwest on Highway 36.

This chapter divides the Denver area into six general regions: **LoDo/Central Denver** refers to "lower downtown," the heart of the city, including Coors Field and various warehouses-turned-brewpubs, as well as nearby neighborhoods such as Civic Center and Capitol Hill; **Northwest/Highlands** is a fast-growing, heavily Hispanic part of town with tons of restaurants at the intersection of 32nd Avenue and Lowell Boulevard, Sloan's Lake park, and numerous old Victorian houses; **City Park** is a relatively small area east of downtown, but it's notable for tourist attractions such as the Denver Zoo and the Denver Museum of Nature & Science, as well as the sprawling park itself; **Cherry Creek** is perhaps Denver's fanciest area, with beautiful old houses and a giant, high-end mall; **South Denver** refers to the entire southern part of the city, including the university and neighborhoods such as Hampden and Wellshire; and **Greater Denver** includes the suburbs, from Aurora to Broomfield to Greenwood Village.

SAFETY

Denver has its share of gang, drug, and crime problems, but police are fairly aggressive and most neighborhoods are safe. As always, use caution at night, lock your car doors, and don't walk alone. The emergency number, of course, is 911, or call 720/913-2000 for less pressing police or fire issues.

Sights

LODO/CENTRAL DENVER

Although Landry's Restaurants bought the **Downtown Aquarium** (700 Water St., 303/561-4450, www.downtownaquarium.com, 10 A.M.–10 P.M. Sun.–Thurs., 10 A.M.–11 P.M. Fri.–Sat., $13) in March 2003 and installed a seafood restaurant on the first floor—the new owners didn't acknowledge the irony—the former Ocean Journey Aquarium retains much of its original spirit. It's still packed with fish of all shapes, sizes, and colors, several octopi, manta rays, sharks, and two tigers who occasionally scratch a massive log to tatters. The changes by Landry's recently became obvious, though: The paths to the exhibits are tighter, more streamlined, with more cheap stuff to buy along the way, the snack bars are smaller and less convenient, and the huge tank of sea otters and foam kids' playground are gone. It is less expensive and open later, however.

A trip to the Denver Public Library's 540,000-square-foot **Central Library** (10 W. 14th Ave., 720/865-1111, 10 A.M.–9 P.M. Mon.–Tues., 10 A.M.–5:30 P.M. Fri.–Sat., 1–5 P.M. Sun.) is a lot less boring than you'd think. Built in the 1950s and renovated a decade ago, the complex includes a three-story atrium, a bunch of interesting sculptures (including a giant horse on a chair outside), and weirdly shaped windows that give it a fort-like ambience. Inside, look for expansive collections of American West art, books, maps, memorabilia, and original paintings by Frederic Remington, Albert Bierstadt, and others. The children's room is stocked with all the Dr. Seuss you could ever want, and the periodicals room carries almost every major magazine.

Denver's public library system is also superb, with tiny branches all over the city offering broad selections of magazines and children's books and videos. Of note, in the Five Points area, is the **Blair-Caldwell African-American Research Library** (2401 Welton St., 720/865-2401, http://aarl.denverlibrary.org, 10 A.M.–

Denver Public Library

7 P.M. Mon.–Wed., 10 A.M.–5 P.M. Fri.–Sat.), which has rare collections of Black Panther leader Eldridge Cleaver's writings along with interesting documents about black settlers in the Old West.

The **U.S. Mint** (320 W. Colfax Ave., 303/405-4761, www.usmint.gov, 9 A.M.–3 P.M. Mon., 8 A.M.–3 P.M. Tues.–Fri., free) is literally where the money is. One of four official U.S. mints, Denver's branch produces 14 billion coins per year and maintains the country's second-biggest gold supply. The gift shop, across the street at the Tremont Center, sells commemorative coins, and walk-up tours are available, although in the post-9/11 world many restrictions apply. Check the website to see what you can and can't bring in.

The centerpiece of Mayor Robert Speer's "City Beautiful" campaign in the early 20th century, **Civic Center** (Bannock St. to Broadway, Colfax Ave. to 14th Ave., 303/331-4060) is three blocks of grass and trees, along with a recently renovated Greek amphitheater and 1920s-era Old West statues such as *Bronco*

Buster. It's a beautiful part of the city, and festivals such as Cinco de Mayo and Taste of Colorado run here every spring and summer, but be careful walking around at night. Crime can be heavy in this part of town.

The 375-foot, 20-story **Daniels and Fisher Tower** (1601 Arapahoe St.) was the third-tallest building in the United States in 1910, when developer William Cooke Daniels built it next to his five-story department store. Although the city razed the store in the 1970s, preservationists kept the tower intact, and it's now a historic site that doubles as an office building. Its clock is 16 feet tall.

(Denver Botanic Gardens

The gardens (1005 York St., 720/865-3500, www.botanicgardens.org, 9 A.M.–5 P.M. mid-Sept.–Apr., 9 A.M.–8 P.M. Sat.–Tues. and 9 A.M.–5 P.M. Wed.–Fri. May–mid-Sept., $7.50 winter, $8.50 summer) make up a serene 23-acre spot filled with 32,000 kinds of plants from all over the world. Check out the "cloud forest tree," inside the Tropical Conservatory, which looks like a huge green giant about to give somebody a bear hug. The gardens are also the best place in town to see an outdoor concert; artists from folk-rocker Richard Thompson to country chanteuse k.d. lang have played here.

Museums

The **Denver Art Museum** (100 W. 14th Ave., 720/865-5000, www.denverartmuseum.org, 10 A.M.–5 P.M. Tues.–Sat., noon–5 P.M. Sun., $8) is just a notch or two below the world-class level of New York's Guggenheim or the Art Institute of Chicago, with works by Georgia O'Keeffe, Claude Monet, Pablo Picasso, and numerous other masters. The Institute of Western American Art is one of the most comprehensive of its kind, including Frederic Remington's bronze *The Cheyenne* and Charles Deas's *Long Jakes.* The museum is also a relaxing place to spend some time, both inside and out—a concrete outdoor plaza leads to the public library next door. The building's $90.5 million expansion, designed by architect Daniel

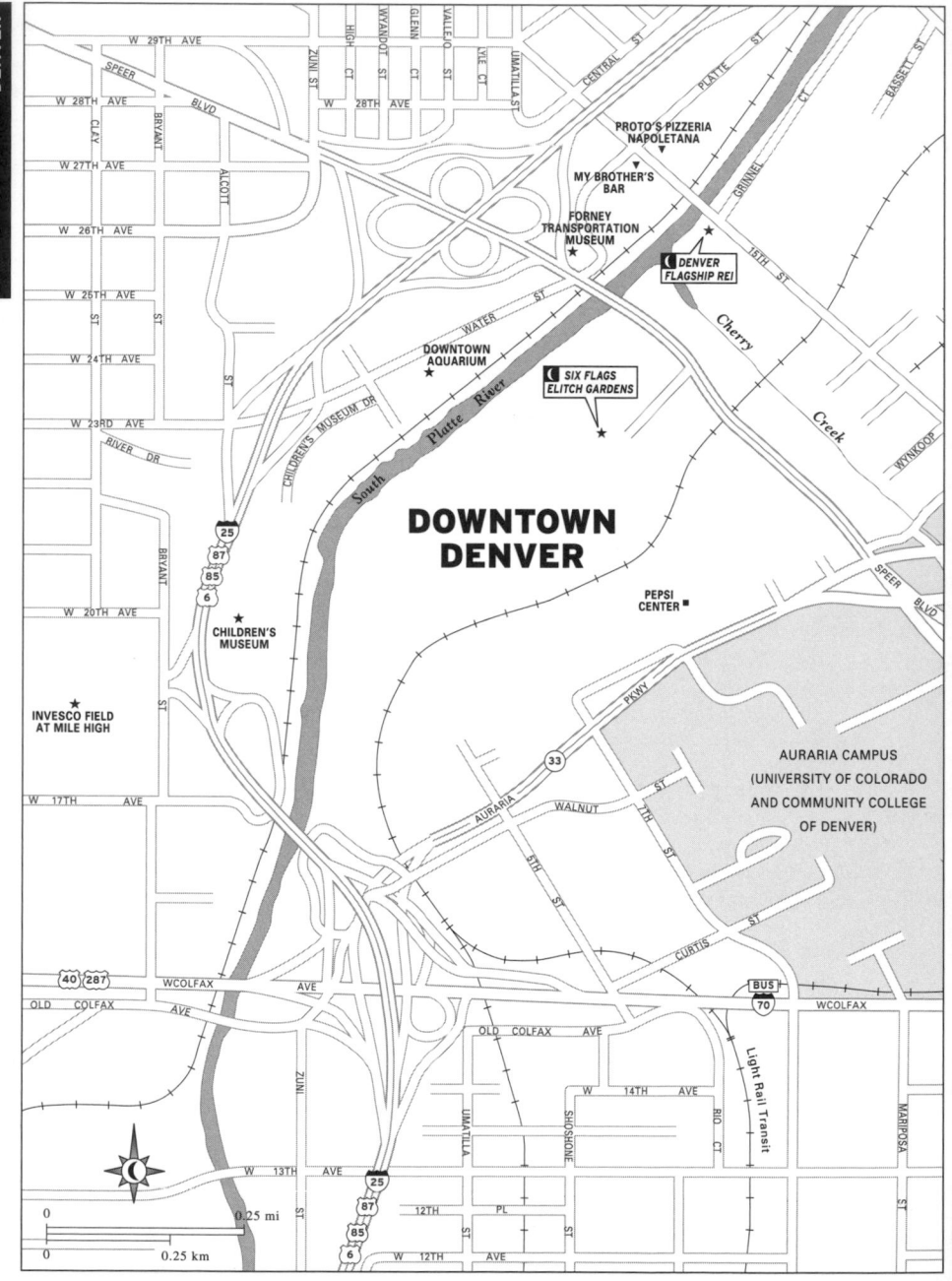

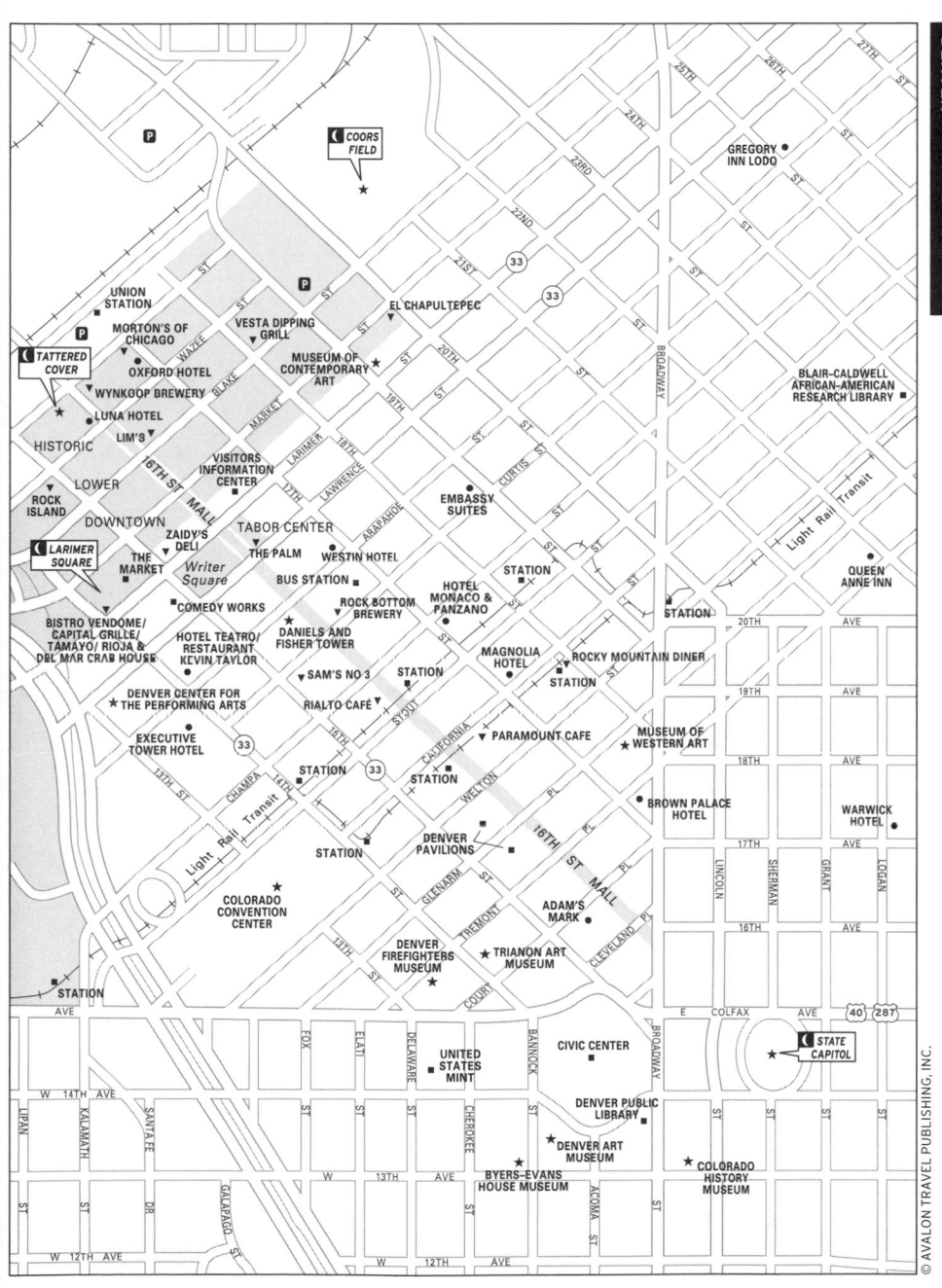

FIVE POINTS

Jazz giants Charlie Parker, Duke Ellington, and Lionel Hampton were regular attractions at Five Points clubs in the 1940s, and the northeast-of-downtown neighborhood along Welton Street remains the city's cultural African-American center today. Although the neighborhood, bounded by Park Avenue, Downing Street, Stout Street, and Tremont Place, has suffered from diminished influence – there's no major club anymore, and the historic Rossonian Hotel is no longer open for business – Five Points is a growing section of restaurants, barber shops, boutiques, and a bank.

Attractions include the **Black American West Museum** (3091 California St., 303/292-2566, www.blackamericanwest. org), the **Cleo Robinson Dance Ensemble** (119 Park Ave. W., 303/295-1759, www. cleoparkerdance.org), and the informal **Juneteenth Festival,** an annual party that draws 150,000 to 200,000 people to the neighborhood, in commemoration of the day Texas released all slaves two years after the Emancipation Proclamation.

Libeskind, who's heading up the World Trade Center reconstruction in New York City, is scheduled to open in fall 2006.

Built in 1883 by William Byers, publisher of the *Rocky Mountain News* and an important founder of Denver as we know it, the **Byers-Evans House Museum** (1310 Bannock St., 303/620-4933, 11 A.M.–3 P.M. Tues.–Sun., $3) maintains the furnishings of its original residents. Byers sold it in 1889 to William G. Evans of the Denver Tramway Company, and his family kept it elegant for 80 years. Tours and a short film are available.

The **Colorado History Museum** (1300 Broadway, 303/866-3682, www.coloradohistory.org, 10 A.M.–5 P.M. Mon.–Sat., noon–5 P.M. Sun., $5) digs into every aspect of the state's past—from Paleoindians to gold miners in covered wagons to the ski-pioneering 10th Mountain Division. The best display is Colorado TimeScape, a 10-by-8-foot map and timeline that plays out the region's 10,000-year history in scale models, lasers, and artifacts. To find the museum, look for the huge colorful mural of miners and Native Americans outside.

The **Denver Firefighters Museum** (1326 Tremont Ave., 303/892-1436, www.denverfirefightersmuseum.org, 10 A.M.–4 P.M. Mon.–Sat., $4) was the city's first firehouse, built in 1909, and today houses artifacts such as hoses, alarm bells, and trucks—plus photos tracing the history of firefighting, from rickety old wagons to modern red trucks. Of course, visitors can slide down the pole.

Denver philanthropist and society maven Molly Brown is best remembered for her role on the Titanic—or, perhaps, Kathy Bates's role in *Titanic.* The **Molly Brown House Museum** (1340 Pennsylvania St., 303/832-4092, 10 A.M.–3:30 P.M. Tues.–Sat. and noon–3:30 P.M. Sun. Sept.–May, 10 A.M.–3:30 P.M. Mon.–Sat. and noon–3:30 P.M.Sun. June–Aug., $6.50) documents her life with her wealthy husband, J. J., in this opulent stone-and-sandstone home. Eventually, after the couple separated, Brown rented the building to families and stayed at the Brown Palace whenever she returned to Denver. She died in 1932, and the still-furnished house is open for tours.

The **Children's Museum of Denver** (2121 Children's Museum Dr., 303/433-7444, www.cmdenver.org, 9 A.M.–4 P.M. Mon.–Fri., 10 A.M.–5 P.M. Sat.–Sun., $7) is a high-class, hands-on city kids' museum, with a tree-decorated, pillowy playground in the basement for infants and a fire truck, basketball court, and grocery store for bigger kids upstairs. The exhibits aren't super-high-tech, but they keep the target market busy.

For the time being, the **Museum of Contemporary Art/Denver** (1275 19th St., 303/298-7554, www.mcartdenver.org, 11 A.M.–5:30 P.M. Tues.–Sat., noon–5:30 P.M. Sun., $5) displays its light-and-shadow mazes, wine-glass chandeliers, and other works by mostly Colorado artists in a small downtown building. The museum's permanent facility, expected to be

the recently renovated Denver Art Museum

Eraser. (It climbs higher than 10 stories, drops abruptly, goes upside-down, and hits speeds of 60 miles per hour.) Kids love the place, especially given tie-in rides with Bugs Bunny and Batman and an elaborate new adventure water park. Grownups—well, those whose minds don't need erasing—can hold hands on the 100-foot-tall Ferris wheel overlooking Denver and the Rockies.

State Capitol

One of the most distinctive sights in the city, the gold-leaf-domed State Capitol (200 E. Colfax Ave., 303/866-2604, tours 9:15 A.M.–2:30 P.M. Mon.–Fri.) was built in 1886 out of granite, white marble, onyx, sandstone, and other materials unique at the time to Colorado. The legislature usually convenes January–May, and people can watch from third-floor viewing areas. Also check out the rotunda—which is sporadically open to the public these days—for great views of the city. Tours are usually available by appointment.

CITY PARK

Many experience this 314-acre park (17th Ave. and Colorado Blvd., 720/913-0696) by visiting the zoo or the Museum of Nature & Science, then jumping back in the car to return home. But the park itself is a beautiful, quiet, kite-flying spot, with a public golf course, tennis courts, a large lake (and several smaller ones), flower gardens, and various fountains. The city first acquired the property in 1881.

The **Denver Zoo** (2300 Steele St., 303/376-4800, www.denverzoo.org, 10 A.M.–5 P.M. daily Oct.–Mar., 9 A.M.–6 P.M. daily Apr.–Sept., $11 summer, $9 winter) is a great city zoo, with a pair of elephants at the center, monkeys of every conceivable shape, age, and size, and an elaborate aquatic section full of polar bears and fish. It's spread out, so bring comfortable shoes and a stroller for the kids—who will probably insist on rides on the animal-themed carousel and mini-train.

Cramming many levels of science and history under one roof, the recently renovated and expanded **Denver Museum of Nature &**

about 25,000 square feet, is scheduled to open in late 2006 at 15th and Delgany Streets.

Among the revelations at the **Black American West Museum and Heritage Center** (3091 California St., 303/292-2566, www.blackamericanwest.org, 10 A.M.–5 P.M. daily June–Sept., 10 A.M.–2 P.M. Wed.–Fri. and noon–5 P.M. Sat.–Sun. Sept.–June, $6): One of the first Colorado miners to discover gold, Henry Parker of Idaho Springs, was African American; the all-black 10th Cavalry was instrumental in helping Teddy Roosevelt capture San Juan Hill in 1898; and black families headed west like everybody else in the late 1800s, establishing all-black cities throughout Colorado.

Six Flags Elitch Gardens

This popular amusement park (2000 Elitch Circle, 303/595-4386, www.sixflags.com/parks/elitchgardens, hours vary, $38), which opened in 1890 as a zoological park in northwest Denver, relocated downtown in 1995 and is now famous for rides such as the Mind

© MELISSA KNOPPER

Colorado State Capitol in Denver

Science (2001 Colorado Blvd., 303/322-7009, www.dmns.org, 9 A.M.–5 P.M. daily, $10) has two superb anchoring exhibits—Space Odyssey, which lets visitors ride in actual moon-visiting spacecraft, and the dinosaur-filled Prehistoric Journey. The IMAX theater is worth the additional price, and before leaving, be sure to look into the rear of the museum, where the third floor overlooks perhaps the best view of the Rockies in the city.

HIGHLANDS/NORTHWEST

A little less congested than the celebrated Elitch Gardens, **Lakeside Amusement Park** (4601 Sheridan Blvd., 303/477-1621, www.lakeside-amusementpark.com, hours vary by season, $1.50) stars the 90-second, wooden-car Cyclone, along with throwback rides such as Tilt-a-Whirl, Wild Chipmunk, and Rock-o-Plane.

The park was built in the mid-1800s, and toddlers particularly love its non-scary kids' park.

All that's left of the old **Elitch Gardens** site is a modest theater and a small pavilion built in 1925. Although Edward G. Robinson, Grace Kelly, Jessica Tandy, and numerous others have performed here, the location is better known these days for its weekly summer farmers markets and other community events. Contact the Historic Elitch Gardens Theatre Foundation at 303/477-3006.

GREATER DENVER

For a city obsessed with souped-up cars and "cruising" streets such as Federal Boulevard, the small **Forney Transportation Museum** (4303 Brighton Blvd., 303/297-1113, www.forneymuseum.com, 9 A.M.–5 P.M. Mon.–Sat., $7) provides sleek historical perspective. The six-cylinder, six-wheel, bright-yellow Model H6A is a Barcelona-built luxury car, supposedly for a king of Greece in the early 1920s. There's also a Rolls Royce, a locomotive, and a train car known as "Big Boy."

The **Museo de las Americas** (861 Santa Fe Dr., 303/571-4401, www.museo.org, 10 A.M.–5 P.M. Tues.–Sat., $4) opened in the early 1990s in a rapidly growing, heavily Latino neighborhood. Long-standing exhibitions include statues and pottery from Mexico and South America before the Europeans showed up, and a display of 20th century painter David Alfaro Siqueiros's brightly colored works.

The main attraction of the peaceful **Butterfly Pavilion** (6252 W. 104th Ave., Westminster, 303/469-5441, www.butterflies.org, 9 A.M.–5 P.M. daily, $8) is a greenhouse room filled with plants and butterflies of all colors and sizes (not to mention caterpillars and cocoons). It also has an iguana, fish in a pond, various large insects, huge plastic grasshopper statues, starfish available for petting, and other hands-on stuff for kids.

Sports and Recreation

SPECTATOR SPORTS

No matter how many Stanley Cups the Colorado Avalanche win, Denver will always be a football town—quarterback John Elway's two Super Bowl victories in the late 1990s merely confirmed it. **Invesco Field at Mile High** (1701 Bryant St., 720/258-3333, www.invescofieldatmilehigh.com), where the **Denver Broncos** play, is a steel-and-glass monolith that replaced the classic old Mile High Stadium. The stadium is a comfortable, well-maintained place to watch a game (or the occasional rock concert), and the concessions snacks tend to be more diverse than just hot dogs and beer.

The **Colorado Avalanche,** 1996 and 2001 Stanley Cup champions, play at the **Pepsi Center** (1000 Chopper Circle, 303/405-1100, www.pepsicenter.com), across the parking lot from Elitch Gardens downtown. The Pepsi Center also houses the **Denver Nuggets,** an NBA team that was one of the worst in the league for much of the 1990s, but, thanks to dynamic young forward Carmelo Anthony, seems to be turning around. Nuggets games are oddly designed to entertain non-basketball fans, with prominent cheerleaders, a daredevil mascot named Rocky, games, and contests during every conceivable break in the action. The Pepsi Center also plays host to the Colorado Crush (arena football), Colorado Mammoth (lacrosse), Rapids (soccer), and big-name concerts such as Eminem, Bruce Springsteen, and Paul McCartney.

When the Avs were on hold during the NHL strike, local fans adopted the University of Denver's Pioneers as their beloved hockey team—they recently became the seventh team in NCAA history to win two straight titles. They play at the college's **Magness Arena** (2240 Buchtel Blvd., 303/871-7403), a rowdy bowl of a sports arena that doubles as a concert venue—Christina Aguilera, Jane's Addiction, the Pixies, Sting, and Luis Miguel have performed here in recent years.

Coors Field, where the Colorado Rockies play in Denver's LoDo neighborhood

(Coors Field

Denver fans usually have room in their hearts (and pocketbooks) to support three major sports franchises—in recent years, the Nuggets were the odd team out. But if the Colorado Rockies' mediocrity of recent years continues, the team that brought baseball to LoDo and Coors Field (2001 Blake St., 303/762-5437, www.colorado.rockies.mlb.com) will likely take their place. This Major League Baseball park, built in 1995, is all purple, black, and brown, with a classic ambience and excellent snacks.

GOLF

The golf courses in Denver aren't as world-renowned as their counterparts in, say, Vail or Aspen, but some of them have won awards and they're convenient for weekend travelers. The par-72, 6,318-yard **City Park** (2500 York St., 303/295-2095) has an acre-and-a-half lake. **Foothills** (3901 S. Carr St.,

303/989-3901), opened in 1933, is one of the city's highest-traffic courses. **Overland** (1801 S. Huron St., 303/777-7331) was built in 1895 and was the Denver Country Club for years; today it's known for high trees and narrow fairways. **Willis Case** (4999 Vrain St., 303/455-9801) is an OK course, but the views of Denver and the Rockies are incredible. **Evergreen** (29614 Upper Bear Creek Rd., Evergreen, 303/674-4128) is the only city-run course outside of Denver. The 27-hole, putting-oriented **Kennedy** (10500 E. Hampden Ave., 303/751-0311), along Cherry Creek, has serious water hazards. One of the most challenging courses in town, **Wellshire** (3333 S. Colorado Blvd., 303/692-5636) has two holes known as "Amen Corner."

Just outside Denver, the **Omni Interlocken Resort** (500 Interlocken Blvd., Broomfield, 303/438-6600, www.omnihotels.com/golf/denver/index.html) has three nine-hole courses designed by 1981 U.S. Open champion David Graham and his partner, Gary Panks. The John Elway Celebrity Classic Golf Tournament, a big deal in these parts, is held here every year. In Littleton, a suburb just south of the city, the **Arrowhead Golf Course** (10850 W. Sundown Trail, Littleton, 303/973-9614) overlooks Roxborough State Park and has some of the most beautiful golf-course scenery in the state, if not the country. It also offers luxurious (if unnecessary) touches like GPS systems on the carts.

HIKING AND CYCLING

The **Denver Parks Department** (201 W. Colfax Ave., Dept. 601, 720/913-0696, www.denvergov.org/Parks) operates more than 200 parks, including massive crown jewels such as the flowery, 165-acre **Washington Park** (701 S. Franklin St., 303/698-4962) and the urban 314-acre **City Park** (17th Ave. and York St.). The parks are generally well kept, often with elaborate flower arrangements, and often with tennis courts, baseball diamonds, and jogging paths.

The **Cherry Creek Trail** is a paved path that connects from Cherry Creek Reservoir along the creek to the network of concrete paths in downtown Denver. The **Highline Canal** is a quiet, tree-lined, paved path that runs 66 miles through Douglas, Arapahoe, and Denver Counties—it starts south of Highway 470 and Wadsworth and ends at the Rocky Mountain Arsenal in northeast Denver.

Once a horribly polluted area ostracized by city officials and residents, the **Platte River Greenway** underwent a massive cleanup effort in the mid-1970s that continues today. The best spot to "jump in" is at **Confluence Park** just behind REI across I-25 from Invesco Field, a pretty little spot where the river turns into rapids and forms a small pool (with a wooden bridge). Kayakers and dogs love it here, and the Platte River extends in three directions—east to the suburbs, west to Invesco Field at Mile High, and south to LoDo. The surrounding cement paths are great for biking and walking.

In Broomfield, west of Denver, **Matthews-Winters Park** is a forest-and-wildlife-heavy park ideal for hikers and mountain bikers, extending to Red Rocks Park and the town of Golden. To get there, take I-70 to Highway 26, turn south and drive about a tenth of a mile to the park entrance. Also in Jefferson County is **Deer Creek Canyon,** a 1,881-acre park that was once a campground for wandering Utes and Jesse James. To get there, take I-70, turn south on C-470 to Kipling, exit south to South Deer Creek Canyon Road, turn west to Grizzly Drive, and go about a quarter-mile to the parking lot. South of the city, in Littleton, **Chatfield Park** (11500 N. Roxborough Park Rd., 303/791-7275) has a reservoir, a marina, and, in late August, the **Rocky Mountain Balloon Festival** (www.rockymountainballoonfestival.com).

Denver is stuffed with bike shops, including **Mob Cyclery** (4272 Tennyson St., 303/477-4460, www.mobcyclery.com), in northwest Denver, which has all the usual equipment and a staff that's friendly rather than snobby or overworked, and **Wheat Ridge Cyclery** (7085 W. 38th Ave., 303/424-3221, http://ridewrc.com/site/intro.cfm), a larger place with far more bikes than Mob Cyclery, but still with helpful employees, particularly in the service department.

FITNESS

Denver has tons of health clubs, all over the city, but start with the 29 **Denver Recreation Centers** (720/913-0693, www.denvergov.org/Recreation), which charge $125 per year for access to swimming pools, basketball courts, weight-lifting equipment, classes, and childcare programs. The most impressive center is the **Colorado Athletic Club** (1630 Welton St., 303/623-2100, www.coloradoac.com), a 40,000-square-foot facility that truly pampers its clients, with tanning beds, massage chairs, and saunas to go with the cutting-edge weight-training equipment and basketball court. Similarly high-quality, but even more convenient for downtown employees, is the **Athletic Club at Denver Place** (1849 Curtis St., 303/294-9494, www.acdp.com), two blocks away from the 16th Street Mall, with a basketball court inside a covered second-floor bridge overlooking LoDo.

About 10 minutes from central Denver, the **Lakeshore Athletic Club—Flatiron** (300 Summit Blvd., Broomfield, 303/729-2582, www.lsac-flatiron.com) is, at 100,000 square feet, more than twice the size of the downtown Colorado Athletic Club, with an NBA-sized basketball court, 50-foot rock-climbing wall, junior Olympic-sized pool, and tons of classes for kids and adults (from yoga to healthy cooking).

Entertainment and Nightlife

The centerpiece of Denver entertainment and culture is the **Denver Performing Arts Complex** (14th St. and Curtis St., 303/893-4000, www.denvercenter.org), a collection of 11 large and small theaters (11,260 seats in all) spread over four city blocks. With a huge, curved, glass "ceiling" covering much of the gray-brick complex, the center dominates downtown Denver even on nights without a popular show. Built in 1974 and run by the Denver Center for the Performing Arts, the complex's anchors are the in-the-round Boettcher Concert Hall, the ornate Temple Hoyne Buell Theatre, and the new (in mid-2005) Ellie Caulkins Opera House. Among the attractions over the years: Disney's *Lion King;* a four-year run of *I Love You, You're Perfect, Now Change; Always… Patsy Cline;* Lyle Lovett; Jerry Seinfeld; *Hello Dolly* with Carol Channing; Penn and Teller; the ballet and opera seasons; and, of course, the Colorado Symphony Orchestra. The main promoter for theatrical productions here is **Denver Center Attractions,** which imports many of the big touring shows to Denver.

THEATER

While it's tough to make it as an actor or director in Denver, the theater scene is supportive, talent rises quickly to the top, and there are enough stages (in all genres, from comedy to drama) to maintain a diversity of mainstream and truly weird productions. The **Denver Center Theatre Company** (Denver Performing Arts Complex, 1245 Champa St., 303/893-4000, www.denvercenter.org) has booked acclaimed Broadway-style shows such as *The Immigrant* and *It Ain't Nothin' but the Blues* to the biggest theaters in town, particularly the four-stage Helen Bonfils Theatre Complex.

The recently restructured and upgraded **Denver Civic Theatre** (721 Santa Fe Dr., 303/309-3773, www.denvercivic.com) brings Broadway-style plays and musicals to town, including *Brooklyn, Newsical,* and even racy stuff like *Puppetry of the Penis.* The theater also plays host to singers and comedy troupes on off-play-nights.

On a smaller scale, the **Bug Theatre Company** (3654 Navajo St., 303/477-5977 or 303/477-9984, www.bugtheatre.org), in a 1912 nickelodeon movie house, is at the center of this scene, sponsoring regular, improv-oriented events such as *Freak Train,* in which actors of all levels stand up to give hilarious impromptu performances. Opened in 1971, when Chicano theater was a relatively new

DENVER'S MUSIC SCENE

Rock, jazz, and blues fans accustomed to the bursting weekends of New York, Chicago, Los Angeles, and Austin, Texas, endure a temporary letdown upon relocating to Denver. They have a right to be disappointed: A month's worth of musical entertainment here is equivalent to a weekend in those places. But have some patience, and pick your spots. Every single major touring act, with rare exceptions, winds up in Denver or Boulder before long, owing to the city's proximity halfway between Chicago and L.A. (Where else are bands going to play? Salt Lake City? Cheyenne?) And on the club level, the city maintains a "scene" for almost every genre—blues, jazz, punk, folk, and hippie jamming music have venues of their own, and while Denver is unlikely to become "the next Seattle" and spawn its own style, its diversity is a plus.

RED ROCKS AND BIG TENTS

Summer is the best time of year for music lovers, as the inimitable Red Rocks Amphitheatre and the suburban Coors Amphitheatre fill up with superstar acts, while the midsize downtown Fillmore Auditorium and the tent-covered Universal Lending Pavilion draw the smaller, Elvis Costello-sized names. If you're a true live-music lover, though, don't lose sight of clubs like the Bluebird, El Chapultepec, and Herman's Hideaway—they thrive in spring and fall, and their shows can be both intimate and star-powered. *The Denver Post* and the *Rocky Mountain News* do a good job of chronicling these scenes, especially in their Friday sections, but pick up *Westword* (www.westword.com) for more thorough listings, critics' picks, and reviews of local music. Here's a run-down of music venues:

The single best place to see a show is **Red Rocks Amphitheatre** (2901 Ship Rock Rd., Morrison, 303/640-2637, www.redrocksonline.com), where the acoustics are almost as breathtaking as the scenery. Bands from the Beatles to U2 have performed legendary shows here, and every summer the crowded, general-admission, 9,000-capacity amphitheatre snags a solid half dozen amazing acts—depending on your age, if you're from Denver, you're probably still talking about R.E.M., local heroes Big Head Todd and the Monsters, B.B. King, the Pretenders, Paul Simon, Bonnie Raitt, or Sonic Youth.

Far less charming, in the south suburbs, is **Coors Amphitheatre** (formerly Fiddler's Green, 6350 Greenwood Plaza Blvd., Greenwood Village, 303/220-7000), which handles more customers at a time and has hosted everything from all six Lollapaloozas to Jay-Z and 50 Cent to Ringo Starr's all-star band. Hosting concerts year-round is the downtown **Pepsi Center** (1000 Chopper Circle, 303/405-1100, www.pepsicenter.com), which gets the Bruce Springsteens, Shakiras, and Aerosmiths, and the **Denver Coliseum** (4600 Humboldt St., 303/295-4444, www.denvercoliseum.com), a less-slick sports arena that has hosted Nirvana, George Jones, and Slipknot over the years and remains a central hub for Spanish-language pop, folk, and rock music, including Los Tigres del Norte.

HISTORIC VENUES, ROCKIN' BANDS

Denver is blessed with three terrific midsize theaters where major musicians play regularly: the **Paramount Theatre** (1621 Glenarm Pl., 303/825-4904), which opened in 1930 and has a beautiful old Wurlitzer organ to go with a classic interior and a comfortable, carpeted lobby; the **Fillmore Auditorium** (1510 Clarkson St., 303/837-0360, www.fillmoreauditorium.com), a lovingly refinished, chandelier-topped, former ice-skating rink (in the 1910s), hockey arena (in the 1940s), and heavy-metal club (in the 1990s), which draws some of the biggest bands in the city; and the **Ogden Theatre** (935 E. Colfax Ave., 303/830-2525, www.nipp.com), down the street from the Fillmore, which is grungier but has an excellent sound system and also draws top acts regularly. The remodeled **Gothic Theatre** (3263 S. Broadway, Englewood, 303/788-0984, www.gothictheatre.com) is famous for hosting punk, metal, and grunge shows throughout the 1990s—memorably, Nirvana, the Red Hot Chili Peppers, the Butthole Surfers, and the Pixies played here; the venue isn't quite as influential as it used to be, but it still draws alternative-rock and punk bands. The circa-1917 **Bluebird Theatre** (3317 E. Colfax Ave., 303/322-2308, www.nipp.com) is sort of a mini-Ogden, a nicely refinished, intimate place to see The Wedding Present or Slim Cessna's Auto Club.

During summers, the **Universal Lending Pavilion** (1700 7th St., 303/405-6080, www.universallendingpavilion.com), in the Pepsi Center parking lot, has sponsored James Brown, John Mayer, Elvis Costello, and many others underneath a big white tent.

Club-wise, the city has at least one venue for almost any kind of music you can name. The legendary jazz venue is **El Chapultepec** (1962 Market St., 303/295-9126), which has hosted Ella Fitzgerald, Sarah Vaughan, Frank Sinatra, Tony Bennett, Chet Baker, Wynton Marsalis, and hundreds of others since it switched from mariachi to jazz music after it opened in the 1950s. Owner Jerry Krantz, who serves only beer and disallows dancing, told the *Rocky Mountain News* that members of U2 stopped by in 1992 with underage girls in tow—and Krantz told them to get lost. A more recent addition to Denver's jazz circuit is **Dazzle** (930 Lincoln St., 303/839-5100), which has mirror-lined walls, modern performers (including many locals), and excellent Sunday brunches.

APPROVED BY RAMONES FANS

Punkers love the **Lion's Lair** (2022 E. Colfax Ave., 303/320-9200, www.lionslair.com), where bands play on a raised stage behind a bar literally at the center of the room – I

saw an incredible show there once by British pub-rocker Graham Parker. Also punk-leaning: the **Aztlan Theatre** (974 Santa Fe Dr., 303/573-0188) and the venerable **Cricket on the Hill** (1209 E. 13th Ave., 303/830-9020, www.cricketonthehill.com). Revered in the 1980s and 1990s as a punk club called Seven South, the **Hi-Dive** (7 S. Broadway, 720-570/4500, www.hi-dive.com) reinvented itself in 2003 as a hipster hangout with a backdrop of DJs, local stars like Dressy Bessy, and up-and-coming national acts like Slim Cessna's Auto Club.

The center of the folk-and-bluegrass (which is to say, "acoustic music") scene is the **Swallow Hill Music Hall** (71 E. Yale, 303/777-1003 or 877/214-7013, www.swallowhill.com), a 2,000-member organization that has put on live shows and classes since the 1960s.

Country line-dancers, or just people who like to take in the occasional Willie Nelson or Tanya Tucker show, flock to the **Grizzly Rose** (5450 N. Valley Hwy., 303/295-2353, www.grizzlyrose.com), an old-school country club where everything's made of wood. Faith Hill, Tim McGraw, Brooks and Dunn, and Garth Brooks, to name just a few, stopped here on their way to the top.

Finally, for plain old rock 'n' roll – by which I think of a Dave Alvin show in the early 1990s, with the Skeletons as his backup band, which kicked my behind all over the floor – **Herman's Hideaway** (1578 S. Broadway, 303/777-5840, www.hermanshideaway.com) has a warm, beer-drinking vibe. Local heroes Big Head Todd and the Monsters and the Subdudes, among others, have made it their home base.

But even big-city snobs know Denver isn't the only place to see live music. Boulder is filled with excellent clubs and theaters, and world-class clubs and festivals are in Telluride, Fort Collins, Lyons, Nederland, and many other places. If you're planning to stay awhile, check out as many as you can.

phenomenon in the United States, **El Centro Su Teatro** (4725 High St., 303/296-0219, www.suteatro.org) explores issues of mortality and religion with productions such as *Death and the Maiden* and *The Miracle at Tepeyac.* The **Hunger Artists Ensemble Theatre** (721 Santa Fe Dr., 303/893-5438, www.hungerartists.org) refers not to a feed-hungry-actors organization but a group of ambitious theater people who've put on critically acclaimed shows all over the city (from the Mercury Café to Denver Civic Theatre) since 1979. Its reach stretches from James Joyce (whose *The Dead* is an annual holiday production) to Steve Martin (whose *The Underpants* is billed "never underestimate the power of a glimpse of lingerie").

Even smaller—so small that it bills itself as "the runt stepchild of small nonprofit theaters"—is **Germinal Stage Denver** (2450 W. 44th Ave., 303/455-7108, www2.privatei.com/~gsden/index.htm), which formed in 1974 and tackles Tennessee Williams, Eugene O'Neill, Albert Camus, and other masters in a tiny theater on the northwest side. The **Buntport Theatre** (717 Lipan St., 720/946-1388, www.buntport.com) puts on small comedic productions such as *Titus Andronicus: The Musical!* and the weekly "sitcom" *Magnets on the Fringe.* The **Mizel Center for Arts and Culture** (350 S. Dahlia St., 303/316-6360, www.mizelcenter.org) is a large Jewish cultural facility that often produces plays in its 300-seat theater—recently, the two-woman show *Poignant Irritations* focused on the life of Gertrude Stein.

The **Country Dinner Playhouse** (6875 S. Clinton St., Greenwood Village, 303/799-1410 or 800/630-1026, www.countrydinnerplayhouse.com) supplements its all-you-can-eat buffet with productions such as the '60s spoof *Beehive* and occasional Broadway-type shows.

CLASSICAL MUSIC AND DANCE

The Denver Performing Arts Complex is pretty much one-stop shopping for the high-class musical arts—including the **Colorado Symphony Orchestra** (303/623-7876, www.coloradosym-phony.org), which plays at various locations throughout the state; **Opera Colorado** (695 S. Colorado Blvd., Ste. 20, 303/893-4100 or 800/641-1222, www.operacolorado.org), which goes for the big names, like *The Marriage of Figaro* and *Julius Caesar*; and the **Colorado Ballet** (1278 Lincoln St., 303/837-8888, www.coloradoballet.org), founded as a ballet school in 1951.

DANCE CLUBS

Throbbing, electronic, updated disco clubs are alive and well in Denver, especially downtown—and the dance scene revolves around the venerable **Rock Island** (1614 15th St., 303/443-2227, www.rockislandclub.com), specializing in dark, gothic DJs, the occasional live band, and multitudes of kids packing the sidewalks on all-ages nights; the **Deadbeat Club** (4040 E. Evans Ave., 303/758-6853), at which a variety of DJs play almost exclusively electronic music; and the **Funky Buddha Lounge** (776 Lincoln Ave., 303/832-5075, www.funkybuddhalounge.com), built on The Ginger Bar, a heated outdoor patio, and multiple dance nights, from swanky lounge music to '80s pop.

BARS

Although it's not quite as self-contained as Boulder's Pearl Street "Mall Crawl," LoDo has a critical mass of bars and brewpubs to sustain anybody for one solid night of debauchery. Begin with the **Wynkoop Brewing Co.** (1634 18th St., 303/297-2700, www.wynkoop.com), where owner John Hickenlooper began his political career (before becoming mayor in 2002), which serves dozens of distinctive brews, notably the signature RailYard Ale and something called Captain Hickenlooper's Flying Artillery Ale.

Old Chicago (1415 Market St., 303/893-1806, www.oldchicago.com) is part of a Colorado chain, and the Boulder outlet is a smidgen better, food-wise, but the pool tables, televised sports, central location, and superb pizza make it one of LoDo's most popular bar-restaurants. Part of the same chain is the **Rock Bottom**

El Chapultepec is a hip place to see live jazz.

Brewery (1001 16th St., 303/534-7616, www.rockbottom.com), with several locations in the Denver area, but none as convenient as this one, on the 16th Street Mall.

Attached to the Courtyard by Marriott hotel on the 16th Street Mall, the **Rialto Café** (934 16th St., 303/893-2233, www.rialtocafe.com) is a well-managed, easygoing pub-restaurant with steaks and appetizers. Beer enthusiasts prefer **Falling Rock Taphouse** (1919 Blake St., 303/293-8338, www.fallingrocktaphouse.com), which serves a kajillion brews from all over the world. On the hipster side, the Miami-style **Mynt Lounge** (1424 Market St., 303/825-6968, www.lotusentertainment.net) serves fruity martinis in addition to the usual drinks.

For red-and-white drinkers, the **Paris Wine Bar** (1553 Platte St., 303/455-2451) supplements its selections with cheese and fruit plates. Also, consider branching to the Colfax Avenue drinking district, including **Irish Snug** (1201 E. Colfax Ave., 303/839-1394), which as per Irish tradition refers to the one-person drinking booth on the premises. Or

pick your own spot by scouring *Westword*'s Best-of-Denver listings (www.westword.com/bestof/index.html).

In the suburbs, **The Purple Martini** (8000 E. Belleview Ave., Ste. D30, Greenwood Village, 303/779-0091) is known for its numerous kinds of $4 martinis and a waitstaff scantily clad in leather; **C.B. & Potts** (6575 Greenwood Plaza Blvd., Greenwood Village, 303/770-1982, www.cbpotts.com/Englewood.asp), a spin-off of a popular Fort Collins joint, has large burgers and friendly waitpeople; and **LoDo's Bar and Grill** (8545 S. Quebec St., Highlands Ranch, 303/346-2930) attempts to bring the downtown Denver feel to the suburbs, but why its clientele can't simply drive to the real LoDo instead, I can't say.

COMEDY

Comedy took a hit locally after 9/11, but it has since bounced back, thanks to a cluster of resilient, creative theaters. The **Impulse Theatre** (1634 18th St., 303/297-2111, www.impulsetheatre.com) is sort of the local version of

Chicago's Second City. **Bovine Metropolis Theatre** (1527 Champa St., 303/758-4722, www.bovinemetropolis.com) is young and hungry, and the comedians who star in the ACME sketch and improv shows are some of the best talent in town. **Comedy Works** (1226 15th St., 303/595-3637, www.comedyworks.com) snags traveling B-plus-list comedians such as Tommy Chong and *Saturday Night Live* alumnus Darrell Hammond.

EVENTS

Denver's mild weather, views of the Rockies, and clean, laid-back downtown make it a natural fit for festivals, and the roster of annual events has been growing since the LoDo renaissance in the early 1990s.

An annual two-week extravaganza of hootin', hollerin', and celebratin' the beef industry, the January **National Western Stock Show** (Denver Coliseum, 4655 Humboldt St., 303/297-1166, ext. 810, www.nationalwestern.com) is one of the most surreal country-and-western rodeo events you'll ever attend.

Every year in May, celebrants from all over the city flock to Civic Center Park for a huge **Cinco de Mayo** party. But the late June **LoDo Music Fest** (3309 Blake St., 303/295-1195, www.denverfestivals.com), whose headliners have included James Brown, Tower of Power, and X over the years, is in limbo, according to its organizers, and may or may not return in future summers.

In early July, the **Cherry Creek Arts Festival** (3rd Ave. and Steele St., 303/355-2787, www.cherryarts.org) draws hundreds of thousands of people to see the works of 200 artists, and once you're bored of the various

high-end paintings, ceramics, glass, and sculpture, hit the mall across the street.

The most spectacular event is the late September–early October **Great American Beer Festival** (Colorado Convention Center, Welton St., 303/447-0816 or 888/822-6273, www.beertown.org), which serves more than 1,600 different beers from 320 U.S. breweries in one-ounce sample cups. The **Denver International Buskerfest** (303/295-1195), also in September, packs the 16th Street Mall with jugglers, magicians, comedians, and tightrope walkers.

The early December **Parade of Lights** (www.denverparadeoflights.com) gets everybody all excited—except the grumpy drivers who have to pass through congested downtown on their way to almost anywhere else.

Smaller extravaganzas of all types play out at Denver-area parks: The **Rocky Mountain Balloon Festival** (www.rockymountainballoonfestival.com) launches colorful hot-air balloons at Chatfield State Park (11500 N. Roxborough Road, Littleton) for an entire late-August weekend; the late-July **Colorado Dragon Boat Festival** (303/722-6852, www.coloradodragonboat.org) celebrates Asian culture at Sloan's Lake Park (West 17th Avenue and Sheridan Boulevard) with funky, decorative boat races, tons of food, and colorful dancing and music; and the **Denver Black Arts Festival,** at Sonny Lawson Park (2300 Welton Street), celebrates local African-American culture with music, dance, and theater events. Check the **Denver Parks and Recreation** website (www.denvergov.org/Parks_Recreation) for schedules—particularly in the summer.

.Shopping

LODO/CENTRAL DENVER

The main shopping areas downtown are 16th Street Mall and Larimer Square, but record-store fanatics swear by **Twist & Shout** (300 E. Alameda Ave., 303/722-1943, www.twist-andshout.com), whose workers are knowledgeable and passionate and remind music fans why it's more fun to flip through racks than click through the Apple iTunes Store; **Wax Trax** (638 E. 13th Ave., 303/831-7246, www.waxtraxrecords.com), a little more hip and focused on cutting-edge punk and techno titles; and **Jerry's Record Exchange** (312 E. Colfax Ave., 303/830-2336, www.jerrysrecordexchange.com), a hole-in-the-wall joint on Capitol Hill where the grizzled cashiers are surprisingly nice under their gruff exteriors.

Even if you're not a celebrity, **Rockmount Ranchwear** (1626 Wazee St., 303/629-7777, www.rockmount.com) is worth a visit for the super-hip western jackets, hats, belts, boots, and many other leather-and-fringe items. As the aggressively self-marketing Denver fixture likes to point out, rock stars from Elvis Presley to Bruce Springsteen, and movie stars from Dennis Quaid to Tom Hanks have modeled the distinctive brand on stage and in films.

🅒 Larimer Square

When miners first settled in Denver, Larimer Square (bounded by Market and Lawrence Streets and 14th and 15th Avenues, 303/685-8143, www.larimersquare.com) was the central part of town with the first bank, a bookstore, a dry-goods store, and racy Gahan's Saloon, allegedly the site of back-room poker games and a basement speakeasy in the 1920s. Today, the area is a clean and easily accessible bar-and-restaurant district with some of the best shopping in Denver—chains like **Ann Taylor** (1421 Larimer St., 303/892-0478, www.anntaylor.com) are here, as well as distinctive local outlets such as the cowkid-fashion **Cry Baby Ranch** (1422 Larimer St., 303/623-3979 or 888/279-2229, crybabyranch.com) and the high-end wom-

en's-clothing boutique **Eve** (1415 Larimer St., 720/932-9382, www.eveinc.com). There's practical stuff, too, including a **UPS Store** (1550 Larimer St., 303/825-8060, www.theupsstore.com) and a **Rocky Mountain Chocolate Factory** (1512 Larimer St., 303/623-1887, www.rmcf.com). Depending on your definition of "practical."

16th Street Mall

Around the corner from Larimer Square is the 16th Street Mall (16th St. from Broadway to Wynkoop St., 303/534-6161, www.downtowndenver.com/bid/16thstmall.htm), a gray-brick, 16-block, pedestrian-only strip of hotels, restaurants, and shops. A free city bus operates regularly, which is a huge bonus, and even if some of the local high school students get a little boisterous at times, the mall is a great place to shop and hang out.

the gray-brick 16th Street Mall

Many of the stores are chains, but **Writer Square** (1512 Larimer St., www.writer-square.com) has originals such as the **City Flower Store, Triage Clothing,** and **Gallery One.** Also on the mall is **Denver Pavilions** (500 16th St., 303/260-6000, www.denverpavilions.com), a four-level plaza anchored with a multiplex movie theater and megachains such as Barnes & Noble, Gap, Virgin Megastore, and the restaurant Maggiano's Little Italy. The **Tabor Center** (1201 16th St., 303/572-6868, www.taborcenter.com), between Arapahoe and Larimer Streets, is a tall, glass-enclosed mall-within-a-mall including an ESPN Zone and Cheesecake Factory.

CHERRY CREEK MALL

Denver's biggest mall is Cherry Creek Mall (3000 E. 1st Ave., 303/388-3900, www.shopcherrycreek.com), a high-class joint with mostly top-of-the-line stores—Burberry, Saks Fifth Avenue, The Sharper Image, and (my personal favorite) the only Apple Computer Store in the city.

◖ Tattered Cover

This Cherry Creek fixture (2955 E. 1st Ave., 303/322-7727, www.tatteredcover.com) restores book-lovers' faith that the entire literary industry hasn't shifted to Barnes & Noble and Borders. (Not that there's anything wrong with those!) Its two outlets—one at the west end of the 16th Street Mall, and the original in the Cherry Creek Mall area—have a sink-into-the-couch ambience, along with regular local-author signings, coffee and pastries, and kids' activities. The book collection is almost intimidatingly huge, with an entire large room devoted to maps and travel (with an emphasis on Colorado, of course), and the best magazine racks in the city. The Cherry Creek location has a fourth-floor restaurant, **The Fourth Story** (303/322-1824) (get it?), serving fish, seafood, wine, martinis, and occasional live jazz music.

HIGHLANDS/NORTHWEST

The Highlands neighborhood is known for its restaurants, but shopping is an unexpected

bonus. A few blocks from the 32nd and Lowell intersection, **Frolik on 32nd** (3715 W. 32nd Ave., 303/458-5575, www.frolikon32nd.com), a women's-clothing boutique in a Victorian house, carries trendy new brands, from $40 Manitoba polar bear T-shirts to Tessuto dresses and Cosabella lingerie. Also in the area is **Babareeba!** (3629 W. 32nd Ave., 303/458-5712), which sells vintage dresses, purses, and jewelry, plus zebra-print blouses and leopard-print caps. But the emerging northwest Denver shopping district is at 44th Avenue and Tennyson Street, where stores such as **The French Flat** (3931 Tennyson St., 720/941-9309, www.frenchflatantiques.com), with its colorful antiques and old photos, could soon rival their LoDo counterparts.

◖ Denver Flagship REI

The REI store (1416 Platte St., 303/756-3100, www.rei.com/stores/denverflagship) is not only a huge warehouse building visible when driving along I-25, it's the flagship for the outdoor-supply chain, with more tents, fishing rods, bicycles, camping stoves, and freeze-dried peas and corn than you could ever possibly want. The store includes a nice climbing wall, a Starbucks, and a third-floor, stream-themed jungle gym for entertaining the kids. Behind the store is the Platte River Greenway, a pretty little spot.

SOUTH DENVER

As with all big cities, Denver has its share of furniture stores, from the huge, traditional, downtown warehouse **Kacey Fine Furniture** (201 Auraria Pkwy., 303/571-5123, www.kacey.com) to the quirky, old-and-new **Paris Loft** (1530A 15th St., 303/571-5638), which lets groups of 10 or more people book private shopping nights. The big antique district is South Broadway, between 1st Avenue and Evans Street, and the **Denver Antique Mall** (827 Corona St., 303/813-1113) is as good a place to start as any.

GREATER DENVER

The next-best mall in the Denver area, after Cherry Creek and 16th Street, is **Colorado**

Mills (14500 W. Colfax Ave., Wheat Ridge, 303/384-3000, www.coloradomills.com), with all the big chains, from Borders to Starbucks. Other fine places to carry a credit card: **Prime Outlets at Castle Rock** (5050 Factory Shops Blvd., Castle Rock, 303/688-2800), about halfway between Denver and Colorado Springs on I-25; **FlatIron Crossing Mall** (1 W. FlatIron Circle, Broomfield, 720/887-9900 or 800/278-1237, www.flatironcrossing.com), with a high-class food court, a dinosaur playground for kids, and an excellent selection of gumball machines, in addition to a Borders Books, Foley's, and Nordstrom; and **Park Meadows Mall** (8401 Park Meadows Center Dr., Littleton, 303/792-2533, www.parkmeadows.com), which has Nordstrom, Dillard's, and JCPenney.

Accommodations

LODO/CENTRAL DENVER
Under $100

The rooms at the **Capitol Hill Mansion Bed & Breakfast Inn** (1207 Pennsylvania, 303/839-5221, www.capitolhillmansion.com, $95–175) are almost as charming as their names: the Elk Thistle Suite, the Shooting Star Balcony Room, the Paintbrush Room, and the Pasque Flower Room, all with vivid touches like a 28-foot alpine-tree mural and a four-poster canopy bed. If you have $455 to kill, or two other couples to share with, consider reserving the entire third floor—a seriously luxurious experience, including a balcony and a whirlpool tub.

Usually, naming rooms after famous painters or musicians is a gimmick, but the **Queen Anne Bed & Breakfast** (2147-51 Tremont Pl., 303/296-6666 or 800/432-4667, www.queenannebandb.com, $95–155) decorates the Alexander Calder Suite, for example, with red, yellow, and blue paintings from the artist himself, along with herky-jerky bedspread colors and diagonally arranged antique furniture. The Norman Rockwell Suite, of course, is more traditional. All 14 of the rooms have writing desks and piped-in classical music, a few have fireplaces, and the overall effect is quirky and artsy.

"As comfortable as you remember grandma's house to be" is the motto of the **Holiday Chalet B&B** (1820 E. Colfax Ave., 303/321-9975 or 800/626-4497, www.bbonline.com/co/holiday, $94–145), and family heirlooms and lacy curtains back it up. In an 1896 Victorian building, the inn has 10 rooms, decorated with elaborate flower-print patterns, antiques, and wicker chairs in the lobby. Sightseeing buses stop out front, a hint that the chalet's clientele tends to be on the older side.

With six rooms named after famous composers—that's Handel, Vivaldi, and Debussy, by the way, not Lennon and McCartney or Jones and Strummer—the **Adagio Bed & Breakfast Hotel** (1430 Race St., www.adagiobb.com, 303/370-6911 or 800/533-3241, $85–175) is in a large 1880s mansion a little removed from downtown. Visitors to City Park attractions like the Denver Zoo will find this the most convenient hotel in town. Everybody else will need a car.

Befitting its name, the **Executive Tower Hotel** (1405 Curtis St., 303/571-0300 or 800/525-6651, www.exectowerhotel.com, $99–109) has basic rooms with generic bedspreads and floor patterns and almost nothing on the walls. Its resources go instead to an on-site fitness center, including one of the largest pools in downtown Denver, an outdoor tennis court, and two indoor racquetball courts.

$100-150
Luxury hotels in downtown Denver are usually large and filled with amenities, but **The Luna Hotel** (1612 Wazee St., 303/572-3300 or 866/724-5862, www.thelunahotel.com, $129–299) has just 20 modern and cozy rooms in its red-brick-facade building at the center of LoDo. No children allowed.

Concentrating on the business customer, **The Warwick Hotel** (1776 Grant St., 303/861-2000, www.warwickdenver.com, $119–149) has 219 extra-large rooms, Internet dataports, and wireless access throughout the hotel, a decent restaurant (Randolph's), and a marble-and-antique elegance.

The Oxford Hotel (1600 17th St., 303/628-5400 or 800/228-5838, www.theoxfordhotel.com, $149–189) is a five-story, red-brick building that truly looks like it came from 1891, when it was built by the same architect who designed the Brown Palace. The rooms are a mixture of art deco and Victorian, with reds and blues all over the place, and in addition to the usual in-room high-speed Internet access and CD players, the hotel's driver will take you out in a hotel Cadillac.

The Burnsley (1000 Grant St., 303/830-1000 or 800/231-3915, www.burnsley.com, $129–149) was a hotel and jazz club in the 1960s, and loyal touring jazz musicians continue to stay here after gigs—the Roy Haynes Quintet, trumpeter Nicholas Payton, and singer-pianist Freddy "Nat's Brother" Cole are among the guests proudly listed on the hotel's webpage. The rooms are all suites, which means they're large and pricey, although the "studio suites" are just 520 square feet and somewhat more affordable.

Although it's part of a (small) chain, the **Magnolia Hotel** (818 17th St., 303/607-9000 or 888/915-1110, www.magnoliahoteldenver.com, $119–199) is one of Denver's most distinctive hotels. Built in a 1906 downtown structure, its rooms are rich in red and brown, large, and thoughtful with fireplaces and perfect spots for baby cribs. Harry's Bar is a swanky, neon spot for drinking martinis.

In a horizontal brick-and-wood building, the **Gregory Inn LoDo** (2500 Arapahoe St., 303/295-6570 or 800/925-6570, www.gregoryinn.com, $119–199) was the last home in Denver to switch from electricity to gas lighting; today its webpage boasts of "the leading edge of fiber optic communications, high-speed computer linkups, and liquid crystal television

projection systems." The eight rooms (plus a more expensive carriage house) are festooned with antiques. None are so old and mysterious as the grave marker underneath a locust tree outside: Kate A. Priole, 19, born in 1886, two years after the home was built. Inn employees can't say why Kate, and not her parents, is buried here.

$150-200

Where the Brown Palace has the pedigree and the Hotel Teatro has the style, **Adam's Mark** (1550 Court Pl., 303/893-3333 or 800/444-2326, www.adamsmark.com/Denver, $184) has the size (and some of that other stuff, too). One of the 25 biggest hotels in the country, the Mark is tall and wide, with 1,225 rooms and 133,000 square feet of meeting space. Although I'm not a fan of the singing waitpeople in the Bravo! Ristorante, I definitely support the Concorde Club, the luxurious top two floors of the hotel, providing a cocktail hour, continental breakfast, hors d'oeuvres, and desserts.

Over $200

The **(Brown Palace** (321 17th St., 303/297-3111 or 800/321-2599, www.brownpalace.com, $235–315) opened in 1892 in a triangular (and brown) high-rise at the center of the city. It has since served Teddy Roosevelt (who wanted a "tub of ice water"), Dwight D. Eisenhower, and countless rock stars, actors, and prime ministers. I once watched as the entire Los Angeles Lakers team, including Shaquille O'Neal and Kobe Bryant, got off a bus and walked to their rooms. Don't let "old" scare you off—the lobby is filled with cozy, vintage couches, waitpeople serving drinks, and wireless Internet access, and the rooms declare not "frilly bed-and-breakfast" but "modern comfort for the business traveler."

With light-colored, almost glowing, rooms, the modern but stately **(Hotel Teatro** (1100 14th St., 303/228-1100 or 888/727-1200, www.hotelteatro.com, $220–390) borrows ambience from the Denver Center Theatre Company across the street (part of the Denver

Performing Arts Complex). The lobby is filled with black-and-white photos of old theater productions, along with props and costumes. One of Denver's top chefs runs two high-end eateries here—Restaurant Kevin Taylor and the healthy-Italian Prima (which replaces Taylor's recently closed Bistro Jou Jou).

The **(Hotel Monaco** (1717 Champa St., 800/990-1303, www.monaco-hotel.com, $230) at first seems like a throwback, located in the 1917 Railway Exchange Building. But it proves super-modern, with pink-and-red-striped lobby walls, an explosion of bright colors in the rooms, and suites named after rocker John Lennon and jazzman Miles Davis. Lonely? Request a goldfish from the front desk.

Directly next to the historic Daniels and Fisher clock tower, at the center of the 16th St. Mall, the recently renovated **Westin Tabor Center** (1672 Lawrence St., 303/572-9100, www.starwoodhotels.com/westin, $249–446) has an indoor-outdoor pool overlooking the Rockies, large rooms with wide beds, concierges who will provide complimentary tickets to weekend Denver Performing Arts Complex shows, and an old-school-fancy, star-pampering, steak-and-seafood restaurant called The Palm.

The **Hyatt Regency Denver** (650 15th St., 303/436-1234, http://denverregency.hyatt.com/hyatt/hotels/index.jsp, $294–314), a tall, rectangular building with 1,100 rooms, opened

in late 2005, with excellent views of the city to go with a classy restaurant (Altitude) and the usual Hyatt stuff. A Hilton is also expected to spring up downtown sometime in 2007.

SOUTH DENVER
$150-200
Loews Denver Hotel (4150 E. Mississippi Ave., 303/782-9300, www.loewshotels.com/hotels/denver, $159–209) one-ups the name-dropping Brown Palace by recalling past guests such as President George W. Bush, Sting, and the New York Giants. The 11-story hotel is old-fashioned Italian, with large classic murals, marble columns, and a facade made of glass and black metal. Despite conveniences like a health club and the Tuscany restaurant, it's a little out of the way, so guests will almost certainly want to rent a car if they're planning to explore downtown Denver.

GREATER DENVER
$100-150
The **Omni Interlocken Resort** (500 Interlocken Blvd., Broomfield, 303/438-6600, www.omnihotels.com, $129–229) is a massive complex off Highway 36 between Denver and Boulder, with 390 rooms, 34,000 square feet of meeting space, and all the trimmings—a highly rated golf course, high-speed Internet in every room, a spa and health club, and an outdoor pool and whirlpool. A little generic, but the views are great.

Food

LODO/CENTRAL DENVER
Snacks, Cafés, and Breakfast
Rocky Mountain Diner (800 18th St., 303/293-8383, www.rockymountaindiner.com, 11 A.M.–10 P.M. Mon.–Thurs., 11 A.M.–11 P.M. Fri.–Sat., 11 A.M.–9 P.M. Sun.) serves comfort food for every meal (try the meatloaf), but it's most famous for Sunday brunch, with pancakes for $8 and *huevos* for $7. "Imagine walking into a diner 100 years ago," boasts the

website, and the wood-brown decor makes a case for it.

(The Market (1445 Larimer Square, 303/534-5140, 6 A.M.–11 P.M. Mon.–Sat., 6 A.M.–10 P.M. Sun.) is the unofficial food anchor of Larimer Square, serving just about everything you could want, deli-style—pastries of all types, sandwiches, potato salad, beef and poultry dishes, natural sodas. Avoid the lunch rush, when it's so packed you can barely move, but otherwise it's a great spot to sit on a rickety wire chair and read a book all afternoon.

Pete's Kitchen (1962 E. Colfax Ave., 303/321-3139, www.petesrestaurantstoo.com/ petesKitchen.html, 24 hours daily) is a classic diner—Mayor John Hickenlooper's favorite, in fact—with a neon sign depicting a jovial, white-hatted chef flipping pancakes. Even if you sit at the counter for the renowned breakfast burritos (or omelets or pancakes), expect a long wait.

Casual

Gloriously basic and cozy, **◖ My Brother's Bar** (2376 15th St., 303/455-9991, 11 A.M.– 2 A.M. Mon.–Sat.) is down the street from REI and serves non-greasy fries and burgers (both beef and buffalo), sandwiches, and, naturally, beer. It's open until 2 A.M., and the tree-covered back porch is the perfect summer drinking spot.

Sam's No. 3 (1500 Curtis St., 303/534-1927, www.samsno3.com, 6 A.M.–9 P.M. Mon., 6 A.M.–10 P.M. Tues.–Thurs., 6 A.M.–midnight Fri., 7 A.M.–midnight Sat., 7 A.M.10 P.M. Sun.) has a menu almost as thick as the phone book, with an emphasis on green chile-covered burritos and potato-filled breakfast skillets. (The "No. 3" refers to original owner Sam Armatas's third of five Coney Islands; his son and grandsons reopened the restaurant in 1998.)

A onetime downtown fixture that relocated to Cherry Creek, then spun off a second restaurant downtown, **Zaidy's Deli** (1512 Larimer St., 303/893-3600, 6:30 A.M.–3 P.M. daily) is the kind of Jewish deli that serves chicken matzoh ball soup and brings a bowl of free pickles to the table.

And speaking of pickles, the **◖ Spicy Pickle Sub Shop** (988 Lincoln St., 303/860-0730, www.spicypickle.com, 10:30 A.M.–7 P.M. Mon.–Thurs., 10:30 A.M.–6 P.M. Fri., 11 A.M.– 6 P.M. Sat.–Sun.) is a Colorado franchise that walks all over Subway and Schlotsky's—try the Sausalito turkey on whole wheat. Also, order an extra-tall beverage because the pickles really are spicy.

A number of local food critics have located

Larimer Square in the heart of LoDo

© MELISSA KNOPPER

Denver's best burger at **CityGrille** (3575 S. Yosemite, 303/694-0454, www.citygrille.com, 11 A.M.–midnight Mon.–Thurs., 11 A.M.– 1 A.M. Fri.–Sat., 2 P.M.–midnight Sun.), which offers a giant steak burger ($8) along with a variety of salads and deli sandwiches.

A grocery store, not a restaurant, **Spinelli's Market** (4621 E. 23rd Ave., 303/329-8143, 9 A.M.–7 P.M. Mon.–Fri., 8 A.M.–6 P.M. Sat., 9 A.M.–3 P.M. Sun.) has nonetheless been serving some of the city's best sandwiches since it opened in a questionable area in 1994. Booming today—both neighborhood and market—Spinelli's is a sort of community center, the kind of place where you'd advertise for a bassist for your band on the wall out front. The meats and cheeses are fresher than Safeway or King Sooper even on Spinelli's worst day.

Modeled after the Place Vendôme square in Paris, **Bistro Vendôme** (1424-H Larimer Square, 303/825-3232, www.bistrovendome.com, 10 A.M.–2 P.M. and 5–10 P.M. Sun., 5–10 P.M. Tues.–Thurs., 10 A.M.2 P.M. and 5–11 P.M. Fri.–Sat.) is as French as anything you'll find in Denver and a lot more easygoing than France itself. Chef Eric Roeder's goal is "French soul food," and he achieves this with dishes such as rabbit blanquette with truffles and fava beans ($21). You expected maybe grits and collard greens?

Racines Restaurant (650 Sherman St., 303/595-0418, www.grdeating.com/racines, 7 A.M.–11 P.M. Mon., 7 A.M.–midnight Tues.– Fri., 8 A.M.–midnight Sat., 8 A.M.–11 P.M. Sun.) has a massive menu of salads, steaks, fajitas, and seafood, but its greatest strength is dessert—15 items, from peach cobbler and banana cream pie to a famous brownie parfait with almost as many strawberries as pieces of brownie.

Steakhouses

It's hard to walk a step in central Denver without running into a decent steakhouse—among the best are: **The Palm Restaurant** (1672 Lawrence St., 303/825-7256, www.thepalm.com, 11 A.M.–11 P.M. Mon.–Fri., 5–11 P.M. Sat., 5–10 P.M. Sun.), in the Westin Hotel; the **Buckhorn Exchange** (1000 Osage St., 303/534-9505, www.buckhorn.com, 11 A.M.–2 P.M. and 5:30–9 P.M. Mon.–Thurs., 11 A.M.–2 P.M. and 5–10 P.M. Fri., 5–10 P.M. Sat., 5–9 P.M. Sun.); and **Denver ChopHouse & Brewery** (1735 19th St. #100, 303/296-0800, www.rockbottomrestaurantsinc.com, 11 A.M.–close daily). But I recommend **The Capital Grille** (1450 Larimer St., 303/539-2500, www.thecapitalgrille.com, 11:30 A.M.–2:30 P.M. and 5–10 P.M. Mon.– Thurs., 11:30 A.M.–2:30 P.M. and 5–11 P.M. Fri., 5–11 P.M. Sat., 4–9 P.M. Sun.) for its dry-aged steaks, plus creative high-class appetizers like caviar and pan-fried calamari with cherry tomatoes. And while **Morton's of Chicago** (1710 Wynkoop St., 303/825-3353, 5:30–11 P.M. Mon.–Sat., 5–10 P.M. Sun.) is one of the larger chain steakhouses, that just means its employees are really, really good at bringing slabs of raw porterhouse and filet mignon to your table before cooking it with béarnaise sauce or *au poivre*.

Asian

With its neon sign and plain-brick location on South Broadway, **Imperial Chinese** (431 S. Broadway, 303/698-2800, www.imperialchinese.com, 11 A.M.–10 P.M. Mon.–Thurs., 11 A.M.–10:30 P.M. Fri., noon–10:30 P.M. Sat., 4–10 P.M. Sun.) looks from a distance like a fast-food joint. It's actually one of the nicest Chinese restaurants in Denver, with goldfish and fountains gleaming in a large, red room and some of the best spring rolls and dumplings in town. They're not kidding when they say the sesame chicken ($10) is spicy.

Tuk Tuk Thai Wraps (605 Grant St., 303/988-5885, www.tuktukrocks.com, 11 A.M.–9:30 P.M. daily), named for a three-wheeled taxi service in Thailand, is your basic Thai restaurant—pad thai ($6), panang chicken ($5), and the like. Only everything is wrapped in a flour tortilla. Top it off with an iced Thai coffee.

Two of the best sushi restaurants in town are **Sushi Den** (1487 S. Pearl St., 303/777-0826, www.sushiden.net, 11:30 A.M.– 2:30 P.M. and 4:30–10:30 P.M. Mon.–Thurs., 11:30 A.M.–2:30 P.M. and 4:30 P.M.–midnight Fri., 4:30 P.M.–midnight Sat., 5–10:30 P.M. Sun.), which has employees to regularly handpick fresh fish in Japan and ship it to Denver, and **Sushi Tazu** (300 Fillmore St., 303/320-1672, www.sushitazu.com, 11:30 A.M.–2:30 P.M. and 4:30–10 P.M. Mon.–Thurs., 11:30 A.M.– 2:30 P.M. and 4:30–11 P.M. Fri., 11:30 A.M.– 11 P.M. Sat., noon–10 P.M. Sun.), which serves rice balls, halibut, and the standard sushi stuff with just the right feel and proportions.

Mexican/Southwestern

"Modern Mexican" is the catchphrase at **(Tamayo** (1400 Larimer St., 720/946-1433, www.modernmexican.com/tamayode, 11:30 A.M.–2:30 P.M. and 5–close Mon.–Fri., 5–close Sat.–Sun.), owing to owner-chef Richard Sandoval's style, both here and at New York City's Pampano and San Francisco's Maya. Some find this white-tablecloth restaurant a little pretentious in a heavily Hispanic city filled with all kinds of Mexican restaurants. But the guacamole ($8) and margaritas are truly among the best in town, and I can't get enough of the corn-covered *pechuga adobada* chicken breast ($19) and the fruit-filled *empanadas* for dessert.

Mezcal (3230 E. Colfax Ave., 303/322-5219, 11 A.M.–2 A.M. Mon.–Fri., 10 A.M.–2 A.M. Sat.–Sun.) is a Tijuana-style restaurant with a super-hip bar that specializes in local-hero chef Sean Yontz's tamales and $1 tacos, plus what the *Rocky Mountain News* calls "one of the finest house margaritas in Denver." The kitchen is open late.

Italian

Although chef Jennifer Jasinski moved on in 2004 to open Rioja, her innovations live on at the Hotel Monaco's **Panzano** (909 17th St., 303/296-3525, www.panzano-denver.com, 7–10 A.M., 11 A.M.–2:30 P.M., 5–10 P.M. Mon.–Thurs.; 7–10 A.M., 11 A.M.–2:30 P.M., 5–11 P.M. Fri.; 8 A.M.–2:30 P.M., 5–11 P.M. Sat.; 8 A.M.–2:30 P.M., 4:30–9:30 P.M. Sun.), whose elaborate menu includes a risotto and *fagioli borlotti,* plus multiple interpretations of mussels, chicken, mushrooms, and everything else that goes with pasta. The pastry-dominated Sunday brunch is also excellent.

Speaking of chef Jasinski, **《 Rioja** (1431 Larimer St., 303/820-2282, www.riojadenver.com, 5–10 P.M. Mon.–Tues., 11:30 A.M.–2:30 P.M. and 5–10 P.M. Wed.–Thurs., 11:30 A.M.–2:30 P.M. and 5–11 P.M. Fri., 11 A.M.–2:30 P.M. and 5–11 P.M. Sat., 11 A.M.–2:30 P.M. and 5–10 P.M. Sun.) is her attempt to reproduce Panzano according to her own personal style—everything's homemade, notably the mozzarella in prosciutto and oven-baked chicken.

Denver's top three pizza joints are (in this order, and if you don't believe me, go find your own): **Basil Doc's** (various locations, including 2170 E. Virginia, 303/778-7747, www.basil-docspizzeria.com, 4:30–10 P.M. daily), which has thin, gushy crusts, small chunks of fruity tomatoes in the sauce, unusually fresh ingredients, and offbeat, mildly spicy flavorings befitting the restaurant name; **BeauJo's** (2710 S. Colorado Blvd., 303/758-1519, www.beaujos.com, 11 A.M.– 9 P.M. Sun.–Thurs., 11 A.M.–9:30 P.M. Fri.–Sat.), whose thick crusts (perfect with honey) might have topped this list if the quaint wooden-wall ambience of the Idaho Springs outlet were somehow harnessed in the South Denver or Westminster location; and **Proto's Pizzeria Napoletana** (2401 15th St., 720/855-9400, 11 A.M.–10 P.M. daily), which lets you watch as the cooks shove the super-thin crusts and salad-fresh ingredients into the huge ovens.

Seafood

In the basement on Larimer Square, the **Del Mar Crab House** (1453 Larimer St., 303/825-4747, www.delmardenver.com, 11:30 A.M.–10 P.M. daily) serves seafood, seafood, seafood—Maine lobsters, Maryland crab cakes, Alaskan halibut.

Upscale

Run by another Denver celebrity chef, Frank Bonanno, **《 Mizuna** (225 E. 7th Ave., 303/832-4778, www.mizunadenver.com, 5–10 P.M. Tues.–Sat.) is a mixture of French, Italian, Asian, and American styles, with a particular emphasis on butters and creams (but not in a fatty kind of way). The secret ingredient in the Macaroni and Cheese appetizer ($15) is lobster. Bonanno, by the way, also runs **Luca D'Italia** (711 Grant St., 303/832-6600, www.lucadenver.com, 5–10 P.M. Tues.–Sat.), which twists traditional Italian dishes with unexpected ingredients—chicken liver ravioli ($8), for example, or rabbit three ways ($19).

Venerable **Restaurant Kevin Taylor** (1100 14th St., 303/820-2600, www.restaurantkevin-taylor.com, 5–10 P.M. daily) rests on the 15-year reputation of its namesake chef (who also runs Dandelion in Boulder and Palettes in the Denver Art Museum). The titles tell the story: roasted broken arrow ranch axis venison, with black truffle brioche pudding and caramelized apples ($36). It's in the Hotel Teatro downtown.

Some say the concept overwhelms the actual food at **《 Vesta Dipping Grill** (1822 Blake St., 303/296-1970, www.vestagrill.com, 5–10 P.M. Sun.–Thurs., 5–11 P.M. Fri.–Sat.), where almost everything on the menu comes in small bites with a variety of fruity, spicy, and creamy salsas and sauces. I love the place. It recalls Spanish *tapas* and Asian *dim sum,* only with more flavors (try the pineapple basil salsa and the Blake St. barbecue sauce together and listen to your tongue explode) and different things (chips and pita) for dipping.

CHERRY CREEK
American

The heart of **Cherry Cricket** (2641 E. 2nd Ave., 303/322-7666, www.cherrycricket.com, 11 A.M.–midnight daily) is steak and burgers— beware the "very well done," in which "moderation is thrown to the wind." But the lengthy menu also includes a hot meatloaf sandwich ($7), beef burritos ($8), and many-sized bowls of pork-filled green chile.

Owned by Charles Master, son of Mel Master, who owns Mel's down the street, **Brix** (3000 E. 3rd Ave., 303/333-3355, 4 P.M.–midnight Mon.–Sat., 4–10 P.M. Sun.) strips comfort food down to its essence—"a rather special hot dog" (with a large pickle, of course), chocolate pudding with whipped cream, beef stew, fish and chips, and the like. Following the family bloodline, **Mel's Restaurant and Bar** (235 Fillmore St., 303/333-3979, www.melsbarandgrill.com, 11:30 A.M.–2:30 P.M. and 5:30–10 P.M. Mon.–Thurs., 11:30 A.M.–2:30 P.M. and 5:30–10:30 P.M. Fri.–Sat., 5–9 P.M. Sun.) is also comforting, but in a fancier way, with roasted salmon cakes ($12) and rock shrimp ceviche-stuffed avocado ($14). Burgers, too.

Italian

Amore (2355 E. 3rd Ave., 303/321-2066, www.amoredenver.com, 11 A.M.–2 P.M. and 5–10 P.M. Mon.–Thurs., 11 A.M.–2 P.M. and 5–11 P.M. Fri.–Sat., 10 A.M.–2 P.M. and 5–10 P.M. Sun.) is a cozy Italian bistro where the owner occasionally wanders the restaurant to mingle with the customers. Seafood is the specialty, but I once had a tremendous *ravioli con asparagi* ($17) with sautéed sweet corn, and equally great minestrone soup.

HIGHLAND/NORTHWEST

I admit to a certain bias when writing about Highlands, the northwest Denver neighborhood about a mile and a half from LoDo. My family bought a house here in late 2001, near the intersection of Lowell Boulevard and West 32nd Avenue, where no less than 15 restaurants, from a corporate Chipotle to the distinctively local Julia Blackbird's, sit within a few hundred yards. Although weighed down with gangs and crack in the early 1990s, the neighborhood made a comeback with the Internet boom, and its solid 19th-century Victorian homes, proximity to downtown, and foundation of immigrant families make it unlikely to fall again anytime soon. (Or so housing prices would indicate.) The cuddly coffee shop Common Grounds and down-to-earth deli Heidi's took root a decade ago, and stroller-pushing hipsters have long since followed.

Breakfast, Cafés, and Snacks

Mayor John Hickenlooper is one of the many local businesspeople who hold meetings at the homey coffee shop **⟨⟨ Common Grounds** (3484 W. 32nd Ave., 303/458-5248, 6:30 A.M.–10 P.M. Mon.–Thurs., 6:30 A.M.–11 P.M. Fri.–Sat., open later during summer). Show up early for the foil-wrapped breakfast burritos, then commandeer a spot near the piano. Kids love the board games in the back room.

Denver Bread Company (3200 Irving St., 303/455-7194, 10 A.M.–6 P.M. Mon.–Fri., 9 A.M.–5 P.M. Sat.) is a brick-walled Highlands fixture that contains no comfy couches for customers to enjoy their fragrant homemade loaves. So grab the sourdough, rye, focaccia, and Swedish peasant breads to go.

Casual

Once a biker bar, **Mead Street Station** (3625 W. 32nd Ave., 303/433-2138, www.meadststation.com, 11 A.M.–midnight Mon.–Sat.) is a dark, loud, smoky neighborhood joint that just happens to have great food—try the portobello mushroom wraps ($8) and the vegetarian chili ($5). Live bands play occasionally.

Heidi's Brooklyn Deli (3130 Lowell Blvd., 303/477-2605, www.heidisbrooklyndeli.com, 7 A.M.–10 P.M. daily) has seven Denver locations, but none more prominent than this one, the quirky white centerpiece of the bustling 32nd-and-Lowell restaurant district. The bread and bagels are baked fresh daily—try the ciabatta—the plastic-wrapped brownies and muffins are surprisingly fresh, and the ice cream is a nice bonus. The only drawback is the service; why thriving Heidi's doesn't spend the money for more sandwich-makers, especially during the lunch rush, is a mystery to all Highlands residents. Go during off-hours.

Mexican/Southwestern

Down the street from North High School, in the rising Potter Highlands neighborhood, ((**Taqueria Patzcuaro** (2616 W. 32nd Ave., 303/455-4389, 11 A.M.–8:30 P.M. daily) is cheap (entrées are $3–10), greasy, totally no-nonsense, and delicious. The basic burritos, enchiladas, and mouth-burning green salsa, along with thick guacamole and a variety of fish, pork, beef, and chicken, are a match for the wooden tables and chile-stained menus.

Jack-N-Grill (2524 Federal Blvd., 303/964-9544, 9 A.M.–9 P.M. Mon.–Fri., 9 A.M.–10 P.M. Sat.–Sun.) lost a smidgen of charm when it expanded its building and modernized its facade on the side of bustling Federal Boulevard. But it didn't lose any burrito heft—these things are gigantic, sloppy with cheese and the house-specialty green chile, and the freshly cooked chiles rellenos and enchiladas are among the best in town.

Never mind the strawberry lemonade arriving in fluorescent pink cups. **Julia Blackbird's New Mexican Café** (3617 W. 32nd Ave., 303/433-2688, 11 A.M.–3 P.M. and 5–9 P.M. Tues.–Sat.) is worthy of discerning, Latino-populated northwest Denver. The feta-cheese-and-pinto-bean-covered enchiladas are spicy, but not as spicy as the incredible salsa, which comes with fresh blue-and-yellow corn chips and which my family takes home by the carton. The restaurant recently relocated into a room twice the size, down the street, but probably could use even more space.

Brazilian

((**Café Brazil** (4408 Lowell Blvd., 303/480-1877, 5–10 P.M. Tues.–Sat.) is a colorful little restaurant with fruity, spicy salsas and appetiz-ers (the black bean soup is especially great) that match the owners' enthusiasm and the boisterous conversational buzz you notice as soon as you step inside. The entrées can be a little expensive, but the jumbo shrimp and fried bananas are certainly worth the splurge. Make reservations in advance or you won't get in, especially on a weekend.

Italian

((**Parisi** (4401 Tennyson St., 303/561-0234, 11 A.M.–9 P.M. Mon.–Sat.) once was a small Italian market, selling pre-made frozen pizzas and gourmet meats and olives in a nondescript room across the street from a Safeway. But it recently moved to 44th Avenue and Tennyson Street, a growing district several blocks from 32nd and Lowell, and today it anchors the entire neighborhood. Its menu is long and diverse, from eggplant-and-portobello panini sandwiches to a smooth risotto Milanese. Two tips: They'll give serious dirty looks if you try to make pizza substitutions, and show up before 6 P.M. to avoid long lines.

American

Don't make the tourist mistake of walking through the front door at **Bang!** (3472 W. 32nd Ave., 303/455-1117, 5–10 P.M. Tues.–Sat.); the way in is a narrow alley just west of the pastel-colored facade. Weird layouts aside, the house specialty is high-end comfort food, such as meatloaf and gingerbread.

Denver isn't known for its barbecue, but the bright-red **Brickyard BBQ** (4243 W. 38th Ave., 303/561-4875, 11 A.M.–9 P.M. daily) has a nice sauce, plus the usual trimmings of ribs, chicken, baked beans, white bread, and corn. Plus, the musical and photographic themes of Billie Holiday and Louis Armstrong create a nice atmosphere—even if it isn't enough to make you feel like you're eating in Texas or Louisiana.

Upscale

The most high-end restaurant on the 32nd Avenue corridor, **Highland's Garden Café** (3927 W. 32nd Ave., 303/458-5920, www.highlandsgardencafe.com, 11 A.M.–2 P.M. and 5–9 P.M.

Tues.–Fri., 5–9 P.M. Sat., 10 A.M.–2 P.M. and 4–8 P.M. Sun.) serves pan-seared halibut, vegetarian five-cheese lasagna, and grilled quail inside a beautiful, roomy old house and adjoining, tree-lined patio.

SOUTH DENVER
Asian
South Federal Boulevard is a hidden vault of Asian restaurants in Denver, and while the service and ambience don't quite approach the Chinese and Thai restaurants closer to downtown—many of them are located in nondescript strip malls—the food is generally superb. **Ocean City Seafood Restaurant** (1098 S. Federal Blvd., 303/936-1000, 11 A.M.–midnight daily) has the usual Chinese dishes but adds surprising menu touches like oysters and honey walnut shrimp. **JJ Chinese Restaurant** (1048 S. Federal Blvd., 303/934-8888, 11:30 A.M.–midnight Wed.–Mon.) will scare the bejeesus out of you by responding to a crab order by fishing a live one out of a tank—but it's worth it. And so is the calamari. **(Pho 79** (781 S. Federal Blvd., 303/922-2930, 9 A.M.–9 P.M. daily) is a super-cheap (entrées are in the $5 range) traditional Vietnamese place to get warm chicken broth and vegetable-filled rice-noodle bowls, with or without hunks of meat.

American
Dedria and Joe Catalano of **Nonna's Chicago Bistro** (6603 Leetsdale Dr., 303/399-2000, 11 A.M.–2:30 P.M. and 5–8:30 P.M. Mon.–Thurs., 11 A.M.–2:30 P.M. and 5–10 P.M. Fri., 5–10 P.M. Sat., 5 –8:30 P.M. Sun.) owned restaurants in Littleton and Greenwood Village before opening this Italian comfort-food place that specializes in hot, homemade bread and thick red sauces. *5280* magazine's editors awarded Nonna's "Top Spaghetti and Meatballs" in summer 2005.

Indian
(India's Restaurant (3333 S. Tamarac Dr., 303/755-4284, 11:30 A.M.–2:15 P.M. and 5:30–9 P.M. Mon.–Thurs., 11:30 A.M.–2:15 P.M.

and 5:30–9:45 P.M. Fri., noon–2:15 P.M. and 5:30–9:45 P.M. Sat., 5:30–9 P.M. Sun.), in a strip mall, has beautifully spiced and frustratingly filling dishes—from tandoori chicken to coconut shrimp curry, with green and red sauces perfectly capturing sweet and spicy. Show up for the lunch buffet, if only for the garlic naan bread.

Mexican
El Noa Noa Restaurant (722 Santa Fe Dr., 303/623-9968, 9 A.M.–10 P.M. daily) is a standard Mexican restaurant—burritos, guacamole—with two major distinctions. First, the margaritas. Second, the patio garden.

Ethiopian
Denver has several superb Ethiopian restaurants, all of which teach American diners an entirely new way of eating: Rather than using spoons, they scoop up the main dishes with their fingers and a squishy kind of bread known as *injera*. The two best are **Abyssinia Market Café Ethiopian Restaurant** (4116 E. Colfax Ave., 303/316-8830, 4–10 P.M. Mon.–Thurs., 11 A.M.–10 P.M. Fri.–Sun.), which emphasizes garlic and ginger spices, and **Arada** (3504 E. Colfax Ave., 303/329-3344, 11 A.M.–11 P.M. daily), which is tasty, but its real edge is quantity (huge piles of lamb wot, ground beef, and liver dulet, and a very heavy spinach dish).

Dessert
The beloved **Bonnie Brae Ice Cream** (799 S. University Blvd., 303/777-0808, 11 A.M.–10 P.M. Mon.–Thurs., 11 A.M.–11 P.M. Fri.–Sun.) has been drawing long lines since 1986 for its heavy, sugary ice cream, from apple pie to triple-death chocolate to, yes, vanilla.

GREATER DENVER
Denver's suburbs aren't as far away as you'd think—Wheat Ridge is just a 10-minute drive from LoDo, and Englewood is practically indistinguishable from much of south Denver. And while none of the surrounding towns has the restaurant volume of the big city, each has at least one or two places worth a meal.

Tiny Parker is the last place you'd expect to find an upscale Japanese-and-French (yes, Japanese *and* French) restaurant, but **Junz** (1121 S. Dransfeldt Rd., Ste. 100, Parker, www.junzrestaurant.com, 720/851-1005, 11:30 A.M.–2:30 P.M. and 5–9 P.M. Sun.–Thurs., 11:30 A.M.–2:30 P.M. and 5–9:30 P.M. Fri.–Sat.) pulls off the unique combination. It serves sushi and filet mignon ($24), chicken teriyaki ($15) and lamb chops with rosemary potatoes ($22). All are excellent.

Although **Bloom** (1 W. Flatiron Circle, Broomfield, 720/887-2800, www.foxrestaurantconcepts.com/bloomco.html, 11 A.M.–3 P.M. and 5–9 P.M. Sun.–Thurs., 5–10 P.M. Fri.–Sat.) is a chain restaurant in a suburban shopping mall, it's the best chain restaurant in a suburban shopping mall. The green-apple martinis are an excellent way to psych yourself up for the meal, and my favorite dish is bow-tie pasta with chicken, spinach, and sun-dried tomatoes.

With appetizers of *kado* (pan-fried squash and pumpkin), *homus,* and *dal* (lentils), and straightforward entrées like chicken and lamb, the Afghan restaurant **Kabul Kabob** (11002 E. Yale Ave., Aurora, 303/750-6020, 11 A.M.–2:30 P.M. and 4:30–9 P.M. Mon. and Wed.–Thurs., 1:30–10 P.M. Fri., 11 A.M.–10 P.M. Sat., noon–8 P.M. Sun.) has an enthusiastic staff, Turkish coffee in lieu of alcohol, and some of the best baklava in town (as *5280* magazine attests).

Also in Aurora is **Café Paprika** (13160 E. Mississippi Ave., Aurora, 303/755-4150, 11 A.M.–3 P.M. and 5–9:30 P.M. Mon.–Thurs. and Sat., 4–9:30 P.M. Fri.), one of the best Middle Eastern restaurants in the Denver area, which makes its hummus, baba ghanoush, and chicken, lamb, and fish *tajines* available for take-out.

Seared tuna peanut butter and jelly. That's right, seared tuna peanut butter and jelly. For this dish, at **Opus Restaurant** (2575 W. Main St., Littleton, 303/703-6787, www.restauranteur.com/opus, 11 A.M.–2:30 P.M. and 5–10 P.M. Mon.–Thurs., 11 A.M.–2:30 P.M. and 5–11 P.M.

Sat., 9 A.M.–2:30 P.M. Sun.), *Westword* food critic Jason Sheehan praises head chef Michael Long's "necessary revolutionary spirit of New American cuisine." The menu is incredibly long, careening through eggs Carolina (with pecan biscuits, ham, and gravy, $11), mushroom escargot tart (with blue cheese, garlic, and spinach, $11), and French-fried Florida lobster ($35).

Located in a suburban strip mall, **240 Union** (240 Union Blvd., Lakewood, 303/989-3562, www.240union.com, 11 A.M.–3:30 P.M. and 5–10 P.M. Mon.–Thurs., 11 A.M.–3:30 P.M. Fri., 5–10:30 P.M. Sat., 5–9 P.M. Sun.) has a huge dining room and an almost-as-large open kitchen and a knack for spicy chipotle sauces. The entrées are mostly fish and beef, but curveballs like Israeli couscous ($14), baba ghanoush ($8), and Sichuan duck pizza with shiitake mushrooms ($11) add to the broadly international feel.

Twin Dragon Restaurant (3021 S. Broadway, Englewood, 303/781-8068, www.twindragonrestaurant.com, 11 A.M.–9:45 P.M. Mon.–Thurs., 11 A.M.–10:15 P.M. Fri., noon–10:15 P.M. Sat., 4:30–9:45 P.M. Sun.) is in many ways like every other Chinese restaurant—noodle bowls, egg rolls, egg foo yong—but it's also a rare gem whose take-out food is just as hot and flavorful as its sit-down meals.

TV Cuisine (4980 Kipling St., Wheat Ridge, 303/432-9264, 11 A.M.–9 P.M. daily), or "Thai and Vietnamese," is well known for its generous portions—coconut milk, lemongrass, *tom ka gai* soup, and so forth.

Greenwood Village is basically a bunch of office buildings and the outdoor Coors Amphitheatre, but, of course, office workers and rock 'n' roll roadies have to eat. The **Cool River Café** (8000 E. Belleview Ave., Suite C10, Greenwood Village, 303/771-4117, http://coolrivercafe.com/Denver/index.htm, 11 A.M.–10 P.M. Mon.–Thurs., 11 A.M.–11 P.M. Fri.–Sat.) has pool tables and a cigar-and-cognac lounge, plus steak, seafood, poultry, and what *5280* considers the best smoked-pork sandwich in the city.

Information and Services

The main number for Denver's city government is 720/913-4900, and www.denvergov.org has numerous resources, from parks to police. Also helpful is the **Denver Chamber of Commerce** (1445 Market St., 303/534-8500, www.denverchamber.org) and the **Denver Tourism Guide** (www.denver.org). The city's major newspapers include the *Rocky Mountain News* (www.rockymountainnews.com), *The Denver Post* (www.denverpost.com), and the alternative weekly *Westword*, plus neighborhood publications such as the *North Denver Tribune*.

Getting There and Around

Denver International Airport (DIA, 8500 Pena Blvd., 303/342-2000, www.flydenver.com) opened in 1995 as a state-of-the-art hub for almost every major airline. Its early controversies, like a shaky baggage system and traffic-slowing toll roads, are almost completely resolved, and DIA, built on 53 square miles with fancy-looking tepee structures on top, is one of the most comfortable and easiest major airports in the United States. Little touches like windmill art in the train tunnels and decent restaurants in the food courts make all the difference to weary and occasionally frightened travelers.

Within Denver, the **Regional Transportation District** (RTD, 1600 Blake St., 303/628-9000, www.rtd-denver.com) is an effective bus service—RTD is not as reliable, or relied-upon, as bus networks in Chicago or New York City, but at $1.50 for a monthly pass you can't beat the price.

As for traffic and congestion, Denver's highways aren't nearly as bad as those in Los Angeles, Chicago, or Washington, D.C., but they have their moments, especially during rush hour. The **Transportation Expansion Project,** or T-REX, has congested the roads for the last several years, but its light-rail service and various other benefits are expected to be completed in September 2006.

All the major car-rental companies, including Hertz, Budget, Enterprise, Avis, and Alamo, have outlets in Denver. Contact them at DIA. The rental-car website, containing all the phone numbers, is www.flydenver.com/gt/rental.asp, and the airport's ground transportation staff can be reached at 303/342-4059 or 800/247-2336.

Morrison

With a population of 427, Morrison is hardly a teeming mountain metropolis. But it does have Red Rocks Amphitheatre, which many traveling musicians consider the most spectacular outdoor arena in the United States—the Beatles and U2, to name just a few, have played legendary shows here. Founded in 1874 as a railroad town—it was supposed to be an important hub but wound up as a last stop—Morrison is tiny and beautiful and its "downtown" area is filled with restaurants and shops catering to concertgoers. Thanks to Red Rocks, it's also a haven for hikers and cyclists.

(A CONCERT AT RED ROCKS AMPHITHEATRE

Red Rocks (2605 Red Rocks Park Rd., 303/697-5968, www.redrocksonline.com) is the site of numerous rock 'n' roll happenings—perhaps most famously, U2's June 5,

© AMY STOREY

Red Rocks Ampitheatre is one of the top concert venues in the country.

1983, concert in which singer Bono declared, "This song is not a rebel song; this song is 'Sunday, Bloody Sunday.'" (The show became legendary after U2 turned it into an album and concert video called *Under the Blood Red Sky*.) The Beatles, Bruce Springsteen, the Pretenders, R.E.M., Sonic Youth, Wilco, Norah Jones, and others too numerous to mention have performed here in their prime, and almost every one comes away marveling at the giant sandstone boulders surrounding the stage and the natural quality of the acoustics.

SPORTS AND RECREATION

Red Rocks Park (5 A.M.–11 P.M. daily, free), surrounding the concert amphitheater, is great

for hikers and cyclists—the 1.4-mile Trading Post trail goes straight up, and while the evening primrose and deer herds are nice to look at, the actual rocks are the main draw. Nearby is **Dinosaur Ridge** (16831 W. Alameda Pkwy., 303/697-3466, www.dinoridgc.org, 9 A.M.–5 P.M. Mon.–Sat., noon–5 P.M. Sun., free), a visitors center where, in 1877, scientists discovered 145 million-year-old brontosaurus, diplodocus, stegosaurus, and other fossils. The ridge has guided tours, classes, and a gift shop. Across from the park is **Mt. Falcon Park** (Hwy. 8, Morrison exit), with a slew of easy-to-find trails, trees, and water.

The *other* big attraction in tiny Morrison is **Bandimere Speedway** (3051 S. Rooney Rd., 303/697-6001, www.bandimere.com), an official course for National Hot Rod Association championship drag racing during the summer, plus events from motorcycling to extreme snowmobiling throughout the year.

FOOD

Inspired by Bent's Fort, the 1830s trading post on the Santa Fe Trail, Samuel P. Arnold built a fort-like home here in 1962 and installed a restaurant on the lower floor—**The Fort** (19192 Highway 8, 303/697-4771, www.thefort.com, 5:30–10 P.M. Mon.–Fri., 5–10 P.M. Sat., 5–9 P.M. Sun.), which serves hefty slabs of beef, poultry, and game (in the $35–50 range, along with an irresistible dish called peanut butter stuffed jalapeños *escabeche*.

INFORMATION AND SERVICES

The **Town of Morrison** (321 Highway 8, 303/697-8749, http://town.morrison.co.us/contact.php) will answer most of your questions, even about Red Rocks.

Golden

Once a rival to Denver for territorial capital status in Colorado—this was in the 1860s—Golden has since slipped into a comfortable zone as a sleepy mountain town with plenty of heavy industry and jobs. The most interesting of these are at the Coors Brewery, built in 1873, and the engineering-oriented Colorado School of Mines, emblazoned with a giant "M" on the side of a mountain. It's easily accessible from both Boulder (about 20 miles via Highway 93) and Denver (20 miles via Highway 58), and its historical sites are among the richest in the greater Denver metropolitan area.

SIGHTS

Everything in Colorado seems to be named after Coors—baseball's Coors Field, the outdoor Coors Amphitheatre, the University of Colorado's Coors Event Center, onetime U.S. Senate candidate Pete Coors, and, especially, the **Coors Brewery** (13th St. and Ford St., 303/279-6565, www.coors.com, 10 A.M.–4 P.M. Mon.–Sat.), which Prussian-born Adolph Coors founded here in 1873. The brewery offers free 30-minute tours throughout weekdays, and, yes, those over 21 are given free samples at the end. Some 250,000 take these tours every year, which seems like a lot until you consider the company sells 32.7 million *barrels* (that's 31 gallons each) of beer per year.

The mountainside **Colorado School of Mines** (1500 Illinois St., 303/273-3000, www.mines.edu) has a world-class mineral-engineering program, which isn't exactly what makes it a fun campus to visit. (And *The Princeton Review* recently named it the campus with the unhappiest students.) In addition to the hijinks of hard-partying engineers, CSM has a **Geology Museum** (303/273-3823, 9 A.M.–4 P.M. Mon.–Sat., 1–4 P.M. Sun., free), containing 50,000 minerals and fossils of every shape, size, color and international origin. Also on campus is the **U.S.G.S. Earthquake Information Center** (1711 Illinois St.,

303/273-8430, tours 9–11 A.M. and 1–3 P.M. Tues.–Thurs., call first to schedule), which quickly determines data about the world's earthquakes and sends out information to the relevant agencies everywhere.

Buffalo Bill's Gravesite and Museum (987½ Lookout Mountain Rd., 303/526-0747, www.buffalobill.org, 9:30 A.M.–5 P.M. daily May–Oct., 9 A.M.–4 P.M. Tues.–Sun. Nov.–Apr., $3) is the final resting spot of Col. William F. "Buffalo Bill" Cody, the Old West trapper, frontiersman, and Civil War scout who starred in plays about his own exploits. The museum, on top of Lookout Mountain, has incredible views, and some people visit this area just for the hiking—numerous trails are at the top of Lookout Mountain, as well as the **Jefferson County Nature Center** (700 Jefferson County Pkwy., 303/271-5925).

Any kid who ever picked up a Thomas Train will enjoy the **Colorado Railroad Museum** (17155 W. 44th Ave., 303/279-4591 or 800/365-6263, www.crrm.org, 9 A.M.–5 P.M. daily, $7), in an 1880s-style depot stocked with a 317-ton Burlington locomotive, a 1937 stainless-steel observation car from the Santa Fe Super Chief, various vintage equipment, an art gallery, and a gift shop.

Golden has many other historic areas. **Heritage Square** (between I-70 and W. 6th Ave. on U.S. 40, 303/279-2789, noon–5 P.M. Tues.–Fri., noon–6 P.M. Sat.–Sun., hours vary by season) re-creates a late-1800s village in Victorian style (in addition to its alpine slide). The **American Alpine Club** (710 10th St., 303/384-0110) has a 17,000-volume library devoted to all things mountain. **Clear Creek History Park** and **Astor House Museum** (822 12th St., 303/278-3557, www.clearcreekhistorypark.org) make up a complex with an 1860s-era replica prospectors' park and Victorian-style 1890s-era hotel. And **12th Street** is a National Historic District of late-19th-century brick buildings, including the **National Guard Armory** at 13th and Arapahoe.

ENTERTAINMENT

Golden's **Buffalo Rose** (1119 Washington Ave., 303/278-6800, www.buffalorose.net) is a classic mountain bar, with wooden walls and furniture and diehard Broncos fans who loyally show up every Sunday in the fall. It's also a surprisingly great concert venue, drawing up-and-coming local bands (mostly of the jam-rock or acoustic-folk variety) and excellent has-beens such as The Fixx and Molly Hatchet.

INFORMATION AND SERVICES

The **City of Golden** (1445 10th St., 303/384-8151, http://ci.golden.co.us/Index.asp) website is focused on water lines and planning-board meetings, but it's somewhat useful for visitors.

Central City/Black Hawk

Until 1991, these twin mountain towns were quaint, historic, Old West mining areas—they celebrated and replicated the 1880s, when somebody discovered gold in western Kansas territory and prospectors in raggedy tents spilled into the area known as Gregory's Gulch. But by the mid-20th century, long after the miners disappeared, both towns were in decline, with little money to maintain buildings and roads.

Low-stakes gambling—meaning you can't bet more than $5 on one hand—rescued Central City and Black Hawk from permanent Ghostville. Suddenly, given the growing number of corporate casinos, huge hotels, and buffet-style restaurants, the towns were tourist destinations, with the added bonus that visitors could go to historic sites such as the Central City Opera House or the Thomas House Museum.

Although some anti-gambling crusaders continue to criticize Central City and Black Hawk for selling out to vice and establishing a "poor tax" on Colorado residents, it's obvious the towns are revitalized. Their main drags have old-fashioned candy and souvenir shops and capture the spirit of debauched miner settlements. Plus, the casinos are well-kept, the gambling is fun, and country-and-imitator bands provide the cornball entertainment. Central City was initially the dominant gambling area, but its sibling town has since taken over much of the business—and that may change again, given a giant boulder that fell onto the center of a key highway in mid-2005, rerouting traffic back to Central City.

SIGHTS

Despite the large casinos and busloads of slot-machine players, both Black Hawk and Central City are acutely aware of their history as Colorado mining towns—historic buildings and districts are everywhere, notably the **Mountain City Historic Park** (Gregory St., Black Hawk, 303/582-5221, free), a collection of 12 historic, Victorian and Gothic homes that were moved to accommodate the casinos.

Built in 1878 for (temporarily) rich miners, the **Central City Opera House** (124 Eureka St., Central City, 303/292-6500, www.centralcityopera.org) hit hard times in the early 1900s, when the gold rush ended. In 1932, local volunteers refurbished and reopened the house—its first opera was *Camille,* starring Lillian Gish, and it has been open ever since for productions such as *The Ballad of Baby Doe* and *Gabriel's Daughter.* The large stone building, with its curved front doors and second-floor balcony, and famous performers' names carved into the red seats, is worth visiting even if you're not an opera fan. There's no dress code, by the way—business attire is more than acceptable.

The **Gilpin County Historical Society Museum** (228 High St., Central City, 303/582-5283, www.coloradomuseums.org/gilpin.htm, 11 A.M.–4 P.M. daily, $5) is a

© STEVE KNOPPER

In recent years, Black Hawk has gone from sleepy tourist town to bustling mini-Las Vegas.

two-story stone building that functioned as a school for miners' kids beginning in 1870—and continued through the 1960s. Its exhibits re-create a doctor's office and barbershop from the old days, and display kerosene lamps and scale models of local mills. Also part of the complex is the **Thomas House Museum** (228 High St., Central City, 303/582-5283, www.colora-domuseums.org/thomasho.htm, 11 A.M.–4 P.M. daily, $5), an 1874 frame building where Ben and Marsha Thomas lived in the 1920s and beyond.

Although the **Teller House** (120 Eureka St., Central City, 303/582-5283, 10 A.M.–5 P.M. daily Memorial Day–Labor Day, call for nonsummer hours) has fallen into disuse in recent years, the 1872 building is perhaps the most impressive in the Central City-Black Hawk region. Built by former senator and U.S. Secretary of the Interior Henry Teller, it was once a lavish hotel—Teller's friend Ulysses S. Grant stayed here, and was reputed to have been irritated by the solid-silver path mine owners laid en route to the entrance. (Grant supposedly took a different path.)

ACCOMMODATIONS

Many of the larger casinos offer lodging, including the **Fortune Valley Hotel & Casino** (321 Gregory St., Central City, 303/582-0800, $80–129), which has 118 rooms and is the largest hotel in the region. But while they're adequate for a night or two on a gambling vacation, visitors may choose to stay at some of the nicer properties, including several bed-and-breakfasts, in both Central City and Black Hawk.

Chateau L'Acadienne (325 Spring St., Central City, 303/582-5209, $60–94), in an 1870s brick-and-stone building restored to its original Victorian ambience, has three rooms at the center of town. The **After Supper Bed and Breakfast** (101 Marchant St., Black Hawk, 303/582-5787, www.aftersupper.com, $75–115) has two guest rooms, an elaborate garden, and a nice view from a cliff.

FOOD

Inside The Lodge casino, the **White Buffalo Grille** (240 Main St., Black Hawk, 303/582-1771, www.thelodgecasino.com, 5–9 P.M. Tues.–Thurs. and Sun., 5–10:30 P.M. Fri.–Sat.) is one of the few nice restaurants in the area

DENVER

(which is to say, other than the cattle-call buffets). Its menu is pretty basic, with steak and salmon dishes in the $19–23 range and appetizers ranging from buffalo wings to crab cakes.

INFORMATION AND SERVICES

Try the **Central City Visitors Center** (216 Main St., 303/582-3345) for information. For more on Central City and Black Hawk—heavy on casino advertisements—check their webpages at www.centralcitycolorado.com and www.blackhawkcolorado.com, respectively. The official Black Hawk government website is more sparse: www.cityofblackhawk.org.

GETTING THERE AND AROUND

Twisty, steep, narrow mountain highways take drivers to Black Hawk and Central City. From Denver, drive west on I-70 toward the Eisenhower Memorial Tunnel, then head north on Highway 279 from Idaho Springs. Central City will be on your left, while Black Hawk is a mile up the road. From Boulder, head west to Nederland—a good area to stop for lunch or dinner—then follow the many hairpin curves along Highway 119 to Black Hawk. Denver and Boulder cabs and limousines are available to shuttle gamblers, but beware of snowstorms.

THE COLLEGE TOWNS: BOULDER AND FORT COLLINS

The time to nap in the car is not when you're on I-36, heading west from Denver to Boulder. After twisting through the suburban sprawl of Westminster, Broomfield, Louisville, Lafayette and Superior, the highway leads up one final steep hill, then... BAM. A breathless panorama of the Rocky Mountain foothills, with Flagstaff Mountain rising out of the red-roofed University of Colorado campus, is to your left. The flat-headed Longs Peak is in the distance to your right. This view is exactly why so many people—almost 100,000, at last census—settle in tranquil, soothing Boulder.

The outdoor activities are obvious just from one glance at the city, but once you start driving around the foothills, the Front Range, and spectacular wilderness areas like Rocky Mountain National Park and Grand County, it's hard to overcome an addiction to clean air and mountain scenery. Plus, when locals feel they've had enough of CU, Fort Collins and Colorado State University are just 40 minutes north. Boulder's only Achilles' heel is its lack of diversity—the African-American population hovers in the low single digits and Latinos tend to populate Denver and its surrounding suburbs. And housing prices are so exorbitant that only members of a certain socioeconomic level, generally speaking, can afford to live here.

PLANNING YOUR TIME

It only takes a few days to get a feel for Boulder, with its combination of college hangouts, yuppie shops on the Pearl Street Mall, mountain scenery, and perfectly paved biking trails. Any of the hotels will do for a weekend, and while

COURTESY OF THE NATIONAL PARK SERVICE

HIGHLIGHTS

◖ **Pearl Street Mall:** With buskers climbing tightropes, kids playing on frog and snail statues, some of the best shops, bars, and restaurants in Colorado, and a red-brick ambience that attracts tourists, locals, and beggars alike, Boulder's downtown mall is just as vibrant as it was when it opened in 1977 (page 72).

◖ **Chautauqua Park:** The grassy park is a great place to play Frisbee or just laze around underneath the foothills for an afternoon, and the hiking trails, restaurant, and concert hall are an elegantly down-home combination—plus, you can rent cabins (page 73).

◖ **Flagstaff Mountain:** Drive up a steep road of hairpin curves for the city's most renowned restaurant (Flagstaff House) and panoramic views of Boulder (page 74).

◖ **Bolder Boulder:** This Memorial Day footrace has three parts—one for world-class, competitive runners; one for regular citizens (some of whom are pretty fast); and one for wheelchair racers. The streets close and most of Boulder comes out to watch if they aren't running (page 76).

◖ **A Show at Boulder Theater:** The distinctive marquee just off the Pearl Street Mall hints at the grandeur inside this 1906 former opera house, which continues to grab big-name concerts and excellent second-run movies despite competition from the Fox Theatre on the Hill (page 79).

◖ **Rocky Mountain National Park:** It's hard to adequately describe this 265,000-acre nature preserve of gigantic mountains, green meadows, intimidating snow-filled tundra, and endless hiking trails, campgrounds, and picnic areas, but let's just say it's one of the most beautiful spots in Colorado (page 93).

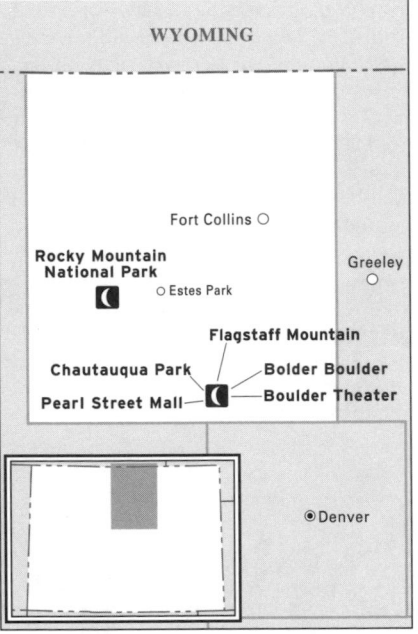

LOOK FOR ◖ TO FIND RECOMMENDED SIGHTS, ACTIVITIES, DINING, AND LODGING.

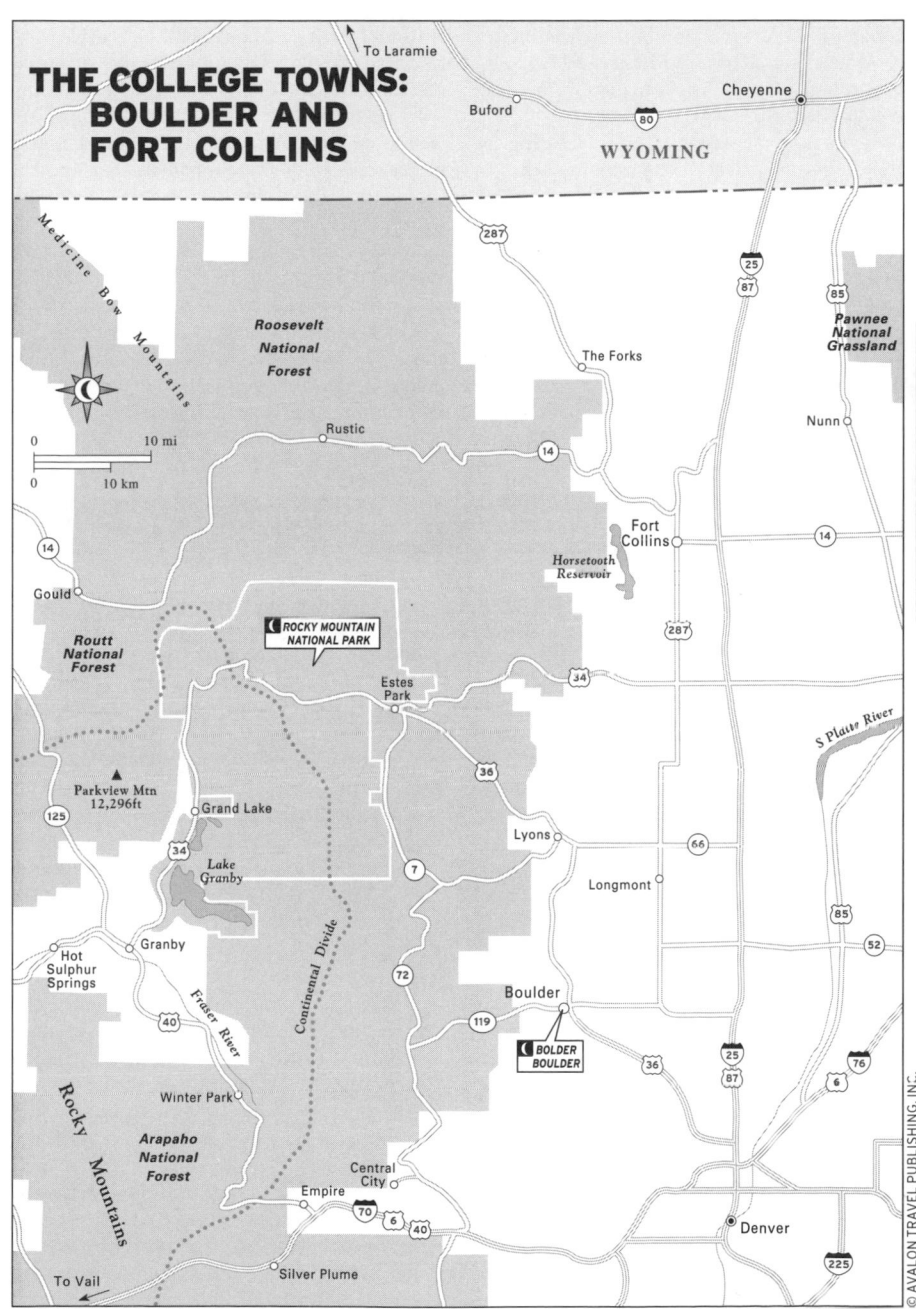

THE COLLEGE TOWNS: BOULDER AND FORT COLLINS

To Laramie

Buford

Cheyenne

WYOMING

287

25
87

85

Roosevelt National Forest

The Forks

Pawnee National Grassland

Nunn

Rustic

14

0   10 mi

0   10 km

Medicine Bow Mountains

14

Fort Collins

14

Gould

Horsetooth Reservoir

Routt National Forest

ROCKY MOUNTAIN NATIONAL PARK

287

Estes Park

34

S Platte River

36

▲ Parkview Mtn 12,296ft

Grand Lake

125

Lyons

66

34

Lake Granby

7

Longmont

Granby

Hot Sulphur Springs

85

52

40

Fraser River

72

Boulder

Continental Divide

119

BOLDER BOULDER

36

25
87

76

6

Winter Park

Arapaho National Forest

Rocky Mountains

Central City

Empire

70   6   40

Denver

To Vail

Silver Plume

225

some feel pressured to get into the mountains as soon as possible, Boulder is a relaxed city that more than rewards lazy days on outdoor restaurant patios.

If you have more time, consider splitting the trip between mountain excursions, hikes in Chautauqua Park, and a sampling of the surprisingly world-class restaurants clustered around the Pearl Street Mall. Just be careful not to fall in love with the city, or you'll wind up giving up your high-powered career in New York or Los Angeles, buying Birkenstocks, and living here (while complaining about crowds) forever.

Boulder's downtown hotels make a perfect base to explore the many sights in northern Colorado. **Estes Park** and the nearby **Rocky Mountain National Park** are about a half-hour drive from the city; hikers and mountain-climbers should plan to spend at least a weekend in that area (the local hotels and restaurants in Estes Park are well above functional, if not luxurious). The tiny hippie town **Nederland** is half an hour into the mountains, and well worth visiting, although many locals consider it a pit stop en route to mountain sightseeing towns such as **Georgetown** and **Idaho Springs** or the ski resorts farther west along I-70. **Fort Collins,** home of Colorado State University and an easygoing college town, is about a one-hour drive north of Boulder. Other pretty, mountain day trips include **Grand Lake, Hot Sulphur Springs,** and **Granby,** all within about 45 minutes of Boulder.

Boulder and Vicinity

Since the 1960s, Boulder has become known throughout the state as "The People's Republic of Boulder," as hippies put down roots, transformed into yuppies, and started driving Saabs with "Visualize Whirled Peas" stickers between the Wild Oats and Celestial Seasonings Tea outlets. Although the college campus is far more famous for partying skiers than political activism, Boulder is by far the state's most liberal (and certainly most environmentalist) city—although ex-CU football coach Bill McCartney formed the stadium-sized, conservative-Christian men's group Promise Keepers here in 1990. Equally notorious are its weird quirks, from the annual Kinetics Sculpture Challenge, in which thousands head to Boulder Reservoir to race their homemade contraptions while wearing elaborate costumes, to the buskers, balloon twisters, tightrope walkers, artists, beggars, and bar-crawling college students who populate the tourist-friendly Pearl Street Mall.

HISTORY

Boulder's incredible mountain scenery has been a magnet for civilizations, businesses, students, and tourists for centuries, from the Arapahos in the early 1800s to European settlers and gold-seekers who arrived during the "Pikes Peak or bust!" movement in 1858 to the University of Colorado in 1877.

"Boulder City" became a town, officially, in 1859, and it immediately became the county's fastest-growing region. Thanks to CU's role as a picturesque economic, intellectual, and social center, and the city's smart purchases of Chautauqua Park, at the base of the Flatirons, and open space west of Boulder, entities such as the National Center for Atmospheric Research and IBM set up headquarters here in the early 1960s. Although Boulder has attempted to limit growth since 1959, growth happened anyhow.

Beaded, pot-smoking hippies flooded the area in the 1960s, and bars (The Sink), concert halls (Tulagi), and rock 'n' roll bands (the Astronauts) sprang up to accommodate them. They were the first group to give CU its reputation as a ski-bum party school, despite occasional protests of the Vietnam War and a countercultural attitude that reflected the activism in Berkeley and Ann Arbor at the time. Local businesses established the colorful "Hill" area to cater to the 6,000 students who attended by the late 1800s.

the red-brick outdoor Pearl Street Mall

The Pearl Street Mall opened downtown in 1977, the same year the city adopted the Danish Plan, the most powerful of many longtime laws intended to protect views of the mountains and prevent the kind of sprawl that would later afflict Denver and its suburbs. But the anti-growth laws backfired, to an extent, as Boulder expanded by 19,000 people and 27,000 jobs from 1980 to 1995. Residents spilled into nearby Louisville, Lafayette, and Niwot, and housing prices jumped almost to San Francisco levels. But despite all these problems, Boulder remains as beatific as ever, and it's a great place to grow up, work, or visit.

ORIENTATION

Boulder is in a bowl, surrounded by the Flatiron mountains on the Front Range. It's an easy half-hour drive from Denver, west on U.S. 36, and it's the central city in a rich open-space area including Estes Park, Grand Lake, and Rocky Mountain National Park to the north, Louis-ville, Lafayette, and Superior to the south, and Fort Collins, Longmont, Loveland, and Niwot to the east and northeast.

SAFETY

Although Boulder has in recent years dealt with violence, gangs, and racial harassment like any other city, it remains one of the safest metropolitan areas in Colorado. It's the kind of place where people leave their car doors unlocked while they run into stores, although the local police probably wouldn't recommend it. Solo walkers and bikers should be careful to stay in well-lit areas after dark. The **Boulder Police Department** (1777 Broadway, 303/441-3090, www.ci.bouldcr.co.us/police) is still reeling from its bumbling investigation of the JonBenet Ramsey murder in December 1996, but its officers are friendly and receptive and are generally happy to answer all tourists' questions.

SIGHTS
University of Colorado

The 30,000-student **University of Colorado at Boulder** (CU, 303/492-1411, www.colorado.edu) is infamous as one of the nation's top party schools, with high-profile scandals of recent years involving football players, alleged sexual assaults, and various other activities and government investigations. (Although CU dropped off the *Princeton Review*'s nonscientific party-school rankings in 2005.) I myself have indulged in a few CU parties over the years—none involving football players or illicit behavior, but several with rousing games of Quarters and Viking Master—and can attest that it's one of the most fun and relaxed institutions on earth. It's also surprisingly strong, education-wise, with a Nobel Prize–winner (Eric Cornell) on the physics faculty and excellent departments in science, journalism, and music (the huge Norlin Library isn't shabby, either).

CU, founded in 1877, is also a great place to hang around. Centered on the **Norlin Quadrangle,** a wide, grassy area where students chill out on sunny afternoons, it's filled

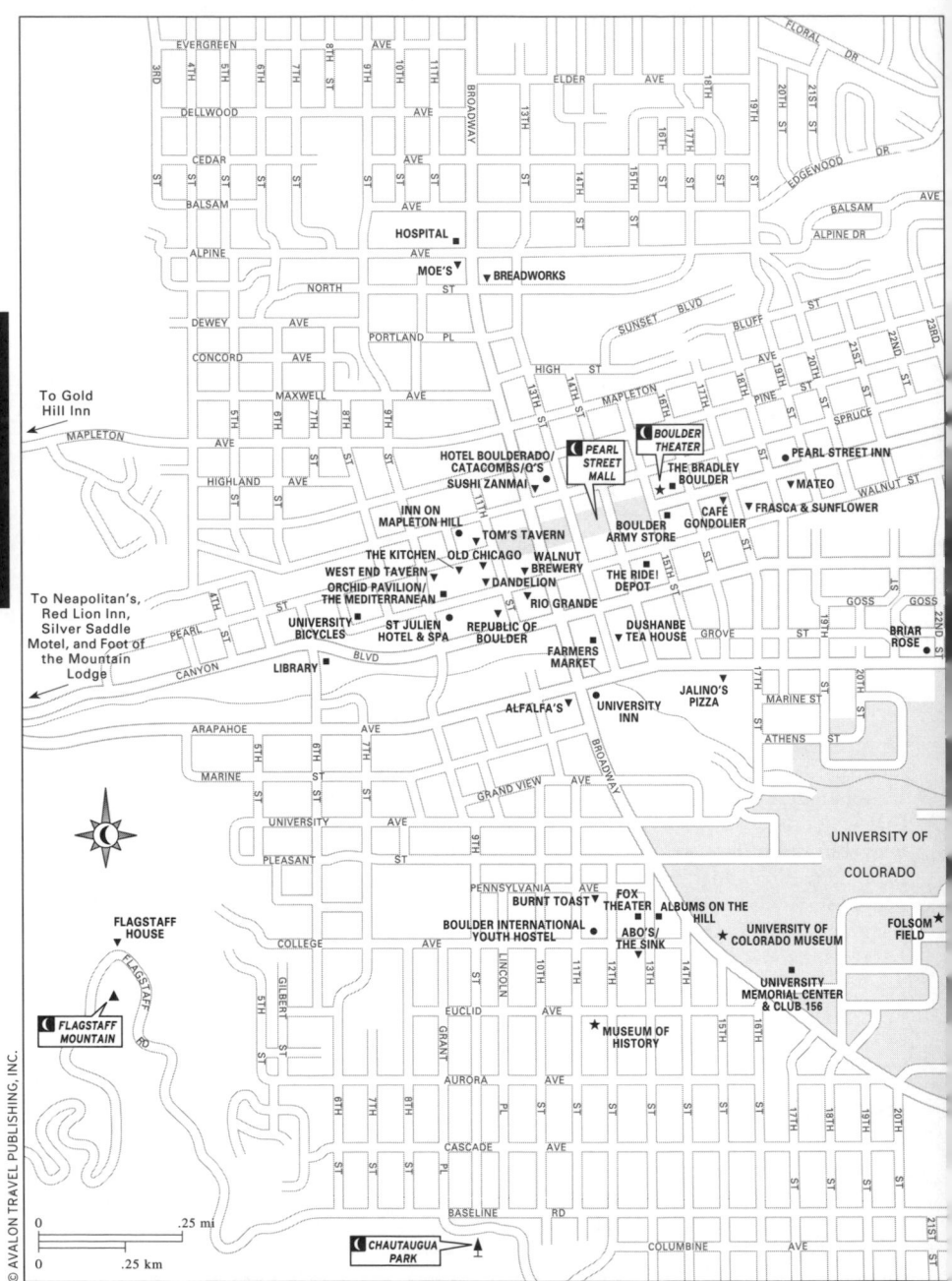

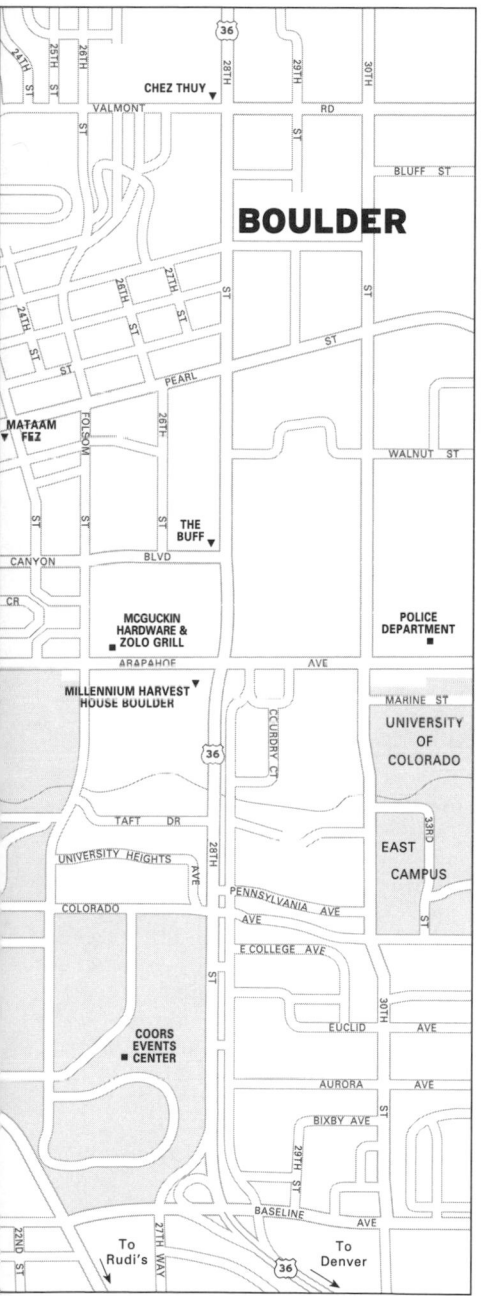

with impeccable cement walkways and buildings with red-tiled, Italian-style tops that are strikingly visible from the hills and mountains around Boulder. The **University Memorial Center** and its fountain-dominated plaza is just south of the Quad, and its movies, cafeteria, and bowling alley (complete with the live-music Club 156 and numerous video and pinball games) are open to the public as well as students.

If you're in the mood to take a break from bowling and beer to study local history, the **University of Colorado Heritage Center** (Old Main, 303/492-6329, www.cualum.org/heritage, 10 A.M.–4 P.M. Mon.–Fri., 10 A.M.–2 P.M. Sat., free) sponsors exhibits on Shakespeare, bison, bats, and other important stuff. The **University of Colorado Museum** (Henderson Building, 303/492-6892, http://cumuseum.colorado.edu, 9 A.M.–5 P.M. Mon.–Fri., 9 A.M.–4 P.M. Sat., 10 A.M.–4 P.M. Sun., $3) has more than four million artifacts, mostly of the dinosaur-and-fossil variety.

Fiske Planetarium (southwest of the CU Events Center, 303/492-5002, www.colorado.edu/fiske/home.html, 8 A.M.–5 P.M. daily, free) has been putting on laser shows (check out Pink Floyd, dude, it's cosmic) and astronomy workshops and lectures for decades in a domed building that's surprisingly roomy on the inside. Nearby is **Sommers-Bausch Observatory,** an amazing star-gazing spot that includes a 24-inch reflector and other gigantic university-owned telescopes. It often puts on lectures and observation sessions after the shows at Fiske.

CU's social center is **University Hill** (13th St., between Pennsylvania St. and College Ave.), also known as "The Hill," a cement playground for concert-goers, album-buyers, pizza-and-ice-cream-eaters, souvenir-shoppers, and people who like wandering into The Sink to see the cartoon depictions of ex-student Robert Redford and other luminaries. University Hill actually refers to the fraternity-heavy neighborhood that surrounds The Hill, and it gets loud and raucous on weekend nights—which can be a plus or a minus depending on your age and attitude.

Fiske Planetarium is a world-class observatory at the University of Colorado.

© STEVE KNOPPER

Downtown

The **Boulder History Museum** (1206 Euclid Ave., 303/449-3464, www.boulderhistorymuseum.org, 10 A.M.–4 P.M. Tues.–Fri., noon–4 P.M. Sat., $5), founded by *Daily Camera* publisher A. A. "Gov" Paddock in the 1940s, displays more than 30,000 objects dating from the 1800s to the present. Some of the best stuff involves costumes, like black ladies' boots and round pillbox hats of previous Boulder eras.

Surrounding the mall are rows of downtown Victorians that command huge real-estate prices. (One of them, at 1619 Pine St., is where *Mork and Mindy* filmed, and some 1980s TV aficionados still make pilgrimages there.) The **Downtown Boulder Historic District** (Spruce between 10th and 16th Streets, Walnut Street between Broadway and 9th Street, Pearl between 9th and 16th Streets) encompasses a bunch of late-19th-century rock-and-brick buildings with Roman and Italian architecture, and the **Mapleton Historic District** (Broadway, Pearl Street, 4th Street, and Dewey Street) includes the 1899

Inn at Mapleton Hill and the 1903 Lewis-Cobb House.

◖ Pearl Street Mall

The Mall (Downtown Boulder Business Improvement District, 1942 Broadway #301, 303/449-3774, www.dbi.org), which extends down Pearl Street from 10th Street to 15th Street, opened in 1977 as a pedestrian-only response to the then-flourishing Crossroads Mall a few miles to the east. Over the years, the red-brick, five-block area has exceeded even the most ambitious city planners' expectations, drawing tourists by the thousands and street performers who walk tightropes, strum Neil Young songs on their guitars, paint portraits, and tie balloons into animal shapes for kids. The mall's former businesses remain as famous as their living counterparts—the Blue Note nightclub drew legends from punk trio Husker Du to comedian Robin Williams in the 1980s, Pearl's and Potter's were notorious college bars, and the New York Deli was a great sandwich shop whose facade was prominently featured on *Mork and Mindy.* Remaining are fixtures such as Old Chicago, the Boulder Theater, and the Walnut Brewery, as well as world-class shops Boulder Bookstore, Peppercorn, and others, not to mention chains like Abercrombie & Fitch. For years, the mall has been locked in a competition with Crossroads; in the early 1990s, Crossroads was so dominant that many mall shops were forced to close. More recently, Crossroads became a ghost town, then closed, but it's scheduled to reopen in fall 2006 as "Twenty Ninth Street."

Contact **Historic Boulder** (2275 30th St., 303/444-5192, www.historicboulder.org, 9 A.M.–4 P.M. Tues.–Fri.) for guided tours and other historic information.

The **Boulder Museum of Contemporary Art** (1750 13th St., 303/443-2122, www .bmoca.org, 11 A.M.–6 P.M., $4) is in a comfortable orange-brick building near the farmers market a few blocks from the mall. It puts on striking exhibitions of international artists such as Brooklyn-based, comic-book-style painter Casey McGlynn, as well as dance concerts and other events.

Chautauqua Park

This walking, Frisbee-playing, picnicking, and afternoon-napping area is literally in the shadow of Flagstaff Mountain; the large, grassy park is at the bottom, along Baseline Road, and it gets more rocky and forest-y as it rises into the foothills. Locals love the hiking-and-biking trails, there's a great old restaurant on the park grounds, and the wooden Chautauqua Auditorium is, as many performers have observed, like spending some time inside a giant acoustic guitar. For information on events, and to some extent the park, contact the Colorado Chautauqua Association (900 Baseline Rd., 303/442-3282, www.chautauqua.com).

North Boulder

Mo Siegel discovered a certain kind of wild herb in Boulder around 1969, and the first teas from his **Celestial Seasonings** (4600 Sleepytime Dr., 303/581-1202 or 800/434-4246, www.celestialseasonings.com) came out shortly thereafter—notably the Red Zinger brand in 1971. Today, Siegel's tea empire is corporate-owned and serves some 1.2 billion cups of tea per year, although it remains a landmark on Sleepytime Drive in southeast Boulder. The company offers tours, including the factory, where eight million tea bags come out every day; an herb garden; the intensely scented Mint Room; and a gift shop. And free samples.

Foothills

The website refers to "the west end of Table Mesa drive," but that hardly does the location of the **National Center for Atmospheric Research** (NCAR, 1850 Table Mesa Dr., 303/497-1000, www.ncar.ucar.edu, 8 A.M.–5 P.M. Mon.–Fri., 9 A.M.–4 P.M. Sat.–Sun., free) justice—it's literally on the edge of a cliff, in a complex of boxy, orange, I. M. Pei–designed buildings with the foothills as

© STEVE KNOPPER

the National Center for Atmospheric Research in the southwest part of Boulder

a magnificent backdrop. NCAR itself is a federal research center that studies the sun, the earth's atmosphere, and above all, the weather; tours and exhibits include a telescopic camera, and tornado and lightning demonstrations. The outdoor "weather trail" has various hands-on science exhibits—kids eat this stuff up—in addition to the excellent views.

◖ Flagstaff Mountain

Continue driving past Chautauqua Park, west on Baseline Road, straight into this steep mountain, where the switchbacks and U-turns go straight uphill. Flagstaff is mostly famous for its crystal-clear views of the entire city—get your bearings by picking out the red-topped University of Colorado buildings on your right—but is also home to Boulder's fanciest restaurant, Flagstaff House. During the holidays, the city lights up a giant star on the side of the mountain, and mischievous types occasionally like to mess with it, cutting wires or changing its shape into various slogans.

Elsewhere

The **Leanin' Tree Museum of Western Art** (6055 Longbow Dr., 303/530-1442 or 800/777-8716, www.leanintreemuseum.com, 8 A.M.–4:30 P.M. Mon.–Fri., 10 A.M.–4 P.M. Sat.–Sun., free) started with four 1949 Christmas cards depicting cowboys and their horses. It has since expanded to a massive greeting-card business that ships more than 30 million a year, all out of this boxlike building south of Boulder, with a bronze statue out front and a museum of Old West paintings and sculpture inside, along with a sculpture garden.

SPORTS AND RECREATION

Before venturing into Boulder's many parks and miles of open space, contact the **City of Boulder Open Space & Mountain Parks** (303/441-3440, www.osmp.org), which has trail maps, weather and safety information, and helpful experts on hand to answer questions.

Hiking and Cycling

Everything you've heard about Boulder's repu-

view of the University of Colorado from Flagstaff Mountain

© STEVE KNOPPER

tation as an outdoor-sports city is true: Where hikers and cyclists in, say, Chicago have to drive miles out of town to find a scenic trail, around here they're everywhere. Tour de France cyclists and Olympic runners have trained in Boulder for decades, and even the paved city streets have clearly marked bike lanes, along with (mostly) respectful drivers who look in all directions before turning.

When all else fails, walk or ride west into the mountains. Just about any road will do. West of Broadway, Mapleton Avenue leads to **Sunshine Canyon,** a pretty, tree-lined ride among pricey, secluded homes, and the site of a popular 3.5-mile-loop trail called **Mt. Sanitas,** plus smaller, more casually scenic trails such as **Red Rocks** and **Boulder Falls; Lee Hill Road,** on the north side of town, goes into Boulder Heights, a steep route (not for squeamish cyclists) filled with hairpin turns and perfect city views; **Canyon Boulevard** goes straight into Boulder Canyon, a relatively easy bike ride; and, most popular, Baseline Road becomes **Flagstaff Mountain,** with a trailhead to the 1.5-mile **May's Point,** beginning at Summit Road, as well as **Boy Scout Trail,** at Sunrise Amphitheater. Flagstaff Road also accesses **Walker Ranch,** about 8 miles west of town, a difficult, 7.5-mile bike ride with great mountain views.

Eldorado Canyon State Park (9 Kneale Rd., Eldorado Springs, 303/494-3943, dawn–dusk daily, $6 per vehicle in summer, $5 per vehicle in winter) is most famous for its **rock climbing**—it has more than 500 routes, and the granite mountain edges are packed with dangling adventurers when the weather is mild. It's also known for incredible views of mountains, rocks, canyons, and vistas; trout fishing and kayaking in South Boulder Creek; bird-and-wildlife-watching just about everywhere; and more than 40 picnic sites, although camping isn't allowed. It's especially great for hiking, with locally renowned trails such as **Rattlesnake Gulch,** a 3-mile walk that shows the Continental Divide, and **Fowler,** which goes past the abandoned tracks of the 19th-century Colorado-Southern-Utah railroad and the burned-down (in 1912) Crags Hotel.

The park's trails are also open to cyclists and snowshoers; the canyon is 8 miles south of Boulder, near the intersection of Colorado 93 and Colorado 170. The park entrance is west of Eldorado Springs.

A network of trails spreads from **Chautauqua Park** to Flagstaff Mountain, Saddle Rock, and Green Mountain, and they range from easy jaunts to steep and somewhat technical paths through sharp rocks and bumpy dirt paths. All have spectacular views: My favorite is **Royal Arch,** just under a mile each way, which passes pretty Tangen Spring before shooting straight up to the naturally occurring arch and great views of the city. Also popular is the 7-mile **Mesa Trail,** a long, up-and-down path leading through forests and meadows, all under the mountains.

The paved and well-maintained **Boulder Creek Path** is one of the city's best attributes, a 9-mile artery connecting Fourmile Canyon (to the west) with the flat intersection of Arapahoe Avenue and Cherryvale Road (to the east).

© STEVE KNOPPER

At the base of the Flatirons, Chautauqua Park is a great place to hike.

Along the way, it passes downtown Boulder. (I used to bike it every day from my apartment near CU to my job at the *Daily Camera* downtown.) Be careful during rush hour, including sunny Saturdays and Sundays, because the flood of bikers, in-line skaters, joggers, walkers, baby-stroller-pushers, and CU football fans can make for grumpy congestion.

Brainard Lake (about 60 miles west of Boulder, off Highway 102, near the Peak-to-Peak Highway) takes hikers into the Indian Peaks Wilderness via several trails, notably the 8-mile (round-trip) **Mount Audubon,** overlooking the entire range of snowcapped peaks, and the 5-mile **Blue Lake,** a difficult path directly underneath the 13,000-foot-tall Mount Toll.

Left Hand Canyon, northwest of Boulder, is a paved road that snakes between the foothills and displays plenty of views. It leads to tiny towns like Rowena and Ward and numerous hidden hiking trails. To get to Left Hand, take Broadway north from Boulder, then turn left on Lee Hill Road; go about 5 miles straight up the mountain, past several hairpin curves, then down the other side; turn left at the first stop sign, Left Hand Canyon Road.

My parents, who've hiked at least once a week in Boulder since 1982, have a favorite walk—Nugget Hill, about a mile west of the Lee Hill and Left Hand Canyon Drive intersection, about a mile outside Rowena. You'll see a rusty gold storage box, which marks the trailhead; the dirt path goes about 1,500 feet up, past several mines and an abandoned family cemetery.

Other good hiking-and-biking routes in Boulder include the forest-heavy **Switzerland Trail** (5 miles west of Broadway on Canyon Boulevard, then turn right onto Sugarloaf Road and right again on Sugarloaf Mountain Road), a gentle up-and-down path that was once a narrow-gauge railroad track; the **Marshall Mesa/Community Ditch Trail,** which begins in South Boulder, just east of the Broadway-Marshall Drive intersection, and goes about 2.5 miles each way, past coal-mining ruins, forest and mountains, and occasional wildlife (horned owls are fairly common); and the 14-mile **East Boulder & Teller Farm Trails** (off Arapahoe Ave., about 7 miles east of downtown), which in lieu of mountains and canyons contains flat, swampy marshes, perfect for **bird-watching** in the Gunbarrel Farm area.

Near Lyons, about 14 miles north of Boulder along the Peak-to-Peak Highway, **Hall Ranch** is a wildlife habitat with several hiking trails as well as great horned owls, golden eagles, ruby-crowned kinglets, mountain lions, elk, and bighorn sheep in plain view. Try the 3.7-mile **Bitterbush Trail** or the 2.2-mile **Nelson Loop.** The entrance is off Highway 7, about a mile west of Lyons.

Cyclists can rent and repair bikes at several stores all over Boulder. **University Bicycles** (839 Pearl St., 303/444-4196 or 800/451-3950) opened in 1985 and frequently hires competitive (but not snobby) riders who know their way around goosenecks and sprockets.

☾ Bolder Boulder

You can't swing a shoelace without hitting a jogger in Boulder, and that's in part thanks to the Bolder Boulder (303/444-7223, www.bolderboulder.com), a Memorial Day 10-kilometer footrace in three stages—the early one for elite runners around the world, a more lackadaisical later one for citizens, some of whom dress up in goofy costumes, from Father Time to Elvis Presley, and a wheelchair race. Meandering through the city, from a bank near Iris Avenue and 30th Street through the Pearl Street Mall area up a hill to the University of Colorado, the race began in 1979 with 2,700 people and today attracts more than 50,000. Many people walk, although I have a yearly tradition of sleeping through it.

Fishing

Despite its outdoor-recreation reputation, Boulder isn't a major fishing hot spot, although **Walden and Sawhill Ponds** (north of Valmont Dr. on N. 75th St.) are collections of 20 small bodies of water, some of which are stocked with bluegill, pumpkinseed, and yellow perch. The **bird-watching** here is excellent—check out the songbirds and raptors. For fishing equipment, tours, and advice, try **Rocky Mountain Anglers** (1904 Arapahoe Ave., 303/447-2400, www.rockymtanglers.com), known for its experienced guides.

Golf

Boulder County has two major courses: **Flatirons** (5706 Arapahoe Ave., 303/442-7851, www.flatironsgolf.com), open since 1933, and **Indian Peaks** (2300 Indian Peaks Trail, Lafayette, 303/666-4706), 10 miles east of Boulder but worth the trip to play in view of several 14,000-foot peaks. Both are 18 holes.

Skiing and Snowshoeing

Pretty much wherever you can walk, you can take a pair of cross-country skis or snowshoes, so feel free to explore Chautauqua Park, Flagstaff Mountain, Brainard Lake, and Left Hand Canyon this way. The **Boulder Outdoor Center** (2707 Spruce St., 303/444-8420 or 800/364-9376, www.boc123.com) rents equipment and provides expertise on trails, directions, and laws and permits.

Water Sports

"The Res," or **Boulder Reservoir** (5100 51st St., 303/441-3468, www.ci.boulder.co.us), is Boulder's lone major body of water—it won't satisfy visitors from the coasts, but it's a pretty fun place to hang out. Sailboating, canoeing, swimming, fishing, and barbecuing are kosher here, but the predominant sport (especially among local high school students) is sitting on the loose gravel beach observing members of the opposite sex. The dirt path around the reservoir is a nice walk on sunny days.

Kayaking is popular in numerous local streams, from the Boulder Creek Path (which has surprisingly choppy currents) to Left Hand Canyon to the South Platte River. The **Boulder Outdoor Center** (2707 Spruce St., 303/444-8420 or 800/364-9376, www.boc123.com) is an excellent resource for this sort of thing.

Boulder Creek is also open to a nutty, do-it-yourself local sport—tubing—in which swimmers sit in giant, puffed-up car inner tubes and navigate currents, rocks, and cement walls. I tried this once and, despite my buddies' pleas

© STEVE KNOPPER

"Tubing" Boulder Creek is a popular local water sport.

JAM BANDS

The Grateful Dead was one of the most influential rock bands of all time, and through endless concerts until guitarist Jerry Garcia died in 1995, it spread the seeds of improvisational music all over the world. These took root in the early 1990s, when similarly improvisational bands such as Phish, Blues Traveler, the Dave Matthews Band, and the Samples became hugely popular among a crowd of neo-hippies who attended concerts and danced for hours in a nonstop twirling motion.

Boulder, with its college crowd and laid-back mountain atmosphere, became ground zero for this "jam band" scene. From the Samples and Big Head Todd and the Monsters to early-1990s local club acts like Acoustic Junction and the Reejers, the scene shifted from small clubs to large venues – by the early 2000s,

homegrown bands Leftover Salmon and String Cheese Incident graduated to national recognition, selling out venues all over the United States and even racking up CD sales. Meanwhile, established national acts like Matthews, who once opened for the Samples, continue to sell out regularly at Red Rocks Amphitheatre and elsewhere.

Although many such bands don't like being lumped into the hippie-Grateful Dead-jamming category, and their styles are diverse and occasionally revolutionary, they share an improvisational quality. It's not uncommon for a song to stretch to more than 15 or 20 minutes on stage, driving Ramones fans a little crazy, but these bands pack festivals like Bonnaroo, in Manchester, Tennessee, drawing 90,000 people a year.

to "lift up your back!" bounced my back on rocks, resulting in large red welts down my vertebrae. The aforementioned buddies have never let me hear the end of it. If you're more agile in cold water, the **Conoco** (1201 Arapahoe Ave., 303/442-6293) sells tubes for $12; the creek is just a block away from the gas station.

Spectator Sports

CU is a Division I college, and it fields competitive teams in soccer, golf, tennis, volleyball, and, naturally, skiing. But the sport that owns Boulder residents' hearts is football—fans are still sore about the national championships that got away in the early 1990s, although they pack **Folsom Field** regularly to root against arch-enemies such as Nebraska and Oklahoma. The basketball Buffs (traditionally mediocre) and Lady Buffs (traditionally pretty good) play at the **Coors Events Center.** For tickets to all the sports—and directions to the arenas and stadiums—call 303/492-8337.

ENTERTAINMENT
Nightlife

Boulder's live music scene has been thriving since the 1960s, when a local surf band, the Astronauts, briefly attempted to challenge the Beach Boys for national dominance. Since then, artists from the Eagles to Firefall to ex-Byrd Richie Furay to Big Head Todd and the Monsters have lived here (some temporarily), and clubs from the late, lamented Tulagi to the still-thriving Fox Theatre continue to draw big touring names away from Denver. The predominant musical style is hippie jamming music, including local stars like String Cheese Incident and national vagabonds like the Dead and Dave Matthews Band, but Boulder has pockets of folk, blues, bluegrass, country, and punk fans as well. Nirvana performed at a small club here in 1989.

CU's student-run **Program Council** (303/492-7704, www.colorado.edu/program-council) sponsors many live shows, some of which are just as great as the ones you'd see at the Boulder Theater or Denver's Fillmore Auditorium. **Club 156,** inside the University Memorial Center, is a tiny, brick-walled lounge that famously played host to the Red Hot Chili Peppers and Toad the Wet Sprocket in their early days. Also in the UMC, the **Glenn**

Miller Ballroom is a large room that snags bigger names; rapper Ice-T and his heavy-metal band, Body Count, once nearly tore the paint off the walls in front of Miller's benign, grinning portrait. **Macky Auditorium,** a few blocks away on campus, is also an excellent place to see a show.

Several blocks from CU, **Chautauqua Music Hall** (900 Baseline Rd., 303/442-3282, www.chautauqua.com) has a summer music series that's the best in town. Many of the concerts are of the soft and classical variety, but Los Lobos, Randy Newman, John Prine, Michelle Shocked, Richard Thompson, and other folk and rock acts show up on a regular basis.

About 10 miles northeast of Boulder, the **Left Hand Grange Hall** (197 2nd Ave., Niwot, 303/444-4640) is a tiny facility that runs somewhat regular folk and bluegrass concerts, some by ex-members of Boulder's renowned but sadly broken-up 1980s bluegrass act Hot Rize.

With one of the country's biggest party colleges as the clientele, Boulder is a city of late-night brewpubs and taverns, with raucous see-and-be-seen happy hours and frequent live-music backdrops. Just off Pearl Street, the **Walnut Brewery** (1123 Walnut St., 303/447-1345) is an upscale brewpub with numerous different kinds of beer, some of which come from the huge silver vats stored in the back. It's often crowded, especially on nights when small bands play on a platform above the front door.

Other bars that are part of the "mall crawl": **The Walrus** (1911 11th St., 303/443-9902), a downstairs joint with underwhelming food, cheap beers in tall glasses, and a decent jukebox; the **Rio Grande Mexican Restaurant** (1101 Walnut St., 303/444-3690), which has superb margarita specials, better-than-average food and snacks, and the most beautiful of the beautiful people; **The Foundry** (1109 Walnut St., 303/447-1803, www.foundryboulder.com), a onetime hipster live-music nightclub until it switched to pool, pool, and more pool in the mid-1990s; the **Corner Bar** (2115 13th St., 303/442-4880), a relaxing indoor-outdoor bar in the Hotel Boulderado; **Catacombs Bar** (2115 13th St., 303/442-4344), a basement bar that lives up to its name, especially when gritty local blues bands play in a cavelike room; the **West End Tavern** (926 Pearl St., 303/444-3535), with a rooftop bar overlooking the mountains; and the **Republic of Boulder** (1095 Canyon Blvd., 303/443-1460, www.republicofboulder.com), a homier, less yuppie-oriented alternative to the Walnut Brewery.

Up on the Hill, **The Sink** (1165 13th St., 303/444-7465, www.thesink.com) is as wild as it was when Robert Redford partied here in the 1960s. If you must scrawl graffiti on something, make it the ceiling, rather than the hallowed artwork.

Catering to an older clientele, **The Broker** (555 30th St., 303/444-3330, www.boulderbroker.com) has a dark bar—Bentley's Lounge—where countless karaoke singers have warbled over the years.

(A Show at Boulder Theater

Although it surrenders many big shows to the Fox Theatre, this 1906 former opera house

The Boulder Theater has housed numerous rock 'n' roll concerts over the years.

(2032 14th St., 303/786-7030, www.boulder-theater.com) has a neon marquee, a renovated ceiling, and comfortable old chairs on the main floor and balcony. Its "house act" since the early 1990s has been *E-Town*, a music-and-environment variety show hosted by former Hot Rize bassist Nick Forster and his wife, Helen—and brings big names like James Taylor, Los Lobos, Lyle Lovett, and others onstage for a few songs with Forster's crack band. The theater itself has regular movie nights as well as national touring acts.

Fox Theatre

The Fox Theatre (1135 13th St., 303/447-0095, www.foxtheatre.com) was a movie house on the Hill for decades until some adventurous local promoters turned it into the city's premier live-music club. In the early 1990s I saw Sheryl Crow, the Gin Blossoms, Uncle Tupelo, and many others here on their way up, and while the club's moneymaking acts are jam bands, its owners aim for diversity, including heavy metal, punk, folk, and hip-hop.

Performing Arts

The **Boulder Philharmonic Orchestra** (2995 Wilderness Pl., Ste. 100, 303/449-1343, www.peakarts.org) performs pieces by Brahms, Tchaikovsky, Stravinsky, and others, mostly at CU's Macky Auditorium.

Boulder's Dinner Theatre (5501 Arapahoe Ave., 303/449-6000 or 800/448-5501, www.theatreinboulder.com) is a nice meal with a bunch of singing people in the background—performing classic Broadway plays like *The Music Man* and *Forever Plaid.*

CU has a superb **College of Music** (Imig Building, 18th St. and Euclid Ave., 303/492-6352, www.colorado.edu/music); check the schedule for year-round concerts by faculty, students, and guests in many genres. They take place at the Music School as well as Macky Auditorium and other CU halls.

Events

Since 1980, the **Kinetic Sculpture Challenge** (Boulder Reservoir, 5100 51st St.) in early May has attracted goofy engineers and masochistic athletes for a competitive morning of zooming over dry land, paddling through Boulder Reservoir, and attempting not to sink in stinky, quicksand-like mud. The idea is to build the best nonmotorized craft by hand, and teams make up names like "Whizzers of Oz," "Inbredibles," and "Radioactive Sushi." A panel of local celebrity judges picks the best-costumed teams. Alcohol pretty much fuels everything.

The **Boulder Creek Festival** (between Canyon Blvd. and Arapahoe Ave., and 9th and 13th Streets, 303/652-4942, www.bouldercreekfestival.com) is a typical city art fair, with crafts, games, and small rides for kids, but it's in a great location, in the park near City Hall along Boulder Creek.

The website for the world-class **Colorado Shakespeare Festival** (Mary Rippon Theatre, University of Colorado, www.coloradoshakes.org) depicts the bard sailing through the sky on a skateboard, which gives you a clue of how classics like *Twelfth Night* and *Othello* come across on stage. The Mary Rippon Theatre is a cozy "in the round" area in the middle of campus, and Shakespeare's words are perfect when the July and August nighttime breeze hits you just the right way—although sirens and other traffic noise from nearby Broadway and Arapahoe Avenue can be distracting.

The **Colorado Music Festival** (900 Baseline Rd., 303/449-1397, www.coloradomusicfest.org), from late June through early August, is a classical and chamber-music extravaganza that combines traditional pieces with selections from *West Side Story,* fiddle performances from bluegrass musician Mark O'Connor, and other off-the-beaten-path styles.

Tiny Lyons is a mountain haven for yearly music festivals, in part because **Planet Bluegrass** (500 W. Main St., Lyons, 303/823-0848, www.planetbluegrass.com), which runs the Telluride Bluegrass Festival, relocated here years ago. The company's biggest Lyons festivals are the **Rocky Mountain Folks Festival,** the third week in August, starring Arlo Guthrie, Steve Earle, and Joan Armatrading, and

THE BIG WHEEL RALLY

Early one summer morning in 1993, my friend Jim and I walked out of a bar on the Pearl Street Mall when we spotted about a dozen full-fledged adults slamming into each other while riding Big Wheels. We immediately remembered these plastic tricycle contraptions from our youths in the 1970s, and as *Daily Camera* reporters, we set to interviewing the participants and writing a feature story.

Today, thanks to the efforts of leader Matt "Captain Obvious" Armbruster, who wears an impressive gold cape and silver helmet, the **Almost-Annual Matt Armbruster Memorial Big Wheel Rally** has become a semi-regular tradition at downtown Boulder institutions (the kind that serve beer, that is). Armbruster's fleet gathers at, say, the Republic of Boulder, then spends the night driving up and down various bar staircases.

Armbruster soups up some of these Big Wheels himself and sells them for charity. The rally is open to anybody with an above-average sense of humor and a threshold for pain. For information, check out www.bigwheelrally.com.

RockyGrass, which draws new bands and legends such as Doc Watson in late July. On a smaller scale, **Lyons Good Old Days** (www.musicinlyons.com) sponsors various local artists, from jazz to rock to bluegrass, in Sandstone Park (4th and Railroad avenues) all summer.

SHOPPING

For years, Boulder had two malls: the **Pearl Street Mall** (Pearl St. from 9th St. to 15th St., 303/449-3774, www.dbi.org) and Crossroads Mall, but after a brief period of dominance in the early 1990s, Crossroads succumbed to the nearby FlatIron Crossing in Broomfield. The situation may soon reverse, however, because major national chains such as The Gap have moved out, perhaps signaling rough times ahead for Pearl Street. And **Twenty-Ninth Street,** with a Home Depot and movie multiplex, is scheduled to rise up from Crossroads' ashes (on 28th St. from Arapahoe Ave. to Pearl St.) by fall 2006.

Pearl Street

As for Pearl Street—meaning the mall and its several surrounding blocks—the shopping is still magnificent, if you like tourist-oriented knickknacks and high-priced clothing, with one-of-a-kind stores such as **Color Me Mine** (1938 Pearl St., 303/443-3469, www.boulder.colormemine.com), a do-it-yourself ceramics studio; **Alpaca Connection** (1326 Pearl St., 303/447-2047 or 800/868-3265, www.alpacaconnection.com), which sells distinctive Peruvian rugs and sweaters; and the funky T-shirt store **Where the Buffalo Roam** (1320 Pearl St., 303/938-1424, www.wherethebuffaloroam.com).

The mall's best stores are (on the west side) **Boulder Bookstore** (1107 Pearl St., 303/447-2074 or 800/244-4651, www.boulderbookstore.com), a friendly, wood-floored, two-story, somewhat cramped literary fixture that has withstood challenges from Barnes & Noble, Borders, and many others over the years, and (toward the east side) **Peppercorn** (1235 Pearl St., 303/449-5847 or 800/447-6905, www.peppercorn.com), a fruity-candle-smelling kitchen-and-bathroom store where I and every single person I knew in high school bought Mother's Day presents for four straight years. Bongo the Balloon Man generally ties his monstrous pink-and-green creations for adoring kids outside Peppercorn.

Specialty bookstores in the Pearl Street area include: **Trident Booksellers** (940 Pearl St., 303/443-3133), a used store that has sold coffee and dog-eared New Age books to bohemian customers for decades; **High Crimes** (946 Pearl St., 303/443-8346, www.highcrimesbooks.com), formerly the Rue Morgue, which

© STEVE KNOPPER

The Farmers Market, near downtown Boulder, is open Saturday mornings in the summer.

focuses exclusively on mystery titles, old and new; and, in a tiny nook east of the Mall, the **Beat Book Shop** (1713 Pearl St., 303/444-7111), which will never compete with Barnes & Noble but has an irresistible collection of Allen Ginsberg's writings and a box of used vinyl records that range from punk to jazz to psychedelic rock. It's sometimes closed at weird times.

I've bought gas masks, camping equipment, hiking boots, and random artifacts over the years at the **Boulder Army Store** (1545 Pearl St., 303/442-7616), just east of the mall, once a desolate area but now a high-end shopping district with Borders Books as an anchor.

For kids' toys, my 3-year-old regularly gets lost—in the best possible way—at **Grandrabbit's Toy Shoppe** (2525 Arapahoe Ave., 303/443-0780, www.grtoys.com), which has just about every kind of stuffed animal you can imagine, as well as sticker and coloring books, DVDs, models, trains, balls, and assorted stocking-stuffers.

Art Galleries and Shops

Boulder has numerous art galleries and arty stores, including: **Art Mart** (1222 Pearl St., 303/443-8291, www.artmartonline.net), which caters to a hippieish clientele, selling hammocks, tie-dyed T-shirts, and Chinese earrings; **Art Source International** (1237 Pearl St., 303/444-4079 or 800/304-5029, www.rare-maps.com), a map store that doesn't tell you where to go but stocks old globes and rare parchments; the **Boulder Arts & Crafts Cooperative** (1421 Pearl St., 303/443-3683, www.boulderartsandcrafts.com), which since 1971 has sold (mostly) locally made pottery, ceramics, paintings, leather, and jewelry; and the **Smith Klein Gallery** (1116 Pearl St., 303/444-7200, www.smithklein.com), selling a variety of different styles, from large pewter statues to hand-blown glass designs.

Farmers Market and Natural Foods

The **Boulder County Farmers Market** (13th St. between Canyon Blvd. and Arapahoe Ave.,

303/910-2236, www.boulderfarmers.org, 8 A.M.–2 P.M. Sat. early April–early Nov., 4–8 P.M. Wed. early May–early Oct.) is not only a great place to buy locally grown fruits, vegetables, and flowers, it's an excuse to drag yourself out of bed and get outside on sunny Saturday mornings. It's in a perfect location near the mall and various parks; kids love it.

Away from the mall, **Wild Oats** (1651 Broadway, 303/442-0082, www.wildoats.com) has been a health-food fixture at the corner of Broadway and Arapahoe Avenue for decades, and it anticipated the Whole Foods boom in organic markets by several decades. (Whole Foods, of course, eventually moved to Boulder, in the crowded strip mall at Pearl Street between 28th and 30th Streets.) The company has announced, though, that by late 2006 it will relocate to the new Twenty-Ninth Street mall.

Other Interesting Shops

McGuckin Hardware (2525 Arapahoe Ave., 303/443-1822 or 800/558-6753, www.mcguckin.com) was a local Home Depot long before Home Depot existed. Absolutely everything is here, from nails to spray paint to plants of all types, and clerks in green aprons are happy to help you navigate the occasionally intimidating maze of aisles and high shelves.

University Hill has several interesting shops, although most are geared to students. (Step into one of the several tattoo-and-piercing boutiques for fashion or terror, depending on your age.) My favorite record store in Colorado is **Albums on the Hill** (1128 13th St., 303/447-0159, www.albumsonthehill.com), in a basement dungeon filled with new and used CDs, a roomful of LPs, and a staff knowledgeable in every genre. The **Colorado Bookstore** (1111 Broadway, 303/444-6604, www.colorado.bkstore.com) is geared toward students, of course, but it's surprisingly practical for civilians looking for art and writing supplies and CU paraphernalia.

ACCOMMODATIONS
Under $100

Pawnee Campground (Brainard Lake Rd., 5 miles west of Highway 72, Ward, 970/295-6600, $14) is part of Brainard Lake Recreation Area, about 17 miles west of Boulder, which means it captures the high-mountain splendor of Indian Peaks Wilderness. Hiking trails are everywhere.

The family-run **Foot of the Mountain** (200 W. Arapahoe Ave., 303/442-5688 or 866/773-5489, www.footofthemountainmotel.com, $80–85), near the Arapahoe Avenue path up Boulder Canyon, is a fairly basic motel made of wood, with striking red highlights near the cabin doors.

$100-150

The **Millennium Harvest House Boulder** (1345 28th St., 303/443-3850 or 866/866-8086, www.millenniumhotels.com, $109–175) has for years been the city's largest hotel, and while it's part of a national chain and isn't particularly distinctive inside, it's a comfortable stop for business travelers. Its outdoor restaurant and patio, just a few hundred feet from Boulder Creek, make it prime real estate for weddings, conferences, and class reunions.

The **Bradley Boulder** (2040 16th St., 303/545-5200 or 800/858-5811, www.thebradleyboulder.com, $145–195), formerly Coburn House, is a 12-room bed-and-breakfast with a stone fireplace (and fireplaces in the rooms)—as well as a business-oriented hotel with 1,500 square feet of meeting space and wireless Internet service everywhere. Just down the street from the Pearl Street Mall, it's also conveniently located, with a bread-and-fruit breakfast and free health-club services at the nearby Pulse fitness center.

A widowed dressmaker opened the **C Inn on Mapleton Hill** (1001 Spruce St., 303/449-6528 or 800/276-6528, www.innonmapletonhill.com, $108–184) as a boarding house in 1899, and while the clientele is a little more affluent these days, the inn's bright-red Victorian elegance remains the same. With four-corner beds and super-soft flowery comforters, plenty of wicker antique furniture, and a black retriever named Mandy, the inn is Boulder's quintessential bed-and-breakfast.

The **Colorado Chautauqua Association** (900 Baseline Rd., 303/442-3282, www.chautauqua.com, $102–224) owns 99 apartment-style cottages with long porches at the edge of Chautauqua Park, off Baseline Road near the bottom of Flagstaff Mountain. The association rents 60 of them year-round, although some are slightly run-down—but hey, in 1898 they were canvas tents, so don't complain.

In tiny Niwot, the town named for Arapaho chief Niwot, about 10 miles northeast of Boulder on the Diagonal Highway, the **Niwot Inn** (342 2nd Ave., Niwot, 303/652-8452, www.niwotinn.com, $139) has spare, quiet rooms named for various Colorado 14,000-foot peaks. (There's no Longs Peak room, although that fourteener is the nearest to this location.) It has conveniences like high-speed Internet access in the rooms, but really, if you're planning to spend significant time in Boulder, the inn is a little inconvenient—and don't even think about it if you're not planning to rent a car.

$150-200

The **Briar Rose B&B** (2151 Arapahoe Ave., 303/442-3007 or 888/786-8440, www.briarrosebb.com, $149–169) has 10 nicely furnished rooms named after Colorado mountain peaks. Lest you forget this is Boulder, it has a meditation room and offers an organic breakfast.

Over $200

The **(Hotel Boulderado** (2115 13th St., 303/442-4344 or 800/433-4344, www.boulderado.com, $195–275) is a local classic that takes up half a city block and makes you feel like you've stepped into the Old West upon entering the lobby. The red-brick structure looks modern from the outside, but the lobby has a huge cherry-wood staircase, stained-glass ceiling, and flowery carpets and wallpaper, and even the bathrooms recall the hotel's 1909 origins. The Catacombs bar, which has live blues bands on several nights, is downstairs, and Q's Restaurant is next to the lobby.

Boulder's newest hotel, the **St. Julien Hotel and Spa** (900 Walnut St., 720/406-9696, www.stjulien.com, $245–285), opened in March 2005 near the old public library. With a fancy restaurant (Jill's), bar (T-Zero), and spa, it's likely to challenge the Boulderado's almost 100 years of local lodging dominance.

Just outside Ward, in the mountains near the Peak-to-Peak Highway, the **(Gold Lake Resort & Spa** (3371 Gold Lake Rd., 303/459-3544, www.goldlake.com, $255–375) is a magnificent mountain-and-lake spot to pamper yourself. It's a complex of small, wooden cabins with old-fashioned stoves and shower stalls made out of rock, as well as spa and tepee facilities and a looped path around the large lake. Ice skating is available in the winter, and the crisp mountain air matches the silence. On the grounds is the upscale **Alice's Restaurant,** which has great bread and soup to go with duck, fish, and venison entrées.

FOOD
Snacks, Cafés, and Breakfast

The second-floor **Burnt Toast Restaurant** (1235 Pennsylvania Ave., 303/440-5200, 7 A.M.–3 P.M. and 5:30–9 P.M. Tues.–Sun., 7 A.M.–3 P.M. Mon.) is a favorite for college students recovering from the previous night of debauchery. It's laid-back to the extreme. The service is surprisingly good, though, as are standard breakfast dishes like steak and eggs, potatoes, and, yes, toast. It serves dinner as well, just not on salsa-dancing Mondays.

The bottom line of **Breadworks** (2644 N. Broadway, 303/444-5667, www.breadworks.net, 7 A.M.–7 P.M. Mon.–Sat., 7 A.M.–6 P.M. Sun.) is bread, of course, from baguettes to batards to challah, but its sandwiches, homemade soups (including several organic kinds), and desserts make the hippieish restaurant a great place to hang out. For breakfast and lunch, **Moe's Broadway Bagel** (2650 Broadway, 303/444-3252, 6 A.M.–7 P.M. daily) eclipsed the Bagel Bakery sometime in the early 1990s and has been serving its thick, homemade, and very tasty breakfasts to most of Boulder ever since.

The Buff (1725 28th St., 303/442-9150, 6:30 A.M.–2 P.M. Mon.–Fri., 7 A.M.–2 P.M. Sat.–Sun.) is a one-story breakfast classic that's part of the Best Western near the corner of Canyon Boulevard and 28th Street. It's your basic eggs-toast-bacon—with, befitting its host city, an emphasis on vegetarian dishes and organically grown ingredients.

Casual

Millions—no, it has to be *zillions*—of college students with the munchies have stopped by **Abo's on the Hill** (1110 13th St., 303/443-3199, www.abosinc.com, 11 A.M.–2 A.M. daily) for a huge slice of New York-style, crunchy pizza, slapped onto a white paper plate with plenty of available grated cheese and spices. Abo's has slowly grown into a Colorado chain, with several locations in the Boulder-Denver area, although its longtime fixture on the Pearl Street Mall closed a few years ago.

Opened in 1923, **The Sink** (1165 13th St., 303/444-7465, www.thesink.com, 11 A.M.–10 P.M. daily) is a mythical CU bar and restaurant and Hill anchor that is still best known for providing beer and pizza to Robert Redford when he was a student in the late 1960s. Although it changed names briefly in the 1980s—my pal Jonathan and I ate the last-ever pizza of the Herbie's Deli era—it's The Sink for good, with above-average burgers, sandwiches, and pizza, a bar that stays packed until 2 A.M., an often-raucous outdoor patio, and large, weirdly friendly bouncers.

I've been eating the all-you-can-eat spaghetti special (now on Sunday and Monday nights) at **Café Gondolier** (1738 Pearl St., 303/443-5015, www.cafegondolier.com, 11:30 A.M.–9 P.M. Mon., 11:30 A.M.–10 P.M. Tues.–Fri., 4:30 A.M.–10 P.M. Sat., 4:30–9 P.M. Sun.) since roughly 1982, and the restaurant's long, squishy noodles, red sauce, and sausage-based minestrone soup haven't changed a bit since then. The silver-metal beast of an espresso machine dates to 1903 and was the first of its kind in Boulder.

◖ Jalino's Pizza (1647 Arapahoe Ave., 303/443-6300, 10:30 A.M.–1 A.M. Sun.–Thurs., 10:30 A.M.–2 A.M. Fri.–Sat.), across the street from Boulder High School, is a hidden gem in a city renowned for its restaurants—the pizza

has thin crust and a spicy sauce, with thick cheese and a huge topping selection, and it's the most reliable pizza delivery in Boulder.

Locals sometimes dismiss **Orchid Pavilion** (1050 Walnut St., 303/449-4353, www.orchid-pavilion.com, 11:30 A.M.–10 P.M. Mon.–Thurs., 11:30 A.M.–11 P.M. Sat.–Sun.), which has served the same juicy chicken dishes, thin egg rolls, and mustard sauce hot enough to clear your sinuses since the late 1980s, but the Chinese restaurant down the steps and across the street from the *Daily Camera* is always reliable—and, during lunch (till 3 P.M.), very affordable.

The Mediterranean (1002 Walnut St., 303/444-5335, www.themedboulder.com, 11 A.M.–3 P.M. and 5–10 P.M. Mon.–Wed., 11 A.M.–3 P.M. and 5–11 P.M. Thurs.–Sat., 5–10 P.M. Sun.), just west of the Pearl Street Mall on Walnut Street, is a hipster hot spot with a crowded bar and front-room dining area, but the food makes it well worth the occasionally long wait for a table. The menu is *tapas*-heavy, with changing fish and pizza specials as well as superb chicken and beef mainstays.

Yes, **Old Chicago** (1102 Pearl St., 303/443-5031, www.oldchicago.com, 11 A.M.–2 A.M. daily) is part of a Denver-based national chain, and there's nothing spectacular about the menu for this western Pearl Street Mall fixture. But the clientele is a comfortable combination of drinkers sampling hundreds of beer brands in the bar and families eating thick-crust pizza and big cookies with ice cream in the restaurant.

The **West End Tavern** (926 Pearl St., 303/444-3535, 11:30 A.M.–1:30 A.M. daily) has been famous for years for its rooftop deck overlooking the mall and the mountains. It has always been better than average for basic bar food like burgers and fries, but owner Dave Query recently upgraded the menu, adding all-star comfort-food dishes like macaroni and cheese and mahimahi sandwiches.

Run by longtime Colorado chef Thuy Le, a native of Vietnam, **Chez Thuy** (2655 28th St., 303/442-1700, www.chezthuy.com, 11 A.M.–9 P.M. Mon.–Thurs., 11 A.M.–10 P.M. Fri.–Sat., 5–9 P.M. Sun.) looks at first like a kitschy Asian restaurant (check out the plastic flowers, statues, and bead curtains near the entrance), but its long menu is diverse and elegant. The yam-heavy Vietnamese curry stew ($9) is the house specialty, but Buddha Delight ($7), with vegetables and tofu, is one of many varied choices.

The Japanese seafood dishes at **Sushi Zanmai** (1221 Spruce St., 303/440-0733, 11:30 A.M.–2 P.M. and 5–10 P.M. Mon.–Fri., 10 A.M.–midnight Sat., 5–10 P.M. Sun.) are pretty excellent, but few show up solely for the food. Karaoke night is every Saturday, and Boulder residents excel at making idiots of themselves; far more humorous and quasi-professional than the customers are the sushi-bar chefs, who sing while they chop up the raw fish. Also check out the sake bar next door, **Amu** (1221 Spruce St., 303/440-0807, 5:30–10:30 P.M. Tues.–Sat.), also serving Japanese entrées.

As with Sushi Zanmai, customers show up at **Mataam Fez** (2226 Pearl St., 303/440-4167, http://mfez.bizland.com, 5:45–9 P.M. daily) for the musical entertainment—a host of beautiful belly-dancers—but Moroccan dishes like vegetarian couscous and grilled lamb brochettes keep them in their seats.

When I was in high school and college and gorged myself with burgers, figuring they could easily be worked off later, I ate at least once a week at **Tom's Tavern** (1047 Pearl St., 303/442-9363, 11 A.M.–10 P.M. Mon.–Thurs., 11 A.M.–11 P.M. Fri.–Sat., noon–8:30 P.M. Sun.). Anchoring the west end of the Pearl Street Mall, the darkened diner has the best burgers in town—although the **Dark Horse** (2922 Baseline Rd., 303/442-8162, 11 A.M.–2 A.M. daily) is up there, a beautiful greasy-spoon oasis in a sea of yuppie bistros, chain cafés, and corporate brewpubs.

In a large yellow house in Lafayette, one of the suburb-like small towns east of Boulder along U.S. 36, **Efrain's** (101 E. Cleveland St., Lafayette, 303/666-7544, 11 A.M.–9 P.M. daily) is perhaps the best Mexican restaurant in Boulder County. It's a friendly, family-style kind of place, with excellent blue-corn enchiladas and chips and salsa. There's another location in east Boulder (63rd St. and Arapahoe Ave.).

the Boulder Dushanbe Teahouse

Upscale

It may seem a little random to have a fancy restaurant from Tajikistan at the center of Boulder, but the **Boulder Dushanbe Teahouse** (1770 13th St., 303/442-4993, www.boulderteahouse.com, 8 A.M.–9 P.M. Sun.–Thurs., 8 A.M.–10 P.M. Fri.–Sat.) grew out of the Dushanbe, Tajikistan, mayor's 1987 announcement of sister-city ties. The teahouse took a while to build—40 artisans from all over the once-Persian country spent three years hand-carving its complex ceramic decorations and hand-painting its ceiling, tables, and columns. Today, it's a full-service restaurant, with an international menu of Spanish seafood pimienta ($12), Chinese plum pork ($11), and German flank steak ($14).

(Flagstaff House (1138 Flagstaff Rd., 303/442-4640, www.flagstaffhouse.com, 6–9:30 P.M. Sun.–Fri., 5–9:30 P.M. Sat.) has always been the gold standard of Boulder fine dining, and even though chef Mark Monette replaced his father, founder Don Monette, in 1985, very little has changed. Dishes include Maine lobster ($59) and Hawaiian big-eye tuna ($36). Supplementing the elegance is one of the best mountain views of Boulder.

Regularly listed among the city's best restaurants in local magazines and newspapers, **(Zolo Grill** (2525 Arapahoe Ave., 303/449-0444, 11 A.M.–10 P.M. daily) is southwestern and fancy—but neither too southwestern nor too fancy. Casual dishes like smoked cheese enchiladas offset the white-tablecloth decor, and elegant dishes like tortilla crusted and seared ahi tuna offset the funky, Boulder-style modern art on the walls and the occasionally raucous, 100-tequila bar.

If co-owner and former celebrity chef Hugo Matheson's dishes are good enough for Mick Jagger, Sting, and Pink Floyd, they're certainly good enough for Boulder—**The Kitchen** (1039 Pearl St., 303/544-5973, www.thekitchencafe.com, 8–11 A.M., 11:30 A.M.–5 P.M., and 5:30–9 P.M. Mon.–Fri., 9 A.M.–2 P.M. and 5:30 P.M.–10 Sat.–Sun.) is a relatively new, cozy little Pearl Street restaurant that serves a mean eggplant-and-olive antipasti as well as pork, lamb, steak, and salmon entrées.

Local food critics have raved about **Frasca** (1738 Pearl St., 303/442-6966, www.frascafoodandwine.com, 5:30–10 P.M. Mon.–Sat.) since it opened in 2003, because its elaborately named meals (hand-cut tagliatelle with Colorado sweet corn, oregano and piave cream and Long Family Farm shaved pork leg with red plums, pancetta, and "sugo naturale") go perfectly with the on-site sommelier's wine selections.

The word "organic," in Boulder, used to refer to natural-hippie restaurants like the long-closed Harvest, but at **Sunflower** (1701 Pearl St., 303/440-0220, www.sunflowerrestaurant.net, 11 A.M.–2:30 P.M. and 5–10 P.M. Tues.–Fri., 10 A.M.–3 P.M. and 5–10 P.M. Sat., 10 A.M.–3 P.M. and 5–9 P.M. Sun.), chef Jon Pell effectively uses the term to mean fresh, creative, and different. The desserts are incredible—chocolate nirvana ($7) is barely an exaggeration—and main courses like buffalo steak ($25) and coriander sea scallops ($24) are almost as rich. Note that "organic" doesn't necessarily mean "vegetarian."

The small, Provence, France-style bistro **Mateo** (1837 Pearl St., 303/443-7766, 11:30 A.M.–2 P.M. and 5–9 P.M. Mon.–Thurs., 5–10 P.M. Fri.–Sat.) can be noisy and crowded if too many people are eating (or drinking in the bar) at once, but it's worth trying if only for the amazing french fries, which actually taste like potatoes.

Inside the Hotel Boulderado, **Q's Restaurant** (2115 13th St., 303/442-4880, www.qsboulder.com, 6:30–11 A.M., 11:30 A.M.–2 P.M., and 5–10 P.M. Mon.–Fri., 7 A.M.–2 P.M. and 5–10 P.M. Sat.–Sun.) is both funky and stately, with a green-and-white ceiling, pillars, and stained-glass windows, and a menu that stretches from foie gras to chicken tortilla soup. With an outdoor patio and huge windows in the dining room, it's also the perfect spot for Pearl Street people-watching.

DaGabi Cucina (3970 N. Broadway, 303/786-9004, www.dagabicucina.com, 5–10 P.M. daily) is a little hard to find—it's behind the Lucky's Market on Broadway, north of Iris Avenue—but with the exception of

BOULDER AND FORT COLLINS

downtown's more casual Café Gondolier it's pretty much Boulder's only traditional Italian restaurant. The linguini with fresh clams ($14) and the risotto with rock shrimp ($15) are among the best dishes.

To get to **Gold Hill Inn** (401 Main St., 303/443-6461, www.goldhillinn.com, 6–9 P.M. Wed.–Sun. May and Oct., 6–9 P.M. Wed.–Mon. June–Sept.), take Mapleton Avenue through Sunshine Canyon, straight up, until you come to this rickety dirt-road town at the intersection of the excellently named Lickskillet Drive. It's in an old log cabin—which perfectly fits its surroundings—but the food inside is Flagstaff House-worthy. The six-course meal ($29) includes your choice of lamb venison, roast pork loin, salmon, roast duck, or broiled, smoked trout.

With its fireplace, tree-branch chairs, and wooden dècor, **Alice's Restaurant** (3371 Gold Lake Road, Ward, 303/459-3544, www.goldlake.com/dining.html, 11 A.M.–2 P.M., 5–8:30 P.M. Fri., 10:30 A.M.–2 P.M., 5–8:30 P.M. Sat.–Sun.), part of the Gold Lake Resort & Spa outside tiny Ward, has perhaps the most soothing ambience of any restaurant in the Boulder area. The entrèes are mostly duck, venison, and fish dishes—chicken and turkey are almost never available—and super-luxurious when mixed with wine.

INFORMATION

The **City of Boulder** (1777 Broadway, 303/441-3090, www.ci.boulder.co.us) is packed with parks and recreation resources, as well as city services and general details. The **Boulder Convention & Visitors Bureau** (2440 Pearl St., 303/442-2911 or 800/444-0447, www.bouldercoloradousa.com) is more geared toward tourists and business travelers. The **University of Colorado** can be reached at 303/492-1411 and www.colorado.edu.

Boulder has a surprisingly large number of newspapers for a midsize city: the *Daily Camera* (www.dailycamera.com) is the morning daily; the *Colorado Daily* (www.coloradodaily.com) focuses on CU but also covers local news; the *Boulder Weekly* (www.boulder-

weekly.com) is sort of a mini-*Westword* focusing on Boulder; and CU's student-run *Campus Press* (www.campuspress.colorado.edu) is often informative. Most of these publications, as well as *Westword* and various trade weeklies, pile up in the vestibules of local record stores, restaurants, grocery stores, and theaters.

The **Nederland Chamber of Commerce** (303/258-3936 or 800/221-0044, www.nederlandchamber.org) gives information about pretty much every business in town. The local weekly is the *Mountain Ear* (www.mountainear.com).

GETTING THERE AND AROUND

In addition to the standard RTD buses (1400 Walnut St., 303/442-7332, www.rtd-denver.com), which serve the entire city as well as Denver and points between, Boulder has a superb mini-transportation system. Colorful shuttles known as Hop, Skip, Jump, and others are quick and easy rides. For more information, contact the **City of Boulder Transportation**

COURTESY OF THE NATIONAL PARK SERVICE

Don't miss the view of Rocky Mountain National Park on the way to Nederland.

Division (1739 Broadway, 303/441-3266, www.ci.boulder.co.us/goboulder/html/transit).

Denver International Airport is still the best way to get to Boulder (you'll need a car or a bus, of course) from out of town. But a few mini-airports, such as **Jeffco** (www.airnav.com/airport/BJC) accommodate smaller planes and private pilots.

NEDERLAND

Some say Boulder is the quintessential hippie town, having discovered marijuana and the Grateful Dead in the 1960s and never let go. But Boulder has transformed into a city with more to life—for the most part—than where the next round of snacks will come from. So where have all the hippies gone? To "Ned," this tiny ex-mining town at the intersection of Highways 72 and 119, surrounded by placid hills and valleys. The people who live here are taking a break from civilization, in a good way, and their restaurants are great.

Sights

The 55-mile **Peak-to-Peak Highway** begins in Estes Park (as Highway 7) and twists through several tiny mountain towns—notably sleeping-dog-in-the-road Ward and gambling meccas Central City and Blackhawk—before intersecting with I-70, just west of Idaho Springs. Built in 1918, the highway winds through some of the most scenic terrain in Colorado, including Rocky Mountain National Park, Arapahoe and Roosevelt National Forests, and the Indian Peaks Wilderness Area. Views of the scenic Continental Divide pop up unexpectedly along the way. It's a narrow, mostly two-lane, paved road, and the easiest way to access it is in Nederland, where Highway 119 comes in from Longmont and Niwot.

Skiing

Here is the part of *Moon Colorado* where I confess that I cannot ski. I've tried twice at **Eldora Mountain Resort** (Hwy. 119, five miles west of Nederland, 303/440-8700, www.eldora.com), and each time involved stumbling off the lift at the top, with irritated grumbles

and catcalls from the experienced skiers below. My vast network of skiing sources assures me that Eldora, despite its reputation as a beginner's stop en route to Winter Park, Vail, or Aspen, is fun and relaxed, with plenty of powder. The resort reports Eldora gets 300 inches of snow per year, the summit is 10,800 feet above sea level, the sharpest vertical drop is 1,400 feet, the longest run is three miles, and there are 50 miles of skiable terrain totaling 680 acres.

Hiking and Biking

Just south of Rocky Mountain National Park and blending with Roosevelt National Forest to the east, **Indian Peaks Wilderness** is almost 77,000 acres with a range of triangular, 13,000-foot granite peaks for a backdrop. The park is filled with hiking trails, although the parking areas are small and it's a little hard to get to some of them. For more information, contact the **Boulder Ranger District** (2140 Yarmouth Ave., 303/541-2500), which is in charge of backcountry camping permits.

Entertainment

The **Pioneer Inn** (15 E. 1st St., 303/258-7733) is a live-music club on the mountain circuit that includes Golden's Buffalo Rose and the Mishawaka Inn near Fort Collins. Most of the bands that play here are of the hippie-jamming variety, but it snags strong local talent as well. In an early-1900s building, the **Acoustic Café** (95 E. 1st St., 303/258-3209, www.acousticcafe.net) snags a quieter variety of musical entertainment to go with homemade sandwiches and coffee.

Accommodations

Nederland is more popular as a pit stop en route to Central City, Blackhawk, Rocky Mountain National Park, and Boulder than a tourist destination, so few non-chain hotels have sprung up over the years. There is one excellent campground in the vicinity: **Kelly-Dahl** (Hwy. 119, three miles south of Nederland, 877/444-6777, $14), near gambling casinos *and* excellent hiking trails.

Food

The wooden-booth Italian fixture ❰ **Neapolitan's** (1 W. 1st St., 303/258-7313, www.neapolitansrestaurant.com, 4–9 P.M. Mon.–Thurs., 11 A.M.–9 P.M. Fri.–Sun.) is a required pit stop for drivers on the Peak-to-Peak Highway. The pizza is superb—homemade, medium thickness, fresh ingredients, tangy sauce—and the pasta dishes and cheesy garlic bread are almost as good.

Black Forest Restaurant (24 Big Springs Dr., 303/279-2333 or 303/582-9971, www.blackforestrest.com, 11 A.M.–9:30 P.M. daily) is a German eatery that looks the part—big, triangular roof, building trim out of *Pippi Longstocking*, and menu items like Hungarian goulash and wiener schnitzel. It's maybe not the best place to stop on a quick drive, but you might crave the protein after a day at Eldora.

Estes Park and Rocky Mountain National Park

Estes Park is the entry point to some of the most magnificent mountain-and-valley country in Colorado—Rocky Mountain National Park, a wilderness area with hundreds of miles of trails, as well as beautiful high-altitude lakes, the 14,000-foot-tall Longs Peak, and several "thirteeners"—but the town itself is surprisingly *un*-magnificent. Except for the huge Stanley Hotel (itself a bit run-down these days), the old hotels are nothing special, most of the non-fast-food restaurants are of the burger-and-billiards variety, and the tourist-trap stores sell a combination of polished gemstones and kids' toys.

The town is a fine detour en route to the national park, but its lack of elegant food and lodging discourages long stays, especially in the winter, when most tourists have moved on to the ski resorts.

Although Native Americans were the first to live here, Estes Park's first white settler was hunter Joel Estes, who stumbled upon the mountain valley in 1859 and relocated his family to two log cabins in order to build a cattle ranch. Word spread among Estes's friends, and by 1877 the Irish Earl of Dunraven had built a hotel for European visitors. Stanley Steamer inventor F. O. Stanley took over as the primary developer at the turn of the 20th century; sick with tuberculosis, he built his massive white Stanley Hotel in 1909.

The Stanley became famous in the 1980s, after Stephen King stayed here and was inspired to write a portion of *The Shining*, although the famously creepy Jack Nicholson film wasn't filmed in Estes Park. After two major floods, Estes Park became known "The Gutsiest Little Town in Colorado."

SIGHTS

Among the exhibits in the small **Estes Park Museum** (200 4th St., 970/586-6256, www.estesnet.com/museum, 10 A.M.–5 P.M. Mon.–Sat. May–Oct., 10 A.M.–5 P.M. Fri.–Sat. and 1–5 P.M. Sun. Nov.–Apr., free) is an actual Stanley Steamer automobile, in honor of F. O. Stanley and his hotel, as well as a log cabin and various photos and postcards from the old days.

Founded in 1883, the **MacGregor Ranch Museum** (180 MacGregor Ln., 970/586-3749, www.macgregorranch.org, 8:30 A.M.–3 P.M. Mon.–Fri., free) displays the original family's personal paintings, clothing, and rock collections in a historic house on a huge ranch underneath Longs Peak.

SPORTS AND RECREATION
Fishing

Nearby Rocky Mountain National Park is where to go for hiking, biking, snowshoeing, and the like, but Estes Park has the **Big Thompson River** (east of town on U.S. 34) and **Peter's Pond** (510 Moraine Ave., 970/586-5171, www.etonnant.com/catch_wild_trout). For equipment, maps,

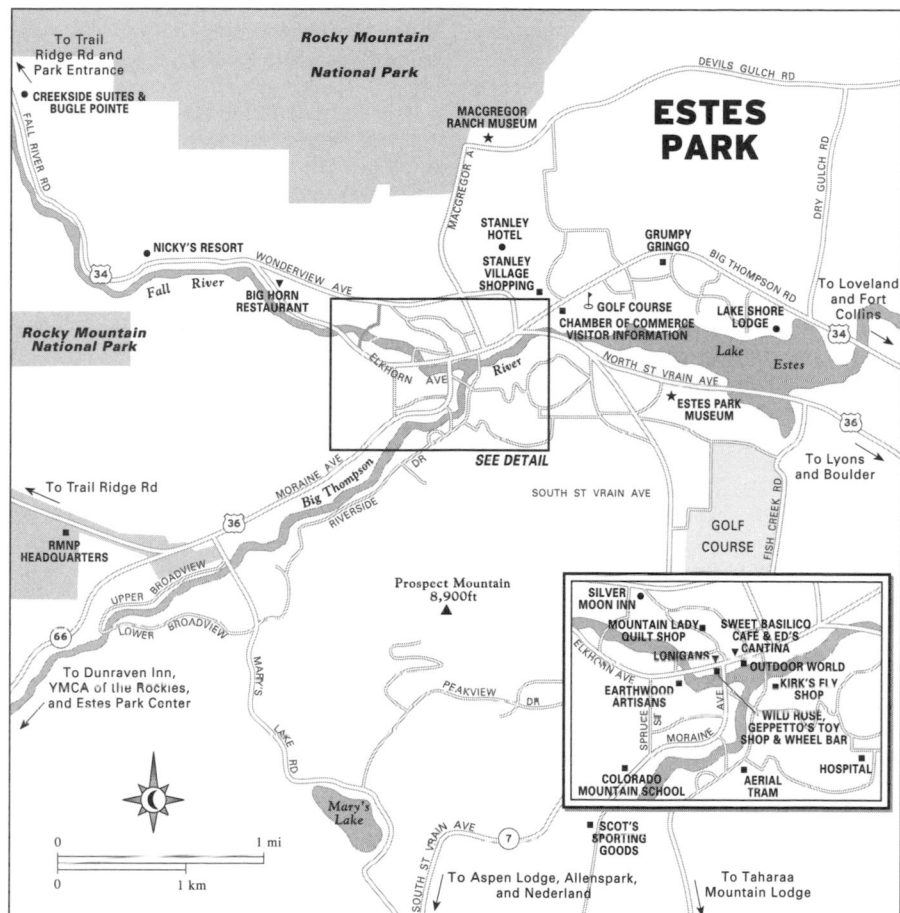

and tour information, contact **Rocky Mountain Adventures** (1117 N. Highway 287, 970/493-4005 or 800/858.6808, www.shoprma.com), which also focuses on the Cache La Poudre River.

White-Water Rafting
The Cache La Poudre River begins in Estes Park and flows fairly ruggedly into the Fort Collins area, and **Rapid Transit Rafting** (800/367-8523, www.rapidtransitrafting.com) tags along, providing the proper guides, rental rafts, equipment, and lessons.

Golf
The **Estes Park Golf Club** (1080 S. Saint Vrain, 970/586-8146, www.estesvalleyrecreation.com/18holegolf.html) has a park district-run 18-hole course that's scenic and no-nonsense—unless you count the occasional deer, elk, or coyote wandering onto the greens.

ENTERTAINMENT AND NIGHTLIFE
Although Wall of Dogs and Ricky and the Red Hot Voodoo Devils are unlikely to challenge the Rolling Stones for national live-concert

dominance, local bands' shows at **Lonigans** (110 W. Elkhorn Ave., 970/586-4346, www.lonigans.com) are usually raucous, bluesy, and fun. Decent bar food, too. Townie bars like the **Wheel Bar** (132 E. Elkhorn Ave., 970/586-9381) are scattered along Elkhorn, inviting tourists to step in for some pool, darts, or a glimpse of sports on television.

SHOPPING

The Estes Park shopping district centers on Elkhorn Avenue, the town's main drag, with all the Christmas knickknacks, kids' toys, wooden wildlife sculptures, and shiny rocks you could ever want. Some of the more unique shops include the **Mountain Lady Quilt Shop** (205 Park Lane, 970/586-5330, www.mtnladyquilt.com), which has nice stuff; **Earthwood Artisans** (145 E. Elkhorn Ave., 970/586-2151, www.earthwoodartisans.com), a large gallery of pottery, photographs, paintings, and many other styles, mostly by local artists; and **Geppetto's Toy Shoppe** (160 W. Elkhorn Ave., 970/586-5709), a requisite stop for embattled parents tired of saying no to their kids as they wander down Elkhorn in search of food.

ACCOMMODATIONS
Under $100

On an 860-acre ranch with tall hills for sledding and backcountry skiing, the **Estes Park Center/YMCA of the Rockies** (2515 Tunnel Rd., 970/586-3341 or 303/448-1616, www.ymcarockies.org, $91–143) has four lodges and several log cabins. It's the most affordable lodging in town for large groups, and the conference dining rooms have all-you-can-eat buffets.

$100-150

Upon viewing the **Stanley Hotel** (333 Wonderview Ave., 970/586-3371 or 800/976-1377, www.stanleyhotel.com, $119–600), underneath a huge mountain peak overlooking the town of Estes Park, you might be tempted to stare through a door and declare, "*Honey,* I'm *home.*" But Jack Nicholson, who delivered that line in *The Shining,*

never filmed in this massive white building, which F. O. Stanley, of Stanley Steamer automobile fame, built while dying of tuberculosis in the early 1900s. The hotel remains an ornate tourist fixture, with red carpets on the floor, wide staircases, large windows that show off the best mountain views, and a restaurant that's the perfect wedding location. The only downfall is that the hotel is, well, old, and feels like it.

The **Aspen Lodge at Estes Park Ranch Resort and Conference Center** (6120 Hwy. 7, 970/586-8133 or 800/332-6867, www.aspenlodge.net, $129) is on an 82-acre ranch of meadows and evergreens that are almost always open for guest hikers, snowshoers, and, of course, horseback riders. The ranch has an on-site livery, with horses available for all different riding levels. As for the 52-room lodge itself, it's a giant log cabin with a fireplace in the cowboy-style lobby. Be careful when exiting your room onto the wooden balcony, however; my wife and I once locked ourselves out and had to ask a bride, who was preparing for her wedding on the ranch in 15 minutes, to let us back in through her room.

The green-roofed **Lake Shore Lodge** (1700 Big Thompson Ave., 970/577-6400 or 800/332-6867, www.lakeshorelodge.com, $129–209) is great for hiking and mountain-viewing—the steps down from the hotel's deck lead directly to the 3.7-mile Lake Estes Trail, a pretty walk, and the outdoor patio at the Silverado Restaurant overlooks both the lake and the mountains.

$150-200

The best part about the **Taharaa Mountain Lodge** (3110 S. St. Vrain, 970/577-0098 or 800/597-0098, www.taharaa.com, $170–325) is the happy hour, in front of a stone fireplace beyond the lobby. The lodge is a larger-than-usual bed-and-breakfast with helpful owners, Ken and Diane Harlen, who patiently answer questions. Large windows let in plenty of blue sky and mountain views.

Creekside Suites (1400 David Dr., 970/577-0068 or 800/349-1003, www.creeksidesuites.com, $165–185) is a collection of wooden suites with decks overlooking the Fall River. Some of the rooms are small, but most have fireplaces and whirlpools. Many other local hotels and condos are along Fall River, including **Bugle Pointe** (1480 David Dr., 970/586-1151 or 888/925-9260, www.bugle-pointe.com, $175–195 for a one-room condo) and **Silver Moon Inn** (175 Spruce Dr., 970/586-6006 or 800/818-6006, www.estes-park.com/silvermoon, $130–170), a two-story, ski-resort-style hotel.

FOOD

There's nothing wrong with a good tourist-trap burger joint with beer and pool—**Ed's Cantina** (362 E. Elkhorn Ave., 970/586-2919, 11 A.M.–11 P.M. daily)—is one of many such restaurants clustered around Estes Park's main drag, Elkhorn Avenue. But the one-room Italian restaurant **Sweet Basilico Café** (401 E. Elkhorn Ave., 970/586-3899, 11 A.M.–10 P.M. daily) is an exception, geared to fine-diners en route to Rocky Mountain National Park. The homemade dishes include lasagna and excellent minestrone soup. Grab a table in the window and watch all the tourists.

Other upscale Estes Park eateries include the **Wild Rose** (157 W. Elkhorn Ave., 970/586-2806, 11 A.M.–10 P.M. daily), which has a long wine list to go with a European menu of seafood, pasta, and steak; **Nicky's Resort** (1350 U.S. 34, 970/586-5376, 7:30 A.M.–10 P.M. daily), a Greek-style steak restaurant with a wooden interior to match the mountain ambience outside; and the **Dunraven Inn** (2470 Highway 66, 970/586-6409, 5–9 P.M. daily), an Italian place a few miles from town specializing in seafood and steaks.

◖ ROCKY MOUNTAIN NATIONAL PARK

With flat, 14,000-foot Longs Peak standing watch over a landscape of massive mountains, as well as meadows, lakes, and wilderness, the 265,000-acre Rocky Mountain National Park is one of Colorado's most exhilarating attractions and a user-friendly nature preserve with 359 miles of meticulously crafted trails. Its valleys are "only" about 8,000 feet high, but the elevations shift abruptly; Longs Peak is the sole fourteener, and more than 75 mountain peaks rise beyond 12,000 feet.

The park has endless nooks and crannies for the three million hikers, rock climbers, campers, and picnickers who visit every year, and they're all consistently rewarded with clean mountain air; sightings of elk, deer, coyotes, eagles, and many other kinds of wildlife; and row upon row of summer wildflowers.

Although it didn't become a national park until the U.S. established it in 1915, the area formed tens of thousands of years ago when active volcanoes and moving glaciers left mountains, valleys, and tundra behind. (Even in the dead of summer, it can be extremely cold as you walk or drive higher up the mountains, so be sure to pack accordingly.) A variety of Native American tribes lived and hunted here for centuries, until gold miners took over in the late 1800s; remnants of both civilizations can still be found in the park.

The easiest way to get into Rocky Mountain National Park is **Trail Ridge Road** (U.S. 34), a paved, 48-mile highway that peaks at 12,183 feet and rises dramatically above the trees, straight into 11 miles of alpine tundra that often includes unexpected patches of snow. (This is where you might have to switch from the air conditioner to the heater in your car.) Bring a camera for the incredible roadside views. Most of the road is open all year, but the central stretch is usually closed from mid-October to late May.

Almost as scenic is 9-mile **Bear Lake Road** (beginning at the **Moraine Park Museum,** off U.S. 36, 970/586-1206, 9 A.M.–4:30 P.M. daily), which overlooks Longs Peak and numerous waterfalls en route to the pretty lake and its surrounding trails. The road and parking lot are often cluttered with cars, so consider stopping 3 miles past the museum to take a U.S. Park Service shuttle.

The 11-mile **Old Fall River Road** (from Fall River to Alpine visitors centers) is sort of a shortcut, but a tough one—one-way, unpaved,

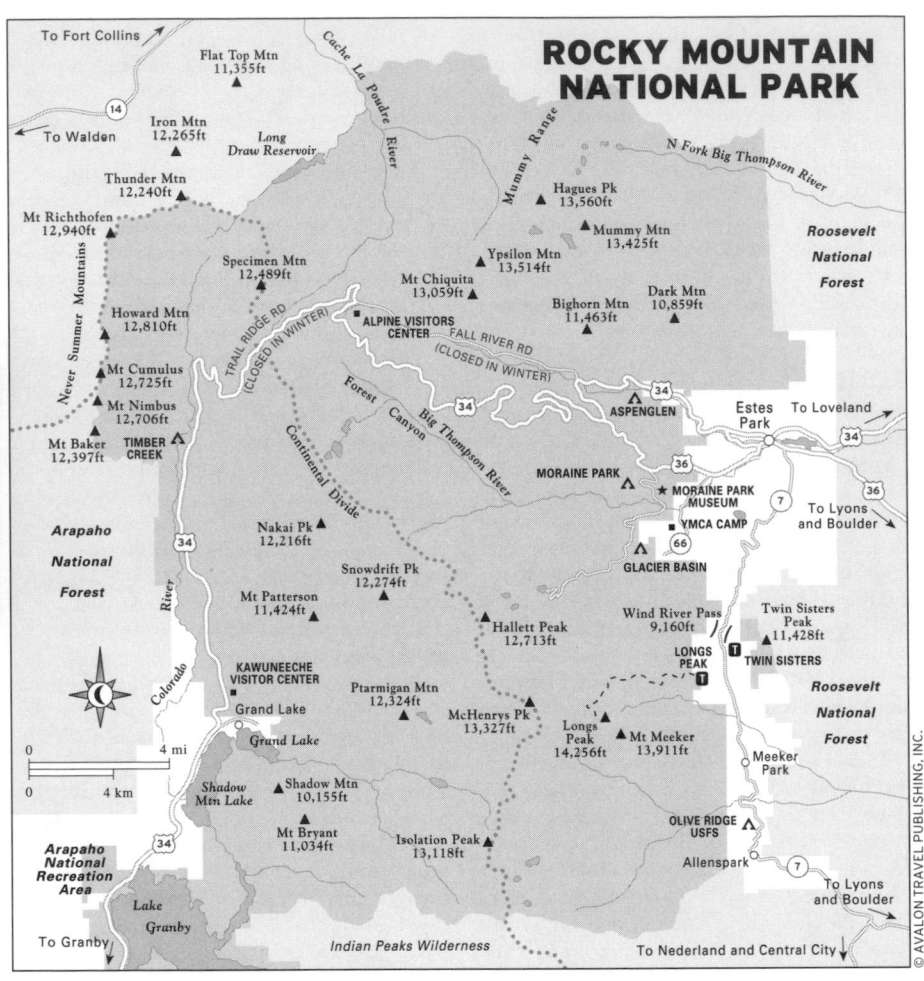

ROCKY MOUNTAIN NATIONAL PARK

15 miles per hour maximum, with no RVs allowed. The views from near-12,000-foot Fall River Pass and potential detours into relaxing Horseshoe and Willow parks are worth it if you can stand the driving conditions. Four-wheel drive is helpful.

The park's visitors centers are **Alpine** (Fall River Pass, at Trail Ridge Rd. and Old Fall River Rd., 970/586-1206); **Beaver Meadows** (U.S. 36, 3 miles from Estes Park, at the park entrance, 970/586-1206); **Fall River** (U.S. 34, 5 miles west of Estes Park, at the park's Fall River entrance, 970/586-1206); and **Kawuneeche** (U.S. 34, 1 mile north of Grand Lake, at the park entrance, 970/586-1513). (**Lily Lake** is closed indefinitely.) Check the park website at www.nps.gov/romo/index.htm for hours, as they vary from season to season.

It costs $20 per car for a week at the park, or $10 for bicyclists and motorcyclists. For maps and other information, try the **Rocky Mountain Nature Association** (970/586-0108, www.rmna.org).

© STEVE KNOPPER

There are many ways to climb 14,000-foot-high Longs Peak – by foot, bike, or car.

Sports and Recreation

Cycling isn't allowed in the park—just on 23 miles of the paved Trail Ridge Road—but **hiking** trails are everywhere. The park can get amazingly crowded, especially in the summer, so if you're looking for seclusion, or at least a walk without running into people, contact park officials at 970/586-1206 for maps and advice.

The park's most famous trail is **Longs Peak** (Hwy. 7, near the park's southeast corner, about 6 miles north of Allenspark), which is Colorado's version of Mount Everest (well, minus the sherpas and life-threatening elevations). The 8-mile trip begins at 9,400 feet of elevation and climbs to more than 14,200 at the summit, and it's one of the most technically difficult climbs in the state; some hikers have died while climbing, so be sure to equip yourself with windbreakers, water, and pre-hike calls to local rangers for conditions. There are shorter and (in some cases) less strenuous routes up the mountain, including the 4-mile trails to **Chasm Lake** and **Twin Sisters Peaks,** both one-way, moderately difficult, and totally worth it for the breathtaking views. But there's nothing like looking down from the Longs summit.

Of the miles and miles of hiking trails within the park, among the best and most popular are **Bear Lake** (Bear Lake Rd., 11 miles from the Beaver Meadows Visitors Center), a 0.6-mile loop that meanders around the base of two large mountains and overlooks the lake and waterfalls; **Coyote Valley** (5 miles north of the Kawuneeche Visitors Center), an easy one-mile trail with elk and moose as frequent guest stars; the **Colorado River Trail** (on the park's west side), a 3.7-mile one-way walk that goes along a onetime stagecoach road into an abandoned gold-mining town, Lulu City; and the 5-mile, one-way **Ouzel Lake** (off Hwy. 7, 2 miles northwest of Allenspark, at the Wild Basin Ranger Station parking lot), along the frantic, waterfall-like North St. Vrain Creek, leading toward several lakes toward the end.

Rock climbers have flocked to the park for decades, particularly the east side of Longs

one of the many scenic pleasures of Rocky Mountain National Park

Peak, where difficult alpine-wall climbs like **The Diamond** (accessible from the mountain trailhead) have become so crowded that enthusiasts have stopped telling their friends about it. Another popular climbing destination within the park is **Lumpy Ridge** (off MacGregor Ave. in Estes Park), a huge chunk of granite that makes veterans rapturous. For gear, maps, and advice, go to the **Colorado Mountain School** (341 Moraine Ave., 970/586-5758 or 888/267-7783, www.cmschool.com).

Most of the hiking trails open in the summer are accessible in the winter for backcountry **skiers** and **snowshoers.** Call the park for weather conditions—avalanches happen now and then in this terrain—before heading out, and be sure to bring at least one partner. **Outdoor World** (156 E. Elkhorn Ave., 970/586-2114 or 800/679-3600, www.rmconnection.com) rents equipment and gives tips.

With lakes everywhere, **fishing** is also common in the park; **Kirk's Fly Shop** (230 E. Elkhorn Ave., 970/577-0790 or 877/669-

1859, www.kirksflyshop.com) rents rods, tackle boxes, and other equipment and provides guided tours, including some with llamas (yes, llamas) carrying your packs.

Accommodations

There are no hotels in Rocky Mountain National Park—you'll have to stay in nearby Estes Park for luxury, or at least indoor plumbing—but several campgrounds are among the best in the state. They include: **Aspenglen** (near Estes Park at the east entrance); **Glacier Basin** (Bear Creek Rd., 5 miles south of U.S. 36); **Longs Peak** (Hwy. 7, 9 miles south of Estes Park); **Moraine Park** (Bear Lake Rd., just south of U.S. 36); and **Timber Creek** (Trail Ridge Rd., 12 miles west of the Alpine Visitors Center). All campgrounds are $20 a night, although some are cheaper in the fall, when the running water is turned off; check details by calling 800/365-2267.

Backcountry camping is plentiful, but it requires a permit, available by calling 970/586-1242.

INFORMATION

For general information on Estes Park, the **Municipal Building** (170 MacGregor Ave., 970/577-3800, www.estesnet.com) has a variety of boilerplate details for locals and visitors. Something called the **Estes Park eWelcome Center** maintains a helpful website at www.estes-park.com, and the local chamber of commerce is at 800/443-7837 and www.estesparkcvb.com.

Grand County

GRAND LAKE

On the west edge of Rocky Mountain National Park, Grand Lake has been a high-class tourist area since miners discovered gold in nearby mountain towns in the late 1800s. It has three huge lakes, including Grand Lake itself, the largest non-manmade body of water in Colorado. For centuries, though, the Utes avoided what they called "Spirit Lake." They believed rival tribes, after massacring the men and pushing rafts of women in children into the lake to capsize and die, created evil spirits from the lake mists.

Grand Lake, thankfully, hasn't had a Ute massacre in years—just plenty of fishing, sailing, and golf. And tourism. The shops here have an Old West feel, like those in nearby Estes Park, but travelers can tell by the lack of Christmas knickknacks that the shopping district is fairly substantive for a tourist town.

Sights

At 69 miles and just one way, the **Colorado River Headwaters & Scenic Byway** is a little inconvenient for drivers who just want to get from Rocky Mountain National Park to Steamboat Springs. But travelers with a couple of hours to kill should experience it for the scenery—mountains, canyons, springs, lakes, a weirdly out-of-place desert, and, of course, the Colorado River, which runs parallel. The byway begins as U.S. 34 in Grand Lake, heads southward to Granby, then curves west through Hot Sulphur Springs, Kremmling, and Radium before ending in State Bridge. From there, look for Highway 131 north, which runs into U.S. 40 and, ultimately, Steamboat Springs. There's a good map at www.coloradodirectory.com/maps/coriver.html.

Sports and Recreation

According to the Grand County Tourism Board, the Grand Lake area has 1,000 miles of streams, 1,000 acres of lakes, and 11,000 acres of reservoirs—most of which contain many different kinds of trout and salmon. The three main lakes are Grand Lake and the bigger reservoirs Lake Granby and Shadow Mountain Lake, and they're all open to ice fishing, sailing, canoeing, and other water sports. On Lake Granby, the **Beacon Landing Marina** (County Rd. 64, one mile away from U.S. 34, 970/627-3671, www.beaconlanding.us), in business since 1952, offers guided **fishing** trips and rents rods, reels, and boats (as well as providing a place to launch them, of course).

In addition to ice fishing, Grand Lake is famous for its **snowmobiling**—and has a decent reputation for cross-country skiing and snowshoeing as well. The area has 150 miles of groomed snowmobiling trails—as well as another 150 for bushwhackers—and several companies that rent the vehicles. One of the best is **On the Trail Rentals** (1447 County Rd. 491, 970/627-0171 or 888/627-2429, www.onthetrailrentals.com).

Cross-country skiers and **snowshoers**—not to mention hikers and bikers—find numerous trails, groomed and otherwise, in nearby Arapahoe National Recreation Area, Rocky Mountain National Park, and Indian Peaks Wilderness Area. For access to 18 miles of groomed trails, check out the **Grand Lake Recreation District** (1415 County Rd. 48, 970/627-8872). For equipment rental, the **Grand Lake Touring Center** (U.S. 34, a quarter mile west of Grand Lake at County Rd. 48,

BOULDER AND FORT COLLINS

970/627-8008, www.grandlakecolorado.com/ touringcenter) has a low-key ski shop.

The city-run **Grand Lake Golf Course** (1415 County Rd. 48, 970/627-8008 or 800/551-8580, www.grandlakegolf.com) has 18 holes, as well as tennis courts and a restaurant.

Nightlife

The **Rocky Mountain Repertory Theatre** (Town Park, 970/531-8559, www.rockymountainrep.com) has been producing local plays, including a regular lineup of youth productions, for decades. Recent shows include *Annie Get Your Gun* and *Beauty and the Beast.*

Shopping

Grand Avenue is the main drag for tourists and shoppers. Among the best galleries and stores are **Jackstraw Mountain Gallery** (1030 Grand Ave., 970/627-8111, www.jackstrawgrandlake.com), specializing in watercolor and oil paintings, and selling digital prints; **Humphrey's Cabin Fever** (1100 Grand Ave., 970/627-8939), selling a range of home products, from home furnishings to clothes; and **Grand Willow Dry Goods & Garden Finery** (801 Grand Ave., 970/627-0092), for upscale, homemade home and garden items.

Accommodations

The **Rapids Lodge** (209 Rapids Lane, 970/627-3707, www.rapidslodge.com, $75–155) is in a secluded house on the Tonahutu River, with classic bed-and-breakfast-style rooms, many with old-fashioned pattern wallpaper, four-poster beds, and snowshoes hanging on the walls. The large, dark-wood lodge has seven rooms, and several smaller log cabins are available as well.

The **Inn at Grand Lake** (1103 Grand Ave., 970/627-9234 or 800/722-2585, www.innatgrandlake.com, $100–140) is a wide and wooden inn with second-floor balconies in view of the mountains and the lake. A massage-therapy company is on the premises, as is the Sagebrush BBQ & Grille.

The **Western Riviera** (419 Garfield St., 970/627-3580, www.westernriv.com, $100–

150) is the only Grand Lake motel on the lake itself. It's not the most fancy joint in the world—the rooms are basic and the second-floor balconies have plastic deck furniture—but you can't beat the location.

Mountain Lakes Lodge (10480 U.S. 34, 970/627-8448, www.mountainlakeslodge.com, $75–145) has 10 log cabins built in 1950, as well as the three-bedroom Little Log House, in the middle of the woods about four miles from town. The rooms are funky and a little strange, with huge log beds and various sports pictures on the walls. A "good caster" can actually fish from the outdoor room deck, according to the lodge website.

Directly next to Rocky Mountain National Park, the pine-built **Grand Lake Lodge** (15500 U.S. 34, 970/627-3967 or 303/759-5848 (winter only), www.grandlakelodge.com, $85–175) has rented several small cabins since the 1920s—Henry Ford once stayed here, and one of the cabins is named after him. Although it's not super-luxurious, the lodge is worth it for its proximity to Grand and Shadow Mountain Lakes.

Food

Inside the Inn at Grand Lake, the **Sagebrush BBQ & Grille** (1103 Grand Ave., 970/627-1404 or 866/900-1404, www.sagebrushbbq.com, 11 A.M.–9:30 P.M. Sun.–Thurs., 11 A.M.–10 P.M. Fri.–Sat.) displays 1883 iron jail doors on the walls and has some of the best burgers (including vegetarian ones) in town. It also serves seafood, pork, burritos, and, of course, barbecue.

GRANBY

Never mind that Granby is a ranching town in the mountains near Winter Park and Rocky Mountain National Park, or that several rodeos are staged here every year. What most Coloradoans associate with Granby these days is a bulldozer. In June 2004, a 51-year-old muffler-shop owner, Marvin Heemeyer, was reportedly upset about a local zoning-board decision and all but destroyed the town with a 75-ton, armor-plated bulldozer he rigged himself. After demolishing several Agate Avenue businesses,

© STEVE KNOPPER

BOULDER AND FORT COLLINS

the scenic route from Winter Park to Granby

including a general store and the local newspaper office, Heemeyer ended the carnage by shooting himself to death.

It's a freaky story, even more so because Granby, founded in 1905, is an otherwise uneventful mountain town at an elevation of 7,935 feet, famous for its cowboy culture and history as a major lettuce-production hub. There's not much here, other than ranches and mountain views, but Granby is conveniently located, within a few miles of several major ski areas, Rocky Mountain National Park, and Hot Sulphur Springs.

Sports and Recreation

Colorado State Forest State Park (56750 Hwy. 14, 53 miles north of Granby, near Walden, 970/723-8366, www.coloradoparks.org) is almost 71,000 acres of wilderness with 50 miles of clearly marked **hiking** trails and spots to watch elk, antelope, moose, and buffalo. The mountain views here are terrific, thanks especially to the Medicine Bow range, which hits 12,000 feet at some plateaus.

Bird-watching is the primary sport in Granby—other than rodeo—and the **Windy Gap Reservoir** (U.S. 40 and Highway 125, about two miles west of Granby, 970/725-6200, free) has a wildlife area where it's possible to spot pelicans, eagles, swans, and many others.

Anglers are generally better served with the three massive lakes of nearby Grand Lake, but some of the connecting waterways, such as the **Colorado River,** are great for **fishing.** Other places to fetch a giant trout or two are the **Fraser River** and **Willow Creek.** For fishing information—on Lake Granby, Grand Lake, and Shadow Mountain Reservoir, in addition to the Granby spots—contact the **Beacon Landing Marina** (1026 County Rd. 64, 970/627-3671).

The **SolVista Ski Area & Golf Club** (999 Village Rd., two miles south of Granby, 970/887-2709 for golf, 800/757-7669 for skiing, www.solvista.com) is the only resort in Colorado to give equal billing to both skiing and golfing. The ski resort is a little invisible, given that Winter Park and Mary Jane are just

15 minutes north, but its 220 inches of snow per year, summit elevation of 9,202 feet, 406 acres of skiable terrain, and a balanced mix of trails for beginners and experts make it an unexpected pleasure. Golf-wise, the club has 18 holes alongside the pretty Fraser River.

The other Granby golf facility is the **Grand Elk Ranch & Club** (1321 Ten Mile Dr., 877/389-9333), an 18-hole, par-71 course designed by Craig Stadler and Tripp Davis in 2002.

Accommodations

The **C Lazy U Guest Ranch** (3640 Hwy. 125, 970/887-3344, www.clazyu.com, $2,700 per week, three nights minimum) emphasizes horseback riding—there's a 12,000-square-foot indoor riding area—but also offers a pool, tennis and basketball courts, trap-shooting, and hayrides. The lodge is a large wooden building on a 1919 ranch, and it's so luxurious that even celebrities show up with their kids.

Food

The **Longbranch Restaurant** (185 E. Agate Ave., 970/887-2209, 11 A.M.–9 P.M. Sun.–Fri., noon–9 P.M. Sat.) has an Old West theme—dig the wagon wheels!—despite an unusual predisposition for German food amid the American and Mexican dishes. More family-oriented is **Remington's** (52 4th St., 970/887-3632, 6:30 A.M.–10 P.M. Tues.–Sat., 11 A.M.–10 P.M. Mon.), with a wide variety of entrées, from enchiladas to trout to bacon double cheeseburgers.

INFORMATION

The **Grand Lake Area Chamber of Commerce** (970/627-3372) runs a somewhat finicky webpage at www.grandlakechamber.com. And while its focus is real estate, www.grandlakecolorado.com has helpful tourism information as well.

The **Greater Granby Chamber of Commerce** is at 970/887-2311 or 800/325-1661, www.granbychamber.com. The Granby newspaper, the *Sky-Hi News* (www.grandcountynews.com/skyhinews/skyhinews.htm), recovered from its brush with the bulldozer and continues to publish once a week.

HOT SULPHUR SPRINGS

With a population of 521, Hot Sulphur Springs is a cattle-ranching town with some of the best scenery in tiny Grand County—the Continental Divide, Colorado River, and various tree-lined meadows and hills are within striking distance. But the town's best quality is something the Utes and Arapahos discovered some 9,000 years ago: the springs themselves, which the Utes named "big medicine" and "healing waters." The pools, ranging 104–126°F, are best experienced at the local spa and resort.

Sights

The **Grand County Historical Association** (110 E. Byers Ave., 970/725-3939, www.grandcountymuseum.com) operates three museums: the **Pioneer Village Complex** (U.S. 40, east end of Hot Sulphur Springs, 10 A.M.–4 P.M. Wed.–Sat. in winter, 10 A.M.–5 P.M. Tues.–Sat. and 1–5 P.M. Sun. in summer, $4), which is in a brick 1924 school building and displays Old West tools and artifacts; the **Cozens Ranch and Stage Stop Museum** (U.S. 40, between Winter Park and Fraser, 10 A.M.–4 P.M. Wed.–Sat., $4), named for the Canadian-born sheriff of Central City and showing various original ranch-house wallpaper and carpet pieces; and the **Heritage Park Museum** (Kremmling, 17 miles west of Hot Sulphur Springs, 970/725-3939, call for appointments), in an 1885 two-story log building recently relocated from nearby Wolford Mountain Reservoir.

Accommodations

The **Hot Sulphur Springs Resort & Spa** (U.S. 40, 20 miles west of Grand Lake, 970/725-3306 or 800/510-6235, www.hotsulphursprings.com, $98–225) has 21 natural mineral springs, some in standard outdoor pools and some at the bottom of rocky holes. The 17 motel rooms and one large 1840s log cabin are wooden and minimalist, with just beds and showers, no telephones or TVs.

The **Riverside Hotel** (509 Grand Ave., 970/725-3589, $58), in a 1903 building near the Colorado River, is crammed with classic furnishings, such as a huge lobby fireplace and numerous plants. Its dining room is similarly old-timey and quaint, with a piano and the best steaks in town.

Latigo Ranch (Kremmling, about 17 miles west of Hot Sulphur Springs, 970/724-9008 or 800/227-9655, www.latigotrails.com, $2,100 per person per week) is one of the few secluded mountain lodging properties in Colorado that encourages parents to bring their kids. The horseback-riding and hiking trails wind around lakes and meadows and overlook mountains and forests, and the log-cabin rooms have old-fashioned metal fireplaces and comfortable chairs and couches.

Information

The **Grand County Visitors Center** (www .rkymtnhi.com/Visitors/Towns/Hotsulphur) site has excellent information on Hot Sulphur Springs, a town so small it doesn't have its own webpage. For details on the springs themselves, contact the resort at 970/725-3306 or www.hotsulphursprings.com.

Fort Collins

Home of both Colorado State University and a wide-open swath of farms and ranches, Fort Collins is a 126,000-resident college town that lacks the loopy yuppies of Boulder and the conservative red-staters of fellow northern Colorado towns like Greeley and Fort Morgan. It's on the Cache La Poudre, a tree-lined river that flows from Rocky Mountain National Park and the Front Range, so it attracts outdoor enthusiasts of all types, and at 60 miles north of Denver it's the perfect combination of isolated and populated.

Fort Collins came into being in 1862, when U.S. soldiers arrived to watch over the Cherokee Trail and the Overland Stage Line, but the "old fort" lasted only four years. Its future arrived in 1860, when settlers created an irrigation ditch for the Cache La Poudre; farmers, ranchers, and a major railroad followed shortly thereafter. CSU opened in 1870 with 25,000 students, and although the student body has shrunk somewhat since then, the college provides the city's largest number of jobs.

Today, Fort Collins is a medium-sized city with a downtown area (historic Old Town Square) that resembles Boulder's University Hill, with all the pierced-nosed kids, sweatshirt-wearing alumni, and microbreweries, microbreweries, and more microbreweries that implies.

SIGHTS

Old Town Square (Mountain Ave. and College Ave.) was a business district in the late 1800s; some of the few remaining original buildings include a drugstore, Old Grout, on the corner of Mountain and College. A National Historic District, the square is known today as the center of college life, with a lively mix of bars and restaurants, shops and galleries. One of the best-known buildings is the sandstone **Avery House** (328 W. Mountain Ave., 970/221-0533, www.poudrelandmarks.com, 1–3 P.M. Sun. and Wed., free), named for original Fort Collins streetbuilder, bank founder, and agricultural pioneer Franklin Avery, who built this family home in 1879.

The **Fort Collins Museum** (200 Mathews St., 970/221-6738, www.ci.fort-collins.co.us/museum, 10 A.M.–5 P.M. Tues.–Sun., noon–5 P.M. Sun., free) has three late-1800s buildings in its courtyard and a main gallery of sugar-beet-farming artifacts and a mud wagon. Andrew Carnegie coughed up $12,500 to fund the museum's sandstone building, originally the city's public library, in 1904.

The **Environmental Learning Center** (3745 E. Prospect Rd., 970/491-1661, www.cnr.colostate.edu/elc), run by Colorado State's Natural Resources department about three miles east of campus, preserves 212 acres of forest and

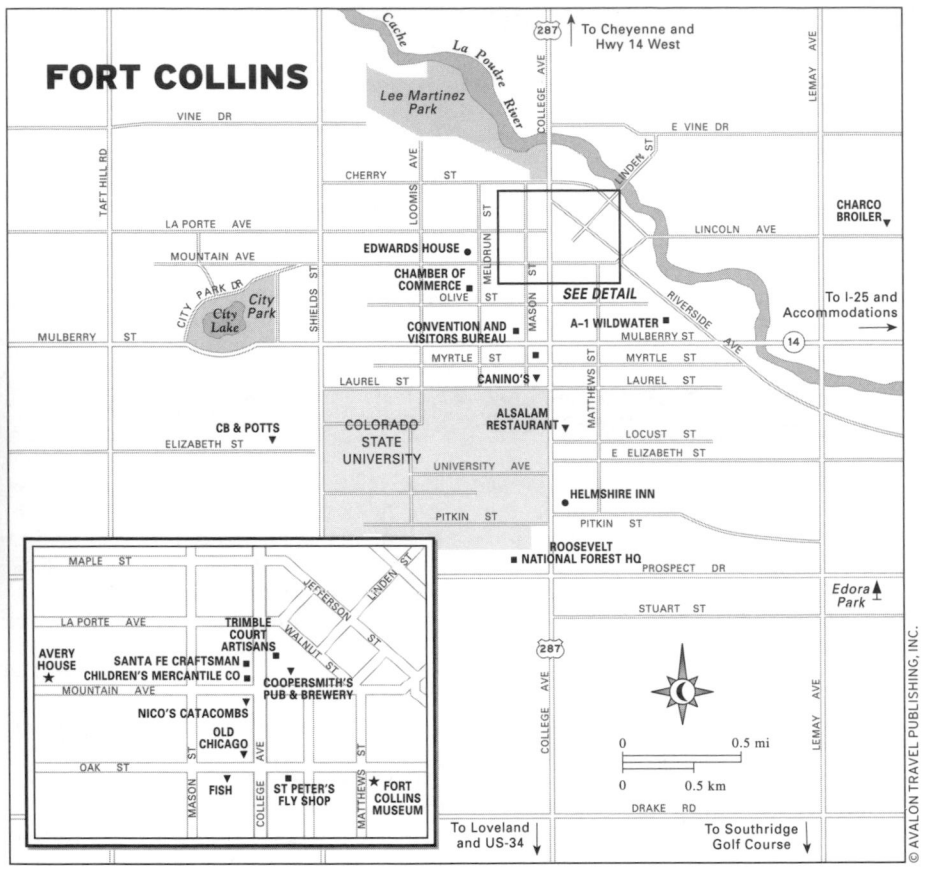

© AVALON TRAVEL PUBLISHING, INC.

grassland for local hikers and wildlife-watchers. There's an information center and a 1.2-mile trail, and staff members are on hand for guided tours and questions. Also on the premises is the Rocky Mountain Raptor Program, a haven for a variety of birds.

It's a little random that the St. Louis company **Anheuser-Busch** (2351 Busch Dr., 970/490-4691, www.budweisertours.com/docs/ftcolns.htm, 10 A.M.–4 P.M. Thurs.–Mon. Oct.–May, 9:30 A.M.–4:30 P.M. daily June–Aug., 10 A.M.–4 P.M. daily Sept., free) runs brewery tours in Fort Collins, but this is one of five tour locations in the United States. Fort Collins is also a huge microbrewery town, and

several of those give tours as well—the **Odell Brewing Co.** (800 E. Lincoln Ave., 970/498-9070, www.odellbrewing.com, free), which in the late 1980s sold its homebrews out of the back of a truck, is the most interesting.

Noted in the goofy-American-traveling-attractions bible *Roadside America*, **Swetsville Zoo** (4801 E. Harmony Rd., 970/484-9509, dawn–dusk daily, free) is ex-farmer Bill Swets's menagerie of dinosaurs, ducks, and robots constructed from scraps of old cars and farm machines. Do not miss the Autosaurus II, a fully operable monstrosity with huge eyes, a tongue, and a 351 Ford engine.

SPORTS AND RECREATION
Hiking and Bicycling

Fort Collins isn't far from Rocky Mountain National Park and the foothills of Boulder, of course, but its own 2,500-acre, waterfall-strewn **Horsetooth Mountain Park** (4200 W. County Rd. 38, 970/679-4570, www.larimer.org/parks/Htmp.htm) is a local hiker-and-biker paradise, climbing from 5,430-foot Horsetooth Reservoir to 7,255-foot Horsetooth Rock. It has 27 miles of trails.

Also at 2,500 acres, **Lory State Park** (708 Lodgepole Dr., 970/493-1623) has 25 miles of trails, for hikers, bikers, and horseback riders—it's a great spot for looking at wildlife, birds, and wildflowers, too. It's on the northwest side of Horsetooth Reservoir. Try the 1.7-mile **Arthur's Rock Trail**; the views of the reservoir and the mountains at the top are worth the difficult uphill stretch.

Other good trails in the Fort Collins area: **Poudre River** (N. Taft Hill Rd., near the Environmental Learning Center on E. Drake Rd.), which goes along the river for about 8 miles; **Spring Creek** (W. Drake Rd., at the intersection of the Poudre Trail), a 6.6-mile path that goes through many parks, including Southwest Community Park; and **Foothills** (along Horsetooth Reservoir, beginning at Dixon Reservoir), a 5.8-mile trip through rough terrain. For more information on these trails, as well as parks and a bike map, contact the city's **Parks and Recreation Department** (214 N. Howes St., 970/221-6640, www.ci.fort-collins.co.us/recreation).

Fishing

The 6.5-mile-long **Horsetooth Reservoir** (north of Fort Collins, on County Rd. 38E, west of Harmony Rd. and Taft Hill Rd., 970/498-7000, www.co.larimer.co.us/parks/Horsetooth.htm) includes the massive Horsetooth Rock, which, according to native legend, was once a giant slayed by heroic Chief Maunamoku. It's the best fishing spot in the area, and also has facilities for boating, water-skiing, and picnicking.

Other excellent fishing holes: the **Cache La Poudre River,** which passes through Fort Collins between the Rockies and the South Platte River, and **Red Feather Lakes,** about 30 miles northwest of the city, north of the intersection of Rist Canyon Road and Manhattan Road. Fort Collins is also home of the superb **St. Peter's Fly Shop** (202 Remington St., 970/498-8968), whose guided tours (not to mention tips and information) span northern Colorado and part of Wyoming.

White-Water Rafting

The Cache La Poudre River can get pretty choppy as it descends from Rocky Mountain National Park to the Fort Collins area, and **A-1 Wildwater** (317 Stover St., 970/224-3379 or 800/369-4165, www.a1wildwater.com) gives tours for all the degrees of white-water-rafting difficulty, from placid to wild.

Golf

The **Collindale Golf Course** (1441 East Horsetooth Rd., 970/221-6651, www.ci.fort-collins.co.us/golf/collindale.php) is a city-run, 18-hole course that occasionally sponsors local qualifying matches for the U.S. Open. The clubhouse is new, the course is spread out, and the lessons are first-rate.

Spectator Sports

Colorado State University operates in the shadow of the University of Colorado at Boulder, but its Rams occasionally bludgeon the Buffaloes. Although the college competes in volleyball, basketball, baseball, and swimming, its most popular sport is football—**Hughes Stadium** (800/491-7267) is the home of the Rams.

NIGHTLIFE

Although it's part of a Denver-area chain, Fort Collins's **C.B. & Potts** (1415 W. Elizabeth St., 970/221-5954) has far more character—and better buffalo wings—than its counterparts. **Coopersmith's Pub & Brewery** (5 Old Town Square, 970/498-0483, www.coopersmithspub.com) is the college-leaning pub alter-ego of the pool hall and pizza joint across the nearby walkway. If you can get in, the teeny-tiny **Town**

Pump (124 N. College Ave., 970/493-4404) has some of the city's best atmosphere.

For live music, the **Mishawaka Amphitheatre** (13714 Poudre Canyon, 970/482-4420, www.mishawakaconcerts.com) is one of those cozy little mountain clubs, like the Buffalo Rose in Golden, and it attracts mostly local performers, although national acts such as David Grisman and Marc Cohn have headlined in recent years. In Fort Collins itself, **Avogadro's Number** (605 S. Mason St., 970/493-5555, www.avogadros.com) has been booking bands since 1971; recent acts include folk singer Lucy Kaplansky and the jazzy James Scott Band.

SHOPPING

Fort Collins's two main shopping districts are Old Town Square and Foothills Mall. **Old Town Square** (Mountain Ave. and College Ave.) has funky little boutiques and shops such as the gem-and-fossil-selling **Nature's Own** (201 Linden St., 970/484-9701), the southwestern jewelry-and-pottery gift store **Santa Fe Craftsman Inc.** (118 N. College Ave., 970/224-1415), and the toy store **Children's Mercantile Company** (111 N. College Ave., 970/484-9946). **Foothills Mall** (215 E. Foothills Pkwy., 970/226-5555, www.shopfoothills.com) is anchored by Mervyn's, Sears, JCPenney, and Foley's.

The city's best-known art gallery is **Trimble Court Artisans** (118 Trimble Court, 970/221-0051, www.trimblecourt.com), which has operated here since 1971 and grown to a co-op of 50 artists (mostly local) who contribute pottery, paintings, jewelry, stained glass, and other media.

ACCOMMODATIONS

Fort Collins has one hotel from roughly every major chain, from Hilton to Best Western, and unlike Boulder or Denver, just a few are unique, locally owned hotels or bed-and-breakfasts.

A beautiful Victorian home built in 1904, **◖ Edwards House B&B** (402 W. Mountain Ave., 970/493-9191 or 800/281-9190, www.edwardshouse.com, $95–165) has high ceilings, wooden floors, stained-glass windows, a large

wooden staircase, excellent breakfast, whirlpools and claw-foot tubs in the rooms, and all the other amenities you'd expect from a bed-and-breakfast—only a little more solid, as if the inn were of a piece with the large surrounding trees.

The rooms at the business-oriented **Fort Collins Plaza Inn** (3709 E. Mulberry St., 970/493.7800, www.plaza-inn.com, $50–100) are pretty basic, like what you'd find at a Marriott or Holiday Inn, but the inn's real advantage is a large indoor-outdoor heated pool, as well as sauna and hot tub. An alternative at the same price is the **Mulberry Inn** (4333 E. Mulberry St., 970/493-9000 or 800/234-5548, www.mulberry-inn.com, $48–125), with hot tubs in every room and an outdoor pool.

The 800,000-acre **Roosevelt National Forest** (2150 Centre Ave., 970/295-6600, www.fs.fed.us/r2/arnf/recreation) has 53 campgrounds on more than 1,000 sites in various locations, most with running water, toilets, picnic tables, and grates for making fires.

FOOD

Students have been dining with their parents—and making them pay—at **Nico's Catacombs** (115 S. College Ave., 970/482-6426, www.nicoscatacombs.com, 5–9:30 P.M. Mon.–Thurs., 5–10 P.M. Fri.–Sat.) since 1973. The chefs prepare various steaks ($32–36) at your table, and seafood dishes like the lobster-and-goat-cheese-wonton appetizer ($13) are almost as substantial as the giant cuts of meat.

Fish (150 W. Oak St., 970/224-1188, 11 A.M.–9 P.M. Mon.–Thurs., 11 A.M.–10 P.M. Fri.–Sat.) is an upscale but affordable seafood (duh) restaurant.

Canino's (613 S. College Ave., 970/493-7205, 11 A.M.–9 P.M. Sun.–Thurs., 11 A.M.–10 P.M. Fri.–Sat.) is Fort Collins's predominant Italian restaurant, in a classic old house, with homemade desserts to go with the usual pasta and eggplant parmigiana dishes.

The **Charco Broiler** (1716 E. Mulberry St., 970/482-1472, 6–10 P.M. daily) is one of those old-school steakhouses with a dark 1970s ambience. It used to be one of Fort Collins's best restaurants, and while it's not exactly hip and modern these days, it's still possible to get a more-than-decent meal.

Alsalam Restaurant (822 S. College Ave., 970/484-3198, 11 A.M.–9 P.M. Mon.–Thurs., 11 A.M.–10 P.M. Fri., noon–9 P.M. Sat.) is a great family-run Middle-Eastern restaurant with kabobs, lamb shanks, hummus, and falafel.

In Severance, about 16 miles southeast of Fort Collins, the only famous attraction is the Rocky Mountain Oyster, known more technically as—and there's really no elegant way of saying this—bull testicles. The delicacy has achieved quite the statewide reputation in recent decades, but one of the first to serve it was **Bruce's Bar** (345 1st St., Severance, 970/686-2320, 10 A.M.–10:30 P.M. Sun.–Thurs., 10:30 A.M.–midnight Fri.–Sat.), a well-known regional stop.

INFORMATION

The **City of Fort Collins** (300 LaPorte Ave., 970/221-6505, www.ci.fort-collins.co.us) is particularly helpful with parks-and-recreation listings, but its website is also a key stop for local residents. Travelers may find **The Fort Collins Convention & Visitors Bureau** (3745 E. Prospect Rd., 970/491-3388 or 800/274-3678, www.ftcollins.com) more useful. The local newspaper is the *Coloradoan* (www.coloradoan.com), and it posts dining listings and restaurant reviews online; a new independent weekly newspaper, the *Fort Collins Weekly* (www.fortcollinsweekly.com), is opinionated and somewhat comprehensive. For CSU information, contact the college (College Ave., 970/491-1101, www.colostate.edu).

BOULDER AND FORT COLLINS

THE SKI TOWNS (EVEN IF YOU DON'T SKI)

Since the first ski resort, Howelsen Ski Hill, opened in Steamboat Springs almost a century ago, those long slats attached to people's feet have defined Colorado's identity and propped up its massive tourism industry. What's the appeal, for the 11 million visitors to the state's 25 ski resorts every year? Just the opportunity to stand on the edge of a giant, snow-covered bowl, with evergreen-covered skylines in the distance, impossibly fresh air in their faces and a bumpy plunge from a 12,000-foot mountain in front of them.

Most of Colorado's best-known ski areas bunch up around I-70, near the Continental Divide, the backbone of the Rocky Mountains. Aspen, Vail, Keystone, Winter Park, Breckenridge, Steamboat Springs, and Arapahoe Basin, just to name the best-known resorts, have for decades created a local culture. Nearby University of Colorado is a haven for hard-partying ski bums, and hippie rock bands such as String Cheese Incident and Leftover Salmon perfectly capture the laid-back mentality of the knit-cap-and-hiking-boot set. (For a while, punk-rocking snowboarders threatened to puncture this culture, but 'boarders and skiers have in recent years come to a sort of détente—almost all Colorado ski areas now offer snowboarding lessons.)

Each resort has a well-defined personality—Vail and Aspen attract the ritziest clientele and have the high-priced shopping districts to prove it, while A-Basin has far fewer frills to go with its amazing mountain views, and the City of Denver—owned Winter Park is full of unpretentious townie bars and restaurants. Expect crowds during the high seasons, from roughly November through February, especially when the sun is out

© STEVE KNOPPER

HIGHLIGHTS

❰❰ Wheeler Opera House: The cultural heart of Aspen since 1889, the Wheeler continues to bring great entertainment to town, from bluegrass to blues to independent films (page 111).

❰❰ Snowmass Mountain: Each of Aspen's four mountains has its advantages, but none is as diverse as Snowmass, with its trails for beginners and experts alike (page 120).

❰❰ Vail Mountain: Skiers argue endlessly about the virtues of Aspen over Steamboat Springs, A-Basin over Copper Mountain. But everybody agrees Vail's 3,000-acre Back Bowls are incomparable (page 124).

❰❰ Arapahoe Basin: A locals' favorite, A-Basin is the highest ski area in the U.S., staying open through June or July; "Beachin' at the Basin" is Colorado's largest tailgate party (page 150).

❰❰ Mount Evans Scenic and Historic Byway: Other than Pikes Peak, this is the only 14,000-foot-high mountain in the U.S. open for automobile traffic; the views are worth it (page 162).

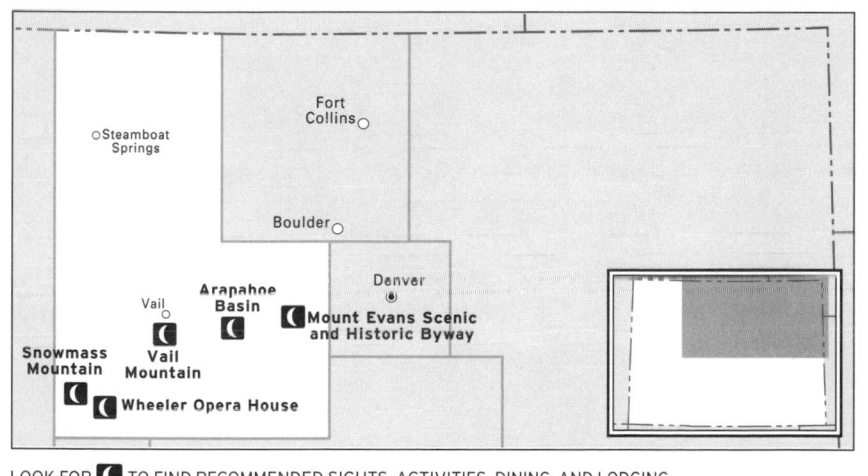

LOOK FOR ❰❰ TO FIND RECOMMENDED SIGHTS, ACTIVITIES, DINING, AND LODGING.

after a large snowfall. But Coloradoans know to avoid the crush and look for off-season deals.

The best of these happen away from ski season, in April and October, when hotels and restaurants are amazingly cheap and the weather remains nice enough for hiking and cycling excursions. In addition to the slopes and moguls, the High Rockies are filled with breathtaking forests and parks, such as the White River National Forest in Aspen and the Devil's Thumb Ranch north of Winter Park. (White-water rafting, sailing, hot-air ballooning, and hang gliding are just some of the other popular summer sports in these parts.)

PLANNING YOUR TIME

Spending time in all the major Summit County ski areas—that is, the ones along I-70, not counting Telluride several hours to the southwest—will require at least a few weeks and a willingness to drive vast distances. Most out-of-state skiers pick their favorite resort and stick with it for a long weekend; they often take shuttle buses from Denver International Airport or nearby towns such as Boulder and Colorado Springs. Once you're there, the resorts are pretty much self-contained, and you'll be able to get the food, entertainment, and,

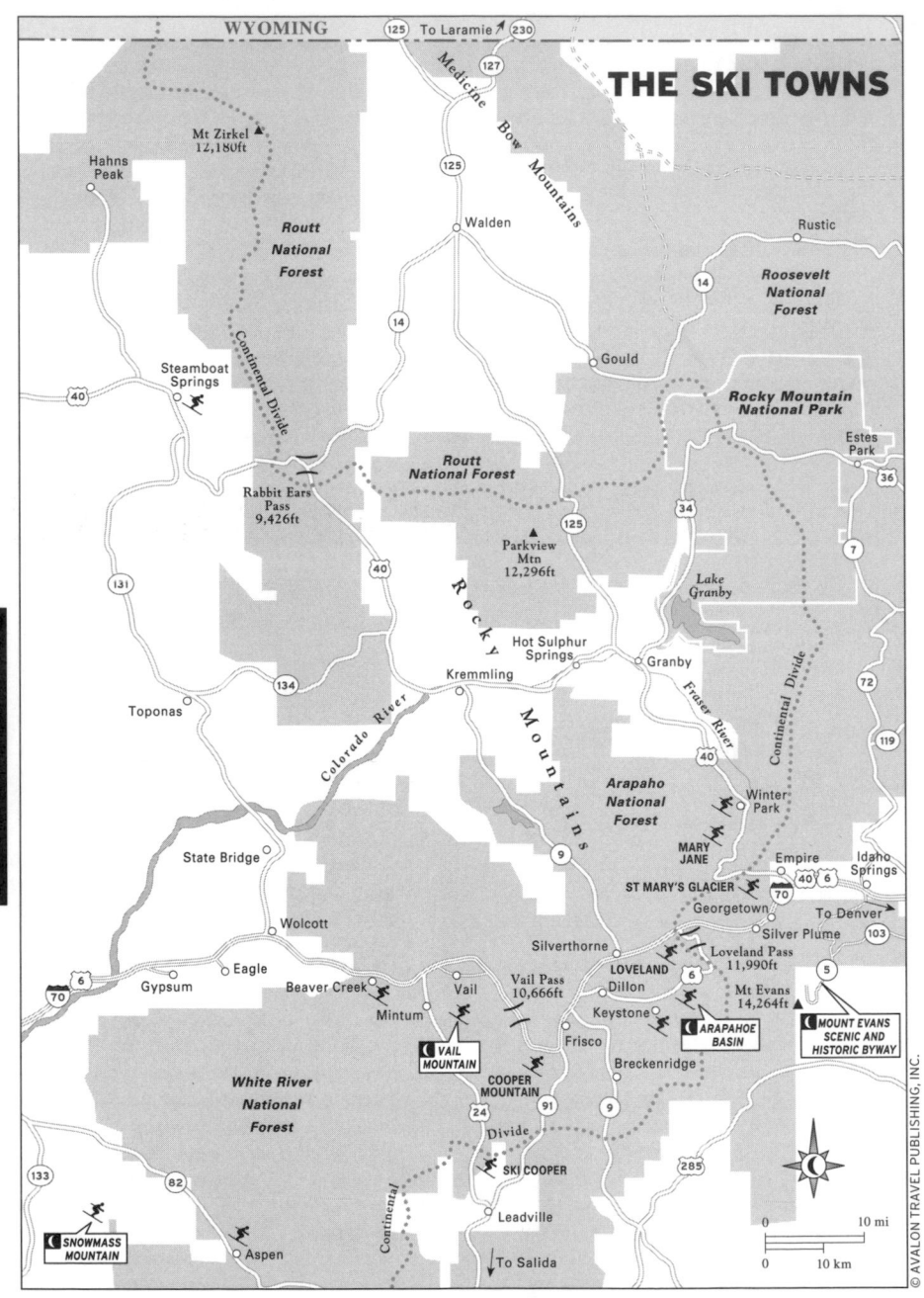

THE SKI TOWNS

of course, skiing you need within walking or shuttle-bus distance.

More ambitious trips, hitting several areas, require greater planning. The most manageable strategy is to drive from the airport—and you'll definitely need a car, some maps, and weather reports—and begin the trip on the eastern edge of the Rockies. Check out Idaho Springs (and its surprisingly great restaurants) and Georgetown (which has superb views and the nearby Mount Evans), then make your first stop in Keystone (and hit Arapahoe Basin just a few miles away). Skiers will want to plan full days at each resort; explorers and hikers may find it easier to wander around a bit before moving to the next area.

Winter Park is about an hour off I-70, so it's almost certain to be a separate trip. Then get back on I-70, head west, and cover the Dillon/Silverthorne, Frisco, and Copper Mountain areas before settling in Vail. Beaver Creek is half an hour to the west, and save time for an evening trip to perfect little Minturn.

Note that the climate in the Rockies is far more extreme and unpredictable than in Denver or Boulder, so pack a mixture of outfits even in the heart of summer or winter. And check driving conditions in advance; it's not uncommon for a snowstorm to slow I-70 to a crawl around the Eisenhower Tunnel. There are other routes back to the airport, but they all involve tinier and more vulnerable mountain roads.

Aspen and Vicinity

While wandering the streets of downtown Aspen, glance at the housing prices in the realtors' windows. They're incredible—mountain hamlets in the tens of millions of dollars. And they show why Aspen is among the most beautiful and most overcooked cities in Colorado's Rocky Mountains. The city has a charming downtown area filled with hipster hotels and gourmet restaurants, and it's located directly beneath four towering mountains—Snowmass, Aspen Highlands, Aspen Mountain, and Buttermilk. But with home prices averaging $4 million, it's one of the most expensive cities in the U.S., so celebrities such as Jack Nicholson, Kevin Costner, Kurt Russell, Goldie Hawn, and Chris Evert are among the elite few who can live there.

But Aspen is also an irresistible place to visit because it gets the best of everything in Colorado. No single hotel in the state, and almost none in the country, is as luxurious as the Little Nell. The country's best chefs and sommeliers have migrated to restaurants of incredible diversity and quality, from the sushi-specializing Matsuhisa to the Asian-and-Southwestern Syzygy. The bars are inviting, the town square centers on the serene Aspen Fountain, and if you have the time and money, there's no better place to wander, whether it's through the town square or in the surrounding mountain wilderness.

Town & Country magazine recently called Aspen Mountain—the one that looms directly over the city, with the Silver Queen Gondola—"the great equalizer." It doesn't matter how much money you have or how well you're dressed as long as you're a skier who can navigate the slippery drops and complex masses of trees and steep moguls. That's true, and Aspen Mountain's 11,000-foot views of the city are stunning enough to impress skiers, hikers, and shoppers of any socioeconomic level. But the city has over the past 140 years taken on the identity of a rich person's town, and some out-of-town skiers and Coloradoans deliberately avoid its overwhelming fashion consciousness and high prices in favor of A-Basin or Winter Park.

People who've never been to Aspen may envision streets lined with gold and fur coats in every window. They should visit. It's also oddly laid-back, and even the snootiest restaurants and hotels aim to make guests relax, rather than be uptight, in their tuxedos and cocktail dresses. Plus, the great gonzo journalist Hunter S. Thompson, who killed himself in

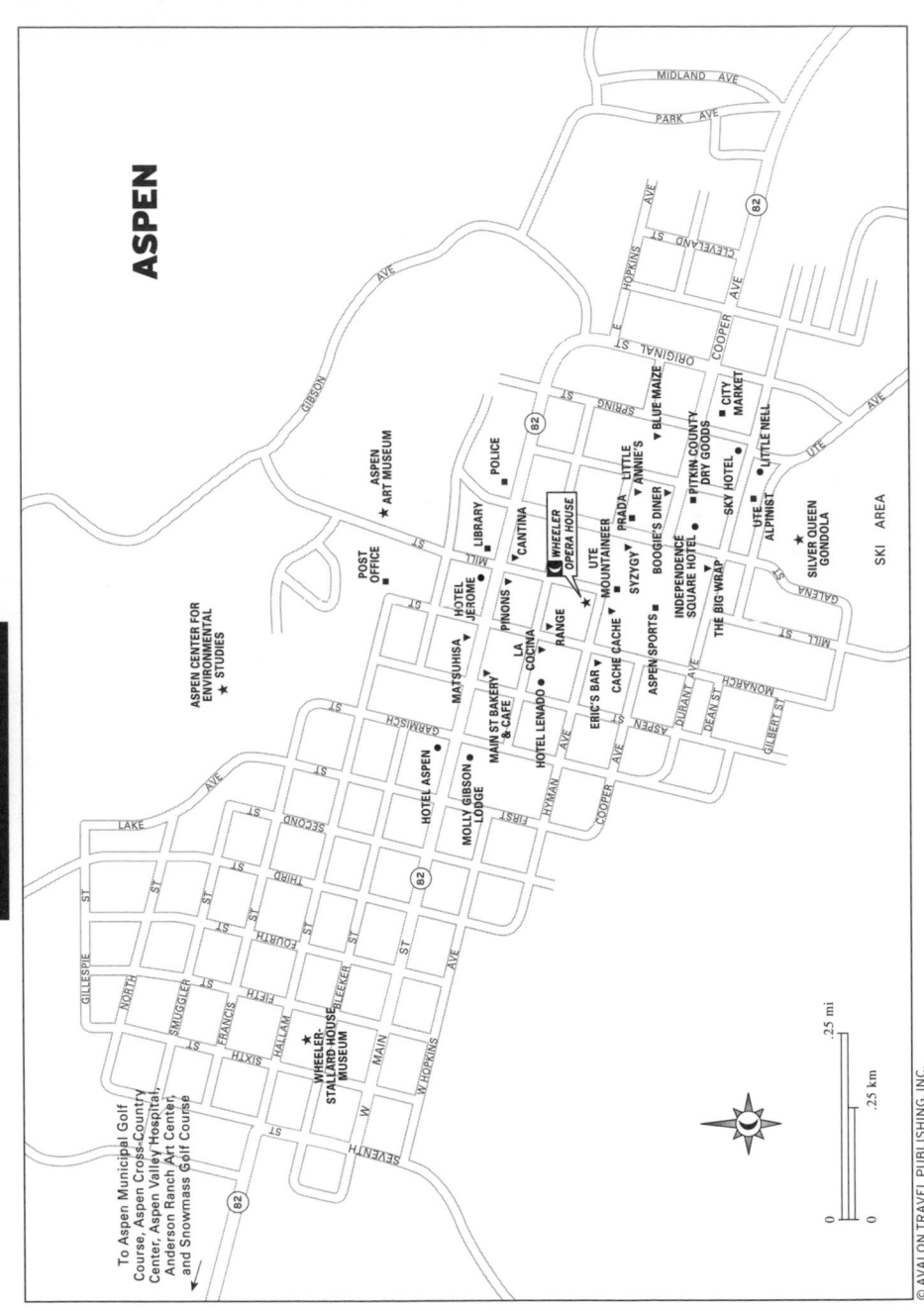

ASPEN

© AVALON TRAVEL PUBLISHING, INC.

February 2005, lived in nearby Woody Creek for decades. So how pretentious can it be?

Despite sticker-shock prices on gas and food, it's still possible to find good deals, like the ultramodern Sky Hotel (especially in the off-season) and the superb downtown Mexican restaurant La Cocina.

HISTORY

Although the Utes first discovered the Aspen region, calling it "Shining Mountain," silver miners arrived in the 1870s, attempting to strike it rich during the Colorado gold rush. Twenty years later, though, the U.S. government demonetized silver and the poor sap who subsequently discovered a 2,350-pound nugget was out of luck. Aspen descended into relative poverty for the next five decades—even Jerome B. Wheeler, the Macy's department store magnate who built the Wheeler Opera House and the Hotel Jerome, declared bankruptcy in 1901—but it discovered a far richer substance to replace silver in the 1930s.

Snow became Aspen's primary business around 1936, and while World War II delayed investors' plans for a major ski area, out-of-town industrialists founded Aspen Skiing Corp. within a decade. Condominiums boomed throughout the region in the 1960s, and Snowmass grew into a resort of its own; by the 1970s, Aspen had developed a worldwide reputation for high-class skiing. Developers and celebrities have moved to town ever since, and as a result Aspen's outdoor charms have become out of reach for almost everybody.

SIGHTS

One of several houses built by founding father Jerome B. Wheeler, the **Wheeler-Stallard House Museum** (620 W. Bleecker St., 970/925-3721 or 800/925-3721, www.aspenhistory.org/wsh.html, 1–5 P.M. Tues.–Sat.) is an 1888 Victorian building that frequently undergoes renovations and updates. The high-class Spirit of Aspen exhibit, which includes a full-floor tribute to late local singer-songwriter John Denver, is open most of the year.

The **Aspen Art Museum** (590 N. Mill St.,

970/925-8050, www.aspenartmuseum.org, 10 A.M.–6 P.M. Tues.–Sat., 10 A.M.–7 P.M. Thurs., noon–6 P.M. Sun.) emphasizes modern art, such as (in a recent exhibit) Donald Judd's minimalist *Green Desk with Two Chairs*. Tours are available, and its Art After Hours program is free (and an excellent place to meet people) 5–7 P.M. Thursdays.

❰ Wheeler Opera House

It's appropriate that Aspen's best-known historical sight is named for a wealthy New Yorker. Wheeler arrived in 1883 to get a piece of the silver-mining boom, and he wound up building a good portion of the town, including his own home, the Hotel Jerome, the Wheeler Bank, and this still-ornate building. When built, it had crimson velvet drapes, gold plush seats, and a silver-star-studded azure ceiling. Today, after a $4.5 million renovation completed in 1984, it's open for about 300 events a year, including the U.S. Comedy Arts Festival, which draws big names, from Conan O'Brien to a reunited Cheech & Chong, every February. The house (320 E. Hyman St., 970/920-5770, www.wheeleroperahouse.com) is open for individual concerts and events—check the website—and tours (usually at 1 P.M. Mon.–Thurs. and Sat.–Sun.).

SPORTS AND RECREATION
Downhill Skiing and Snowboarding

Since 1950, when Olympic skier Dick Durrance took a job at the Aspen Skiing Co. and brought the FIS World Championships to town, Aspen has been prime territory in a state that knows its chutes and moguls. Aspen's resort is actually four mountains—Snowmass (see the *Snowmass* section), Buttermilk, Aspen Highlands, and Aspen Mountain (or Ajax, the big one that overshadows the town). They're all within 14 miles of each other, and together they encompass 4,993 acres of ski trails.

With a summit elevation of 11,200 feet, **Aspen Mountain** is known for its massive bumps and expert runs. (It has zero trails for beginners.) The longest run is three miles, and

THE BASICS OF SKIING

1. **Lift tickets.** Depending on the resort – as with everything else, Aspen is more expensive than, say, Arapahoe Basin – lift tickets will run about $71 for a one-day pass. But truly, only suckers pay that amount. Scan local newspapers, as well as websites for *Westword, The Denver Post*, the *Rocky Mountain News*, and others, for deals and coupons. Also, contact resort hotels in advance for lift-and-lodging packages. Consider, too, skiing during off-season periods – Christmas week tends to be packed and expensive, while it's a serious seller's market (Keystone lift tickets are $39!) in April.

2. **Lessons.** Every resort has a Ski & Snowboard School, with group and private lessons for kids (usually over 3) and adults (all skill levels). Some resort lessons are basic – train 'em and herd 'em to the lifts – while those at Steamboat and Vail have instructors who know hundreds of languages and may have competed on a super-high level. Again, rates depend on season and resort, but $100 for a one-day group lesson (including lift ticket and lunch) is about average.

3. **Renting equipment.** Every resort has its own rental shop, which is usually a bit more expensive than the "unsanctioned" shops lining the surrounding area. I'd recommend stopping at an outside town – for example, the outlet malls at Dillon or Silverthorne, if you're heading to Breckenridge or Keystone – for better deals. Some of the big sporting-goods names are Christy Sports (877/754-7627, www.christysports.com) and Gart Sports (www.gartsports.com), and I swear you won't miss shops like this in a ski town. Forty bucks a day for skis, poles, and boots, or $30 for a snowboard, is about average.

some of the groomed paths take skiers almost directly into town. Although the mountain has eight lifts, the Silver Queen Gondola goes from bottom to top in 14 minutes, and many skiers, after spending the morning on high-up Ruthie's Road or Buckhorn, break for lunch at the mountainside restaurant Bonnie's. Shrines to Jimi Hendrix, Elvis Presley, John Denver, and Jerry Garcia are among the wacky snow-covered sights.

Many consider **Aspen Highlands** the best skiing mountain not only in Aspen but the entire state. Locals worship it for the frighteningly steep and bumpy Highland Bowl, Olympic Bowl, and Steeplechase runs. Its disadvantage used to be old, poky lifts, but today it has four, including three high-speed quads. The Highlands has far more beginner runs than Aspen Mountain, including the short and popular Red Onion and Exhibition, and there are seven restaurants on the mountain, notably Cloud Nine Alpine Bistro. The majestic views of the Maroon Bells and Pyramid Peak cannot be described appropriately here.

Buttermilk, site of ESPN's Winter X Games for six straight years, is sort of the reverse image of Aspen Mountain. The runs are predominantly for beginners, and there are no expert trails whatsoever. The Ski & Snowboard School is also here, areas are available for kids, and the mood is considerably less intense and show-offy than the other Aspen mountains. Snowboarders are especially welcome on Buttermilk—Aspen Mountain didn't even allow snowboarders until 2001—as The Crazy T'Rain Park has 25 rails and 40 jumps.

The **Ski & Snowboard School** has 1,100 pros from all over the world, and it offers lessons to skiers of all ages and skill levels. The typical group lesson is $115, but private lessons (call 877/282-7736 to set something up) are more expensive, as are advanced lessons and courses tailored to women and other special groups. The **Aspen Skiing Company** (800/525-6200, www.aspensnowmass.com) operates the ski area at all four mountains; information on the website comes directly from the company. For equipment rental, the resort recommends **Aspen/Snowmass Four-**

Aspen's gondola is functional (for skiers) in the winter, but purely scenic in the summer.

Mountain Sports (five locations at the base mountains, 970/920-0980) and **D&E Ski & Snowboard Shop** (520 E. Durant Ave., 970/920-2337), but I'd encourage you to find better deals at the many sporting-goods stores in the area. **Aspen Sports** (408 E. Cooper Ave., 970/925-6331, www.aspensports.com) and **Pomeroy Sports** (614 E. Durant Ave., 970/925-7875, www.pomeroysports.com) have wide selections and helpful staff.

Cross-Country Skiing

Hut-to-hut skiing, in which backcountry aficionados follow up-and-down trails for several days in a row and sleep at small cottages in the woods, is particularly big in Aspen. The best outlet is the **10th Mountain Hut & Trail System** (1280 Ute Ave., Ste. 21, 970/925-5775, www.huts.org), which presides over hundreds of miles of trails in the wide area between Vail Valley and Aspen. These include the **Alfred A. Braun Hut System,** which goes from the Ashcroft Ski Touring Center to the Maroon Bells-Snow-

mass Wilderness. The 10th Mountain website also provides a wealth of information about trailheads such as Hunter Creek and Lenado, which go up steep mountain paths. Snowshoes are allowed on these trails, but snowmobiles are discouraged.

For guided tours and other information, try the **Aspen/Snowmass Nordic Council** (Box 10815, 970/429-2039, http://aspennordic.com/), which maintains the Roaring Fork Valley's 48 miles of groomed trails. The **Aspen Cross-Country Center** (39551 W. Hwy. 82, 970/925-2145) gives lessons, and the **Ute Mountaineer** (308 S. Mill St., 970/925-2849, www.utemountaineer.com) rents equipment.

Hiking and Mountain Biking

Surrounding Aspen, the forest includes alpine valleys such as Maroon Creek, Castle Creek, and Hunter Creek, all of which are open to hikers and cyclists (mostly in spring and summer). The most difficult biking trail is 12,000-foot **Independence Pass,** a superstrenuous, 10-mile, straight-up-a-mountain path that points at the end (with more down-hills) into Leadville. Another breathtaking trail is **Maroon Bells,** a 10-mile hike that starts at 10,000 feet and winds up at a 14,156-foot summit. (To get there, take Maroon Creek Road almost 10 miles to the parking area; pack for snowy weather, even in spring.) Less difficult is the 16-mile **Rio Grande Trail,** which follows the Roaring Fork River through thick forest to Woody Creek; look for the trailhead near the Aspen Post Office. For maps and other information, check in with the **Forest Service** (806 W. Hallam St., 970/925-3445) or the **Aspen Parks Department** (585 Cemetery Lane, 970/920-5120). Also, **Ajax Bike & Sports** (635 E. Hyman Ave., 970/925-7662) is one of several local sporting-goods stores that rents bicycles, and **Blazing Adventures** (Snowmass Village, 970/923-4544 or 800/282-7238, www.blazingadventures.com) leads guided tours for all skill levels.

Golf

Befitting a town with amazing scenery, great weather, and wealthy residents, Aspen has several acclaimed private courses: **Maroon Creek** (10 Club Circle, 970/920-1533), designed by Tom Fazio and filled with creeks and ponds at the base of Buttermilk Mountain; **Aspen Glen** (0545 Bald Eagle Way, Carbondale, 970/704-1905, www.aspen-glen.com), designed by Jack Nicklaus and located along the Roaring Fork River; **Roaring Fork** (100 Arbaney Ranch Rd., Basalt, 970/927-9100), also designed by Nicklaus and built along the Roaring Fork; and **River Valley Ranch** (303 River Valley Ranch Dr., Carbondale, 970/963-3625, www.rvgolf.com), 520 acres at the base of Mount Sorpis.

Aspen also has one public course: **Aspen Municipal** (39551 Hwy. 82, 970/925-2145), with 18 holes and a nice restaurant.

Other Outdoor Sports

Visitors from the coasts will find the Roaring Fork Valley surprisingly **fish-packed.** The primary rivers are the Frying Pan, Roaring Fork, and Colorado. White-water **rafting** is available through **Blazing Adventures** (Snowmass Village, 970/923-4544 or 800/282-7238, www.blazingadventures.com).

ENTERTAINMENT AND NIGHTLIFE

Aspen's primary musical entertainment is of the classical and chamber variety: **Aspen Music Festival and School** (2 Music School Rd., 970/925-9042, www.aspenmusicfestival.com) draws hordes of college-student prodigies to woodsy residence halls every June and August. The concerts they put on are affordable and often revelatory. **Wheeler Opera House** (320 E. Hyman St., 970/920-5770, www.wheeleroperahouse.com) has a diverse summer schedule of jazz, pop, and opera concerts. The early September **Jazz Aspen Snowmass** (970/920-4996, www.jazzaspen.com) isn't as stuffy as its name, booking rock, country, and pop artists such as James Brown, Macy Gray, and Lyle Lovett to go with the standard jazz combos. The mid-June **Aspen Food & Wine Classic** (www.foodandwine.com/ext/classic) draws renowned chefs from all over the world for wine tastings, cooking classes, and other events. Around the same time of year, in Snowmass Village, the **Annual Chili Pepper and Brewfest** (www.snowmasspress.com/chili.html) shows off 40 microbreweries to go with an International Chili Society competition and national music acts such as Spearhead.

Aspen's bars are world-class, even when they're not as celebrity-packed and luxurious as the nearby restaurants and hotels. The **J-Bar** (330 E. Main St., 970/920-1000), inside the Hotel Jerome, is a laid-back place to hang out, attracting tons of locals, with beer and burgers that rival any eatery in town. Another excellent hotel bar, this one of the hipster variety, is the Sky Hotel's **39 Degrees** (709 E. Durant Ave., 970/925-6760), which has round, fluffy couches and a huge flat-panel television for sports enthusiasts. **Eric's Bar** (315 E. Hyman Ave., 970/920-6707) is far homier, with an emphasis on malt Scotch. And most famous of all is the **Woody Creek Tavern** (2 Woody Creek

Plaza, Woody Creek, 970/923-4585), whose primary comforts are a few pool tables, beer, comfort, and an opportunity to raise a glass to late regular Hunter S. Thompson.

For all its other social qualities, Aspen isn't much of a live-music town, although local bands and writers are always trying to pump up some kind of "scene." The loss of Whiskey Rocks, a club in the St. Regis Hotel until 2004, hasn't helped in this attempt. Still kicking are the **Main Street Bakery** (201 E. Main St., 970/925-6446), which plays host to acoustic folk and bluegrass bands on Wednesday nights, and **Syzygy** (520 E. Hyman Ave., 970/925-3700), which has excellent (if quiet) jazz. Over in Basalt, the **Two Rivers Café** (156 Midland Ave., 970/927-3348) is attempting to reinvent itself as a sort of Whiskey Rocks, Part II.

SHOPPING
Shopping in Aspen, as *The New York Times* calls it, is a "mix of the insanely expensive (movie stars) and the insanely inexpensive (ski bums)." I've yet to see anything that can be reasonably described as "insanely inexpensive" in Aspen, but the article's example—**Susie's Limited** (623 E. Hopkins Ave., 970/920-2376)—is as good a place as any to find such deals as a $30–60 ski jacket or sweater.

Clothing
The insanely expensive is much easier to find: The **Prada Store** (312 S. Galena St., 970/925-7001), which opened in the former Planet Hollywood building with a $700,000 renovation in 2002, immediately started drawing celebrities such as Ivana Trump, Nikki and Paris Hilton, and Monica Lewinsky. At one point, according to *The Denver Post*, it sold a $14,160 mink sleeping bag. The family-owned-for-years **Pitkin County Dry Goods** (520 E. Cooper Ave., 970/925-1681) isn't nearly as ostentatious, but it has sleek menswear and hipster women's clothing, jewelry, and purses. For shoe enthusiasts, **Bloomingbirds** (304 S. Galena Ave., 970/925-2241) has a high-end mix of tennis, formal,

and ski. **Funky Mountain Threads** (409 E. Hyman Ave., 970/925-4665) sells brightly colored clothing and jewelry by local artists, as well as candles and incense.

Galleries
Aspen's galleries are also among the best in the region, and there are dozens of them in a small area: The **David Floria Gallery** (312 S. Mill St., 970/544-5705) has a huge roster of top new artists, from Joseph Scheer and his large butterflies to James Surls and his jittery bug sculptures. The **Huntsman Gallery of Fine Art Ltd.** (410 E. Hyman Ave., 970/920-1910) shows owner Don Huntsman's bronze Reggie Jackson and Marcel Marceau sculptures along with the work of 40 prominent artists.

Antiques
Another high-end vein to tap is antiques, notably **Fetzer's Interiors and Fine Antiques** (8435 County Rd. 113, Carbondale, 970/384-2305), which has been specializing in 18th and 19th century European imports for 45 years, and **Paris Underground** (205 S. Mill St., 970/544-0137, www.parisunderground.com), which carries furniture, pottery, and chandeliers by 1930s and 1940s French designers.

Ski Equipment
Super-fashionable skiers go to **Performance Ski** (408 S. Hunter St., 970/925-8657), where Cindy Crawford and other big names are said to have shopped, and **Pomeroy Sports** (614 E. Durant Ave., 970/925-7875), a family-run store that caters to both top athletes and beginners craving personal attention.

ACCOMMODATIONS
There's just no getting around it: Hotels in Aspen are *expensive,* especially during ski season and major weekend holidays. Fractional ownership, in which somewhat rich guests can pay for permanent lodging shares, is the new thing—the St. Regis Resort has tried it, and the Little Nell and Hyatt Grand Aspen reportedly have plans in the works. And, of course, there are condos.

$150-200

It's not absolutely necessary to pay $500 a night for an Aspen hotel room, as the **Limelite Lodge** (228 E. Cooper Ave., 970/925-3025 or 800/433-0832, $180–275) proves. Luxury isn't a big priority here, but location is—the tree-lined, wooden building is a short walk from the gondola. It also has two pools and two whirlpool tubs. A rare (at least, in Aspen) combination of low cost and high quality, the **Boomerang Lodge** (500 W. Hopkins Ave., 970/925-3416 or 800/992-8852, www.boomeranglodge.com, $180–255) has private balconies in almost every room, plus an outdoor pool with an indoor pool-viewing area. One disadvantage: It's somewhat removed from mountain views.

Over $200

The **Hearthstone House** (134 E. Hyman Ave., 970/925-7632 or 888/925-7632, www.hearthstonehouse.com, $239–259) is in a two-story building with flat, angular architecture reminiscent of Frank Lloyd Wright. The rooms are almost as nice-looking, and they take on a certain glow when you factor in the mountain views. Also on the premises is The Aspen Club & Spa. The Hearthstone is part of a network of quaint lodges and bed-and-breakfasts from the **Gems of Aspen** (866/770-8358, www.gemsofaspen.com), which also includes the **Little Red Ski Haus** (118 E. Cooper Ave., 970/925-3333 or 866/630-6119, www.littleredskihaus.com, $209–309), one of the town's first bed-and-breakfasts, in a late-1880s Victorian.

The **Aspen Meadows Resort** (845 Meadows Rd., 970/925-7790 or 800/452-4240, www.aspenmeadows.com, $215–307) has large rooms with balconies that overlook the mountains and the Roaring Fork River. It's also the headquarters of the Aspen Institute, a longtime nonprofit group that organizes influential public-policy seminars. (Former CNN executive Walter Isaacson is in charge these days).

The **(Sky Hotel** (709 E. Durant Ave., 970/925-6760 or 800/882-2582, www.theskyhotel.com, $319–369) is new and modern, in stark contrast to the rustic Little Nell and the mainstream St. Regis. Hipsters hang out at the curvy outdoor pool and party in the hot-tub area late at night; the rooms have touches of bright red and green to go with the cream-colored walls and beds, and tall, cartoonish white chairs are in the lobby, along with board games for kids.

It's probably best to get a fireplace room at the **Molly Gibson Lodge** (101 W. Main St., 970/925-3434 or 888/271-2304, www.mollygibson.com, $375), as the basic guest rooms are nondescript. But it's a nice place in a mountain location three blocks from downtown, with a heated outdoor pool, whirlpool tubs, and complimentary wireless access throughout the hotel.

Hotel Lenado (200 S. Aspen St., 970/925-6246 or 800/321-3457, www.hotellenado.com, $335–395) has two kinds of rooms, the very basic Larkspur, with shared balconies, and the deluxe Smuggler, with four-corner wooden beds. The Smuggler is far preferable, with in-room hot tubs and (in some cases) private balconies and wood-burning stoves. Either way, it's in a central location next to the town's Whitaker Park and worth trying out.

Many say the **(Little Nell** (675 E. Durant Ave., 970/920-4600, www.thelittlenell.com, $625–775) is the best hotel between the coasts, and its pampering is beloved among guests. In a city where the pool of talented, experienced hotel workers isn't nearly as big as, say, New York or Los Angeles, the Nell grabs all of them. "What do you need?" is a common refrain among the staff. In addition to that, it's beautiful: Even the standard rooms have gas fireplaces and down sofas (and some have balconies), and if you can afford the $1,500 to $3,500 for a suite, the mountain views are unlike any in the Rockies.

A few notches down from the Nell, but still very nice, is **The St. Regis Resort** (315 E. Dean St., 970/920-3300 or 888/454-9005, www.stregisaspen.com, $765–1,615), which is at the base of Aspen Mountain. It recently underwent a major renovation, adding the 15,000-square-foot Remede Spa, plus the St. Regis Residence Club Aspen, which sells fractions of a residence for $300,000 to $1.5 million apiece. Pocket change!

Built in 1889, the 🌑 **Hotel Jerome** (330 E. Main St., 970/920-1000 or 800/331-7213, www.hoteljerome.com, $575–610) takes the down-home Colorado approach to luxury Aspen hotels, with a genuine Wild West ambience throughout the building, with moose heads on the walls and numerous crystal chandeliers. Locals in cowboy boots love the place for its hard-drinking ambience, especially in the J-Bar, an inexpensive and homey little place with excellent burgers.

FOOD

Yes, Aspen is ridiculously expensive, and the average human probably couldn't survive there for more than a few weeks. But while every visitor ought to have a solid $200 meal (with wine) at the Century Room or Matsuhisa or Range, it's surprisingly affordable to get by for a few days on J-Bar burgers, The Big Wrap sandwiches, and Main Street Bakery & Café pastries. An excellent resource is the website of *Aspen Times Weekly* (www.aspentimes.com, click on "dining"), in which critic Christina Patterson never takes too seriously the luxuries so prominent in this glittery town.

Snacks, Cafés, and Breakfast

The **Main Street Bakery & Café** (201 E. Main St., 970/925-6446, 7 A.M.–4 P.M.) is on every travel writer's "Aspen on the cheap" list. For as little as $5 an entrée, it serves pastries, cakes, and croissants, plus homemade soups and granola. While it's locally famous for breakfast, it also serves lunch and dinner. Mountain views, too.

Casual

Aspen Times Weekly readers annually pick **La Cocina** (308 E. Hopkins Ave., 970/925-9714, 5–10 P.M. daily) as the town's best Mexican restaurant, and as an added bonus, it's affordable enough to eat there several times a week. The chips are free, the burritos, enchiladas, and fajitas are a stomachful, the outdoor patio is filled with trees and a big stone fountain, and

the hustling, bustling waitpeople are attentive and friendly.

The aggressive 1950s rock 'n' roll themes make **Boogie's Diner** (534 E. Cooper St., 970/925-6111 or 888/245-8121, www.boogiesaspen.com, 11 A.M.–10 P.M.) as much of a gimmick as a restaurant—ever been to Ed Debevic's in Chicago?—but it's a fun place to eat dinner, and the half-pound burgers anchor a diverse (and even vegetarian) menu.

Little Annie's Eating House (517 E. Hyman Ave., 970/925-1098, 11:30 A.M.–10 P.M.) competes with the Hotel Jerome's J-Bar for the "best burger" prize, and **The Big Wrap** (520 E. Durant Ave., 970/544-1700, 10 A.M.–6 P.M. Mon.–Sat.) has tortilla-covered healthy sandwiches that inspire this scene at the *Times Weekly* offices: "Every time the intercom crackles with 'Big Wrap in the front office,' the sound of a half dozen pairs of feet resounds through the rickety building." Try the hummus-and-Greek-veggie-salad wrap ($6).

Upscale

The 🌑 **Century Room** (330 E. Main St., 970/920-1000, www.hoteljerome.com/croomfacts.html, 6 P.M.–10 P.M. daily), like its host, the Hotel Jerome, artfully combines gourmet food with a sort of rustic Old West feel. And it has a hand-carved fireplace. One signature dish is the Colorado lamb duet: horseradish-crusted rack of lamb chops and osso buco with toasted farro and barley risotto, caponata, and nicoise olive-lamb jus.

Run by Charles Dale, the chef behind the late haute restaurant Renaissance, **Range** (304 E. Hopkins Ave., 970/925-2402, www.rangerestaurant.net, 11:30 A.M.–2 P.M. Mon.–Fri., 5:30–10 P.M.daily) is as casual as a $36-steak joint can be. Dale uses mostly local ingredients, including Alaskan salmon and Colorado lamb, and meals such as Kobe meatloaf and roasted range chicken are filling and comforting at the same time.

🌑 **Montagna** (675 E. Durant Ave., 970/920-4600, 7–10:30 A.M., 11:30 A.M.–2 P.M. and 6–10 P.M. daily), in the Little Nell, is a one-of-a-kind luxury restaurant around which out-of-town visitors plan entire vacations. Master sommelier Richard Betts, presiding over a 15,000-bottle wine cellar, is one of the best in the country. The menu's charms range from white river trout and bacon cassoulet ($34) for dinner, chicken noodle soup ($10) for lunch, and an $18 brunch that includes the best oatmeal you ever tasted. Also, try the sticky buns.

Piñons (105 S. Mill St., 970/920-2021, 5:30–9:30 P.M. daily), named after New Mexico's state tree, is an American-style restaurant with Southwestern decor, serving elk, pork, and beef tenderloins. Lobster strudel is a specialty of chef Rob Mobillian, and the appetizers range from potato-crusted scallops to Beluga caviar.

Cache Cache (205 S. Mill St., 970/925-3835 or 888/511-3835, www.cachecache.com, 5:30–10:30 P.M. daily) is so well known for its use of garlic, rosemary, and vinaigrettes that it's almost impossible to get a table, even midweek. Every menu item has some kind of oddly perfect flavoring: The calf's liver is in caramelized onion sauce, the pork tenderloin is in apple-brandy sauce, and even the filet mignon comes with Dijon-peppercorn sauce.

Blue Maize (308 S. Hunter St., 970/925-6698, www.bluemaize.com, 5:30–10 P.M. daily) is so called not because of its Southwestern and Latin-American emphasis but because the owner attended the University of Michigan. It's high class, and simply reading the menu will make you hungry: The grilled elk tenderloin comes with cranberry pasilla sauce and sautéed asparagus ($23). But it's also unpretentious enough to have a kids' menu, carnival-style multicolored walls, and side dishes like corn on the cob and garlic mashers.

Aspen imported **Matsuhisa** (303 E. Main St., 970/544-6628, www.nobumatsuhisa.com, 6–10 P.M. Mon.–Sun.), the namesake of chef Nobu Matsuhisa, after his restaurants earned acclaim in Beverly Hills, Malibu Beach, and New York City. It's famous for sushi, but entrées such as the halibut cheeks with pepper sauce ($29)—supplemented, of course, with miso soup—are superb alternatives for the fear-of-raw-fish set.

At **Ajax Tavern** (685 E. Durant Ave., 970/920-9333, www.ajaxtavern.com, 11:30 A.M.–10 P.M. daily), the extensive dinner, lunch, and brunch menus are almost secondary to the extensive wine list and cocktails. Its drink-serving outdoor deck has all the standards, plus a few originals like "jet fuel" (with Skyy vodka, Absolut Peppar, jalapeño-stuffed olives, and a spot of Tabasco). The Little Nell Bar once stood at this location, overlooking Ajax Mountain.

Regularly named one of the best restaurants in Aspen, **Syzygy** (520 E. Hyman Ave., 970/925-3700, 6–10 P.M. daily) captures all the little things that take an eatery to the next level—perfectly arranged flowers on the table, live jazz that's just the right volume, miniature waterfalls, and, oh yes, the food. Chef Martin Oswald, an expert in cooking game, combines Asian and Southwestern influences into dishes like hazelnut-crusted lamb loin.

INFORMATION AND SERVICES

The ski resort's website, www.aspensnowmass.com, has information about everything from live music to hotels. Or call 800/525-6200 or 970/925-1220. The **Aspen Chamber Resort Association** (800/670-0792, www.aspenchamber.org) has an elaborate website geared toward travelers. Aspen's weekly newspaper is very sophisticated for a small town, including well-written restaurant reviews: the *Aspen Times* (www.aspenalive.com). The ski resort also maintains a separate Snowmass website: www.snowmass.com, or call 800/923-8920.

GETTING THERE

Aspen is almost a 2.5-hour drive west from Denver International Airport, and once you're there, the Roaring Fork Valley region is so self-contained it's hard to wander around and explore the rest of the Rockies. In part, that's why Aspen has become such a destination town. To get there, take I-70 west to Glenwood Springs, then turn left (southeast) and backtrack along Highway 82 to get to Aspen. Especially in winter, the high, curvy highway can be treacherous.

DRIVING TIPS IN THE MOUNTAINS

Snowy mountain roads, even big ones like I-70, are unsuspectingly dangerous in Colorado. Highway crews can be slow to react with plows after blizzards, so icy conditions are common—and even if stretches of blacktop look dry, "black ice" can fool even the savviest of mountain drivers. Obviously, it's safer in warmer weather, but beware of unexpected hairpin curves and icy patches in the high country. Some tips:

- Slow down in the winter. Plan in advance and allow extra time to arrive. And if the sports car behind you is following too close, ignore it—and find a safe shoulder to pull over and let faster traffic pass.

- Avoid sudden moves.

- In the mountains, deer and other animals can leap in front of cars at all times, so pay attention to the deer crossing signs and drive slowly enough to stop.

- Pass only when you're absolutely certain it's safe. Pay attention to the Do Not Pass signs and the straight and broken lines on the highway. Make sure you have a clear vision of the entire road before doing so. When in doubt, don't do it. Entering the opposing lane at the wrong time can be catastrophic.

- Avoid cruise control, especially when it's slippery.

- When it's icy, pump the brakes to stop, rather than slamming on them.

- When driving downhill in slippery conditions, try to avoid braking on snowy or icy patches. It's best to find what looks like a dry spot and slow yourself down there. However, you should be going slowly enough so this doesn't become a factor—and never be afraid to brake if you feel you're in an unsafe situation.

- Downhill, if you're driving 30-40 miles per hour, slow yourself down by shifting into a lower gear (this works with both automatic and manual transmissions).

- Don't tailgate.

- Make sure your car has good tires. Experts recommend buying tires with the worst possible driving conditions in mind; also, tread depth in snowy conditions should be three-sixteenths of an inch.

- Use your brights at night, but if it's foggy or snowy, turn them off to avoid confusing reflections.

If you need further information, check with local governments in mountain towns. The Summit County Chamber of Commerce (800/564-0371) gives tips on local tire dealers. For **road conditions** call 303/639-1111, or watch for the blue radio signs on the highway.

THE SKI TOWNS

Also, be sure to gas up along I-70, as Aspen's prices are among the most expensive in the state—sometimes as much as 50 cents per gallon more than Denver. Snowmass is about 14 miles northeast of Aspen along Highway 82.

A popular alternate route to Aspen is I-70 to U.S. 24, just east of Copper Mountain, then passing through Leadville before turning right onto Highway 82 into Aspen. It makes for a slightly longer trip, but many Denver-to-Aspen regulars swear by the Old West ambience and friendly restaurants of Leadville. It's also a nice change of pace from the crowded Interstate highway.

Most affluent visitors and residents—which is to say, a lot of people—indulge in the **Aspen/ Pitkin County Airport** (0233 E. Airport Rd., 970/920-5384), three miles from the city of Aspen and six from Snowmass Village. It has service from United Express, Northwest, and America West. Punters can fly into Denver, Colorado Springs, or Grand Junction airports, rent a car and take I-70 to Highway 82.

GETTING AROUND

Free shuttle buses serve all four Aspen mountains during the day, and the **Roaring Fork Transit Authority** (Rubey Park, Durant St.,

970/925-8484) provides free and convenient city buses within the city during the day and $3 buses between Aspen and Snowmass Village from evening until night.

SNOWMASS

Since it opened in 1967, Snowmass Village and its one-mountain ski area have always been a sleepier alternative to ritzy Aspen. Residents have come to like it that way, which is why many opposed a $400 million plan in early 2005 to build a long-in-the-works base area. It passed a local election, which means that over the next two decades, the Aspen Skiing Co. owner and Canadian ski-resort developer Intrawest Corp. will add 600 hotel rooms and 65,000 square feet of commercial space to the resort village.

These changes are likely to give Snowmass the identity it has lacked for almost 30 years, but they're also likely to transform the town from a townie-oriented, best-kept-secret type of resort that has more in common with Copper Mountain than Aspen or Vail. Then again, Snowmass has been building up to this transformation for years, with additions to its resort area in the mid-1990s and an opening of super-expert ski runs that attract more death-defying snowboarders and extreme skiers than laid-back beginners.

█ Snowmass Mountain

For skiers, Snowmass is the fourth and largest mountain in the Aspen-Snowmass range, and while 6 percent of its runs are geared to beginners, its specialty is expert-only terrain. With the Winter X Games coming to the Aspen area on a regular basis in recent years, a new group of extreme snowboarders and skiers have come to dominate the mountain, and the resort responded by opening acres of terrain on the high-up Cirque's Burn Side Cliffs. The new runs, including Leap 'n' Land, Gluteus, and Triple Jump, have huge cliff drops and complement such expert standbys as the Hanging Valley Wall.

But with 3,100 acres of ski trails on the mountain, Snowmass has a variety of runs for just about every type of skier and skill level. The most popular of six distinct areas is Big Burn, for intermediates, which seems endless and open. Toward the bottom of the mountain are numerous short and smooth runs for beginners and kids. Snowboarders, who've long worshipped Snowmass for its bumps and ski-lift accessibility, should check out the pipes in the Coney Glades area.

Snowmass also is an excellent setting for cyclists and hikers—in some ways, better than Aspen. During summer, the ski-resort mountains open to various bike trails, including Village Bound (for beginners) and Sam's Knob (for experts), both of which require trips up the ski lift. "Discovery Zones," for mountain bikers and BMX riders alike, are located inside the Snowmass Village Mall.

Entertainment and Nightlife

The **Blue Door** (100 Elbert Ln., 970/923-8338), in the Silvertree Hotel, supplements its après-ski happy hours and pub food with DJs, a large dance floor, and Sunday-night karaoke. **Cirque Café** (125 Daly Ln., 970/923-8686) is Snowmass Village's hippest spot, with frequent live music and a nice outdoor deck.

Accommodations

A stumpy box of a building, the **Stonebridge Inn** (300 Carriage Way, 800/213-3214, www.stonebridgeinn.com, $219–239) exemplifies the difference between Aspen and Snowmass—Aspen's best hotels are elaborately luxurious, while Snowmass's best is functional and convenient. It's two blocks from the Village Mall, the rooms are comfortable but nothing fancy, and it has all the amenities you need, like a heated outdoor pool and a cozy bar and restaurant. Side by side, the **Pokolodi Lodge** (25 Daly Ln., 970/923-4310 or 800/666-4556, www.pokolodi.com, $154–174) and the **Snowmass Inn** (67 Daly Ln., 970/923-2819 or 800/635-3758, www.snowmassinn.com, $144–154) are within 100 yards of the slopes and immediately next to the village. They're basic and affordable, and ensconced in the mountains, making for excellent views. (The

Naked Lady Pub, a locals' favorite, is in the Snowmass Inn.)

Also in keeping with Snowmass's personality—comfort over luxury—is the higher-end **Silvertree Hotel** (100 Elbert Ln., 970/923-3520 or 800/837-4255, www.silvertreehotel.com, $370–485), which has the feel of a Marriott, only with better scenery and several bars and restaurants in the lobby. The town's most charming hotel, though, is the **Snowmass Mountain Chalet** (115 Daly Lane, 970/923-3900 or 800/843-1579, www.mountainchalet.com, $255–294), a 64-room bed-and-breakfast-style lodge with log furniture, a lobby fireplace, and complimentary breakfast.

Food

Krabloonik (4250 Divide Rd., 970/923-3953, www.krabloonik.com, 11 A.M.–2 P.M. Mon.–Fri. and 5:30–9 P.M. daily Thanksgiving–mid-Apr., 6 P.M.–close Fri.–Sat. mid-June–Sept.) is unique in the Aspen-Snowmass area, mainly because its full title is "Krabloonik Restaurant and Kennel." Yes, while guests in this serene log-cabin restaurant dine on the house-specialty wild mushroom soup ($5), 200 sled-pulling huskies eat dog food in the kennel next door. (They're available for sled tours throughout the area.)

Good Italian restaurants are hard to find in the mountains, and **Il Poggio** (73 Elbert Ln., 970/923-4292, 5:30–10 P.M. daily) is the kind of casual pasta specialist that wouldn't seem out of place in the heart of New York or Chicago. It does great things with garlic, and the sweet-potato ravioli ($16, in a hazelnut cream sauce with goat cheese) is a highlight.

Originally located in a tent next to the Aspen Grand Hotel, **Butch's Lobster Bar** (970/923-4004, www.butchslobster.com, 6–9:30 P.M. daily) moved to Snowmass Village in 1992 and continues to serve, well, lobster—a "small" one-pounder is $28, a medium one-and-a-half pounder is $39, and beyond that the bar charges $25 per pound. For those squeamish about food with claws, ex-Cape Cod lobster-catcher Butch Darden's highly popular bar

also serves seafood, barbecued ribs, and New York strip steak.

LEADVILLE

Many travelers know Leadville as the quaint little mountain town with friendly old cafés and restaurants that they pass through en route to Aspen. It also gave Colorado some of its most famous characters, from the mining-era couple Horace and Baby Doe Tabor to the Old West outlaw Doc Holliday.

As the story goes, Kansas farmer Horace Tabor moved his wife and son to what would become Leadville to take advantage of the mining boom. He opened a grocery store, and in 1878, two German immigrants showed up and asked Tabor to "grubstake" them for their future silver discoveries. He gave them $17, and within months they'd each made $10,000.

Tabor used this money to make his fortune and become the symbolic master of the mining boom. He bought the Matchless Mine, developed a fortune worth a reported $3 million, and fell in love with a new Leadville resident, divorcee Elizabeth Bonduel McCourt Doe. Before long, Tabor was asking his wife, Augusta, for a divorce. Against her wishes, he married "Baby Doe" in 1882.

The story, one of the most famous in Colorado history, ends in tragedy. Congress repealed the Sherman Silver Act in 1893, dissipating Tabor's fortune and those of countless others. Tabor became destitute and begged Baby Doe on his deathbed (according to the history section of Leadville's website) to "hold on to the Matchless as it will pay millions again"—although some dispute those were actually his words. The mine never paid millions again, and Baby Doe died of a heart attack in her icy cold Matchless Mine cabin.

The ostentatious Baby Doe and Tabor, who became a U.S. Senator, have since been immortalized in the opera *The Ballad of Baby Doe,* among many other fictional works. Leadville is now a quaint tourist town, a sort of gateway from Denver to Aspen, but the original Matchless Mine (and Baby Doe's shack) still exist in historical-museum form.

THE SKI TOWNS

Sights

The **Matchless Mine** (557 County Rd. 3, 719/486-4918, www.matchlessmine.com, 9 A.M.–4:30 P.M. daily Memorial Day–Labor Day, 10 A.M.–4 P.M. Thurs.–Mon. Labor Day–Memorial Day) preserves the original cabin where Baby Doe died in 1935—some say she froze to death, but historical records show it was actually a heart attack. The mine is more or less as it was, and an on-site museum exists primarily to sell books and videotapes about the Tabor story. Also obsessed with Tabor-family history is the **Tabor Opera House** (308 Harrison Ave., 719/486-8409, www.taboroperahouse.net, 10 A.M.–5 P.M. Mon.–Sat.), once so regal it drew performers such as Harry Houdini, John Philip Sousa, and Oscar Wilde. The **Augusta Tabor Home** (116 E. 5th St., 719/486-2092) was a happy place for a few years when Horace and loyal Augusta first lived here, but Horace took off for mistress Baby Doe in 1881. Branching beyond the Tabor family, the **National Mining Hall of Fame & Museum** (120 W. Ninth St., 719/486-1229, www.mininghalloffame.org, 9 A.M.–5 P.M. daily in summer, 10 A.M.–4 P.M. Mon.–Fri. in winter) has a walk-through replica of an 1880s mine, a miniature model Colorado railroad, and a Hall of Fame honoring dozens of miners past. The **Heritage Museum** (9th St. and Harrison Ave., 719/486-1878, 10 A.M.–6 P.M. May–Oct.) displays Victorian furniture of the time and a model replica of the town's 1896-era "palace of ice."

The scenic **Leadville, Colorado, and Southern Railroad** (326 E. 7th St., 719/486-3936, www.leadville-train.com) follows the Arkansas River between the tiny towns of Leadville and Climax along the Continental Divide. The depot is an 1893 building filled with historical artifacts and a gift shop.

Sports and Recreation

It's a little nuts to travel all the way to Colorado and ski at the dinky **Ski Cooper** (U.S. 24, about nine miles west of Leadville, 719/486-3684 or 800/707-6114, www.skicooper.com), but the slopes are rarely crowded, and the four

lifts serve 400 skiable acres (a Sno-Cat delivers backcountry skiers to 2,400 more available acres). Backcountry skiers should consider the Mineral Belt Trail, opened in 2000, a 12.5-mile loop around Leadville with views of two large mountain ranges and stops at various historic mining areas. Also, the **Piney Creek Nordic Center** (U.S. 24, 719/486-1750, www.tennesseepass.com/skiing) offers backcountry skiing lessons and access to trails halfway between Leadville and Minturn off U.S. 24. Billing itself as the highest golf course (elevation-wise) in North America, the nine-hole **Mt. Massive Golf Course** (259 County Rd. 5, 719/486-2176, www.mtmassivegolf.com) is miles from the nearest condo or even building.

Accommodations

Leadville is a great one-night stopover on the way to Aspen or Snowmass, with several excellent bed-and-breakfasts in the town's historic district. The best is the **Ice Palace Inn Bed & Breakfast** (813 Spruce St., 719/486-8272, www.icepalaceinn.com, $99–159), built from material rescued from the original, 1895-era Ice Palace that once towered over Leadville. Today, owners Giles and Kami Kolakowski stock the rooms with antiques and plush beds, and offer free German apple pancakes and other breakfast delights in the just-as-plush dining room.

Not quite as luxurious as the Ice Palace, but worth visiting, are the **Apple Blossom Inn** (120 W. 4th St., 719/486-2141 or 800/982-9279, www.theappleblossominn.com, $69–179), with stained-glass windows and fireplaces in many of the rooms; and **Peri & Ed's Mountain Hideaway** (201 W. 8th St., 719/486-0716 or 800/933-3715, www.mountainhideaway.com, $49–159), surrounded by pine trees with mountains in the distance.

Food

For upscale diners willing to travel to a yurt via cross-country skis, snowshoes, or snowmobile, the **Tennessee Pass Cookhouse** (Route 24, 719/486-8114, www.tennesseepass.com/cookhouse, lunch at noon, 1:30 P.M. Sat.–Sun., dinner at 5:30 P.M. daily) has four-course meals ($60) of elk tenderloin, rack of lamb, salmon, chicken, and vegetables. In downtown Leadville, The **Grill Bar and Café** (715 Elm St., 719/486-9930, 4–9 P.M. daily, lunch Sat. and Sun. in the summer) has a (usually packed) patio overlooking Mount Massive, and the Martinez family's margaritas, green chile, and hand-roasted peppers from Hatch, New Mexico, are well worth a stopover meal.

Events

The weirdest event in Leadville is the International Pack Burro Race, which began in 1949, when people presumably still asked burros to carry all their heavy stuff. The race, a surreal part of Leadville's early-August **Boom Days** (www.leadville.com/boomdays) celebration, demands that participants lead burros over a 21-mile course, some of which goes over the 13,183-foot Mosquito Pass summit. Oh, and the burros carry 35-pound packs.

Vail and Vicinity

It's possible to spend a few days in Aspen and have the time of your life without even thinking about skiing. Not so with Vail. Yes, there are luxurious things here—a few of the hotels, restaurants, and shops are the best in the Rockies—but the entire culture revolves around preparing for the slopes, skiing, and relaxing afterward. Skiers will find no problem with that arrangement; the resort's back bowls and tree-filled basins have been world-renowned even before President Gerald Ford visited here in the 1970s. But non-skiers, especially in winter, may find Vail Resorts' "company town" overcrowded and obsessed with moguls and goggles.

Vail has been the white-gold standard for skiing since the resort opened in 1962, in what was once practically a ghost town. Although business dipped somewhat after 9/11, leading to a desperate plunge into deals and bonus amenities, its charm and luxury remain intact. The central Vail Village area is a heavy concentration of fireplace-equipped lodges and restaurants with hopping outdoor patios, and it's fun to wander around even when the skiers come clomping back from the slopes over the central, wooden, covered bridge. The new Adventure Ridge (on the side of a mountain and accessible only via the Eagle Bahn Gondola) is a late-night family fun center with a bar, restaurant, laser tag, and "thrill sleds."

The resort isn't as hoity-toity as Aspen, but the shopping has become almost as important

(and expensive) as the skiing. "Ski-in/ski-out" restaurants and lodges are right up against the mountains, so customers barely have to take their skis off to take a break.

The Vail resort is the anchor of Vail Valley, the broad area around I-70 that includes Eagle, Beaver Creek (a super-high-class resort that rivals Vail's skiing), Minturn, Arrowhead, and Edwards. The White River National Forest surrounds the area, and local entrepreneurs provide mountain biking, horseback riding, rock climbing, hot-air ballooning, and, yes, llama trekking. The area can be tourist-heavy in summer, especially during festivals such as the Teva Mountain Games, the Brews and Chili Festival, and the Annual Vail Jazz Party, so watch for off-season deals.

HISTORY

If not for imperialistic explorers and gold miners, the Utes might still be frolicking around the mountains of Vail, peacefully enjoying the region's dramatic peaks and valleys. Scratch that—they'd probably be making tons of money off skiing, just as Vail Resorts does today. But as the story goes, Irishman "Lord" George Gore and American Jim Bridger bushwhacked into Vail in the 1850s, paving the way for miners and railroad men to suck out the gold and silver and transport it to civilization beyond the Rockies. More and more miners showed up and pushed the Utes off the land; the vengeful Utes set fire to thousands of

THE SKI TOWNS

acres of trees, causing severe deforestation that happened to be just right for skiing.

Eventually the miners took off and left the bruised valley for sheep farmers. It stayed quiet until 1939, when construction engineer Charlie Vail built Highway 6 from Denver. But even then, Vail was a sleepy mountain town until World War II, when the U.S. Army's 10th Mountain Division used the area's backcountry trails for survival training. Some of those troops returned after the war, as veterans, including Pete Seibert, who with several partners carried out a lavish plan to build a ski resort. They started building in 1962.

The officially incorporated Town of Vail arrived four years later—along with the first gondola in the U.S., two double chairlifts, and, before long, restaurants, hotels, and a medical clinic. Its reputation as a ski area exploded worldwide in the mid-1970s—thanks to the Utes' choppy, bumpy, tree-lined paths—and sometime resident Gerald Ford became president in 1974. Like the rest of Colorado's ski-resort towns, Vail has become much more sophisticated (some would say corporate) since then, adding more and more trails, year-round gondolas and chairlifts, tennis tournaments, and hot-air balloon rides.

SIGHTS

The small **Colorado Ski Museum** (231 S. Frontage Rd. E., 970/476-1876, www.skimuseum.net, 10 A.M.–5 P.M. Tues.–Sun.), on the third floor outside the Vail Village parking garage, is one of the few local attractions that rarely draws long lines. Which is a shame, because the snowboarding and skiing histories presented here, along with the equipment and clothes of U.S. Olympic heroes such as Billy Kidd and Nelson Carmichael, put the lifts and moguls outside into perspective. I wasn't aware, for example, that inventor Tom Sims built the first snowboard in 1963 and later used one as a stuntman in the 1984 James Bond movie *A View to a Kill*. Also, the first-ever snowboard competition was in nearby Leadville.

Given the underwhelming nature of his presidency, the many Vail buildings named after Gerald R. Ford can seem comical at first. (The man skied there in the 1970s, for heaven's sake; he didn't win any Olympic luge medals!) Nonetheless, the **Betty Ford Alpine Gardens** (183 Gore Creek Dr., 970/476-0103, www.bettyfordalpinegardens.org, dawn–dusk daily) is a sprawling park filled with mountain-grown flowers of every type, from roses and hyacinths to *hymonoxy grandiflora*. Even if you're not big into flower classification, the waterfalls and rock gardens are worth wandering around during spring and summer.

SPORTS AND RECREATION
《 Vail Mountain

Colorado skiers constantly debate the particulars of resorts—Keystone's night trails or Breckenridge's expert runs? Copper Mountain's convenience or Aspen's luxury? But Vail transcends all arguments. The mountain is 11,500 feet high, with 193 trails over 5,289 acres, and it ranges from the seven naturally formed and beautifully bumpy Back Bowls to the long, steep Front Side, which caters to beginners but

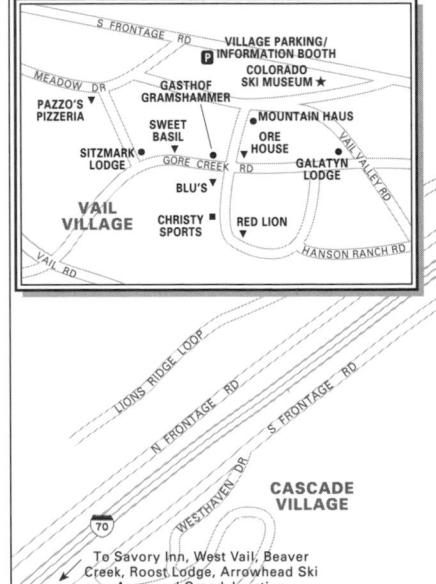

has a few expert trails. The tree-filled Blue Sky Basin has only 645 acres, but no matter how many skiers show up on a given day at Vail, they're always secluded and almost eerily quiet. High-speed lifts, too, mean few bottlenecks.

Vail can be a bit tricky to traverse, and it doesn't look like much when you first encounter the mountain from the base area. But the higher up you go, the more complex the chutes and moguls become. "It can take an hour to get to where you want to be on the mountain, but once you're there, it's incredible," says Ryan Anderson, a Denver native and 15-year Colorado skiing and snowboarding veteran.

Beginners should plan to stick with the Front Side, notably the Lost Boy trail, which seems to last forever and has great views of the mountain range. (Conversely, beginners should avoid the Back Bowls and Blue Sky Basin, which have exactly zero acres of green trails.) Experts should proceed immediately to the mountain's east side, notably the Prima and Highline trails, which are filled with sharp bumps and log chutes. Check the resort website at www.vail.snow.com for lift information, directions, and weather reports.

The **Vail Ski and Snowboard School** (LionsHead and Golden Peak, 970/479-4330 or 800/475-4543, www.vail.snow.com/info/mtn/adult.asp) gives private and group lessons for all skill levels, and 850 instructors speak 30 different languages. The two sales offices are at the bases of LionsHead and Golden Peak. And Vail Village is, naturally, packed with ski-and-snowboard rental shops—try **Christy Sports** (293 Bridge St., 970/476-2244 or 877/754-7627, www.christysports.com) or **Vail Sports** (227 Wall St., 970/479-0600, www.vailsports.com), which has several central locations throughout the resort.

Other Winter Sports

Vail Resorts offers lessons and rentals for many different skiing activities—cross-country, Telemark, and Nordic, plus snowshoeing and snowmobiling. For lessons, which run about $65 for three hours, call 970/479-3210. If you plan to venture on your own, be careful; not

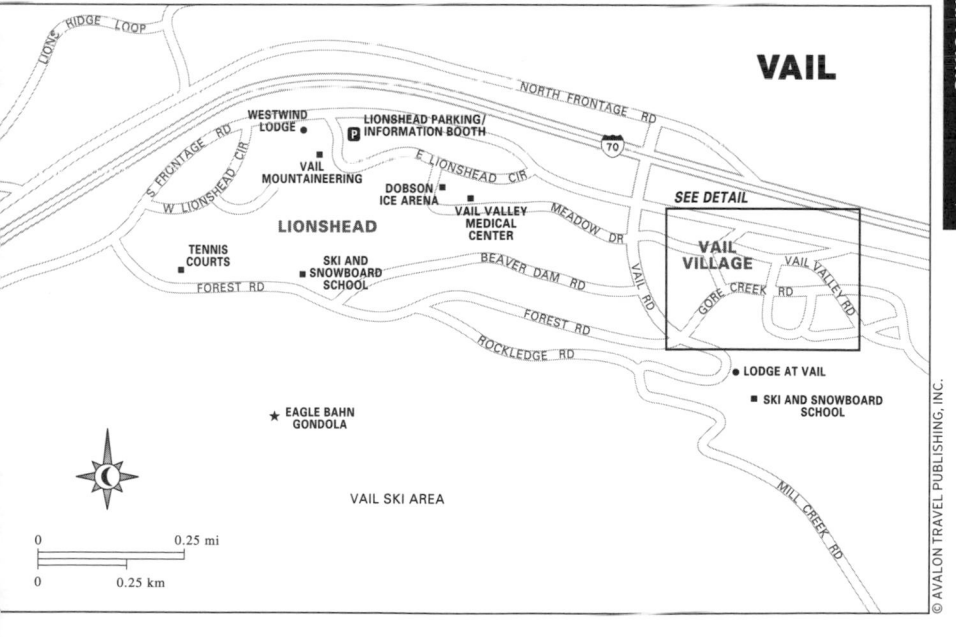

© STEVE KNOPPER

Vail Mountain is 11,500 feet high, with arguably the best skiing in Colorado.

everything that looks like a ski trail is really a ski trail. The **Holy Cross Ranger District** (24747 U.S. 24, Minturn, 970/827-5715), **Eagle Ranger District** (125 W. 5th St., Eagle, 970/328-6388), and **Colorado Avalanche Information Center** (303/275-5360) give free advice on safety and directions.

The **10th Mountain Hut Association** (1280 Ute Ave., Ste. 21, Aspen, 970/925-5775, www.huts.org) offers tours on trails all around Summit County, including Vail Pass (which has a trailhead at an elevation of 10,580 feet) and Commando Run (which is accessible by car near Mill Creek but easier by gondola). Also, **Paragon Guides** (970/926-5299 or 877/926-5299, www.paragonguides.com) offers backcountry skiing and hut-to-hut tours that last 3–5 days each. Snowmobile rentals are available via **Nova Guides** (719/486-2656 or 888/949-6682, www.novaguides.com), which also runs the nearby Pando Cabins.

Vail's **Activities Desk** will direct you to the right arena: 970/476-9090.

Bicycling and Hiking

Hundreds of miles of biking and hiking trails run in and out of Vail Valley, including many on Vail Mountain itself—start with the pretty, one-mile Eagle's Loop. Later, step up a few notches in difficulty and take Kloser's Klimb, a steep hike up 1,000 miles of elevation. Then go straight down six miles from Eagle's Nest through groves of Aspen trees. Just outside of Vail, down I-70 about five miles to the northeast, is the entrance to Eagle's Nest Wilderness, hundreds of acres of snowcapped peaks, beautiful lakes and creeks, and aspen and spruce-fir trees. For bicycle rentals (as well as tours and repairs), try **Vail Bike Tech** (555 E. Lionshead Circle, 877/269-0448), near the Eagle Bahn Gondola. Vail Mountain trail information is at www.vail.snow.com (click on "summer" at the bottom and look for recreational activities), and call the **Dillon Ranger District** (680 Blue River Pkwy., Silverthorne, 970/468-5400) or the **Holy Cross Ranger District** (24747 U.S. 24, 970/827-5715) about outside-the-town hikes and bike rides.

Golf

Vail has more than 18 golf courses, including some at hotels and lodges such as the **Sonnenalp Golf Club** (20 Vail Rd., 970/477-5370, www.sonnenalp.com). The **Vail Golf Club** (1778 Vail Valley Dr., 970/479-2260) is at 8,200-foot elevation, which means the ball will fly 20 percent farther (in theory), and has an 18-hole, par-72 course.

NIGHTLIFE

Sanctuary (333 Bridge St., 970/479-0500, www.taproomvail.com/sanctuary) is partly a dance club and partly a cozy après-ski drinker's haven with a central fireplace. It works on both counts, with Monday-night football crowds and bachelorette parties alike. (It's on the penthouse floor of another bar, The Tap Room.) Dancers at **Club 8150** (143 E. Meadow Dr., 970/479-0607, www.club8150.com) get so aggressive that locals refer to it as a "bouncing floor"; DJs spin records and live bands occasionally fill the joint, too.

EVENTS

The **Bravo! Vail Valley Music Festival** (970/827-5700, www.vailmusicfestival.org), late June through early August, started with a handful of people and musicians in 1987 but has grown to crowds of more than 60,000 people. Among the attractions: the Dallas Symphony Orchestra and the New York Philharmonic.

Held in late July and early August at the Gerald R. Ford Amphitheatre, the **Vail International Dance Festival** (970/845-8497, www.vvf.org/dance.cfm) began in 1989 with the Bolshoi Ballet Academy. It continues to focus on ballet, although the Fly Dance Company, a Houston hip-hop-and-breakdancing outfit, give it a fun, modern edge.

Late spring's **Vail Film Festival** (970/333-9689, www.vailfilmfestival.org) is hardly Cannes, or even Telluride, but it draws a nice selection of up-and-coming movie premieres, including 2004's acclaimed *Before Sunset*.

SHOPPING

Not surprisingly, most of Vail's top shops are geared to skiers, and in Vail Village, it's hard to swing a pole around without whacking into a boot store. Among the most prominent are **Pepi Sports** (231 Bridge St., 970/476-5206, www.pepisports.com), which makes a big point of shaping footwear to fit your foot, and **Charter Sports** (660 W. Lionshead Pl., 970/476-8813, www.chartersports.com), in the Lion Square Lodge.

Vail is a cornucopia of high-end galleries and shops—and while it's not as shopping-conscious as its pricey neighbor, Aspen, tourists often come here just for the stores. Among them: the fine-jewelry **Currents** (285 Bridge St., 970/476-3322), the fur-coat-and-leather-boots **Gore Range Mountain Works** (201 Gore Creek Dr., 970/476-7625, www.grmw.com), the Italian-clothing **Luca Bruno** (183-3C Gore Creek Dr., 970/479-0050), and the **Masters Gallery at Vail** (100 E. Meadow Dr., 970/477-0600), which sells many colorful and vivid paintings by artists such as James Jensen and Carrie Fell.

ACCOMMODATIONS

Vail's best hotels are crowded in the central part of town—mostly Vail Village and Golden Peak—and some of the best are within a few hundred yards of the slopes. Some hotels and lodges (such as the economical Roost Lodge, in West Vail) are in alternative areas, but in general, if you want to avoid the ski-season crush of downtown Vail, it's best to try outlying areas such as Minturn or Beaver Creek. Skiers know to factor in high-season lodging prices, and lift-ticket packages are often the best deals. Prices drop dramatically in the off-season. And don't ignore condos. They're everywhere.

$100-150

In West Vail, a little removed from the main part of town, the **Roost Lodge** (1783 N. Frontage Rd., 970/476-5451 or 800/873-3065, www.roostlodge.com, $129–139) is an affordable option for the non-fur-coat-and-Stetson set. It's convenient, especially given the chain restaurants and supermarkets within walking distance, but be prepared for uneven front-desk

© STEVE KNOPPER

After they're through on the mountain, most skiers relax in Vail Village.

service and a loudly coughing hotel-to-town shuttle.

$150-200

In case Vail didn't look enough like an Austrian ski village, the **Gasthof Gramshammer** (231 E. Gore Creek Dr., 800/610-7374 or 970/476-5626, www.pepis.com, $195–245) has the old-script lettering and women in Bo Peep outfits (at least, as depicted on the webpage) to correct the oversight. Run since 1964 by former Olympic skier Pepi Gramshammer and his wife, Sheika, the brightly colored inn has a party atmosphere, with happy-hour skiers populating an outdoor patio even in the middle of winter.

Over $200

The Lodge at Vail (174 E. Gore Creek Dr., 970/476-5011 or 800/367-7625, http://lodgeat-vail.rockresorts.com, $441–915) had been open for exactly one month when the first gondola opened on Vail Mountain in 1962—and things have worked out pretty well for both the skiing industry and the lodge ever since. It's prime real estate, just a few steps from the slopes in

Vail Village, and the best rooms have superb views of the mountain. There's also a heated outdoor pool, hot tubs, high-speed Internet access, and The Wildflower, one of the best restaurants in Vail.

The **Galatyn Lodge** (365 Vail Valley Dr., 970/479-2418 or 800/943-7322, $295) emphasizes luxury, convenience, and privacy; it's at the center of Vail Village, but its stone-covered building doesn't broadcast itself to the crowds outside. (Unlike, say, the Gasthof Gramshammer, which screams, "Look at me!") The rooms are large and colorful, with air-conditioning, high-speed Internet access, DVD players, and fully equipped kitchens.

For those with enough vacation time to tackle southwest-French fusion and crustaceans in addition to Vail Mountain, **Savory Inn and Cooking School of Vail** (2405 El-liott Ranch Rd., 970/476-1304 or 866/728-6794, www.savoryinn.com, $279) is, yes, a cooking school in addition to a high-class log-cabin hotel. (Note the big fireplace in the lobby and the overflowing comforters in the rooms.) One disadvantage is its location, removed from the slopes in West Vail, but for off-season and non-skiing visitors, it's perfect.

Another comfortable lodge at the center of Vail Village is **Mountain Haus** (292 E. Meadow Dr., 800/237-0922 or 970/476-2434, www.mountainhaus.com, $285–545), whose fat, inviting lobby couches and armchairs hint at what to expect inside. Many of the rooms have stone fireplaces and balconies.

The **Sitzmark Lodge** (183 E. Gore Creek Dr., 970/476-5001 or 888/476-5001, www.sitzmarklodge.com, $215–297) is probably the town's best deal if ski-slope proximity is your primary concern. It's in Vail Village, ensconced between slopes, restaurants, and shops, and the prices aren't out of control. The rooms work just fine, like a more personable Marriott, and amenities like the year-round outdoor pools are a nice touch.

FOOD
Snacks, Cafés, and Breakfast
Although **Blu's** (193 E. Gore Creek Dr., 970/476-3113, 9 A.M.–11 P.M.) is a pricey lunch-and-dinner establishment known for its something-for-everybody menu, including ribs, chicken-fried steak, tuna, and lasagna, I particularly recommend the brunch, which is both light and filling, especially the oatmeal with a cup of brown sugar on the side.

Casual
Vail's pizza options are surprisingly strong, particularly the **Bada Bing Gourmet Pizza Company** (1000 Lionsridge Loop, 970/477-2232, 5–10 P.M.), which has a kids' menu and does both takeout and delivery (thus saving countless of hippie skiers from relying on Domino's or Pizza Hut after extreme late-night partying). **Pazzo's Pizzeria** (122 E. Meadow Dr., 970/476-9026, 8 A.M.–11 P.M.) is perfectly located in Vail Village, just between the covered bridge and the parking lot, so it's almost always packed without even trying. The pizza is a little greasy and the service uneven on crowded nights, but the sandwiches are excellent and it's a great place to relax, meet people, and not have to venture too far from the slopes.

When last I ventured to the **Red Lion** (304 Bridge St., 970/476-7676, www.theredlion.com, 11 A.M.–10 P.M.), a guitarist was covering the Eagles' "Hotel California" on the jammed outdoor patio in the middle of winter. I'll withhold comment on Eagles cover bands, but the food here is perfect for skiers on a budget—wings, microbrews, burgers, fries, onion rings. The location is perfect, too, at the center of Vail Village, just steps from the slopes and hotels.

Upscale
In The Lodge at Vail, **Wildflower** (174 E. Gore Creek Dr., 970/476-5011, 6–10 P.M. Tues.–Sun.) is one of the few gourmet restaurants to match the quality of high-class joints like Denver's Mizuna or Aspen's Century Room. The menu is diverse and eclectic—try the foie gras and duck confit terrine as an appetizer—and the outdoor patio is gorgeous, especially in the summer.

The only thing holding back the **Larkspur** (458 Vail Valley Dr., 970/479-8050, 11:30 A.M.–9:30 P.M. daily) is its location (inside the ski-in/ski-out Golden Peak Lodge), adjacent to a hotel lobby of boot-clomping skiers and screaming parents and kids. If you're looking for a peaceful meal, be sure to get a table as far into the restaurant as possible, with a full view of the nearby slopes; the food ranges from salmon to veal to beef. Also, there's a smaller Larkspur toward the entrance of the hotel that serves deli-style snacks and quick breakfast.

Sweet Basil (193 E. Gore Creek Dr., 970/476-0125, www.sweetbasil-vail.com, 11:30 A.M.–2:30 P.M. and 5:30–10 P.M. daily) is thicker and more luscious than even the best of Vail's gourmet restaurants—the fish isn't just fish, it's pan-roasted swordfish with tempura green beans and herb olive oil mashed potatoes. The apple pie isn't just apple pie, it's caramel apple tart with dark rum and ginger ice cream.

The **Game Creek Restaurant** (Game Creek Bowl, 970/479-4275, 5:30–8 P.M. Tues.–Sat. in winter (and private lunch), 6–8 P.M. Thurs.–Sat. and 11 A.M.–2 P.M. Sun. in summer) isn't exactly a quick walk from your hotel; it involves gondola and Sno-Cat rides straight up

THE SKI TOWNS

the mountain, into the Game Creek Bowl. More foie gras here, along with lamb chops, filet mignon, and a dessert whose name alone creates a sort of Pavlovian response: roasted chestnut ganache cake.

INFORMATION

Check www.vail.snow.com before making a trip here for any reason—its main thrust is the ski slopes, of course, so it has powder and weather updates, but the site is also filled with lodging and food information. Call 970/479-2226 for Town of Vail information, 877/204-7881 for Vail Resorts, or 970/476-4888 for area weather. The Beaver Creek ski resort has a comprehensive webpage, including dining and lodging listings, at www.beavercreek.snow.com. The **Town of Minturn** (302 Pine St., 970/827-5645, www.minturn.org) will help you get away from crowded, expensive Vail and Beaver Creek.

GETTING THERE

Even before you see the first green Vail sign off I-70, you'll notice the condominiums. They're everywhere in Vail, and the actual ski village isn't until the second exit. That's where visitors will want to go; a huge parking garage is on the outskirts of the village, and while it fills up during prime ski times, it's almost always possible to find a spot. The third exit is West Vail, which is more of a regular town, with supermarkets, affordable restaurants, gas stations (although the gas prices are a good 30 cents higher per gallon than those of Denver or Boulder), and the reasonably priced but Holiday Inn–like Roost Lodge.

Over the years, Vail's surrounding towns have developed a charm and personality of their own. Beaver Creek, a few miles west down I-70, is a gated resort that caters to luxury tourists; park in a garage, get off an elevator, and run into a row of art galleries with small $7,500 paintings and $8,500 sculptures. Although Minturn, off I-70 between Vail and Beaver Creek, has doggedly tried to protect its rural-town feel, developers are on the warpath; for now, its down-home restaurants and inns are the best places in Vail Valley to es-

cape. And the quality of Edwards's restaurants has recently grown to match the quantity of its condos.

Vail has its own airport, the **Vail/Eagle County Airport** (970/524-9490 or 877/204-7881, www.eaglecounty.us/airport/), which serves 13 U.S. cities and six major airlines. For the independently wealthy, there's also the **Vail Valley Jet Center** (871 Cooley Mesa Rd., Eagle, 970/524-7700, www.vailvalleyjetcenter.com).

GETTING AROUND

Vail Valley Taxi and Transportation (877/829-8294, www.vailtaxi.com) offers 24-hour shuttle service between the towns in Vail Valley and also goes to the Vail/Eagle County Airport. And the **Vail Resorts Express Shuttle** (970/496-8245) takes skiers from Vail to Keystone or Breckenridge and back. Another shuttle, based in Beaver Creek, stops every 20 minutes at various points around the resort as well as Arrowhead, Avon, and Bachelor Gulch; call 970/949-1938 for a schedule. A bus service goes between Vail and Beaver Creek (970/328-3520), and taxis, which may well be the most affordable option, are available upon request (970/524-5555). Taxis and shuttles are also available from Denver International Airport.

BEAVER CREEK

Since it opened in 1980, Beaver Creek has never tried to be the next Vail. It's too many miles west down I-70, for one thing, and buried within the town of Avon. But it has more than discovered its niche—luxury and class. The skiing is designed with all three skill levels in mind, with Beaver Creek Mountain summit available purely for beginners, and the shops, hotels, and restaurants are several steps in elegance up from, say, Blu's in downtown Vail Village. Just know what you're getting into before you go; even the red-brick strip of art galleries immediately outside the central parking area can induce serious sticker shock.

Beaver Creek is a sort of gated community; driving in through Avon off I-70, you have to identify yourself to a guard in a booth. The resort is more self-contained than even Vail or Keystone, and it has the feel of a super-outdoor-mall, complete with a network of escalators and a charming ice-skating rink in the middle of one of the plazas. The ski trails of Beaver Creek link to Bachelor Gulch and Arrowhead, both of which are in quaint surrounding towns on the same level of luxury. (Check out the home prices!)

Sports and Recreation

Many skiers trek to Beaver Creek when Vail is mobbed, but that standard operating procedure hardly does the resort's slopes justice. Beaver Creek's 109 trails—not counting the 25 at Bachelor Gulch and 12 at Arrowhead—are equally distributed for beginners, intermediates, and black-diamond experts. Its deceptively steep Birds of Prey course, which starts at an elevation of 11,427 feet, was the site of four men's World Cup races in late 2004 and 2005, and its Grouse Mountain runs are legendarily (and strenuously) bumpy.

Skiing the village-to-village route from Beaver Creek to Bachelor Gulch to Arrowhead and back again is one of the area's great charms. Bachelor Gulch generally has better powder but not as many expert runs, while Arrowhead is three resorts removed from Vail, so it's hardly ever filled with people.

Beaver Creek's **Ski & Snowboard School** (800/475-4543) gives lessons (in the $150 range, but many packages are available) for all skill levels. Kids, women, snowboarders, Nordic-skiers, and downhill racers can choose from a variety of classes, clinics, and private lessons. For rental equipment, try **Beaver Creek Sports** (111 Beaver Creek Plaza, 970/845-5400 or 970/476-9457, www.beavercreeksports.com), which also rents bikes for the many area trails. It's probably easiest to reserve a rental-and-lift-ticket package online in advance.

The resort's best backcountry ski trails—more than 20 miles of them—are at **McCoy Park,** which is accessible from the Strawberry Park Express lift (number 12). Snowshoes are allowed on the lift. Warning: Although there are equal numbers of beginner, intermediate,

and advanced tracked trails, there are many uphills and it's easy to get exhausted at 9,840 feet. The **Beaver Creek Nordic Sports Center** (1280 Village Rd., 970/845-5313, 8:30 A.M.– 4 P.M. daily Dec.–Apr.) rents cross-country skis and snowshoes and can answer questions about local trails.

One of the Beaver Creek Village Plaza central charms is the year-round **ice-skating** rink, just past the strip of art galleries beyond the parking garage. A Zamboni polishes the 150-by-65-foot rink every three hours, and $10 rental skates are available at a nearby booth. Contact the rink at 970/845-0438.

The **Red Sky Golf Club** (1099 Red Sky Rd., Wolcott, 970/477-8400 or 866/873-3759) is a swanky private joint with segments designed by pros Tom Fazio and Greg Norman. Also on the premises is the prestigious **Chuck Cook Golf Academy** (970/477-8400 or 866/873-3759), run by an expert who has coached Payne Stewart, Tom Kite, and others. The **Beaver Creek Golf Club** (103 Offerson Rd., 970/845-5775) isn't quite as breathtaking as Red Sky, but it's a decent course with nice views. Robert Trent Jones Jr. designed the 18-hole course. Some hotels have golf facilities, too, including the four-course **Club at Cordillera** (2206 Cordillera Way, Edwards, 970/926-2200 or 800/877-3529, www.cordillera-vail.com).

Deciding whether to **hike** in Vail or Beaver Creek is a tossup—the only difference is Vail tends to be more crowded during the spring and summer. As in ski season, Beaver Creek's big draw is the **Village-to-Village Trail,** a three-mile one-way hike through aspen trees (with views of the Gore Range beyond the forest). To get there, take Village Road beyond Beaver Creek, and the trailhead is just past Elk Track Road on the right; after walking to Bachelor Gulch, you can turn around or call from the Ritz Carlton to arrange a shuttle pickup.

Beaver Creek Mountain itself has 50 miles of hiking-and-biking trails, including the popular **Beaver Lake Trail** and new **Royal Elk Trail,** both of which are easy jaunts to Beaver Lake.

The **Beaver Creek Information Center** (970/845-9090) has more information on trails, and $59 bike rentals are available at the base of the Centennial Express Chairlift; call 970/845-5400. The **Beaver Creek Hiking Center** (970/845-5373, open spring and summer) provides guided hikes.

Entertainment and Nightlife

The **Vilar Center for the Arts** (68 Avondale Ln., 888/920-2787 or 970/845-8497) is a 530-seat theater at the center of Beaver Creek Village (just down the escalator from the ice-skating rink). It gets big names, but mostly of the genteel variety: singer Madeline Peyroux, Michael Flatley's *Lord of the Dance,* bluegrass singer Del McCoury, and various Broadway-style theater and dance acts.

Shopping

The art galleries along the red-brick path from the parking garage to the Beaver Creek Village have window-shopping prices that may well blow your mind. The **Sportsman's Gallery Ltd. & Paderewski Fine Art** (Beaver Creek Plaza, 970/949-6036) has an $8,500 bronze elk and a small Ogden M. Pleissner watercolor of a yellow-and-orange mesa for $7,500. **J. Cotter** (Market Square, 970/949-8111) specializes in fine art and jewelry, and displays a two-foot-tall purple-crystal rock. Beyond the path, **Pismo Fine Art Glass** (45 W. Thomas Pl., 970/949-0908, www.pismoglass.com) sells hand-blown glass collections that twist into exotic shapes, like Brian Brenno's *Blue Hat with Turquoise Flower* for $800. A unique store in Beaver Creek, though, is **Christopher & Co.** (0105 Edwards Village Blvd., 970/926-8191, www.christopherco.com), which has a gigantic stash of vintage entertainment and art posters, from a pen-and-ink French Buster Keaton handbill to scenic mountain images from many different eras and locations.

Accommodations

Beaver Creek hotels are extremely expensive, but plenty of cheaper deals are available up the highway, in Vail, Minturn, Edwards, and Eagle.

Just to make everything as confusing as possible, the ◖ **Ritz-Carlton Bachelor Gulch in**

Beaver Creek (0130 Daybreak Ridge, Avon, 970/748-6200, www.ritzcarlton.com/resorts/bachelor_gulch/overview/default.asp, $459–5,000) is actually in Avon. But everything else is easy to figure out at this beautiful, sprawling building that's as big as a town and nestled underneath a mountain. There's a private golf club, the Red Sky, on the premises, as well as a spa (sorry, a "co-ed rock grotto") and various one-of-a-kind accoutrements. For example: The hotel makes its own Labrador retriever, Bachelor, available for hikes, and its "Key to Luxury Package" ($540) includes one-day use of a new Mercedes-Benz (plus a tank of gas).

The incredible mountain views distinguish the **Park Hyatt Beaver Creek Resort & Spa** (136 E. Thomas Pl., Avon, 970/949-1234, http://beavercreek.hyatt.com/property/index.jhtml, $570–685) from every other Hyatt. It also has a "storyteller" who sits around the huge lobby fireplace and reads books to guests in the winter.

"Luxury lodging" reads the sign on the front of the **Poste Montane** (76 Avondale Rd., 970/845-7500 or 800/497-9238, www.postemontane.com, $510–695), and it's a believable claim. The white building, topped with brown, wooden roofs, is directly at the bottom of the Beaver Creek shopping area and escalators, and visitors wander out wearing cowboy boots and Stetsons. The rooms are huge and bathrobes are available.

The Charter at Beaver Creek (120 Offerson Rd., 970/949-6660, www.thecharter.com, $370–540) is a beautiful property, both inside and out, with dark-blue roofs and elegant flowery bedspreads and thick mattresses in even the smallest of rooms. (Which is to say, two beds.) It has a spa, pool, three restaurants, and excellent views of the resort, ski slopes, and multitude of trees.

In addition to a prime location among the trees on the resort slopes, **The Pines Lodge** (141 Scott Hill Rd., 970/845-7900 or 866/605-7625, http://pineslodge.rockresorts.com/info/rr.asp, $299–349) has a sort of quiet dignity—ski-boot heaters are in all the rooms, and some have incredible panoramic mountain views.

© STEVE KNOPPER

Beaver Creek is Vail's sibling city, with pricey malls and a great ice-skating rink.

The Grouse Mountain Grill is one of the resort's best restaurants.

The **Lodge & Spa at Cordillera** (2206 Cordillera Way, Edwards, 970/926-2200 or 800/877-3529, www.cordillera-vail.com, $295–395) has sadly gone the way of Watergate—nice place to stay, but nobody will think of it as merely a place to stay ever again. This is where police arrested basketball star Kobe Bryant in summer 2003 for allegedly raping a young employee. (Charges were later dropped.) It's a decent hotel—a long, white complex on the side of a mountain with four restaurants and four golf courses.

The **Beaver Creek Lodge** (26 Avondale Ln., 970/845-9800 or 800/583-9615, www.beavercreeklodge.net, $420–525) has always been a decent place to stay, in the European mode with large rooms and a central location. But owner Richard Kessler recently gave it a multimillion-dollar facelift, and suddenly it's a condo-lodge filled with red suede lobby curtains and even grommets. The rooms have fireplaces and wireless Internet access.

Food

A ranching and farming community in the 1880s, the town of Edwards, a few miles west of Beaver Creek off I-70, has developed a reputation for diverse and affordable restaurants. Among the more interesting ones: **Sato** (0105 Edwards Village Blvd., 970/926-7684, 5–10 P.M. daily, 11:30 A.M.–2:30 P.M. Mon.–Fri.), one of the only sushi joints in the region; **The Gashouse** (34185 Hwy. 6, 970/926-3613, 11 A.M.–10 A.M. daily), an old log-cabin steakhouse with serious happy hours; **Fiesta's New Mexican Café and Cantina** (57 Edwards Access Rd., 970/926-2121, 10:30 A.M.–10 P.M. Mon.–Fri., 7:30 A.M.–10 P.M. Sat.–Sun.), which combines Mexican and New Mexican food into one blue-corn enchilada; and **Juniper** (97 Main St., 970/926-7001, 5–10 P.M. daily), at which chef Mike Irwin's idea of "comfort fusion" is roasted butternut squash soup with ginger.

Located just past the red-brick gallery path from the parking lot to the resort village, authentic-Italian **Toscanini** (Beaver Creek Village, Avon, 970/845-5590, 5:30–9:30 P.M.

daily) is relatively affordable—the Chilean sea bass is $32—despite the preponderance of women in fur coats who file out after dinner.

The **Grouse Mountain Grill** (141 Scott Hill Rd., 970/754-7200, 5–10 P.M. daily) is inside the Pines Lodge, in the middle of a forest on the side of its namesake mountain. Although it serves fancy fish and duck dishes, its house specialties are of the slabs-of-meat variety—elk rib chop, beef tenderloin steak, and New York strip, all in the mid-$30 range. As with the rooms, the mountain views are awesome.

Vista (48 E. Beaver Creek Blvd., Avon, 970/949-3366, www.vistarestaurant.com, 5–9:30 P.M. daily) has the entrées and white-linen air of an upscale restaurant, but it's built on a homey bar with a big wine list and has down-home touches like a kids' menu that kids actually like.

All the restaurants around here have an elk dish, but try the Big Hat Ranch Elk Ragout ($19). Beaver Creek founder George Townsend supposedly built the log-cabin structure that houses **Mirabelle** (55 Village Rd., 970/949-7728, www.mirabelle1.com, 1–9 P.M. Mon.–Sat.) as the town's first residence in the early 1880s. It's still a beautiful building, with hardwood floors and elegant rugs, and it adds French touches like foie gras and Dover soul meunière ($45) to what is otherwise a typically diverse menu of elk, chicken, steak, and seafood.

To get to **Beano's Cabin** (Larkspur Bowl, 970/949-9090, 5 P.M.–close early Dec.–early Apr.), on the side of the Grouse Mountain, diners must hail a Sno-Cat and sleigh in the winter or a shuttle van or wagon ride (or even a horse) in the summer. Try the pan-seared pheasant breast or the Colorado lamb loin. Caution: *The Denver Post* ripped the place for its excessive kid-friendliness, so plan accordingly.

In addition to the woodsy scenery and the food—try the veal loin and mustard-crusted veal breast ($32) or the wood-oven-roasted lobster ($45)—the main thing you need to know about **Splendido** (17 Chateau Ln., 970/845-8808, www.splendidobeavercreek.com) is it has a piano bar. And a good pianist.

tiny Minturn in Vail Valley

MINTURN

The streets of this century-old mining-and-railroad town are invitingly quiet even on a Saturday night during ski season. It's just a few exits west of Vail off I-70, on a pretty spot beneath the hills where Gore Creek and the Eagle River intersect. And it's an oasis between always-mobbed Vail to the east and super-affluent Beaver Creek to the west. The shops and galleries are quaint, the Minturn Inn is a little out of the way but well worth searching for, and the restaurants are among the best in the area.

Minturn became a town in 1904, long before Vail was incorporated, and workers settled here for years before the railroads closed, mining died out, and skiing took over as the region's major industry. Today it's a quaint footnote, but one well worth trying out. Don't be surprised if you sidle up to The Saloon for a beer and find two Hummers parked outside and several pairs of ski boots and ski poles leaning against the 1901 building out front.

Accommodations

Built in a 1915 log-cabin home and refurbished by an enterprising ski-bum couple in 1995, the (◖ **Minturn Inn** (442 Main St., 970/827-9647 or 800/646-8876, www.minturninn.com, $149–169) has huge rooms and beds in wooden, comfortable rooms with lots of space and large beds and couches. It's a friendly local spot, with owners Tom and Cathy Sullivan almost always on hand for a chat in the lobby kitchen.

Food

Don't let the name of the **Minturn Country Club** (131 Main St., 970/827-4114, 5–10 P.M.) fool you: "The only thing missing is the golf course," goes the slogan. From the outside, it looks like a wooden-walled dive, with pool tables and old framed pictures. But the cook-your-own steak dinners are a steal at $12, and chicken and fish are available.

Also deceptively dive-looking is **The Saloon** (142 N. Main St., 970/827-5954, www.minturnsaloon.com, 3:30–11 P.M. daily), in another wooden structure that (according to various legends) has housed gambling rings and basketball games since it was built in 1901. It has sit-down food of the upscale Mexican variety on one side, drinks on the other, and various stuffed mooseheads and Gerald R. Ford Invitational Golf Tournament posters all over the walls.

The diner-style **Turntable Restaurant** (160 Railroad Ave., 970/827-4164, 7 A.M.–9 P.M. Mon.–Sat., 7 A.M.–1:30 P.M. Sun.) doesn't get much attention in the travel guides, but it's cheap, fast, and equally adept with burgers and shakes as with burritos and green chile.

Shopping

Galleries and shops line Main Street in Minturn, and while some of them are expensive, they're a break from the eye-popping prices of, say, Beaver Creek. Especially fun in a woodsy-tourist kind of way is the **Eagle River Trading Company** (161 Main St., 970/827-9262), which announces, "This Ain't No Museum! This Junk is for Sale!" on a sign outside. It's filled with wooden Indian heads and cowboy posters.

THE SKI TOWNS

Breckenridge

Exactly 393 people lived in Breckenridge in 1960, and residents feared the area just west of the Continental Divide would dwindle into a ghost town. But a year later, the Rounds and Porter Lumber Company, of Wichita, Kansas, received a permit to build a ski area, and within a few months, 17,000 visitors had showed up to ride the one two-chair ski lift. Breck has grown steadily ever since, and while nine companies, including Aspen and Vail resorts, have owned the resort, it continues to expand—the base area, long a frustrating clump of nothing, will soon add a gourmet restaurant, a hotel, condos, and shops. The one constant during boom and bust years has been incredible Tenmile Range backdrops, easily accessible from downtown.

For skiers, Breckenridge has always been a contradiction. The mountain's four peaks, all of which are around 13,000 in elevation, are challenging and fun, especially for expert skiers, but navigating them through a complex maze of narrow "catwalks" can be frustrating. Breckenridge officials, however, are touting the recently inaugurated Peak 7 as a solution to these problems—and the breathtaking views on the new run overlook the 14,000-foot Grays and Torreys peaks. Still, for many Denver residents and Denver International Airport tourists, the base is a little too far and the ski-lift lines a little too long to be worth it.

Also, Breckenridge was one of the first Colorado resorts to embrace the once-renegade sport of snowboarding, sponsoring a major national competition in 1986 and continuing to tailor runs for one-board visitors. (Some 'boarders, however, complain about navigating the many paths between the runs.)

The town of Breckenridge, with its 100 restaurants, 500 hotels, and 2,300 condos, is among the most diverse and affordable of all the Summit County resort areas. From the pizza-and-burger joint Downstairs at Eric's to the tony and beautiful Café Alpine, not to mention reasonable prices and wide-open areas

for parking and walking, the tourist experience is top-notch. Breckenridge is also a big area for history buffs—gold was first discovered here in 1887, and the Washington Gold Mine is one of several artifacts from that era offering tours; also, the 12-block downtown Breckenridge district has more than 250 historic buildings.

Perhaps more than any other Summit County ski area, Breckenridge thrives in spring and summer as well. It's on the Colorado River, and fishing, kayaking, and whitewater-rafting opportunities are numerous. Plus, there's a golf club and about a zillion festivals, from Genuine Jazz to the Toast of Breckenridge.

HISTORY

Believe it or not, some people still show up in Breckenridge for reasons other than skiing, mountain biking, hiking, or feasting in local bars and restaurants. Of all the Summit County ski towns, Breckenridge has the most historical riches—350 such structures, including 250 in the National Register of Historic Places.

Breckenridge became an official town in 1859, when somebody discovered gold in the hills and miners from all over the U.S. rushed to become part of the boom. By 1860, the town had more than 8,000 miners and merchants and an actual bar, the Gold Pan Saloon, which continues to operate downtown. At the turn of the 20th century, miners erected a Methodist church, a railroad, a boarding house, and a school, and sent a four-boat Navy expedition down the Blue River to the Colorado, hoping to find a water passage to the Pacific. (It didn't work.) Miners discovered the town's biggest gold nugget, at 13.5 pounds, in 1887.

Gradually, through the early 20th century, mining of gold, silver, lead, zinc, and other metals slowed down, especially when U.S. officials demanded that metal be melted down and sent to help in World

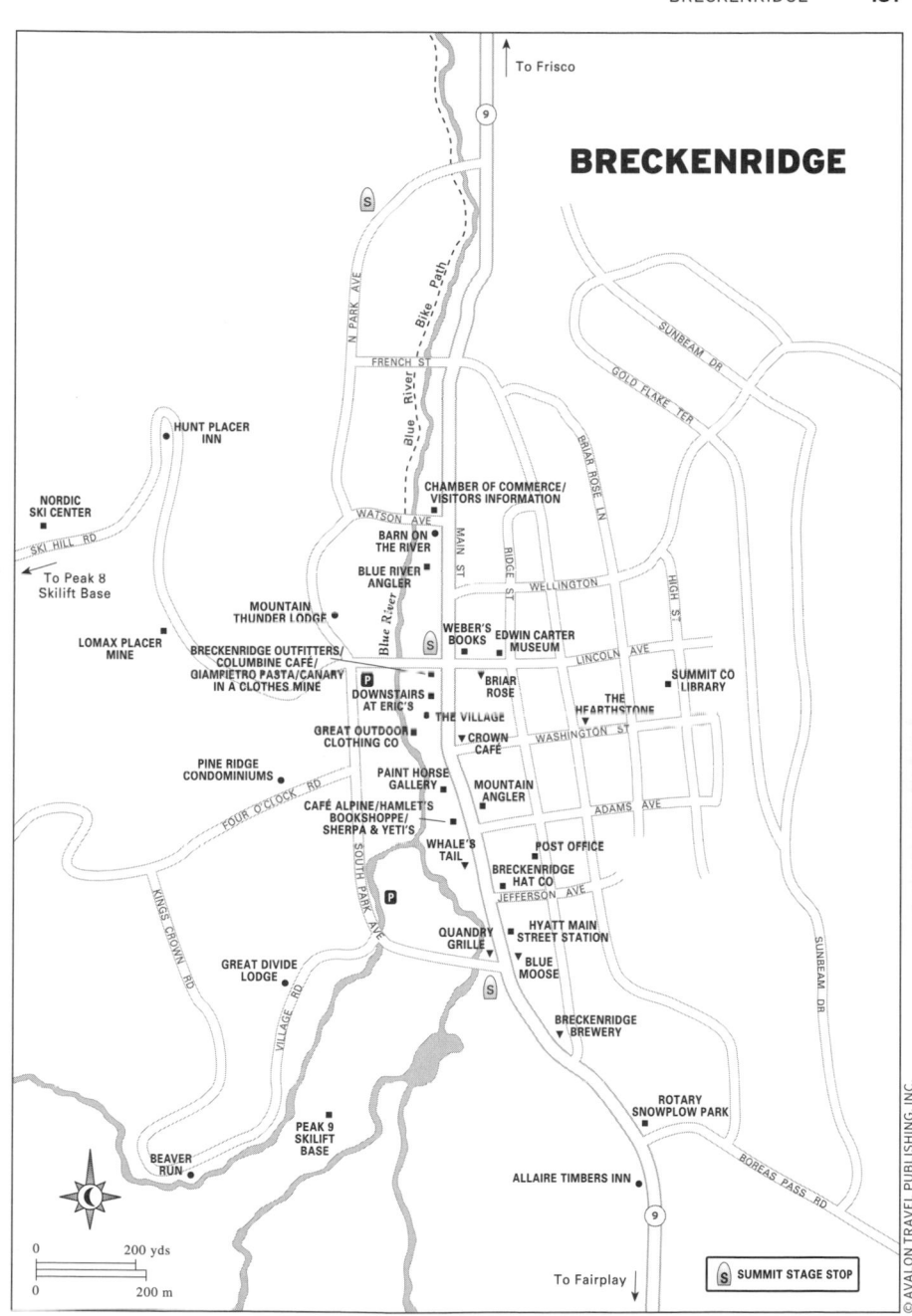

To Frisco

9

S

BRECKENRIDGE

S

N PARK AVE

Bike Path

Blue River

FRENCH ST

SUNBEAM DR

GOLD FLAKE TER

HUNT PLACER
INN

NORDIC
SKI CENTER

SKI HILL RD

To Peak 8
Skilift Base

LOMAX PLACER
MINE

MOUNTAIN
THUNDER LODGE

BRECKENRIDGE OUTFITTERS/
COLUMBINE CAFÉ/
GIAMPIETRO PASTA/CANARY
IN A CLOTHES MINE

WATSON AVE

CHAMBER OF COMMERCE/
VISITORS INFORMATION

BARN ON
THE RIVER

BLUE RIVER
ANGLER

Blue River

MAIN ST

RIDGE ST

BRIAR ROSE LN

WELLINGTON

HIGH ST

WEBER'S
BOOKS

S

EDWIN CARTER
MUSEUM

LINCOLN AVE

SUMMIT CO
LIBRARY

P

DOWNSTAIRS
AT ERIC'S

GREAT OUTDOOR
CLOTHING CO

BRIAR
ROSE

THE VILLAGE

CROWN
CAFÉ

THE
HEARTHSTONE

WASHINGTON ST

PINE RIDGE
CONDOMINIUMS

FOUR O'CLOCK RD

PAINT HORSE
GALLERY

CAFÉ ALPINE/HAMLET'S
BOOKSHOPPE/
SHERPA & YETI'S

MOUNTAIN
ANGLER

ADAMS AVE

KINGS CROWN RD

SOUTH PARK AVE

WHALE'S
TAIL

P

VILLAGE RD

GREAT DIVIDE
LODGE

QUANDRY
GRILLE

POST OFFICE

BRECKENRIDGE
HAT CO

JEFFERSON AVE

HYATT MAIN
STREET STATION

BLUE
MOOSE

S

BRECKENRIDGE
BREWERY

SUNBEAM DR

BEAVER
RUN

PEAK 9
SKILIFT
BASE

ALLAIRE TIMBERS INN

ROTARY
SNOWPLOW PARK

BOREAS PASS RD

9

To Fairplay

| 0 | 200 yds |
| 0 | 200 m |

S SUMMIT STAGE STOP

THE SKI TOWNS

War II. The Country Boy Mine was among the last to close, after a flood in 1945, and residents deserted the town—just 393 people were left in the early 1960s.

But skiing took over in 1961, even before the completion of I-70, and the industry became successful enough to prop up Breckenridge for the next four decades. Early creaky lifts gave way to a high-speed "quad" lift in 1981, and for the 1999–2000 season, the resort peaked with 1,441,000 visitors.

SIGHTS

When people refer to Breckenridge's **Historic District,** they usually mean the 12-square-block area of downtown with Main, High, and Washington Streets and Wellington Road as the borders. While touring this area, you may note that one thing hasn't changed—miners hung out in the same buildings and streets that townies and tourists use today.

The 40-year-old **Summit Historical Society** (970/453-9022 www.summithistorical.org) offers summer walking tours (at 10 A.M. on sporadic days in June, August, and September) of historical sites in downtown Breckenridge, including the Alice G. Milne House and the W. H. Briggle House, along with the school, courthouse, and churches. Although the society focuses on all the mining towns in Summit County, it takes particular interest in Breckenridge, with tours of the Washington Mine, Edwin Carter Museum, and Rotary Snowplow Park.

Had it existed in 1859, People for the Ethical Treatment of Animals would have surely enlisted Edwin Carter, a gold rush miner who noticed that Summit County deer and bison were growing strange deformities. He attributed the mismatched antlers and two-headed calves to chemicals used for placer mining, a technique for extracting gold from stream beds. Eventually, Carter switched from mining to naturalism and traveled all over the Rockies collecting samples and learning taxidermy. His work helped scientists learn about the adverse effects of mining on local wildlife, and his log-cabin home (filled with 3,300 full-sized specimens of bears, bison, elk, and others) became his office and public museum. Before his death in 1900, he made arrangements to sell his collection to what would become the Denver Museum of Nature and Science. The **Edwin Carter Museum** (111 N. Ridge St., 970/453-9022, 10 A.M.–1 P.M. Wed. and 1–4 P.M. Tues., Thurs., Fri.) contains few of those specimens, but it has lots of information about his life.

In the 1880s, the **Washington Mine** (465 Illinois Gulch Rd., 970/453-9022, tour at 1 P.M. Tues.–Sat. late June–Labor Day) was one of the largest mines in an area crawling with them—30 men worked here in five main gold-and-silver-ore shafts stretching more than 10,000 feet underground. It was heavily active through about 1905 and stayed open on and off until the 1960s, when the local mining industry effectively died out (and gave way to the ski industry). Tickets are available at various Breckenridge sites, including the Information Cabin (309 N. Main St.); the mine itself is about a 20-minute drive from downtown. Other historic mines in or near town include the **Lomax Placer Mine** (301 Ski Hill Rd., 970/453-9022, tour at 1 P.M. Tues.–Sat. late June–Labor Day) and the still-operating-for-tourists **Country Boy Mine** (0542 French Gulch Rd., 970/453-4405 to arrange tours).

Rotary Snowplow Park (Boreas Pass Rd. at French St., 970/453-9022) contains a 108-ton snowplow, built in 1901, with intimidating blowing-and-cutting fans that once cleared narrow railroad tracks. These monstrosities were so big that a half dozen steam-driven locomotives had to push them up Boreas and Fremont passes. Although the cabin is restored, the plow no longer operates, so don't get any big ideas about driving it down Main Street.

The graves at the circa-1882 **Valley Brook Cemetery** (near the Airport Road-Valley Brook Road intersection, free) include that of Baby Eberlein, whose remains were moved here from Breckenridge's first cemetery in 1997. Most of the hand-carved headstones are unmarked, and they likely belong to miners too poor to pay for their own burials.

© STEVE KNOPPER

Breckenridge is the perfect ski resort, falling somewhere between luxury and down-home comfort.

SPORTS AND RECREATION
Downhill Skiing and Snowboarding

With a capacity of almost 37,000 skiers taking 27 lifts up the four peaks, skiing and snowboarding are Breckenridge's primary cultural, recreational, and financial base. Experts are fiercely loyal to the runs, choosing Breck over its more basic neighbor Arapahoe Basin and the more glamorous Vail—some feared the newly opened Peak 7 would be swamped with beginners, but it has its share of difficult 45-degree slopes.

The primary complaint about Breck is navigating the narrow cross-country "catwalks" that connect the runs on the front of the mountain. This is especially pronounced among snowboarders, who have come to love the resort for its long-standing support of the younger sport but can't stand the leg-cramping "cross-country snowboarding" required to traverse the catwalks. But the recently built six-passenger SuperChair, among other lifts, has helped skiers reach the back of the mountain, filled with wide-open bowls and tree-filled runs.

According to difficulty, Breckenridge's downhill skiing trails break down like this: easiest, 15 percent, including a portion of the Four O'Clock, which at 3.5 miles is the area's longest run; more difficult, 33 percent, including seven new runs on Peak 7; most difficult, 20 percent, including the bumpy Pika, Ptarmigan, and Forget-Me-Not trails; and expert, 32 percent, with the tree skiing of Peak 9 and the South Side of Peak 10, a desolate spot filled with bumps and glades.

Note that the one-day walk-up rate for lift tickets during the high season is $71, but scour the local newspapers and websites for deals. Many of the town's lodges offer packages and, of course, season passes are excellent deals for frequent skiers. Child-care facilities are available for all ages at the Peak 8 **Children's Center** (970/453-3258) and the Peak 9 **Village Child Care Center** (970/496-7449). And many businesses along Main Street rent equipment; believe me, you won't have trouble finding deals on the slopes or in town.

The resort's **Ski & Ride School** (970/453-3272 or 888/576-2754) has programs for beginners of all ages and also offers private lessons. It's best to reserve a slot in advance.

For weather and snow updates on Breckenridge, check www.breckenridge.snow.com and click on "weather reports." Also, the resort records regular snow reports at 970/453-6118, or call 970/453-5000 for general information.

Cross-Country Skiing and Other Snow Sports

Nordic skiing, which most people know as "cross-country," is big in Breckenridge, especially given the off-the-slope trails that link the downhill runs together. The **Breckenridge Nordic Center** (970/453-6855) is on Peak 8 with plenty of groomed trails; the **Gold Run Nordic Center** (Clubhouse Dr., 970/547-7889, www.townofbreckenridge.com/nordic/index.cfm), with nine miles of trails, also rents skis and provides lessons.

Of course, backcountry skiers can choose from an almost unlimited terrain of mountain trails. Just be careful, especially in tricky weather conditions, and check out the trails in advance by calling the Dillon Ranger District (970/925-5775).

For hut-to-hut skiers, the **Summit County Huts Association** (524 Wellington Rd., 970/453-8583, www.summithuts.org) makes four tiny cabins available for skiers to spend the night while on a run.

A number of companies throughout the area give **snowmobiling** and **dog-sledding** tours—try **Good Times Adventures** (6061 Tiger Rd., 970/453-7604, www.goodtimesadventures.com), **Tiger Run Tours** (0056 County Rd. 450, 970/453-2231, www.tigerruntours.com), or, for general information, the **Summit Activities Center** (970/547-1594, www.breckenridgeactivities.com). Santa Claus wannabes should contact **Nordic Sleigh Rides** (373 Gold Flake Ct., 970/453-2005, www.nordicsleighrides.com) or the **Country Boy Mine and Breckenridge**

Sleigh Rides at Gold Run Nordic Center (970/453-4405, www.brecksleighrides.com, www.countryboymine.com).

Ice-Skating

Breckenridge has two ice-skating options: **Maggie Pond,** at the Village at Breckenridge, and the **Stephen C. West Indoor and Outdoor Ice Arenas** (0189 Boreas Pass Rd., 970/547-9974). Both rent skates.

Hiking and Biking

Yes, it is possible to enjoy yourself outside in Breckenridge while wearing plain old shoes or boots. Hundreds of miles of hiking and biking trails, of all levels of difficulty, snake through the Central Rockies, and the Breckenridge options include: **Sapphire Point Overlook,** half a mile, beginning on Swan Mountain Road between Breckenridge and Keystone, with superb views of Dillon Reservoir and the mountains; **Peaks Trail,** 10 miles, a plunge from Breckenridge to Frisco; **Spruce Creek Trail,** 3.1 miles, which allows four-wheel-drive vehicles for half the trail; **Gold Hill Trail,** 3.1 miles, off Highway 9 between Frisco and Breckenridge, a challenging up-and-down path that overlooks the Blue River Valley and Tenmile Range; and **Quandary Peak,** 3 miles, which goes straight up, well above 14,000-foot elevation, a long, difficult hike with views of Grays and Torreys Peaks at the top.

Many information-center employees and hotel concierges will give out trail maps and may even know something about the terrain. Or try **Daniel's Cabin Information Center** (309 N. Main St.) or the **Breckenridge Activity Center** (Blue River Plaza, 970/453-6018).

If it goes really fast up and down hills, chances are it's a sport and Breckenridge offers some form of it. Silverthorne's **Colorado Bike & Ski Tours** (970/668-8900, www.coloradobikeandski.com) gives tours (and instruction) for snowshoers, rock climbers, hikers, rafters, kayakers, off-road drivers, and cyclists. The guides are experienced and some of the routes include lodging.

Fishing

Most visitors think of Colorado as a dry, land-locked state—and truthfully, nobody will mistake Breckenridge for San Francisco or Norfolk, Virginia, anytime soon. But the bodies of water can be even more exhilarating because you don't expect to encounter them. The town is directly on the Colorado River, and **Maggie Pond** is one of thousands of miles of lakes, streams, and reservoirs with fishing options. For lessons, equipment, and tours, there's **Blue River Angler** (209 N. Main St., 970/453-9171, www.blueriveranglers.com), **Mountain Angler** (311 S. Main St., 970/453-4665, www.mountainangler.com), and **Breckenridge Outfitters Inc.** (100 N. Main St., 970/453-4135).

Golf

Jack Nicklaus designed the town's sloping 27-hole course in 1985, then added another nine holes in 2001. As Colorado Rockies pitchers will sadly attest, balls fly faster and straighter in high altitudes than they do at sea level, so enjoy the long whacks—and the surrounding views. The **Breckenridge Golf Club** (0200 Clubhouse Dr., 970/453-9104, www.breckenridgegolfclub.com) is at an elevation of 9,324 feet.

Fitness

The **Breckenridge Recreation Center** (880 Airport Rd., 970/453-1734, www.townofbrecknridge.com/pr_center.cfm) is a typical public-gym complex, with racquetball and basketball courts, aerobics classes, weight machines, and two indoor swimming pools. At 69,000 square feet, it's the first building you see on the way into town off Highway 9.

ENTERTAINMENT AND EVENTS

Summit County has a live-music scene built primarily around hippie skiers and jamming rock 'n' roll bands, and Breckenridge entered the club world a few years ago with **Sherpa & Yeti's** (320 S. Main St., 970/547-9299), which regularly packs the place with hip-hop acts and dance DJs, plus local bands and occasional national touring acts like Fishbone, once-notorious rappers 2 Live Crew, and the country-punk act Split Lip Rayfield. Also a well-known restaurant dating to the 1850s, the **Gold Pan Saloon** (103 N. Main St., 970/453-5499) regularly puts on DJs and Colorado bands. The **Blue River Bistro** (305 N. Main St., 970/453-6974) has live jazz on weekend nights, and **The Whale's Tail** (323 S. Main St., 970/453-2221) sometimes puts on live comedy and music.

Note that a sizable portion of Breckenridge's tourism crowd is college students and young international visitors, many of whom like to stay up all night drinking mountain brews. (Colorado ski resorts, still reeling from years of post-9/11 tourism drops, have recently been aggressively aiming their marketing campaigns at outside-the-U.S. skiers.) Bars for this scene include the **Breckenridge Brewery** (600 S. Main St., 970/453-1550) and the martini-and-cigar **Cecelia's** (520 S. Main St., 970/453-2243).

The **Breckenridge Music Festival** (www.breckenridgemusicfestival.com) is spread out among several venues—mostly the downtown Riverwalk Center—between June and September. It stars the Breckenridge Music Festival Orchestra, which is diverse enough to handle symphony pieces, patriotic July Fourth anthems, and sometimes even big-band swing. In January, if eerie ice princesses give you pleasure, try **The Budweiser International Snow Sculpture Championships,** but if Norse gods of snow are more your thing, there's the **Ullr Festival,** which includes a wacky costumed parade down Main Street and other cold-weather events.

SHOPPING

Breckenridge, especially a five-block section of Main Street, is a picturesque shopping area marketing to all types of skiers: a T-shirt shop is just a few doors down from a sign advertising "teak and mink." Expensive knickknacks and bumper stickers with slogans about how it's better to fall off a ski slope than to fall off your living-room sofa are available everywhere, along with more practical (and familiar) businesses such as Sunglasses Hut and Starbucks.

Prices at ski towns are generally a little higher than average, but Breckenridge shops are reasonable compared to some of the other Summit County resorts.

For a small mountain resort town with a population of just 2,408, Breckenridge sure has a lot of shops—258 in all, from galleries of horse paintings to vegetable-based glycerin soaps. One of the best is the **Paint Horse Gallery** (226 S. Main St., 970/453-6813), including, yes, paintings of horses (and a lot of Navajo weavings and sculpture of them as well). **Canary in a Clothes Mine** (114 S. Main St., 970/547-9007) is a high-end alternative to the many goofy T-shirt shops along Main Street; a fancy, hillbilly-style "True Love" T-shirt costs $54, and a hand-painted Virgins Saints and Angeles Jesus and Mary Belt is a steal (well, for some people) at $178. The town is just too small for a Barnes & Noble or Borders, but cozy bookstores in colorful Victorian houses more than suffice: Try **Weber's Books** (100 S. Main St., 970/453-4723) and **Hamlet's Bookshoppe** (306 S. Main St., 970/453-8033).

Outlets for practical skiwear are everywhere—try the eight ski-area locations of **Breckenridge Sports** (970/453-3000) or the one location of **Great Outdoor Clothing Co.** (211 S. Main St., 970/547-2755)—but for impractical skiwear the best option is **Breckenridge Hat Co.** (411 S. Main St., 970/453-2737), which sells mullet wigs, Christmas-tree hats, and Rastafarian ski-helmet covers.

ACCOMMODATIONS

With 2,300 condos and 500 hotels, Breckenridge is equipped for almost any tourism surge—and given post-9/11 travel declines, the No Vacancy signs aren't as bright as they were in the booming late 1990s. Rates during the peak seasons—January to March and late June to early September, plus holidays—tend to be the highest, but scan the newspapers and websites for package deals. Summer (Memorial Day through late September) can also be crowded and pricey due to local festivals and

picnicking Rocky Mountain tourists. The best month for skiers is April, a surprisingly snowy month in recent years, with deals on lodging, lift tickets, and restaurants. Other good-deal months are June, September (which benefits from 70-degree late Indian summers), and October, which is often balmy in Colorado and has the best travel deals of all.

The town offers central reservation information at http://gobreck.com (click on "Lodging") and at 888/251-2417 (inside the U.S.) or 00-800/2720-0000 (outside the U.S.).

$100-150

Strategically located for history buffs—it's on an actual mining claim from the 1850s and is next door to the Summit Historical Society's miner tribute Lomax Placer Gulch—**Hunt Placer Inn** (275 Ski Hill Rd., 970/453-7573 or 800/472-1430, www.huntplacerinn.com, $135–218) has three suites and five regular rooms. All have private balconies, and while the wooden floors and ornate shelves give the rooms a certain antique feel, the ambience is basic and functional.

$150-200

The beloved B&B **[** **Barn on the River** (303B N. Main St., 970/453-2975 or 800/795-2975, www.breckenridge-inn.com, $149–289) has spectacular scenery on the bank of the Blue River, with the mountains in the background. The four queen rooms include fireplaces, and all have private balconies.

The **Hyatt Main Street Station** (505 S. Main St., 970/547-2700, $176–351) may look like a standard Rocky Mountain condo from the outside (note the green and brown wood panels), but it goes out of its way to provide cozy luxury—gas fireplaces, large kitchens, and whirlpool spas are in every room. Watch for deals during the off-season.

A classic log-cabin ski lodge with mountain views from the main-deck hot tub, the **Allaire Timbers Inn** (9511 Hwy. 9, 970/453-7530 or 800/624-4904, www.allairetimbers.com, $175–255) fills up its 10 rooms (from basic lodge rooms to suites) quickly during ski season. The stone fireplaces, door-to-door coffee delivery, four-poster beds (in some rooms), and short walk to Main Street give it a friendly, practical feel.

Beaver Run Resort and Conference Center (620 Village Rd., 970/453-6000 or 800/265-3560, www.beaverrun.com, $180–210) is owned by the Premier Resorts chain and feels a little corporate, but it offers ski-in/ski-out access to the Beaver Run Super Chair and the Quicksilver Six lifts at the base of Peak 9. Not a lot of frills, but 500 rooms and seven restaurants are on the premises, including the Copper Top.

The spa is the main draw at **The Lodge & Spa at Breckenridge** (112 Overlook Dr., 970/453-9300 or 800/736-1607, www.thelodgeatbreck.com, $169–243), which is a little removed from town and the ski slopes but over-compensates with extra luxury. Most of the standard rooms have mountain views—which is to say, spectacular views overlooking the Continental Divide—and the suites are panoramic.

Over $200

The Village at Breckenridge (535 S. Park Avenue, 970/547-5725 or 800/379-6517, http://villageatbreckenridge.com, $300–360) is the monster place to stay in Breckenridge, as it's sprawled out on 14 acres at the base of the ski resort and a 10-minute walk from the Main Street shops and restaurants. It has a variety of rooms, from small, no-frills studios to large three-bedroom luxury condo suites, all with ski-in/ski-out access to the six-person Quicksilver Super6 chairlift. On the premises are hot tubs, the Blue Sage Spa, an indoor pool, two restaurants (the Park Avenue Pub and Le Bistro de Paris), a ski school for adults and children, and even The Village at Breckenridge Fly Fishing School. It's not particularly creative to simply book a room at The Village, but it's simple, usually available, and convenient.

The **Great Divide Lodge** (550 Village Rd., 970/547-5725 or 888/906-5698, www.greatdividelodge.com, $300–360) is a smaller but just-as-modern alternative to The Village at Breckenridge, with 208 rooms in a rectangular, tree-lined building 50 yards from the ski resort's Peak 9 base. The hot-tub area overlooks the mountains, but the key reason for staying here (at least in the winter) is location.

Mountain Thunder Lodge (50 Mountain Thunder Dr., 970/547-5725 or 888/268-8376, www.mtnthunderlodge.com, $300–360), like The Village and the Great Divide Lodge, is run by Vail Resorts—but it's a little more removed from the slopes than those two properties. The wooden lodge has an old-school log-cabin quality, and its primary luxuries are in-room stone fireplaces, outdoor hot tubs, and a large heated pool (with surrounding heated decks). A shuttle takes guests to the slopes.

The primary advantage of **Pine Ridge Condominiums** (400 Four O'Clock Rd., 800/333-8833, www.pineridge.com, $330–399) is its proximity to ski trails—many of the slope-side units are located directly on the popular Four O'Clock ski run. Each unit has a hot tub, washer-dryer, and full kitchen, but if you're looking for rustic mountain charms you'd probably be better off at, say, the Allaire Timbers Inn. Keep an eye out for specials: During some event and off-season weekends, rooms can be as cheap as $119.

The six-bedroom, three-fireplace **Williams House** (303 N. Main St., 970/389-5761, riverridgerentals.com, $1,800) and the one-bedroom, Jacuzzi-equipped **Willoughby Cottage** (305 N. Main St., 970/389-5761, riverridgerentals.com, $400) are under new management as of summer 2004—as full rental houses.

FOOD

For a small ski town, Breckenridge is crammed with restaurants—more than 100 in all, from greasy breakfast to fancy breakfast to sportsbar lunch to high-end, super-eloquent, multicourse dinner.

Snacks, Cafés, and Breakfast

The Crown Café and Tavern (215 S. Main St., 970/453-6022, daily 10 A.M.–11 P.M.) serves coffee and breakfast all day and basics like lasagna and tuna salad for meals, but its specialties are the sweet stuff—try the baked

THE SKI TOWNS

brie with chipotle raspberry sauce, then tour the pastry case. Not as delectable but just as functional (and more affordable) are the **Blue Moose** (540 S. Main St., 970/453-4859, 7 A.M.–1 P.M.) and the **Columbine Café** (109 S. Main St., 970/547-4474, 7:30 A.M.–1:30 P.M. Mon.–Fri., 7:30 A.M.–3 P.M. Sat.–Sun.), both of which serve breakfast, along with coffee, dessert, and sandwiches.

Casual
After a day on the bright-white slopes, walking into the dungeon-like sports bar **Downstairs at Eric's** (111 S. Main St., 970/453-1401, 11 A.M.–midnight daily) might cause temporary blindness. But the disconcerting feeling quickly passes, and the cheerful waitpeople, 120 brands of beer, televisions suspended everywhere (if you're interested in that sort of thing), and old-school video games give this Main Street fixture charm. The food is affordable and very solid, from buffalo burgers to pizza. For the latter dish, though, you might want to go with an expert: **Giampietro Pasta & Pizzeria** (100 N. Main St., 970/453-3838, 11 A.M.–10 P.M. daily). The **Quandry Grille** (505 S. Main St., 970/547-5969, 11 A.M.–10 P.M. daily) has $5 lunch and $10 dinner specials in its barn-shaped building next to pretty Maggie Pond, and the fare is basic burgers, fries, and burritos.

Upscale
Café Alpine (106 E. Adams Ave., 970/453-8218, 5–8:30 P.M. daily) is one of those white-tablecloth restaurants with Spanish *tapas* for appetizers and orange-cardamom crème brûlée

with white chocolate dipped cat's tongue cookie for dessert. In between is a variety of grilled grouper, softshell crabs, smoked chicken breast, and pasta.

Voted "Top Dinner for the Whole Family" in *5280* magazine, **The Hearthstone** (130 S. Ridge St., 970/453-1148, 5 P.M.–close) is in a 100-year-old Victorian and has a wine list that seems miles long. Its menu is an elegant mix of comfort food (try the three-onion soup) and exotic experiments (granola-crusted elk chop)—plus an affordable prime rib dish for the kids. **Pierre's Riverwalk Café** (137 S. Main St., 970/453-0989, 5:30–9:30 P.M. Tues.–Sat., 5:30–9 P.M. Sun.) has 100 wines and the entrées to go with them—trout, scallops, duck breast, lamb, that sort of thing.

INFORMATION
Several official Breckenridge websites contain useful information on the ski area, the town, and lodging, restaurants, shopping, and other amenities: www.breckenridge.com, www.gobreck.com, and www.townofbreckenridge.com. For general inquiries, call 970/453-2913.

GETTING THERE
I-70 connects to Highway 9 in the Dillon/Silverthorne area, and the two-lane route is considerably more icily treacherous than the interstate. Take Highway 9 south into Breckenridge, and keep going until it turns into Main Street. You can't miss the ski area in the snowcapped mountains in front of you, to the right, and Main is a row of shops, restaurants, and galleries several blocks long. Street parking is available, but pay attention to the signs.

Keystone

For years, hard-core skiers considered Keystone a fun but tourist-heavy resort that never gets quite enough snow, notable for perhaps a brief stop on the way to Copper Mountain or Breckenridge. Millions of dollars in renovations have changed that mentality in recent years: "This isn't the same place you remember from that icy nightskiing experience a decade ago," opines *Ski* magazine. A $4.5 million snowmaking system took care of the ice problem; the resort expanded its acreage considerably and added several bowls above the tree line geared to expert skiers. Another $1 million brought restaurants, bars, and hipster nightclubs to the River Run base area.

Skiing-wise, Keystone has three peaks: Keystone Mountain, North Peak, and the Outback. Although Keystone Mountain, geared for beginners, once dominated the resort, its upgrades and changes in recent years have attracted numerous experts, including training members of various U.S. ski teams. Its major distinction from other resorts is night-skiing—the resort keeps 15 halogen-lamp-lighted trails open at night and sponsors events such as moonlight snowshoe tours and "36 Hours at Keystone," attracting snowboarders and skiers who don't mind the weird shadows that mysteriously appear on the moguls.

Both River Run and Lakeside Village are affordable and heavy on the tourists, and restaurants such as the mountaintop Alpentop Stube and the super-fancy Champeaux have high-class food to match the views. The Keystone Ranch, built in the 1930s, is a self-contained mountain playground (including a golf course), and decades of tourists have come to associate the entire resort with the ranch experience. Note that many cost-conscious skiers avoid shopping at the villages entirely, opting instead to park in Dillon or Silverthorne, about 20 miles away, and take reasonably priced shuttles to the base mountains.

Keystone summers are eventful as well,

and the resort enthusiastically rents mountain bikes for its hundreds of miles of trails, some of which overlook the magnificent Grays and Torreys Peaks. It's also just removed from the Colorado River, which in tandem with the small Keystone Lake means boating, whitewater-rafting, fishing, and kayaking. Check out the River Run Blues and the Bluegrass & Beer festivals, in July, as well.

SPORTS AND RECREATION
Skiing and Snowboarding

Unlike Breckenridge, Aspen, or Vail, Keystone is a village built for the ski industry. Upon arriving in town for the first time, you might wonder where all the shops and restaurants have gone—and the answer is "up the slopes." Some of the town's best amenities, such as the 11,444-foot-high Alpenglow Stube restaurant and the Outpost Lodge, are accessible only via ski lift.

The skiing itself sometimes gets a bad rap from locals and experts, who perceive Keystone as prime territory for families and beginners—the resort's Incubator Beginner Park, on the Freda's Way run about halfway up North Peak, has basic rails and rollers for the less coordinated. Also, the **Keystone Snow University** (970/496-4170), at the base Mountain House, offers lessons for adults and classes and day-care programs for kids from 2 months to 14 years old. But in truth, Keystone's easiest trails make up just 19 percent of the three peaks; more difficult runs account for 32 percent and most difficult runs are almost half. (The resort has 2,870 acres of total skiable terrain, a huge increase due to the improvements of recent years.)

Keystone is also known for its night skiing, offered on 15 trails at the A-51 Terrain Park (also the site of the beginner park halfway up North Peak). The lighted runs are surprisingly technical, including a 400-foot super pipe, a spot for difficult jumping, and tricky tree-line runs for both skiers and 'boarders. Hours vary, so check www.keystone.snow.com before making night plans.

In recent years, Keystone has invested millions of dollars into adding lifts and updating the snowmaking machines. Some Keystone skiers swear by the central North Peak, filled with long drops unencumbered by trees and crowds; others prefer more technical terrain such as the twisty Bergman Bowl and the steep and rocky Erickson Bowl. Thanks to rugged Sno-Cat vehicles, it's easier than ever before to access these bowls, high atop North Peak with views of Grays and Torreys Peaks in the distance. Bypassing North Peak is a little tricky, involving a gondola transfer or two, but for experts searching for difficult runs, The Grizz and Bushwhacker on the dense Outback mountain are the places to be.

The easiest way to buy lift tickets is online, by going to keystone.snow.com, then clicking "Winter Accommodations" and "Lift Tickets." As usual, watch the local papers and ask at your hotel for package deals. The **Children's Center** (River Run, 800/255-3715) has day-care accommodations for kids between 2 months and 6 years old—and has a special learn-to-ski program for 3-year-olds.

Keystone Sports (Mountain House, 970/496-4398) is one of many centrally located stores—another is **River Run Rentals** (970/496-3617 or 970/496-4619, www.rentskis.com)—that rents skis and equipment and sells winter clothing. It's in both the Mountain House base area and River Run village. The average price is about $20 (or more than $36 for higher-end packages), but deals are more common in Dillon or Silverthorne, or even Denver or Boulder.

The Keystone website, www.keystone .snow.com, has a "Snow Report" on every page.

Cross-Country Skiing

Keystone's **Nordic Center** (River Course Clubhouse, 970/496-4275) offers lessons and rental equipment. The center is at the edge of 45 miles of White River National Forest trails. In addition to skiing, the center focuses on skating, snowshoeing, tubing, and Telemarking.

Golf

The hub of Keystone golf is **Keystone Ranch** (1239 Keystone Ranch Rd., 970/496-4250), a sprawling, beautiful area filled with trees and a nine-acre lake. It also has some of the resort's best lodging (at the Keystone Ranch condos) and food (the Keystone Ranch restaurant). The club's par-72, 7,090-yard course, designed by Robert Trent Jones Jr. in 1980, is fairly traditional on the first nine holes, but it switches to more mountainous terrain on the second. Another course, the Keystone River Course, opened in 2000 and winds on the back nine through dense forest. Both courses have amazing mountain views, but the Keystone River Course overlooks the Continental Divide.

Ice-Skating

The frozen, five-acre Keystone Lake is "the largest Zamboni-maintained outdoor skating rink in North America," according to the resort website, and any superlative involving a Zamboni is fine by me. Seriously, the lake is spectacular, the air is clear, and skates and hockey sticks are available for reasonable rental fees. Call 800/354-4386.

Fishing

Keystone Resort offers fly-fishing lessons (800/354-4386), although they're on the pricey side. Also pricey is **Summit Guides** (Lake Village, 970/468-8945 or 866/468-8945, www.summitguides.com), which sells equipment and gives wading and floating tours throughout Summit County (including Keystone).

ENTERTAINMENT AND NIGHTLIFE

For foosball, local rock bands on most nights, and free Pabst Blue Ribbon beer, **The Goat Soup and Whiskey Tavern** (Hwy. 6, 970/513-9344, www.thegoattavern.com) is a longtime favorite for the younger ski crowd. Also serving live music on a regular basis is **Parrot Eyes** (River Run, 970/496-4333), a Mexican restaurant that goes heavy on the margaritas, and **Great Northern Tavern** (River Run, 970/262-2202, www.gntavern.com), more of a brewpub.

From 9:30 P.M.–1:30 A.M. nightly, **Greenlight** (River Run, 970/496-3223) transforms from a mild-mannered snack bar and après-ski hangout to a throbbing disco-ball dance club.

EVENTS

Keystone has no major entertainment draw à la the Telluride Bluegrass Festival or the Breckenridge Music Festival, but October's **Wine in the Pines** (http://cpco.org/wineinthepines/index.html) brings some 1,000 people to sample more than 500 vintages. The benefit for Cerebral Palsy of Colorado includes a gourmet food tasting and a winemaker's dinner.

SHOPPING

Most of Keystone's stores are in the **River Run** condominium district, not far from the ski lifts, but others are scattered throughout Lakeside Village, the Mountain House base area, and elsewhere in town. (Many residents and day-trippers, however, opt for the outlet stores in nearby Dillon and Silverthorne.) Among the gems: **Cassiopeia of Keystone** (River Run, 970/513-6649), a touristy shop specializing in bath products and home decor, specifically Waterford crystal; the **Twisted Pine Fur & Leather Co.** (River Run, 970/468-0988, www.ttpine.com), which is hardly the most politically correct store in the mountains but will undoubtedly appeal to luxury-lovers; and the local chain **Gorsuch Ltd.** (River Run, 970/262-0459, www.gorsuchltd.com), which rents equipment and sells stylish ski jackets and corny snowflake sweaters.

ACCOMMODATIONS

With more than 1,500 lodging units, **Keystone Resort** (run by Vail Resorts, 970/845-2500 or 888/222-9324, www.vailresorts.com, www.snow.com) has a lock on the market. But it does a pretty good job, offering diverse properties such as the 1880s Ski Tip Lodge and the golf-centric Keystone Ranch, along with a wide range of restaurants and outdoor activities and a shuttle that stops at most properties and the ski area. Many

of the hotels, apartments, and condos listed here belong to the resort. The resort is divided up into seven basic areas—East, North, and West Keystone, all somewhat removed from the slopes; Mountain House, the "base cam" at the bottom of the ski area; Keystone Ranch, golf-course territory; and Lakeside and River Run Villages, both centrally located "towns" equally close to amenities and the slopes. (These are given in lieu of addresses as locations below.)

For many Keystone skiers, location is the most important criteria when picking a lodge. Some of the more central (and affordable) properties include **Gateway Mountain Lodge** (East Keystone, 888/222-9298, $119), which for convenience has a liquor store on the premises; **Aspen Ridge** (North Keystone, 888/222-9298, $179), condos with superb views from the Tenderfoot Mountain Ridge; and **Riverbank Condominiums** (River Run, 888/222-9298, $170–200). Note that many condos require a five-night minimum, although shorter stays may be available during the off-season.

The resort's general lodging number is 877/753-9786, or (for international travelers) 970/496-4500.

$100-150

Not to be confused with the Ski Tip Condominiums, **Ski Tip Lodge** (0764 Montezuma Rd., 970/496-4386 or 888/222-9298, www.skitiplodge.com, $115–159) was a stagecoach stop in the 1880s. Keystone founders Max and Edna Dercum (whose names also begat one of the local mountain peaks) bought it in the 1940s as a private home and turned it into an early ski lodge. Although Keystone Resort bought the lodge in the 1970s, it's still intimate and quaint, with individually decorated rooms, a central fireplace, and an acclaimed restaurant.

The **Inn at Keystone** (Mountain House, 888/222-9298, $106–130) is a basic but inexpensive hotel on Highway 6, with a jazz bar and restaurant on hand. It's closer to nightclubs such as The Goat and the Snake River Saloon than it is to the slopes, but it's within 300 yards of the Mountain House base area.

$150-200

At the center of Keystone Village, the **Keystone Lodge Hotel** (Keystone Village, 888/222-9298, $179) aims for luxury (check out the spa, sauna, and indoor-outdoor pool) above the intimate charm of the Ski Tip Lodge. Every room has a nice view of Keystone Mountain and the Snake River. It's also incredibly convenient, with ice skating and bike rental within a short walk and the slopes within a short shuttle ride.

Over $200

Keystone Ranch (Keystone Ranch, 888/222-9298, $500–1,000) is the prime spot for golfers, immediately next to the Robert Trent Jones Jr.-designed course, but renting a house in this area is fairly pricey. **Cabin in the Pines** (North Keystone, 888/222-9298, $385) is a woodsy condominium complex with three-bedroom units.

FOOD
Casual

The Mountain House ski-area base underwent renovations in late 2003, and family-oriented quickie restaurants such as **Bite Me Pizza** (Mountain House, 970/496-4020, 7:30 A.M.–9 P.M. daily) sprang up for skiers whose 3-year-olds are unable to sit still for a six-course Alpenglow Stube meal. The pizza isn't bad at all. Neither is the beer. Also, the **Timber Ridge Food Court** (North Peak, 970/496-3156, 9 A.M.–3 P.M. daily), at the top of prime skiing territory, has a variety of quick-and-cheap hamburger and Asian noodles dishes (the food isn't anything special, but you can't beat the convenience—or the views).

It's unlikely that many Irish immigrants live in Keystone, but the **Cala Inn** (40 Cove Blvd., 970/468-1899, 11:30 A.M.–midnight daily) is one of those classic Irish joints with shepherd's pie and fish and chips to go with unlimited Guinness.

Upscale

Dinner prices can easily get to the $100 range,

not counting the lengthy wine list, but the **Alpenglow Stube** (North Peak, 970/496-4132 or 800/354-4386, 11 A.M.–1:30 P.M. daily, 5:30–10 P.M. Wed.–Sun.) is worth it for the scenery alone. It's a North Peak gondola ride up to 11,444 feet, with a six-course meal of super-elegant dishes like duck foie gras and roast chestnut and butternut squash tartlet. They also let you replace your ski boots with slippers—and no, this isn't a typo—warmed in the oven.

Real-life cowboys probably don't come to the **Keystone Ranch** (21996 Hwy. 6, 970/496-4161 or 800/354-4386, 5–8:30 P.M. Mon.–Sat.) golf-course restaurant anymore—I'm pretty sure Roy Rogers and Dale Evans didn't eat foie gras trio sautéed with pumpkin oil—but the Old West paraphernalia and decor is fun to look at. Located in a 1930s cattle-ranch homestead, the restaurant offers six-course meals with boar and buffalo specialties.

As comfortable and welcoming as the surrounding bed and breakfast, the **Ski Tip Lodge** (0764 Montezuma Rd., 970/496-4950 or 800/354-4386, 5:45–8:30 P.M. Thurs.–Mon.) turns mahimahi, roast prairie quail, and veal into high-class comfort food. The fixed-price dinners are slightly more affordable than those at the Alpenglow Stube, but from the fireplace to the rich coffee and dessert (best eaten in the lounge), the Ski Tip is as soothing as a post-ski hot chocolate.

The Alpenglow Stube and Ski Tip Lodge are great, but **Champeaux** (Lakeside Village, 970/496-3740 or 800/354-4386, 5:30–10:30 P.M. daily), in the Keystone Lodge, is one of the rare French restaurants in Summit County. Wines are specifically picked out to go with certain menu items—try the beef tournedos and the roasted garlic and forest mushroom fettuccine—and the only thing un-French about the experience is the panoramic view of Keystone Lake and Snake River Valley.

INFORMATION

Just about everything Keystone—ski area, town, lodging, shopping—falls under the Keystone Resort umbrella (970/496-2316 or

877/625-1556, http://keystone.snow.com). This makes for one-stop shopping, although if you have a question about a particularity that's not part of the website package, stumped resort phone operators can be a little impatient.

GETTING THERE AND AROUND

Keystone is tucked at the bottom of Loveland Pass, just removed enough from I-70 to make the drive interesting during a blizzard. From Denver, take I-70 west through Georgetown and Idaho Springs, but turn east on Highway 6 (at the Silverthorne/Dillon exit) a few miles before hitting the Eisenhower Tunnel. After passing the Loveland ski area, the beautiful Loveland Pass (overlooking the Continental Divide), and Arapahoe Basin, continue on the narrow, twisty, two-lane highway until you plunge into Keystone. Compared to Vail or Breckenridge, the town itself is a little hard to spot—just green-and-brown wooden condo buildings everywhere. It's only about nine miles from Breck up Highway 9, making a two-resort vacation simple.

The small and self-contained Keystone has its own little bus stop, serving most of the condos, hotels, restaurants, and ski shops in the area. To check the pickup locations and schedule, call 970/496-4200.

LOVELAND SKI AREA

Few out-of-towners travel all the way to Colorado to ski at the **Loveland Ski Area** (I-70, exit 216 near Georgetown, 800/736-3754 or 303/571-5580, www.skiloveland.com)—for one thing, there's no lodging—but day-tripping locals swear by this 13,010-foot-tall mountain that averages 400 inches of snow. Opened in 1936, the mountain rises above the Continental Divide, which means great scenery, and while the lifts can be poky and the wind intense, it gets some of the best powder in the region. Nine lifts service more than 80 runs, an equal mixture for beginners (Loveland Valley) and experts (Loveland Basin). Rental shops and a ski school (303/571-5580) are easily accessible from the base area, and parking is plentiful. Loveland Pass, directly up Hwy. 6, has a scenic area overlooking the Continental Divide about 10 miles from the ski area. Whether you're skiing or

THE SKI TOWNS

© STEVE KNOPPER

Loveland Pass

exploring, the area makes for a nice stop en route to Keystone or Breckenridge.

◖ ARAPAHOE BASIN

If Vail and Aspen are for skiers serious about their clothes, A-Basin is for skiers serious about their partying. It's the tallest ski area in the U.S., with a base elevation of 10,780 feet and a summit of 13,050 feet; it's Summit County's first ski area, built in the 1940s, and maintains its rickety charm; and due to its elevation and a relatively new snowmaking machine, it stays open later than any other Colorado resort. As a result, locals fill the parking lots for "Beachin' at the Basin" tailgate parties through June or July.

Aside from an on-site cafeteria and bar, A-Basin itself has almost nothing by way of restaurants or hotels. Its clientele tends to be day-trippers up from Boulder or Denver, or out-of-town visitors who've settled in nearby Dillon or Silverthorne and shuttled between their hotel and the base.

Most visitors to the old-school resort will find it unsurprising that Arapahoe Basin began with just one sturdy tow rope for a ski lift. And to get to the bottom of the rope, skiers had to ride in a U.S. Army weapons carrier. Which was pulled by a four-wheel drive vehicle. This was in 1946, and the resort still seems like a throwback.

Sports and Recreation

Beyond the bring-your-own mentality, A-Basin offers few frills aside from its internationally known extreme runs. (One longtime Colorado skier calls it "scary-ass terrain.") Best known is the Pallavincini, thought to be the longest and steepest in Colorado, but it's filled with double-black diamond (which is to say, expert) runs that attract locals who aren't so obsessed with drinking hot chocolate in the lodge afterward. It's also just west of the Continental Divide—almost on top of it—and the views are excellent.

The $200-per-person **Ski School** (970/496-7007) promises groomed runs for beginners ("or your money back!"). Lift tickets tend to be affordable here, and the slopes aren't as crowded as those of Vail or Steamboat Springs. Rental equipment is available at the base area. For more information, call 970/468-0718 or visit www.arapahoebasin.com.

Getting There

Driving to A-Basin can be tricky in bad weather, as it involves a trip up the twisty, two-lane Highway 6 (after exiting I-70) to Loveland Pass. The base area is at the very bottom of the steep highway. Just six miles beyond the area is Keystone, so skiers from that resort may want to venture to a different experience.

Dillon, Silverthorne, and Frisco

DILLON AND SILVERTHORNE

Most ski-resort regulars drive past suburban-looking twin towns Dillon and Silverthorne and think "cheap shopping." Both have huge factory outlets with many name brands and are generally more affordable than the shops populating nearby resort base areas and tourist districts. Both are also worth a stop—and not just for the many convenient chain hotels, restaurants, and ski-slope park-and-ride shuttles. Silverthorne (pop. 3,500) is along the Blue River and has many parks and out-of-the-way spots for anglers and kayakers. The 125-year-old Dillon (pop. 2,800) is best known for the 9,000-foot-high, marina-equipped Lake Dillon, a favorite for sailboaters, and its history as a stagecoach stop in the 1880s.

History

In the 1950s, Denver gave Dillon an ultimatum: Everybody move, or you'll drown. Drought had struck Denver, the capital city 70 miles to the east, so its water board decided to dam the Blue River. This turned out to be a massive undertaking. Townspeople had to sell their property and move by 1961. Workers cut a 1,700-foot-long tunnel out of solid rock, built a shaft 233 feet deep, and submerged the town under 150 feet of water. (The dam, located underneath Lake Dillon, is no longer visible, but you can see the location by driving east from Frisco to Dillon on Dam Road.) That was the *third* time Dillon moved.

Dillon became a town in 1883, when stagecoach riders established a trading post in the region (then as now, the town was a prime midpoint for city dwellers traveling to pretty mountain towns). The town first moved closer to the Utah and Northern Railroad; later, it moved to be near the Blue, Ten Mile, and Snake Rivers. Its third move was to the shore of the Denver Water Board's reservoir. And that's where the town—which swells to 5,200 people in the winter, thanks to condos and hotels—stands today.

Silverthorne's history is slightly less colorful. Its name comes from Judge Marshal Silverthorn, who in 1880 made a gold-mining claim called the Silverthorn Placer on what would become the town of Silverthorne. The border between the two towns is blurred, so many passersby refer to them interchangeably.

Sports and Recreation

Unburdened with the crush of downhill skiing, Dillon and Silverthorne can focus on other ways of enjoying the Rockies in the winter. Cross-country skiers can spread out on miles of trails at Silverthorne's **Nordic Center** (at the Raven Golf Course, 2929 Golden Eagle Rd., open Dec.–Mar.). Silverthorne has an **ice-skating park** (Hwy. 9 and Hamilton Creek Rd., open Dec.–Jan.).

As for outdoor recreation, Dillon's best draw is the picturesque **Lake Dillon,** on the edge of Dillon and Frisco. Its marina rents sailboats and other crafts, and even oceanfront snobs from San Francisco and Boston will find the 26 miles of shoreline a relaxing way to spend a non-snowy afternoon. For **anglers,** the lake is packed with brown and rainbow trout. (The marina also offers **sailing** lessons, but call in advance at 970/468-5100 or go to www.dillonmarina.com.)

THE SKI TOWNS

© STEVE KNOPPER

Lake Dillon has a marina for sailboats and is a prime spot for fishing.

Although the best golf courses in the area are in Keystone, a just-as-scenic and not-so-pricey option is the **Raven Golf Club at Three Peaks** (2929 Eagle Rd., Silverthorne, 970/262-3636, www.ravengolf.com), a tree-and-lake-filled 18-hole course designed by Alister Mackenzie.

Summit County is also **mountain-biking** heaven: Many of the region's 40 miles of trails begin in Dillon or Silverthorne and circle around Frisco, Breckenridge, and other scenic spots; contact the **Summit County Chamber of Commerce** (246 Rainbow Dr., 970/262-0817 or 800/530-3099, www.summitchamber.org).

Shopping

Many visit the Silverthorne-Dillon area purely for the mall-type shopping—common in big cities and suburbs, but an unexpected luxury in the middle of a Rocky Mountain blizzard. The **Silverthorne Factory Stores** (145-L Stephens Way, 970/468-9440 or 866/746-7686, www.silverthornefactorystores.com) has 50 outlets split up into three "villages" on opposite sides of I-70; Tommy Hilfiger and the Gap are to the north, while Nike and Levi's outlets are to the south.

Accommodations

Many of the hotels in Dillon and Silverthorne are of the Holiday Inn variety—and some tourists prefer these rates to the much higher ones in nearby Keystone and Breckenridge—but there are a few bed-and-breakfasts nestled between the hills and lakes. The **Mountain Vista Bed and Breakfast** (358 Lagoon Ln., Silverthorne, 970/468-7700 or 800/333-5165, $45–135) is a centrally located, no-frills hotel with three rooms.

Food

The **Dillon Dam Brewery** (100 Little Dam St., 970/262-7777 or 866/326-6196, www.dam-brewery.com, 11:30 A.M.–midnight daily) is a brewpub with pretty much everything you could want on the menu (try the San Luis pepper duck, $19) and several kinds of homemade beers. For steaks of all shapes and sizes (and, yes, chicken and fish), the **Historic Mint** (347 Blue River Pkwy., Silverthorne, 970/468-5247, www.mintsteakhouse.com, 4:30–10 P.M.) lets you cook slabs on 1,100-degree, flaming rocks. Located in a square, can't-miss, white building, the restaurant has been here since 1862 and has the antiques and decor to prove it.

FRISCO

Although it doesn't draw as many I-70 travelers as neighboring Dillon and Silverthorne, let alone booming resort areas like Vail or Breckenridge, Frisco is a woodsy mountain town with decent hotels and restaurants. First discovered by the Utes, Frisco was overrun with beaver-trapping mountain men in the early 1800s; the gold rush later that century brought mines, railroads, hotels, saloons, and people. The boom ended in 1918, and the Great Depression lowered the population to exactly 18 people. "Frisco persevered," its website reads, "and by 1946 the population had increased to 50." Thanks to ski traffic, it's up to 2,800 today.

History

The **Frisco Historic Park** (Frisco Historical Society, Main St. and 2nd St., 970/668-3428, 11 A.M.–4 P.M. Tues.–Sat. in winter, 11 A.M.–4 P.M. Tues.–Sun. during summer) is a 10-building district anchored on the old Frisco Schoolhouse (which today houses a museum). Some of the buildings, including the gazebo Ches' Place, are open for public tours. Just don't commit any crimes against history or you'll land in The Historic Jail.

Sports and Recreation

Despite the misleading name, **Frisco Bay** isn't a standalone body of water—it's part of the Dillon Reservoir—but it does have its own marina on the east end of Main Street. The town of Frisco has sailboat rental and storage information (970/668-5276, ext. 3042).

Accommodations

Don't be put off by the huge moose head hanging above the stone fireplace in the **Hotel Frisco** (308 Main St., 970/668-5009 or

800/262-1002, http://hotelfrisco.com, $125); it just contributes to the woodsy quality of this bed-and-breakfast on Main Street. Huge foothills are visible right outside the front door, and the hotel's Main Street location is at the center of Frisco's historic district. Also, the website claims the only complimentary high-speed Internet access in Summit County (although I suspect that's an exaggeration).

Food

Open since the 1940s, the **Blue Spruce Inn** (20 Main St., 970/668-5900, 4 P.M.–2 A.M. daily) specializes in large steaks (and the occasional fish or chicken dish). Its homey bar has chicken wings a-plenty, and somebody named "Doowop Denny" plays during happy hour every Sunday afternoon.

Silverheels at the Ore House (601 Main St., 970/668-0345, www.silverheelsrestaurant.com, 4–10 P.M. daily) is a great place to get $9 salmon crab cakes. Despite its nautical theme, including a Wednesday sushi night, Silverheels is best known for inexpensive and basic dishes, from pork chops to stuffed rellenos. Also on the affordable side are **Fiesta Jalisco** (450 Main St., 970/668-5043, 10:30 A.M.–10 P.M. daily), a homey Mexican joint, and the **Backcountry Brewery** (720 Main St., 970/668-2337, www.backcountrybrewery.com, 11 A.M.–10 P.M. daily), a nightlife party-time kind of place that serves burgers, wraps, pizza, and, of course, beer.

For breakfast, don't miss the **Log Cabin Café** (121 Main St., 970/668-3947, 6 A.M.–2 P.M. Mon.–Fri., 7 A.M.–2 P.M. Sat.–Sun.), in a 1908 log cabin, serving classic breakfasts like Summit County-renowned three-egg omelets. It's also open for lunch and dinner. Finally, the **Alpine Natural Foods Deli** (301 Main St., 970/668-5535, 8 A.M.–8 P.M. Mon.–Sat., 9 A.M.–7 P.M. Sun.) is a friendly little Whole Foods–style supermarket with a bonus: an amazing deli in the back with super-fresh meats, breads, vegetables, and cheeses. It's a great quick place to stop off I-70 between the ski resorts and Denver (look for the blue highway sign).

COPPER MOUNTAIN

Chuck Lewis built Copper Mountain on 280 acres in 1971, and thanks to three huge mountain peaks, thousands of miles of ski trails, and a word-of-mouth reputation that attracts non-snobby skiers, it has since expanded to 2,433 acres. Growth has slowed down in recent years, though, as owners realized Copper's deficiency in the ski-resort competition with towns like Vail and Winter Park was its lack of a surrounding city.

Intrawest Corp. has changed all that, funneling more than $500 million into the resort since 1997, and building the pedestrian village Burning Stones Plaza, with high-priced condominiums and restaurants. The new "village" area isn't really a city in the Vail sense, but it has nice touches like ice-skating rinks and sledding hills. Copper Mountain is simple to find, along I-70 about seven miles west of Frisco.

Sports and Recreation

Copper remains one of the best-laid-out ski areas in the state, with three peaks, all more than 12,000 feet high, and a total of 2,400 ski acres. The runs are conveniently removed from each other so experts on the bumpy eastern side and beginners in the Union Creek area don't collide at the bottom.

A full-day adult lesson at the **Ski & Snowboard School** (866/841-2481, www.coppercolorado.com) costs $89, and separate classes are available for snowboarders and kids. The resort also provides rental equipment (866/416-9876) that's fairly reasonable, especially compared to Aspen or Vail.

Aside from skiing, Copper's other two big outdoor sports are cycling and golf. **Mountain bikers** can rent steeds at **Gravitee** (The Village at Copper, 970/968-0171) and use the resort's American Eagle lift to access trails such as the moderate Shrine Pass (including a nine-mile drop) and the more advanced Searle Pass. Golfers can try the 18-hole, par-70, Pete and Perry Dye–designed **Copper Creek Golf Club** (Wheeler Pl., 970/968-3333), which starts underneath towering pine trees and meanders into an abandoned mining-town area.

Nightlife

Most Copper denizens of the night rotate between a few hot spots: **Endo's Adrenaline Café** (The Village at Copper, 970/968-3070), which has DJs and a dance floor and promises "body shots and dancing on the bar nightly!"; **JJ's Rocky Mountain Tavern** (102 Wheeler Circle, East Village, 970/968-3062), with live music Wednesday through Saturday and drink specials; the **Storm King Lounge** (The Village at Copper, 970/968-2318), specializing in martinis; and **Jack's Slopeside Grill** (The Village at Copper, 970/968-2318), also with live music on a regular basis.

Shopping

Hang around the shops at Copper Mountain for a while and you'll notice a theme—skiing. **The Mountain Adventure Center** (The Village at Copper, 970/968-2318, ext. 45621) rents and sells high-quality ski equipment and winter clothing. The **Surefoot Boot Fitting Co.** (The Village at Copper, 970/968-1728) expands its repertoire from ski boots to cowboy boots. **Giggleworks** (The Village at Copper, 970/968-2574) has hard candies and toys and is a great place to find gifts to bring home to the kids you left behind.

Accommodations

Copper Mountain Resort (209 Ten Mile Circle, 970/968-2882 or 800/458-8386, www.coppercolorado.com, $213–337) is pretty much the only game in town, lodging-wise, but it makes up for the lack of choice with high quality rooms and amenities—try the Cirque, a new building with three pools, French architecture, and washer-dryers in every room. The relatively new Village at Copper is the centerpiece area,

near most of the restaurants and shops, but the East Village is closer to the mountain. Resort guests can buy $10-a-day passes to the Copper Mountain Athletic Club, which has a huge indoor pool, spas, steam rooms, and saunas. Be sure to ask about lift-ticket packages.

Food

While booming music and a huge, grizzled ski-in/ski-out crowd won't make anyone mistake **Endo's Adrenaline Café** (The Village at Copper, 970/968-3070, 10:30 A.M.–8 P.M. Mon.–Fri., 10:30 A.M.–9 P.M. Sat.–Sun.) for a New York City chophouse, the sandwiches are gigantic and the food is better than you'd expect. Somewhat classier than Endo's is **Alexander's on the Creek Restaurant** (The Village at Copper, 970/968-2165, www.alexandersonthecreek.com, 5:30–10 P.M. daily), which serves Colorado specialties like elk tenderloin and seared duck breast.

JJ's Rocky Mountain Tavern (102 Wheeler Circle, East Village, 970/968-3062, www.jjstavern.com, 10:30 A.M.–10 P.M. daily) has the feel of a brewpub, but the food is far better than you'd expect—try the gourmet Thai pizza, with shrimp, snowpeas, and pineapple.

INFORMATION

The Silverthorne traveler's line is at 888/635-2515—or go to www.silverthorne.org. Dillon is 970/468-2403 or www.ci.dillon.co.us. Also try the **Town of Frisco** (1 Main St., 970/668-5276, www.townoffrisco.com). **Copper Mountain** isn't a town, but the ski resort has all the information you'll need (209 Ten Mile Circle, 866/841-2481 or 888/219-2441, www.coppercolorado.com).

Winter Park

Revered for its treacherous moguls and expert ski runs, the five-mountain Winter Park is a step up from spare, townie-oriented resorts such as Copper Mountain and Arapahoe Basin. It's also due for serious renovation; owner Intrawest Corp. announced $50 million plans to expand the beginner's area to 50 times its original size. But loyal Winter Park fans worry that 1) Intrawest will do away with Colorado's only Nordic ski jumps besides Steamboat Springs and 2) that somebody will smooth out the moguls. Bumper stickers throughout the Front Range read: "Save Our Bumps." (The bumps are probably safe, though.)

Of Winter Park's five mountains—Winter Park, Mary Jane, Vasquez Cirque, Vasquez Ridge, and Parsenn Bowl—Mary Jane is the most respected, especially for its long mogul runs and steep chutes. The City of Denver–owned resort is also the

exact midpoint between snooty Aspen and Vail and the lower-key Arapahoe Basin and Copper Mountain. Its mountainside resort village, which was being aggressively renovated in 2005, includes low-key but elegant condos, hotels, and restaurants (including the Zephyr Mountain Lodge and local favorite Deno's Mountain Bistro), and affordable shops.

Created in 1940, the ski resort overwhelms the nearby town of Winter Park, which encompasses 7.5 square miles and has 662 full-time residents. The town is well worth visiting, especially during spring and summer, when crowds keep away and hundreds of miles of trails are wide open for cyclists and hikers. The resort, which has 50 miles of its own trails, is on the eastern edge of town, and a shuttle runs between town and resort throughout ski season. Many opt to stay at nearby (and smaller) Fraser as well.

THE SKI TOWNS

© STEVE KNOPPER

Winter Park has tall, treacherous ski mountains and a restaurant-and-hotel district downtown.

SPORTS AND RECREATION
Downhill Skiing and Snowboarding

Winter Park itself is the most diverse of the resort's three ski areas, with runs for all skill levels and terrain parks and a half pipe for expert skiers and 'boarders. Its $2 million Groswold's Discovery Park, at 20 acres, is popular for beginners and riders trying to avoid extreme twists, trees, and bumps. Mary Jane ("No Pain, No Jane") is world-renowned for its seemingly endless mogul runs and steep chutes—almost all geared towards experts. Vasquez Ridge is the opposite extreme; it's a little out of the way, accessible via the Pioneer Express lift, but many leisurely skiers prefer long, easygoing runs like Stagecoach and Sundance.

Of the 2,762 total acres of skiing at Winter Park, Mary Jane (which opened in 1976) has the longest runs, including some at 4.5 miles. It's also the tallest mountain, at 12,060 feet. And at the very top of the mountain it has the Parsenn Bowl, which has incredible views and is especially popular after a blizzard.

Winter Park's ski school is open to adults and children, and gives private and group lessons. (A half-day adult session is $62.) Several shops at the ski area rent equipment for skiers and 'boarders: West Portal Rental (970/726-1662), at the base of the mountain, also offers free overnight storage, and The Jane Shop (970/726-1670) is based exclusively at the Mary Jane base area.

Finally, the base area is home to the **National Sports Center for the Disabled** (970/726-4112, www.nscd.org), which began in 1970 as a ski lesson for young Denver amputees. It has since grown to thousands of members of all ages, and offers a variety of ski and snowboard programs in the winter.

Information about Winter Park's ski area, along with lodging, food, recreation, and other activities, is on www.skiwinterpark.com. Or call 303/316-1564 or 970/726-1564.

Cross-Country Skiing

It's not uncommon, while driving toward Winter Park on I-70 or U.S. 40 during a heavy snowfall, to see backcountry skiers and snowboarders schlepping their equipment along the side of the road. Use these trails at your own risk, as many of them are unexplored and unmarked. For skiers preferring more organized cross-country trips, there's the **Devil's Thumb Ranch** (3530 County Rd. 83, Tabernash, 800/933-4339), 7 miles from Winter Park, with about 75 miles of groomed trails through the woods. (A day pass is $15.) The YMCA-run **Snow Mountain Ranch** (1101 County Rd. 53, Granby, 970/887-2152, www.ymcarockies.org) opens in October, closes in April, and offers about 62 miles of backcountry-skiing trails, including two that are open at night. Both areas provide equipment and are open to snowshoers.

Use extreme caution when tackling **Berthoud Pass** (U.S. 40, www.berthoudpass.com), once a classic Colorado ski area built in 1937. Its lifts have long been removed, the base lodge will soon be gone, and what's left are 65 trails spread

© STEVE KNOPPER

MARY JANE
extremely colorado

The Mary Jane ski resort, near Winter Park, goes by the unofficial slogan "No Pain, No Jane."

over 1,200 acres. "Please do not ski this area without the proper gear and knowledge," reads the website, listing zero percent of beginners' trails, 26 percent expert, and 74 percent advanced. South of Winter Park off the highway, Berthoud Pass is affiliated with the **Boulder Outdoor Center** (2707 Spruce St., 800/364-9376, www.boc123.com), which rents equipment and provides trail information.

Hiking and Biking

Winter Park Resort shifts from skiers to cyclists in the summer, offering the Zephyr Express chairlift to the mountain summit—and 50 trails of varying difficulty. (They're marked similarly to the ski trails, with green Fantasy Meadow and Tunnel Hill trails for beginners and black Mountain Goat and Icarus trails for more experienced riders.) The resort offers lessons, guided tours, and equipment rental; call 800/729-5813. Also, two summer events focus on mountain bikers: the **Mountain Bike Capital USA Weekend** (800/903-7275, www.mountainbikecapitalusa.com), in late June, with contests and tours, and the **American Red Cross Fat Tire Classic,** a two-day charity competition that's laid-back and open to all ages. A chairlift ride with a bike costs $16.

Beyond the resort are more than 600 miles of trails for cyclists and hikers, only they're spread out and hard to find if you don't prepare beforehand. An easily accessible trailhead for casual hikers and cyclists is at the intersection of U.S. 40 and Winter Park Drive; it leads to paths including Moffat Road, an old railroad route with some of the ties still embedded in the dirt road. **Winter Park Guide** (970/887-0776, www.winterparkguide.com) will send you a trail map for a fee.

Golf

The **Pole Creek Golf Club** (6827 County Rd. 5, 970/726-8847) has several high-elevation courses, including the tree-lined Meadow, Ranch, and Ridge, which at 9 holes each are available for 18-hole combinations. **Grand Elk** (1321 Ten Mile Dr., Granby, 877/389-9333)

was designed by ex-PGA hero Craig Stadler and is a more standard 18-hole course near the woods.

NIGHTLIFE

Winter Park has in the past had clubs devoted to live music and dance floors, but these days musical entertainment is more likely as an appetizer in bars and hotels, such as Deno's or the Ranch House Restaurant at Devil's Thumb. One nightlife staple remains: **The Pub** (78260 U.S. 40, 970/726-4929) has excellent happy hour specials and is known to draw the younger, post-ski crowd.

ACCOMMODATIONS
Under $100

The **Winter Park Mountain Lodge** (81699 U.S. 40, 970/726-4211 or 866/726-5151, www.winterparkhotel.com, $84–139) is the first hotel you see upon driving into Winter Park on I-70. It's large and boxy, with mountains all around, and the rooms are purely functional.

Although the **Sundowner Motel** (970/726-9451, www.thesundownermotel.com, $80–130) has more in common with a Best Western than a Hyatt Regency, it's at the center of town and is sort of a tradition among price-conscious local skiers.

Also centrally located, the **Gasthaus Eichler** (78786 U.S. 40, 970/726-5133, $79–150) has the look of a corny European hotel (complete with dark-brown trim and flags), but it's actually quite nice, with Jacuzzis in every room and excellent package deals including rooms and one of the three on-site restaurants. (Dezeley's may be the most elegant, but the Fondue Stube is the most fun.)

The **Rocky Mountain Inn** (15 County Road 72, 970/726-8256, 866/467-8351, www.therockymountaininn.com, $53–119) is a hotel and hostel with private rooms on one floor and dorm rooms on the other. It's not the most luxurious lodge in Colorado ski country, but it allows people to experience the Rockies on a tight budget.

About 30 miles from Winter Park, just off

I-70 on the way up U.S. 40, the **Peck House** (Empire, 303/569-9870, www.thepeckhouse.com, $60–105) claims to be the state's oldest hotel. Built in 1860, the building was once a destination spot for mining-boom tourists, including P. T. Barnum and Ulysses S. Grant, and its Old West charm remains. The rooms have a timeless quality, some all in red and others with quaint pattern wallpaper.

$100-150

The **Anna Leah B&B** (1001 County Rd. 8, Fraser, 970/726-4414, www.annaleah.com, $100–160) is Winter Park's best combination of price and luxury, with five beautiful little rooms, all with mountain views (the hotel is next to the Continental Divide) and some with whirlpool baths. It's a little removed from the main drag, six miles away in Fraser, and tends to fill up during ski season.

Vintage Hotel (100 Winter Park Dr., 970/726-8801 or 800/472-707, www.vintagehotel.com, $135–205) has the look and feel of a Radisson or a Marriott, but skiers swear by it for the heated outdoor pool, tavern, and ski shop on the premises. The rates are very reasonable, even during high season.

The **Inn at SilverCreek** (62927 U.S. 40, 800/926-4386, www.sclodging.com, $129) sacrifices location—it's about 20 miles from the ski resort—for amenities. Its 342 rooms are tall, with a modern feel, and it has a heated outdoor pool, racquetball and outdoor volleyball courts, a beauty shop, exercise facilities, and a complimentary shuttle to the resort.

$150-200

From the moment you walk into the lobby and spot the stone fireplace, huge picture windows overlooking the mountains, and log-built everything, the **Wild Horse Inn** (536 County Rd. 83, 970/726-0456, www.wildhorseinn.com, $160–245) screams, "Rocky Mountains!" It has three cabins, seven rooms, and tiny luxuries like in-house massages and chess sets near the fireplace.

Over $200

With the **Zephyr Mountain Lodge** (201 Zephyr Way, 970/726-8400 or 877/754-8400, www.zmlwp.com, $295–311), you're paying for location—it's the only Winter Park lodging at the base of the ski area. As a result, most of the rooms have mountain views, and the small outdoor hot-tub area draws a hard-partying ski-bum crowd.

FOOD

Winter Park's restaurants are hardly in the foie-gras-and-caviar class of its culinary neighbors, such as Vail, Aspen, and even Breckenridge, but they have a casual, townie feel, and many serve first-rate pub food.

Snacks, Cafés, and Breakfast

Although it doesn't look like much in its Park Plaza strip-mall location, the **Base Camp Bakery and Café** (78437 U.S. 40, 970/726-5530, 7 A.M.–4 P.M. Wed.–Mon.) is a quickie place that serves excellent sandwiches and baked goods. **Carver's Bakery and Café** (93 Cooper Creek Way, 970/726-8202, 7 A.M.–1 P.M. Sat.–Thurs.) is another great breakfast joint, especially notable for its blueberry pancakes.

Casual

Deno's Mountain Bistro (78911 U.S. 40, 970/726-5332, www.denosmountainbistro.com, 11:30 A.M.–11 P.M. daily) is a Winter Park institution with a colorful past—previous owners recall keeping a gun under the bar in case the tough, sleeping-in-the-trunks-of-their-cars, ski-bum crowd became too rowdy. Today, Deno Kutrumbos's 1900s-era restaurant is best-known for its huge wine list, although the joint, like much of the town, is in need of a renovation.

Upscale

The stone floors, walls, and fireplace at **The Lodge at Sunspot** (Zephyr Express Lift, 970/726-1444, hours vary per restaurant) hint at the relaxed mountaintop feel of this restaurant area at the top of the Zephyr Express Lift. The Provisioner is a buffet with sliced turkey and ham, and the Coffee Shop & Bakery serves drinks and scones, but the main draw is The Dining Room, with its multicourse menu ($59) of elk, beef, deer, or fish. The **Devil's Thumb Ranch House Restaurant and Saloon** (City Rd. 83, 970/726-5633 or 800/933-4339, www.devilsthumbranch.com, 5–9 P.M. Sun.–Mon. and Wed.–Sat., 11:30 A.M.–1:30 P.M. Sat.–Sun.) has a distinct Rocky Mountain flavor, like the 3,700-acre guest ranch it sits on. Antelope and steak are big here, but the menu goes for variety, with fish and turkey as well as an extensive children's menu. It's about a 15-minute drive west of Winter Park.

INFORMATION

Information about Winter Park's ski area, along with lodging, food, recreation, and other activities, is on www.skiwinterpark.com. Or call 303/316-1564 or 970/726-1564. The **Town of Georgetown** (404 6th St., 303/569-2555 or 888/569-1130, www.town.georgetown.co.us) is a good resource for local services, as is the **City of Idaho Springs** (303/567-4421, www.idahospringsco.com).

GETTING THERE AND AROUND

To get to Winter Park, take I-70 west from Denver—Idaho Springs is the first major mountain town before U.S. 40, which leads north to Winter Park. Just a few miles west of the U.S. 40 exit, also off I-70, is Georgetown. Both Idaho Springs and Georgetown are dinky towns, excellent for a quick stop.

The first town you reach after exiting the interstate is Empire, a tiny mountain town with a gas station. A word about Empire: Don't speed as you pass through town. (Trust me.) Upon arriving in Winter Park, the resort is on the immediate left, while the town is farther up U.S. 40 and lasts for about a mile.

Winter Park is also accessible via the **Ski Train** (303/296-4754), which advertises scenery "seen only by train passengers and goat herders." It starts at Denver's Union Station and goes 67 miles, past historic mining sights and 29 tunnels.

Once in Winter Park, there's a free town shuttle called "The Lift" (970/726-4163), which stops at most hotels and condos and, of course, the ski area.

GEORGETOWN

After climbing all over the Colorado Rockies in a vain search for gold, prospector George Griffith finally had his "eureka!" moment in 1859. For years after that, "George's Town" was miner territory, and travelers from all over the world dislodged more than $200 million in gold, silver, copper, and lead. Today, Georgetown is a tiny, quiet mountain town where sightings of bighorn sheep and reasonably priced condominiums provide the most excitement—but many of the abandoned mineshafts and brick buildings remain, so it's possible even now to roughly imagine what those gold-mining days must have looked like.

The town is far less exciting today, although it serves as a pretty introduction for first-time Rocky Mountain visitors headed up I-70 to Steamboat Springs, Vail, Aspen, and the rest. Check out the restaurants while you're here, and some of the reasonably priced hotels aren't bad, either.

Sights

In the late 1960s, it was a massive undertaking to carve the **Eisenhower Memorial Tunnel** (www.dot.state.co.us/Eisenhower/welcome.asp) just west of Georgetown along I-70; it's a hole 55 feet wide and 45 feet high through solid mountain rock underneath the Continental Divide. The project began in spring 1968, but it quickly bogged down due to weather conditions and worker inefficiency at 11,000-foot altitudes. The first tunnel was supposed to open three years later, but it was delayed until 1973; its twin didn't open until 1979. At some point during the $108 million project, one of its 1,140 workers declared: "We were going by the book, but the damned mountain couldn't read." Until the Eisenhower was completed, travelers had to navigate the far-more-treacherous Loveland Mountain Pass, which even today is a twisty, two-lane road that's frightening during the snow season. The square, two-lane tunnel, planned as early as 1937 despite geologists' concerns about cutting into the rock, has essentially given Denverites and other visitors easy access to the heart of the Colorado Rockies. Without it, the ski-resort towns are lost.

The town's biggest tourist attraction is the **Georgetown Loop Historic Railroad** (I-70, exit 226 near Silver Plume, 888/456-6777, www.georgetownlooprr.com, $17), a 1929 steam locomotive that pulls a narrow-gauge train on six miles of track from Georgetown and Silver Plume. It's not as scenic as, say, the Durango & Silverton Narrow Gauge Railroad in southwestern Colorado, but the tree-filled hills are pretty and the massive bridge makes for a dramatic trip.

British-born William A. Hamill, the town's best-known silver baron, lived in **Hamill House** (3rd St. and Argentine St., 303/569-2840, 10 A.M.–5 P.M. daily Memorial Day–Sept., noon–4 P.M. weekends Oct.–Dec.) after it was built in 1867 (it was expanded in 1979). Hamill's high-class tastes extended to the walnut woodwork, hand-painted wallpaper, and marble fireplaces, and **Historic Georgetown Inc.** (303/569-2840 or 303/569-2111, www.historicgeorgetown.org) has restored and preserved these original artifacts.

The **Hotel de Paris** (6th St. and Griffith St., 303/569-2311, 10 A.M.–5 P.M. daily Memorial Day–Labor Day, 10 A.M.–5 P.M. weekends Labor Day–Memorial Day) was one of the fanciest hotels and restaurants in Colorado during the miner era. French miner Louis Dupuy bought the building, originally a bakery, and expanded it into a hotel in 1970 after an accident cut his mining career short. Today it's a museum.

Accommodations
The **Georgetown Mountain Inn** (1100 Rose St., 800/884-3201, www.georgetownmountaininn.com, $69) has 33 rooms, each with distinctive style and decorations—the Colorado Room has pine walls and a steel drawing of the Georgetown Loop Railroad on the

bed headboard, and the Antique Room is filled with elegant but slightly spooky paintings and curvy lamps from the miners' days.

Silver Heels Guest Suites (506 6th St., 303/569-0941 or 888/510-7628, www.silverheelsguestsuites.com, $125–145) are two apartment rooms (the Merry Widow and Baby Doe suites) above the Buckskin Trading Co. in downtown Georgetown. Both rooms are hard to snag in the high season, so make reservations early.

Food
The **Red Ram Restaurant** (604 6th St., 303/569-2300, 11 A.M.–9 P.M. daily) is in the Fish Block Building, built in the late 1880s during the Clear Creek silver-mining boom. The burgers are huge, the fajitas are plentiful, the beer is available, and that's pretty much all you need to know about the menu.

The **New Prague Restaurant** (511 Rose St., 303/569-2861, 5–9 P.M. Wed.–Sun, winter, 11:30 A.M.–2 P.M., 5–9 P.M. daily, summer) is a European version of the Red Ram, with cabbage, sauerkraut, and Bohemian crepes standing in for the burgers and ribs.

IDAHO SPRINGS
The first mountain town you hit while driving I-70 west from Denver, Idaho Springs seems like a touristy miner district at first—but certain things about it are breathtaking and addictive. To some skiers and mountain-town explorers, for example, a trip to the high country isn't complete without a thick-crust pizza at the downtown BeauJo's. And up Highway 103, just beyond Echo Lake, is the Mt. Evans Scenic and Historic Byway, a 28-mile drive straight up a 14,265-foot peak with views of the Front Range.

First discovered by the Ute and Arapaho tribes—who considered the local hot springs sacred healing waters—sleepy Idaho Springs became a new kind of town when George Jackson discovered gold in the creeks. It's hard to believe, just by looking at the black-and-white Old West photos in the town's Heritage Museum and Visitors Center, that local miners once provided $2 million worth of gold ore to the U.S. Mint.

Sights

In addition to the **Heritage Museum and Visitors Center** (2060 Miner St., 303/567-4382, www.historicidahosprings.com, 9 A.M.–4 P.M. Mon.–Sat., 10 A.M.–4 P.M. Sun.), several Idaho Springs sights celebrate the town's legacy as a late-1800s miners' metropolis. The most popular is the **Phoenix Gold Mine** (Trail Creek Rd., 303/567-0422, www.phoenixmine.com, 10 A.M.–6 P.M. daily), which bills itself as the oldest running family-owned gold mine and allows visitors to keep any of the gold fragments they unearth in the old sand-and-bucket style.

The **Argo Gold Mill and Museum** (2350 Riverside Dr., 303/567-2421, 9 A.M.–6 P.M. daily mid-Apr.–mid-Oct.), too, relives the good old days—specifically 1913, when miners completed the 22,000-foot Argo Tunnel to transport gold from the mine to buyers in outlying areas. The mill sold more than 100 million dollars of ore at a time when prices were $18–35 per ounce; the tunnel closed in the 1940s, after an accident left four miners dead.

The **Charlie Tayler Water Wheel** (City Hall Park, on the south side of I-70), at the base of Bridal Veil Falls, was built in 1890 by a miner who attributed his longevity to never bathing or kissing women. The **Underhill Museum** (1416 Miner St., 303/567-4709, www.historicidahosprings.com, 11:30 A.M.–2:30 P.M. daily, free) is an information center and gift shop in a building once owned by Colorado surveyor and mining engineer James Underhill and his wife, Lucy. Finally, the entire **Miner Street** has the wooden-building feel of an Old West boom town, with the Victorian buildings to prove it.

Built into the side of a mountain between 1903 and 1911, **Indian Springs Resort** (302 Soda Creek Rd., 303/989-6666, www.indianspringsresort.com, 7:30 A.M.–10 P.M. daily) remains a great place to take a bath—or a hot tub in a "geo-thermal cave," or a steam, or a mud bath. Chief Idaho of the Utes was said to have called the baths "the healing waters of the great spirit."

St. Mary's Glacier looks like a glacier only after a particularly wet summer and cold winter. It's accessible to hikers—those who want to wander less than a mile to the base for a

© STEVE KNOPPER

Charlie Tayler built this water wheel in Idaho Springs.

THE SKI TOWNS

view of the lake, those who want to see the Continental Divide from a much higher, more bumpy summit, or those who want to climb the 13,294-foot James Peak in the distance. A sign on the 10-mile drive to the base reads "injuries and fatalities occur each year" and shouldn't be ignored: In the early '90s, a fisherman was trapped in bad weather and had to cut off his own leg.

Is St. Mary's really a glacier? "It is pretty small and if we lived in Alaska, we probably would not call it a glacier," David Bahr, a scientist with the University of Colorado's Institute of Arctic and Alpine Research, told *The Denver Post* in 1998. "But since we live in Colorado, we take what we can get." Note that the lakes are private, parking is available only in a small lot north of the glacier trail, and fishing is illegal. Property owners in the nearby towns of Alice, St. Mary's, and Winterland are extremely particular about this sort of thing and regularly push the Forest Service to discourage tourists.

"Oh My Gawd Road" is so-named not because of the New Yorkers who drive through here on the way to Vail or Aspen but because its 2,000-foot climb straight uphill is filled with treacherous curves. Just as it did in the 1870s, when it was built, the road takes fortune-seekers from Idaho Springs (exit 241 off I-70) to Central City and Black Hawk (which today are popular low-stakes gambling towns).

(Mount Evans Scenic and Historic Byway

This 28-mile byway climbs to a 14,265-foot summit with some of the greatest mountain views in all the Rockies—the entire Front Range and the Continental Divide are visible here. On the way up, you'll pass Echo Lake (10,600

feet), Lincoln Lake (11,700 feet), and Summit Lake (12,830 feet), along with trailheads leading to 100 miles of hiking and mountain-biking paths. It's also a great area for nature-lovers, as the Mount Goliath Natural Area, between Echo and Lincoln Lakes, has bristlecone pines, flag trees, and other plants characteristic of this region. Oh, and if you see a bighorn sheep (with curly horns) or a white mountain goat, for God's sake, don't chase it—they bite and ram, and rangers charge a fine for feeding them.

Although the byway closes from mid-September through Memorial Day, it's worth getting out during winter for a glimpse of snowdrifts as high as 75 feet on the road. To get to the byway, drive I-70 west from Denver, take exit 240 in Idaho Springs, and follow Highway 103 to Echo Lake. The **U.S. Forest Service Clear Creek Ranger's Station,** off Highway 103 in Idaho Springs, has more information about the mountain.

Food

There's Chicago pizza, New York pizza, Italian pizza, and, thanks to **(BeauJo's** (1517 Miner St., 303/567-4376, www.beaujos.com, 11 A.M.– 9 P.M. Sun.–Thurs., 11 A.M.–11 P.M. Fri.–Sat.), "mountain pizza." The crusts are thick (and best served with honey), the cheeses blend perfectly, and the napkin drawings on the walls are fun for kids. Even the football players from my high school were unable to pass "The Challenge," a 14-pound hamburger-and-sausage pie for $64. First-time Idaho Springs visitors are required to visit BeauJo's, but if you've eaten too many pizzas there in a short period of time, a nice alternative is the **Buffalo Restaurant & Bar** (1617 Miner St., 303/567-2729, www.buffalorestaurant.com, 11 A.M.–10 P.M.), which serves burgers, black bean chile, fajitas, and other things—all buffalo, of course.

Steamboat Springs

When Norwegian Carl Howelsen set up a wooden ski jump in Steamboat Springs in 1912, he had no idea he was inventing a multimillion-dollar Colorado tourism industry and indulging people's wintertime obsessions all over the world. It's not hard to see what drew him to the place. Located in the Yampa River Valley, the former ranching and farming (but not mining!) community is about an hour removed from I-70 and has some of the most awesome Rocky Mountain views in Summit County.

The town, at an elevation of almost 7,000 feet, is known as "Ski Town USA." Its sprawling Steamboat Mountain Village has a variety of restaurants (the crab-and-elk Café Diva and the coffee-and-bagel Mocha Molly's nicely capture both sides of the economic food spectrum), hotels (try the Home Ranch if you have the money, or the Best Western Ptarmigan Inn if you don't), and diversions such as Strawberry Park Natural Hot Springs, about seven miles outside of Steamboat.

Note that unlike most of the ski areas along I-70 and the Continental Divide, Steamboat is a trip unto itself. Even travelers to Aspen and Vail will have an easy time hitting other resorts or making diversionary side trips on the way up; in Steamboat, once you're there, you pretty much stay there. (Unless, of course, you have several weeks to kill on a vacation.) Note also that Steamboat, in the summer, has a surprising number of horseback-riding facilities.

HISTORY

The Utes were believed to have lived in this region as early as the 1300s, but it didn't officially become "Steamboat Springs" until 1865, when three French fur-trappers traveled down the Yampa River and heard what sounded like a paddle-wheel steamer. It turned out to be a gurgling mineral spring.

THE SKI TOWNS

© STEVE KNOPPER

Steamboat Springs is known as "Ski Town USA."

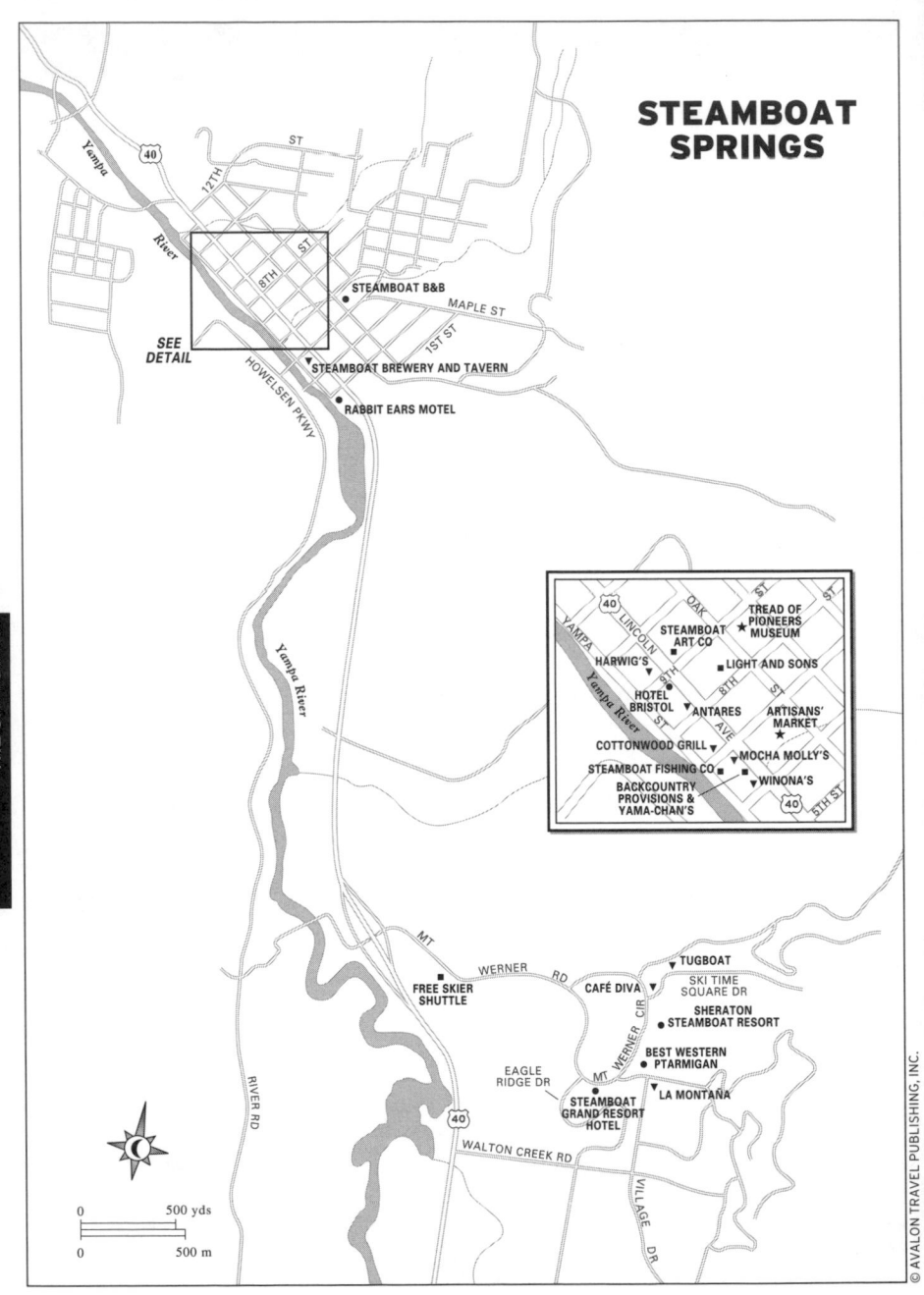

STEAMBOAT
SPRINGS

SEE
DETAIL

STEAMBOAT B&B

MAPLE ST

STEAMBOAT BREWERY AND TAVERN

RABBIT EARS MOTEL

Yampa River

TREAD OF
PIONEERS
MUSEUM

STEAMBOAT
ART CO

LIGHT AND SONS

HARWIG'S

HOTEL
BRISTOL

ANTARES

ARTISANS'
MARKET

COTTONWOOD GRILL

STEAMBOAT FISHING CO

MOCHA MOLLY'S

WINONA'S

BACKCOUNTRY
PROVISIONS &
YAMA-CHAN'S

TUGBOAT

FREE SKIER
SHUTTLE

CAFÉ DIVA

SKI TIME
SQUARE DR

SHERATON
STEAMBOAT RESORT

BEST WESTERN
PTARMIGAN

EAGLE
RIDGE DR

LA MONTAÑA

STEAMBOAT
GRAND RESORT
HOTEL

WALTON CREEK RD

RIVER RD

0   500 yds

0   500 m

© AVALON TRAVEL PUBLISHING, INC.

THE SKI TOWNS

Nine years later, hunter James Harvey Crawford discovered the Yampa Valley region, staked a claim, and brought his family to Steamboat. The town grew slowly after that—a newspaper here, a general store and hotel there—and mail carriers figured out how to traverse the difficult snowy cliffs on skis and snowshoes. The growth accelerated irreversibly in 1913, when Norwegian visitor Howelsen arrived in 1912 and started "ski-jumping" off a wooden platform—and teaching local kids how to do the same.

Borrowing from Howelsen, local ranch-family heir Jim Temple spearheaded the Steamboat Ski Area, which opened in 1961 with a creaky lift known as the Cub Claw. By the late 1960s, Steamboat was equipped with five new chairlifts, a restaurant on top of Thunderhead Peak, ski-patrol buildings, and other facilities—which locals called the "million-dollar building boom." The constant is champagne powder, a naturally occurring light-and-dry snow that's so distinctive the resort actually copyrighted the name.

SIGHTS

Although it's not as comprehensive as Vail's Colorado Ski Museum, the **Tread of Pioneers Museum** (800 8th St., 970/879-2214, 11 A.M.–5 P.M. Tues.–Sat., $5 for out-of-country residents) has a history-of-skiing exhibit to go with its displays on Routt County pioneer life, Native American artifacts, and a large vintage firearms collection. It's in a 1908 Queen Anne–style Victorian home with authentic early-1900s furniture and decor.

The **Steamboat Springs Health & Recreation Center** (Lincoln Ave. and 3rd St., 970/879-1828, 5:30 A.M.–10 P.M. Mon.–Fri., 7 A.M.–9 P.M. Sat., 8 A.M.–9 P.M. Sun.) is the granddaddy of Rocky Mountain hot springs, with an 82-degree, Olympic-sized lap pool, a 350-foot water slide, and three hot pools registering from 98 to 103 degrees. The downtown complex offers fitness equipment (including newfangled weight-lifting machines and treadmills), yoga and kickboxing classes, and more than 100 hot springs.

Strawberry Park Natural Hot Springs

(County Rd. 36, seven miles west of Steamboat, 970/879-0342, 10 A.M.–10:30 P.M. Sun.–Thurs., 10 A.M.–midnight Fri.–Sat.) isn't quite as popular as the Health & Recreation Center, and it isn't quite as well maintained, but discreet chicanery is encouraged. Guests can bring their own beverages—3.2 percent alcohol or less is allowed—and kids under 18 aren't allowed after 6 P.M. The thermal pools reach as high as 105 degrees, and guests are guaranteed soaks of at least an hour. In the winter, a separate company, **Sweet Pea Tours** (970/879-5820, www.strawberryhotsprings.com/sweetpeasummer.html, $25), carts hot-springs visitors along snowy roads (many of which require chains for cars during the winter).

SPORTS AND RECREATION
Downhill Skiing and Snowboarding

The **Steamboat Ski Resort** (2305 Mount Werner Circle, 970/879-6111, www.steamboat.com) is a range of six different mountains, with altitudes of more than 10,000 feet at the summits,

Norwegian ski pioneer Carl Howelsen created one of the world's first ski jumps at this hill.

© STEVE KNOPPER

and 142 trails spread over 65 miles—including Mavericks, a 650-foot-long, 50-foot-wide pipe with 15-foot walls. The resort is known for its snowfall, which regulars call "champagne powder," and the tree-filled, bumpy terrains are diverse and fun. If Winter Park does away with its ski jumps, as some fear, the 15 trails of Steamboat's **Howelsen Ski Area** (845 Howelsen Pkwy., 970/879-4300) will be the only run for aspiring jumpers in Colorado.

In addition to the champagne powder—which can get a little *too* deep after a blizzard for some skiers' tastes—Steamboat's biggest draws are tree-lined terrain, wide runs for cruisers, fast lifts, and near-oppressive sunshine. One of the best spots for tree skiing is Twistercane, a short but rough stretch of aspens between the black-diamond Twister and Hurricane runs. Although the runs are fast and smooth, they're not long, so take full advantage of quads like the Storm Peak and Sundown. For snowboarders, the recently pumped-up Mavericks Superpipe is, at 650 feet, the longest in North America.

Warning to the least experienced: Of the 142 ski trails on 2,939 acres, just 13 percent are for beginners.

Olympic skier Billy Kidd directs the **Steamboat Springs Ski & Snowboard School** (800/299-5017), which offers a range of group and private lessons for adults, kids, and skiers with special needs. Kidd's **Performance Center** takes a high-tech, high-attention approach to expert lessons—instructors use handheld cameras to study skiers' strengths and weaknesses, and the ratio of students to teachers is just six to one. Although many sports-equipment stores rent skis and snowboards in town, **Steamboat Central Reservations** (970/879-0740 or 877/237-2628) is one-stop shopping for all ages and skill levels.

Cross-Country Skiing

The **Steamboat Ski Touring Center** (Clubhouse Dr., 970/879-8180, www.nordicski.net) is a family-owned backcountry-skiing school and shop with access to several excellent trails around Steamboat.

Elkhorn Outfitters (37399 N. Hwy. 13, 970/824-7392) makes 15 miles of groomed trails (for snowshoeing and inner-tubing as well) available to a total of eight skiers per day, and serves lunch and rents equipment. One disadvantage: It's 15 miles north of Craig, about 40 minutes west of Steamboat, so a long shuttle ride is part of the deal. Also renting equipment is **Ski Haus** (U.S. 40 and Pine Grove Rd., 970/879-0385). For more information on backcountry and Nordic skiing, contact Steamboat Central Reservations at 877/237-2628.

Hiking and Biking

The **Medicine Bow/Routt National Forest** area is 2.2 million acres of parks and forest land extending from Steamboat Springs through southern Wyoming. Among the many official and unofficial routes for hikers and mountain bikers is the **Mountain View Trail,** a moderate 6-mile trek connecting Mount Werner to Long Lake and giving access to another 25 miles of summer hikes. The easiest way to get there is by riding the resort's Silver Bullet Gondola to Thunderhead and following trailhead signs to the top.

Also close by are the massive **Fish Creek Falls,** the **Mt. Zirkel Wilderness Area,** and **Steamboat** and **Pearl** lakes.

During summer, the resort's 50 miles of ski trails—particularly on the Thunderhead part of the mountain—transform into 50 miles of mountain-biking trails. Lift tickets are available for the gondola for $8, and the resort's main ticket office (877/237-2628) rents bikes and gives cycling lessons and clinics.

Golf

The nine-hole **Steamboat Golf Club** (West U.S. 40, 970/879-4295) has water and pond hazards, and a stream actually cuts through one of the fairways. Designed by Robert Trent Jones Jr., the 18-hole course at the **Sheraton Steamboat Golf Club** (2200 Village Inn Court, 970/879-1391, www.sheratonsteamboatgolf.com) has views of the Flat Top Mountains in the distance and occasionally attracts uninvited bears and other wildlife.

Horseback Riding

Tons of ranches are in the Steamboat Springs area, which means tons of horseback riding—the 1,000-acre **Del's Triangle 3 Ranch** (55675 Routt County Rd. 62, Clark, 970/879-3495, www.steamboathorses.com) gives rides to all ages (well, 6 years and older) during summer and winter. **Saddleback Ranch** (37350 Routt County Rd. 179, 970/879-3711) offers two rides a day along with calf-roping demonstrations.

NIGHTLIFE

Steamboat's primary place to catch live bands is **The Tugboat Grill and Pub** (1860 Mt. Werner Rd., 970/879-7070), a local fixture with great happy-hour specials and a relaxed après-ski vibe that attracts a younger crowd.

SHOPPING

Steamboat's shopping areas are confined to the ski-resort base village (which has Ski Time Square, Gondola Square, and Torian Plum Plaza), **Old Town Square** (7th St. and Lincoln Ave.), and the five-block downtown. Of these, the last area has the most unique and affordable shops, including the **Steamboat Art Company** (903 Lincoln Ave., 800/553-7853, www.steamboat-art.com), with $475 photos of old-time skiers and pewter martini glasses; **F.M. Light & Sons** (830 Lincoln Ave., 970/879-1822), a clothing store that opened in this very spot in 1905; and **Into the West** (807 Lincoln Ave., 970/879-8377), where the proprietor is U.S.-ski-team-member-turned-furniture-maker Jace Romick.

ACCOMMODATIONS
Under $100

The motel with the strange pink bunny on the sign, the **Rabbit Ears Motel** (201 Lincoln Ave., 970/879-1150 or 800/828-7702, www.rabbitearsmotel.com, $79–119) has basic and luxury rooms, some overlooking the Yampa Valley. Opened in 1952, the Rabbit Ears isn't exactly in its renaissance phase, but it's centrally located (although it's three miles from the base area, the free city bus stops nearby), fun, and affordable.

$100-150

Hotel Bristol (917 Lincoln Ave., 970/879-3083 or 800/851-0872, www.steamboathotelbristol.com, $129–189) is a pretty little lodge with 24 rooms, including colorful wool blankets and sharp Old West paintings and photos. Then-police chief Everett Bristol built the place in 1948; it was a bed-and-breakfast for years.

The **Steamboat B&B** (442 Pine St., 970/879-5724 or 877/335-4321, www.steamboatb-b.com, $129–159) is affordable, within walking distance of the ski area. The rooms are white and almost glowing, giving the property a modern feel, although it's in a Victorian that was once a church. Each of the rooms overlooks some major piece of scenery, including Howelsen Hill, Emerald Mountain, and Sleeping Giant Mountain.

$150-200

The Steamboat Grand Resort Hotel and Conference Center (2300 Mt. Werner Circle, 970/871-5500 or 888/613-7349, www.steamboatgrand.com, $194–233) is a massive mountainside hotel with 327 rooms at the base of the ski mountain. With a pool, exercise center, and 17,000 feet of meeting space, it's a favorite of business visitors.

Over $200

Relais & Chateaux's **Home Ranch** (54880 Routt County Rd. 129, Clark, 970/879-1780, www.homeranch.com, $400–500) isn't for spontaneous locals or day skiers—the Old West-style complex requires a two-night minimum stay, and it's a few miles north of Steamboat. But it's amazingly charming and comfortable, with beds and tables made out of logs, a fully stocked refrigerator (and cookie jar) in the lobby, and, of course, horseback riding almost any time of day. The restaurant is one of the area's best.

The **Sheraton Steamboat Resort & Conference Center** (2200 Village Inn Court, 970/879-2220, $239–279) looks great in a photo, just a few hundred yards from Steamboat's base ski area. The town's only ski-in/ski-out lodging per se, the resort complex includes four restaurants, including a Starbucks, the fancy Sol Day Spa, the Morningside Tower (with 23 luxury condos), and a seven-hole golf course.

Don't let the hotel-chain name on the sign keep you away: The **Best Western Ptarmigan Inn** (2304 Apres Ski Way, 970/879-1730 or 800/538-7519, $208–228) has the best spot in town, at the base of the Mount Werner/Steamboat ski area. It's all about the skiing, with complimentary valet ski storage, an onsite ski shop, a daily après-ski happy hour, and slopeside dining at the Snowbird Restaurant and Lodge.

FOOD
Snacks, Cafés, and Breakfast
Mocha Molly's (635 Lincoln Ave., 970/879-0587, 6 A.M.–7 P.M. Mon.–Thurs., 6 A.M.–9 P.M. Fri.–Sun.) is the kind of quick-breakfast-burrito joint every ski resort needs. It has comfortable couches, custom coffee roasts (in addition to many other international flavors, all on the honor system, just drop a dollar into the jar), and Internet access. In the same building, Old Town Square, is **Backcountry Provisions** (635 Lincoln Ave., 970/879-3617, 7 A.M.–5 P.M. daily), a crowded deli with a huge sandwich selection.

Winona's (617 Lincoln Ave., 970/879-2483, 7–11 A.M., 11 A.M.–3 P.M. Mon.–Sat., 7 A.M.–1 P.M.Sun.) is a great drop-in breakfast-and-sandwich joint with a long menu, from tofu scrambles ($7) to banana almond pancakes ($5). It reeks of healthfulness.

Casual
La Montana (2500 Village Dr., 970/879-5800, www.la-montana.com, 5–9:30 P.M. daily) has 25 kinds of tequila and almost as many flavors of margarita, but its major selling point is basic Tex-Mex food. Some of the entrées can be a little pricey (like the scallops Veracruz, for $27), but the basic enchiladas are $13, the fish tacos are $16, and the kids' menu is the deal you'd expect. Tip: Fill up on the guacamole sauce. **Yama-Chans** (635 Lincoln Ave., 970/879-8862, 5:30–10 P.M. Sat.–Mon.,

11:30 A.M.–2 P.M. Tues.–Fri., 5:30–10 P.M. Sat.), Steamboat's first-ever sushi restaurant, is extremely popular, so try to avoid showing up exactly at 6 P.M.

Upscale
Café Diva (1855 Ski Time Square, 970/871-0508, www.cafediva.com, 5:30–10 P.M. daily) opened in 1998 as a white-tablecloth kind of place that serves foie gras and chocolate fondue along with regional standards like elk tenderloin and duck confit. Its location, not far from the ski lifts, gives it an automatic crowd.

Housed in the 1880s-era Harwig Building—which includes a built-in wine cellar with 10,000 bottles—**(L'Apogee** (911 Lincoln Ave., 970/879-1919, www.lapogee.com, 5 P.M.–2 A.M.) offers a dish for every conceivable eating preference. If you don't eat the veal oscar ($29), there's always the New Orleans jambalaya ($19) or the pistachio chicken ($24). **Harwig's Grill** (970/879-1980) is in the same building—the former Harwig's Saddlery and Western Wear—and it's known for wines by the glass, French and Asian dishes, and desserts.

"Roast elephant garlic" is a telling menu item at **Antares** (57 8th St., 970/879-9939, 5:30 P.M.–close daily), a beautifully flavored restaurant that reflects chef Paul LeBrun's Asian, French, and Indian influences. The building, a Victorian in the downtown First National Bank, has sturdy wood floors and stone fireplaces. The bar has 27 kinds of vodka, and the martinis are especially popular.

Chefs Michael Fragola and Peter Lautner bring their elegant Asian-food expertise to **Cottonwood Grill** (701 Yampa St., 970/879-2229, www.cottonwoodgrill.com, 5:30–9:30 or 10 P.M. daily, depending on time of year), which serves a variety of Thai (pork tenderloin), Chinese (Peking duck), Cambodian (hot pot), and other dishes (Yampa Valley lamb pot stickers). Don't forget the sake.

INFORMATION
The main Steamboat number is 970/879-6111, but www.steamboat.com will tell you

just about all you need to know. For updated snow reports, call 970/879-7300, and for lodging reservations, try 877/237-2628.

GETTING THERE AND AROUND

Steamboat is accessible via I-70, driving west from Denver, like most of the other ski resorts, but it's surprisingly far away—three or four hours depending on weather. In snowy conditions, the trip up U.S. 40 from Winter Park can be treacherous, so handle the hairpin curves and steep declines with care. From I-70, take exit 232 to U.S. 40, and follow it almost 100 miles beyond Empire and Winter Park.

Some of the hotels provide their own town shuttles, but the best local-transportation deal is the SST (970/879-3717), a free shuttle that runs 7 A.M.–1:45 A.M. daily between the resort, condos, grocery stores, restaurants, and hotels.

THE SKI TOWNS

GRAND JUNCTION AND THE DINOSAURS

If northwest Colorado has an unofficial capital city, it's Grand Junction, which appears in the middle of nowhere on the map—Telluride is several hundred miles south, Denver is a four-hour drive east, and the closest ski resorts are the dinky ones in touristy Glenwood Springs and Grand Mesa. Although it's flat and quiet, with far more churches than nightclubs, Grand Junction is part of the Grand Valley, a rich outdoor area of massive mesas, gnarled sandstone formations, tall, natural arches, dry canyons, and scenic lakes.

The Grand Valley is at the Colorado and Gunnison Rivers, near the Little Bookcliffs (flat, steep mountains that look a little like the Grand Canyon and extend for miles), the 10,000-foot-tall Grand Mesa and its surrounding national forest, and the 23,000-acre Colorado National Monument. Few visitors come to this region for the nightlife—or even the hotels, which skew plain and modest—but the cycling, cross-country skiing, and accompanying mountaineering outfits are world-class. Try the REI outlet in Grand Junction or Summit County Mountaineering in downtown Glenwood Springs.

Because of its mild weather and rich soil, the Grand Valley is a major agricultural outpost, with farms, ranches, and orchards everywhere. Grapes became a huge part of the harvest in the late 1800s; the state's first winery, Ivancie, opened in 1968; and quiet Palisade has grown into the state's primary vineyard region.

There's one other unexpected attraction in northwest Colorado: dinosaurs. They roamed this part of the world millions of years ago,

© STEVE KNOPPER

HIGHLIGHTS

◖ Colorado Canyons National Conservation Area: With the Black Ridge Canyons Wilderness on the inside, this outdoor paradise west of Grand Junction was created in 2000 and encompasses red-rock cliffs, waterfalls, and natural arches and spires. Great for hiking and biking. (page 181).

◖ Kokopelli's Trail: Bring a bike and three or four days' worth of free time—and get in shape. Beginning west of Grand Junction, the 135-mile trail, very rocky in parts, climbs from 4,400 to 8,500 feet of elevation, rubbing against the Colorado River, en route to Moab, Utah (page 181).

◖ Colorado National Monument: A sort of mini-Grand Canyon, with twisted, reddish rocks that arch over roads and recall Morrison's Red Rocks Park and Colorado Springs' Garden of the Gods, Colorado National Monument is filled with trails, bike paths, and huge, flat mesas (page 184).

◖ Dinosaur Journey: The best part of this Fruita museum—not to be confused with Dinosaur National Monument to the north—is the robotic arms that let you experience shambling dinosaur movements directly (page 184).

◖ Little Bookcliffs Wild Horse Range: More than 30,000 acres of breathtaking canyons and plateaus aren't enough—about 115 wild horses, from pintos to roans, browns to palominos, run free in this sprawling range thanks to a long-ago act of Congress (page 187).

◖ Grand Mesa National Forest: With the 11,000-foot Leon Peak, the beautifully blue Butts Lake, and several excellent hiking and biking trails, the Grand Mesa is one of the state's most dramatic outdoor enclaves (page 193).

◖ Dinosaur Quarry: The scenery and hiking are amazing on the Colorado side of the two-state Dinosaur National Monument park, but the Utah side has this quarry, where 1,500 stegosaurus, tyrannosaurus rex, and other fossils are embedded in a wall and visitors can hunt for thousands more (page 197).

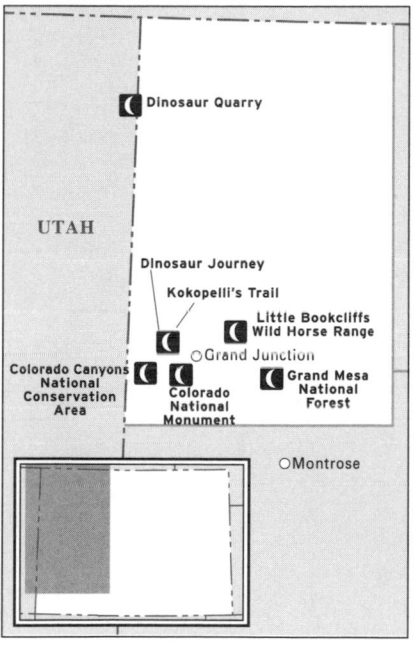

LOOK FOR ◖ TO FIND RECOMMENDED SIGHTS, ACTIVITIES, DINING, AND LODGING.

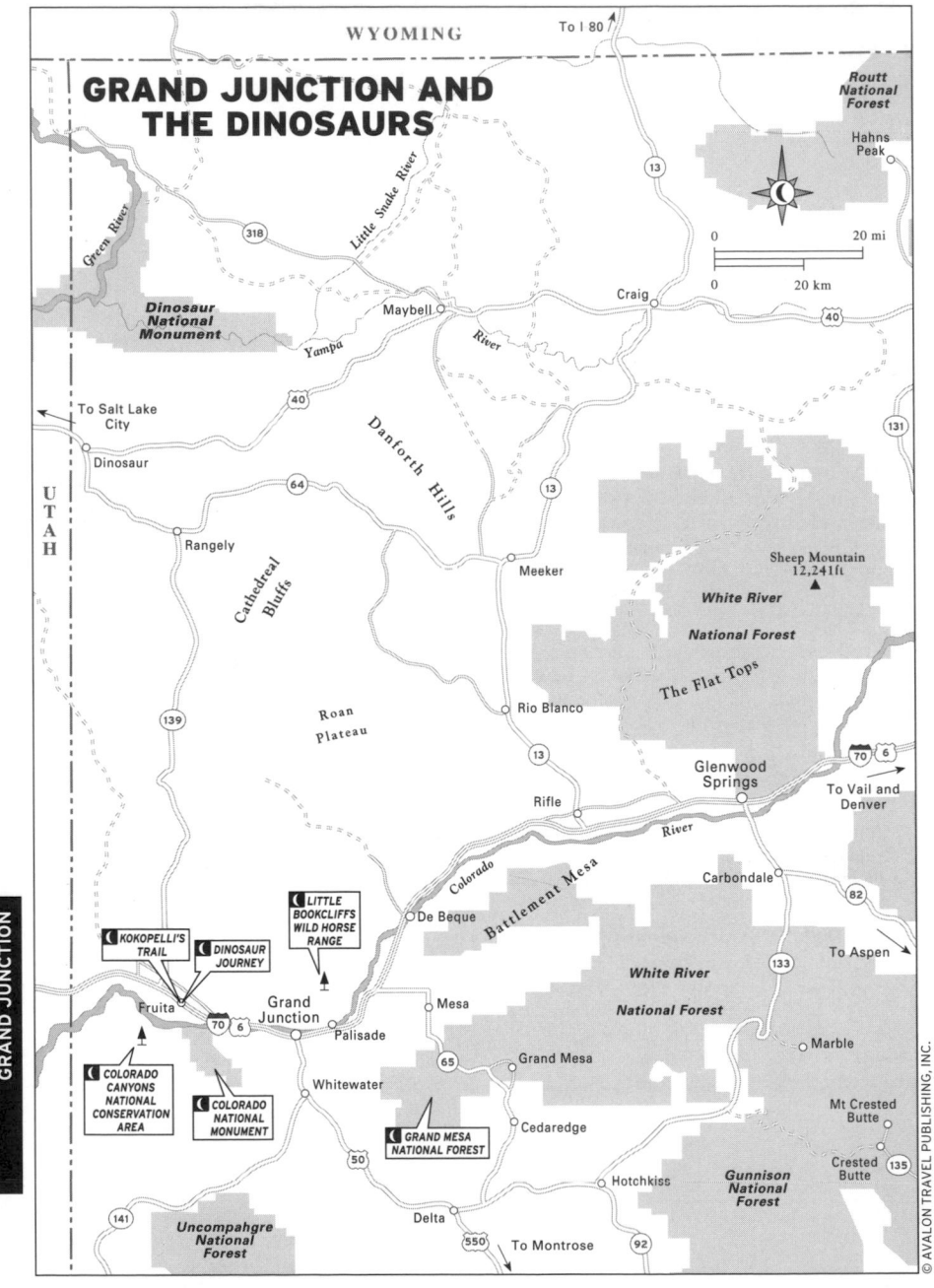

GRAND JUNCTION AND THE DINOSAURS

WYOMING

To I 80

Routt National Forest

Hahns Peak

Green River

318

Little Snake River

13

0   20 mi

0   20 km

Dinosaur National Monument

Maybell

Yampa River

Craig

40

To Salt Lake City

Danforth Hills

131

Dinosaur

64

13

U T A H

Rangely

Cathedral Bluffs

Meeker

Sheep Mountain 12,241ft

White River

National Forest

The Flat Tops

Roan Plateau

Rio Blanco

139

13

Glenwood Springs

70 6

Rifle

To Vail and Denver

River

Colorado River

Battlement Mesa

Carbondale

82

LITTLE BOOKCLIFFS WILD HORSE RANGE

De Beque

To Aspen

KOKOPELLI'S TRAIL

DINOSAUR JOURNEY

White River

National Forest

133

Grand Junction

Mesa

Fruita

70 6

Palisade

Marble

COLORADO CANYONS NATIONAL CONSERVATION AREA

COLORADO NATIONAL MONUMENT

Whitewater

65

Grand Mesa

Mt Crested Butte

GRAND MESA NATIONAL FOREST

Cedaredge

Crested Butte

135

50

Hotchkiss

Gunnison National Forest

141

Uncompahgre National Forest

Delta

550

To Montrose

92

GRAND JUNCTION

© AVALON TRAVEL PUBLISHING, INC.

leaving behind fossils and bones. Dinosaur National Monument is a scenic hiking area at the northwest tip of the state; on the Utah side, it turns into a museum and outdoor playground for amateur paleontologists and kids obsessed with stegosauri and pterodactyls.

PLANNING YOUR TIME

The stretch of I-70 from Denver to Grand Junction is about four hours long, and Glenwood Springs, Rifle, and Palisade are pleasant stopovers along the way. (Glenwood Springs is also a sort of gateway to Aspen, and many skiers who don't want to pay Aspen's high hotel and restaurant rates book lodging at the Hotel Colorado or the Hotel Denver.) Cedaredge,

Grand Mesa, and Delta bunch up along Highway 65, south of Palisade.

Some of the many entrances to Colorado National Monument are within 10 miles of Grand Junction's western edge, and the town of Dinosaur, adjacent to Dinosaur National Monument, is about 80 miles north on the up-and-down Highway 139. The trip from Dinosaur to Steamboat Springs, including Craig at just about the midpoint, is three hours straight uphill, and you'll notice the altitude shift. My wife and I took a two-day, 13-hour drive from Denver to Grand Junction to Dinosaur to Steamboat, staying at the Doubletree Grand Junction, and had a nice time. Some of the long stretches of Highway 139 and U.S. 40 are a little boring, though.

Glenwood Springs

The last ski town for travelers heading west on I-70 from Denver, Glenwood Springs is perfectly situated between Aspen to the south, Vail to the east, and Grand Junction to the west. It has a tiny ski resort, but the town is far more famous for its namesake springs—two natural hot pools, one of which is 405 by 100 feet, both in a giant tourist-trap area near the regal but worn Colorado Hotel.

Due to its proximity to high-end, non-kitschy Aspen, you'd think Glenwood Springs would be a ritzy kind of mountain town, the way it was from the late 1800s to the mid-20th century, when Teddy Roosevelt and Al Capone used to stay downtown. It's actually modest and tourist-oriented, with the large hot-springs pool on one side of town and a strip of low-key shops and cafés on the other. Both historic hotels, the Colorado and the Denver, show their age, and travelers wishing for more luxury should proceed to Aspen.

HISTORY

The Utes considered the springs sacred for centuries, and, after fiercely protecting their land from other tribes, they happened upon ailing explorer Richard Sopsis, a U.S. military cap-

tain, and took him to the springs for healing in the 1860s. A decade later, silver miners from nearby Leadville flooded the town, displaced the Utes, and colonized it for themselves. The springs' reputation grew quickly in American culture as well: Annie Oakley and Doc Holliday visited here in the 1880s, but Holliday, suffering from tuberculosis, died about six months after he showed up.

By 1893, thanks to the Denver and Rio Grande Railroad and the luxurious, swimming-pool-equipped Hotel Colorado, Glenwood Springs became a resort town for travelers en route to California. Some of these big-money visitors stayed permanently, and for years Glenwood Springs' polo teams won national titles.

Just to show how things have changed over 150 years, the hot springs are now a popular spa; formerly the Yampah ("big medicine" in Ute) Valley Springs, they're known today as the Hot Springs Pool.

SIGHTS

Hot Springs Pool (401 N. River St., 970/945-6571, 800-6571, or 800/537-7946, www.hotspringspool.com, 7:30 A.M.–10 P.M. daily, $12)

GRAND JUNCTION

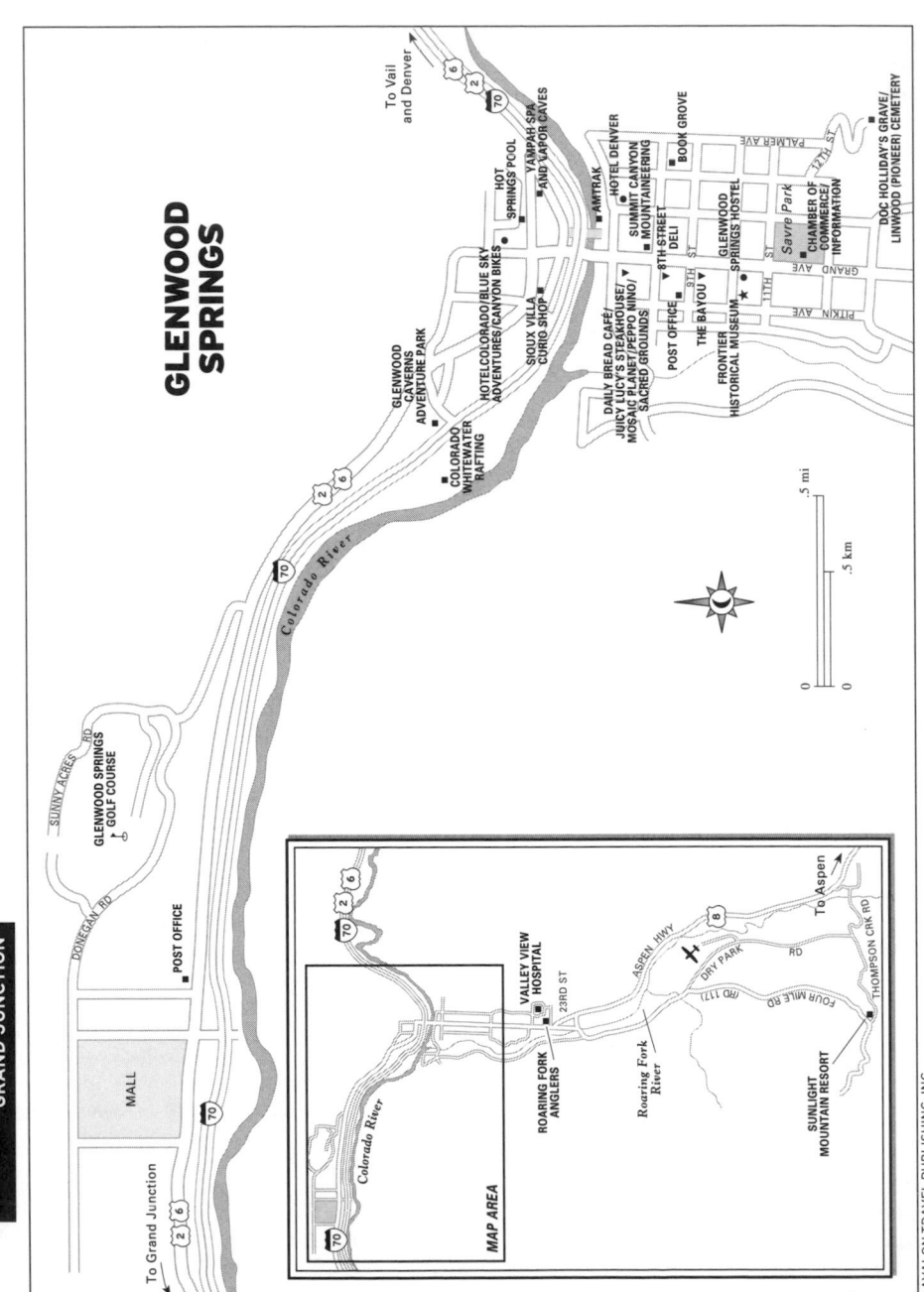

GLENWOOD SPRINGS

To Vail and Denver

VAMPAH SPA AND VAPOR CAVES

HOT SPRINGS POOL

AMTRAK

HOTEL DENVER

SUMMIT CANYON MOUNTAINEERING

BOOK GROVE

PALMER AVE

8TH STREET DELI

GLENWOOD SPRINGS HOSTEL

CHAMBER OF COMMERCE/ INFORMATION

Sayre Park

DOC HOLLIDAY'S GRAVE/ LINWOOD (PIONEER) CEMETERY

9TH ST

GRAND AVE

PITKIN AVE

GLENWOOD CAVERNS ADVENTURE PARK

HOTELCOLORADO/BLUE SKY ADVENTURES/CANYON BIKES

SIOUX VILLA CURIO SHOP

DAILY BREAD CAFÉ/ JUICY LUCY'S STEAKHOUSE/ MOSAIC PLANET/PEPPO NINO/ SACRED GROUNDS

POST OFFICE

THE BAYOU

FRONTIER HISTORICAL MUSEUM

COLORADO WHITEWATER RAFTING

Colorado River

.5 mi

.5 km

SUNNY ACRES RD

GLENWOOD SPRINGS GOLF COURSE

DONEGAN RD

POST OFFICE

MALL

To Grand Junction

VALLEY VIEW HOSPITAL

ROARING FORK ANGLERS

23RD ST

ASPEN HWY

DRY PARK

To Aspen

THOMPSON CRK RD

RD

FOUR MILE RD (RD 117)

Roaring Fork River

SUNLIGHT MOUNTAIN RESORT

Colorado River

MAP AREA

© STEVE KNOPPER

Glenwood Springs' biggest tourist attraction is the Hot Springs Pool.

is built around two natural pools, heated constantly to almost 100 degrees Fahrenheit. The large one is longer than a football field, while the small one is just 100 feet. The pools aren't quite as sacred as they were in the days of the Utes, or when luminaries like Doc Holliday and Annie Oakley showed up in Glenwood Springs to experience their healing qualities. Given the 107-room lodge on the premises, plus a spa, shops, and miniature golf, the pool is among the biggest tourist attractions in western Colorado. Go during the off-season to avoid crowds. To check out the pool before indulging, climb the large footbridge overhead and spy on all the swimmers.

The **Yampah Spa & Salon** (709 E. 6th St., 970/945-0667, www.yampahspa.com, 9 A.M.–9 P.M. daily, $12), subtitled "The Hot Springs Vapor Caves," turns yet another Ute tradition into modern tourism. The three underground caves get hotter and hotter—at a top temperature of 125 degrees Fahrenheit—until you feel like the stresses have seeped out of your pores. Of course, the salon offers all the beauty products and spa treatments one could possibly want.

Glenwood Caverns Adventure Park (5100 Two Rivers Plaza Rd., 800/530-1635, www.glenwoodcaverns.com, 9:30 A.M.–8 P.M. daily, $18) is a gigantic theme park built on the natural caves and mazes of the Glenwood Caverns and Fairy Caves, which opened as a tourist attraction in 1887. It takes 127 steps to get down, so make sure you're in shape before descending. To get to the cave entrance, take the 4,300-foot-long Iron Mountain Tramway gondola, which floats over the Rockies and brushes the tops of trees. The cave gives tours of varying lengths and intensity, and the Panorama Trail is a nice outdoor walk (in the summer) or snowshoeing trip (in the winter). New attractions include the 3,400-foot Alpine Coaster; a 1,300-foot Giant Swing; and a 32-foot climbing wall.

The **Frontier Historical Museum** (1001 Colorado Ave., 970/945-4448, www.glenwoodhistory.com, 11 A.M.–4 P.M. Mon.–Sat. May–Sept., 1–4 P.M. Mon. and Thurs.–Sat.

GRAND JUNCTION

Oct.–Apr., $3) documents the fascinating history of Glenwood Springs, from the time Captain Sopsis "discovered" the springs with his Ute encounter to Doc Holliday's ultimate demise here in 1887. (Holliday, for the record, is buried in Linwood Cemetery, just east of the town. Nobody knows the exact location of his grave.) The museum contains 5,000 photos from the Old West days and offers guided tours and a gift shop.

SPORTS AND RECREATION
Skiing and Snowboarding
Skiing had been an off-and-on sport in Glenwood Springs since 1940, and it truly took hold in the mid-1960s, when the **Sunlight Mountain Resort** (10901 County Rd. 117, 970/945-7491 or 800/445-7931, www.sunlightmtn.com) opened about 10 miles up Four Mile Road. Today it's hardly the biggest resort in northern Colorado, but it has 67 trails, 470 acres of ski terrain, vertical drops of 2,010 feet, and a collection of steep runs known as Extreme Sunlight. The summit is almost 9,900 feet, more than 4,000 feet higher than the town of Glenwood Springs, and the incredible views at the top are of Mount Sopsis and the Elk Mountain Range. Bonus for cross-country skiers: 20 miles of trails through a valley between Sunlight Mountain and Williams Peak.

Although it's at the center of downtown, the **Sunlight Mountain Ski and Bike Shop** (309 9th St., 970/945-9425, www.sunlightmtn.com) is affiliated with the ski resort.

Water Sports
The Colorado River flows in and around Glenwood Springs—particularly through 16-mile Glenwood Canyon, on I-70 just east of town—and the rapids rage quite nicely during spring and summer. Several local outfits offer guided tours, including **Rock Gardens** (1308 County Rd. 129, 800/958-6737, www.rockgardens.com), which has both easygoing scenic family tours and hardcore trips for adventure travelers; **Colorado Whitewater Rafting** (2000 Devereux Rd., 970/945-8477 or 800/993-7238, www.colo-

the Colorado River, on the eastern edge of Glenwood Springs

© STEVE KNOPPER

GRAND JUNCTION

radowhitewaterrafting.com), which has full-day, half-day, and short kids' trips; and **Blue Sky Adventures** (319 6th St., 970/945-6605 or 877/945-6605, www.blueskyadventure.com), in the Hotel Colorado.

Fishers, swimmers, kayakers, and other lake-going types should contact the local **Division of Wildlife Office** (50633 Hwy. 6/24, 970/947-2920), which provides information about all kinds of outdoor sports in the area. Also helpful in the fishing department is **Roaring Fork Anglers** (2114 B Grand Ave., 970/945-0180, www.alpineangling.com), which rents equipment and provides guided tours and fly-tying classes.

Mountain Biking

The White River National Forest isn't far from these parts, and many choose to bring their own bikes or rent equipment in Glenwood Springs before heading down to the trails of Aspen. Otherwise, try **Canyon Bikes** (526 Pine St., 970/945-8904 or 800/439-3043, www.canyonbikes.com), in the Hotel Colorado, for rentals and trail advice.

EVENTS

Strawberry Days (Sayre Park, Highland Park, and Grand Ave., 970/945-6589, www.strawberrydaysfestival.com) is a three-day, late-June festival with all the trimmings—parade, local bands, pancake breakfast, the 5K "Strawberry Shortcut" run, food court, art, crafts, and something called the Valley View Hospital Auxiliary Pie Day.

SHOPPING

The touristy area of Glenwood Springs centers on the hot springs, near the Hotel Colorado and the Hotel Denver, where a huge bridge overlooks the city. But the best shopping is a few blocks away, along 9th Street, an area of comfortable, modern cafés and tourist and townie stores alike.

Two charming bookstores—**Through the Looking Glass** (816 Grand Ave., 970/945-5931) and **Book Grove** (801 Blake Ave., 970/384-0992, www.bookgrove.com)—specialize in used and out-of-print titles. **Mosaic Planet** (720 Grand Ave., 970/384-2126) is a bohemian store that sells colorful clothes from various cultures.

ACCOMMODATIONS

Built in 1806 as an art deco palace on the corner, the **Hotel Denver** (402 7th St., 970/945-6565 or 800/826-8820, www.thehoteldenver.com, $84–139) has a three-story atrium and (in most rooms) views of the springs outside. Like the Hotel Colorado, it has a historic charm that screams "famous people once stayed here!"—but it hasn't been appropriately restored in years. Several interesting historical artifacts are in the lobby, including an 1885 Weber piano, a tile floor laid in 1921, and an old grandfather-style clock that has stood here since the 1930s. The lower rooms are the cheapest, but they're a little noisy due to the train station next door. The Glenwood Canyon Brewing Company, for food and beer, is on the first floor.

Not far from the Sunlight Mountain Resort, the **Sunlight Mountain Inn** (10252 County Rd. 117, 970/945-5225 or 800/733-4757, www.sunlightinn.com, $65–149) is a woodsy New West lodge with fireplaces in many of the rooms (and the lobby) and plenty of room to store your skis and poles. Some of the packages include nearby horse-riding trails, skiing, snowmobiling, and hot springs coupons.

Once the most luxurious place to stay between New York City and Los Angeles—Al Capone, Teddy Roosevelt, William Taft, Molly Brown, Doc Holliday, and assorted other luminaries and gangsters stayed here in the late 1800s—the **◖ Hotel Colorado** (526 Pine St., 970/945-6511 or 800/544-3998, www.hotelcolorado.com, $139–479) is on the National Registry of Historic Places and retains much of its elegance from the old days, although its fanciness has worn down over the years. Known as the "grande dame" after it was built in 1893, the hotel was famous for its Italian-style design and various elaborate waterfalls and shooting fountains. Imported Italian wallpaper, antiques, and interesting black-and-white portraits of former

GRAND JUNCTION

© STEVE KNOPPER

Built in 1893, the Hotel Colorado has provided rooms for Teddy Roosevelt and Al Capone.

guests Capone, Roosevelt, and others almost reproduce the Old West ambience, but more modern adventurers will appreciate the convenient lobby locations of Light Circle Massage, Canyon Bikes, and Blue Sky Adventures. The indoor-outdoor restaurant on the main floor is charming, and it has a $45–55 three-course dinner theater.

FOOD

Owned by Kurt Wigger, whose actor friend Michael Douglas occasionally drops by and leaves his vegetables on the plate, the Swiss-themed **Sopris Restaurant** (7215 Hwy. 82, 970/945-7771, 5–10 P.M. daily) specializes in veal with mushrooms, plus escargot and other seafood dishes—often slathered with the owner's butter sauce. Open since 1974, the restaurant is in a distinctive red building.

Peppo Nino (704 Grand Ave., 970/945-9059, 5–10 P.M. Wed.–Mon.) is a traditional Italian restaurant that does a great job with the basics—lasagna, veal, calamari, wine, desserts. With a gigantic breakfast-and-lunch menu

ranging from burritos to omelets to granola to a zillion kinds of toasts, **Daily Bread Café** (729 Grand Ave., 970/945-6253, 7 A.M.–2 P.M. Mon.–Fri., 8 A.M.–2 P.M. Sat., 8 A.M.–noon Sun.) specializes in mushroom bisque ($7) and deli sandwiches ($6).

The Bayou (919 Grand Ave., 970/945-1047, 11 A.M.–10 P.M. Sun.–Thurs., 11 A.M.–midnight Fri.–Sat.), relocated recently to a historic downtown building, is perhaps the only New Orleans-style restaurant in the mountains of Colorado, and it's a good one—specializing, of course, in gumbo, étouffée, blackened fish and chicken, red beans and rice, and menus describing certain spices as "hurt me." Mardi Gras masks hang on the wall, the staff provides goofy entertainment, and you can raise a glass to the ailing Crescent City.

8th Street Deli (205 8th St., 970/945-5011, 7 A.M.–6 P.M. daily) is an easygoing and somewhat hippie-ish deli that seats just eight people and has breakfast burritos, sandwiches, and desserts. (The salad dressings are homemade.) A little bigger is **Sacred Grounds** (725 Grand

Ave., 970/928-8804, 7 A.M.–8 P.M. daily), one of those roomy delis that chalk-prints its huge menu across several blackboards. "Build Your Own Sandwich" is usually a straightforward instruction, but here it involves numerous kinds of cheeses, vegetables, wraps, spreads, and breads. The homemade brownies are delicious.

Also basic—in the best sense of the word—is **Juicy Lucy's Steakhouse** (308 7th St., 970/945-4619, 11 A.M.–9:30 P.M. Sun.–Thurs., 11 A.M.–10 P.M. Fri.–Sat.), just underneath the bridge on the touristy side of town. It has the feel of a Boulder brewpub, if a little older, but its 14-ounce New York sirloin ($28) and center-cut pork chop ($17) are about as far from vegetarian-friendly Boulder as you can get.

INFORMATION

Glenwood Springs' **Chamber of Commerce** is at 1102 Grand Avenue; call 970/945-6589 or check out www.glenwoodchamber.com. The local paper is the *Glenwood Springs Post Independent* (www.postindependent.com).

GETTING THERE AND AROUND

Ride Glenwood Springs (970/384-6400, www.ci.glenwood-springs.co.us/transpo/1a-1.htm, 7 A.M.–7 P.M. Mon.–Fri., 8 A.M.–5 P.M. Sat., 9 A.M.4 P.M. Sun.) is a bus service that hits most of the central spots in town. Also, the **Roaring Fork Transportation Authority** (970/925-8484, www.rfta.com/summer/valley.html) provides a shuttle between Aspen, Snowmass, Glenwood Springs, and several of the smaller towns in between.

If you have a small plane and know how to fly it, try **Glenwood Springs Airport** (970/618-0778, www.glenwoodspringsairport.com).

Grand Junction and Vicinity

As a midsize agricultural town far removed from Denver and Colorado Springs, Grand Junction is the kind of place that advertises "relaxed pace" and "friendly people." In short, the town is a little boring.

But in almost every direction is an adventure—the Grand Mesa, to the south, is a flat-topped, 10,000-foot-tall mountain; the Bookcliffs, to the north, have the feel of an inverted Grand Canyon, 2,000 feet tall, red, yellow, and completely flat, stretching 100 miles into Utah; and even the Palisade orchards and vineyards, to the east, have a certain cherry-and-apricot-filled natural beauty. These outdoor sights make Grand Junction a hot spot of mountain biking, hiking, showshoeing, and fishing.

Grand Junction's history is rooted in the "Meeker massacre," a clash between 1870s reformer Nathan Meeker (whose namesake town is still about 100 miles northeast of the city) and resentful Utes that resulted in 11 dead white men. Whites demanded retribution and Ute leaders agreed to a compromise—a retreat beyond Colorado's western borders. After that, freed from pesky Indians, settlers formed new cities, including Grand Junction, so-called for its location at the Grand (now Colorado) and Gunnison Rivers.

The city's founders, Kansas politician George Crawford and Michigan attorney James Bucklin, assembled the Grand Junction Town Company in 1881, and within a year they'd installed a local newspaper, a mayor, aldermen, and a major railroad. With no Utes around, nearby miners felt comfortable stopping in the city, and some of them stayed to farm sugar beets and build farms and ranches. Thanks to more sophisticated Grand Valley irrigation systems, locals exported crops of apricots, cherries, and grapes.

Grand Junction has boomed and busted a few times since then—in the 1900s, oil and uranium drillers set up wells along the Western Slope, and the city was a key stopover for these new businesspeople. The market continued through the bust of the early 1960s;

GRAND JUNCTION

hiking, museums, and tourism have since taken over. Although its population is only 40,000, Grand Junction is the largest town between Denver and Salt Lake City.

SIGHTS

The Art Center (1803 N. 7th St., 970/243-7337, www.gjartcenter.org, 9 A.M.–4 P.M. Tues.–Sat., $2) shows 300 works focusing on Colorado and the West, with an emphasis on historic Native American artifacts. The exhibitions are usually Southwestern-style—colorful paintings of Colorado National Monument and other mountain-desert concoctions—but now and then brilliantly weird works like Paul Pletka's bird skeletons creep in.

The **Museum of Western Colorado** (462 Ute Ave., 970/242-0971, www.wcmuseum.org, 9 A.M.–5 P.M. Mon.–Sat., noon–4 P.M. Sun., $5.50) deals with many angles and time periods of the Old West, from a 1921 fire truck to a firearms exhibit of Winchesters, carbines, pistols, and a 15th-century Spanish cannon. An education tower has geology and weather exhibits at the top, but many make the climb just for the views.

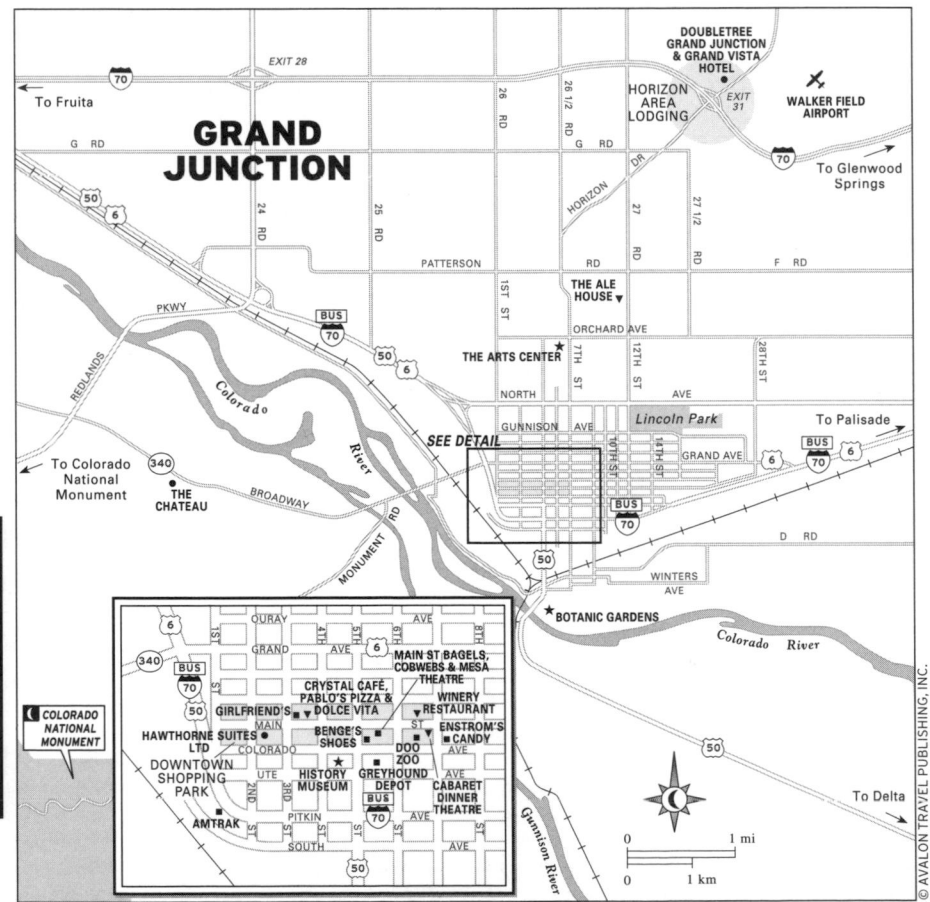

GRAND JUNCTION

© STEVE KNOPPER

The Bookcliffs, in and around Grand Junction, have the feel of an inverted Grand Canyon.

From 1896 to 1923, the Red Cross Land and Fruit Company ran a 243-acre, 22,000-tree farm of apples, pears, and peaches that dominated Grand Junction's economy and geography. It has long since closed, but preservationists bought four acres of it in 1980 and turned the site into the **Cross Orchards Living History Farm** (3073 F Rd., 970/434-9814, www.wcmuseum.org/crossorchards.htm, 9 A.M.– 4 P.M. Tues.–Sat. May–Oct., closed winters, $4), which shows much of the original farm equipment and 19th-century kitchen and pantry facilities.

Colorado Canyons National Conservation Area

Created in 2000, this 122,240-acre forest-and-valley area (2815 H Rd., 970/244-3000) extends from western Colorado into Utah. Its centerpiece is the Black Ridge Canyons Wilderness, a picturesque area of red-rock cliffs, waterfalls, rocks, and natural arches and spires. (And deer, mountain lions, and bighorn sheep, if you're really, really quiet.) Operated by the

Bureau of Land Management, the massive area is about 10 miles west of Grand Junction and popular with hikers and cyclists.

SPORTS AND RECREATION
Kokopelli's Trail

A gnarly 135-mile bike trip that begins about 15 miles west of Grand Junction and cuts straight into Moab, Utah, Kokopelli's Trail is a three- to four-day trip that's part steep bushwhacking and part smoothed-out Jeep roads. It climbs from 4,400 to 8,500 feet, and rubs against the Colorado River before shooting back up and dropping down into Utah's canyons. To get to the trailhead, go west on I-70 out of Grand Junction and exit at Luoma; turn left at the top, take the next right, turn left at the truck station, and go about half a mile until you can park along the road. This area—particularly Fruita, just west of Grand Junction—is a haven for mountain biking.

The **Colorado Plateau Mountain Bike Trail Association Inc.** (970/241-9737 or 970/244-8877, www.copmoba.com) is a long-running

GRAND JUNCTION

group of cyclists that sets up and maintains trails in the areas and sponsors biking events. For rentals and guided local tours, try **Over the Edge Sports** (202 E. Aspen Ave., Fruita, 970/858-7220, www.otesports.com).

ENTERTAINMENT AND EVENTS
Nightlife
The Ale House (2531 N. 12th St., 970/242-7253, www.breckbrew.com, 11 A.M.–2 A.M. daily) is part of the statewide Breckenridge Brewery chain and draws a late-night clientele. The menu is high-end bar food—nachos, chicken wings, sandwiches, all very good—and, of course, beer, including a signature brew.

Events
The city's biggest music festival is the late-June **Country Jam** (800/780-0526, www.country-jam.com), which draws gigantic mainstream-country acts such as Big & Rich, Montgomery Gentry, and (well, sort of country) ZZ Top. The three-day festival draws Stetson-wearers from all over the West, so plan for traffic (and reserve hotels early) during that weekend.

Entertainment
Main Street is filled with interesting restaurants, cafés, and shops, but everything seems to close around 8 or 9 P.M., even on the weekends. The exceptions are the **Cabaret Dinner Theatre** (701 Main St., 970/255-0999, www.thecabaret.net), which has local actors in well-known productions like *The Full Monty,* and **The Mesa Theater and Club** (538 Main St., 970/241-1717, www.mesatheater.com), which snags midlevel national music acts like the Young Dubliners and (!) Warrant and attracts a healthy regimen of kids out front on otherwise-boring nights. Also downtown: weird street art! If it's still around, check out *Jesus Head,* a self-explanatory sculpture about as big as your fist, which creeped me out when I wandered Main Street not long ago.

The **Grand Junction Symphony Orchestra** (970/243-6787, www.gjsymphony.org) gives concerts all year, including special events like kids' shows.

SHOPPING
Downtown Grand Junction is hardly the Pearl Street Mall in Boulder, but it has a comfortable, historic feel, and shops such as the outdoor-outfitting **Summit Canyon Mountaineering** (641 Main St., 970/243-2847), the self-explanatory **Champion Boots and Saddlery** (545 Main St., 970/242-2465), and the imported-clothing **Mosaic Planet** (315 Main St., 970/263-0499) nicely supplement the area's available outdoor activities.

Particularly unique: **Enstrom's Candy** (200 S. 7th St., 970/683-1000, www.enstrom.com), a Colorado chain specializing in nutty toffee; the funky **Girlfriends** (316 Main St., 970/242-3234), which has couches to go with clothes and gifts; **Cobwebs** (558 Main St., 970/245-0109), a kitschy antique shop; and **Benge's Shoes** (514 Main St., 970/242-3843), which sells plenty of hipster brands (like Diesel and Mephisto) despite being the second-oldest shoe store (or so they say) in Colorado.

ACCOMMODATIONS
Glenwood Springs, Aspen, and even Redstone, just a few miles east along I-70, are known for their distinctive luxury hotels, but Grand Junction is mostly chains—you're more likely to find a La Quinta or Comfort Inn than a bed-and-breakfast. As a result, the best places to stay are the high-end chains.

The eight-story **Doubletree Grand Junction** (43 Horizon Dr., 970/241-8888, www.doubletree.hilton.com, $99–129), formerly an Adam's Mark, has 273 rooms and high-end amenities like wireless Internet, a horseshoe pit, and a 5,000-square-foot ballroom downstairs. It's sort of *the* place to stay in Grand Junction although it's a little plain and (in places) needs work. (A multimillion-dollar renovation plan is reportedly in the hotel's near future.)

Another chain hotel, nothing special, but comfortable and reliable, is the **Hawthorne Suites L.T.D.** (225 Main St., 970/242-2525 or 800/527-1133, www.hawthorne.com, $99–239), a centrally located, relatively new brownstone with a free breakfast buffet and all the basic amenities (including high-speed Internet access).

The Grand Vista Hotel (2790 Crossroads Blvd., 970/241-8411 or 800/800/7796, www.grandvistahotel.com, $79) is a six-story building with an indoor and outdoor pool and a lobby lounge with karaoke every Thursday and Saturday night.

The Chateau (2087 Broadway, 970/255-1471 or 866/312-9463, www.tworiverswinery.com, $79–145) is better known as Two Rivers Winery, but it's also a French-style bed-and-breakfast directly underneath the Bookcliff Mountain Range. The winery produces chardonnay, merlot, cabernet sauvignon, and riesling and hopes to hit 10,000 cases soon.

The **Tomorrow Hill Bed & Breakfast** (945 24 Road, 970/255-8080, 877/258-8080, www.tomorrowhillfarm.com, $75) is on an eight-acre farm built in 1995 but designed to look like a farm built in 1890. The rooms are fine—with wireless Internet access, even—but the views of Colorado National Monument and general on-the-farm spirit are the main draw. Check out the windmill.

FOOD

Befitting a meat-and-potatoes kind of city, **The Winery** (642 Main St., 970/242-4100, 5–9 P.M. Mon.–Fri., 5–10 P.M. Sat.–Sun.) specializes in steak and chicken dishes—nothing fancy—and a fine-dining experience that includes stained-glass windows, brick walls, and plants.

 Dolce Vita (336 Main St., 970/242-8482, 11 A.M.–10 P.M. Sun.–Fri., 11:30 A.M.–10 P.M. Sat.) is perhaps the best restaurant in town, a family northern-Italian restaurant that serves wine-marinated portobello mushrooms and scaloppini chicken with angel-hair pasta, grilled red onions, a brandy cream sauce, and (the surprise ingredient) strawberries.

The restaurant part of the Tomorrow Hill Bed & Breakfast, the **Crystal Café & Bake Shop** (314 Main St., 970/242-8843, www.tomorrowhillfarm.com/CrstlCafe.html, 7–10:15 A.M. and 11 A.M.–1:45 P.M. Mon.–Fri., 8 A.M.–noon Sat.) is known for a super-sweet breakfast menu of apple pancakes and banana-nut French toast, but its dinners of steak and seafood are worth trying as well.

Across the street from Dolce Vita, **Pablo's Pizza** (319 Main St., 970/255-8879, www.pablospizza.com, 11 A.M.–8:30 P.M. Sun.–Thurs., 11 A.M.–9 P.M. Fri.–Sat.) has a knack for unusual flavor combinations—try the roasted garlic, walnut, and goat cheese pesto, the pepper-and-sausage Big Daddy's Rajun Cajun, and the peanut-sauce-and-shrimp Bangkok Express.

Main Street Bagels Artisan Bakery & Café (559 Main St., 970/241-2740, www.mainstreetbagels.net, 6:30 A.M.–4 P.M. Mon.–Thurs., 6:30 A.M.–5:30 P.M. Fri.–Sat., 6:30 A.M.–2 P.M. Sun.) is a rare bohemian enclave in a conservative city. The chai, bagels, and cinnamon rolls are homemade, and it's a Wi-Fi hot spot (for wireless-Internet laptop users, that is).

INFORMATION

The **Grand Junction Chamber of Commerce** (360 Grand Ave., 970/242-3214, www.gj-chamber.org) has tons of information about the city, and the **Grand Junction Visitor & Convention Bureau** (740 Horizon Dr., 800/962-2547, www.visitgrandjunction.com) is helpful as well. The *Grand Junction Daily Sentinel* (www.gjsentinel.com) is the local metro paper.

The **Delta City Hall** (4th St. and Main St., 970/874-7566, www.deltaco.org) is a great resource for locals, but travelers will probably prefer the **Delta Area Chamber of Commerce** (301 Main St., 970/874-8616, www.deltacolorado.org).

Try the **Palisade Chamber of Commerce** (319 Main St., 970/464-7458, www.palisadecoc.com) for basic city services. The **Rifle City Hall** (202 Railroad Ave., 970/625-2121, www.rifleco.org) is geared more toward locals than visitors, but it's somewhat helpful. Between the **Town of Meeker** (www.meeker-colorado.com) and the **Meeker Chamber of Commerce** (710 Market St., 970/878-5510, www.meekerchamber.com), travelers should get just about anything they need to know about this small historic town.

The **Moffat County Visitors Center** and **Craig Chamber of Commerce** share a

GRAND JUNCTION

website at www.craig-chamber.com (or visit 360 E. Victory Way, or call 970/824-5689). The **Cedaredge Chamber of Commerce** (245 W. Main, 970/856-6961, www.cedaredgecolorado.com) shares a website with the town government. The **Town of Fruita** (325 E. Aspen Ave., www.fruita.org) is somewhat more sparse.

GETTING THERE

The easiest way to get to Grand Junction is by flying into the **Walker Field Airport** (2828 Walker Field Dr., 970/244-9100, www.walkerfield.com), with 19 departures a day, mostly via major airlines, and serving primarily western Colorado and eastern Utah. **Grand Valley Transit** (970/256-7433, www.grandvalleytransit.com) is a bus service that stops throughout the city.

◖ COLORADO NATIONAL MONUMENT

A sort of mini-Grand Canyon, with gnarled, reddish rock formations that recall Colorado Springs' Garden of the Gods or Morrison's Red Rocks Park, Colorado National Monument is a 20,500-acre haven for hikers, bikers, wildlife-watchers, and campers. Its main artery is the narrow 23-mile Rim Rock Drive, which seems to have the perfect mesa-top, valley, or canyon view at the edge of every hairpin curve.

Credit for exploring the monument's many trails (most famously the **Canyon Rim Trail** above Wedding Canyon) goes to John Otto, saluted on a plaque as "trail builder, promoter, and first custodian"—in 1911, he became the first modern explorer to preserve the area. Today it's run by the **National Park Service** (Fruita, on the western edge of Grand Junction, 970/858-3617, www.nps.gov/colm, $5), and the 6,000-foot-high mesas and cliffs and complex horizontal sandstone formations are worth a long visit.

The **Visitors Center** (970/858-3617) is about four miles into the monument area and gives out maps of the many trails.

Sights

With nine massive natural arches that extend from natural sandstone and cliffs that rise 500

The 23-mile Rim Rock Drive is the main road in Colorado National Monument.

© MELISSA KNOPPER

to 700 feet from the ground, **Rattlesnake Canyon** (King's View Rd., west of Colorado National Monument, 970/244-3000, www.co.blm.gov/gjra/rattlesnakearches.htm, free) is a great, uncrowded spot for a nature walk. It's just a little hard to get in. The easiest entrance—one that doesn't involve floating down the Colorado River and climbing up a canyon—is a 13-mile drive along the rugged Black Ridge Access Road, which takes you to the trailhead. (Don't even think about it during rain or snow.) And four-wheel-drivers can get here from the high end of Rim Rock Road. Maps are available from the nearby Bureau of Land Management.

◖ Dinosaur Journey

Across from the western monument site, this "paleontologist's playground" (550 Jurassic Ct., Fruita, 888/488-3466, www.dinosaurjourney.org, 9 A.M.–5 P.M. daily, $7) is just off I-70 a few miles west of Grand Junction. Run by a company that specializes in robot dinosaur replicas, the elaborate museum is more

MIKE THE HEADLESS CHICKEN DAYS

Every September the serious people of Fruita, a small town just north of Colorado National Monument, gather downtown to drink beer, eat chicken, drive in car shows, and dance in contests. The occasion? A Wyandotte rooster from 1945 who legendarily lived for 18 months after farmer Lloyd Olsen – whose wife Clara demanded chicken for dinner – swung an ax and chopped off his head.

This miracle of science (the explanation goes that the ax missed Mike's brain stem and a clot formed to stop him from losing too much blood) draws thousands of people to experience Mike the Headless Chicken Days. Colorado's nuttiest and most macabre festival this side of Nederland's annual Frozen Dead Guy Days, Mike the Headless Chicken Days operates under this inspirational motto: "It is a great comfort to know you can live a normal life, even after you have lost your mind." PETA is apparently not invited.

For more information on the festival, contact Mike the Headless Chicken Days headquarters (325 E. Aspen Ave., Fruita, 970/858-3663, www.miketheheadlesschicken.org).

---

impressive than even the dinosaur exhibits in Dinosaur National Monument to the north. Its life-size fossil reconstructions of dilophosaurus, utahraptors, and tyrannosaurus rexes are animated so visitors can control them with buttons and levers. On-site paleontologists work in a lab that's open to public viewing, and the interactive kids' exhibits include an earthquake simulator.

Accommodations

Aside from small, plain, chain motels, the **Saddlehorn Campground** (Colorado National Monument, 970/858-3617) is the primary "lodging" in the area—it has 80 sites, including flush toilets and sinks, and allows charcoal grills but no wood fires. Located in a piñon forest near the visitors center, the site has pretty valley views.

Food

Nearby Fruita is no metropolis, and the restaurants are mostly of the Subway-Wendy's-McDonald's variety, but the **Fiesta Guadalajara Restaurant** (103 U.S. 6/50, 970/858-1228, 11 A.M.–10 P.M. Mon.–Thurs., 11 A.M.–11 P.M. Fri.–Sat., 11 A.M.9:30 P.M. Sun.) is a family Mexican joint worthy of its southwestern location—the chiles rellenos and fajitas come in huge portions.

DELTA

Almost 50 miles south of Grand Junction, on the Gunnison River near the picturesque Escalante Canyon, Delta is a small (population 3,900) agricultural town known for its orchards and several large Main Street murals painted in the 1980s. (Thus the nickname "City of Murals.") Although it has a couple of OK restaurants and chain hotels, it's not exactly a tourist trap, and many visitors prefer nearby Cedaredge.

Sights

The Ft. Uncompahgre Living History Museum (205 Gunnison River Dr., 970/874-8349, www.deltafort.org, 10 A.M.–4 P.M. Mon.–Fri. Apr.–Oct., $5) is on the site of a heavy-traffic 1828 fur-trading post. As a small-town museum, it's pretty elaborate, with a "trade room" including furs, guns, knives, and beads, a "hide room" that once stored deer and beaver skins, and guides dressed as settlers, traders, Native Americans, and cowboys.

Accommodations

The **Riverwood Inn and RV Park** (677 U.S. 50 N., 970/874-5787 or 888/213-2124, www.riverwoodn.com, $52) is a one-story, 14-room hotel that's a step above the chains in the area. Half of the rooms overlook the Gunnison River.

NORTHWEST COLORADO WINERIES

- **Amber Ridge Vineyards,** 3820 G. 25 Rd., Palisade, 970/464-5314, www.corleyvineyards.com

- **Canyon Wind Cellars,** 3907 N. River Rd., Palisade, 970/464-0888, www.canyonwindcellars.com

- **Carlson Vineyards,** 461 35 Rd., Palisade, 970/464-5554, www.carlsonvineyards.com

- **Colorado Cellars Winery,** 3553 E Rd., Palisade, 800/848-2812, www.coloradocellars.com

- **Confre Cellars,** 785 Elberta Ave., Palisade, 970/464-1300

- **DeBeque Canyon Winery,** 3943 Hwy. 6, 1.5 miles east of Palisade, 970/464-0550

- **Garfield Estates Vineyard and Winery,** 3572 G Rd., Palisade, 970/464-0941, www.garfieldestates.com

- **Grande River Vineyards,** 787 Elberta Ave., Palisade, 970/464-5867, www.granderiverwines.com

- **Graystone Winery,** 3352 F Rd., Clifton, 970/523-6611, www.graystonewine.com

- **Plum Creek Winery,** 3708 G Rd., Palisade, 970/464-7586, www.plumcreekwinery.com

- **Reeder Mesa Vineyards,** 7799 Reeder Mesa Rd., Whitewater, 970/242-7468, www.reedermesawines.com

- **Rocky Mountain Meadery,** 3701 G Rd., Palisade, 970/464-7899 or 800/720-2558, www.wic.net/meadery

- **St. Kathryn Cellars,** 888 Elberta Ave., Palisade, 970/464-9288 or 877/464-4888, www.st-kathryn-cellars.com

- **Two Rivers Winery,** 2087 Broadway, Grand Junction, 970/255-1471, www.tworiverswinery.com

- **Whitewater Hill Vineyards,** 220 32 Rd., Grand Junction, 970/434-6868, http://whitewaterhill.com

Food

The **Delta Fireside Inn** (820 Highway 92, 970/874-4413, www.deltafireside.com, 11 A.M.–2 P.M. and 4–9 P.M. Mon.–Thurs., 4–10 P.M. Fri.–Sun.) is not for even borderline vegetarians—there are isolated pasta-and-sauce dishes, but the heart of the menu is steak (an eight-ounce prime rib is $17), chicken ($11–16), and various seafood and pork entrées.

PALISADE

Unless you're a wine enthusiast, you might have no idea upon driving past dinky Palisade, from Glenwood Springs west to Grand Junction on I-70, that this is the winery capital of Colorado. Seventy-five percent of the state's vineyards are here, most give tours, and, as a bonus, the blink-and-you'll-miss-it kind of town has tan-and-red mesas in every direction and the Colorado River charging past the railroad tracks.

A longtime agricultural town, 2,600-resident Palisade was renowned even among the Utes for its rich soil. It began to produce peaches, cherries, and, of course, grapes, after the U.S. Reclamation Department built irrigation canals, including a Colorado River dam that created the Highline Canal and several large ditches. Today, the mild weather makes for a 182-day growing season—perfect for peaches.

Sights

Palisade's "Vinelands" area has more than a dozen wineries, specializing in a wide range of wines—rieslings, chardonnays, merlots, cabernet sauvignons, and Budweisers. (Just kidding on that last one.) The four wineries listed here have no tasting fees, although Plum Creek charges $2 per person for groups with more than 15 people (and adds that they get the savings back via discounts on wine).

© STEVE KNOPPER

Most of Colorado's wineries are in tiny Palisade.

One of the best Palisade marketers is **Carlson Vineyards** (461 35 Rd., 970/464-5554 or 888/464-5554, www.carlsonvineyards.com, 10 A.M.–6 P.M. daily), a down-home place where "wine is not treated as the nectar of snobs"— names like Prairie Dog Blush and Cougar Run Fat Cat Muskrat reinforce the point.

Founded in 1978, **Colorado Cellars Winery** (3553 E Road, 970/464-7921, www.coloradocellars.com, 9 A.M.–4 P.M. Mon.–Thurs., noon–4 P.M. Sat.) is the state's oldest and largest vineyard, specializing in peach, raspberry, plum, and cherry wines, along with something called Roadkill Red.

The website for **Garfield Estates Vineyard and Winery** (3572 G Rd., 970/464-0941, www.garfieldestates.com, 11 A.M.–5 P.M. daily) delivers an impassioned defense of rosé—it's not just "white zin," don't you know, because it has "more complexity than many whites but not the heavy tannins of a full blown red."

Most renowned in the area is probably **Plum Creek Winery** (3708 G Rd., 970/464-7586, www.plumcreekwinery.com, 9:30 A.M.–6 P.M.

daily Apr.–Oct., 10 A.M.–5 P.M. daily Nov.–Mar.), which boasts of all the gold, double-gold, and silver medals its 1998 Cabernet Franc, 1992 Grand Mesa, and numerous others have won over the years.

The **American Spirit Shuttle** (970/523-7662 or 888/226-5031, www.gisdho.com, 1–5 P.M. Sat., $130 for groups of 1–5 people) offers driving tours of many of the Palisade and Grand Junction wineries.

(Little Bookcliffs Wild Horse Range

The Little Bookcliffs Wild Horse Range (2815 H Rd., eight miles northeast of Grand Junction, 970/244-3000, www.co.blm.gov/gjra/lbc, free) is 30,261 acres of low, rocky canyons and high, flat plateaus that rise from 5,000 to 7,421 feet. And one other thing: wild horses. About 115 of them—bays, blacks, grays, pintos, roans, browns, and palominos—are running free, like a sequel to *The Black Stallion.* They're mostly descendants of horses who fled nearby ranches over the last two centuries; some have blood

GRAND JUNCTION

that can be traced to 1800s Native American tribes or, even earlier, to Spanish traders. Thanks to schoolchildren writing to their representatives, Congress passed the "Wild, Free-Roaming Horse and Burro Act" in 1971, which is why hiking, biking, and mountain climbing in this massive area can be so dramatic. There you are, walking along, and a wild horse appears out of nowhere.

Entertainment and Events

Palisade's many orchards come together every August for the **Palisade Peach Festival** (3rd St. and Main St., among other locations, www.palisadepeachfest.com, $2), which claimed an 18,000-person attendance in 2004. You've never seen so much fuzz in your life, and vendors set up booths for barbecue, corn, and pancakes—plus, there's an afternoon car show.

The **Grande River Vineyards** (I-70, exit 42, 970/464-5867, www.granderivervineyards.com) sponsors relatively big-name blues, country, folk, and flamenco music stars—bluesman Tommy Castro headlined on Memorial Day 2005—throughout the summer. Its festival is called **Heard It Through the Grapevine.**

Accommodations

With the exception of The Orchard House— The Garden House Bed & Breakfast, sadly, has closed—the lodging in Palisade is generally small, plain, and motel-style. For good deals, try the **Mesa View Motel** (424 W. 8th St., 970/464-0539, $39–47) and the **Palisade Wine Country Inn** (588 W. 1st St., 970/464-1498, www.palisadewinevalleyinn.com, $99–129).

Most of the rooms at **The Orchard House Bed & Breakfast** (3573 E 1/2 Rd., 970/464-0529, www.theorchardhouse.com, $80–95) have views of the Grand Mesas and the Bookcliffs—but the best place to enjoy the scenery is from the long porch on this large, triangular house. The rooms are named for pets; Zoe's Room, inspired by a cat, has a pencil-post bed and soothing green-and-cream fabrics.

Food

The **Palisade Café** (113 W. 3rd St., 970/464-0657, 8 A.M.–2 P.M. daily) is a basic breakfast-and-lunch restaurant—omelets and sandwiches of all kinds—with paintings on the walls and a homey atmosphere. And pie. Plenty of pie.

In an old brick building, the **(Slice O' Life Bakery** (105 W. 3rd St., 970/464-0577, 8 A.M.–5 P.M. Tues.–Fri., 8 A.M.–3 P.M. Sat.) is Palisade's biggest claim to fame (other than the wineries, of course). Locals rave about the homemade baked goods, from sweet rolls to fruitcakes, and it serves sandwiches for lunch.

RIFLE

Like many of the small towns near Grand Junction, Rifle is a hub for mountain bikers, hikers, cross-country skiers, and hunters—Teddy Roosevelt came here in 1901 to hunt bears—without a whole lot to do in town. Well, there is one thing: Drop by a bar and start an argument with locals about how the town got its name. One of many legends has it that an explorer in the 1800s left his rifle leaning on a tree. Upon his return to camp, he realized his error and wrote "Rifle" on the only map anybody had. The name stuck.

The scenery surrounding Rifle is incredible—mesas, cliffs, sagebrush parks, woodlands of piñon and juniper trees, the Elk Mountains, Gore Range, Grand Mesa, and Flat Tops. Trails are everywhere, and it's common to pass cars toting bikes, skis, and, yes, rifles.

Sights

Rifle Falls State Park (Highway 325, 14 miles north of Rifle, 970/625-1607, www.coloradoparks.org/index.html) is named for a triple waterfall that goes over limestone cliffs. Within the cliffs are dark and scary caves— bring a flashlight, especially if you plan to explore a famous 90-foot room beneath the falls. The surrounding area is a 100-acre state park; it first opened in 1883 to local ranchers, and by 1910 the Rifle Hydroelectric Plant had split the waterfall into three streams. Consider visiting in winter, when the falls create ice crystals on the vegetation.

Ice and rock climbers swear by the 1,305-acre **Rifle Gap State Park** (Highway 325, nine miles north of Rifle, 970/625-1607, www.coloradoparks.org/index.html, $5), beneath the thick Grand Hogback sandstone, which is filled with waterfalls and caves. It also has a 350-acre reservoir, popular among boaters, fishers, swimmers, divers, and windsurfers (and ice fishers and skaters in the winter). Art-history trivia: Renowned outdoor artists Christo and Jeanne-Claude built an orange curtain that stretched across the entire valley in 1971; winds knocked it down, they rebuilt it a year later, and the second curtain lasted just 24 hours. So, there's no curtain anymore, but a commemorative site on Rifle Creek recalls the huge environmental display.

The **Rifle Falls Fish Hatchery** (11466 Highway 325, 970/625-1865, 7 A.M.–4:30 P.M. daily, free), run by the Colorado Division of Wildlife, produces the most trout in the state. It's open for viewing but not fishing.

Sports and Recreation

Mountain-biking trails spread like tentacles from Rifle into the surrounding mountains and cliffs. The town recommends a trail three miles north of town, off JQS Road, which is on Highway 13 north of I-70—look for a small break in the guardrail. The rocky dirt road goes seven miles up the Roan Cliffs, overlooking Rifle at the top. Numerous Jeep trails and narrow biking roads are also off JQS Road. The **Rifle Information Center** (200 Lions Park Circle, 970/625-2085 or 800/842-2085, www.riflechamber.com), on the Colorado River, provides detailed mountain-biking trail maps.

Also, watch the main Rifle webpage—www.rifleco.org—for information about races and group biking events. **Roan Cliff Chaos**, in mid-July on the JQS Road trails, is a popular one.

Several local shops rent bikes and equipment and give trail information—the city recommends **Colorado Custom Cycles** (230 Railroad Ave., 970/625-6188, www.coloradocustomcycles.com).

The easiest place to find fish is outside the Rifle Information Center, next to the Colorado River at 200 Lions Park Circle, and many local shops will set you up a littler farther inside the rapids. **Boating** and **fishing** are big at the trout-and-bass-packed Rifle Gap State Park, which has a paved boat ramp.

The Rifle area is disproportionately packed with outdoors-type stores: **Big Mountain Outfitters** (120 W. 4th St., 970/625-4239), **Timberline Sporting Goods** (101 E. 3rd St., 970/625-4868), and **Up Close on the River** (1060 Grand Ave., Silt, 970/876-2665, www.upcloseontheriver.com).

Three miles north of Rifle, the 18-hole **Rifle Creek Golf Course** (3004 Hwy. 325, 970/625-1093, www.riflecreekgolf.com) is in the shadow of the Hogback Range and has plenty of trees and water hazards. It also has the **Columbine Restaurant** (970/625-9201, www.columbinerestaurant.net), which tops off an easy day of golf with plenty of wiener schnitzel ($13), steak, chicken, and trout.

Accommodations

Rifle's lodging is mostly low-end chains and low-overhead motels, so most visitors will probably want to stay in nearby Grand Junction or Glenwood Springs. But there is one campground: Although you probably won't want to set up a tent underneath the 60-foot triple waterfall—and probably not in the limestone caves underneath the falls, either—**Rifle Falls State Park** (5775 Highway 325, 970/625-1607, $12–18) is a photogenic place to camp. Swimming is available in the creek, but call first to find out whether electricity and heat are available where you plan to stop.

Food

As with hotels, Rifle is mostly chains (and fast-food ones at that). But there are a few distinctive local joints, including **Tortilleria La Rocca II** (119 W. 3rd St., 970/625-4777, 9 A.M.–9 P.M. daily), a reasonably priced Mexican restaurant with the usual tacos and tamales and a butcher shop on the premises.

MEEKER

The 2,200 people who live in Meeker must be pretty thrilled that their town is forever linked with the word "massacre." But such is history. The Meeker Massacre began with journalist and teacher Nathan C. Meeker, a well-known reformer of the 1800s who'd founded the town of Greeley and wanted to convert the Utes into the white vision of church-attending farmers. The Utes didn't respond well to his advances, and in September 1879, Meeker requested reinforcements from the U.S. Army.

The Utes ambushed Major Thomas Thornburg, who was on his way to Meeker's White River area with a relief contingent, killing him and 13 of his troops. The Utes continued into Meeker's agency and slaughtered not only the would-be reformer but 11 other men—and took several women and children captive and burned down Meeker's agency. The women and children were released after 23 days, but the damage was done; the "Utes must go!" movement became more shrill and powerful overnight, and the Utes lost their bargaining leverage. By 1880, Chief Ouray agreed in Washington to move his people to Utah.

The town of Meeker as we know it began three years later, when the U.S. government established a fort and sold it to local settlers. Today, three of these log cabins house the White River Museum in downtown Meeker. A marker commemorating the massacre site is on Highway 64, four miles west.

Located about halfway between I-70 and U.S. 40, on the west end of the White River National Forest, Meeker is like many small northwestern Colorado towns—a haven for outdoor activities, but not much else. The hiking, fishing, horseback riding, rafting, snowmobiling, and, especially, hunting, are popular, given the proximity to the White River forest, the Flat Tops Wilderness, and the White River Valley.

Sights

The photo near the front door of the **White River Museum** (565 Park St., 970/878-9982, www.meekercolorado.com/museum.htm,

9 A.M.–5 P.M. Mon.–Fri. and 10 A.M.–5 P.M. Sat.–Sun. May–Oct., 11 A.M.–4 P.M. Fri.–Sat. Nov.–Apr., free) was taken three years after the U.S. military left Meeker in the late 1880s. The museum's three log cabins were a barracks until the government sold them to settlers; today, they're filled with photos (including many of doomed reformer Nathan Meeker and his family), period dresses, hats, jewelry, and, um, a Victorian wreath made of human hair. Perhaps most historically important is the actual plow with which Meeker dug up the Utes' pony racetrack, which led to the Meeker Massacre.

The **Flat Tops Trail Scenic Byway** (U.S. Forest Service, Blanco District, 317 E. Market St., 970/878-4039, www.meekercolorado.com/byway.htm) is an 82-mile passage through the ranches, mines, lakes, and woodlands of the original (set aside in the 19th century) White River Plateau Timberland Reserve. It's a pretty drive, from Meeker to Yampa, and hits just a few small towns in between, so be sure the gas tank is full before you take off. Also, the road gets slippery and treacherous when it rains.

Entertainment and Events

It's a little slow around here—the Telluride Bluegrass Festival is several hundred miles south—so residents get disproportionately excited about the **Meeker Classic Sheepdog Trials** (970/878-5510, www.meekersheepdog.com), a five-day, early-September celebration of really smart dogs who tell sheep what to do. The winner gets $20,000, so you'll see some of the best fetching, outrunning, and herding in the world, and some expert human whistling as well. A pancake breakfast, art contest, crafts, and various dog-therapy workshops are on hand.

Accommodations

Built in 1896, **The Meeker Hotel and Café** (560 Main St., 970/878-5255, www.themeekerhotel.com, $40–80) is a brick structure filled with elk and mule deer trophies and a vivid lobby painting of the Meeker Massacre. Its 24 rooms include a few large suites, and they're all colorful and orderly, with beds matching the meticulously patterned wallpaper. The café is as historic as the hotel, having served Billy the Kid, both President Roosevelts, and Gary Cooper, and it continues to emphasize heavy comfort food like chicken-fried steak and mashed potatoes with gravy.

The family-owned **(Sleepy Cat Guest Ranch** (16064 County Rd. 8, 970/878-4413, www.sleepycatguestranch.com, $75–120) has both standard motel rooms and more luxurious log cabins, including one with a fireplace marketed to honeymooners. Its restaurant serves the big-appetite stuff—steak, prime rib, Rocky Mountain trout, and all the wine and beer you can drink.

Food

The hotel restaurants (at the Meeker and the Sleepy Cat Guest Ranch) are the best in town, but the **Market Street Bar and Grill** (173 1st St., 970/878-3193, 7–11 A.M. and 5–9 P.M. Mon.–Fri., 7–11 A.M. and 5–8 P.M. Sun.) is a throwback family restaurant with a wooden interior and western-style antiques and paintings. Again, comfort food is the norm—steaks, seafood, and pie.

CRAIG

A city of 8,100 people, Craig is tantalizingly close to Colorado's most popular ski areas, particularly Steamboat Springs, about a 45-minute drive to the east. Craig itself, however, is flat and filled with nothing. Well, that's not totally true—the **Grand Old West Days** bring bull-riding, bands, and a parade to town every Memorial Day, and the Museum of Northwest Colorado has an interesting collection of guns and other cowboy memorabilia.

But as with Rifle, Rangely, Palisade, and other small towns in northwest Colorado, Craig is also a popular spot for outdoor recreation—particularly hunting and fishing in the Yampa and Green Rivers and Trappers Lake. Otherwise, it's a long, empty drive down U.S. 40 between Dinosaur and Steamboat Springs, so think of Craig as a last-ditch gas-and-snacks option.

And if you're really desperate for scenery, the three-smokestack **Craig Station** is the largest coal-fired energy plant in Colorado. It's about six miles south of town.

Sights

In the city park downtown, early-1900s mining-and-railroad magnate David Moffat's greenish-black **Marcia Car** (U.S. 40, 970/824-5689, free), named for his daughter, is available for tours and private viewings. Recently restored, the car once transported Moffat up and down his Denver Northwestern & Pacific Railroad line to inspect the construction. Although Moffat planned to extend the line to Salt Lake City, he and his investors fell short of funds and had to stop in Craig—nonetheless, from 1913 to 1947 it was known as the Denver & Salt Lake Railroad.

The **Museum of Northwest Colorado** (590 Yampa Ave., 970/824-6360, www.musnwco.org, 9 A.M.–5 P.M. Mon.–Fri., 10 A.M.–4 P.M. Sat., free) is yet another Colorado museum that delves into the romantic Old West days of cowboys and outlaws, miners and ranchers. This one's specialty is cowboy gear—chaps, saddles, spurs, guns, and other memorabilia from Bill Mackin's 50-year-old collection. Another striking artifact is the bronze statue (by Sheridan, Wyoming, artist Jerry Smiley) of local gunfighter James Robinson, whose tall hat and casual manner capture the lazy-eyed renegade spirit of those times.

The **Browns Park National Wildlife Refuge** (1318 Hwy. 318, 970/365-3613) is about 30 miles west of Craig, 53 miles northwest of the Maybell intersection of U.S. 40 and Highway 318, and the pretty waterfall-and-canyon area is somewhat infamous for having hid Butch Cassidy and other Wild West outlaws. The 13,455-acre area is along the Green River, and its main function is to provide a habitat for Great Basin Canada geese and ducks. It's a great place for **bird-watching**—golden eagles and peregrine falcons occasionally fly overhead—as well as spotting antelope, bighorn sheep, and elk.

Sports and Recreation

The Yampa River is just one of the **fishing** spots (mostly pike and trout) around Craig—one good vantage point is east on U.S. 40 for seven miles. For more information on this or the Green River, Freeman Reservoir, Trappers Lake, Lake Avery, Elkhead Reservoir, or any of the other bodies of water in the area, contact the **Sportsman Information Center** (360 W. Victory Way, 970/824-3046). For fishing and hunting license and map information, try **Craig Sports** (124 Victory Way, 970/824-4044, www.craigsports.com).

The well-maintained, tree-filled, 18-hole **Yampa Valley Golf Course** (2179 Highway 394, 970/824-3673) doubles as a cross-country skiing zone in the winter.

Accommodations

The Holiday Inn is the primary place to stay in Craig, and many prefer to go all the way to Steamboat Springs rather than deal with a nondescript chain hotel. Campers have a better option: **Freeman Reservoir Campground** (Hwy. 13, 12 miles north of Craig, 970/824-5689, $12), which has 17 campsites, running water during some parts of the year, and easy access to many hiking and biking trails.

Food

The **Bad to the Bone BBQ & Grill** (572 Breeze St., 970/824-8588, 11 A.M.–9:30 P.M. daily) is a plainspoken ribs-and-burgers place that more or less captures Craig's culinary experience. The **Golden Cavvy** (538 Yampa Ave., 970/824-6038, 6 A.M.–9 P.M. daily) is a cheap, everything-on-the-menu kind of restaurant on the site of a hotel that burned down years ago. (Its huge fireplace remains.) House specialty: fried stuff.

CEDAREDGE

This town of 1,200 people is the midpoint between the flat, Grand Canyon-like mesas to the north and the rounder, greener, and taller San Juans a little farther to the south. It's tiny and easy to blip past on the map, but it also has 300 lakes, an elevation of 6,100 feet and

the mild, orchard-friendly climate to go with it, and (like many small towns in northwestern Colorado) a huge variety of mountain-biking trails.

Fifteen minutes south of Cedaredge—along Highway 65, also known as the Grand Mesa National Scenic and Historic Byway—is the Grand Mesa, a flat-topped mountain that extends from 10,000 to 11,000 feet above sea level. The scenery is incredible: Rainbows and dramatic sunsets are common, the San Juans are in the distance, and the elevation makes everything cool, even as late as June or July, so bring a coat.

Sights

Pioneer Town (Hwy. 65, 970/856-7554, www.cedaredgecolorado.com/pioneer_town/ptown.html, 9 A.M.–4 P.M. Mon.–Sat. and 1–4 P.M. Sun. Memorial Day–Sept., $5) is a 23-building, wooden-sidewalk area two blocks south of downtown that re-creates frontier life in the late 1800s. There's a working blacksmith shop (just in case your horse's feet get tired), a railroad depot, a schoolhouse, a fruit-packing shed, several ranch silos, a saloon, and the popular Doris Doll and Toy House.

Sports and Recreation

The **DeerCreek Village Golf Club** (500 SE Jay Ave., 970/856-7781, www.deercreekvillage-golf.com/main.html) is an 18-hole course (that is, two nines) with the Grand Mesa in the distance and lots of trees and water. On-site is one of the few decent restaurants in town, **The Grill at Deer Creek Village** (500 SE Jay Ave., 970/856-7782), in view of the course, with a nice wine list to go with house specialties like steak and seafood pasta.

Shopping

The Apple Shed (250 S. Grand Mesa Dr., 970/856-7007 or 888/856-7008, www.appleshed.net/) is a complex of shops and galleries, with an emphasis on local artists—most notably the owner, Connie Williams, who does watercolor landscapes and abstract acrylics. The shops are of the seasonal knickknack variety, including tiny snowmen, teapots, and Christmas stockings.

Accommodations

I personally would not have thought to combine a llama-breeding farm with a bed-and-breakfast, but the **((Cedars' Edge Llamas B&B** (2169 Hwy. 65, 970/856-6836, www.llamabandb.com, $75–100) has both llamas and rooms, so why not? Aladdin, Emma, Mini T, and others cost roughly $250 each to take home, although as of this writing all but one were sold out. And if that isn't enough scenery, the bed-and-breakfast is within viewing distance of the Black Canyon of the Gunnison National Park and the Grand Mesa National Forest. The rooms are colorful, with many blues and peaches, and breakfast in bed is available.

The **Aspen Trails Campground** (19975 Hwy. 65, 970/856-6321, $15), three miles north of town, specializes in motorcycle rallies, so if you're lost in this area and happen to stumble upon a bunch of llamas and Harley riders, that's a sign you're in Cedaredge. There's a central fireplace, camper cabins, RV sites, a tent area, and a gift shop.

Food

Cedaredge is not known for its gourmet dining, but **Highway 65 Burgers** (1260 S. Grand Mesa Dr., 970/856-4465, 10:30 A.M.–9 P.M. daily) is a classic burger joint with the usual styles and trimmings—bacon with cheese, hickory, malts, ice cream, and fries.

GRAND MESA

Although this part of Colorado is dry and hot, a trip up the 11,000-foot Grand Mesa, the world's largest flat-topped mountain, leads to a dramatically different world. The sagebrush gives way to spruce and fir trees, the heat disappears and lakes pop up in every direction, and what was a bumpy desert turns into a sportsperson's paradise of fishing holes, hiking trails (try the 10-mile Crag Crest), and 13 campgrounds.

In the Utes' days, the 50-square-mile area encompassing Grand Mesa was known as "Thunder Mountain"—until the U.S. government herded the Utes to Utah and southwestern Colorado reservations in the 1880s. The Grand Mesa became an official national forest in 1892, by decree from President Benjamin Harrison.

Sports and Recreation

World-class skiers probably wouldn't plan a trip around **Powderhorn Ski Resort** (Hwy. 65, 20 miles south of I-70, 970/268-5700, www.powderhorn.com), but it's a great unexpected place to drop in if you happen to be traveling in the area during winter. The resort has 510 acres, with a summit elevation of almost 10,000 feet, four lifts, and trails for all skill levels. The ski trails run along the contours of the mesa. There's also resort lodging: **The Inn at Wildewood** (48371 Quakie St., Mesa, 970/268-5170, www.powderhorn.com/stay-wildewood.html, $65–119).

((Grand Mesa National Forest

The best-known **hiking-and-biking** trail in this 346,219-acre forest (2250 U.S. 50, Delta, 970/874-6600, www.fs.fed.us/r2/gmug/) is the Crag Crest National Recreation Trail, a 10-mile loop that curves around three lakes (with others on the outside)—bring a camera for the spectacular view of Butts Lake, a glittering, blue, one-mile body of water surrounded by fir, spruce, and aspen trees. As for the mesa itself, its lava indentations can inspire geologists for hours. Consider hiking the 11,234-foot Leon Peak, on the forest's eastern edge, which is the Grand Mesa's tallest point and overlooks Gunnison Peak, the West Elk Mountains, and the San Juan Range, among other things.

To get to the trailhead from I-70, take the Highway 65 exit and go south about 35 miles to Forest Road 121, turn left, drive another 2.5 miles, bear left, and watch for signs about a mile ahead. Note that lightning is common on this popular trail, and it can get cold even when the weather below indicates otherwise. For maps and other information, contact the Ranger District (970/242-8211).

GRAND JUNCTION

The forest has some of the best **fishing** in Colorado—mostly rainbow trout, but also brook and cutthroat. There are 300 lakes, so it's hard to pick one, but the 10,000-foot-high **Carson Lake** (from Highway 65 south, take Rim Drive Road southwest three miles to Carson Lake Road and follow it for about two miles) has 12-inch cutthroat and some rainbow.

Contact the **Colorado Division of Wildlife** (711 Independent Ave., Grand Junction, 970/255-6100, http://wildlife.state.co.us/fishing) for maps, licenses, and information on conditions and laws.

Accommodations

Unlike the rest of northwest Colorado, the Grand Mesa area has several quaint, elegant inns and resorts; if you're planning to visit Colorado National Monument or Grand Junction, consider using this area as a base. Perhaps the best is **❰ Mesa Lakes Resort** (Hwy. 65, 12 miles south of Mesa, 970/268-5467 or 888/420-6372, $45–115), a log cabin next to a lake (fishing gear is available at the resort) in the middle of a forest. Several miles of groomed cross-country skiing trails are on the site, and the lodge serves prime rib nightly with live country singers in the background.

Also overlooking a lake—actually two, both filled with trout—is the **❰ Spruce Lodge Resort** (20658 Baron Lake Dr., 16 miles north of Cedaredge, 970/856-6240 or 800/850-7221, $100–200), built in 1956. It's in the forest itself, among a clump of spruce trees, and has 11 cabins, most with kitchens. Also on the premises are the new Over the Top Restaurant and snowmobile rentals.

The Grand Mesa National Forest has 13 full-service campgrounds, but perhaps the most striking is **Vega State Park** (15247 N. 610th Rd., 12 miles east of Collbran, 970/487-3407, $12), which is in an alpine meadow next to a high-elevation lake. The park is big with hikers, cyclists, cross-country skiers, and snowmobilers, and the complex has four campgrounds, one of which is just for tents. Call first to find out which areas have electricity and heat—don't worry, none of them have phones or television sets.

Rangely and Dinosaur

RANGELY

Although Rangely didn't officially become a town until 1947, it has been a thoroughfare for Fremont Indians, Utes, Spanish explorers en route from Mexico to California, early-American pioneers and cattle-herders, and, after World War II, so many new oil-men that they had to live in makeshift trolley cars.

The oil boom has long since died out, and Rangely's popularity has slowed to a trickle—mostly history buffs searching for Native American artifacts, off-road mountain bikers heading to the Raven Rims and other trails, coyote-and-elk-watchers, and outdoor enthusiasts looking for a mesa or sandstone cliff. About 2,100 people live in the city, and most travelers come for the accessibility to parks and mountains.

Sights

The **Canyon Pintado National Historic District** (beginning three miles south of Rangely on Highway 139, 970/878-3800) took its name (which means "Painted Canyon" in Spanish) in 1776, when traveling missionaries discovered Native American glyphs and art on the rocks. They're pretty extraordinary—Utes and Fremonts "pecked" them onto the sides of mountains using large rocks, and some resemble hands and bowls popping out of tiny urns. Tribes carved them between the years 600 and 1300, and the elaborate artwork distinguishes this district, which stretches roughly 15 miles along Highway 139, from the surrounding Douglas Creek Valley. Contact the **Rangely Chamber of Commerce** (209 E. Main St., 970/675-8476, www.rangely.com/pintado.html) to find out where all the glyphs are.

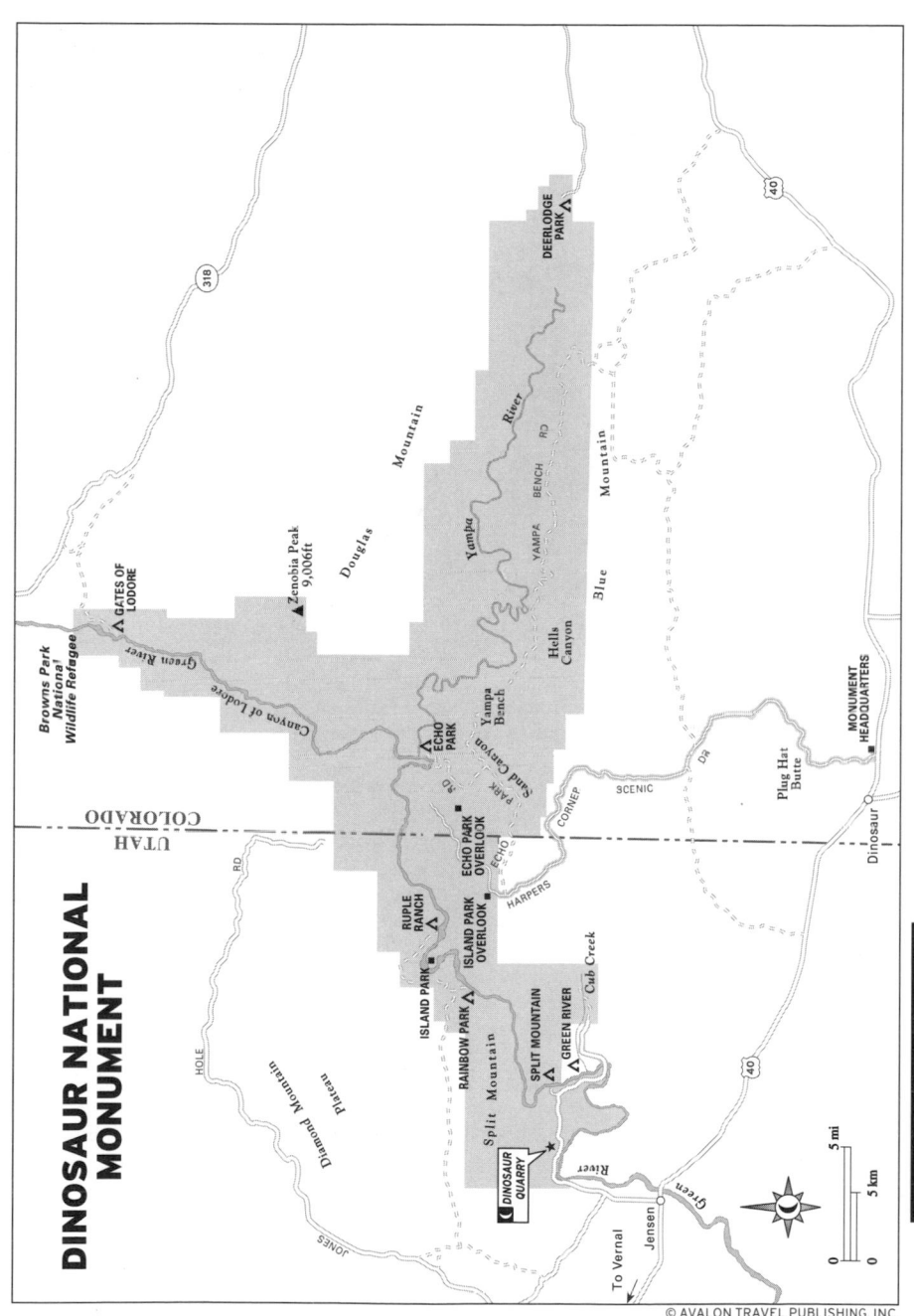

DINOSAUR NATIONAL MONUMENT

DEERLODGE PARK

Mountain

Yampa River

BENCH RD

YAMPA BENCH

Blue Mountain

Zenobia Peak
9,006ft

Douglas

GATES OF LODORE

Green River

Browns Park
National
Wildlife Refuge

Canyon of Lodore

Hells Canyon

ECHO PARK

Yampa Bench

Sand Canyon

RD

PARK

ECHO

CORNEP

SCENIC

RD

Plug Hat Butte

MONUMENT HEADQUARTERS

COLORADO

UTAH

ECHO PARK OVERLOOK

HARPERS

Dinosaur

RD

RUPLE RANCH

ISLAND PARK OVERLOOK

ISLAND PARK

HOLE

Cub Creek

Split Mountain

RAINBOW PARK

SPLIT MOUNTAIN

GREEN RIVER

Diamond Mountain Plateau

DINOSAUR QUARRY

Green River

To Vernal

Jensen

JONES

40

318

40

5 mi

5 km

0

0

GRAND JUNCTION

© AVALON TRAVEL PUBLISHING, INC.

© STEVE KNOPPER

The scenery on the Colorado side of Dinosaur National Monument is remarkable.

Sports and Recreation

Kenney Reservoir (Hwy. 64, five miles east of Rangely) is on the White River, directly below the 20-year-old Taylor Draw Dam. It's stocked with black crappie, channel catfish, and rainbow trout—and if you happen to catch an endangered pikeminnow, Colorado Division of Wildlife park officials request that you throw it back immediately. **Fishing** at the reservoir requires a license, available at the **Rangely Chamber of Commerce** (209 E. Main St., 970/675-8476, www.rangely.com/kenney.html); for fishing reports and other information, the Division of Wildlife is at 303/291-7534.

Accommodations

Super-cheap hotel chains and bargain motels are the standard in Rangely, so for lodging I'd recommend Grand Junction, about an hour's drive south. Campers can stay at the relatively new **Buck 'N' Bull RV Park & Campground** (2811 E. Main St., 970/675-8335, $10), which has hookups for electricity and water and is near Kenney Reservoir and the Canyon Pintado National Historic District.

Food

Cowboy Corral (202 W. Main St., 970/675-8986, 6 A.M.–9:30 P.M. Mon.–Sat., 7 A.M.–9:30 P.M. Sun.) is an old-school family restaurant with an equal emphasis on American (which is to say, burgers) and Mexican (which is to say, burritos) food. More traditionally Mexican is **Los Tres Potrillos** (302 W. Main St., 970/675-8870, 11 A.M.–9 P.M. Mon.–Sat.), which complements its tacos and fajitas with wall-hanging sombreros and pottery. The **Pinyon Seed Bakery** (511 E. Rangely St., 970/675-2022, 5 A.M.–8 P.M. Mon.–Fri., 5 A.M.–2 P.M. Sat.) has home-baked pastries, muffins, and doughnuts, plus deli sandwiches and pizza for lunch.

DINOSAUR

Dinosaur itself is a tiny town with a couple of small restaurants, a large and run-down green dinosaur statue, a Visitors Center, and a couple

GRAND JUNCTION

DINOSAURS IN COLORADO

Dinosaur Quarry, in Dinosaur National Monument, marks the area where early-20th-century paleontologist Earl Douglass discovered thousands of bones and reassembled them to determine what the 165 million-year-old monstrosities looked like. Many of the species he uncovered were traced to what is now Colorado and other western states, including:

*   **Apatosaurus:** The 34-ton, 75-foot-long, skinny-necked brontosaurus first showed up in Morrison; excavators in the National Monument found a skull from it in the early 1900s.

*   **Camarasaurus:** Also known as "chamber lizard," this 35- to 60-ton species has a "small version" and a "large version." Both are huge and were discovered in Garden Park.

*   **Diplodocus:** Discovered in Garden Park, this tall, skinny dinosaur was 75-85 feet long and weighed "only" 13 tons.

*   **Stegosaurus:** Another of the best-known dinosaurs—at least, to kids who read books about them and watch The Flintstones reruns—stegosaurus was relatively small but protected itself from sharp-toothed munching with hard spines along its back. It was first found in Morrison, where Red Rocks Park houses a dinosaur exhibit today.

*   **Ceratosaurus:** Also found in Garden Park, this meat-eating dinosaur had a rare horn.

For more information on these and other dinosaurs, check out Dinosaur National Monument's official website (www.nps.gov/dino/dinos.htm).

of shops. It's mostly famous for its proximity to **Dinosaur National Monument** (www.nps.gov/dino/index.htm), a sprawling area of incredible mountain hikes and 1,500 genuine dinosaur fossil bones on the Colorado-Utah border.

The monument is not the kind of place you can pass through on a side trip from Grand Junction or Moab. The **Dinosaur Quarry** is on the Utah side, about a 20-minute drive from the town of Dinosaur, and completely inaccessible during the winter. The Colorado side is mostly superb **hiking** and scenery, particularly trails like Echo Park Drive and the Canyon of Lodore, but the trailheads aren't immediately evident, and many visitors will need to spend some time talking to the monument's rangers.

◖ Dinosaur Quarry

The quarry is on the Utah side (Hwy. 149, seven miles north of Jensen, Utah, 435/781-7700, www.nps.gov/dino) and is perhaps best known as "the place with all the dinosaur bones." It began in 1909, when paleontologist Earl Douglass explored northeastern Utah,

came across thousands of bones, and shipped them to a Pittsburgh museum for display. Fascinated, President Woodrow Wilson named the site Dinosaur National Monument; within a few years, the National Park Service started work on the quarry. Today, more than 1,500 fossil bones are embedded in a rock layer on a wall of the quarry's Visitors Center; imprints of bones are visible throughout the quarry grounds. The bones belonged to 11 kinds of dinosaurs, roughly half of the species found in North America—stegosaurus, dryosaurus, allosaurus, camptosaurus, and others who lived roughly 150 million years ago, during the Jurassic Park era.

The Colorado side of Dinosaur National Monument has little to do with dinosaurs, but it's terrific for hiking, biking, and camping. Again, the trails aren't suitable for in-and-out side trips, but the monument offers many guided tours and information for bushwhacking—try **Journey Through Time,** a 62-mile Harpers Corner Road drive that hits numerous scenic overlooks on the Blue Mountain Plateau, Echo Park, and the Yampa Bench.

GRAND JUNCTION

Some hikes, drives, and bike rides, including Ruple Point Trail and the path to Echo Park, take all day and are completely inaccessible during bad weather. Another good tour—this one, you have to take yourself—is the 11-mile **Tour of the Tilted Rocks,** leading through extremely scenic areas and a few Native American history sites.

Accommodations

Neither Dinosaur nor its nearest town, Rangely, has much by way of cozy hotels, so consider staying in Grand Junction to the south or Craig to the east. Sleep-on-the-ground types should try **Green River Campground** (Cub Creek Rd., five miles east of Dinosaur Quarry, on the Utah side, 970/374-3000, www.nps.gov/dino), with almost 90 tent areas and plenty of shade—although during high tourism season it may be hard to find a spot. It's five miles from the Visitors Center, so the location is perfect for campers of all ages who want to sit through classes or seminars during their vacations.

Food

The **Massadona Tavern Steak House & RV Campground** (22927 E. U.S. 40, 20 miles east of Dinosaur, 970/374-2324, 11 A.M.–8 P.M. Mon.–Thurs., 11 A.M.–9 P.M. Fri.–Sat.) is one-stop shopping for many campers—the tavern has burgers and steaks (of course) and is a little hard to find.

B&B Family Restaurant (120 Brontosaurus Blvd., 970/374-2744, 7:30 A.M.–8 P.M. daily) is indicative of the entire town of Dinosaur—fun but run-down, with Flintstones-inspired Brontoburgers and Plateosaurus steaks. (As far as I know, the meat doesn't come from actual dinosaurs.)

INFORMATION

The **Town of Rangely** (209 E. Main St., 970/675-8476, www.rangely.com) has information about the town itself in addition to the dinosaur monument and other nearby activities.

As for Dinosaur, the Colorado side's **Visitors Center** (U.S.–40, two miles east of Dinosaur, 970/374-3000, 8 A.M.–4:30 P.M. daily Memorial Day–Labor Day, 8 A.M.–4:30 P.M. Mon.–Fri. Labor Day–Memorial Day, free) has knowledgeable employees who can help you navigate the hard-to-find trails, plus dinosaur souvenirs.

THE SAN JUAN MOUNTAINS

The northern Rocky Mountains get all the press in Colorado, but the San Juans, which provide the majestic backdrops for Telluride, Ouray, Silverton, Lake City, and Pagosa Springs, are worth the long and often harrowing drives southwest from Denver. The San Juans encompass about 12,000 square miles, or roughly one-eighth of the state, and are made of numerous "fourteener" peaks, such as Uncompahgre and Wetterhorn, just northeast of Ouray. They're part of a two-million-acre national forest filled with hiking trails and ski slopes, but they're more spread out and less compact than their northern-mountain neighbors. Every time I drive through the San Juans, en route to the Telluride Bluegrass Festival or an overnight in pretty Ridgway, I'm overwhelmed by the valleys, plains, small lakes, and red-and-yellow flat peaks. Certain parts have the look and feel of the Badlands in South Dakota, even though they're in a whole different world.

The San Juans, though, aren't all there is to southwest Colorado—Crested Butte is the northern tip of this region, and it has its own namesake mountain, a hulking, pyramid-shaped peak that provides some of the state's best (if most isolated) skiing. The Four Corners area, in the far southwest corner of the state, is so-called because you can touch Colorado, New Mexico, Arizona, and Utah at the same time. The area's mesa-and-canyon scenery rivals the chunks of Rocky Mountains in Aspen or Vail. The Black Canyon of the Gunnison National Park, with a 12-foot-thin stretch of river visible far down a mesa cliff, is at the edge

HIGHLIGHTS

◖ Redstone Castle: John Cleveland Osgood is the early-1900s coal-and-railroad magnate behind this 42-room mansion, which dominates a gem of a one-road tourist town south of Aspen and north of Crested Butte (page 211).

◖ Telluride Ski Resort: Two thousand-foot drops down the majestic San Juan Mountains, trails perfectly groomed for experts and beginners, and a free gondola make Telluride some of the best (and perhaps most underrated) skiing in the state (page 217).

◖ Bridal Veil Falls: With a funky 19th-century power station at the top, this tall waterfall is the first thing you notice upon driving into Telluride (page 218).

◖ Ouray Ice Park: Make sure your carabiners are tight when scrambling up these massive manmade ice cliffs on the edge of a historic mining town (page 227).

◖ Black Canyon of the Gunnison National Park: Hold tight to the railing as you stare from the North or South Rim straight down mesa cliffs into a 40-foot-wide river at the bottom; only the best kayakers paddle below (page 233).

◖ Durango & Silverton Narrow Gauge Railroad: The prettiest commute in Colorado involves a two-hour, 45-mile trip from Durango to Silverton (and back) via 1920s-era locomotives that once hauled ore out of the San Juans (page 239).

◖ Mesa Verde National Park: Perhaps the finest ghost town in the world, the large and scenic park is home to abandoned cliff dwellings from the A.D. 1200 civilization of Anasazi (page 244).

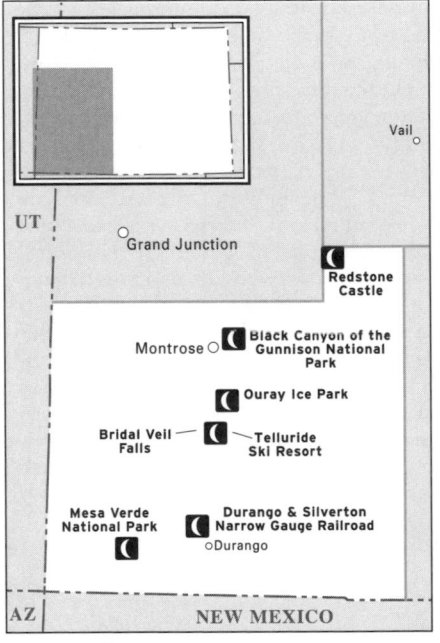

LOOK FOR ◖ TO FIND RECOMMENDED SIGHTS, ACTIVITIES, DINING, AND LODGING.

of a spectacular park area with several reservoirs, all open for fishing and boating.

Also fascinating is the area's history. Creede, in the eastern shadow of the San Juans, is where Jesse James's killer, Bob Ford, was shot and killed, and historic gold-and-silver-mining towns such as Ouray and Lake City are such serene tourist areas these days that it's easy to forget the violent mayhem that went on in the Old West. Four Corners, including Durango, Cortez, and Mesa Verde National Park, is filled

with elaborate Native American ruins—in some cases entire abandoned towns that have been carefully archaeologically preserved.

Finally, of course, there's skiing—the resorts in Telluride and Crested Butte are world-renowned, and the lesser-known hills near Durango and Pagosa Springs have the added advantage of being uncrowded. One tip: If you're driving south from Aspen, stop in tiny, touristy Redstone and have a picnic by the river.

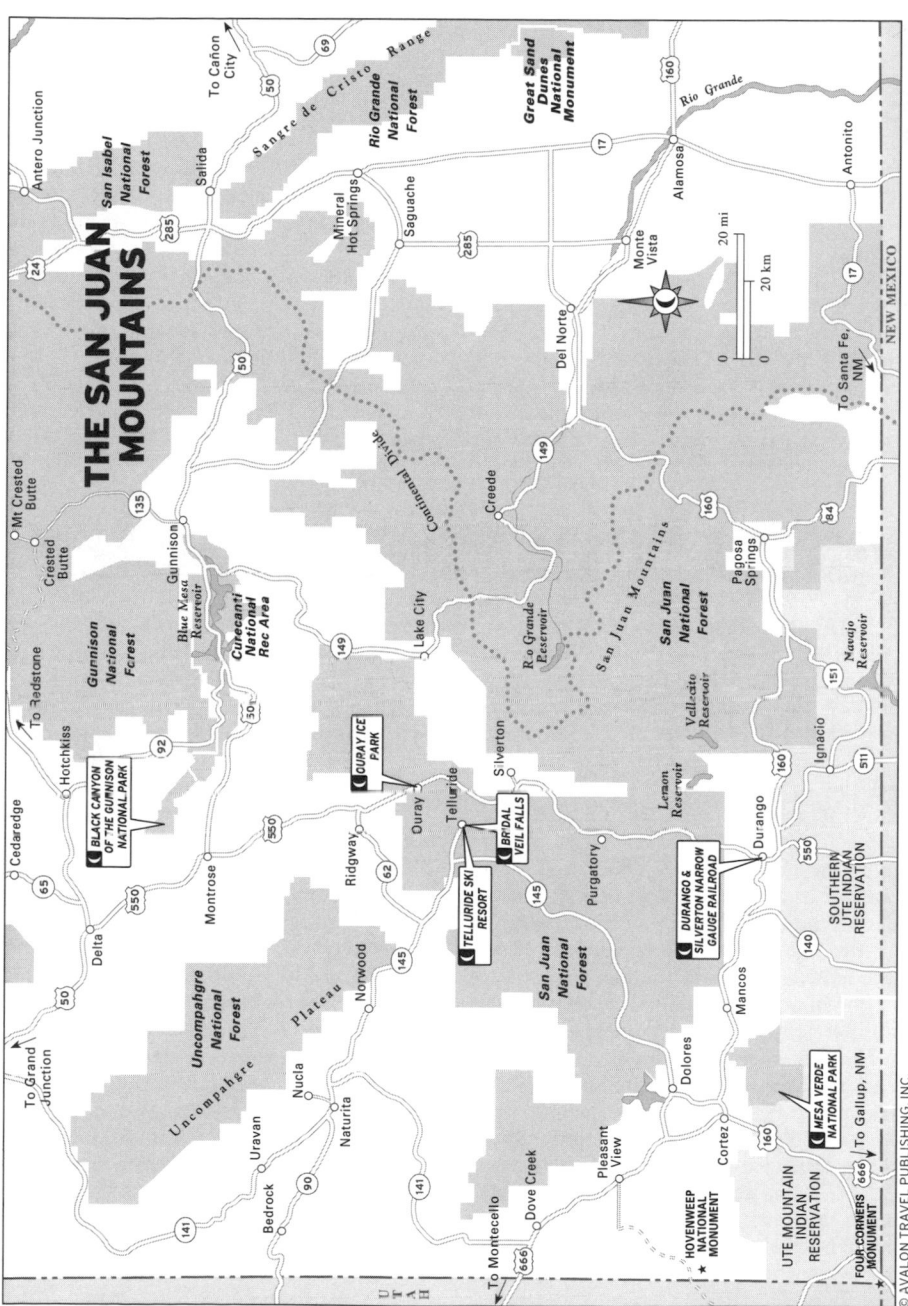

THE SAN JUAN MOUNTAINS

To Cañon City

69

50

Sangre de Cristo Range

Rio Grande National Forest

Great Sand Dunes National Monument

160

Rio Grande

17

Antero Junction

285

San Isabel National Forest

Salida

Mineral Hot Springs

Saguache

Alamosa

Monte Vista

Antonito

17

24

285

285

Del Norte

To Santa Fe, NM

NEW MEXICO

THE SAN JUAN MOUNTAINS

Mt Crested Butte

135

Crested Butte

Gunnison

149

Creede

San Juan Mountains

Pagosa Springs

160

84

20 mi

20 km

0   0

To Redstone

Gunnison National Forest

Blue Mesa Reservoir

Curecanti National Rec Area

Lake City

Rio Grande Reservoir

San Juan National Forest

151

Navajo Reservoir

Continental Divide

Hotchkiss

92

50

149

Silverton

Vallecito Reservoir

Ignacio

160

511

Cedaredge

BLACK CANYON OF THE GUNNISON NATIONAL PARK

OURAY ICE PARK

Lemon Reservoir

Durango

Southern Ute Indian Reservation

65

550

Montrose

550

Ridgway

Ouray

Telluride

BRIDAL VEIL FALLS

Purgatory

DURANGO & SILVERTON NARROW GAUGE RAILROAD

550

Delta

62

TELLURIDE SKI RESORT

145

140

50

Uncompahgre National Forest

Norwood

145

San Juan National Forest

Mancos

To Grand Junction

Plateau

Nucla

Uncompahgre

Naturita

Dolores

MESA VERDE NATIONAL PARK

To Gallup, NM

Bedrock

90

Cortez

160

Uravan

141

Dove Creek

Pleasant View

Ute Mountain Indian Reservation

666

141

To Montecello

666

HOVENWEEP NATIONAL MONUMENT

FOUR CORNERS MONUMENT

UTAH

To Santa Fe, NM

© AVALON TRAVEL PUBLISHING, INC.

PLANNING YOUR TIME

The small airports of Durango, Montrose, and Gunnison are mostly reliable, but they serve small carriers, and in nasty weather conditions it's probably best to fly into Denver International Airport. From Denver, Telluride is roughly a six-hour drive by car—the most direct route is U.S. 285 southwest to tiny Poncha Springs, then west on the super-scenic U.S. 50, which passes Monarch Pass, the Continental Divide, pretty Blue Mesa Reservoir, and the hills and valleys of Curecanti National Recreation Area (Black Canyon of the Gunnison National Park is just a short drive up Highway 347). From Montrose, go south on U.S. 550 through Ridgway and Ouray and follow the signs to Telluride.

To get to Crested Butte, in the summer, the fastest and easiest route is I-70 west to Glenwood Springs, then south on Highways 82 and 135, the last leg of which becomes bumpy and difficult. You'll cross Kebler Pass, although it's closed in the winter, which makes Crested Butte the most isolated major ski resort in the state—to get there from Denver, the indirect route of U.S. 285 south to U.S. 50 west to Highway 135 north is one of the few good options. These are the main highlights of southwest Colorado, although pit-stop towns such as Pagosa Springs (east of Durango), Gunnison (south of Crested Butte), Cortez (near the Four Corners, west of Durango), and Redstone (along Highway 82 en route to Crested Butte) have their charms as well.

Crested Butte and Vicinity

"The last great ski town," as locals call it, is a relaxed little historic area that lionizes its gold-mining years just as hard-partiers are streaming down the slopes in kilts, pink-bunny costumes, or no clothes at all. It's one of Colorado's most beloved ski resorts, but it's hard to get to, especially when ski conditions are best—heavy snowfall can close Kebler Pass, along Highway 135, 110 miles south of Aspen, forcing travelers to use the longer, unpaved Highway 82 or 133 or other tricky roads. Such woodsy seclusion has hit the resort hard in recent years; while Crested Butte real-estate sales were up 127 percent in 2004, ski traffic was down.

But in what *Ski* magazine calls "a $50 million gamble," Tim and Diane Mueller, turnaround specialists who own ski areas in Okemo, Vermont, and Mount Sunapee, New Hampshire, bought the resort in late 2003 and have been building condos and boosting Butte skiing ever since.

Like Aspen and Telluride, Crested Butte has turned into a bit of a rich person's playground over the past few years, and its gap between homeowners and ski bums stands to get wider with the Muellers' high-class upgrades.

(Crested Butte actually refers to two separate areas, connected by shuttle bus—the pastel-colored, Victorian-lined, 1880s mountain town that has the feel of a funkier Breckenridge or Steamboat Springs, and the 40-plus-year-old ski resort two miles uphill that's officially known as Mount Crested Butte.)

The town's personality remains far different from hoity-toity Aspen and hippie-swamped Telluride—in addition to naked skiers, Crested Butte is a magnet for extreme sports and mountain bikers. The resort plays host to the **Winter X Games,** the **U.S. Extreme Freeskiing Championships,** and the **U.S. Extreme Boarderfest,** among others, and even in a state renowned for its mountain biking, Crested Butte is consistently where all the cyclists go. You can ride up Pearl Pass, 40 miles up to a 12,700-foot elevation, on a Saturday, and visit the Mountain Bike Hall of Fame & Museum on a Sunday. Just bring lots of water.

HISTORY

When miners discovered $350,000 worth of gold in Washington Gulch, Crested Butte

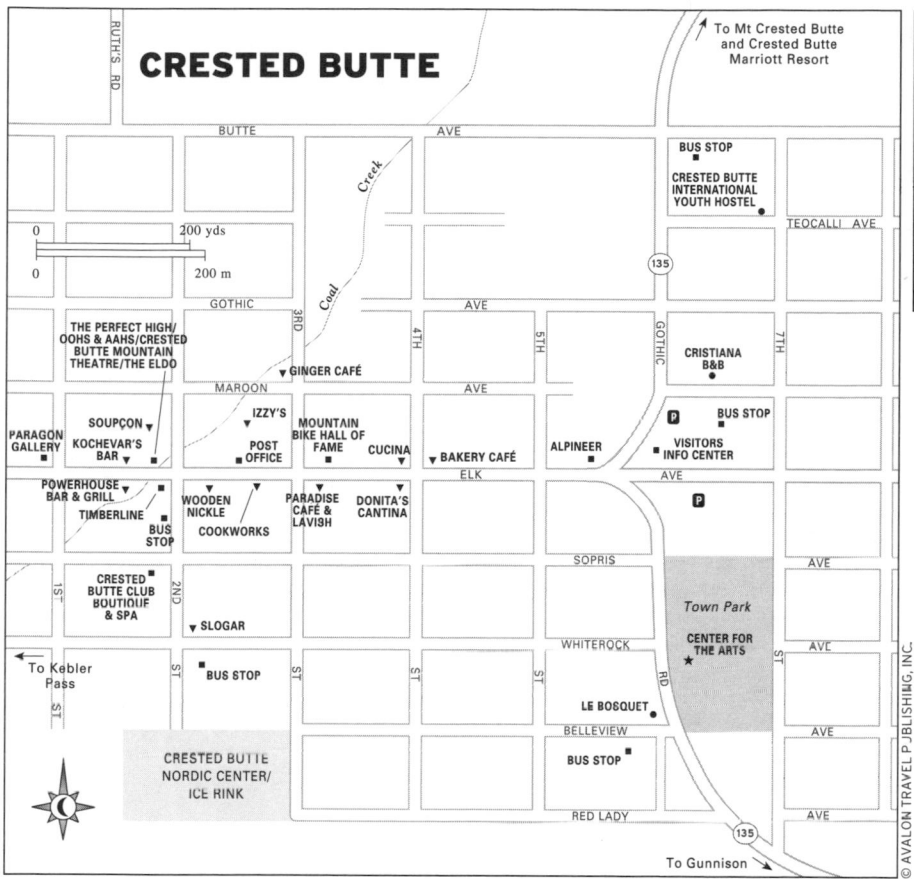

shifted from a roaming ground for Utes, explorers, and fur traders to a key stopover for frantic wealth-seekers. This was in the 1860s, and areas such as Washington and Armstrong Gulches, Crystal River, and Gold Creek produced millions of dollars for gold-panners. Prosperity led to colonization: In 1874, Sylvester Richardson founded the Gunnison agricultural colony, which evolved into Gunnison County, a big ranching area.

The gold boom led to a silver boom in the 1870s and 1880s, and 25,000–40,000 people streamed into town, followed by two narrow-gauge railroads and mining camps of some 3,500 people each. The silver industry busted in 1893, but Crested Butte and its mountain-valley neighbor, Gunnison, survived into the 1950s thanks to their resources of cows and coal. The Mount Crested Butte ski area opened in the early 1960s, ensuring the town would thrive for another four decades, even without gold and silver.

SIGHTS

The town of Crested Butte is about three miles away from the mountain and resort village, and it's worth visiting, particularly in the summer, when the crowds aren't quite so intense. The village is a lovingly preserved National Historic District of colorful Victorian buildings, some of which have retained their identities as saloons and banks. Wandering downtown is a great way to kill a lazy summer Saturday, and the large park along 6th Street often has live music and kids' events.

The best part of the **Mountain Bike Hall of Fame & Museum** (331 Elk Ave., 800/454-4505, www.mtnbikehalloffame.com/home.cfm, 10 A.M.–6 P.M. daily Sept.–Oct. and Dec.–April, 10 A.M.–8 P.M. daily mid-June–Aug., closed Nov. and May, $3) is the old photos showing how the bikes themselves have evolved—from the rubber hose that veterinary surgeon John B. Dunlop attached to his son's bike in 1887 to the V-shaped handlebars of the 1974 Cupertino riders to the sleeker, more engineered rides of today. Located inside the free **Crested Butte Mountain Heritage Museum,** the $3-donation-per-entry Mountain Bike section is as important to cyclists as Vail's Colorado Ski Museum is to downhillers.

SPORTS AND RECREATION
Downhill Skiing

Although 12,162-foot-high **Crested Butte Mountain Resort** (12 Snowmass Rd., 800/810-7669, www.skicb.com) has allowed itself to get a little run-down in recent years, pushing ski traffic to other resorts, its new owners are aggressively renovating the place—and emphasizing beginner and intermediate runs, although the area is famous for its intimidating peaks, advanced and expert terrain, and friendliness toward snowboarders and extreme-sports aficionados. A new base village, Mountaineer Square, is in the works, with 93 planned residences, a spa, and a convention center, and co-owner Tim Mueller tells *Ski:* "There's been an overemphasis on the extreme. We also have good beginner and intermediate terrain. Crested Butte should be marketed more as a family place."

But first, something for the experienced thrill-riders: Extreme Limits, 583 acres of deliberately ungroomed, incredibly steep trails with trees that seem to block every turn. And

Mount Crested Butte is the site of many outdoor activities.

that's just the bowls that are open to the public. For events such as the U.S. Extreme Freeskiing Championships (in early March), mountain officials open routes like The Hourglass and Catch and Release, filled with sharp rocks and unexpected twists. Most of the double-diamond runs are at the top—take the Twister Lift to the High Lift.

For skiers who prefer more humane terrain, the Keystone lift gives access to gentle runs such as Poverty Gulch and Mineral Point; toward the bottom, Houston is easy to find and ride for kids. Both the Paradise and Teocalli lifts lead to intermediate runs—the former with long chutes like Forest Queen and Canaan leading to the East River area, the latter into the half-pipe. Overall, the resort's 1,058 acres of ski trails break down to 15 percent for beginners, 44 percent intermediate, and 41 percent advanced and expert.

Crested Butte's **Ski & Snowboard School** (Gothic Center, 970/349-2259 or 800/600-7349, www.skicb.com) gives lessons for all ages but is especially good for kids from 3 to 16. The resort has on-site ski rental at the Gothic Center, 888/280-5728, but **Crested Butte Ski & Bike Shop** (35 Emmons Loop Rd., 800/301-9169, www.crestedbuttesports.com) is also a good option.

Cross-Country Skiing

With gigantic wilderness areas sprawled in every direction—Maroon Bells–Snowmass, Raggeds, and Collegiate Peaks—Crested Butte's backcountry skiing opportunities are just about unlimited if you're careful. Among them: **Slate River Gulch,** about 4.5 miles from the Gothic Road exit off Highway 135, leading 2 miles from Nicholson Lake (at 8,920 feet) to Oh-Be-Joyful (9,100 feet); **Washington Gulch,** about 2.6 miles from the same Gothic Road exit, which passes empty valleys and tree-filled mountaintops, including Anthracite Mesa, White Rock Mountain, and the breathtaking Snodgrass Mountain; and **Ditch Road,** south of town on Highway 135, off Forest Road 738 near Brush Creek Road, a less-strenuous route near some pretty ranch country. Note that

avalanches aren't common, but they've been known to happen in these parts. The **Alpineer** (419 6th St., 970/349-5210 or 800/847-0244, www.alpineer.com) rents equipment and can answer most questions about weather conditions and routes.

The **Crested Butte Nordic Center** (620 2nd St., 970/349-1707, www.cbnordic.org) maintains a 15- to 20-mile network of groomed tracks that go through the town's historic area, along the East River, and through forests and recreation paths. It also sponsors guided tours, nighttime ski parties, and a 4-mile hike to the Forest Queen Hut in Gothic. You can rent equipment here, too.

Hut-to-hut skiing isn't as formal here as it is, say, in Telluride or Aspen, but **Adventures to the Edge** (88 Aspen Ln., 970/349-5219) leads trips to the Elkton Huts, above Gothic Mountain and Elkton Ridge, a path that includes a steep drop into a ravine and a difficult climb. **Crested Butte Mountain Guides** (970/349-5430, www.crestedbutteguides.com) does guided 3-mile trips to the Forest Queen Hut in nearby Gothic, and the route is far easier, with incredible views of the Maroon Bells–Snowmass Wilderness and Gothic Mountain.

Hiking

It's easy to find hiking in Crested Butte: Return to the aforementioned backcountry-skiing trails in the summer, and start walking. And there are tons of trails beyond that, from the **Upper Loop Trail,** an easy 3.4-mile walk southeast of Mt. Crested Butte on Hunter Hill Road, through aspens and meadows, to the difficult-but-beautiful **Crested Butte Summit Trail,** which begins at the resort visitors' parking area and leads through tall trees and choppy tundra. **Judd Falls** goes two miles from the Gothic Campground, on the north side of town, and the Silver Queen chairlift provides access to numerous trails filled with skiers and 'boarders during the winter.

And watch for wildflowers, particularly in mid-July, when the **Crested Butte Wildflower Festival** (409 2nd St., 970/349-2571, www.crestedbuttewildflowerfestival.com) guides more than 100 different hikes throughout the area, for $10–35 each—botanists are generally the leaders, and the slots tend to fill up quickly.

Mountain Biking

Some say Crested Butte tinkerers came up with the original mountain bike, and while that's impossible to verify, it's easy to observe the unusually high bike-to-car ratio and conclude that this is the mountain-biking capital of the world, or at least Colorado. Rides are everywhere. On a recent summer driving trip down Road 12, over Kebler Pass—which my 3-year-old daughter nicknamed the "Bumpy Cow Road" due to its washboard bumps and cows grazing in the middle of the dirt road—my family passed at least half a dozen huffing-and-puffing cyclists. It's a challenging, spectacular ride, if you're in shape.

Perhaps the most famous local ride is **Pearl Pass,** site of the annual "Klunker Tour" beginning in 1976, when a group of crazed riders took makeshift bikes of fat tires, pedals, a chain, and handlebars up this 40-mile pass from Crested Butte to Aspen. The trail continues to attract cyclists by the dozen—albeit with more sophisticated rides—and most even make it, although the top altitude of 12,700 feet is nothing to take lightly. It's open to cars, too.

Check out the **Mountain Bike Hall of Fame**'s website (www.mtnbikehalloffame.com/crestedbutte.cfm) for descriptions of more than a dozen bike trails, including **Deer Creek,** a steep, almost-18-mile ride beginning in nearby Gothic and weaving through meadows and cow paths straight into Mt. Crested Butte, and the wildflower-filled **Teocalli Ridge,** which begins 2 miles south of Crested Butte, on Brush Creek Road, and climbs up Teocalli Mountain into Middle Brush Creek.

Many local hotels rent bikes, as does **Crested Butte Sports & Ski** (35 Emmons Loop Rd., 970/349-7516, www.crestedbuttesports.com) and the **Alpineer** (419 6th St., 970/349-5210 or 800/847-0244, www.alpineer.com). **Crested Butte Mountain Guides** (970/349-5430, www.crestedbutteguides.com) offers guided tours (some from vans) to trails long and short, easy and hard. And for mountain-biking events, you can't beat late June's **Fat Tire Bike Week** (800/545-4505, www.ftbw.com), which is all about the riding. And the tricks. And the partying.

Fishing

With trout wiggling through the nearby Taylor, Gunnison, and East Rivers, Crested Butte is a surprisingly excellent place for fly-fishing. For reports on conditions and other basic information, visit the Gunnison-Crested Butte Vacations website (www.gunnisoncrestedbutte.com); for equipment, maps, and tour guides, **Three Rivers Resort & Outfitting** (130 County Rd. 742, Almont, 888/761-3474, www.3riversoutfitting.com) is one of several reliable (and knowledgeable) local shops.

Golf

The centerpiece of **The Club at Crested Butte** (385 Country Club Dr., 970/349-6127,

© MELISSA KNOPPER

A common sight along the "Bumpy Cow Road" en route to Crested Butte.

www.theclubatcrestedbutte.com) is a Robert Trent Jones Jr.–designed course—but it also has tennis courts, a swimming pool, a spa, and a high-class restaurant. If you can afford to be a member, you can't beat the views.

ENTERTAINMENT AND EVENTS

Most of the town's numerous outdoor festivals—including the late-July **Crested Butte Music Festival,** the **Tour de Forks** in July and August, and a weekly film series—are arranged through the **Crested Butte Center for the Arts** (606 6th St., 970/349-7487, www.crestedbuttearts.org). The center puts on art exhibits, plays, concerts, and speakers.

The nonprofit **Crested Butte Mountain Theatre** (403 2nd St., 970/349-0366, www.cbmountaintheatre.org) puts on dramas, musicals, and comedies all year, from *Footloose* to *Much Ado About Nothing.*

A number of bars have lively happy hours, including **Kochevar's** (127 Elk Ave., 970/349-6745) and the **Wooden Nickel** (222 Elk Ave., 970/349-6350) steakhouse. For live music on top of cheap booze, **The Eldo** (215 Elk Ave., 970/349-6125) is a microbrewery that snags many of the reggae, bluegrass, folk, and jam bands when they come through town; the sign out front says, "A sunny place for shady people." Over in the mountain village, the **Butte 66 BBQ Roadhouse** (Mt. Crested Butte, 800/544-8448) has a built-in stage for live music (as well as weddings) and is where many skiers begin their partying before shambling closer to town as the night goes on.

SHOPPING

Crested Butte's shopping is on par with Breckenridge or Steamboat Springs—lots of little shops, few of them practical, most geared toward tourists. **Cookworks** (341 Elk Ave., 970/349-7398 or 800/765-9511, www.cookworks.com) is an exception, selling sturdy steel kitchen appliances and cookware. The **Paragon Gallery** (132 Elk Ave., 970/349-6484) is a local artists' co-op that displays Jim

P. Garrison's photography, Bren Corn's jittery, colorful paintings of people, and others.

On the clothing front, **Lavish** (318 Elk Ave., 970/349-1077, www.lavishcb.com) stocks funky, high-end stuff for women—Skaagen watches, Maxx handbags, Hillary Druxman jewelry, and the like. **The Perfect High** (234 Elk Ave., 970/349-0236) sells colorful T-shirts, tank tops, sweatpants, and other hipster clothing for people into jogging, yoga, and lounging around the house eating ice cream. **Oohs & Aahs** (207 Elk Ave., 970/349-0303) specializes in large antique furniture—all very comfortable—and various western knickknacks.

ACCOMMODATIONS
Under $100

The family-owned **Nordic Inn** (14 Treasury Rd., 970/349 5542 or 800/542-7669, www.nordicinncb.com, $93–116) is a homey, European-style, ski-village lodge with large rooms and an outdoor hot tub. The room rates reflect a deliberate lack of frills.

The **Cristiana Guesthaus** (621 Maroon Ave., 800/824-7899, www.cristianaguesthaus.com, $75–90) is the same idea as the Nordic Inn—family-owned, small, wooden, European-style, strategic location down the street from the ski-resort shuttle—but a step down in elegance. It does have a sundeck, sauna, large lobby fireplace, and free continental breakfast.

$100-150

The **Grand Lodge Resort & Suites** (6 Emmons Loop, 888/823-4446, www.grandlodgecrestedbutte.com, $99–209) is perhaps the easiest place in town to find a room during heavy season, with 246 rooms, including 105 suites. When my family visited, we found the rooms to be large and comfortable, the staff friendly, and the views gorgeous, but it was under construction, and the parking lot outside our window was a little noisy.

Eight miles south of town, the **Pioneer Guest Cabins** (Cement Creek Rd., 970/349-5517, $115–155) is a collection of eight streamside, 1930s-era log cabins in Gunnison

National Forest. The smartly decorated cabins use the soothing wood floors and staircases to their advantage, and while staying in one of the four historic cottages is a little like camping in the woods, the four mountain cabins are more luxurious than rustic.

Over $200

A Marriott until 2001, **Club Med Crested Butte** (Mt. Crested Butte, 970/349-8700 or 800/258-2633, www.clubmed.com, $240, closed summers) recently underwent a $6 million renovation—adding a fitness center, whirlpool, on-site masseuse, and upgrades to all 256 rooms. With its all-inclusive family rates and amenities like puppet shows and pint-sized ski lessons, the lodge-and-village's marketing thrust is families, families, families. But even if you don't have kids, the rates (for what you get) and location are pretty good.

Built in 1886, the eight-room **❰ Crested Butte Club Boutique & Spa** (512 2nd St., 970/349-6655 or 800/815-2582, www.crestedbutteclub.com, $200–320) has been a bar, brothel, meeting place for the Knights of the Paythian (a fraternal organization for English and Scottish miners), a wedding hall, National Science Academy headquarters, and finally, in 1988, a hotel—and it still has the original hand-carved bar. It doesn't look like much from the outside—just a white, boxy, two-tiered building—but inside its chandeliers, antiques, wooden staircase, and pink-walled spa make you forget the words "Club Med."

As with most Colorado ski towns, condominiums are often more affordable than hotels—especially if you want to do your own cooking or stay with a large group. The listings at the community website **Visit Crested Butte** (www.visitcrestedbutte.com/condominiums) are up-to-date and reliable.

FOOD
Snacks, Cafés, and Breakfast

In business since the late 1980s, **Paradise Café** (303 Elk Ave., 970/349-6233, 7–11 A.M. daily) specializes in standard breakfast dishes—burritos, skillets, pancakes, French toast, and so forth. Its lunchtime deli sandwiches, burgers, and soups are almost as captivating. Serving excellent deli sandwiches on homemade bread, **Izzy's** (Elk Ave., behind the post office, 970/349-5630, 7 A.M.–2 P.M. daily) is new but becoming well known for its dessert crepes, homemade bagels, muffins, and cookies.

During summers, **Crepe-a-Gogo** (Elk Ave., 970/275-4806, varying hours) serves "French pancakes," from chocolate-and-strawberry to ham-and-egg—out of a small stand in the middle of town.

Casual

In an 1882 building that ran as a saloon during the coal-mining boom, the refurbished **Slogar** (2nd St. and Whiterock St., 970/349-5765, 5–9 P.M. daily) is a local comfort-food fixture—skillet-fried chicken, biscuits, cole slaw, mashed potatoes, and steaks.

The **Buffalo Grille & Saloon** (435 6th St., 970/349-9699, 6–10 P.M. daily) has buffalo everything—steak, ribs, tenderloin—and

The Ginger Café is a good place to grab a quick bite.

© STEVE KNOPPER

beef as well. Not to mention saltimbocca deer medallions.

Cucina (425 Elk Ave., 970/349-7174, 8 A.M.–6 P.M. Mon.–Fri., 8 A.M.–4 P.M. Sat.–Sun.) has a small dining porch inside its pink, barn-like building, but most locals know its strength is in mobility. The garlic-and-herb-roasted chicken, lamb stew, twice-baked potatoes, and various homemade soups, cookies, and cakes are all available in box-lunch form.

Don't let the hideous pink-and-aqua building scare you off: **Donita's Cantina** (330 Elk Ave., 970/349-6674, 5 P.M.–varying closing times, daily) is a loud and usually packed Mexican restaurant that has great salsa, fajitas, and $2 margaritas.

The light-green **Ginger Café** (311 3rd Ave., 970/349-7291, 11 A.M.–10 P.M. daily) has the look of a tiny, one-room Asian restaurant, but many of its dishes have a surprising Indian feel—I had a great spicy mixture of grilled chicken, peppers, and onions.

Upscale

At the base of the Twister chairlift—an elevation of about 10,500 feet—the **Ice Bar & Restaurant** (800/544-8448, 9 A.M.–4 P.M. daily, winters only) is an intimate après-ski eatery that serves decent high-end dishes like blue-corn chiles rellenos stuffed with mesquite-smoked rainbow trout. The outdoor deck is the best drinking spot on the mountain. Other winter-only restaurants on the mountain include the **Paradise Warming House** (near the Keystone lift) and the **Butte 66 BBQ Roadhouse** (next to the Red Lady Express lift).

Brooklyn-born chef Scott Greene may have picked a corny pun name for the log-cabin **Soupçon** (127A Elk Ave., 970/349-5448, www.soupconrestaurant.com, dinners at 6 and 8:15 P.M., closing times vary nightly), but he did cook with Charlie Trotter in Chicago, so diners should give him a pass. Other reasons to do so: pistachio-crusted pheasant breast ($28), a marinated Sonoma quail entrée ($11), and really classy dishes like foie gras and frog legs.

With a green facade that resembles a New York City streetside bistro, **Timberline** (201

Elk Ave., 970/349-9831, 5:30–10 P.M. daily) has three dining areas—including a super-elegant wine cellar—and a high-class menu and wine list. The menu is straight-up fish, beef, and poultry, but the combinations are often unexpected, such as a salmon dish with chanterelle-mushroom sauce.

Le Bosquet (6th and Belleview, 970/349-5808, 5:30–9 P.M. daily) is a French-tinged family restaurant that has operated in Crested Butte since 1976—with nothing extreme on the menu, just rack of lamb, hazelnut chicken, salads, soups, and the like.

INFORMATION

The **Crested Butte Mountain Resort** (12 Snowmass Rd., 800/810-7669, www.skicb.com) maintains weather reports, ski conditions, and a trove of dining, lodging, and nightlife information on its website; the phone operators are fairly helpful, too. Also informative is the **Gunnison-Crested Butte Tourism Association** (221 N. Wisconsin, Gunnison, 970/641-7992, www.gunnisoncrestedbutte.com), **Visit Crested Butte** (www.visitcrestedbutte.com), and the **Crested Butte-Mt. Crested Butte Chamber of Commerce** (970/349-6438, www.crestedbuttechamber.com). The local paper is the *Crested Butte News* (www.crestedbuttenews.com), and the local weekly is the *Crested Butte Weekly* (www.cbweekly.com).

The **Gunnison Country Chamber of Commerce** (500 E. Tomichi Ave., 970/641-1501, www.visitgunnison.com) focuses on Gunnison but has plenty of detail about Crested Butte, as well.

Redstone's official community website is at www.redstonecolorado.com; its community association (303 Redstone Blvd.) has no phone number.

GETTING THERE AND AROUND

Crested Butte is one of the more difficult ski resorts to reach in Colorado, as the easiest driving route—over Kebler Pass Road, south from Aspen along Highway 135—is closed after the first fall snowstorm. That leaves the southern entrance into town—coming in from the opposite direction, north on Highway 135. This approach adds at least an hour, especially in snowy weather, as Denver drivers will have to take U.S. 285 (rather than the much faster I-70), then head west on U.S. 50. No matter how Crested Butte residents try to spin it, the town is a huge pain to reach during ski season.

The aforementioned winter realities aside, the easiest way to get to Crested Butte from out of state remains flying into Denver International Airport, renting a car (or taking a shuttle), and driving in. But connecting flights from Denver to **Gunnison-Crested Butte Regional Airport** (711 W. Rio Grande Ave., Gunnison, 970/641-2304), including United Express and other major carriers, are convenient much of the year.

The free **Crested Butte Town Shuttle** (970/349-7318, 7 A.M.–midnight daily) runs between the town, ski resort, and various condominium locations all day and most of the night.

REDSTONE

Built as a coal-mining area in the late 1800s, serving the regional railroads, Redstone has since transformed into a charming little artist-and-tourist hot spot with a beatific park next to the Crystal River. The town is basically one long block, Redstone Boulevard, with the tourist-trap castle and historic inn on one end and a campground on the other. The boulevard runs along the river, and quaint structures like the one-room museum, ice cream-selling general store, and Highline Foot Bridge are at the center of town.

Sights

You're definitely in Redstone once you see the cave-like **Coke Ovens** on the west side of Highway 133. The Colorado Fuel and Iron Co.'s John Cleveland Osgood constructed these large, beehive, pod-structures in the 1890s, which gave him the ingredients for the Crystal River Railroad, transporting the coke from Carbondale to Pueblo. This area boomed in the mining years, but neither the

The Coke Ovens outside of Redstone were used for coal mining in the late 1800s.

© STEVE KNOPPER

ovens nor the railroad have been in business here for decades.

Once Colorado's third-largest industrial town, **Marble** (www.marblecolorado.org) is today a ghost town about 17 miles south of Aspen, where workers once extracted precious building materials from the Colorado Yule Marble Quarry and sent them to the Lincoln Memorial, in Washington, D.C., and elsewhere. After the **Crystal Mill** closed in the mid-20th century, the workers took off, even though the mill still stands (and is photographed frequently) about eight miles east of the old town, accessible only via four-wheel-drive vehicle. Today, Marble is a quiet and picturesque area amid numerous hiking trails, rivers, and some of the best Rocky Mountain scenery in the state.

At the center of Redstone is the **Redstone Museum,** a one-room log cabin that has no phone number or even staff members, but includes some artifacts in glass cases—like a Redstone Band bass drum, 20th century letters, and silverware and plates from the old Big Horn Inn.

⚑ Redstone Castle

John C. Osgood built this 42-room mansion (58 Redstone Blvd., 970/963-2526, www.redstoneinn.com, call for tour times) for $2.5 million in 1902. Known as Cleveholm Manor at the time, it was one of the most lavish and beautiful estates in the state, and his list of celebrity guests included Teddy Roosevelt, John D. Rockefeller, and Buffalo Bill. It sits on 150 acres, with red roofs on all the towers, as well as a carriage house, barn, and other buildings—inside the castle itself are high-class touches (even for today) such as Persian rugs and Tiffany lamps. But the castle's latest chapter is a sad one: The Internal Revenue Service seized the property in March 2003 after its owners bought the property using money from a fraudulent investor-fraud scheme worth millions of dollars. It went up for auction in 2005, and for now, the nearby Redstone Inn manages the property; be sure to call first before visiting, as it may not open in 2006.

Sports and Recreation

There's no downhill skiing area in Redstone—you'll have to hit Crested Butte, Aspen, or Snowmass for that—but Nordic skiing is available via the **Ute Meadows Nordic Center** (2880 County Rd. 3, Marble, 970/963-5513 or 888/883-6323, www.utemeadows.com/nordic.htm), which maintains 10 miles of groomed trails through the breathtaking Crystal River Valley. The shop on the premises rents equipment, including skis and snowshoes.

Accommodations

Another Osgood construction, the ⚑ **Redstone Inn** (82 Redstone Blvd., 970/963-2526 or 800/748-2524, www.redstoneinn.com, $50–145) was originally a 20-room building that housed workers in the local coal mines and railroads. After Osgood lost his company in a stock war and the mines and ovens closed, he returned, a chastened man, and spent the rest of his life renovating this property. Today, the red-roofed inn has the elaborate Old West charm of the Hotel Colorado in nearby Glenwood Springs—there's a first-floor dining room overlooking a pool, a stately wooden staircase, chandeliers and period wallpaper, and friendly employees.

Over in Marble, the primary hotel is the **Ute Meadows Inn Bed and Breakfast** (2880 County Rd. 3, Marble, 970/963-5513 or 888/883-6323, www.utemeadows.com, $139), which is below a hill and next to the Crystal River; a river-rock fireplace adds to the inn's rustic, secluded ambience.

Food

The Redstone General Store at the center of town sells snacks and ice cream to go with expensive gas, but aside from that and **Redstone Pizza** (167 Redstone Blvd., 970/704-9995, 5–9:30 P.M. Mon.–Wed., 11:30 A.M.–9:30 P.M. Thurs.–Sun.), it's hard to find a decent meal on Redstone Boulevard. Best to stock up in nearby Carbondale, a small, suburban-leaning mountain town about 20 miles north, or better yet, go all the way to Aspen or Crested Butte.

Shopping

One thing Redstone has is lots of galleries and knickknack shops. My daughter loved the teddy bear-filled **Wild Horse Enterprises** (0306 Redstone Blvd., 970/963-8100), a friendly tourist-type store filled with jewelry, antiques, and scratched musical records (I picked up a 1950s gem called *Music for Private Eyes,* by somebody named Ralph Marterie and his Marlboro Men).

GUNNISON

If a helicopter dropped you into the center of Gunnison, you might wonder why anybody visits this 5,300-resident town at all. Aside from a few nice shops, a decent arts-and-theater center, a small college, and a few homey places to eat breakfast and lunch, there's really nothing here. But drive (or bike) a few miles in any direction and you'll see why so many people visit this town—it's less than 30 miles south of Crested Butte, just east of the breathtaking Curecanti National Recreation Area, and at the intersection of the Gunnison River

and Tomichi Creek. As a result, tourists flood the local Comfort Inn and other chains.

In nice weather, plan to fight for hotel space and wait in line for Sunday-morning breakfast, as hunters, fishers, cyclists, and other outdoorspeople have long since realized this is a far cheaper alternative to staying in Crested Butte or Telluride. Other than that, Gunnison is basically a small, pleasant ranching town where the Utes hunted and fished more than 150 years ago. Its most obvious landmark is a giant white "W" (for the local Western State College) on the side of Tenderfoot Mountain, a chunk of hill overlooking the city to the east.

Sights

Although it looks a little ramshackle from the outside, the **Pioneer Museum** (U.S. 50 and S. Adams St., 970/641-4530, 9 A.M.–5 P.M. Mon.–Sat., 1–5 P.M. Sun., $7) is a well-maintained and surprisingly elaborate complex of 1800s buildings and artifacts, including a bright yellow narrow-gauge train engine, an original post office, and various arrowheads,

Blue Mesa Reservoir

© STEVE KNOPPER

dolls, and toys. Ask for directions to **Aberdeen Quarry,** on Beaver Creek a few miles south of town, which supplied granite for the Colorado State Capitol building.

Curecanti National Recreation Area

The first time I took U.S. 285 to U.S. 50 from Denver to Telluride—I had driven I-70 on previous trips—I was unprepared for the majesty of Curecanti National Recreation Area (102 Elk Creek, between Gunnison and Montrose on U.S. 50, 970/641-2337), a collection of three dark-blue reservoirs underneath yellow-and-pink mesas and canyons that rival South Dakota's Badlands. In addition to being a massive fishery of kokanee salmon, the 26-mile-long **Blue Mesa Reservoir** is the largest body of water in the state, and nearby Morrow Point and Crystal Reservoirs aren't bad either.

Sports and Recreation

The Blue Mesa's **Elk Creek Marina** (off the reservoir, 15 miles west of Gunnison, 970/641-0707 or 970/641-5387, www.whresorts.com, May–Sept.) rents various kinds of boats, sells fish-and-tackle equipment and provides guides for fishing tours; there's also a restaurant here called Pappy's. Or do as I did—pull over on one of U.S. 50's side roads overlooking the reservoir and leisurely eat a picnic lunch.

The **Cimarron Visitors Center** (off U.S. 50, about 20 miles east of Montrose, 970/249-4074) is within Curecanti park, and it has the usual information—as well as some fancy old trains and railroad exhibits.

The **Dos Rios Golf Club** (501 Camino Del Rio, 970/641-1482), about a mile and a half west of Gunnison on U.S. 50, has 18 holes and a restaurant.

Entertainment

The **Gunnison Arts Center** (102 S. Main St., 970/641-4029) is a vibrant community center with three gallery spaces, a theater for community and children's productions and the occasional movie, plus space for dance, art, quilting, and book-appreciation classes. The center also presents a free summer "Sundays at Seven" concert in the park a few blocks away.

Shopping

The shopping in Gunnison is on the quirky side, with the occasional toy and book store around the corner from **Traders Rendezvous** (516 W. Tomichi Ave., 970/641-5077), an everything-goes type of place that spreads its elk heads and moose rugs all over the sidewalk on sunny summer mornings. Artier and more seasonal is **Let's Go Country** (234 N. Main St., 970/641-1638), which sells pottery, candles, and various holiday accoutrements.

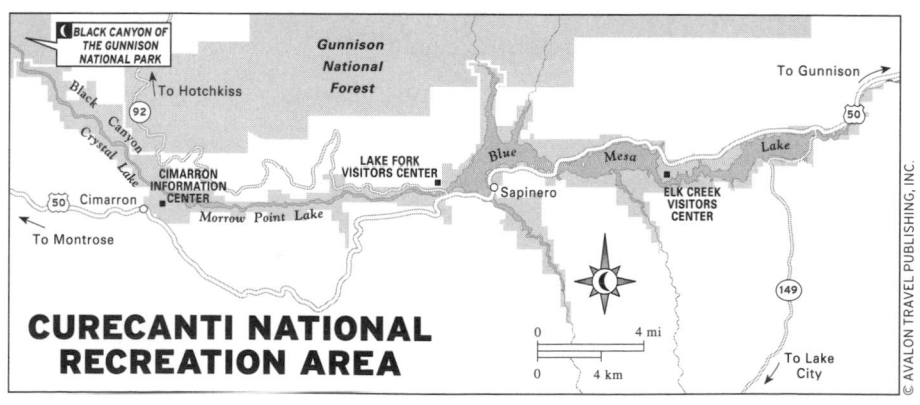

CURECANTI NATIONAL RECREATION AREA

BLACK CANYON OF THE GUNNISON NATIONAL PARK

To Hotchkiss

Gunnison National Forest

To Gunnison

92

Black Canyon

Crystal Lake

CIMARRON INFORMATION CENTER

Cimarron

50

To Montrose

Morrow Point Lake

LAKE FORK VISITORS CENTER

Blue

Mesa

Sapinero

ELK CREEK VISITORS CENTER

Lake

50

To Gunnison

149

To Lake City

0   4 mi

0   4 km

© AVALON TRAVEL PUBLISHING, INC.

Accommodations

Given its proximity to Crested Butte and Telluride, Gunnison has a surprising lack of distinctive, privately owned hotels; when my family stayed here, we picked the Comfort Inn, which is generic and across the street from a Wal-Mart, but it has a pool and large rooms and met our needs.

The **Mary Lawrence Inn** (601 N. Taylor St., 970/641-3343 or 888/331-6863, www.commerceteam.com/mary.html, $79–129) is named after the widow and teacher who operated this blue-green, cube-shaped building for years, beginning in the early 1900s. Renovated almost a century after it was built in 1885, the Mary Lawrence has seven rooms and a hot tub in the gazebo out back.

Food

Gunnison is a small town with a large tourist population during certain times of the year, which means one thing: overcrowded restaurants. Expect to wait in line for any of the three side-by-side restaurants at the corner of North Main and Tomichi Street: the **W**

Café (114 N. Main St., 970/641-1744, 7 A.M.–2 P.M. Thurs.–Tues.), an old-fashioned diner with wood paneling, chicken-fried steak sandwiches ($8), steak and eggs ($10), and breakfast burritos ($8); the **Firebrand Delicatessen** (108 N. Main St., 970/641-6266, 7 A.M.–3 P.M. daily), with homemade soups and deli sandwiches and friendly snapshots all over the walls; and **The Bean** (120 N. Main St., 970/641-2408, 6:30 A.M.–8 P.M. Mon.–Fri., 7 A.M.–8 P.M. Sat.–Sun.), which supplements its coffee, pastries, and sandwiches with cozy couches, sculptures and paintings on the walls, and kids' toys.

For dinner, **Pie-Zan's NY Pizzeria** (730 N. Main St., 970/641-5255, 11 A.M.–9 P.M. daily) serves hand-tossed, New York-style pizza with barely a hint of grease—and delivery is fast. The fancy sit-down place is **Garlic Mike's** (2674 Hwy. 135, 970/641-2493, www.garlicmikes.com, 5–9:30 P.M. Mon.–Sat., 10 A.M.–1 P.M. Sun.), whose signature dish is a pepper-crusted filet mignon in a cognac mustard-cream sauce—and there's also a Sunday champagne brunch buffet.

Telluride and Vicinity

So many hippies have settled in Telluride—with its exhilarating, clean air, 8,237-foot elevation, and waterfall-covered mountains casting shadows over Colorado Avenue—that this utopian middle-of-nowhere town has become a sort of laid-back, southwestern Colorado metropolis. My first trip to Telluride was in 1988, to visit a friend who was taking a break between college and career, and the town was still roomy and relaxed. Colorado Avenue had a few shops and bars, a sizable number of residents wore dreadlocks and the look of having stayed up all night, and the Victorians within a few blocks of downtown were surrounded by open space and muddy culverts. It was totally different in 2005, on my last trip: Sturdy, modern houses had filled in every bit of the downtown open space, high-end restaurants were on every block of Colorado, and the people wandering the streets wore far more jewelry than I remembered.

"The Next Aspen," as some have pejoratively called Telluride over the years, is a bit of an exaggeration (although the town's median home price in 2003 was $902,062). But celebrities such as Gen. Norman Schwarzkopf, Oprah Winfrey, and Donald Trump have moved to the area (at least part-time) in recent years, home prices have skyrocketed, and while hippies continue to peruse the "free box" at the center of town, they're pretty much priced out of the housing market. So while the town's lazy, comforting vibe has given way to a certain sprawl, it's still one of the most magnificent cities in the state, with 14,000-foot Mount Wilson and Bridal Veil Falls literally

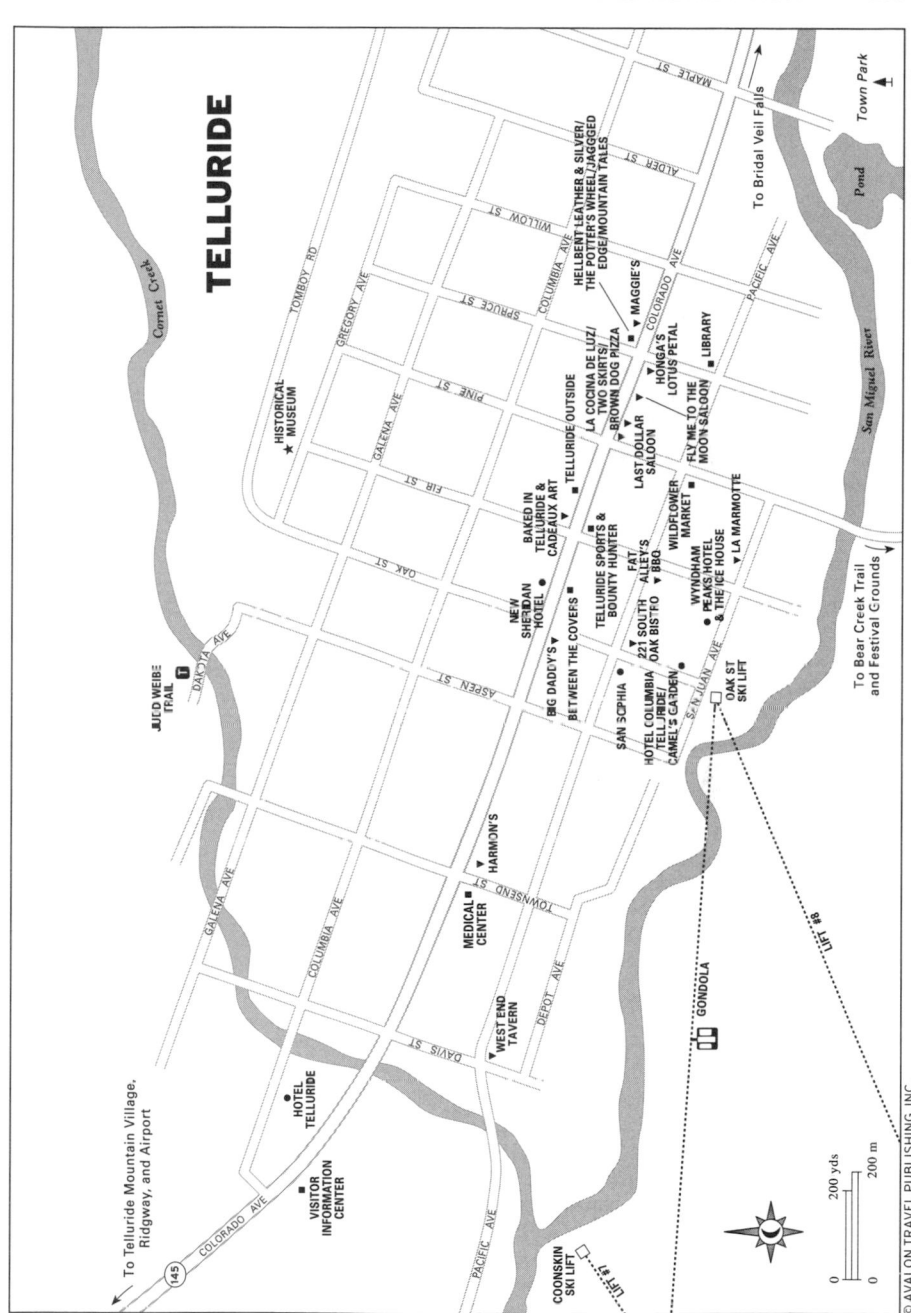

TELLURIDE

Cornet Creek

Tomboy Rd

To Bridal Veil Falls

Town Park

Pond

San Miguel River

MAPLE ST
ALDER ST
COLUMBIA AVE
PACIFIC AVE
WILLOW ST
SPRUCE ST
PINE ST
GALENA AVE
FIR ST
OAK ST
ASPEN ST
DAKOTA AVE
GREGORY AVE
COLORADO AVE

HELLBENT LEATHER & SILVER/
THE POTTER'S WHEEL/JAGGGED
EDGE/MOUNTAIN TALES

MAGGIE'S

LA COCINA DE LUZ/
TWO SKIRTS/
BROWN DOG PIZZA

HONGA'S
LOTUS PETAL

LIBRARY

LAST DOLLAR
SALOON

TELLURIDE/OUTSIDE

FLY ME TO THE
MOON SALOON

BAKED IN
TELLURIDE &
CADEAUX ART

WILDFLOWER
MARKET

LA MARMOTTE

TELLURIDE SPORTS &
BOUNTY HUNTER

FAT
ALLEY'S
BBQ

WYNDHAM
PEAKS HOTEL
& THE ICE HOUSE

NEW
SHERIDAN
HOTEL

221 SOUTH
OAK BISTRO

BETWEEN THE COVERS

BIG DADDY'S

SAN SOPHIA

HOTEL COLUMBIA
TELLURIDE/
CAMEL'S GARDEN

SAN JUAN AVE

OAK ST
SKI LIFT

To Bear Creek Trail
and Festival Grounds

LIFT #8

GONDOLA

200 yds
200 m

HISTORICAL
MUSEUM

JUD WEIBE
TRAIL

HARMON'S

TOWNSEND ST

MEDICAL
CENTER

WEST END
TAVERN

DEPOT AVE

DAVIS ST

GALENA AVE

COLUMBIA AVE

HOTEL
TELLURIDE

VISITOR
INFORMATION
CENTER

PACIFIC AVE

COLORADO AVE

145

To Telluride Mountain Village,
Ridgway, and Airport

COONSKIN
SKI LIFT

LIFT #7

0

at the end of town. My latest trip was in late September, when the leaves had turned bright yellow and snow had fallen in the peaks for the first time; most visitors arrive during ski season, but I highly recommend a trip during this spectacular time of year.

Although Butch Cassidy robbed banks here in the late 1800s, Telluride was a sleepy little nothing town until roughly 1971, when the ski resort opened—and ever since, it has been a haven for skiers of all kinds, hikers, mountain climbers, cyclists, and off-roaders. It's one of those places in Colorado where the weather always seems to be superb—even during a blizzard—and the air is cleaner than any place you've ever been. Leading the annual roster of high-class events is the Telluride Bluegrass Festival, which started in 1974 as a gathering of local bluegrass mavericks and has grown into a four-day institution of bluegrass, country, blues, and rock, from Emmylou Harris to Wilco.

HISTORY

After the Utes hunted here and Spanish explorers stumbled upon and named the San Juan mountains, prospectors drifted here with the 1858 Colorado gold boom—and discovered gold in the San Juans. Telluride's first claim was in 1875, by John Fallon, in Marshal Basin; the town attempted to establish itself as "Columbia" five years later, but the U.S. Post Office denied the name due to the mining camp in Columbia, California. "Telluride" is so-named because: 1) Tellurium is an element associated with gold deposits, although it doesn't exist in this area; or 2) "To Hell you ride!" is what friends, family, and squeamish prospectors told gold-diggers heading for the southwest mountains. Believe your own theory.

For a while in the 1890s, after the railroad came to town, miners from all over the world traveled to the area, boosting Telluride's population to 5,000—along with saloons, gambling dens, and what the official Telluride website calls "a much-heralded red-light district." Butch Cassidy and his "Wild Bunch" showed up to begin a notorious career of bank-robbing (among other things) at the San Miguel National Bank. But the mining boom ended, many locals joined the military during World War I, and by the 1960s, the population had dropped to less than 600. As with Vail and Aspen, however, skiing came to the rescue.

Locals built a ski area out of a ridge in the early 1970s, and by decade's end, entrepreneurs Ron Allred and Jim Wells had figured out how to profit from it—they added a mountain village, snowmaking equipment, new lifts, beginner-focused terrain, and, in 1996, a free gondola. But owing to Telluride's remote location—Denver is at least a five-hour drive in good weather conditions, and who really comes to Colorado through Durango?—the town remained mostly isolated and dominated by locals. Throughout the 1970s, starry-eyed hippies dominated local boards and enacted severe restrictions on growth.

Growth happened anyway, especially after the town built a regional airport in the late 1980s, and Telluride quickly started growing from an out-of-the-way mountain gem to a booming rich person's playground. The housing prices have spun out of control, and as with Aspen, celebrities are some of the few who can afford to live among the population of 2,000. Still, thanks to smaller nearby towns such as Ridgway, Ouray, and Silverton, the area is still popular with hippies and ski bums, and events like its 14 summer festivals and the construction of the Wyndham Peaks Resort and Telluride Mountain Village ensure tourists will be streaming through here for decades to come.

SIGHTS

Like most of the mountain towns in Colorado, Telluride aggressively memorializes its gold-mining heritage—particularly in the 14-building, downtown-centered **National Historic Landmark District** (www.telluride.com/about_telluride/Buildings.asp), including the San Miguel County Courthouse (301 Colorado Ave., built in 1887 as the county's first courthouse), the Rio Grande Southern Railway Depot (Townsend and San Juan, built in 1891 and converted to Harmon's Restaurant

100 years later), and most famously, the totally refurbished **New Sheridan Hotel & Opera House** (231 W. Colorado Ave., built in 1895 with phones and velvet curtains, still a well-known hotel and restaurant).

One of these buildings, the former Miner's Hospital, today houses the **Telluride Historical Museum** (201 W. Gregory Ave., 970/728-3344, www.telluridemuseum.com, 11 A.M.–5 P.M. Tues.–Sat., $5), which has 20,000 historical artifacts and 2,000 photos focusing on the mining era. Guided audio tours are available.

A local historian, Ashley Boling, runs **Historic Tours of Telluride** (970/728-6639, by appointment), covering the aforementioned buildings and many other sights.

SPORTS AND RECREATION

◖ Telluride Ski Resort

The second-greatest quality of this southwestern skiing utopia (800/778-8581, www.tellurideskiresort.com)—after the majesty of the San Juan Mountains and the natural drops of the 2,080-foot Bushwacker and intimidating early-spring bump runs like Mammoth—has always been seclusion. The resort is in the middle of nowhere, a long and twisty five-hour drive from Denver and 65 miles from Durango, the nearest "regular city," and locals and regulars alike have long prized their wide-open terrain, lack of lift lines, and ticket to a hidden world of natural mountain beauty.

But commerce and transportation have been chipping away at Telluride's seclusion for the past 10 or 15 years. In the late 1980s, the Telluride Regional Airport gave skiers a whole new way to reach the resort, and city officials hope to renovate the "notoriously dodgy" airport, as *Ski* magazine calls it, so 100-seat commercial jets can land as well. In recent years, the resort has opened many once-remote areas to lift traffic, including the 12,250-foot-high Gold Hill, previously accessible only to ambitious hikers. And the resort's new owners have pledged to build a 100-room Ritz-Carlton halfway up the mountain from the base area.

Lines or no lines, the skiing remains impec-cable. Telluride's primary downhill areas remain the long, steep, bumpy trails on the north side of the mountain—to get there from town, use Lift 8 to get to Lift 9, which leads to the self-explanatory Spiral Staircase and the bumpy Mammoth. Catering to beginning and intermediate skiers, Gorrono Basin, on the other side of the mountain, includes long cruises like See Forever and The Lookout, as well as the snowboarding Sprite Air Garden Terrain Park. Also making skiers talk in rapturous tones is Prospect Bowl, a huge expansion of the ski area with runs that swerve around trees; it's accessible by several lifts, but many prefer the more rugged "hike-to" approach.

Keep in mind that the town of Telluride and the Mountain Village park are two distinct areas, separated by a mountain. But one of the resort's great advantages is the free gondola, an incredible 2.5-mile, 13-minute ride over ridges and valleys that begins in Telluride and ends in the village (and continues to a remote parking lot). The gondola is open year-round; on a recent trip to Telluride, I rode it at night, in the rain, and the return trip was like descending back into town via the space shuttle. The resort also has several impressive "hike-to" runs beyond the lifts.

Of the resort's 1,700 skiable acres, 24 percent are for beginners, 38 percent for intermediates, and 38 percent for advanced skiers or experts. Sixteen lifts are available, including two gondolas, and the highest peak is Palmyra, which watches over Mountain Village and Telluride at 13,320 feet.

The **Telluride Ski & Snowboard School** (565 Mountain Village Blvd., 970/728-7507 or 800/801-4832, www.tellurideskiresort.com) gives lessons for a variety of skiing types—kids 3 and older, women, groups, and beginners. Full-day group lessons are roughly $100, while full-day individual lessons are about $560.

A number of Telluride shops rent skis, but among the most prominent are **Telluride Sports** (150 W. Colorado Ave., 970/728-4477 or 800/828-7547, www.telluridesports.com) and **Paragon Ski & Sport** (213 W. Colorado Ave., 970/728-4525, www.paragontelluride.com).

Cross-Country and Heli-Skiing

The best skiing away from the mountain begins at the **Telluride Nordic Center** (500 E. Colorado Ave., Town Park, 970/728-1144, 10 A.M.–4 P.M. Sat.–Thurs., 10 A.M.–7 P.M. Fri., winters only), which guides you to 10 miles of groomed trail in the Town Park area. The center rents skis and ice skates and gives cross-country lessons and ski and snowshoe tours. (Note: The center's phone number works only during the winter.)

The **San Juan Hut Systems** (Ridgway, 970/626-3033, www.sanjuanhuts.com) ski route follows the Dallas and Alder Creek Trails, underneath huge peaks in the Mount Sneffels Range, from Telluride to nearby Ridgway and Ouray—with stops at five greenish huts, each with eight padded bunk beds, propane cook stoves and lamps, and no water. (What do you think all that snow outside is for?) Intermediate skiing experience is recommended.

Finally, for well-to-do adventurers who *really* want to get away from crowds, **Telluride Helitrax** (970/728-8377 or 866/435-4754, www.helitrax.net) uses a Bell 407 helicopter to drop skiers into remote locations such as the Hope Lake Basin, 13,000 feet above sea level. It's pricey—numerous packages are available, including a six-run, single-day experience in the $800–900 range—but safe. Telluride Helitrax is the only Colorado company that does heli-skiing, and it claims just one injury in more than 23 years—a well-publicized 1994 incident involving supermodel Christie Brinkley, her friend, and a sputtering copter.

(Bridal Veil Falls

This impossible-to-miss waterfall overlooking Telluride is the easiest and most obviously spectacular **hiking, biking,** and **off-roading** trail in the area, and it begins at Pandora Mill on the east side of town; the trail is about 1.8 miles long.

Hiking

Just north of Telluride, the **Sneffels High Line Trail** is a 14-mile loop that climbs strenuously from about 9,000 to 12,250 feet; the trail takes about seven hours, but it's worth it,

Mount Wilson from Telluride

© STEVE KNOPPER

given the views of the San Miguel Mountains, three fourteeners, Lizard Head Peak, and Dallas Peak. Connecting with the Sneffels Trail is **Jud Wiebe Trail** (north on Aspen Street, near Cornet Creek), a curvy, 3-mile passage that isn't nearly as difficult.

South of Telluride along Highway 145, the 12-mile, hard-and-steep **Lizard Head Trail** straddles the Uncompahgre and San Juan national forests and is worth trying for the classic view of 13,113-foot Lizard Head Peak alone.

Finally, two of the most popular local trails are **Mount Wilson** (11 miles southwest of Telluride on Hwy. 145), which climbs 4,000 feet in 8 miles, including the hard-sloping final 400 feet, and **Bear Creek Falls,** a pretty and easy 2-mile trail beginning at the end of Pine Street.

For information and maps, contact **Uncompahgre National Forest** (2250 U.S. 50, Delta, 970/874-6600, www.fs.fed.us/r2/gmug), the **Ouray Ranger District** (2505 S. Townsend Ave., Montrose, 970/240-5300), or the **Norwood Ranger District** (1150 Forest, Norwood, 970/327-4261).

Biking

In summer, the **San Juan Hut Systems** (Ridgway, 970/626-3033, www.sanjuanhuts.com) hut-skiing service turns into a mountain-bike adventure guide, leading cyclists 206 miles from Telluride to Moab, Utah, with huts every 35 miles. The route is mostly U.S. Forest Service dirt roads, beginning with the San Juan Mountains and ending in Utah's deserts and canyons. Bring a well-exercised body, as vehicles aren't allowed access to the huts.

Imogene Pass, between Telluride and Ouray, is a high, twisty, 17-mile road that some say is a route for courageous mountain bikers. But I'd add "crazy" and "death-defying" to that description.

Ice-Skating

Telluride's Town Park, just before the mountains begin on the far side of town, has a nice ice-skating rink. (Contact the **Telluride Nordic Center,** at 970/728-1144, for rentals; note that the phone number works only during winter.)

Mountain Village also has a free ice-skating pond in winter.

Water Sports

Three major mountain rivers—the San Miguel, Dolores, and Gunnison—are within striking distance of Telluride, as well as plenty of lakes. The rainbow-and-brown-trout-packed San Miguel, west of the city in the Ilium Valley, is especially great for fly-fishing in summer and fall; the hard-to-get-to Gunnison has fees and complicated regulations; and the cutthroat-heavy Dolores, on Highway 145 outside Cortez, is especially challenging.

Five lakes are within 15 miles of the city as well: Alta (9 miles southwest on Highway 145), Priest (12 miles south on Highway 145), Silver (in Bridal Veil Basin), Trout (near Priest), and Woods (12 miles west on Highway 145). For more information, and equipment rental and guided tours, **Telluride Angler** (121 W. Colorado Ave., 970/728-0773) is a terrific resource.

Like many riverside cities in Colorado, Telluride is superb for white-water rafting; try **Telluride Outside** (121 W. Colorado Ave., 970/728-0773 or 800/831-6230, www.tellurideoutside.com) for tours of varying intensity along the San Miguel and Dolores Rivers.

Rock Climbing and Ice Climbing

Because rock climbing wasn't death-defying enough, locals have in recent years invented the sport of ice climbing, which is big in Telluride and nearby Ouray. Both sports are dangerous, but for thrill-seekers they're irresistible in these towns of peaks, crags, cliffs, and boulders. To get started, **Fantasy Ridge Mountain Guides** (28 Village Court, Placerville, 970/728-3546, www.fantasyridge.com) gives lessons and rents equipment (you'll need one seat harness, two hammer holsters, one hard hat, and lots of other stuff). Also giving guided trips is the **San Juan Outdoor School** (917 E. Porphyry, Ophir, 970/728-4101, www.tellurideadventures.com), which recommends at least four people to a group and gives a one-day course for the basics.

Horseback Riding

Longtime wrangler and mustachioed local character Roudy Roundebush of **Ride with Roudy** (970/728-9611, www.ridewithroudy.com) conducts scenic horseback-riding tours from his ranch barn about six miles from Telluride. He gives tours from another ranch, in Norwood, during the winter.

Golf

If you must come to Telluride for golf—as opposed to, say, listening to bluegrass or climbing to a waterfall—the **Telluride Golf Club** (565 Mountain Village Blvd., 970/728-7320, www.tellurideskiandgolfclub.com) has 18 holes and remarkable views of Mounts Wilson and Sunshine.

Hang Gliding

The principals behind **Telluride Soaring** (Telluride Regional Airport, 1500 Last Dollar Road, 970/209-3497 or 970/708-0862, $160/hour) are certified pilots Jeff Campbell and "Glider Bob," who guide one passenger at a time all over the skies of Telluride.

ENTERTAINMENT AND EVENTS
Nightlife

Telluride's bar scene isn't as interesting as it was 100 years ago, when cowboys and gamblers regularly pulled guns on each other, but the mixture of old-school hippies, new-school trust-funders, and tourists looking for a good time makes for lively nights.

For live music and dancing, the **Fly Me to the Moon Saloon** (136 E. Colorado Ave., 970/728-6666) is best known to tourists for booking new country, rock, and bluegrass bands the weekend of the Telluride Bluegrass Festival. It's a dump of a place, with a patched-up ceiling and a tiny, ramshackle stage, but bands play nightly around 10 P.M.; they're mostly local, and mostly of the hippie-jamming persuasion, but every now and then the club scores a major national act on the way up, such as the Derek Trucks Band a few years ago.

Other live-music joints in town: **Big Daddy's** (300 W. Colorado Ave., 970/728-1801) and **Brown Dog Pizza** (103 W. Colorado Ave., 970/728-8046).

For plain old drinking and cavorting, the **Noir Bar** (123 S. Oak St., 970/728-8862), inside The Bluepoint steakhouse a block from the gondola, has a swizzle-stick feel, serving martinis to guests on leather couches near a fireplace. The **West End Tavern** (573 W. Pacific Ave., 970/728-1808, www.telluridetavern.com) has cheap happy-hour specials, decent bar food, and attractive waitpeople. It's in the Johnson House, built in 1913, but if the tavern is doing its job, you won't notice the building.

An old standby is the **Last Dollar Saloon** (100 E. Colorado Ave., 970/728-4800), with a great jukebox and bartenders who know their way around a shot.

Across the mountain, at the Mountain Village, drinking can be had at **Allred's** (565 Mountain Village Blvd., 970/728-7474, www.allredsrestaurant.com), 1,800 feet above the city, with one of the best wine lists in town.

Theater

In addition to being a historic building, the **Sheridan Opera House** (231 W. Colorado Ave., 970/728-6363, www.sheridanoperahouse.com) is the only nice indoor stage in town—so it draws big music names, from hit singers James Taylor and Jimmy Buffett to bluesman John Hammond Jr. to rising country star Dierks Bentley. It's also a renowned theatrical stage, having sponsored productions with actors like Mel Gibson, Patrick Stewart, and Carol Burnett over the years. The opera house is a nonprofit venue, benefiting the **Sheridan Arts Foundation** (110 N. Oak St., 970/728-6363), which brings the stars to town to work with promising young talent.

The **Telluride Repertory Theatre Co.** (970/728-4539, www.telluridetheatre.com) books local actors and productions into the Sheridan Opera House and onto the Town Park stage (and conducts workshops with thousands of schoolkids). **Lizard Head Theatre Co.** (970/728-3133, www.lizardheadtheatre.com), a smaller company, puts on smaller shows, including, recently, *Crimes of the Heart*. The community-run **Telluride Council for the Arts & Humanities** (100 W. Colorado Ave., 970/728-3930, www.telluridearts.com) and the **Ah Haa School for the Arts** (135 S. Spruce St., 970/728-3886, www.ahhaa.org) also run smaller-scale classes and workshops.

Festivals

Telluride has 14 festivals in the summer alone, including the well-known Bluegrass Festival and the Wine Festival (both in late June). Although the film festival's reputation has grown considerably in recent years, the **Telluride Bluegrass Festival** (www.bluegrass.com) remains the festival flagship. It's a spectacular event, with old-school bluegrass heroes such as Ralph Stanley on the same bill as new-school bluegrass experimenters like Bela Fleck and Sam Bush, and rock, country, and pop acts from John Hiatt to Wilco just to bring in the big crowds. Be sure to make hotel reservations long in advance, however; I camped one year just outside of town and could barely find a spot in a muddy, noisy area.

The town is so festival-heavy that residents have declared a weekend in late July "The Nothing Festival." Check out www.visittelluride.com (click on "Festivals & Events") to coordinate dates.

Early September's **Telluride Film Festival** (603/433-9202, www.telluridefilmfestival.org) is a sub–Sundance fest that draws serious film stars to town and broke *Sling Blade* and Ken Burns's *The Civil War*.

The **Wild West Fest** (970/728-6363) in early June brings disadvantaged kids to town for art, theater, and rodeo events; late June's **Telluride Wine Festival** (970/728-3178, www.telluridewinefestival.com) brings numerous master sommeliers to town.

The mid-August **Telluride Chamber Music Festival** (www.telluridechambermusic.com) and early August's **Telluride Jazz Celebration** (www.telluridejazz.com, 970/728-7009) round out the musical offerings.

SHOPPING

Here's the best evidence that Telluride has yet to become the next Aspen (despite two homes on the market for $18 and $19 million, respectively, in early 2005): The shops are still (reasonably) affordable. And few people wear fur coats and Fort Knox jewelry down Main Street.

Open since 1974, the **Between the Covers Bookstore & Coffee House** (224 W. Colorado Ave., 970/369-0967 or 866/728-4504, www.between-the-covers.com) is hardly a well-stocked Barnes & Noble, but it's a great place for browsing, with an emphasis on local authors, tour guides, Colorado history, and relevant titles like Annie Gilbert Coleman's *Ski Style: Sport and Culture in the Rockies.*

Every mountain town that hopes to have any kind of tourist following contains at least one cowboy-hat store, and **Bounty Hunter** (226 W. Colorado Ave., 970/728-0256, www.bountyhuntertelluride.com) is Telluride's. Of course, "cowboy hat" is a little too limiting a description for a store that sells

downtown Telluride

© STEVE KNOPPER

Outback explorers, derbies, and classic brown fedoras. Plus boots.

Noteworthy galleries include **Hellbent Leather and Silver** (215 E. Colorado Ave., 970/728-6246, www.hellbentleather.com), with solid handbags, wallets, belts, and hats, plus silver and gold jewelry; **The Potter's Wheel** (221 E. Colorado Ave., 970/728-4912), with local artists' pottery and sculpture; and **Cadeaux Art** (324 W. Colorado Ave., 970/728-2055), focusing on vintage prints and posters, particularly Old West scenes and late-1800s magazine covers.

For outdoor-type clothing and sporting equipment, **Telluride Mountaineer** (219 W. Colorado Ave., 970/728-6736, www.telluride-mountaineer.com) has knowledgeable guides who can walk you through all your weird adventure excursions, from rock climbing to heli-skiing. **Jagged Edge** (223 E. Colorado Ave., 970/728-9307, www.jagged-edge-telluride.com) is more stylish than rugged, with Tibetan jackets, sports moccasins, Thermoses, and water bottles.

In the Nugget Building, the first to carry modern electricity in the U.S., **Two Skirts** (127 W. Colorado Ave., 970/728-6828) is a pink-bag women's-clothing store that targets women in T-shirts and jeans who occasionally like to wear expensive cashmere.

Telluride is still a hippie town, so dogs are big, and so are their accessories: **Mountain Tales** (224 E. Colorado Ave., 970/369-4240) sells dog goggles for $22 (a bit of detail that made *The New York Times* in summer 2005).

ACCOMMODATIONS
$100-150
More old-fashioned and homey than Telluride's luxury hotels, the **San Sophia B&B** (330 W. Pacific Ave., 970/728-3001 or 800/537-4781, www.sansophia.com, $129–279) is in an elaborate Victorian building with triangular turrets and slanted roofs—with pretty oak woodwork and stained-glass windows in every room. "Telluride's Best Breakfast," claim the owners, and judging from just the name of this dish, see if you disagree: straw-

view of Telluride from the New Sheridan Hotel

© STEVE KNOPPER

berry-stuffed French toast with amaretto crème anglaise.

A huge river-rock fireplace is the most impressive part of the **Mountain Lodge at Telluride** (457 Mountain Village Blvd., 866/368-6867, www.mountainlodgetelluride, $129–569), which is in a perfect location for skiers and has both standard hotel rooms and larger condominiums with kitchens.

$150-200
Built in 1891, rebuilt in 1894 after a fire, and elaborately refurbished in 1995, the **New Sheridan Hotel** (231 W. Colorado Ave., 970/728-4351 or 800/200-1891, www.new-sheridan.com, $175–300) is the best-known and most impressive historical site in a town that continually celebrates its gold-mining past. (Trivia: William Jennings Bryan announced his failed bid for the presidency here in 1896.) It's also a luxury hotel in a sturdy red-brick building, with 32 rooms and corresponding period furniture and antiques; hot tubs are on the roof, the breakfast and pantry pastries are amazing,

and the on-site Chop House is one of the best high-end restaurants in a town full of them. Ask for a third-floor room overlooking Colorado Avenue; I woke up one morning, looked beyond the buildings across the street, and noticed the clouds in the mountains were almost at eye level. During the off-season, particularly September, October, March, and April, the rooms are almost shockingly affordable.

In a brown brick-and-wood building that's a cross between a ski condo and a college dorm, **The Hotel Telluride** (199 N. Cornet St., 970/369-1188 or 866/468-3504, www.thehoteltelluride.com, $189–450) is a nice half-step toward the luxury of Wyndham Peaks or the New Sheridan. The Spa has the usual deep cleansing facials and Swedish massages, The Bistro serves a breakfast buffet, the lobby has comfortable leather sofas and wool rugs, and each of the 59 rooms has something called "The Incredible Bed."

Also in a convenient spot for skiers, the **Inn at Lost Creek** (119 Lost Creek Ln., 970/728-5678 or 888/601-5678, www.innatlostcreek.com, $195–595) is a standard high-end hotel that opened in 1988; its most distinctive feature is the 9545 Restaurant & Bar, which serves highfalutin' dishes like lamb satay vindaloo and has a hefty wine list.

A huge corner hotel downtown, the red-brick **Hotel Columbia Telluride** (300 San Juan Ave., 970/728-0660 or 800/201-9505, $180–350) opened in 1995 with 21 fireplace-equipped rooms, including two penthouse suites, plus a rooftop hot tub and the fancy Cosmopolitan Restaurant. (The nearby gondola is a little noisy, especially in the summer.)

Over $200

◖ **Camel's Garden** (250 W. San Juan Ave., 970/728-9300 or 888/772-2635, www.camelsgarden.com, $275–895) has 35 rooms, suites, and condos that are pink and super-luxurious, with Italian marble bathrooms, balconies, and fireplaces. Whereas most quaint hotels in secluded mountain towns play up the antiques and Old West history, Camel's Garden is thoroughly modern, with immaculate shining

hardwood floors and a facade that looks like a suburban-hipster townhouse complex. It's also home of the Wildflour Market and Catering Co., an upscale restaurant.

Locals complain about the gentrification of Telluride, and the ski-in/ski-out **Wyndham Peaks Hotel & Golden Door Spa** (136 Country Club Dr., 970/728-6800 or 800/789-2220, www.thepeaksresort.com, $385–665) is proof. But who cares? It's literally on a cliff in the middle of Telluride's Mountain Village. The views of Mount Wilson and various other peaks are incredible—you feel like you're standing next to Pete Coors in a beer commercial—and the 174 rooms and suites, 14 penthouse condominiums, and 10 private cabins are filled with CD players, huge down comforters, and terrycloth bathrobes. As for the spa, let's just say the Skier's Salvation Massage is aptly named.

Next to a pond, river, and wetlands, **The Ice House** (310 S. Fir, 970/728-6300 or 800/544-3436, www.icehouselodge.com, $225–390) has a woodsy feel, mostly due to the balconies (and mountain views) in every room. Although it's not as luxurious as the New Sheridan or Wyndham Peaks, The Ice House has the best combination of price and comfort in town.

For condominium information, contact the **Telluride & Mountain Village Convention & Visitors Bureau** (630 W. Colorado Ave., 888/605-2578, www.visittelluride.com).

FOOD
Snacks, Cafés, and Breakfast

The two best things about downtown bakery-deli-and-café fixture **Baked In Telluride** (127 S. Fir St., 970/728-4775, www.toski.com/bakedintel/index.html, 5:30–10 P.M. daily) are 1) the pizza; and 2) it delivers after 5 P.M. Plus, the bread and bagels are homemade, the soup and sandwiches are cheap and plentiful, and the pasta dinners are $7.

Maggie's Bakery & Café (217 E. Colorado Ave., 970/728-3334, 7:30 A.M.–3 P.M. Mon., 7:30 A.M.–6 P.M. Tues.–Sun.) is your basic but rarely disappointing breakfast-and-burger joint, with bacon and eggs for the morning and sandwiches for lunch.

At the base of the gondola, the **Wildflour Market and Catering Co.** (225 S. Pine St., 970/728-0200, 11 A.M.–7 P.M. Mon.–Sat.) has breads of all types (try the cranberry pecan) by a French-trained chef, as well as the usual coffee, pastries, deli sandwiches, homemade soups, and salads.

Casual

Fat Alley's BBQ (128 S. Oak St., 970/728-3985, 11 A.M.–10 P.M. daily) is a haven for Telluride's "Trustafarians"—which is to say, well-off locals who don't want to dump all their trust-fund money on meals at Allred's—and others who need a break from white tablecloths and $800 bottles of wine. The tables are built for families, the beer is cheap, and the pork sandwiches and big plates of ribs are straight out of the South.

Sofio's Mexican Restaurant (110 E. Colorado Ave., 970/728-4882, 7 A.M.–1:30 P.M. and 5–8:30 P.M. Mon.–Fri., 7 A.M.–1:30 P.M. and 5–10 P.M. Sat.–Sun., closed Mon. during the off-season) was almost exactly the same (if slightly more run-down the second time) when I visited in 1992 and 2005. The first time around, its big-burritos-and-chips-and-salsa menu was one of many affordable choices in the downtown area; the latter time, I had to wander the streets, past the Honga's Lotus Petals and La Marmottes, to find something basic and cheap. In both cases, Sofio's paid off.

The **Excelsior Café** (200 W. Colorado Ave., 970/728-4250, 6–10 P.M. Sun.–Thurs., 6–11 P.M. Fri.–Sat.) is a great (if not exactly gourmet) wine bar and restaurant at the center of town, with friendly locals dining at the metal bar and huge picture windows overlooking Colorado Avenue.

Upscale

To get to ◖ **Allred's** (565 Mountain Village Blvd., 970/728-7474, www.allredsrestaurant.com, 5:30–9 P.M. daily), at 10,551 feet above sea level, you need to take a gondola to the top. The views of various 13,000-foot mountains are a bit distracting, but dishes like macadamia-and-hazelnut-crusted soft-shell crab with Himalayan red rice, tropical fruit, and Thai coconut broth should drag your focus back to the table. The head chef is Erich Owen, who used to work at Aspen's Cache Cache.

◖ **Honga's Lotus Petal & Tea Room** (133 S. Oak St., 970/728-5134, 5:30–10 daily) has the best sushi bar in town, plus superb vegetarian and organic chicken and beef dishes. It's Asian fusion, with an emphasis on Thai and Japanese, along with especially potent curry and fruit flavors—and a wide variety of cocktails from all over the world.

Inside the Hotel Columbia Telluride downtown, the **Cosmopolitan** (300 W. San Juan Ave., 970/728-1292, www.cosmotelluride.com, 5–9:30 P.M. daily) is most famous for its coffee-and-donuts dessert—a reference not to Krispy Kreme but southern beignets. The menu is long on fish—lobster corn dogs are more New England seaside bistro than New York City hot-dog stand—but the chicken and pork dishes are excellent as well.

La Marmotte (150 San Juan Ave., 970/728-6232, www.larmarmotte.com, 6–9:30 P.M. daily) is one of those simple and confident French bistros that puts only six entrées on its dinner menu—the spinach-stuffed chicken breast is a highlight.

Southern chef Eliza H. S. Gavin used to cook at Galatoire's, the Cajun fixture on Bourbon Street in New Orleans, but at **221 South Oak Bistro** (221 S. Oak St., 970/728-9507, www.221southoak.com, 6–10 Mon.–Sat.), there's nary a red-beans-and-rice or jambalaya dish on the menu. Rather, the bistro is heavy on fancy fish and steak dishes, such as ruby red trout with spaghetti squash and wild mushroom raviolis ($21). (Maybe it's because Gavin studied in Paris and the Napa Valley as well.) There's a brunch one Sunday a month.

In the 1891 train depot, **Harmon's** (300 S. Townsend, 970/728-3773, 6–9:30 P.M. daily) knows the value of a good bowl of chicken soup to go with the foie gras and Chilean sea bass. The Spago Mexico City–trained chef, James Ackard, has a very tasty knack for combining basic contemporary-American dishes (like potato pancakes) with upscale touches (the potato pancakes are actually made of smoked trout, with watercress and caviar). The chicken soup contains truffle oil.

INFORMATION

Several websites deliver the basics about Telluride. The **Town of Telluride** (113 W. Columbia Ave., 970/728-3071, www.town.telluride.co.us/home/index.asp) has a directory of official phone numbers and sections on parks and recreation, history, and so forth. The **Telluride Ski Resort** (970/728-6900, www.tellurideskiresort.com) includes snow reports, weather maps, and hotel and restaurant listings, as well as a "summer" page on hiking, cycling, and other non-skiing activities. Telluride's tiny newspaper, the *Daily Planet*, is at www.telluridegateway.com; www.telluride.com is a marketing site that emphasizes real estate but is reasonably informative.

The **Ridgway Area Chamber of Commerce** (150 Racecourse Rd., 800/220-4959, www.ridgwaycolorado.com) website is mostly ads, but it posts some details about outdoor activities, food, lodging, and local businesses. The **Silverton Chamber of Commerce** (U.S. 550 and Hwy. 110, 970/387-5654 or 800/752-4494, www.silvertoncolorado.com) has tons of dining, lodging, and outdoor-activity listings. The **Ouray Chamber Resort Association** (1230 Main St., 970/325-4746, www.ouraycolorado.com) maintains a most informative website, with plenty of dining, lodging, and shopping listings.

GETTING THERE AND AROUND

The **Telluride Regional Airport** (1500 Last Dollar Rd., 970/728-5313, www.tellurideairport.com) opened in 1984 and has since expanded to accommodate several major airlines—Frontier, America West, and United, among them. Many connecting flights to Denver International Airport are available.

A free bus service, the **Galloping Goose** (970/728-5700, www.telluride.com/plan_your_trip/Buses.asp, 7:30 A.M.–6 P.M. Mon.–Fri.), loops through downtown Telluride, hitting stops at the gondola plaza, the library, the courthouse, and other central places. **Dial-A-Ride** (970/728-8888, 7 A.M.–12:20 A.M. Sun.–Sat.) is a free shuttle around Mountain Village.

"The most beautiful commute in America," boasts Telluride's website of the gondola, and it's no exaggeration, given the peaceful float over the mountains from downtown to Mountain Village. The eight-passenger "G" cars are open 275 days a year, 7 A.M.–midnight; it's about 10 minutes from Station Telluride (near the corner of Oak and San Juan) to Station Mountain Village, and another minute and a half to Station Village Parking. Passengers can transport bikes in some of the gondola cars.

Both Ridgway and Ouray are small towns en route to Telluride, just a few miles north along U.S. 550. (Follow the signs to Telluride from either town.) Silverton is harder to reach—to get there from Telluride, take Highway 145 south, turn left on County Road D65, left again on County Rd. 8, then U.S. 550 south. **Mountain Limo** (970/728-9606, 888/376-9770, www.mountain-limo.com) arranges van and limousine trips around the Telluride area, including the tiny mountain towns, like Silverton and Ouray.

OURAY

Ouray may look like the prettiest, most placid mountain town in the world, but the man who inspired its name was ambiguous and troubled. Known as "the white man's friend"—for better or worse—Taos, New Mexico-born Chief Ouray was the leader of the Utes beginning in the mid-1800s. He was by all accounts a great, brilliant man, with a beautiful and equally stately wife, Chipeta, and the two were so well-respected that they met personally with U.S. presidents Ulysses S. Grant and Rutherford B. Hayes.

When whites started settling on western land that had belonged to the Utes for decades, Ouray preached compromise and conciliation. He signed treaties for the Utes to give up their land east of the Continental Divide in exchange for better conditions vis-à-vis white

Americans. Many of his people considered him a traitor, and some even tried to kill him, but treaties and negotiations continued. Until 1878. Tensions were high due to conflicts between the Utes and Colorado gold miners, and they peaked when reformer Nathan Meeker tried to push Indians into a utopian farming arrangement like the one he famously set up in Greeley. Many Utes wouldn't take it, and they killed Meeker and seven other whites, took women and children captive, and Ouray intervened on behalf of the hostages. Americans lost sympathy for the Utes, and in 1880 Ouray signed a treaty agreeing to leave Colorado and move to Utah.

Ouray died not long after that, of natural causes, but his small southwestern namesake town, which began in 1875 as gold-mining territory, lives on as a quaint Old West tourist attraction. The Tabeguache Utes lived in this beautiful San Juan Mountains spot for centuries during warm weather, until the miners took it over, building saloons, hotels, bordellos,

The town of Ouray is named after Chief Ouray, the conciliatory Ute Leader of the late 1800s.

© STEVE KNOPPER

and churches in pretty Victorian-style buildings—some of which stand on Main Street today. Mountains edge up against the town, and it's a hot spot for ice climbing.

Sights

The **Million Dollar Highway** is the skinny, treacherous two-lane section of U.S. 550 that veers up and down a mountain from out-of-the-way Ouray to secluded Silverton. Although crews keep it open year-round, it scared the hell out of me when I tried to make it one mid-spring day, when it didn't look especially threatening from the dry vantage point at the bottom. Ouray's section is known as **Red Mountain Pass,** an 1880s toll road for miners dragging gold ore out of town.

Laid-back Telluride hippies and other tourists have been filling Ouray's hot springs for decades—and before that, the Utes saw the natural waters as healing spirits. **The Historic Wiesbaden Hot Springs Spa & Lodge** (625 5th St., 970/325-4347 or 888/846-5191, www.wiesbadenhotsprings.com, $120–175) is an extraordinary hotel built above an underground vapor cave (which is open to visitors as a sort of natural Jacuzzi) that gets its heat during the winter from the adjacent natural hot springs. Those waters range 78–128 degrees Fahrenheit, and it's the most soothing place to stay in southwestern Colorado.

It's not to be mistaken for the **Hot Springs Pool and Fitness Center** (1200 Main St., 970/325-7073, 10 a.m.–10 p.m. daily Memorial Day–Labor Day, noon–9 p.m. daily Labor Day–Memorial Day, $8), a more conventional type of springs that also has exercise equipment in the fitness center.

Box Canyon Falls & Park (southwest Ouray, off U.S. 550, $3) spills thousands of gallons of water every minute from Canyon Creek to a boxy rock formation 285 feet below. It's a pretty spot in a town where everything is a pretty spot, and the visitors center gives interactive geology lessons. A walkway and suspension bridge take you directly under the falls.

The **Ouray County Museum** (420 6th Ave.,

FOUR-WHEEL DRIVING IN SOUTHWEST COLORADO

Rugged mountain roads make for four-wheel-driving paradise throughout much of Colorado, especially in the Southwest, where the San Juans are drier, dirtier, and less explored than their Rocky neighbors to the north. Here are six excellent trails:

* **Dolores:** The drive up Highway 145 to Scotch Creek is filled with muddy holes and leads to serious lake and abandoned-mine territory.

* **Ouray:** The last stretch of County Road 361 (off U.S. 550) into Yankee Boy Basin is four-wheel-only, and the mountain views and wildflowering landscape are terrific.

* **Purgatory:** The route from here to Silverton atop Coal Bank and Molas Passes is an out-of-the-way tour of the area's steepest mountains and deepest valleys.

* **Ridgway:** The gravel County Road 10, just north of Ridgway off U.S. 550, leads to Owl Creek Pass; the views of 11,781-foot-high

Chimney Rock are great, and the drive isn't as strenuous as some other four-wheel passes in the area. Try it in late summer or fall, when the trees are changing color.

* **Silverton:** Several dodgy roads around Silverton lead to historic mining areas around town, including Engineer and Cinnamon Passes.

* **Telluride:** Tomboy Road, beyond North Fir Street, where the National Guard once put an end to a miners' strike, goes over Imogene Pass, a thirteener, and has a nice vantage point overlooking Bridal Veil Falls.

For more information on four-wheel-driving in this area—or to a rent a Jeep or other vehicle—try **Triangle Jeep Rental** (864 Green St., Silverton, 970/387-9990 or 877/522-2354, www.trianglejeeprental.com), one of many companies in the area that parks a bunch of Jeeps-for-rent on the side of the road.

970/325-4576, www.ouraycountyhistoricalsociety.org, 10 A.M.–5 P.M. Mon.–Sat., 1–5 P.M. Sun., $5) was a miners' hospital 1887–1964, and it's easy to imagine patients and doctors roaming the 27 rooms over three floors. Today, the museum concentrates on mining, ranching, and railroading, along with Native American culture and artifacts.

The **Bachelor-Syracuse Mine Tour** (1222 Country Rd. 14, 970/325-0220 or 800/227-8545, www.bachelorsyracuse.com, 9 A.M.–4 P.M. daily mid-May–mid-June and mid-Aug.–mid-Sept. 15, 9 A.M.–5 P.M. daily mid-June–mid-Aug., $16) is a ride on a "trammer" (mine train) about 3,350 feet into Gold Hill, where visitors can pan for gold and learn about the Old West mining days. There's a gift shop, blacksmith shop, and an outdoor café.

Sports and Recreation

Ironton Park has three or four miles of groomed **cross-country skiing** tracks, about

nine miles south of town on U.S. 550. Doing the grooming is the **Ouray County Nordic Council** (970/325-4288, www.ouraytrails.org), a branch of the local Ouray Trail Group, whose members' phone numbers are on the website.

◖ Ouray Ice Park

Recently featured in *Esquire* magazine, ice climbing is the latest Colorado adventure sport for gearheads who can't be bothered with wimpy little excursions like extreme snowboarding. The sport centers on this ice park (Unhcompahgre Gorge, 970/325-4288, www.ourayicepark.com), which the owner of Ouray Hydroelectric bought in 1992, then (after buying insurance, of course) allowed people to spray water all over it and climb to the top. Thanks to imaginative climbers and half-inch PVC pipe, the ice turned into art—blue, shiny, and crystallized—and then a popular sport with 40 different climbing paths in three areas of the city-leased park.

Accommodations

For a town this small, Ouray has a ton of hotels, inns, motels, and bed-and-breakfasts, many of which are elegant and distinctive (although you can, of course, stay at the Best Western Twin Peaks). Most are in historic buildings, and some, like the Beaumont and the St. Elmo, retain their stately ambience.

The 【 **Beaumont Hotel** (505 Main St., 970/325-7000 or 888/447-3255, www.beaumonthotel.com, $180–350), which in its days as the "flagship of the San Juans" served Teddy Roosevelt, Herbert Hoover, and Belgium's King Leopold, opened in 1887 but spent 35 years as a large, boarded-up shack. A renovation began in 1998, and today's version of the Beaumont includes a huge wooden lobby staircase, four-corner beds in the rooms, a salon and spa, and the Tundra Restaurant.

The **Ouray Hotel** (303 6th Ave., 970/325-0500 or 800/216-8729, www.ourayhotel.com, $45–120) isn't quite as refurbished and beautiful as the Beaumont, but it's in a solid Victorian-style corner brick building erected in 1893 and restored a century later.

Another of the many natural hot springs in Ouray—this one in the form of mountainside hot tubs—the **Box Canyon Lodge & Hot Springs** (45 3rd Ave., 970/325-4981 or 800/327-5080, www.boxcanyonouray.com, $110) includes a small, triangular lodge and rooms with free satellite television service and DVD players.

The **China Clipper Inn** (525 2nd St., 970/325-0565 or 800/315-0565, www.chinaclipperinn.com, $85–140) is in a three-story Victorian just below the mountains, but its primary distinction is a nautical theme—all 12 rooms are named after famous clipper ships, from *Witch of the Seas* to *Flying Cloud*. Fortunately, pirates rarely walk the halls at night shouting, "Argh!"

Quaint and fancy, with flower-pattern wallpaper and frilly bedcovers, the **St. Elmo Hotel** (426 Main St., 970/325-4951 or 866/243-1502, www.stelmohotel.com, $120–140) is in a restored, boxy-brick, turn-of-the-20th-century building. It includes the Bon Ton and Buen Tiempo Restaurants.

True to its name, the **Riverside Inn** (1805 N. Main St., 970/325-4061 or 800/432-4170, www.ourayriversideinn.com, $50–95) includes several small wooden cabins adjacent to the Uncompahgre River as well as a fairly standard 18-room lodge. Hiking trails are all over the grounds.

Food

Most of Ouray's best restaurants are in Ouray's best hotels. The Beaumont's **Tundra Restaurant** (505 Main St., 970/325-7040, www.beaumonthotel.com, 6–9 P.M. Mon.–Sat., 10 A.M.–2 P.M. Sun.) serves high-end steak, chicken, and fish from its second-floor perch overlooking Main Street. In the basement of the St. Elmo, the **Bon Ton Restaurant** (426 Main St., 970/325-4951, www.stelmohotel.com, 5:30–9 P.M. daily) is Italian with frills—from pasta primavera to escargot and crawfish tails. And while the restaurant at the **Historic Western Hotel** (210 7th Ave., 970/325-4645 or 888/624-8403, www.historicwesternhotel.com, 11 A.M.–9 P.M. daily) isn't as distinguished as the other two, it's a great family place for burgers and beer.

Shopping

Ouray's Main Street strip has a mixture of practical and arty shopping for various kinds of travelers. Of the surprisingly high number of galleries, the best are the **Ouray Gallery** (518 Main St., 970/325-4110, www.ouraygallery.com), with a nice collection of Colorado painters' works, and **Ouray Glassworks** (619 Main St., 800/748-9421, www.ourayglassworks.com), at which artist Sam Rushing blows his own bowls, hummingbird feeders, and various ornaments.

RIDGWAY

Every time I go to the Telluride area, these days, I like to avoid the "big city" and stay among the dirt roads and one streetlight of Ridgway, about half an hour south of Montrose. It looks like a sleepy mountain area, and although designer Ralph Lauren's Double RL Ranch is just south of town, time passes slowly here—it was once a major western railroad hub and a serious ranching area, but not so much these days.

John Wayne filmed his 1969 movie *True Grit* in Ridgway, and several monuments (including the True Grit restaurant) display Wayne memorabilia. For a cheap, quick trip to the San Juans, stay at the homey Chipeta Sun Lodge and make sightseeing runs to Telluride, Ouray, and Silverton.

Sights

Although the last train left Ridgway in 1951, the tiny, green **Ridgway Railroad Museum** (U.S. 550 and Hwy. 62, no phone number or hours of operation available, www.ridgwayrailroadmuseum.org, drpaulson@sprintmail.com, free) maintains a number of photos and displays about the old days.

Sports and Recreation

It's hard to find sandy beaches in the mountains, but the **Ridgway State Park & Recreation Area** (28555 U.S. 550, 970/626-5822) has a curvy lake filled with rainbow trout, large-mouthed bass, and yellow perch, as well as hiking trails and campsites. The **Ridgway Marina,** a place to rent and launch kayaks, powerboats, and other crafts, was closed due to a contractual issue, but park officials believe it will be open under new management by summer 2006.

Accommodations

I drove to the adobe ◖ **Chipeta Sun Lodge & Spa** (304 S. Lena, 970/626-3737 or 800/633-5868, www.chipeta.com, $157–215) one March weekend for an impromptu two-day trip to Telluride and Silverton, and there were so few other guests that the front desk upgraded me to the second-floor hot-tub suite. Overlooking the San Juans, the room was incredible, and the hippie types who work at the lodge are sweet and helpful. It's a little more crowded, obviously, during high season, but not nearly as crowded as downtown Telluride.

Food

The **True Grit Café** (123 N. Lena, 970/626-5739, www.truegritcafe.com, 11 A.M.–10 P.M. daily) is all burgers, fries, and beer, but with friendly, biker-and-hippie, wooden-wall ambience—complete with John Wayne movie posters and paraphernalia on the wall. Don't waste your time looking for more elegant restaurants in the area, unless you're in the mood to drive to Ouray or Telluride.

SILVERTON

Wander the streets of Silverton in March or April, when most of the skiers have gone home and summer tourists have yet to arrive, and it's a 7-by-12-block, clean-air *Pleasantville* in a valley of 14,000-foot peaks. The 500 townspeople mostly keep to themselves, although they're perfectly polite to visitors, who keep the Greene Street shops and hotels filled during high seasons. While Silverton boomed in the mining days, with 5,000 residents as late as 1912, isolation is a major part of its charm—only way to get here (other than the Durango & Silverton Narrow Gauge Railroad) is via the high hairpin curves of the Million Dollar Highway, the stretch of U.S. 550 that runs north from Durango and south from Ouray.

Sights

The entire downtown area is a National Historic Landmark District, and it's pretty fun to imagine the crowded streets and overflowing saloons of the old days, from the 1880s to the 1910s, when miners left their ramshackle boarding houses to visit brothels on Saturday night and churches on Sunday morning. Among the historic buildings are the 1907 **San Juan County Courthouse** (1557 Greene St.), which still has a gold dome and clock tower; the 1902 **San Juan County Jail** (1559 Greene St.), now the San Juan County Historical Society; and the 1907 **Old County Hospital** (1315 Snowden), a boxy building that houses the *Silverton Standard and Miner* newspaper.

Silverton magazine will send a copy of a walking-tour map if you send $10 to Circle B Publishing Inc. (P.O. Box 705, Ridgway, CO 81432). Or click on "Visitor Information" at the **Silverton Chamber of Commerce & Visitors Center** webpage (www.silvertoncolorado.com).

The most notable thing about the **San Juan County Historical Society** (1559 Greene St., 970/387-5838, www.silvertonhistoricalsociety.org, 9 A.M.–5 P.M. daily) is its location—inside the old county jail, the first building on Court House Square, which was by several accounts consistently full during the mining years. Converted to a museum in 1965, the building's exhibits include old railroad passes, mining equipment, handguns, a re-created schoolroom and kitchen, and, of course, jail cells on the second floor.

The **Old Hundred Gold Mine** (near County Roads 2 and 4-A, about three miles east of Silverton, 970/387-5444 or 800/872-3009, www.minetour.com, 9:30 A.M.–4 P.M. daily mid-May–mid-Oct., $15) opened in 1872 when three German brothers staked their claim to a gold vein called "Number Seven." Although it closed in 1973, the underground mine—45 to 50 degrees at all times—simulates the old days with mine-train rides and gold panning. Another gold-panning spot is the **Mayflower Mill** (Hwy. 110, two miles northeast of Silverton, 970/387-0294, 10 A.M.–5 P.M. daily Memorial Day–Labor Day, $6.50), which closed in 1991.

The **Christ of the Mines Shrine** (on top of Anvil Mountain, three miles north of Silverton) is a 12-ton, white-marble statue carved in Carrara, Italy, and erected as a miners' tribute in 1959. At the time, it was considered a good-luck charm for struggling Silverton. You can reach it by hiking a mile up 10th Street or driving along Shrine Road.

Silverton Mountain

Silverton Mountain (Route 110A, six miles north of Silverton, 970/387-5706, www.silvertonmountain.com) is an exclusive ski resort that climbs from 10,400 feet at the base to almost 12,300 feet at the peak. By "exclusive," I mean it's open only to expert and advanced skiers—and the resort strongly recommends eight-person groups for the steepest and rockiest trails (guides are available). One chairlift serves just 40 people per day, and be sure to read the safety precautions under "General Info" on the website; the high altitudes can be dangerous—the resort recommends ginseng or Viagra (!) to overcome this—weather changes are quick and frequent, and the skiing is "the steepest, most adventure-filled, lift-served skiing this side of Valdez, Alaska."

Also check the **Colorado Avalanche Information Center** (325 Broadway, Boulder, 970/247-8187, www.geosurvey.state.co.us/avalanche) for weather conditions.

Sports and Recreation

Beginning skiers are better off at the weekend-only, town-operated **Kendall Mountain Recreation Area** (1 Kendall Mountain Pl., 970/387-5522, $6), which also has hills for sledders and tubers, and free ice skating at the **Silverton Town Rink** (with skate rentals at the visitors center nearby).

Nordic skiers can veer off the established ski-resort paths at the **St. Paul Lodge** (14665 U.S. 550, 970/387-5367), an old miner's cabin with six rooms for 22 people and several nearby groomed trails. For more information about trails in the area, contact **Silverton Snowmobilers** (970/387-5748, www.silverton-snowmobilers.com).

Silverton Mountain (Route 110A, six miles north of Silverton, 970/387-5706, www.silvertonmountain.com) transforms from a ski resort to an extreme-cycling playground during summer—one of the runs is evocatively known as the Chicken [Expletive Deleted] Drop. It's probably best to bring your own bikes—parking is $22 per day, and scenic lift rides are $15 each—mostly because rental shops are hard to find in this isolated area.

Entertainment

The **Miners Union Theatre** (1069 Greene St., 970/387-5337 or 800/752-4494) plays host to movies, theater events, and a fine-arts youth camp; A Theatre Group is the local company that books all the shows. It's on the second floor of Miners Union Hall, built by, yes, miners (in 1902).

Shopping

The shops of Silverton are generally of the kitschy, touristy variety, so if you want to find practical sweaters or even books, Ouray and Telluride are better bets. The **Blair Street Emporium** (1147 Blair St., 970/387-5323), packed with Christmas decorations year-round, exemplifies this trend.

Accommodations

In a wide, blue 1882 building at the center of Greene Street, the **Grand Imperial Hotel** (1219 Greene St., 970/387-5527 or 800/341-3340, www.grandimperialhotel.com, $60–170) has become a little worn over the years, but it's still the most recognizable and one of the nicest hotels in town.

The **Wyman Hotel & Inn** (1371 Greene St., 970/387-5372 or 800/609-7845, www.thewyman.com, $139–159) is far better maintained than the Grand Imperial, with huge beds, whirlpools in many of the rooms, and a gourmet breakfast (a candlelight dinner is included in more expensive packages).

Also downtown is the **Teller House** (1250 Greene St., 970/387-5423 or 800/342-4338, $64–89), which a prominent brewer built in 1896. It's still one of the best-known hotels in town, but be sure to ask about the facilities before showing up—the "European-style" rooms have shared bathrooms.

The Animas B&B at the Wingate House (1045 Snowden St., 970/387-5520 or 877/387-

5520, www.wingatehouse.com, $59–175) is in a striking blue 1882 building with dogs lounging on the porch and (when guests bring them along, which actually happens) horses and llamas grazing in the yard. It has nice little touches like featherbeds, a lobby piano, and a stained-glass door from the porch.

Food

The top of the 1883 building that houses **Natalia's 1912 Restaurant** (1159 Blair St., 970/387-5300, www.natalias1912.com, 11 A.M.–3 P.M. Mon. and 11 A.M.–9 P.M. Tues.–Sun. May–Oct.) once said "Mattie B's"—a reference to the madam who ran a notorious bordello. Today it's a restaurant with a splashy, red-and-white facade that serves American, Italian, and Mexican dishes and a lunch buffet.

Handlebars (117 13th St., 970/387-5395, 10:30 A.M.–9 P.M. daily May–Oct.) is a boisterous bar and restaurant with Old West knickknacks, from photos to bandannas, hanging all over the walls and ceiling. The food is basic homemade bar fare, like seven types of burgers (including Buffalo Bill's buffalo burger), baby-back ribs, chicken-fried steak, and peach cobbler.

The **Avalanche Coffee House** (1065 Empire St., 970/387-5282, 8 A.M.–3 P.M. Tues.–Sun.) is a homey blue shack of a coffee-and-sandwiches joint that serves espresso and homemade soups to cold and desperate skiers.

Lake City

Lake City is where Colorado's most infamous resident, Alferd Packer, ate his five companions while they were trapped for days in a mountain blizzard in 1874. The six men had left Chief Ouray's camp near what would later become Montrose in February, and Packer's next sighting was two months later, at the Los Pinos Indian Agency, with somebody else's rifle and hunting knife. Authorities arrested him, and it came out that Packer killed one

of his men—in self-defense, he said—and ate him and at least one of the others. Although he was sentenced to murder, a judge reduced it to manslaughter, and Packer served 17 years of a 40-year sentence, living in Littleton until his death in 1907.

Packer has since become sort of a wacky Colorado historical icon, the inspiration for Lake City's Alferd Packer Jeep Tour and Barbecue and the University of Colorado-Boulder's Alferd

Packer Grill. There's even a local monument, the **Alferd Packer Memorial,** on Highway 149 near Lake San Cristobal.

Lake City itself is largely oblivious, these days, to Packer's deadly shenanigans. It's a pretty tourist town of just 250 people, surrounded by the Uncompahgre and Rio Grande forests, and its large National Historic District includes numerous classic Victorian buildings.

SIGHTS

The **Silver Thread Scenic Byway,** or Highway 149, was a mining road in the 1870s and has long since expanded to a modern paved highway. En route to South Fork, about 75 miles to the south, it passes some of southwest Colorado's most beautiful scenery, in the Gunnison and Rio Grande National Forests, as well as several historic mining areas and the Rio Grande valley.

SPORTS AND RECREATION

Fishing

Lake San Cristobal (off Hwy. 149, about five miles south of town) came into being about 700 years ago when something called the Slumgullion Earthflow flowed into the Gunnison River and created a large body of water. The Slumgullion is no longer a threat to the lake, which is plopped inside the Gunnison National Forest and is one of the best fishing spots in the area. Also, while the lakeshore is private property, numerous public trails are nearby, leading to 14,000-foot mountains such as Redcloud, Sunshine, and Handies.

For more information on the forests, hiking trails, and fishing, contact the **Forest Service** (2250 U.S.–50, Delta, 970/874-6600, www.fs.fed.us/r2/gmug). Or, for local fishing equipment, guided tours, and general advice, try **Dan's Fly Shop** (723 Gunnison Ave., 970/944-2281 summer, 970/252-9106 winter).

Hiking

Lake City is close to five 14,000-foot-tall

peaks: Uncompahgre, Handies, Redcloud, Wetterhorn, and Sunshine, all of which have hiking opportunities of varying levels of difficulty. One of the more challenging trails, more than 11 miles long, leads from the Gunnison River to Redcloud Peak to Sunshine Peak; the beginning of the hike is 2.5 miles south of town, on Highway 149. Go about 16.5 miles on Cinnamon Pass Road and look for the trailhead on the right. The elevation climbs quite a bit, so bring water.

ACCOMMODATIONS

Lake City isn't a huge bed-and-breakfast area—neither is nearby Gunnison, for that matter—but there are a couple of decent ones if you can't make it all the way to Crested Butte or Ouray. The **Cinnamon Inn** (426 Gunnison Ave., 800/337-2335, www.cinnamoninn.net, $89–129) is in a well-furnished Victorian house, with rooms named after Chief Ouray and Chipeta, former leaders of the Utes. And the **Old Carson Inn** (8401 Cinnamon Pass Rd., 800/294-0608, $92–140) is sort of the rustic alter-ego to the Cinnamon, in a log cabin in a forest with seven rooms and a wood fireplace.

FOOD

One of the handful of mom-and-pop restaurants in Lake City, the **Crystal Lodge Restaurant** (2175 Hwy. 149, 970/944-2201 or 877/465-6343, www.crystallodge.net, 6–9 P.M. Tues.–Sat., 10:30 A.M.–2 P.M. and 6–8 P.M. Sun.) is underneath the pretty Crystal Peak and has a long wine list to go with steak and seafood dishes and an outdoor deck.

INFORMATION

The **Lake City/Hinsdale County Chamber of Commerce** (800 N. Gunnison Ave., 970/944-2527 or 800/569-1874, www.lakecityco.com) will tell you everything you need to know about local restaurants, hotels, outdoor sports, and Alferd Packer.

Montrose

Every time you drive from Denver to Telluride, you pretty much have to go through Montrose, an ordinary town that's perfectly placed for a pit stop—gas stations, supermarkets, and fast-food restaurants line this stretch of U.S. 50. It's hard to believe so much natural beauty is within a short drive—Black Canyon of the Gunnison National Park, the San Juan Mountains, Curecanti National Recreation Area, and Gunnison River. Utopian mountain towns Telluride, Ouray, Ridgway, and Crested Butte are just down the road. Montrose is an affordable place to stay, though.

Montrose's history is about as eventful as the town itself—with one colorful exception. In 1873, gold-mining wannabes Oliver D. "Pappy" Loutsenhizer, Alferd Packer, and several others showed up in Ute territory en route to what is now Breckenridge, but they ran into Chief Ouray's valley camp. Ouray encouraged them to turn back, which Loutsenhizer and some of his friends did, but Packer and four other men went on. They landed in a Lake City blizzard, where the trapped Packer cannibalized his companions.

Loutsenhizer eventually returned with a friend, and in 1881, the two founded and named Montrose after a duchess in a Walter Scott novel. Within the next 20 years, the railroad and the

Gunnison Diversion Tunnel turned Montrose into a fairly important farming town, specializing in cotton and sugar beets.

SIGHTS

The recently renovated **Ute Indian Museum and Ouray National Park** (17253 Chipeta Dr., 970/249-3098, www.coloradohistory.org, 9 A.M.–4:30 P.M. Mon.–Sat. and 11 A.M.–4:30 P.M. Sun. mid-May–mid-Oct., 9 A.M.–4:30 P.M. Mon.–Sat. mid-Oct.–mid-May, $3) is on the 8.65-acre plot owned by Chief Ouray and his wife, Chipeta, in the 1800s. (Ouray, whose namesake town is about 30 miles south of Montrose, was the diplomatic Ute leader who befriended U.S. officials; he is considered a hero even though his willingness to compromise led to the Utes withdrawing from huge tracts of Colorado land.) Built in 1956, the museum displays thousands of Ute photos and artifacts, and the grounds include a memorial park, Chipeta's crypt, and a plant garden.

The **Montrose County Historical Museum** (Main St. and Rio Grande Ave., 970/249-2085, www.visitmontrose.net/museum.htm, 9 A.M.–4:30 P.M. Mon.–Sat. and 11 A.M.–4 P.M. Sun. mid-May–Sept., $4) is in the onetime Denver & Rio Grande Train Depot and, like many small Old West history museums in Colorado towns, displays wagons, farm tools, railroad memorabilia, Native American artifacts, and musical instruments.

◖ BLACK CANYON OF THE GUNNISON NATIONAL PARK

This unusually steep and scenic park (Hwy. 347, National Park Service, 102 Elk Creek, Gunnison, 970/641-2337, www.nps.gov/blca) gets much of the attention in this area as scenic landmarks go, and it's pretty amazing—a 53-mile cut of the earth that's 1,000 feet wide at the top, with the Gunnison River at the bottom, just 40 feet wide. But it's also a bit of a tourist trap, especially during summer, with a souvenir-selling visitors center, lines for outdoor

MONTROSE

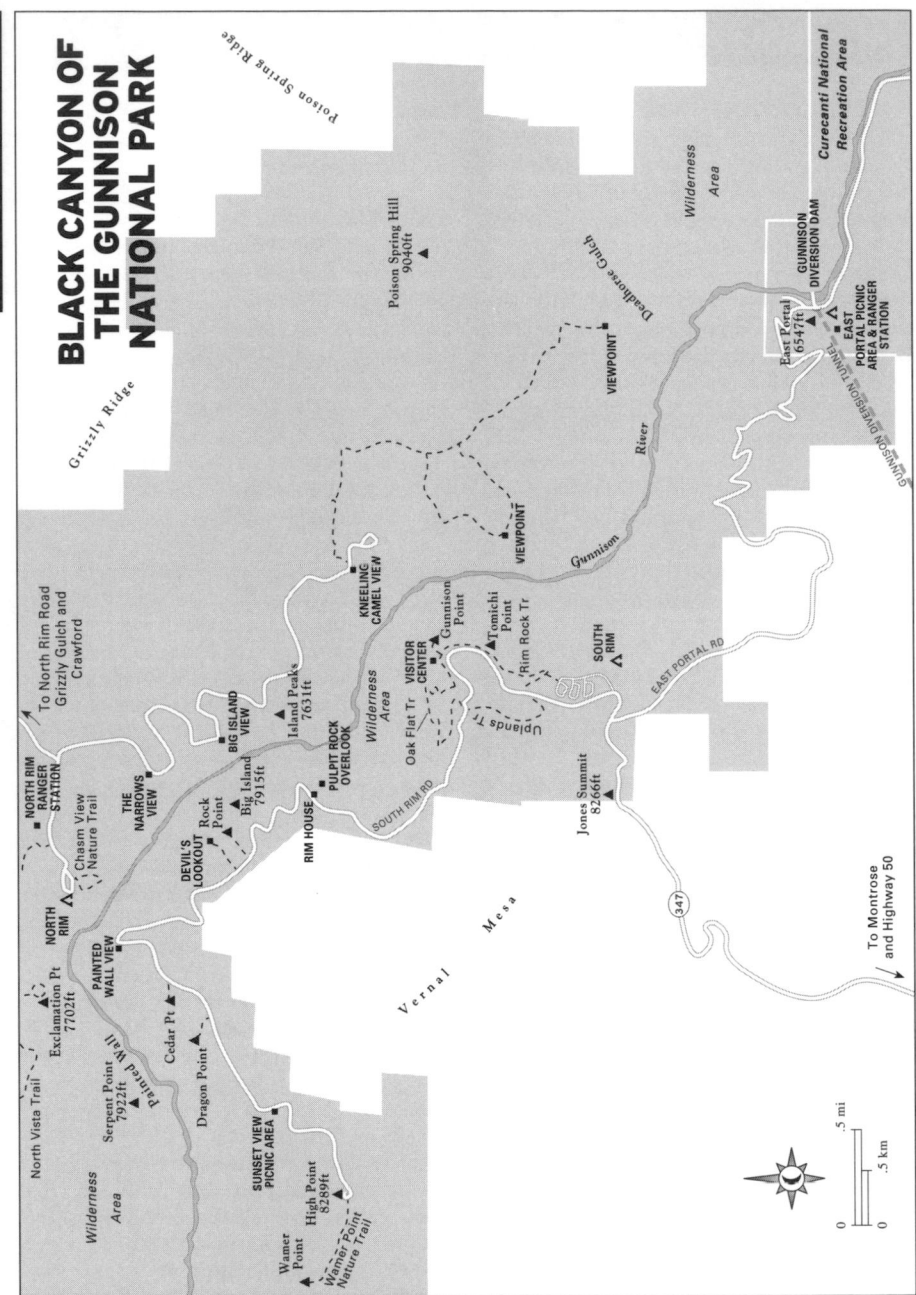

BLACK CANYON OF THE GUNNISON NATIONAL PARK

© STEVE KNOPPER

Ute Indian Museum in Montrose

restrooms, and a few crowded paths leading to points where you can look down the vertigo-inducing mesa cliffs into the sliver of river.

You can check it out via the North Rim or the South Rim; the easiest way is to take Highway 347 north from U.S. 50, then drive about six miles to the visitors center and hit one of the 10 scenic overlooks into the canyon. It's $8 to get in.

SPORTS AND RECREATION
Water Sports
The 14 miles of Gunnison River white water at the bottom of the Black Canyon National Park is not for the squeamish—the thin water passage is for expert **kayakers** only, and even some of those have died trying. The water is cold all the time, the rocks are so close together that you can barely see the sun, poison ivy grows more than five feet high at some points, and the river is exclusively Class IV and Class V. If you must try, though, at least contact the **National Park Service** (102 Elk Creek, Gunnison, 970/641-2337, www.nps.gov/blca/webvc/kayak.htm).

Calmer waters are just west of the park, in the **Gunnison Gorge National Conservation Area** (Bureau of Land Management, 2465 S. Townsend Ave., 970/240-5400). **Canoes** are kosher in this area, and several of Colorado's many white-water-rafting outfits sponsor tours—try **Wilderness Aware Rafting** (Buena Vista, 719/395-2112 or 800/462-7238, www.inaraft.com) or the **Boulder Outdoor Center** (2707 Spruce St., Boulder, 303/444-8420 or 800/364-9376, www.boc123.com).

Fishing
Both the **Black Canyon of the Gunnison National Park** and the **Gunnison Gorge National Conservation Area** contain points where you can fish for brown and rainbow trout on the river. But getting there is hard, involving various four-wheel-drive-only routes and bushwhacking hikes. You'll need a free state fishing license, although the Park Service gives out just a few, to whomever arrives first. It may be worth it: The Colorado Wildlife Commission considers this stretch of the Gunnison

River "gold medal waters," meaning 60 pounds of trout per surface acre. Just be sure not to swim or wade into the river.

Free permits are available through the **National Park Service** (970/641-2337, ext. 205, www.nps.gov/blca). Several local fishing shops provide information, guided tours, and equipment, including **Cimarron Creek** (317 E. Main St., 970/249-0408, www.cimarroncreek.com).

Hiking

Bushwhackers can hike through Black Canyon of the Gunnison Park at any number of self-made trailheads—just be careful—but established (and safer) trails exist with views of both the top and the bottom. The two-mile **Oak Flat Loop** is just west of the park's **visitors center** (970/249-1914), about eight miles west of Montrose on U.S. 50, and descends briefly below the south rim. The easier, three-mile **Exclamation Point** begins on the North Vista Trail, leading due west from the ranger station

© STEVE KNOPPER

Black Canyon has tall, steep cliffs at the top and a narrow stretch of river below.

(on the north side of the park); you'll be able to walk right to the edge of the North Rim and stare 1,800 feet down to the river.

Gunnison Gorge National Conservation Area also has a few excellent hiking trails, including, well, **Gunnison Gorge,** which begins about 9.5 miles north of Montrose on U.S. 550. (Once you get to Falcon Road, turn right, drive 11.1 miles, turn right on Ute Road, and go 2.6 miles to the trailhead.) It's not as breathtaking as the Black Canyon of the Gunnison, but the canyon views are nice.

To hike on local trails, you'll need a free permit from the **National Park Service** (970/641-2337, ext. 205, www.nps.gov/blca).

ENTERTAINMENT AND EVENTS

Although it mostly plays host to weddings and corporate events, the 600-seat **Montrose Pavilion** (1800 Pavilion Drive, 970/249-7015, 800/982-2518) occasionally has dance, music, and theater events. North of Montrose, in tiny Olathe, the early-August **Olathe Sweet Corn Festival** (970/323-6006, 866/363-2676, www.olathesweetcorn.com) is a much bigger deal than you'd think, with big-time performance names (such as country singer Randy Travis) supplementing the pancake breakfast, car show, and other corny events.

SHOPPING

Most of the shopping in Montrose is pretty generic, but the plain-looking **Russell Stover Factory Outlet** (2185 Stover Ave., 970/249-5372, www.russellstover.com) is a gigantic (7,500 square feet!) building filled with chocolate and other gift candies. Disappointingly, there are no Oompa Loompas or other psychedelic, *Charlie and the Chocolate Factory*-style visions, but Stover does manufacture more than 100 million pounds of chocolate, all over the U.S., every year.

ACCOMMODATIONS

Lodging in Montrose consists mostly of chains, but a few low-priced motels are good for a quick stop en route to Telluride, Ouray, Ridgway, or the Four Corners. The **Black Canyon Motel** (1605 E. Main St., 970/249-3495 or 800/348-3495, $65–80) has an outdoor pool, as does the wooden **Country Lodge** (1624 E. Main St., 970/249-4567, www.countryldg.com, $75–85), where John Wayne reportedly stayed while filming *True Grit* in the 1960s.

About six miles from Montrose, the seven-room **Uncompahgre Bed & Breakfast** (21049 Uncompahgre Rd., 970/240-4000 or 800/318-8127, www.uncbb.com, $75) is slightly more quaint than the other area hotels.

FOOD

Montrose is hardly an area around which to plan a gourmet trip, but it has a few distinctive restaurants, including **Amelia's Hacienda** (44 S. Grand Ave., 970/249-1881, www.ameliashacienda.com, 11 A.M.–9 P.M. Mon.–Fri.,

noon–9 P.M. Sat., noon–8 P.M. Sun.), one of the better Mexican restaurants in town.

INFORMATION

The **Montrose Visitors and Convention Bureau** (1519 E. Main St., 970/240-1414 or 800/873-0244, www.visitmontrose.net) has up-to-date dining and lodging listings as well as city services.

GETTING THERE AND AROUND

The **Montrose Regional Airport** (2100 Airport Rd., 970/249-3203, www.co.montrose.co.us/airport/airport.html) services several major carriers, and it's a reliable alternative to Telluride's smaller airport in bad-weather conditions. Within the city, **Montrose Bus Depot** (1360 N. Townsend Ave., 970/249-6673) operates most of the time.

Durango

More of a real city than a scenic mountain hamlet like nearby Telluride, Durango is neither big (population 14,000) nor tall (elevation 6,500 feet) nor amazingly popular with skiers or mountain bikers. But its location on the Animas River (thus the name, which means "water town"), moderate climate, and proximity to four western states makes it a pleasant place to pass through and an affordable place to live.

Durango began as a railroad town. After gold-mining drew thousands of people to the nearby San Juan Mountains, they incorporated Animas City, two miles north of what is Durango today; when the Denver and Rio Grande Railroad showed up within a few years, almost all 2,000 townspeople relocated to the new area. Durango officially became a town in 1881—a booming one, thanks to the railroad, although the 1893 silver crash forced many residents away and the rest into farming and ranching.

Durango lived on as a sleepy city for decades, but tourism gradually began to create

growth, which continues today. The city is near Mesa Verde National Park and the Four Corners area, as well as popular ski resorts such as Telluride and Silverton. Higher-end hotels, restaurants, and rows of tourist shops have sprung up in recent years to supplement the popular Durango & Silverton Narrow Gauge Railroad.

SIGHTS

Some of Durango's downtown area has filled up with chain hotels and restaurants in recent years, but it remains a giant National Historic District: 86 buildings are preserved from the late 19th and early 20th centuries. The primary area is around 12th Street and Main Avenue, with buildings such as the 1895 **Palace Hotel** (429 Main Ave.), the 1882 **Railroad Depot** (4th and Main), the 1887 **Strater Hotel** (7th and Main), and the 1897 **Newman Building** (8th and Main). The second historic area is on 3rd Avenue, two blocks east of Main, with rows of Victorian homes.

The Utes used what is now **Trimble Hot**

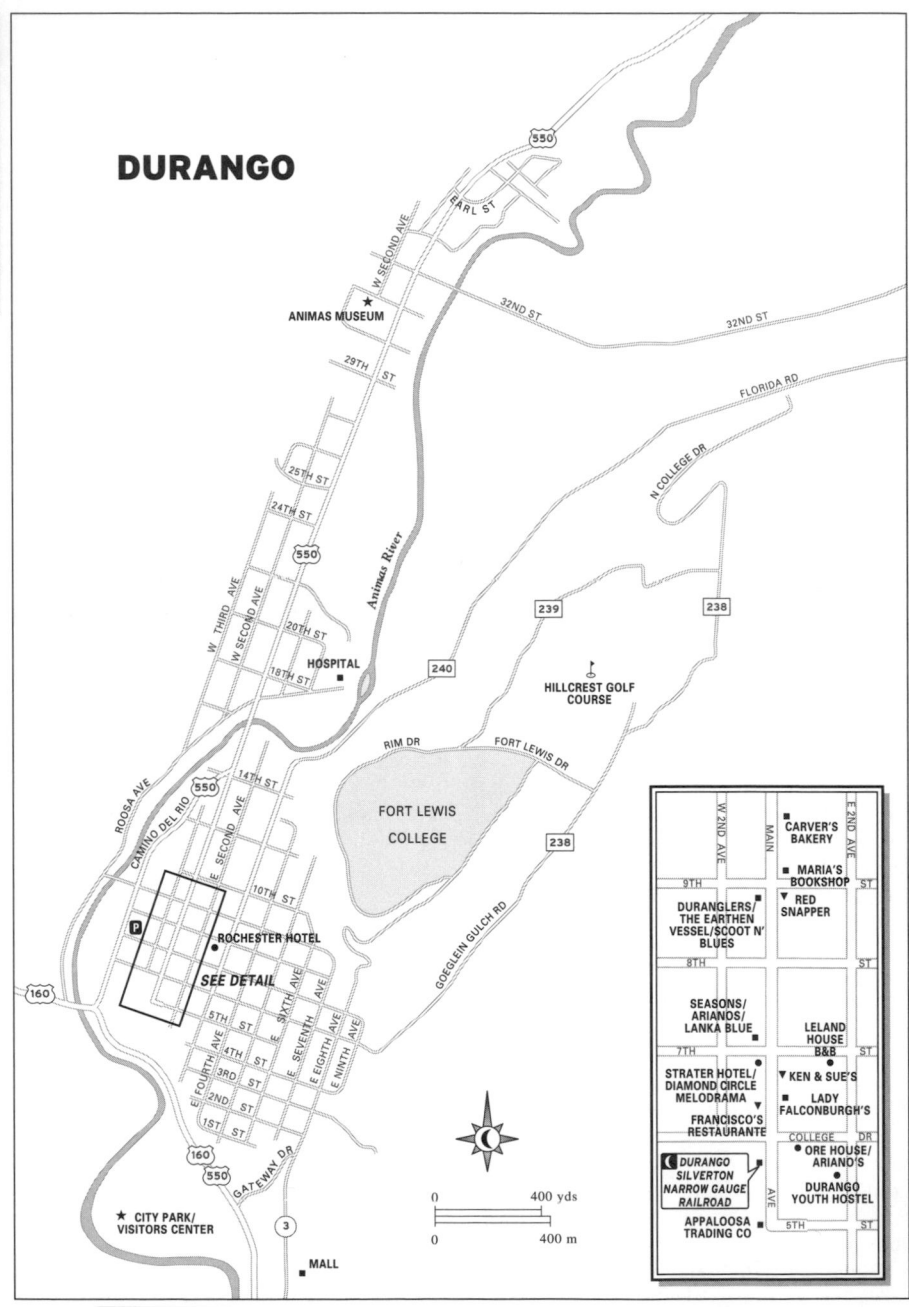

DURANGO

550

EARL ST

W SECOND AVE

★ ANIMAS MUSEUM

32ND ST   32ND ST

29TH   ST

FLORIDA RD

25TH ST

24TH ST

N COLLEGE DR

550

Animas River

W THIRD AVE

W SECOND AVE

20TH ST

18TH ST

■ HOSPITAL

239

238

240

HILLCREST GOLF
COURSE

ROOSA AVE

CAMINO DEL RIO

14TH ST

RIM DR   FORT LEWIS DR

W SECOND AVE

550

FORT LEWIS

COLLEGE

238

GOEGLEIN GULCH RD

E SECOND AVE

10TH ST

P

● ROCHESTER HOTEL

SEE DETAIL

160

SIXTH AVE

E SEVENTH AVE

E EIGHTH AVE

E NINTH AVE

5TH ST

4TH ST
3RD ST
2ND ST
1ST ST

E FOURTH AVE

160
550

GATEWAY DR

★ CITY PARK/
VISITORS CENTER

3

■ MALL

0   400 yds

0   400 m

W 2ND AVE

MAIN

E 2ND AVE

■ CARVER'S
BAKERY

9TH   ST

■ MARIA'S
BOOKSHOP

DURANGLERS/
THE EARTHEN
VESSEL/SCOOT N'
BLUES

▼ RED
SNAPPER

8TH   ST

SEASONS/
ARIANDS/
LANKA BLUE ■

LELAND
HOUSE
B&B

7TH   ST

STRATER HOTEL/
DIAMOND CIRCLE
MELODRAMA

▼ KEN & SUE'S

■   LADY
FALCONBURGH'S

FRANCISCO'S
RESTAURANTE

COLLEGE   DR

◖ DURANGO
SILVERTON
NARROW GAUGE
RAILROAD

● ORE HOUSE/
ARIANO'S

●
DURANGO
YOUTH HOSTEL

AVE

APPALOOSA
TRADING CO

5TH   ST

Springs (6475 County Rd. 203, 970/247-0111, www.trimblehotsprings.com, 8 A.M.–11 P.M. daily in summer, 9 A.M.–10 P.M. Sun.–Thurs. and 9 A.M.–11 P.M. Fri.–Sat. in winter, $11 summer, $9 winter) as "healing waters," and when rheumatism-plagued Frank Trimble settled here in 1884, he claimed to be healed. He also turned the springs into a tourism business that continues to this day—temperatures are as high as 120 degrees Fahrenheit, and Marilyn Monroe is said to have experienced the healing powers. Today, there's an Olympic-sized pool and three "natural therapy pools."

Known as Colorado's "campus in the sky," the 4,500-student **Fort Lewis College** (1000 Rim Dr., 970/247-7010, www.fortlewis.edu) is on top of a mesa, with red-roofed buildings surrounded by various cliffs and mountains. In an expanded and refurbished building with Masayuki Nagase's stone-obelisk *Passage of the Wine* sculpture out front, **The Fort Lewis College Art Gallery** (101 Art Building, 970/247-7167, 10 A.M.–4 P.M. Mon.–Fri.) displays student paintings and sculpture. The college's **Native American Center** (970/247-7221) supports a student population that's (uniquely) 16 percent Native American.

Chimney Rock Archaeological Area (three miles south of Hwy. 160 on Hwy. 151, about 40 miles east of Durango, 970/883-5359 or 970/264-2287 off-season, www.chimneyrockco.org, 9 A.M.–4:30 P.M. mid-May–Sept.) may have been the Anasazis' astronomy observatory 1,000 years ago—more likely, it was an agricultural area, as well as the site of 200 homes and ceremonial buildings, 27 work camps, and 91 other structures. Archaeologists are still figuring this out, but what's certain is Chimney Rock is a beautiful and fascinating 4,100-acre site within the Southern Ute Indian Reservation, with pinkish mesas and weird rock formations in every direction.

Durango & Silverton Narrow Gauge Railroad

The railroad has defined Durango for most of its 125-year existence, so it's fitting that the city's tourism business centers on the Durango & Silverton Narrow Gauge Railroad (479 Main Ave., 970/247-2733 or 888/872-4607, www.durangotrain.com, 8 A.M.–6 P.M. daily May–Oct., $62). This 45-mile line began in 1882 to haul gold and silver ore out of the San Juan Mountains, and it continued running despite the silver crash of 1893 and a devastating Spanish-flu outbreak in Silverton. It closed just before World War II, though, and reopened for tourism in 1947—and movie producers came to the area, filming the train in *Ticket to Tomahawk, Around the World in 80 Days, Butch Cassidy and the Sundance Kid,* and several others. Today, the steam-powered, coal-fired, 1920s-era locomotives pull six passenger cars along a scenic, placid Animas River route at 18 miles per hour; it's perhaps the nicest commute in Colorado, and the layover in mountain-secluded Silverton is more than two hours.

SPORTS AND RECREATION
Hiking and Biking

Durango's trails aren't as renowned as those in Crested Butte or Telluride, but they cut through forests and canyons, with views of La Plata Mountains and the Animas Valley. An easy one is the **Animas Overlook Trail** (north on Main Avenue, left on 25th Street, left at the fork in the road, to a parking area at milepost 7), a half-mile stretch that overlooks the valley. More difficult is **Mountain View Crest** (north on Main Avenue, right on 32nd Street, left on Colorado Road 250, right on Missionary Ridge Road, right on Henderson Lake Road), about 28 miles outside of town, requiring a four-wheel-drive vehicle the last four miles. The uphill nine-mile hike is worth it, with amazing views of Pigeon and Turret Peaks and Chicago Basin in the Weminuche Wilderness.

For more information about hiking local trails—and rock climbing, and other outdoor activities—contact the **San Juan Public Lands Center** (15 Burnett Ct., 970/247-4874, www.fs.fed.us/r2/sanjuan, 8 A.M.–5 P.M. Mon.–Fri.), part of the U.S. Forest Service.

Fishing

Fly-fishing spots are all over the Durango area—in the San Juan River and Weminuche

Wilderness, among others, but perhaps the best known is just below Navajo Dam, about an hour's drive from the city. **Duranglers** (923 Main Ave., 970/385-4081, www.duranglers.com) is one of several local angler shops that sell maps and equipment and offer fishing advice. It gives guided tours, too.

Golf

The Durango area has two major golf courses. The 18-hole, 7,000-yard **Dalton Ranch Golf Club** (589 County Rd. 252, 970/247-7921, www.daltonranch.com) is six miles north of Durango, above the Animas River and below the San Juan Mountains. The public, 18-hole **Hillcrest Golf Course** (2300 Rim Dr., 970/247-1499) is near Fort Lewis College.

ENTERTAINMENT AND EVENTS
Theater

The **Diamond Circle Melodrama & Vaudeville** (699 Main Ave., 970/247-3400, www.diamondcirclemelodrama.com) puts on the kinds of turn-of-the-last-century shows that involve mustache-twirling villains, damsels in distress, and lots of slapstick comedy. Weird and funny. The **Durango Lively Arts Company** (970/382-8584) presents four or five plays every year in various venues, and the 600-seat **Fort Lewis College Community Concert Hall** (1000 Rim Dr., 970/247-7657, www.durangoconcerts.com) puts on music concerts (bluegrass, classical, blues, country, and everything else) and theater.

Events

Just 11 musicians played the first **Music in the Mountains** (www.musicinthemountains.com) in 1987; today the chamber, pops, classical, and orchestra festival has expanded to a three-week extravaganza starring renowned musicians from all over the world. It runs from mid–July to mid–August.

Nightlife

Of the many places to drink until very late at night in Durango, the **Diamond Belle**

Saloon (699 Main Ave., 800/247-4431, www.strater.com/belle.php) is the most surreal—it's an Old West ragtime piano bar, with period music and costumes. According to legend, author Louis L'Amour always stayed in the Strater Hotel room (222) above the Diamond Belle to help set the mood for his novels. More conventional—despite the large murals on the wall—is the European-style tavern **Lady Falconburgh's Barley Exchange** (640 Main Ave., 970/382-9664, www.ladyfalconburgh.com).

Scoot 'N Blues (900 Main Ave., 970/259-1400, www.scootnblues.com) supplements its live local blues bands with plenty of beer to cry in. And the **Bar D Chuckwagon** (8080 County Rd. 250, East Animas Valley, 970/247-5753, www.bardchuckwagon.com) is an old-fashioned (since 1969) barbecue joint with the veteran comedy-and-music troupe Bar D Wranglers as a backdrop.

About 25 miles from Durango, the **Sky Ute Casino & Lodge** (14826 Hwy. 172 N., Ignacio, 970/563-3000 or 888/842-4180, www.skyutecasino.com) has the best low-stakes gambling (blackjack, slots, and so on) in the state if you don't count Black Hawk, Central City, or Cripple Creek.

SHOPPING

Durango's downtown has become increasingly touristy in recent years, and many of the shops and galleries have stepped up their business with the growth. **Maria's Bookshop** (960 Main Ave., 970/247-1438, www.mariasbookshop.com) is a comfortable little store with hardwood floors and not a single employee named Maria. The **Appaloosa Trading Co.** (501 Main Ave., 970/385-1722, www.appaloosadurango.com) sells hand-crafted silver and leather items, from belt buckles to books, and **O'Farrell Handcrafted Hats** (399 Camino Iglesia, 970/259-5900) is the requisite homemade cowboy-hat store (although it sells many different kinds as well).

Gallery-wise, the **Toh-Atin Gallery** (145 W. 9th St., 800/525-0384, www.toh-atin.com) has been selling Navajo rugs and Native American jewelry since 1957. Artist and goldsmith Gary

McVean runs **Lanka Blue Jewelry** (701 Main Ave., 970/247-9448, www.lankablue.com), specializing in gold-and-silver-set *naja* amulets, once believed in Spanish culture to ward off the evil eye. **The Earthen Vessel** (115 W. 9th St., 970/247-1281 or 800/884-1281, www.earthenvessel.com) sells pottery made by Colorado artists.

ACCOMMODATIONS

Built in 1887 by a Cleveland pharmacist, the (**Strater Hotel** (699 Main Ave., 800/247-4431, www.strater.com, $170–250) is a classic red-brick fortress with hand-carved turrets and flourishes; it has survived fires and market crashes, and underwent a massive renovation in the early 1980s. The hotel claims the world's largest collection of Victorian walnut furniture, and while that's difficult to verify, the rooms certainly make a case, with four-poster beds, elaborately patterned love seats, and other antiques.

The **Rochester Hotel** (726 E. 2nd Ave., 970/385-1920 or 800/664-1920, www.rochesterhotel.com, $149–229) is a rectangular brick box of a building that has operated as a hotel in this spot since 1892. Naturally, it plays up the Old West history, with rooms based on Durango-filmed movies such as *Around the World in 80 Days* and *Viva Zapata*—framed Hollywood posters are in each of the 12 rooms, adding to what the owners call the "funky cowboy" look.

The Rochester Hotel's owners, Diane and Kirk Komick, also run the **Leland House B&B** (721 E. 2nd Ave., 970/385-1920 or 800/664-1920, www.leland-house.com, $149–340), across the street in a two-story 1927 brick apartment building. Breakfast is in the Rochester Hotel.

The **Apple Orchard Inn** (7758 County Rd. 203, 970/247-0751 or 800/426-0751, www.appleorchardinn.com, $140–210) is a sprawling complex of a stone-chimney house and six cottages in the middle of the Animas Valley. In addition to a pond (complete with geese) and homemade bread and chocolate-chip cookies, the five-acre property has an outdoor hot tub and rocking chairs and swings on each cottage patio.

FOOD

Seasons (764 Main Ave., 970/382-9790, www.seasonsonthenet.com/Durango, 11:30 A.M.–2 P.M. and 5:30–10 P.M. Mon.–Fri., 5:30 P.M.–10 P.M. Sat.–Sun.) is part of a two-restaurant chain (the other is in Albuquerque) centered on an open kitchen with a wood-burning grill and rotisserie. Locals rave about the mashed potatoes and green chile-covered sweet potatoes, although most of the dinner menu is your basic steak, chicken, and seafood.

Only a baby, relatively speaking, in Old West Durango—the **Ore House** (147 E. College Dr., 970/247-5707, www.orehouserestaurant.com, 5–11 P.M. daily) was established in 1972 and serves gigantic cuts of beef ranging $19–64, as well as lobster and poultry.

The Red Snapper (144 E. 9th St., 970/259-3417, 5–10 P.M. daily) broadcasts "Fresh Seafood Steak & Prime" on its awning, but aficionados know its primary strengths are not steak and prime but oysters, salmon, orange roughy, lobster tail, and shrimp cocktail. The numerous glass fish tanks make you feel hungry and guilty at the same time.

Francisco's Restaurante Y Cantina (619 Main Ave., 970/247-4098, www.franciscosrestaurante.com, 11 A.M.–10 P.M. Mon.–Sat., 9 A.M.10 P.M. Sun.), as you may have surmised, serves Mexican food—which owners Francisco and Claudine Garcia and their kids have been cooking since 1968. The menu is fairly typical—enchiladas, fajitas, and the like—with a few unique touches such as asparagus, potato, and poblano cream soup.

Ken & Sue's Place (636 Main Ave., 970/259-2616, 11 A.M.–2:30 P.M. and 5–10 P.M. Mon.–Fri., 5–10 P.M. Sat.–Sun.) is an Asian-influenced American restaurant with heavy sauces to go with high-end combinations like potato-encrusted trout and lobster ravioli.

Best early in the morning or late at night, **Carver's Bakery and Brew Pub** (1022 Main Ave., 970/259-2545, 6:30 A.M.–10 P.M. Mon.–Sat., 6 A.M.–2 P.M. Sun.) opens with kid-friendly breakfast menus and closes with eight on-tap beers and a comfortable outdoor *biergarten* out back.

Ariano's Northern Italian Cuisine (150 E. College Dr., 970/247-8146, 5:30–10 P.M.) gets everything right about Italy—linguine, trout, chicken, and fettuccine with prosciutto, all with great sauces.

INFORMATION

The **City of Durango** (949 E. 2nd Ave., 970/375-5000, www.durangogov.org) has information on transportation, parks and recreation, and most city services. For travel listings, including dining and restaurants, try the **Durango Area Tourism Office** (111 S. Camino del Rio, 800/525-8855, www.durango.org). The local newspaper is the *Durango Herald* (www.durangoherald.com).

Several local websites provide information on Cortez: the **City of Cortez** (210 E. Main St., 970/565-3402, www.cityofcortez.com), the **Cortez Area Chamber of Commerce** (928 E. Main St., 970/565-3414, www.cortezchamber.org), and the local newspaper, the *Cortez Journal* (www.cortezjournal.com). Also, the **Colorado Welcome Center** (928 E. Main St., 970/565-3414 or 800/253-1616, www.mesaverdecountry.com) is in Cortez City Park at the center of town.

Get information about Dolores at the **Dolores Chamber of Commerce and Visitors Center** (201 Railroad Ave., 970/882-4018, www.doloreschamber.com).

GETTING THERE AND AROUND

The **Durango-La Plata County Airport** (1000 Airport Rd., 970/247-8143, www.durangogov.org/services/airport.html) serves the Four Corners region, via carriers America West Express, United Express, and others. **Durango Transit** (970/259-5438, www.durangogov.org/resident/services/transit.html) runs buses and trolleys well into the night.

PURGATORY VILLAGE

Although it's still known colloquially as "Purgatory," Purgatory Village is actually the ski-town area inside **Durango Mountain Resort,** about 20 miles north of Durango, near the intersection of U.S. 550 and Highway 160. It's a great, friendly little ski area, with an elevation of almost 11,000 feet and trails that start off bumpy but smooth out as you go—as a result, it's perfect for beginners, even if nearby Crested Butte and Telluride skiers scoff. The village is filled with restaurants and bars—as well as the massive Lodge at Tamarron, on 750 acres in the middle of the woods—and the resort has an alpine slide and biking trails in the summer.

Sports and Recreation

Of the 75 ski trails at **Durango Mountain Resort** (1 Skier Pl., 970/247-9000 or 800/525-0892, www.durangomountainresort.com)—40 miles overall—about 23 percent are for beginners, 26 percent advanced and expert, and the rest intermediate. Eleven chairlifts serve the established trails, although the **San Juan Ski Co.** (1831 Lake Purgatory Dr., 970/259-9671 or 800/208-1780, www.sanjuanski.com) gives access to another 35,000 ungroomed acres—a great experience for bushwhackers.

The resort has two places for lessons, the **Adult Adventure School** (970/385-2149) and **Kids Mountain Adventure** (970/385-2149), both of which offer group and individual lessons in the $35–$75 range.

During summer, the resort converts to **mountain-biking** terrain, some of which is pretty hard-core, given the World Mountain Bike Championships were here in 1990. But the 50 miles of trails include plenty of lighter, more scenic territory, and rentals are available on the premises. Contact the resort at 970/247-9000 for more information.

Accommodations

The Lodge at Tamarron (U.S. 550, 18 miles north of Durango, 970/259-2000, $150) is a gigantic cliffside property with rooms of many different sizes, from sleeper-sofa studios to kitchen-equipped condo suites. It has a spa, pool, hot tubs, tennis courts, and **The Glacier Club** (970/382-7800 or 866/375-8300, www.theglacierclub.com), with three nine-hole golf courses amid dramatic views of mesa cliffs.

The resort offers lodging at several properties, most notably the slopeside **Purgatory Village Condominium Hotel** (1 Skier Pl., 800/982-6103, $70–210), including some of the best views in the resort, plus fireplaces in most rooms and a four-bedroom penthouse whose atrium overlooks the Demon ski run. It has several properties, from condos to hotel studios and suites.

Food

The resort itself has several decent-enough restaurants, but to get to the good stuff you have to get out of the village. The **Cascade Grill** (50827 U.S. 550, 970/259-3500, 5:30–9 P.M. Wed.–Sat.), about a mile north of the resort, has grilled elk medallions as well as steak, seafood, and pasta. The **Sow's Ear** (48475 U.S. 550, 970/247-3527, www.silverpicklodge.com/sowsear.htm, 5–9 P.M. daily) is in a condominium complex a mile south of the resort, serving homemade bread and dessert, as well as steak, seafood, pasta, and poultry. It's pretty hard to find oysters on the half shell ($15 for a dozen) anywhere else around here. Live music is on some nights.

CORTEZ

Tiny Cortez is the last town in Colorado en route to the Four Corners—a symbolic area where Colorado, Utah, New Mexico, and Arizona meet—and remains sacred to several Native American tribes that live on nearby reservations.

Cortez itself is one of those Colorado towns that doesn't look like much when you drive through—lots of fast-food restaurants, hotel chains, and old trailer-park-style buildings scattered everywhere—but it's within striking distance of scenic plains, mesas, cliffs, and mountains, and galleries and shops on the main drag. Also, this is Native American country, with dances every week and art-and-rug dealers everywhere.

Cortez's main draw, though, is its proximity to Mesa Verde National Park, which at first glance is just another Colorado nature preserve filled with canyons and mesa cliffs—but what sets it apart is a ghost civilization of Anasazi cliff dwellings, tall and remarkably well preserved, with 200 elaborately detailed rooms that resemble apartments and hotels. Archaeologists have traced their origins to A.D. 550.

Sights

The **Four Corners Monument** (U.S. 160, about 38 miles south of Cortez, www.navajonationparks.org/fourcorners_monument.htm), run by the Navajo Nation, is the only place in the U.S. where people can touch four states at the same time. The brass-and-granite, manhole-like monument reads: "Four states here meet in freedom under God."

The **Cortez Cultural Center** (25 N. Market St., 970/565-1151, www.cortezculturalcenter.org, 10 A.M.–10 P.M. Mon.–Sat. Memorial Day–Labor Day, 10 A.M.–5 P.M. Mon.–Sat. Sept.–May, free) is a boxy building designed and painted in tribute to the Mesa Verde's cliff dwellings. The complex contains a museum, dedicated mostly to Ute, Navajo, and Anasazi culture and heritage, but it also sponsors traditional Native American dances, sells pottery, books, and CDs, and has a cultural park with a tepee.

Hovenweep National Monument (McElmo Route, 970/562-4282, www.nps.gov/hove, 8 A.M.–5 P.M. daily, $3) is a dramatic, 20-mile stretch of canyons and mesas containing six prehistoric villages on the border between Colorado and Utah. Built by the Anasazi some 10,000 years ago, the dwellings are architecturally similar to those at Mesa Verde National Park, and some are built directly on top of boulders and canyon rims. They look precarious, but they've survived since roughly the late 1200s, when an estimated 2,500 people lived here. (Cultural note: The commonly used word Anasazi, in Navajo, means "enemy to our peoples," so many descendants prefer the more neutral term "Ancestral Puebloans.") A Mormon explorer discovered the ruins in 1854, and by 1923, President Warren G. Harding declared the area part of the National Park System.

It's possible to enter the monument from either the Colorado or Utah side—the access roads are only intermittently paved and a little precarious—but many start at the visitors center and Square Tower Group. To get here, take County Road G (McElmo Canyon Road) from Cortez, or Highway 262 (from White Mesa, south of Blanding). The most difficult path is a dirt road from Highway 666 (near Pleasant View).

Sports and Recreation

The views at the 18-hole **Conquistador Golf Course** (2018 N. Dolores Rd., 970/565-9208, www.cityofcortez.com/golfcourse.shtml) are of La Plata Peak, Mesa Verde National Park, and Sleeping Ute Mountain, and golfers should beware the trees on hole 5.

Entertainment

It's pretty far from Black Hawk and Central City around here, so if you're lonely for slot machines and blackjack, the **Ute Mountain Casino** (3 Weeminuche Dr., Towaoc, 970/565-8800 or 800/258-8007, www.utemountaincasino.com) is run by the Ute reservation in nearby Towaoc.

Shopping

Cortez and its surrounding little towns are a great area to pick up Native American knickknacks and artistic works—among the best shops are the **Clay Mesa Art Gallery and Studio** (29 E. Main St., 970/565-1902, www.claymesa.com), which sells homemade plates and bowls with intricate painted designs (out of clay, of course); **Cliffrose High Desert Gardens** (27885 Hwy. 160, 970/565-8994), specializing in hard-to-find plants; and the **Notah Dineh Trading Company and Museum** (345 W. Main St., 800/444-2024, www.notahdineh.com), known for its large hand-crafted rugs, including an elaborate one called *Two Grey Hills*, for which weaving began in 1960.

Accommodations

Cortez isn't exactly known for its luxury hotels—the Best Western and the Comfort Inn are the only places that get three AAA stars in town—but the **Anasazi Motor Inn** (640 S. Broadway, 970/565-3773 or 800/972-6232, www.anasazimotorinn.com, $65) is a pretty entertaining place to hang around. It has live music (mostly local acts) in the lounge, a decent home-cooking restaurant, and a pool.

Food

Again, Arby's and Domino's are the predominant culinary excitement in Cortez, but try the **Homesteaders Family Restaurant** (45 E. Main St., 970/565-6253, www.thehomesteaders.com, 11 A.M.–9:30 P.M. Mon.–Sat.) for steak, seafood, and baby-back ribs.

◖ MESA VERDE NATIONAL PARK

Walking into this 80-square-mile area of right-angle cliffs and deep canyons is like stumbling onto an entire ghost civilization. Here are massive stone villages, complete with buildings, towers, pools, and an odd-shaped checkerboard of rectangular windows and protruding, brick-shaped stones—everything a town would need, that is, except the people. The residents of these cliff dwellings were the Anasazi (also known as Ancestral Puebloans), who built and lived here from roughly A.D. 600 to 1300. The Anasazis took off, inexplicably, in the late 1300s, leaving their empty homes behind, and they went undiscovered until around 1888, when local ranchers came upon the Cliff Palace, Spruce Tree House, and Square Tower House. Eighteen years later, the abandoned dwellings became a national park, and almost 500,000 visitors continue to arrive every year—so it's best to drop by anytime other than summer to avoid crowds.

Mesa Verde (U.S. 160, 970/529-4465, www.nps.gov/meve/home.htm, hours vary according to museum and visitors center, $10 per vehicle) is accessible at a few different points. The **Chapin Mesa Archeological Museum,** the park headquarters, including a U.S. Post Office, is about 20 miles from the U.S. 160 entrance, and the **Far View Visitors Center** is 15 miles from the highway and has paths (and

COURTESY OF THE NATIONAL PARK SERVICE

Mesa Verde National Park

a tram) up the scenic route to **Wetherill Mesa** (open only during the summer) and **Ruins Road** (leading to the magnificent Spruce Tea House ruin). Perhaps the best-known ruin is the **Cliff Palace,** about 15 minutes by foot from the museum.

Accommodations

Within the park, Aramark runs most of the lodging and food areas, including the **Far View Lodge** (Box 277, Mancos, 970/529-4421 or 800/449-2288, www.visitmesaverde.com, $105–126), which has well-furnished (if pretty basic) rooms and balconies that overlook amazing Mesa Verde views and, in the distance, glimpses of three different states (and Colorado, of course). The lodge also has a southwestern restaurant, the Metate Room, and sponsors guided tours and Navajo rug–weaving demonstrations. Roughing-it types will prefer the **Morefield Campground** (four miles from the park entrance, 970/533-1944, www.visitmesaverde.com, $20), open May through mid-October, which has 435 campsites (and a

pancake breakfast) in a grassy area. You might see deer or wild turkeys.

Food

In addition to the Far View Lodge's Metate Room, as well as a marketplace and cafeteria within the park, **Millwood Junction** (U.S. 160 and Main St., Mancos, 970/533-7338, www.millwoodjunction.com, 11 A.M.– 2 P.M. and 5:30–10:30 P.M. Mon.–Fri., 5:30– 10:30 P.M. Sat.–Sun.) is known for its Friday-night seafood buffet, although it also serves steak, chicken, and beer and wine.

DOLORES

The main reason for visiting tiny Dolores, near the southwest corner of the state, is the **fishing**—particularly at **McPhee Reservoir,** which after Blue Sky Reservoir is the largest body of water in Colorado. Other fishing spots are Groundhog Lake, Narraguinnep Reservoir, and the Dolores River. (The latter, formed from a 1968 irrigation dam, runs through the town and is stocked with many kinds of trout.)

The Colorado Division of Wildlife has stocked more than 4.5 million fish in McPhee since 1987, including bluegills, crappies, trout, bass, kokanee salmon, and catfish. It's also a popular boating area, thanks to the **McPhee Marina** (25021 Hwy. 184, 970/882-2257).

Sights

About three miles west of town, the **Anasazi Heritage Center** (27501 Hwy. 184, 970/882-4811, 9 A.M.–5 P.M. daily, $3) collects the results of the Anasazi archaeological efforts of the past several decades. On display are three million artifacts—smaller things like blankets, sandals, and large structures from hands-on corn-grinding instruments to a reconstructed pithouse and actual archaeological sites.

Sleeping Ute Mountain, to the southwest, looks exactly as its name suggests—a gigantic reclining man wearing a headdress. The Utes believed he was a warrior god who helped ward off evil, and that he descended into some kind of coma after being wounded in battle.

The **Galloping Goose Museum** (5th St. and Hwy. 145, 970/882-7082, 9 A.M.5 P.M. daily, free) recalls Dolores's days as an important railroad connection between Durango and Ridgway. This museum is the town's original train depot, including the 72-year-old Galloping Goose #5, a restored narrow-gauge car that carried mail (and occasionally tourists) through the San Juan Mountains from roughly 1932 to 1952.

About nine miles west of Mesa Verde National Park, the **Canyons of the Ancients National Monument** (County Rd. CC, west of the intersection of Hwy. 184 and U.S. 481, 970/882-4811) is a 164,000-acre, mesa-heavy area of 5,000 archaeological sites—the highest concentration of such sites in the United States. Scientists believe the Anasazis hunted and gathered here through about 7500 B.C., and Ute and Navajo tribes lived off the land until European and American settlers showed up in the 1700s and beyond—some of the more substantial evidence includes cliff dwellings and 420-room houses, sacred hot springs, and sweat lodges. Perhaps the most impressive site is the **Lowry Pueblo National Historic Landmark,** in the north part of the monument, a 40-room dwelling built in roughly A.D. 800 and restored in the 1960s to its (perhaps) original form, including large, sacred kiva chambers.

Pagosa Springs

For centuries, Native Americans prayed and conducted fire ceremonies around **The Spring,** in this mild area in the shadow of the San Juan Mountains. It's a collection of 13 tubs known as "healing waters"—medicine men and American settlers swore by them, and today's New Age types insist they're better than ibuprofen. Two hotels in tiny Pagosa Springs provide access to the springs, and while you don't have to book a room to have a soak, both hotels charge a fee.

The (**Springs Resort** (165 Hot Springs Blvd., 970/264-2360 or 800/225-0934, www.pagosahotsprings.com, $125–175) is a sparse, pinkish, adobe-style hotel with a swamp of 18 hot-springs pools of varying sizes in lieu of a backyard. It's a great place to relax, with trees and rocks strewn around the pools,

which go from 83 to 114 degrees Fahrenheit, and an amazing view of the San Juan River.

The big spring, about 50 by 74 feet, is at the **Spa at Pagosa Springs** (317 Hot Springs Blvd., 970/264-5910 or 800/832-5523, www.thespaatpagosasprings.com, $80–125), and the hotel is a little more basic (and inexpensive) than the Springs Resort.

SPORTS AND RECREATION
Downhill Skiing

Many avid Colorado skiers haven't heard of the **Wolf Creek Ski Area** (Hwy. 160, top of Wolf Creek Pass, between Pagosa Springs and South Fork, 970/264-5639, www.wolfcreekski.com), but they're missing out, because this small, middle-of-nowhere area has six lifts, 1,600 acres of trails, a top elevation of almost 12,000 feet, and snowfall averages of more than 465 inches a year.

Golf

The **Pagosa Springs Golf Club** (1 Pines Club Pl., 970/731-4755, www.golfpagosa.com) has three nine-hole courses underneath the San Juan Mountains.

ACCOMMODATIONS

The two hot-springs hotels are the best places to stay in the area, but **Davidson's Country Inn B&B** (Hwy. 160, three miles east of Pagosa Springs, 970/264-5863, www.davidson-sinn.com, $65–100) is one of a few homey, antique-filled inns within striking distance. Davidson's has two log-cabin rooms decorated with family heirlooms and handmade furniture.

FOOD

The **Keyah Grande** (13211 W. Highway 160, 970/731-1160, 6–8 P.M. Fri.–Sat.), inside the Lodge at Keyah Grande, has a 3,000-bottle wine cellar to go with an upscale menu of buttermilk-poached chicken breast and cucumber fettuccine—it's the best hotel restaurant in town.

A few steps down the elegance scale, but still good, are the **Elkhorn Café** (438C Pagosa St., 970/264-2146, 6 A.M.–9 P.M. Wed.–Sun., 6 A.M.–1:30 P.M. Mon.–Tues.), serving sandwiches and burgers, and **Frankie's Sicilian Ristorante & Bar** (214 Pagosa St., 970/264-1800, 5–9 P.M. Tues.–Sun.), Pagosa Springs' best pizza joint.

INFORMATION

Between the **Pagosa Springs Chamber of Commerce** (970/264-2360 or 800/252-2204, www.pagosaspringschamber.com), the **Town of Pagosa Springs** (551 Hot Springs Blvd., 970/264-4151, www.townofpagosasprings.com), and Pagosa.com (www.pagosa.com), you'll find just about everything you need to know before traveling to Pagosa Springs.

North of Pagosa Springs

CREEDE

Just 850 people live today in picturesque Mineral County, of which Creede is the only town, tucked into the east side of the San Juan Mountains. But in 1890, after Nicholas Creede came across a silver vein near the Rio Grande River, its population surged to 10,000. This led to an intense fortune-seeking explosion even by Colorado standards—travelers poured into the county, building "tent towns" such as Amethyst and Jimtown and pulling tons of silver out of the Holy Moses, Last Chance, and Kentucky Belle mines.

Creede wound up exporting more than $1 million in silver by 1892, transporting much of it via Colorado Springs businessman William Palmer's extended railroad line. Then the questionable characters showed up: Bob Ford, who allegedly killed Jesse James, opened a saloon and was killed in a gunfight here. Poker Lulu Swain, known as the Mormon Queen, became one of the town's more infamous call girls. Bat Masterson and Calamity Jane lived here. Opined the *Creede Candle:* "Creede is unfortunate in getting more of the flotsam of the state than usually falls to the lot of a mining camp."

Today's Creede isn't nearly as exciting, but like nearby Salida, Buena Vista, and Gunnison, it's a pit-stop town among numerous outdoor attractions—several fourteeners are within striking distance, notably San Luis Peak, and the Silver Thread National Scenic Byway (Highway 149) leads to pretty North Clear Creek Falls and the sparkling Wheeler Geologic Area.

Sights

Upon its discovery in the early 1900s, locals favorably compared the **Wheeler Geologic**

Area (about 24 miles east of Creede) to Colorado Springs' Garden of the Gods and even the Grand Canyon. Formed 30 million years ago out of volcanic ash, some of which has cemented and some of which remains loose and fragile, the area is filled with mountain-sized, pointy peaks and wild-looking stripes and sandstone-colored patterns. It's pretty hard to get there, though: You drive about 7 miles southeast on Highway 149, then turn north onto Pool Table Road #600 for another 10 miles. Look for the dusty remains of the former Hanson's Sawmill, then drive another 14 miles to the area's fence—but you'll need a four-wheel-drive vehicle for that last stretch. Cars aren't allowed into the area, so bring sturdy hiking boots.

A one-hour drive along Highway 149 north from Creede, **North Clear Creek Falls** is a striking 100-foot waterfall that's frequently photographed due to its proximity to the main road.

The **Creede Museum** (6th St. and San Luis St., no phone, call chamber of commerce at 719/658-2374, www.museumtrail.org/CreedeMuseumHistory.asp, 10 A.M.–4 P.M. daily, free) has an old roulette wheel, a come-hither saloon painting of a woman, a horse-drawn hearse, and other interesting artifacts from Creede's wild days.

The **Underground Mining Museum** (Forest Service Rd. 503 #9, 719/658-0811, www.museumtrail.org/CreedeUndergroundMiningMuseum.asp, 10 A.M.–4 P.M. daily in summer, 10 A.M.–3 P.M. Mon.–Fri. in spring and fall, $5) is a long, flat structure built into the side of a hill, although it never was a working mine. Instead, the exhibits re-create old blacksmith shops and elevator-like "hoists" along with several ore and rock specimens.

Accommodations
Although it's open only May–September, the **Antlers Rio Grande Lodge** (26222 Hwy. 149, 719/658.2423, www.antlerslodge.com, $88) is next to the Rio Grande River about five miles southwest of town. It rents weekly cabins and has spaces for RV camping, but the motel rooms are the best deal—including a porch and a swing, from which you can fish for trout in the river.

Sheepherders drive dozens of fuzzy white animals across the grounds of **Cottonwood Cove** (13046 Hwy. 149, 719/658-2242, www.cottonwoodcove.com, $90–150) a few times a year, adding a surreal touch to the friendly cabins and lodge rooms. The complex, which also allows RV camping, is south of Creede, halfway to South Fork along the highway.

Known as Zang's Hotel in the late 1800s, when Creede had some 100 hotels to accommodate the miners and miscreants, the light-blue **Creede Hotel** (120 N. Main St., 719/658-2608, www.creedehotel.com, $80–95) has four rooms named after notorious local characters—Calamity Jane, Poker Alice Tubbs, Soapy Smith, and Bat Masterson.

The **Wason Ranch** (Hwy. 149, 719/658-2413, www.wasonranch.com, $85–125) is an old horse ranch belonging to explorer and Civil War soldier M. V. B. Wason in the 1800s, and today it rents modern, furnished log cabins along the Rio Grande River.

Food
Most of the restaurants in tourist-heavy Creede are at the hotels—try the Riverside Restaurant in the Antlers Lodge—and the rest are of the down-home variety, mostly burgers and burritos. **Kip's Grill** (101 Wall St., 719/658-0138, 11 A.M.–8 P.M. daily May–Sept.) serves tacos, burgers, and homemade salsa on the back deck of the Tommyknocker Tavern, and **Café Olé** (112 N. Main St., 719/658-2880, 7:30 A.M.–4 P.M. Mon.–Sat.) has homemade baked goods, deli sandwiches, and (on Thursday evenings) pizza.

Entertainment
USA Today named the **Creede Repertory Theatre** (124 N. Main St., 719/658-2540, www.creederep.org) one of the "10 best places to see the lights way off Broadway," and it's easy to see why—the performers are surprisingly talented for such a small town, and the theater rotates a wide variety of well-chosen

productions, from musicals like *Lumberjacks in Love* to mining-history dramas like *Slabtown*.

Information

The **Creede/Mineral County Chamber of Commerce** (719/658-2374 or 800/327-2102, www.creede.com) has a detailed tourist-oriented website full of restaurant and hotel listings and a bunch of interesting history.

DEL NORTE

Once the "Gateway to the San Juans," Del Norte became a town in 1872, after various Native American tribes set up camp here for centuries and the first Spanish explorers arrived with their families in the mid-1800s. It's a tiny town with few hotels or major restaurants for tourists, but plenty of rock climbing, biking, cross-country skiing, and fishing opportunities in the area.

Sights

The **Rio Grande County Museum and Cultural Center** (580 Oak St., 719/657-2847, 10 A.M.–5 P.M. Tues.–Sat. in summer, noon–5 P.M. Tues.–Sat. in winter, donation suggested) focuses on artifacts from the Native American and Spanish-explorer eras—with an emphasis on John C. Frémont's 1848–1849 expedition into the San Juan Mountains, during which 10 explorers died of exposure before the rest were rescued.

Sports and Recreation

Penitente Canyon has transformed over the past century from a worshipping area for the devout Catholic sect known as Los Hermanos Penitente to a Bureau of Land Management-run haven for **rock climbers.** *Climbing* magazine has written about the area, which includes nearby Rock Garden, Sidewinder, and Witches Canyons. To get to the recently renovated area, with new camping facilities, drive about three miles north of town on Highway 112, then follow the signs.

Information

The **Del Norte Chamber of Commerce** is at 719/657-2845 or www.delnortechamber.info.

COLORADO SPRINGS AND THE GREAT SAND DUNES

With Pikes Peak as the eternal tourist attraction, Colorado Springs is the big-city anchor of south-central Colorado—including flat Pueblo to the south, the gambling town Cripple Creek to the west, the Great Sand Dunes National Park to the southwest, and various pretty small-highway drives leading to Salida, Buena Vista, and La Junta. Coloradoans addicted to the axis of Boulder, Denver, and Aspen often scoff at Colorado Springs, with its conservative military-and-family values and corny mining-era tourist attractions, but the scenery is incredible and it has a diversity of restaurants and hotels (notably The Broadmoor) perfect for budget-conscious visitors.

Beyond Colorado Springs, the south-central region is where the Rockies end—and flat cities such as Pueblo (third-largest city in the state) and Alamosa (significantly smaller, with a population of 8,000) have far more in common with the landscape of neighboring New Mexico than the Rocky Mountain ski-resort towns to the north. But many other underrated mountain ranges are just beginning here, from the Sangre de Cristos to the numerous 14,000-foot peaks outside Salida. This region also has a rich Native American and Latin American heritage, as Mexico City immigrants came here in the 1800s by wagon train after they'd explored the southwestern states. Highlights of this area include the Great Sand Dunes National Park, which resembles a lunar landscape and has several 900-foot hills for climbing and "sand-skiing."

© STEVE KNOPPER

HIGHLIGHTS

(Pikes Peak: It isn't the tallest mountain in Colorado, but Colorado Springs visitors will immediately recognize why 1880s gold miners all over the U.S. considered it a snowcapped beacon (page 257).

(North Cheyenne Cañon Park: This 1,600-acre preserve is filled with birds and animals of all types, waterfalls, trees, and all the nature you could possibly want outside of Pikes Peak (page 258).

(Garden of the Gods: Yes, it's a tourist trap, but the large and twisted red-rock formations are perfect backdrops for an impromptu picnic or hiking excursion (page 263).

(Bishop Castle: Colorado's answer to the Mitchell Corn Palace, of Mitchell, South Dakota, is Pueblo resident and amateur turret-builder Jim Bishop's obsession since 1969. Check out the 160-foot tower (page 270).

(Arkansas River White-Water Rafting: While Salida has its watery charms, I recommend the outfitters along the river in nearby Buena Vista, who claim, with some justification, "Best white-water rafting in the state" (page 277).

(Great Sand Dunes National Park and Preserve: Just north of Alamosa, the constantly shifting dunes are a cross between the Grand Canyon and the surface of the moon. Try the sand-skiing (page 278).

(Colorado Gators: Truly, no trip to Colorado is complete without a $50 alligator-wrestling lesson (page 278).

(San Isabel National Forest: A one million-acre area spread through south-central Colorado, this forest includes the beautiful Sangre de Cristo Mountains, Cuchara Pass, and many lakes and peaks full of hiking trails, campgrounds, and nature-watching opportunities (page 280).

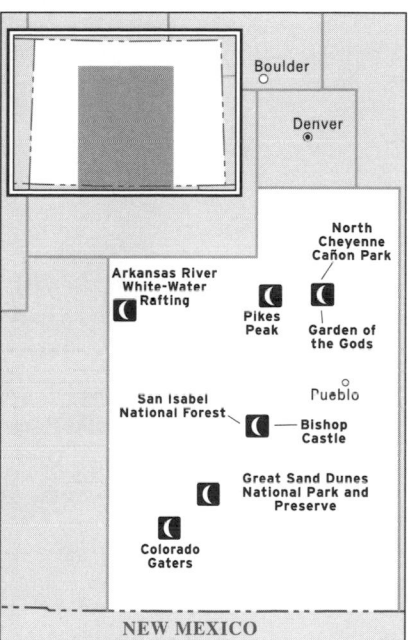

LOOK FOR **(** TO FIND RECOMMENDED SIGHTS, ACTIVITIES, DINING, AND LODGING.

COLORADO SPRINGS

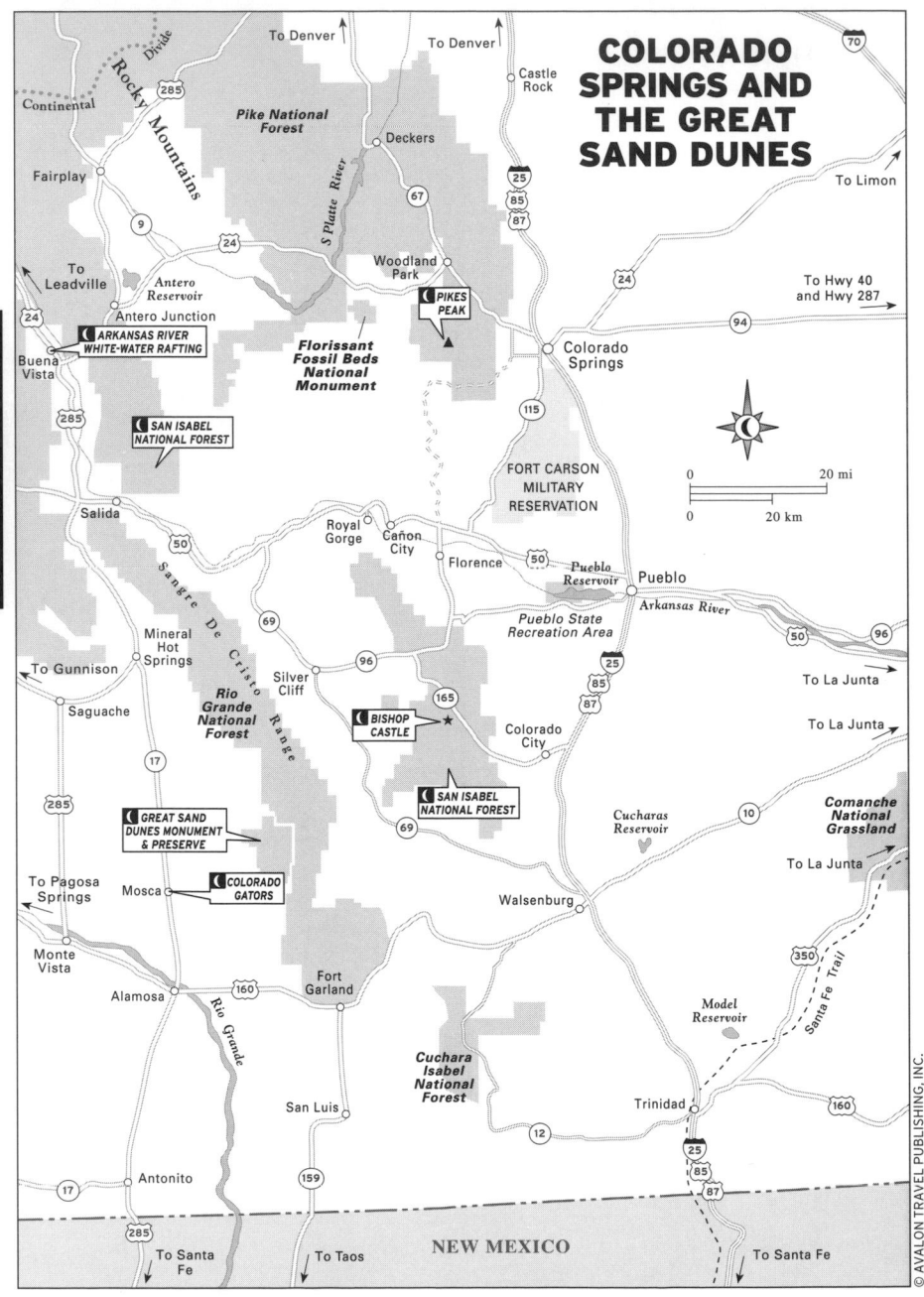

COLORADO SPRINGS AND THE GREAT SAND DUNES

To Denver

To Denver

Castle Rock

Continental Divide

Rocky Mountains

Pike National Forest

Deckers

To Limon

Fairplay

285

9

24

Woodland Park

To Hwy 40 and Hwy 287

To Leadville

Antero Reservoir

Antero Junction

PIKES PEAK

Colorado Springs

94

ARKANSAS RIVER WHITE-WATER RAFTING

Buena Vista

Florissant Fossil Beds National Monument

285

SAN ISABEL NATIONAL FOREST

115

FORT CARSON MILITARY RESERVATION

S Platte River

Salida

50

Royal Gorge

Cañon City

Florence

50

Pueblo Reservoir

Pueblo

Pueblo State Recreation Area

Arkansas River

50

96

0   20 mi
0   20 km

Sangre De Cristo Range

69

96

Mineral Hot Springs

To Gunnison

Saguache

Silver Cliff

165

25
85
87

To La Junta

Rio Grande National Forest

BISHOP CASTLE

Colorado City

To La Junta

17

SAN ISABEL NATIONAL FOREST

Cucharas Reservoir

10

Comanche National Grassland

285

69

To La Junta

GREAT SAND DUNES MONUMENT & PRESERVE

COLORADO GATORS

Walsenburg

To Pagosa Springs

Mosca

350

Santa Fe Trail

Monte Vista

Model Reservoir

Alamosa

160

Fort Garland

Rio Grande

Cuchara Isabel National Forest

Trinidad

160

San Luis

12

25
85
87

17

Antonito

159

NEW MEXICO

285

To Santa Fe

To Taos

To Santa Fe

© AVALON TRAVEL PUBLISHING, INC.

70

25
85
87

24

115

PLANNING YOUR TIME

It's tempting to look at the flat route between Colorado Springs and Trinidad and say, "No problem, I'll just cruise at the 75-mile-an-hour speed limit down I-25 and hit everything in a few days." That may be possible, but you'll miss an entire state's worth of scenic and historic routes. The out-of-the-way highway drives, such as Highway 69 from Walsenburg through Westcliffe to Cañon City, are surprisingly beautiful, with the Wet Mountains on one side and the Sangre de Cristo Mountains on the other. And even tiny towns that look unappealing from the highway—from big Pueblo to tiny Walsenburg—contain interesting historic museums, public art displays, and generally mild-weather biking, hiking, and white-water-rafting areas.

To explore the south-central region by car, plan at least four or five days. Spend a weekend in Colorado Springs, checking out the touristy Garden of the Gods and nearby Cripple Creek; maybe a day or two in Pueblo, pausing for a leisurely tour of downtown; and the remaining days on some of the beautiful drives, including U.S. 50 near the Royal Gorge, Highway 12 between Trinidad and Walsenburg, and the entirety of the Great Sand Dunes National Park outside Alamosa. Come to think of it, take a week.

Colorado Springs and Vicinity

With the U.S. Air Force Academy and Focus on the Family headquarters in the same town, Colorado Springs is the state's conservative counterweight to Boulder, about two hours to the northwest. But regardless of their politics, both cities share one thing in common: spectacular mountain scenery. The 14,110-foot Pikes Peak has drawn tourists from all over the world, notably in 1893, when Katharine Lee Bates climbed to the top in a prairie wagon, then on a mule, and wrote "America the Beautiful."

Founded in 1871, Colorado Springs boomed as a gold-rush town in the 1890s, then boosted its population at the beginning of World War II, when it sold land to the U.S. military. Fort Carson sprang up in the south, and the Air Force Academy opened in the 1950s, the first of several important Air Force facilities, and, later, the North American Aerospace Defense Command, or NORAD. This heavy artillery—along with the heavy views of Focus on the Family, an influential conservative Christian group that gained steam in the early 1990s by opposing "special rights" for gay people—balances out the light mountain air and laid-back tourist hot spots such as Garden of the Gods and The Broadmoor hotel.

Today, six million tourists visit Colorado Springs every year, and while the obvious tourist draws include Pikes Peak, Garden of the Gods, the Cheyenne Zoo, and the U.S. Olympic Training Center, the Springs (population 370,000) has a big-city feel with a diversity of restaurants and shopping.

ORIENTATION

From Denver, Colorado Springs is a straight shot down I-25 south—beware rush hour, though, because the interstate narrows in the Springs, and when there's an accident or bad weather, traffic can back up for hours. The prime business-and-restaurant district is at the center of town, roughly the corners of Colorado and Platte Avenues, with the quiet Acacia Park as the anchor. Touristy spots such as Pikes Peak, Manitou Springs, Garden of the Gods, and Ghost Town line up along U.S. 24 due east of town. To the south, I-25 extends to Pueblo, Walsenburg, and Trinidad and is the main route to Santa Fe, New Mexico.

HISTORY

Like so many regions of Colorado, the Pikes Peak area's first settlers were Native Americans—beginning with the Utes, before A.D. 1300, then Apaches, Comanches, Cheyenne, and Arapaho.

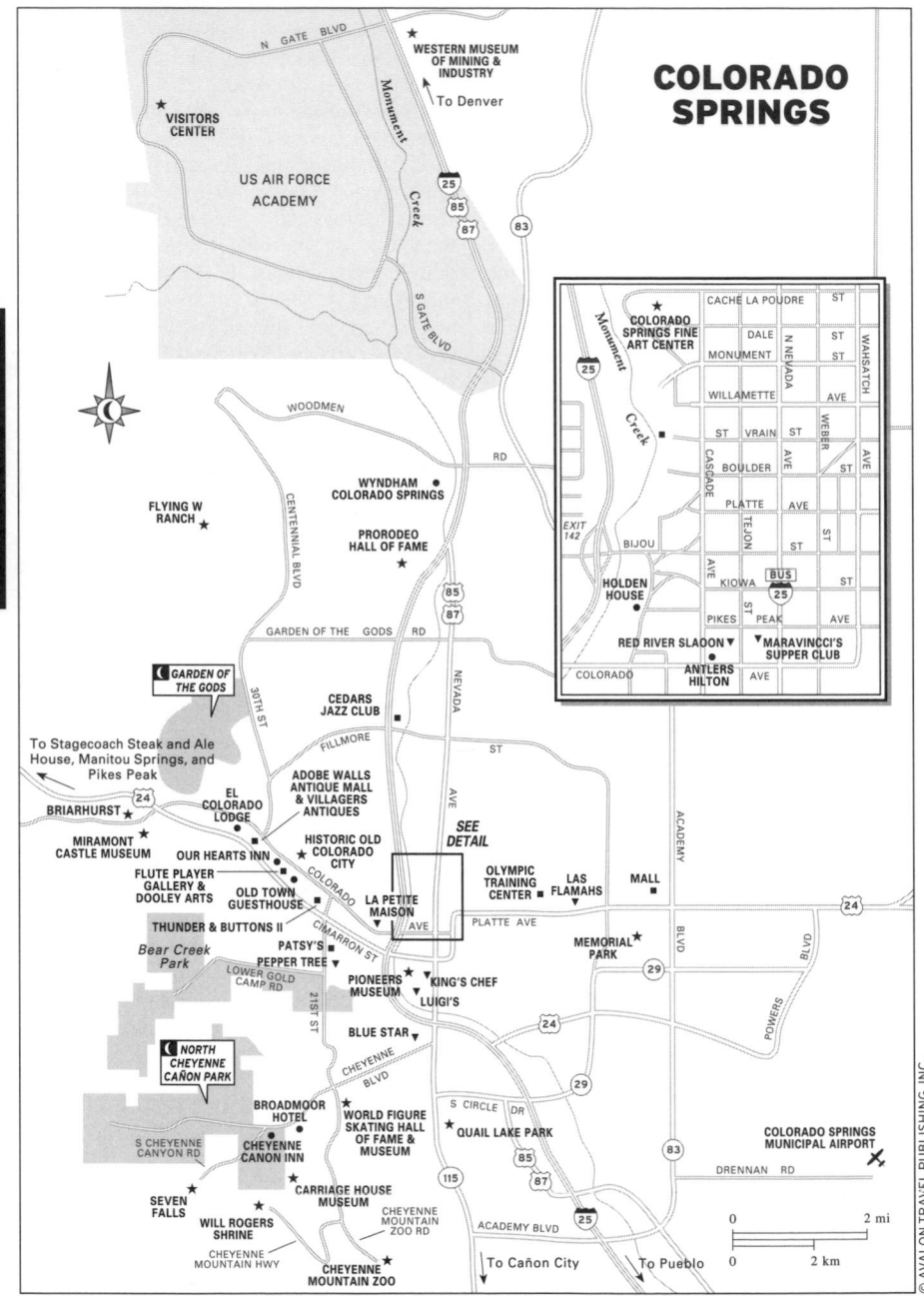

COLORADO SPRINGS

Then the rest of the country started talking about gold. In 1858, during a depression, two groups of prospectors responded to sketchy reports of nuggets in gold mines by flooding the area between what is now Denver and Colorado Springs. Pikes Peak was their beacon, but they landed at Cherry Creek, outside Denver, and successfully panned for "color" a few months later. Thus began the gold rush that established Colorado as a state.

Miners founded Colorado Springs—actually, the area between Colorado Springs and Manitou Springs known as Colorado City—in 1858. But the first to truly develop the town was William J. Palmer, a railroad baron who brought track to the area he called "Fountain City" in 1871. He also bought 10,000 acres and, in his own moral image, designed churches, parks, and playgrounds, leaving the saloons to Colorado City.

The gold rush didn't produce many multimillionaires that year, but Palmer's railroad lured thousands of people (mostly farmers) to Colorado Springs—the population grew from 987 in 1870 to 7,949 in 1880. The city's fortunes went way up, then way down, until the early 1890s, when prospectors discovered massive gold deposits in the nearby Cripple Creek mines, and Colorado Springs began to boom again. Suddenly, it was "Little London," a ritzy mountain town that was especially popular among the British.

After silver replaced gold as the American standard in the 1920s, Colorado Springs went through another bad period, but just before World War II, the city shrewdly offered land to the U.S. military—which built Fort Carson and, later, the Air Force Academy. The Olympic Training Center followed, and in the 1970s and 1980s, Colorado Springs built a tourist industry around its generally mild weather and sights such as Pikes Peak, Garden of the Gods, and the Cheyenne Mountain Zoo.

SIGHTS

For a while, there, the **U.S. Air Force Academy** (I-25, 14 miles north of downtown Colorado Springs, 719/333-1110, www.usafa.af.mil, visitors center 9 A.M.–5 P.M. daily) limited tourist visits due to post-9/11 security issues. Today, several spots are open to the public: the three-level, 17-spire, triangularly modern Cadet Chapel (which occasionally puts on public organ concerts); Arnold Hall (a student center with a performance stage and a cafeteria); and the Field House sports complex (including Clune Arena, where the basketball team plays). Established in 1954, the academy is on 18,000 acres and is filled with military-plane paraphernalia and statues such as a tribute to the Tuskegee Airmen, an African-American unit.

You'll get better-than-usual access to everything via **Gray Line of Denver** (800/348-6877 or 303/289-2841, www.coloradograyline.com, 1:30 P.M. daily, $30), which tours training cadets and a B-52 display, and generously samples the $3.8 million, donation-driven visitors center.

Open since 1978, the **Olympic Training Center** (1750 E. Boulder St., 719/866-4618 or 888/659-8687, visitors center 11 A.M.–6 P.M. Sun., hourly tours 9 A.M.–4 P.M. Mon.–Sat., free) has massive facilities for young athletes hoping to be the next Mary Lou Retton or Pocket Hercules. The Aquatic Center houses the biggest pool you've ever seen, and no, you can't dive in or start lifting weights.

Seven Falls (2850 S. Cheyenne Canyon Rd., 719/632-0765, www.sevenfalls.com, open daily, call for seasonal hours, $3 suggested donation) refers to both the waterfall, which cascades down 181 feet over seven steps on a granite cliff, and the one-mile drive up a scenic canyon. The falls are open at night most of the year—they're elaborately lit during holidays—and there are trails for bikers and hikers.

Cheyenne Mountain Zoo (4250 Cheyenne Mountain Zoo Rd., 719/633-9925, www.cmzoo.org, 9 A.M.–6 P.M. daily Memorial Day–Labor Day, 9 A.M.–5 P.M. daily Labor Day–Memorial Day, $12) is your basic city zoo, only much higher above sea level than usual. It has 500 animals, including an impressive giraffe herd, and the zoo claims the most prolific breeding program in the world, with 185 giraffe births since 1954.

One large building houses an entire

Ghost Town (400 S. 21st St., 719/634-0696, www.ghosttownmuseum.com, 9 A.M.–6 P.M. Mon.–Sat. and 11 A.M.–6 P.M. June–Aug., 10 A.M.–5 P.M. Mon.–Sat. and 11 A.M.–5 P.M. Sun. Sept.–May, $6), including a sheriff's office, jail, saloon, general store, and a central museum (which also has gold panning).

When miners and railroaders turned the Pikes Peak region into a boom town in the late 1800s, the city's tough-talking saloon district was known as "Colorado City," and **Old Colorado City** (History Center, 1 S. 24th St., 719/636-1225, http://history.old-colo.com, 11 A.M.–4 P.M. Tues.–Sat., free) preserves the old buildings, now much gentler galleries and shops.

The **Colorado Springs Pioneers Museum** (215 S. Tejon St., 719/385-5990, 10 A.M.– 5 P.M. Tues.–Sat., free) has 40,000 books, quilts, pottery, a huge Native American collection, and mining and agricultural artifacts. It includes the **Starsmore Center for Local History,** a research library focusing on the Pikes Peak region.

At the front of the **ProRodeo Hall of Fame and Museum of the American Cowboy** (101 ProRodeo Dr., 719/528-4761 or 719/528-4764, www.prorodeo.org/hof, 9 A.M.–5 P.M. daily, $6) stands a statue of Casey "The Champ" Tibbs, who, as the story goes, had a bronze heart welded into his chest containing the words "Ride Cowboy Ride." He's one of more than 160 riders enshrined at this Old West museum, featuring calf-ropers' actual saddles and boots, horses' silver halters, and various art and artifacts. It's easy to spot the museum from the bronco statue off I-25, but call first, as it can close at unexpected times.

A dynamite-blasting machine and actual steam engines are among the explosive highlights of the **Western Museum of Mining and Industry** (1025 N. Gate Rd., 719/488-0880 or 800/752-6558, www.wmmi.org, 9 A.M.–4 P.M. Mon.–Sat., $7), which also has scale models of

The Van Briggle Art Pottery Factory has been open since 1899 in Colorado Springs.

© STEVE KNOPPER

FOCUS ON THE FAMILY

Focus on the Family, located in an impeccable green-and-brown complex on the way into Colorado Springs from Denver, has an altruistic name and a spiritual mission. Its goal, according to child-development specialist and founder James Dobson, is to "turn hearts toward home" using "reasonable, biblical and empirical insights." Since it formed in 1977, the Christian group has grown to 74 ministries with 1,300 employees, and Dobson's radio broadcasts have an audience of 200 million listeners every day.

These are admirable goals, but the group is also one of the most controversial conservative and anti-gay organizations in Colorado, if not the United States. In a characteristic article on the Focus website, one author declares that homosexuality is "wrong, according to God's word."

In an era when evangelical Christians receive much of the credit for President George W. Bush's reelection in 2004, Focus on the Family regularly flexes its political muscle. After courts ruled to remove Terri Schiavo's feeding tube in a highly publicized "right to die" case in early 2005, Focus gave this statement: "Terri Schiavo has been executed, under the guise of law and 'mercy,' for being guilty of nothing more than the inability to speak for herself."

If you're interested in setting up a visit or a tour, contact Focus on the Family (8685 Explorer Dr., 719/531-3328, www.focus.org). Tours are free; check the website for hours, which vary by season and are unavailable during chapel services.

actual Colorado mines and free guided tours every day. Plus real burros!

The **Will Rogers Shrine of the Sun** (4250 Cheyenne Mountain Zoo Rd., 719/578-5367, 9 A.M.–5 P.M. daily Apr.–Nov., 9 A.M.–4 P.M. daily Nov.–Apr., free with zoo admission) is so-named because Broadmoor and Cheyenne Mountain Zoo founder Spencer Penrose was a friend of the great humorist. After Rogers died in a 1935 Alaska plane crash, Penrose erected this oblong, five-story, granite shrine in the zoo.

The **Van Briggle Art Pottery Factory and Showroom** (600 S. 21st St., 800/847-6341, www.vanbriggle.com, 8:30 A.M.–5 P.M. Mon.– Sat.) is a huge deal in the pottery world, as it opened in 1899 and collectors have prized its distinctive ceramic vases and bowls ever since. It's open for tours.

Ravaged by arson in 2000, the **Bear Creek Nature Center** (245 Bear Creek Rd., 719/520-6387, http://adm.elpasoco.com/parks/bcnc.asp, 9 A.M.–4 P.M. Tues.–Sat., $3) reopened two years later with bear-and-coyote-fur exhibits and a huge collection of butterflies and insects. Two miles of woodsy hiking trails surround the small brown complex.

The **Colorado Springs Fine Arts Center** (30 W. Dale St., 719/634-5581, www.csfineartscenter.org, 9 A.M.–5 P.M. Tues.–Sat., 1–5 P.M. Sun., $5) is a big-time art museum, in a tall 1936 building designed by architect John Gaw Meem. Inside are paintings and sculpture by Georgia O'Keeffe, Ansel Adams, and John Singer Sargent, as well as a huge grand-lobby chandelier by Dale Chihuly. The museum is open for drinks and hobnobbing on weekend evenings during the summer.

Pikes Peak

Named for the 1806 explorer Zebulon Pike, Pikes Peak (719/385-7325, www.pikes-peak .com) is not the tallest mountain in Colorado—that would be Mount Elbert—but it has a "purple mountain majesty" unparalleled in the state or the country. When Americans rushed west to search for gold in 1859, they shouted, "Pikes Peak or bust!"

All 14,110 feet of the mountain are open to visitors willing to travel a variety of ways—via the 19-mile, one-hour **Pikes Peak Highway** to the summit; the **Barr Trail,** which climbs 7,000 feet over the course of 13 miles; or the **Pikes Peak Cog Railway** (515 Ruxton Ave.,

Manitou Springs, 719/685-5401, www.cograil-way.com, various times and dates 8:20 A.M.–5:20 P.M., mostly closed in the winter, $28), a 9-mile journey in an 1891-era along a stream. All are scenic routes with views of Colorado Springs, Garden of the Gods, and all kinds of trees and wildlife.

Thousands of crazed runners partake in the **Pikes Peak Marathon** (www.pikespeakmarathon.org), up Barr Trail every August, and events from the Pikes Peak Auto Hill Climb to a New Year's fireworks display celebrate the mountain. At the top is the **Summit House,** which has a gift shop and snack bar and is open 8 A.M.–8 P.M. daily. For driving and weather updates, call 719/473-0208 or 800/318-9505.

The **Pikes Peak RV Park** (320 Manitou Ave., Manitou Springs, 719/685-9459, pikespeakrvpark7@aol.com, $30) is centrally located near a stream and the touristy parts of town.

©STEVE KNOPPER

Pikes Peak

◖ North Cheyenne Cañon Park

North Cheyenne Cañon Park is an almost-as-idyllic-as-Pikes-Peak, 1,600-acre tree-and-valley area that encompasses Helen Hunt Falls, Mount Almagre, and North Cheyenne Creek, along with black bears, mountain lions, deer, kingfisher birds, and broad-tailed hummingbirds.

Hikers should begin with the **Starsmore Discovery Center** (2120 S. Cheyenne Cañon Rd., 719/578-6146, 9 A.M.–5 P.M. daily June–Labor Day, 9 A.M.–4:30 P.M. Wed.–Fri. and 9 A.M.–5 P.M. Sat.–Sun. Apr., May, Sept., and Oct.), which has maps, exhibits, and a climbing wall.

Bird-watchers should try the **Great Pikes Peak Birding Trail** (www.gppbt.org), which begins a mile below nearby Seven Falls; they should also consider coming in May, during the **Hummingbird Festival.**

The **Helen Hunt Falls Visitors Center** (4075 N. Cheyenne Cañon Rd., 719/578-6146 or 719/633-5701, 9 A.M.–5 P.M. Memorial Day–Labor Day) is directly beneath the falls and sells trail maps and nature-history books and sponsors hikes.

SPORTS AND RECREATION

Tourist attractions such as Pikes Peak and Garden of the Gods are renowned for hiking, mountain biking and rock climbing, but they can also be crowded at the best times of day and year. Less congested are Colorado Springs' multitudes of city trails, including a Palmer Park-to-Fountain pathway linking the **Pikes Peak Greenway** (damaged by a flood in 1999 and recently repaired) and the New Santa Fe and Fountain Creek regional trails.

Other city parks include the 165-acre **Blodgett Open Space,** in the northwest part of town, and the 1,680-acre **Cheyenne Mountain State Park,** underneath Cheyenne Mountain, which opened in 2004 near Fort Carson. For more information on city parks, contact the **Parks and Recreation Department** (719/385-5940, or click the "Parks and Recreation" link at www.springsgov.com).

Golfing options include the city-run **Patty Jewett** (700 E. Espanola St., 719/385-6950), an 18-hole, par-72 course whose restaurant has a nice view of Pikes Peak, and the 18-hole, par-71 **Valley Hi** (610 S. Chelton, 719/385-6917), known for its beginner's program and proximity to Pikes Peak and Cheyenne Mountain. Private facilities are at **The Broadmoor** (1 Lake Ave., 719/577-5790), which has trees and sand bunkers underneath the mountains; Nicklaus Design is scheduled to overhaul the 30-year-old Mountain Course by 2006. Finally, the **Colorado Springs Country Club** (3333 Templeton Gap Rd., 719/473-1782) is an 18-hole course built in 1925.

NIGHTLIFE

Colorado Springs is at heart a country-music town, and **⟨ Cowboys** (3910 Palmer Park Blvd., 719/596-1212) is the capital—singer Brad Paisley is one of many acts who have stopped here on the way up. Drinks, food, and two-stepping are taken for granted. On a slightly smaller scale, **Red River Saloon** (32 S. Tejon, 719/955-5664, www.redriversaloon.com) grabs country-oriented local bands almost every night to go with its food specialty, barbecue. (Note that this venue used to be called 32 Bleu and the Tejon Street Bistro.)

Other live-music joints include **Cedars Jazz Club** (3125 Sinton Rd., www.cedarsjazzclub.com, 719/578-5744); **Golden Bee** (1 Lake Ave., 719/577-5776), a piano bar on The Broadmoor grounds; **Thunder and Buttons II** (2415 W. Colorado Ave., 719/447-9888), which hosts blues jams; and **Union Station** (2419 N. Union Blvd., 719/227-7168), an eclectic rock club with battle-of-the-bands events.

The **Loonees Comedy Corner** (1305 N. Academy Blvd., 719/591-0707, www.loonees.com) grabs almost-stars such as Howard G. of HBO's *The Wire.*

SHOPPING
Malls
Colorado Springs is packed with malls. The **Shops at Briargate** (1885 Briargate Pkwy., 719/265-6264, www.theshopsatbriargate.com, 10 A.M.–9 P.M. Mon.–Sat., noon–5 P.M. Sun.) offers Pottery Barn, Ann Taylor, and Wil-

liams-Sonoma. **The Citadel** (750 Citadel Dr. E., 719/591-5516, www.shopthecitadel.com, 10 A.M.–9 P.M. Mon.–Sat., 11 A.M.–6 P.M. Sun.) has 160 stores, including Dillard's and Foley's. A pricey 15-boutique strip, with salons, galleries, and a healthy-food market, is part of The Broadmoor hotel complex at 1 Lake Avenue.

Galleries
The city's art galleries aren't in the same league, quantity-wise, as those in Aspen, say, but a few are worth visiting. **The Flute Player Gallery** (2511 W. Colorado Ave., 719/632-7702, 10 A.M.–6 P.M. Mon.–Sat., noon–5 P.M. Sun.), specializes in southwest Indian jewelry, rugs, and furniture. **Fountain Creek Productions** (3440 Astrozon Pl., 800/433-5858, 8 A.M.–4:30 P.M. Mon.–Fri.) has wildlife sculptures, including marble lamp bases and pewter wolf statues. **Dooley Arts** (2627 W. Colorado Ave., 719/630-3677 or 719/685-9622, www.dooleyarts.com, open by appointment), a husband-and-wife-run gallery, sells lithographs of animals and mountain landscapes.

Antiques
The **American Classics Marketplace** (1815 N. Academy Blvd., 719/596-8585, 10 A.M.–6 P.M. daily) is one-stop shopping for this sort of thing. And, while its garish orange, yellow, and white adobe building screams "tourists!" locals find excellent deals on Navajo rugs and Native American baskets at the **Adobe Walls Antique Mall and Trading Post** (2808 W. Colorado Ave., 719/635-3394, www.adobe-walls.com, 10 A.M.–5 P.M. Mon.–Sat., 11 A.M.–5 P.M. Sun.) And **Villagers Antiques & Collectibles** (2514 W. Colorado Ave., 719/632-1400, 10 A.M.–5 P.M. Mon.–Sat.) sells silver, crystal, linens, rugs, and china.

Stop at **Patsy's** (1540 S. 21st St., www.patsyscandy.com, 719/633-7215) for important traveling necessities such as chocolate, toffee, peanut-butter nuggets, and saltwater taffy.

ACCOMMODATIONS
The Broadmoor is so dominant in Colorado Springs that it sucks all other luxury hotels

COLORADO SPRINGS

out of the market—the only other options are nice but generic chains like the Antlers Hilton and the Wyndham or tiny bed-and-breakfasts such as the Holden House and the Cheyenne Cañon Inn. Bargain-hunters may want to avoid The Broadmoor, but its packages are generally affordable.

Under $100

The 121-year-old **Antlers Hilton Colorado Springs** (4 S. Cascade Ave., 719/955-5600, $99–149) underwent a $7.5 million renovation when it switched chains from the Adam's Mark to the Hilton. The downtown hotel doesn't look like much from the outside—just a boxy, white building—but the mountain views are excellent, and services such as free high-speed Internet access and the Judge Baldwin's microbrewery are a good fit for business customers.

Like the Antlers Hilton and the Embassy Suites, the **Wyndham Colorado Springs** (5580 Tech Center Dr., 719/260-1800, www.wyndham.com/hotels/COSCO/main.wnt, $71–94) is a business-oriented hotel with huge conference-room space and functional rooms befitting the national chain. The mountains are a spectacular backdrop, and owners poured in $15 million for a 2005 renovation.

All 316 rooms at the **Cheyenne Mountain Resort** (3225 Broadmoor Valley Rd., 800/428-8886, www.cheyennemountain.com, $73–119) have private balconies and views of Cheyenne Mountain. Check regularly for packages—some come with free buffets at the Mountain View Dining Room.

Located in an 1880s-era building, the **Cheyenne Cañon Inn** (2030 W. Cheyenne Blvd., 800/633-0625, www.cheyennecanoninn.com, $99–189) has been a brothel, a casino, and the Sunnycrest hotel over the years. Today it's a cozy bed-and-breakfast with a stone fireplace in the lobby.

$100-$150

A classic bed-and-breakfast with flowery pillows, cats roaming the halls, a porch swing, and knickknacks strewn about the lobby mantel and fireplace, the **Holden House** (102 W.

Pikes Peak Ave., 719/471-3980 or 888/565-3980, www.holdenhouse.com, $140) is a family-owned inn in a restored 1902 Victorian.

Over $200

(The Broadmoor (1 Lake Ave., 719/577-5775 or 800/634-7711, www.broadmoor.com, $220–350) isn't so much a luxury hotel as a massive luxury complex, with its own lake, three golf courses, spa, 11 restaurants, and 700 rooms. Its nickname, "the grande dame of the Rockies," seems like hyperbole until you actually stay there—the wide, puffy beds and frilly pillows whisper "sleeep heeere for 15 straight hooours" and the impeccable Cheyenne Lake grounds just about magnetize you to the spot. Built in 1891 as a hotel and gambling casino, it transformed into a resort when Philadelphia entrepreneur Spencer Penrose took it over in 1916; it has been one of the state's best hotels ever since. Try the Charles Court restaurant, which has lake views and 600 wines.

FOOD

Colorado Springs is similar to Boulder in terms of dining variety, although it doesn't have the same number of experimental, exotic, or upscale restaurants. It does have at least one or two strong choices for every ethnicity—Indian, Japanese, Mexican, French, Italian—and the prices are better than those at ski resorts. For more local restaurant information, scan the reviews at the *Gazette-Telegraph* website (www.coloradosprings.com/entertainment/reviews.jsp).

Snacks, Cafés, and Breakfast

Long a local architectural joke, the **King's Chef** (110 E. Costilla St., 719/634-9135, www.kingschefdiner.com, 7 A.M.–2 P.M. Mon.–Fri., 9 A.M.–3 P.M. Sat., 10 A.M.–3 P.M. Sun.) diner is in a purple, red, and yellow metal castle on the side of the road. But the food is serious: killer green chile, plus breakfast and deli sandwiches (the Reuben, at $7, is a great deal).

Casual

The best barbecue joint in town is **Bird Dog BBQ** (5984 Stetson Hills Blvd., 719/596-4900, 11 A.M.–

9 P.M. Mon.–Sat., 11 A.M.–8 P.M. Sun.), in a strip mall near a chain supermarket. The combination plate ($11) is the best deal, and brisket aficionados are advised to shop here before anywhere else in town. The huge blue fish atop **Barracuda Bob's Neighborhood Cabana and Grill** (13860 Gleneagle Dr., 719/481-6446, 11 A.M.–8 P.M. Mon.–Thurs., 11 A.M.–9 P.M. Fri.–Sat.) is somewhat misleading—this colorful "beach attitude" joint serves ribs, Caribbean jerk chicken ($9), and steak tacos, among many other things.

Colorado Springs has numerous affordable ethnic restaurants. **India Palace** (5644 N. Academy Blvd., 719/535-9196, 11 A.M.–2:30 P.M., 5–10 P.M. Mon.–Fri., 5–10 P.M. Sat.–Sun.), with a lunch buffet and the super-spicy lamb *roganjosh* ($12), is the best of five or six local Indian restaurants. **Las Flamahs** (405 N. Union Blvd., 719/636-1177, 7 A.M.–5 P.M. daily) is known for its chiles rellenos and an $8 Mexican buffet. **Sushi Joe** (3478-B Research Pkwy., 719/282-8238, 11 A.M.–2:30 P.M. and 4:30–9 P.M. Tues.–Thurs. and Sun., 11 A.M.–2:30 P.M. and 4:30–10 P.M. Fri.–Sat.) does raw fish and chicken teriyaki pretty well.

The Blue Star (1645 S. Tejon St., 719/632-1086, 11:30 A.M.–10 P.M. Mon.–Fri., 5:30–10 P.M. Sat., 10 A.M.–9 P.M. Sun.) has a casual bar (with excellent burgers) that's open all day and an elegant dinner menu with *tapas* (chicken basil meatballs are $7) and comfort food (like chicken à la king, $17) of American and Asian persuasions.

Upscale

Maravincci's Supper Club (123 E. Pikes Peak Ave., 719/227-7400, 4–10 P.M. Tues.–Thurs., 4:30 P.M.–midnight Fri., 5 P.M.–midnight Sat., 5–11 P.M. Sun.) has a certain who-cares-as-long-as-the-food-is-good charm—pink-and-black walls, four total entrées (including filet of beef Della Casa for $25 and Mediterranean seared fillet of sea bass for $19) and a certain martini that *Gazette-Telegraph* food critic Tom Karpel describes as "a glassful of straight alcohol."

La Petite Maison (1015 W. Colorado Ave., 719/632-4887, 11 A.M.–2 P.M. Mon.–Fri., 5–10 P.M. Mon.–Sat.), in a blue Victorian cottage, has a huge, diverse menu of all kinds of meats, fish, and vegetables—plus a set of casual entrées including that old French standby, the hamburger.

The Margarita at Pine Creek (7350 Pine Creek Rd., 719/598-8667, 11:30 A.M.–2 P.M. Tues.–Fri., 5:30–9 P.M. Tues.–Sat., 10:30 A.M.–2 P.M. Sun.) has basic decor—plants everywhere, tiled floors—and straightforward, elegant Sunday brunch and prix fixe dinners (including one Mexican and two continental choices nightly). Saturday nights, a harpsichordist (yes, a harpsichordist) plays chamber music.

For an over-the-top formal experience—where the waiters wear tuxedos—the **Pepper Tree** (888 W. Moreno, 719/471-4888, 5:30–9 P.M. Mon.–Sat.) specializes in steak (the 14-ounce chateaubriand is $33) and fish (the Chilean sea bass is $26). And I dare you to not book a reservation after reading the name of this dessert: milk chocolate tulip cup filled with berries and cream, on a bed of bittersweet espresso mousse.

INFORMATION

The City of Colorado Springs has a wide-ranging website at www.springsgov.com and a staff helpline at 719/385-2489. The *Colorado Springs Gazette-Telegraph* posts dining reviews and other tourist-friendly information at www.gazette.com. And pick up a free copy of the alternative weekly *Independent* (www.csindy.com), which also has news and snarky reviews of all types.

Although Manitou Springs is usually in the shadow of Colorado Springs, and you can find much information about the area at www.springsgov.com, its primary website is www.manitousprings.org. For Pikes Peak-oriented information, visit www.pikes-peak.com. Or call 719/685-5089 or 800/642-2567.

The Palmer Lake website doesn't have amazingly great tourist information, but try it at www.ci.palmer-lake.co.us or call 719/481-2953.

Cripple Creek's website is thorough and colorful: www.cripple-creek.co.us. Its visitors center (513 E. Bennett Ave.) is at 877/858-4653.

GETTING THERE AND AROUND

The **Colorado Springs Airport** (7770 Drennan Rd., 719/550-1900, www.springsgov.com/AirportIndex.asp) is not only an efficient way to visit the area, but it's often a more affordable option for Denver flights than Denver International Airport. Most of the major carriers fly here.

Like most big cities, Colorado Springs has a large **Transit System** (1015 Transit Dr., 719/385-RIDE) of buses and shuttles.

MANITOU SPRINGS

Built around the nine naturally carbonated springs at the center of town—bring your own cup, as French settlers did in the late 1800s, to enjoy a tasty natural soda pop—Manitou Springs is the small-town addendum to Colorado Springs. While the other Springs is the second-biggest city in Colorado, Manitou is a quaint bed-and-breakfast kind of town full of galleries, tourist parks, and historic sights.

The springs themselves have fallen into disrepair and been restored several times over the years—most recently in the 1980s, which was good timing, because spas and hot springs exploded in popularity the following decade. The local chamber of commerce's **Mineral Springs Foundation** (354 Manitou Ave., 719/685-5089) provides maps and walking tours of the springs.

Sights

Cave of the Winds (off U.S. 24, 719/685-5444, www.caveofthewinds.com, 9 A.M.–9 P.M. daily in summer, 10 A.M.–5 P.M. daily in winter, $16) is a fascinating—and always warm—labyrinth of stalactites, stalagmites, flowers, crystal, and coral. Discovered and rediscovered many times over the centuries, it became a bona fide tourist attraction in 1880, when two boys came upon it during an "Exploring Association" trip and started charging $1 admission. It can be cheesy, though, especially the elaborate summer laser shows.

The **Cliff Dwellings Museum** (U.S. 24, 719/685-5242 or 800/354-9971, www.cliff

You can bring your own cup to sample the actual spring water in Manitou Springs.

© STEVE KNOPPER

dwellingsmuseum.com, 9 A.M.–6 P.M. daily May–Sept., 10 A.M.–4 P.M. daily Dec.–Feb., 9 A.M.–5 P.M. daily Mar., Apr., Oct., and Nov., $8.50) documents a period (as far back as A.D. 1100) when the Anasazi carved elaborate rooms into red-rock cliff homes. These replicas were built in 1906. The museum sponsors traditional Native American dances in the summer.

A long time ago, this was railroad magnate William J. Palmer's town, and his old estate **Glen Eyrie** (3820 N. 30th St., 719/634-0808 or 800/944-4536, www.gleneyrie.org, $60–170 per room) was a 22-room frame house on 2,225 acres filled with red sandstone formations—giving it the nickname "Little Garden of the Gods." Today, it's luxury lodging, with beautiful areas like the blue-and-brown General Palmer's Room, including an antique shower and a hand-carved wooden bed. The many surrounding trails are open to bikers and hikers, as are the volleyball, basketball, and tennis courts.

In 1895, the **Miramont Castle Museum**

(9 Capital Hill Ave., 719/685-1011, www.miramontcastle.org, noon–3 P.M. Tues.–Sun., $6) was the home of French-born Jean Baptiste Francolon, a Catholic priest who lived here with his mother and six servants—they used 28 of the 46 rooms, on 14,000 square feet. Today, many of those rooms are lovingly reproduced after a 2000 renovation, and the exhibits include railroad and vintage-doll collections.

If a CD titled *The Flying W Wranglers Live in Concert with the Colorado Springs Philharmonic* doesn't scare you, the **Flying W Ranch** (3330 Chuckwagon Rd., 800/232-3599, www.flyingw.com, shows at 5 and 8 P.M. Fri.–Sat. Oct.–Memorial Day, 4:30–9:30 P.M. daily Memorial Day–Sept.) may be your kind of place. It's a working cowboy ranch with a chuckwagon supper and nightly entertainment by, yes, The Flying W Wranglers, who are sort of a combination of Riders in the Sky and Wayne Newton with a little Christian music thrown in.

(Garden of the Gods

As the story goes, when two surveyors stumbled upon a valley of towering, twisted, blood-red sandstone formations in 1859, the first declared it a "capital place for a beer garden." Responded the second man: "Beer garden! Why, it is a fit place for the gods to assemble!" Thus the name **Garden of the Gods** (1805 N. 30th St., 719/634-6666, www.gardenofgods.com, 8 A.M.–8 P.M. daily Memorial Day–Labor Day, 9 A.M.–5 P.M. daily Labor Day–Memorial Day, free), which personalizes the big rocks with names like the Kissing Camels and the Siamese Twins. Archaeologists have found bowls and artifacts that prove people lived here more than 3,300 years ago, although it didn't become a park until railroad magnate Charles Elliot Perkins bought 240 acres for a summer home in 1879, then declared it free to the public; his heirs sold it to Colorado Springs with that condition.

History and geology aside, though, the 1,350-acre park is prime territory for **hiking, rock climbing, horseback riding,** and

COLORADO SPRINGS

© STEVE KNOPPER

Garden of the Gods in Colorado Springs

camping (the Garden of the Gods campground is at 3704 W. Colorado Ave., 719/475-9450, $26). Parks officials have in recent years added a Visitors & Nature Center, rock-climbing areas, school programs, and a film titled *How Did Those Red Rocks Get There?*

Shopping

Manitou Springs is the most touristy part of Colorado Springs, so scan the streets for shops and galleries, including **Cripple Creek Dulcimers** (740 Manitou Ave., 719/685-9655, www.dulcimer.net), which sells Appalachian stringed instruments of all kinds (just in case you needed one), and **Nature of Things Chainsaw Art** (347 Manitou Ave., 719/685-0171, www.natureofthingschainsawart.com), which is self-explanatory. The **Business of Art Center** (513 Manitou Ave., 719/685-1861, www.thebac.org, 10 A.M.–5 P.M. Tues.–Sat.) is a community-run collection of studios, galleries, and even a small theater for local artists—it displays everything from high schoolers' photographs to humorous live productions of Hans Christian Andersen stories.

Accommodations

A 20-room boarding house that thrived during the gold-mining boom in the 1850s, **The Cliff House** (306 Cañon Ave., 719/685-3000 or 888/212-7000, www.thecliffhouse.com, $199–345) hung around through the bust and turned into a resort hotel in 1914—Thomas Edison and Clark Gable were among the guests at the time. After a $9 million renovation in the late 1990s, the inn at the base of Pikes Peak has 200 nice-looking rooms, including several elaborately furnished, pastel-colored, marble-decorated suites named for the old-time celebrities who stayed here in the 1910s.

Not to be confused with Redstone Castle, in Redstone, the **Red Stone Castle** (601 South Side Rd., 719/685-5070, www.redstonecastlebandb.com, $140) is in, well, a castle—built in 1890s and maintained by a local family on a 20-acre estate. The two turret rooms are pretty and understated, with old-fashioned decor and hardwood floors, plus views of Garden of the Gods and Colorado Springs.

Food

After the **Craftwood Inn** (404 El Paso Blvd., 719/685-9000, www.restauranteur.com/craftwood, 5:30 P.M.–close) switched from hotel to restaurant in 1940, stars such as Bing Crosby and Cray Grant were known to sit at window tables. It has since closed and reopened (in 1988), and specializes in wild game, from ostrich (a $14 appetizer) to venison ($27) to wild boar ($28), plus signature veggie dishes such as pistachio pesto ravioli ($20 for two as part of a combination plate).

The **Briarhurst Manor** (404 Manitou Ave., 719/685-1864 or 877/685-1448, www.briarhurst.com, 5–9 P.M. Wed.–Mon.) is in a historic pink-sandstone building packed with a huge, old-fashioned staircase, stained-glass windows, and even a vintage church pew. The food is just as distinctive: An à la carte menu includes diamondback rattlesnake ($20), bison carpaccio ($19), and dandelion-green salad ($7).

Although **Adam's Mountain Café** (110 Cañon Ave., 719/685-1430 or 719/685-4370, www.adamsmountain.com, 8 A.M.–3 P.M. daily, 5–9 P.M. Tues.–Sat.) serves three meals a day, it's best known for the three-egg breakfast omelets—avocado, salmon, Santa Fe, and spinach, $8 apiece. Acoustic guitarists play in the evenings and some mornings.

PALMER LAKE

Built as a railroad town in 1871, Palmer Lake has grown (shrunk?) into a tiny hiking-and-biking town just east of the gigantic **Pike National Forest.** Although the population is only 2,000, it fills up every summer with hikers and cyclists, and every winter with snowshoers and cross-country skiers. A 500-foot-wide star, erected on the side of Sundance Mountain, is a Christmas tourist attraction. The town has lit it up annually, throughout December, since 1934.

Sights

In Woodland Park, about 20 miles west of Colorado Springs, the **Rocky Mountain Dinosaur Resource Center** (201 S. Fairview St., 719/686-1820, www.rmdrc.com, 9 A.M.–6 P.M. Mon.–Sat. and 10 A.M.–5 P.M. Sun. Nov.–Mar.; 9 A.M.–6 P.M. Mon.–Thurs., 9 A.M.–8 P.M. Fri.–Sat., 10 A.M.–5 P.M. Sun. Apr.–Oct., $9.50) is run by local paleontologists Mike and J. J. Triebold, who've put many of their fossil collections, including "the world's smallest T. Rex," a pachycephalosaurus, and a mosasaur, on display. The center offers tours and kids' workshops.

Sports and Recreation

Palmer Lake itself was for years too shallow for **fishing,** but local volunteers have recently changed that—at least, when Colorado droughts take the summer off. The lake is next to the Santa Fe Regional Trailhead and El Paso County Park; call 719/481-2953 for directions and information.

The **Santa Fe Regional Trail,** 14 miles of narrow gravel **biking** and **hiking** paths, begins in Palmer Lake and runs through Monument to the border of the Air Force Academy in Colorado Springs. Trailheads are at 3rd Street and Baptist Road in nearby Monument and County Line Road in Palmer Lake.

While the town's reservoirs are closed to swimmers and fishers, the pretty hiking-biking-and-showshoeing **Palmer Lake Reservoirs Trail** is open all year. To get to the Emory Hightower Trailhead, exit I-25 onto Highway 105, go four miles, turn left on South Valley Road, then left again on Old Carriage Road, then look for parking at the bottom of the curve.

Events

The Palmer Lake area, which includes Monument, doesn't have much by way of distinctive hotels, restaurants, or nightlife—but nearby Larkspur has the June–July **Colorado Renaissance Festival** (303/688-6010, www.coloradorenaissance.com), a loopy celebration of medieval times that often recalls *Monty Python and the Holy Grail.* The annual dress-up extravaganza, complete with jugglers, jousters, maidens, and glassblowing artisans, is spread out over several summer weekends.

CRIPPLE CREEK

After gold-rushers cried "Pikes Peak or bust!" in the late 1880s, they found what they were looking for—not at Pikes Peak but in Cripple Creek. Prospector Robert Womack found a small amount of gold ore in 1890, leading to production of $200,000 by the following summer, and the town wound up producing almost $20 million a year by the turn of the century. Cripple Creek was a boomtown for years, and its mining legacy lives on today in both historic mine shafts and modern gold-processing plants.

The spirit of Cripple Creek, though, has completely changed in the age of legal low-stakes gambling. Like fellow small mountain towns Black Hawk and Central City, Cripple Creek is a shell of its former self, with casinos and parking lots taking away from the surrounding mountain views. Then again, gambling is pretty fun, as long as you don't get addicted—or double down on a 4 when the dealer has a 10 showing.

Sights

The **Mollie Kathleen Gold Mine** (Hwy. 67, 719/689-2466 or 888/291-5689, 9 A.M.–4 P.M. daily June–Apr., 9 A.M.–5 P.M. daily May, $15) offers tours into a 1,000-foot-deep mine, more or less maintained as it was in 1891, when Mollie Kathleen Gortner and her family staked their claim. (According to legend, a town official told Mollie that women couldn't stake gold-mining claims, but she got her way by invoking her attorney-husband's name.)

Although gambling and other factors have turned nearby Victor, once a booming gold-rush area, into a depressing ghost town, the **Cripple Creek and Victor Narrow Gauge Railroad** (520 E. Carr St., 719/689-2640, www.cripplecreekrailroad.com, hours vary by season, $9.50) is a fun, old-fashioned, 45-minute-long way to see the historical riches and modern casinos of Cripple Creek.

The **Cripple Creek District Museum** (5th St. and Bennett Ave., 719/689-2634, 10 A.M.–5 P.M. daily June–Sept., 10 A.M.–4 P.M. Fri.–Sun. Oct.–May, $5) is a three-building downtown complex filled with maps, paintings, photos, and other artifacts from the mining era.

Twenty-six miles north of Cripple Creek, in tiny Florissant, the **Florissant Fossil Beds National Monument** (15807 Teller County 1, 719/748-3253, www.nps.gov/flfo, 9 A.M.–5:30 P.M. May–Sept., 9 A.M.–5 P.M. Oct.–Apr., $3 per week) is a huge mountain valley full of petrified redwoods and fossilized insects.

Nightlife

Cripple Creek has around 20 working casinos, many of which have some form of live entertainment, even if it's just the Irish dance band at Creeker's Casino on St. Patrick's Day. Most of the casinos also have restaurants—Las Vegas gamblers will feel right at home at the buffets—and some even have lodging packages. The **Double Eagle Hotel & Casino** (400 E. Bennett Ave., 719/689-5011, www.deca-sino.com), for example, has such contemporary acts as Juice Newton and B. J. Thomas, who, if you're lucky and ask real, real nice, might play "Raindrops Keep Falling on My Head."

Accommodations

Unless you're a casino buffet hound, grab meals in nearby Colorado Springs. Fortunately, there is one quality place to stay near Cripple Creek, the **Victor Hotel** (4th St. and Victor Ave., 719/689-3553 or 800/713-4595, www.victorhotelcolorado.com, $35–50), originally built in 1894, but delayed when excavators found a vein of gold in the foundation. The hotel burned down in 1899, along with the rest of Victor's businesses; owners rebuilt it as a bank, then changed it back into a hotel, although it was vacant for decades. In the early 1990s, the tall, square hotel reopened again with a retro look—exposed brick walls in the rooms, with antique-style radiators and vintage photos.

Pueblo and Vicinity

For a major Colorado city in the Rockies' shadow, Pueblo is surprisingly flat—in both senses of the word. Yes, there are historical sights (including the impressive Rosemount Museum Victorian mansion) and a few outdoor things to do (mountain biking and desert golfing), but compared to the huge mountains, fantastical rock gardens, and tourist traps of Colorado Springs and the bohemian food-and-lodging riches of Boulder, Pueblo is, well, boring. To residents, though, that just makes the area more pleasurable—*Money* magazine has ranked Pueblo in its Top 10 "most livable cities" several times in the past decade, owing to the low cost of living, diversity (its Hispanic population far outweighs those of Boulder and Colorado Springs), and proximity to mountains, golf courses, lakes, and hiking and biking trails.

If you wind up in Pueblo, save time for a long walk around downtown. The ambience is a mixture of urban and rural, and many of the tan-and-brown buildings are part of the **Union** Avenue Historic District** (www.pueblonline.com/unionave), a central area of restaurants and galleries that thrived as brothels and gambling houses during the mining-boom years. And while Pueblo is more plains than mountains, its proximity to **Lake Pueblo** and its central **City Park** with two lakes, playgrounds, and a pool, make it a surprisingly rich outdoor-recreation area. Watch for the **Union Avenue Train,** a black-and-red steam-engine replica complete with coal car and caboose, which shows up at various events and random spots around town.

HISTORY

Although Native American tribes and Spanish explorers tinkered around this area for centuries, Pueblo truly became an American city in 1842, when "The Pueblo" opened as a trading post for travelers from the southern Rockies to Taos, New Mexico, and beyond. At first, American settlers established the post

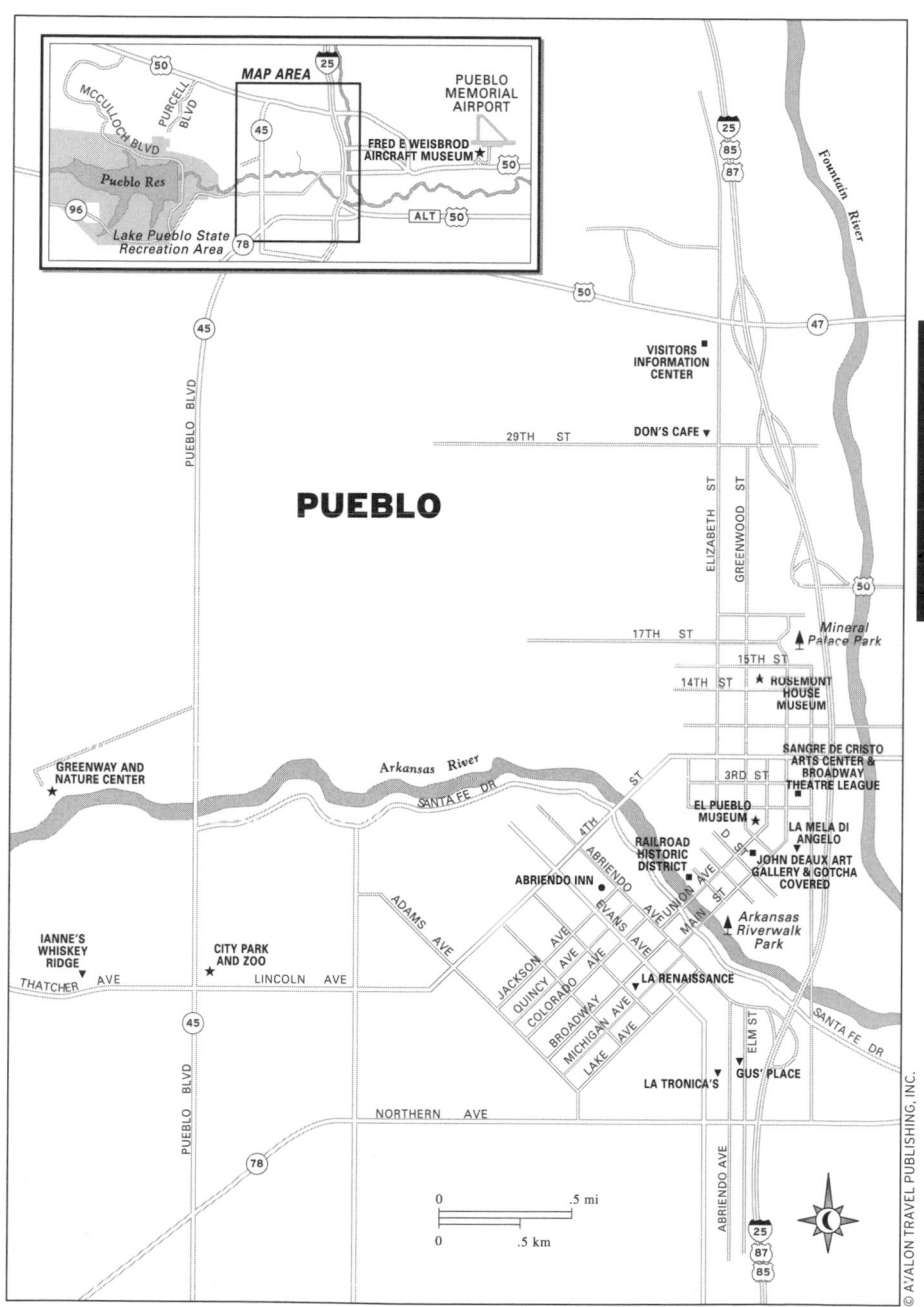

MAP AREA

PUEBLO MEMORIAL AIRPORT

FRED E WEISBROD AIRCRAFT MUSEUM ★

McCULLOCH BLVD
PURCELL BLVD

Pueblo Res

Lake Pueblo State Recreation Area

ALT 50

Fountain River

VISITORS INFORMATION CENTER

29TH ST   DON'S CAFE ▾

PUEBLO

ELIZABETH ST
GREENWOOD ST

Mineral Palace Park

17TH ST

15TH ST

14TH ST   ★ ROSEMONT HOUSE MUSEUM

Arkansas River

SANTA FE DR

GREENWAY AND NATURE CENTER ★

SANGRE DE CRISTO ARTS CENTER & BROADWAY THEATRE LEAGUE

3RD ST

EL PUEBLO MUSEUM ★

LA MELA DI ANGELO ▾

RAILROAD HISTORIC DISTRICT

JOHN DEAUX ART GALLERY & GOTCHA COVERED

ABRIENDO INN ●

ADAMS AVE

ABRIENDO AVE
EVANS AVE
UNION AVE
MAIN ST
D ST

Arkansas Riverwalk Park

IANNE'S WHISKEY RIDGE ▾

CITY PARK AND ZOO ★

THATCHER   AVE

LINCOLN   AVE

JACKSON AVE
QUINCY AVE
COLORADO AVE
BROADWAY
MICHIGAN AVE
LAKE AVE

LA RENAISSANCE ▾

ELM ST
SANTA FE DR

PUEBLO BLVD

LA TRONICA'S ▾   GUS' PLACE ▾

NORTHERN   AVE

0   .5 mi

0   .5 km

ABRIENDO AVE

25
87
85

as competition to a prominent post in Santa Fe, but over the years, various Mexican and U.S. traders took it over and traded whiskey, blankets, and other goods to travelers between Rocky Mountain, New Mexico, and Mexico. Locals also established Fort Pueblo, a small adobe structure, to defend the area.

But Pueblo almost died before it began— in 1854, when colonizing Fort Pueblo settlers asked local Utes to celebrate with them during Christmas. The Americans got drunk, the Utes slaughtered them, and this "Christmas massacre" turned Pueblo into a ghost town (thought to be cursed) for the next 15 years.

The railroad arrived in 1870, and Pueblo became what historians Carl Abbott, Stephen J. Leonard, and David McComb call the "great iron and steel city of the New West." Its manufacturing business competed with Denver, outstripped Colorado Springs, and helped Pueblo grow into the third-biggest city in the state.

SIGHTS

Built for $60,750 in 1893, the **Rosemount Museum** (419 W. 14th St., 719/545-5290, www.rosemount.org, 10 A.M.–4 P.M. Tues.– Sat., closed Jan., $6) is a carefully preserved, 37-room, 24,000-square-foot home-turned-museum with huge Tiffany chandeliers, beautiful oak staircases, a giant stained-glass window known as *Kingdoms of Nature,* and one strange anomaly—the McClelland Collection of World Curiosities, with Lotus shoes and a mummy.

Located in a former trading post built in 1842, the **El Pueblo Museum** (301 N. Union Ave., 719/583-0453, 10 A.M.–4 P.M. Tues.– Sat., $4) is a stockpile of local history, covering railroads, Native American tribes, the Spanish arrival in 1540, businesses, and other developments from prehistoric times through 1900. (For more on this subject, try the **Pueblo Historical Society** (201 W. B St., 719/543-6772, www.pueblohistory.org, 10 A.M.–4 P.M. Mon.–Sat., free), which has a library and gift shop in addition to the exhibits.)

Airplane enthusiasts should extend their layovers at the Pueblo Airport, home of the **Pueblo Weisbrod Aircraft Museum** (31001 Magnuson Ave., 719/948-9219, www.pwam.org, 10 A.M.–

© STEVE KNOPPER

Buell Children's Museum, part of the Sangre de Cristo Arts Center in Pueblo

FOUR GREAT UNEXPECTED DRIVES

Scenic Highway of Legends: Like the Subaru-driving Spanish settlers and Native American tribes before you, take Highway 12 from Trinidad through the San Isabel National Forest, including Cuchara Pass and Cordova Pass. Stop at tiny towns like Cokedale, Segundo, and Stonewall along the way for snacks.

U.S. 50 between Pueblo and Salida: The stretch of highway west of Pueblo, through Cañon City and the Royal Gorge area, begins along the Arkansas River and remains in a pretty mountain valley for most of 100 miles. On the last stretch, as you ease into Salida, the bumpy snowcaps of the Sangre de Cristo mountain range become visible to the south.

Highway 69, from Walsenburg to Westcliffe: If possible, take the long way from Pueblo to Walsenburg, rather than the flat and boring stretch down speedier I-25. This curvy two-lane road passes through the Sangre de Cristos on one side and the Wets (part of the San Isabel National Forest) on the other. The midway point is tiny Westcliffe, a beatific mountain town with a couple of bed-and-breakfasts and small roadside restaurants. Plan about an hour and a half to U.S. 50, then another hour back east to I-25.

Highway 160 from Walsenburg to Alamosa: This 75-mile drive, over 9,413-foot North La Veta Pass, is notable for its mountain views and interesting rock formations. Before you hit Fort Garland, about 50 miles from Walsenburg, you'll see several 14,000-foot mountains to your right, including Little Bear Peak.

COLORADO SPRINGS

4 P.M. Mon.–Fri., 10 A.M.–2 P.M. Sat., 1–4 P.M. Sun., $6), displaying actual military aircraft, including the Boeing B-29 bomber (used extensively in World War II) and a Huey UH-1 helicopter (like the ones you'd see on *M*A*S*H*). The **International B-24 Memorial Museum,** also on the premises, is, in part, a tribute to airmen who trained in Pueblo.

The **Historic Arkansas Riverwalk** (downtown, roughly between Grand, 1st, Victoria, and D Streets, 719/595-0242, www.aboutharp.com) is a 26-acre collection of pedestrian paths along the Arkansas River channel downtown. Bike routes lead to Lake Pueblo, and locally designed art and sculpture line the walkway. While wandering the area, check out the **Pueblo Levee Project** (719/546-0315), a 175,000-square-foot mural that made the *Guinness Book of World's Records* as "World's Largest Mural." Some 1,000 artists have contributed to the sprawling, patchwork painting since University of Southern Colorado students began the impromptu project one night in 1978, and the styles range from graffiti to cartoons. To check it out, take the 1st Street exit from I-25, head south on Union

Avenue, and turn right at the end of the Corona Avenue bridge.

The **Sangre de Cristo Arts Center** (210 N. Santa Fe, 719/295-7200, www.sdc-arts.org, 11 A.M.–4 P.M. Tues.–Sat., $4) has grown over the last three decades from a small, two-building complex to 90,000 square feet of gallery space, with a $2 million budget and a theater. The large, colorful paintings emphasize the Southwest, such as Bettina Steinke's *Early Morning Smile,* of a young Native American woman beaming on a cloudy day. The Buell Children's Museum, adjacent to the museum with bronze statues of kids playing, has make-your-own-art displays.

In La Junta, about 65 miles west of Pueblo, the reconstructed **Bent's Old Fort National Museum** (402 Santa Fe, 719/383-5010, www.nps.gov/beol, 8 A.M.–5:30 P.M. June–Aug., 9 A.M.–4 P.M. Sept.–May, $3) is on the site of William and Charles Bent's original 1833 trading center for plains Indians and trappers. For almost 16 years in the mid-1800s, the fort was among the only Santa Fe Trail settlements between Missouri and Mexico, and was an oasis for travelers scratching through the desert.

Bishop Castle

Bishop Castle (Hwy. 75, 719/485-3040, www.bishopcastle.org, "always open [daylight hours] and always free") is either a genuine Wonder of the World (as its website claims with numerous exclamation points) or one man's loopy lifelong obsession. Jim Bishop started building the medieval architectural collage, whose tallest tower reaches 160 feet, in 1969 using stonemasonry know-how he picked up from books; a group called Friends of the Castle sent out Bishop's first-ever volunteer crew in 1999. The castle is impressive, full of stained-glass windows, turrets, stone-decorated walkways, tall stairways, and a gift shop. And, proclaims the website: "It won't be finished until the morning that Jim doesn't wake up again." Don't leave without picking up a Bishop Castle shot glass.

SPORTS AND RECREATION

The 9,600-acre **Lake Pueblo State Park** encompasses a large reservoir with two marinas and two boat ramps, 400 campsites, and numerous **hiking** and **biking** trails. The **Greenway & Nature Center** (5200 Nature Center Rd., 719/549-2414, www.gncp.org), operated with the University of Southern Colorado, includes miles of trails, a hospital for injured hawks called the **Raptor Center,** volleyball and horseshoe courts, and a restaurant. More information on Pueblo-area parks and recreation is at www.pueblo.org/visitorsguide/recreation.htm.

About 65 miles east of Pueblo, near La Junta, the **Comanche National Grassland** (1420 E. 3rd St., 719/384-2181) is "hikable," but the 440,000-acre area spread throughout southern Colorado is better known for its **wildlife viewing**—rarely seen golden eagles, lesser prairie chickens, and swift foxes live here, along with coyotes, hawks, and wild turkeys.

The main draw of **Picketwire Canyonlands** is its 1,300 naturally preserved dinosaur footprints, which originated in the mud some 150 million years ago. For more information on this area, contact the USDA Forest Service (2840 Kachina Dr., 719/553-1400).

NIGHTLIFE

Gus' Place (1201 Elm St., 719/542-0756, 10 A.M.–close Mon.–Sat., noon–8 P.M. Sun.) is a classic local pub, a re-creation of which once landed at the Library of Congress' American Folklife Center to mark Italian-American history. (The pub is located in what was, years ago, a predominantly Italian neighborhood.) For more genteel live performances, the best venue is the **Broadway Theatre League** (210 N. Santa Fe Dr., 719/545-4721), which has put on *Evita* and *Tommy* and hosted performances by Carol Channing and Marvin Hamlisch (both of whom, undoubtedly, wound up at Gus' Place after their shows).

SHOPPING

The mild weather and proximity to both New Mexico and the Rockies attracts a large community of artists to Pueblo, and many have galleries—Kay Singleton's charcoal and watercolor scenes of southwestern buildings and other sights are on display at **Earth N' Art** (477 S. Clarion Dr., 719/542-5204, www.earthn-art.com). For work by more local artists, the **John Deaux Art Gallery** (221 S. Union Ave., 719/545-8407) is one of several galleries worth visiting. Female clotheshounds, especially those of the teen-age, pink-loving variety, will enjoy the family-run **Gotcha Covered** (230 S. Union Ave., 719/544-6833 or 866/544-6833, www.schwabe2000.com/shoponline).

ACCOMMODATIONS

The hotels of Pueblo are mostly of the Best Western and Marriott variety—some of them aren't bad—but the **Abriendo Inn** (300 W. Abriendo Ave., 719/544-2703, www.abriendoinn.com, $69–165) is one of the classier hotels in south-central Colorado. It has a spiral staircase, stained-glass windows, parquet floors, brass beds, free daily breakfasts, and large whirlpools in the rooms.

FOOD

La Tronica's (1143 E. Abriendo Ave., 719/542-1113, 5–9 P.M. Tues.–Thurs., 5–10 P.M. Fri.–Sat.) has been around since 1943, and

Lyndon B. Johnson is among the dignitaries reputed to have dined here; it retains an old-fashioned quality, with comfort food like steak and fried chicken.

La Mela di Angelo (123 N. Main St., 719/253-7700, 11 A.M.–2 P.M. Mon.–Sat., 5–10 P.M. Fri.–Sat., 5–9 P.M. Mon.–Thurs.) is a relatively new downtown Italian restaurant with a large bar, green-and-red decor, and Dean Martin ballads piped in from the ceiling. The food is excellent, too—try the angel-hair pasta with goat cheese and sun-dried tomatoes.

Ianne's Whiskey Ridge (4333 Thatcher Ave., 719/564-8551, 4:30–9 P.M. Tues.–Thurs., 4–10 P.M. Fri.–Sat., 11 A.M.–9 P.M. Sun.–Mon.) is a family-run Italian fixture between downtown Pueblo and the reservoir. Homemade highlights include chicken piccata, the lobster-and-steak dinner, and various high-quantity-and-quality combinations of pasta and seafood.

La Renaissance (217 E. Routt Ave., 719/543-6367, 5–9 P.M. Mon.–Sat.) has a few vegetarian dishes (including the rellenos, for $12), but everything else is meat—many different kinds of steak, plus chicken, duck, and lamb. It's all very juicy.

INFORMATION

The **Greater Pueblo Chamber of Commerce** (302 N. Santa Fe Dr., 719/542-1704 or 800/233-3446) and the *Pueblo Chieftain* (www.chieftain.com) have put up the extremely useful website www.pueblo.org, which has information about historic sites, restaurants, and art displays.

Cañon City's webpage, www.canoncitycolorado.com, is completely geared to tourists, with information on dining, lodging, and especially the Royal Gorge.

CAÑON CITY

Bizarre but beautiful mountain town Cañon City is known for two things: prisons and a huge hole. The Royal Gorge is a 1,000-foot-deep canyon surrounded by rocky cliffs and treacherous peaks, and simply standing next to it is enough to give you vertigo. As for pris-

ons, Cañon City built its first one in 1871, and today some 7,500 to 8,500 convicts stay at 10 area facilities—including the Super Max, which has housed super-villains such as Ted "The Unabomber" Kaczynski, original World Trade Center bomber Ramzi Yousef, and Oklahoma City bomber Timothy McVeigh. Residents, believe it or not, love the prisons, as they give decent jobs to some 3,500 people.

Beyond those two things, Cañon City is a pretty little mountain town with creeks and fishing ponds throughout the valley west of Pueblo and northeast of the breathtaking Sangre de Cristo mountain range. Its downtown area of shops and galleries is a bona fide historic site, including mostly 1900s-era buildings, and is the place to visit if you're not in the mood for tourist attractions such as the Buckskin Joe Frontier Town and the Museum of Colorado Prisons. Also, the weather is frequently great, even in the winter, and Cañon City has plenty of hiking-and-biking trails, white-water-rafting outlets, and a summer music festival.

Sights

A natural wonder some call the "Grand Canyon of the Arkansas River," the Royal Gorge formed three million years ago from a trickle of water, and its location was once home to dinosaurs. The Utes, among other tribes, set up camp here in the winter, and Spanish missionaries, fur traders, and trappers were among the early settlers. In the late 1800s, after miners discovered silver on the Arkansas, two railroads competed to build lines to cart ore from the high country—the Rio Grande won this "Royal Gorge War," which began with gunshots and ended in court.

There are several dramatic ways to experience the Royal Gorge, beginning with the **Royal Gorge Bridge & Park** (4218 Fremont County Rd., 719/275-7507 or 888/333-5597, www.royalgorgebridge.com, 10 A.M.–5 P.M. daily, $20), an 18-foot-wide bridge, built in 1929 and suspended 1,053 feet up from the bottom. It's a little expensive to get in, and the 360-acre theme park is heavy on hot dogs and cowboy-hat shops, but the views are breathtaking and

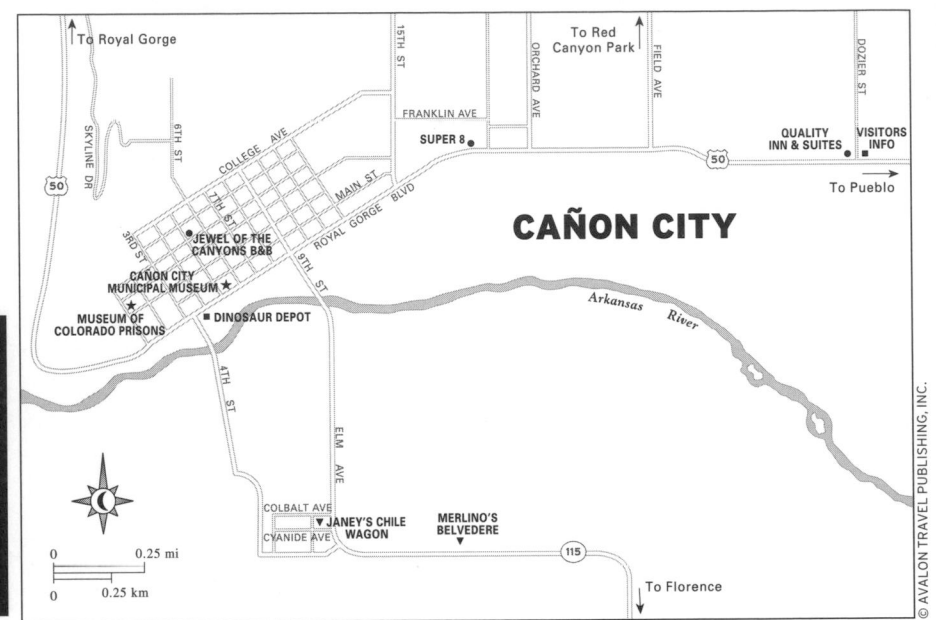

CAÑON CITY

the windy, wobbly walk across the bridge scares hundreds of thousands of visitors every year. To check out the gorge from the bottom, the **Royal Gorge Route Railroad** (401 Water St., 303/569-2403 or 888/724-5748, www.royal-gorgeroute.com, various departure times depending on season, $28.95) is a 12-mile trip through the narrow valley, stopping to linger over the aforementioned suspension bridge and other sights. The railroad, heavily marketed by Cañon City, offers packages such as a "gourmet dinner car," a murder-mystery game, and a ride up front with the locomotive engineer.

Focusing on Cañon City's *other* claim to fame, the **Museum of Colorado Prisons** (201 N. 1st St., 719/269-3015, www.prisonmuseum.org, 8:30 A.M.–6 P.M. daily Memorial Day–Labor Day, 10 A.M.–5 P.M. Fri.–Sun. Oct.–Apr., 10 A.M.–5 P.M. daily May and Sept.–Oct.) has such cheerful exhibitions as the hangman's noose used in the last Colorado execution, a lovingly preserved women's correctional facility from 1935, an actual gas chamber, and a gift shop. The creative visitor

may want to bake a cake with a file in it before stopping by.

The **Buckskin Joe Frontier Town & Railway** (1139 Fremont County Rd. 3A, 719/275-5149, www.buckskinjoe.com, 9 A.M.–6:30 P.M. daily May–Sept., varying hours during the off-season, $12) is an Old West replica, complete with staged gunfights and characters walking around in authentic costumes (but presumably not the authentic *smells* of that showerless era). From the main gate, on the way up to the Royal Gorge Bridge & Park, you can buy tickets to the Royal Gorge Scenic Railway, a three-mile tourist-train trip far above the gorge on a narrow track.

Connoisseurs of both wine and Benedictine monks will enjoy the **The Winery at Holy Cross Abbey** (3011 E. U.S. 50, 719/276-5191 or 877/422-9463, www.abbeywinery.com), with a monastery on the west side of the property and a Napa Valley-style wine-bottling facility on the east side. Visitors can tour both the abbey, which has impressive views of the

You have to pay a fee to view the 1,000-foot-deep-Royal Gorge, outside Cañon City.

Sangre de Cristo range, and the wine making facility, with tasting in the pretty outdoor garden during the summer.

The **Dinosaur Depot** (330 Royal Gorge Rd., 719/269-7150 or 800/987-6379, www.dinosaurdepot.com, varying hours depending on the season, $3) documents the area's *really* old history, when dinosaurs roamed through the gorge. The region has produced many amazing fossils over the years, although some of the most famous ones have relocated to museums in Washington, D.C., and Denver; visitors to this museum will have to settle for a full-size replica of a reproduced stegosaurus skeleton.

Accommodations

The Cañon Inn was once a fixture in this town, and even though it's now a **Quality Inn and Suites** (3075 E. U.S. 50, 719/275-8676 or 800/525-7727, www.canoninn.com, $70–90), it still has the same plainspoken charm as it did when stars John Wayne, Jane Fonda, John Belushi, James Caan, and Corey Haim (Corey Haim?) stayed here over the years. It also has six indoor hot tubs and a heated pool.

More rustic, but centrally located near the gorge, and encouraging of guests with horses, is the **Bandera Bed & Barn** (44784 W. U.S. 50, 719/276-2551, www.banderabedandbarn.com, $75 for the first person, $25 for each additional person). It advertises "hospitality... the cowboy way" and has the saddle-and-wood decor, 11 acres, actual barn, and two horses to prove it.

In a restored 1890 Victorian downtown, the **Jewel of the Canyons Bed and Breakfast Suites** (429 Greenwood Ave., 719/275-0378, www.jewelofthecanyons.com, $60–75) has three rooms with a cozy, turn-of-the-20th-century ambience—including one with a huge, puffy, brass bed.

Food

Le Petit Chablis (512 Royal Gorge Blvd., 719/269-3333, 11:30 A.M.–1:30 P.M. and 5:30 P.M.–close Tues.–Fri., 5:30 P.M.–close Sat.) is a high-class French joint with fresh seafood and pasta dishes, plus homemade bread and pastries. The menu changes daily.

Run by an Italian family that operated

a cider mill and cherry orchard for years in Cañon City, **◖ Merlino's Belvedere** (1330 Elm Ave., 719/275-5558 or 800/625-2526, www.merlinosbelvedere.com, 11:30 A.M.–1:30 P.M. Mon.–Fri., 4:30 P.M.–close Fri., noon–9 P.M. Sat., noon–7:30 P.M. Sun.) has served fettuccine with smoked salmon Alfredo sauce ($16) and manicotti ($14) since roughly 1946. Everything is homemade, and the bakery and pasta shop is a great find even if you don't stop for a meal.

El Caporal (1028 Main St., 719/276-2001, 11 A.M.–9 P.M. Sun.–Thurs., 11 A.M.–10 P.M. Fri.–Sat.), an easygoing Mexican eatery with purple-and-pink tabletops, has a massive menu of all combinations of tacos, enchiladas, burritos, and tostadas. A little greasier and spoonier, but just as spicy, is **Janey's Chile Wagon** (807 Cyanide Ave., 719/275-4885, 11 A.M.–8 P.M. daily), where you can wash down the cheap ($6) enchiladas with Tecate and Corona beer.

Salida and Buena Vista

SALIDA

Downtown Salida is a great place to kill a summer afternoon. For a town of just 5,500 people it has some of the best art galleries in the state, and its colorful downtown district of restaurants, theaters, and little shops is built for tourists—with a little extra artistic oomph from

Downtown Salida is home to some of the state's best art galleries.

pastel-colored restaurants and galleries with life-size, wrought-iron animals spilling onto the sidewalks outside.

Salida's other great advantage is its proximity to extremely tall mountains, particularly the Sawatch Range, which seems to pop out of nowhere as you head north along U.S. 285. The Collegiate Peaks line the half-hour stretch of road from here to equally tiny Buena Vista, and on your left is a series of 14,000-foot peaks, including Mount Shavano, Tabeguache Peak, Mount Antero, and Mount Princeton. In addition to the 15 "fourteeners" surrounding Salida, the Arkansas River runs through town, the Sangre de Cristo Range is to the south, and the climate is so consistently mild that residents have dubbed it the "Banana Belt."

As a result, Salida, which in the late 1800s was a railroad town with legendarily tough saloons and flophouses, is a destination area for hikers, bikers, cross-country skiers, fishers, and white-water rafters. From Buena Vista, it's about 25 miles south on U.S. 285; from Cañon City, it's 50 miles west on U.S. 50.

Sports and Recreation

For truly excellent mountain **fishing,** make a pilgrimage almost any time of year to 14,433-foot-high Mount Elbert, the tallest mountain in Colorado, where the Arkansas River begins, popping and hissing its way down to the rest of

COLORADO SPRINGS

© STEVE KNOPPER

The Sawatch Range contains the three highest mountain peaks in the state.

the fourteeners in the area. The Colorado Division of Wildlife heavily stocks brown trout and rainbow trout here, and while several dozen fishing spots are accessible on the river, some are private.

Rafters will find it difficult to choose between Salida and Buena Vista, both near superb Arkansas River rapids. Tour-guide outfits unique to Salida include **Canyon Marine Expeditions** (105 E. U.S. 50, 800/539-4447) and **Whitewater Encounters** (14825 U.S. 285, 719/530-0937 or 800/530-8362, www.weraft.com).

Salida is also home to a small **ski** area—**Monarch** (23715 U.S. 50, 719/530-5000 or 888/996-7669, www.skimonarch.com), with 55 trails spread out over 670 acres along the Continental Divide. The runs are just about evenly divided among beginners and experts, and it has five chairlifts, but nonetheless, this is a ski area of convenience—few would pick Monarch over Vail or Aspen.

To participate in the two-day, 26.5-mile **Banana Belt Bicycle Weekend,** every Septem-

ber, register with the **chamber of commerce** (406 W. U.S. 50, 719/539-2068). Salida is also a big cycling town, and rentals and equipment are available at **Absolute Bikes** (310 S. Sackett St., 719/539-9295, www.absolutebikes.com).

Shopping

Salida is stocked with antiques shops and art galleries, including **Antiques on First** (140 W. 1st St., 719/539-3353), with lamps, tables, books, a $45 bust of the poet Henry Wadsworth Longfellow, and an old box of acne medicine with the slogan "Rinse Away Your Blackheads." More modern is **Cultureclash** (101 N. F St., 719/539-3118), an art-and-jewelry store with colorful paintings on display. Naturally, Salida has one of those new-agey souvenir shops that sells crystals, T-shirts, wind chimes, and stuffed animals—**Earth's Treasures** (119 F St., 719/539-3904).

Accommodations

Salida is filled with Best Westerns and Econo Lodges, plus the roadside fixture **Woodland**

WHITE-WATER RAFTING TOURS

Don't go into a white-water-rafting trip expecting a cakewalk — it's not like you can pull off to the side of the road, put on some special shoes, and run a river the way you'd hike a trail. First, unless you have a kayak and some experience, you'll need a commercial outfitter to set up the tour and provide the equipment. (There are tons of them on the Internet, and I've listed several throughout this chapter and book.)

Secondly, prepare in advance: Wear a swimsuit, of course, and either tennis shoes or water sandals. Wool socks are OK. Bring waterproof sunscreen and, if you wear glasses, a string or "Croakies." Waterproof cameras, with elastic bands, can be easily attached to lifejackets. Leave everything else — caps, jewelry, cotton clothing, wallets, keys — in the car. The outfitter will provide lifejackets and helmets if necessary.

Finally, call in advance to determine the trip's degree of difficulty. A Class I rapid is calm and easy, for kids and adults alike. Anything higher than a Class IV may require some heavy-duty paddling, so make sure you're in shape. Class VI is for professionals or experienced rafting teams only. Note that the water can be *freakin' cold* at almost all times of year save mid-July through early September, but the white-water-rafting season officially begins around May. Most outfitters will rent wetsuits as well.

Motel, but two properties are more than generic, and worthy of the dramatic mountain scenery surrounding the town. In a brown, triangular house straight out of *The Sound of Music,* the tree-lined **⬛ Tudor Rose** (6720 County Rd. 104, 719/539-2002 or 800/379-0889, www.thetudorrose.com, $80–175) has six rooms with large feather beds and views of several 14,000-foot mountains. More historic is the 1892-era building that houses the **River Run Inn** (8495 County Rd. 160, 719/539-3818 or 800/385-6925, www.riverruninn.com, $100–125), directly on the Arkansas River, with six private rooms and a shared third-floor "dormitory" that costs $30 per person (including breakfast).

Food

Burger Kings are plentiful here, but head to the downtown historic district for the distinctive bistros and wine bars. A mixture of modern (for the healthy food and fancy drinks) and historic (in an 1880s-era building, one of the oldest in Chaffee County), **Dakota's Bistro** (122 N. F St., 719/530-9909, 11:30 A.M.–9 P.M. Tues.–Sun. Memorial Day–Labor Day, 11:30 A.M.–8:30 P.M. Tues.–Sat. Labor Day–Memorial Day) serves steak, lamb, and fish.

Homier (and a little kitschier, in that Country Kitchen kind of way) is the **Country Bounty Restaurant** (W. U.S. 50, 719/539-3546, www.countrybounty.net, 7:30 A.M.–8 P.M. daily Oct.–May, 6:30 A.M.–9 P.M. June–Sept.), which starts with burgers ($6) and fries and moves into elk burgers ($8), salmon-and-broccoli linguini ($15), and Thai-style noodles with grilled vegetables ($11). Check out the gift shop's large collection of porcelain dolls and various angels and lotions.

A far more personal and healthy version of Chipotle Mexican Grill, **Whitewater Wraps** (139 W. 3rd St., 719/530-8992, www.whitewaterwraps.com, 11:30 A.M.8 P.M. Mon.–Sat. Labor Day–Memorial Day, 11:30 A.M.–9 P.M. daily Memorial Day–Labor Day) began as a burrito stand at nearby folk-music festivals and turned into an easygoing, reliable burrito joint (with beer, too).

BUENA VISTA

Although just 2,200 people live in Buena Vista today, it was once the home of 3,000 Utes, explorers believed, and during the gold-mining boom, it had 36 bars. The scenery hasn't changed much—the Collegiate Range, with its eight 14,000-foot mountains, is to the west, and Brown's Canyon, which surrounds a surging stretch of the Arkansas River, is to the south. The town is big with hikers and bikers, and some call it the "capital for white-water rafting in the U.S."

Sights

About 12 miles southwest of Buena Vista, the **Mt. Princeton Hot Springs Resort** (15870 County Rd. 162, Nathrop, 888/395-7799, www.mtprinceton.com) is a hotel-and-restaurant complex built around trickles of 135-degree spring water. The natural pools, used since the days of the Native Americans, are in view of the 14,000-foot mountain ranges.

Formerly the Old Chaffee County Courthouse, site of a violent confrontation between rival Granite and Buena Vista officials in the 1880s, the **Buena Vista Heritage Museum** (506 E. Main St., 719/395-8458, www.buenavistaheritage.org, 10 A.M.–5 P.M. daily, $3) displays miner-era clothing, furniture, and even a piano. Supposedly, the sheriff's wife used it to entertain prisoners in the county jail.

◖ Arkansas River White-Water Rafting

White-water rafting is the thing to do in Buena Vista, and the best place for it is on the **Arkansas River,** home of the sharply dropping Brown's Canyon. The rapids are so intense here that local adventure-sports companies have named them: Zoomflume, Staircase, Devil's Punchbowl, and, my personal favorite, Seidel's Suckhole.

Several outfitters sponsor tours, including **Performance Tours** (115 Gregg Dr., 800/328-7238, www.performancetours.com, $38–259 depending on the duration and length of trip),

Dvorak Expeditions (17921 U.S. 285, Nathrop, 719/539-6851 or 800/824-3795, $50–1,625, with the high price being for elaborate 10-day trips), and **Buffalo Joe's** (113 N. Railroad St., 719/395-8757, www.buffalojoe.com, $41–249 depending on duration and length).

Accommodations

The three-guest-room **Adobe Inn Bed and Breakfast** (303 N. U.S. 24, 719/395-6340 or 888/343-6340, $84–109) is notable for its art, such as the wood carvings on the ceiling of the Indian Room and the adobe fireplace in the lobby.

The **Liar's Lodge** (3000 County Rd. 371, 719/395-3444 or 888/542-7756, www.liarslodge.com, $128–148) is an impressive log structure, with a 25-foot ceiling and a stone fireplace climbing all the way to the top. It's literally on the bank of the Arkansas River.

In nearby Nathrop, the tree-covered, **La Roca de Tiza Bed and Breakfast** (16420 County Rd. 289A, 719/395-8034, www.larocabandb.com, $90–115) is wedged between two 14,000-foot peaks—from a distance, the mountains look like they rise out of the hotel. Also in Nathrop, **Lloyd's Inn** (16260 County Rd. 162, 719/395-8202 or 877/395-8202, www.lloydsinn.com, $95) is on the bank of the pleasant Chalk Creek; fishers will love the catwalk-style, raised dock that extends directly over the creek.

INFORMATION

Contact local chambers of commerce for more information: Buena Vista (343 U.S. 24 S., 719/395-6612) and Salida (406 W. U.S. 50, 719/539-2068 or 877/772-5432, www.salidachamber.org).

COLORADO SPRINGS

Alamosa and the Great Sand Dunes

With a population of 9,500 people, Alamosa is the metropolis of the San Luis Valley, the south-central Colorado plains area that extends about 125 miles north to south and 50 miles wide. It's not the most exciting city in the state, although two centuries ago it was the spot where Pikes Peak discoverer Zebulon Pike was captured and taken prisoner to nearby Santa Fe, then a hostile area outside the United States.

While Alamosa has long been an agricultural center of Colorado, notably for potatoes, and its Adams State College is one of the biggest universities in the region (check out the **Luther Bean Museum and Art Gallery** on campus), it's a sleepy town most notable for its proximity to other spots. Use the city as a base to visit the Great Sand Dunes National Park and Preserve, just to the northeast.

Also near Alamosa are a few tiny but interesting towns—**Antonito,** about 30 miles south on U.S. 285, is home of both the 120-year-old, steam-locomotive **Cumbres and Toltec Scenic Railroad** (587 Terrace, 888/286-2737, www.cumbrestoltec.com, varying hours according to season, $55–70) and the **Conejos River Guest Ranch** (25390 Hwy. 17, 719/376-2464, $85–105), a pretty riverfront lodge whose innkeeper is named Shorty Fry.

SIGHTS

The Alamosa region is a huge draw for **birdwatchers,** with the wet meadows and river oxbows of the **Alamosa National Wildlife Refuge** (9383 El Rancho Ln., 719/589-4021, http://alamosa.fws.gov/AlamosaNWR.html) giving homes to migrating songbirds and water birds, along with mule deer, beaver, and coyotes.

The **Monte Vista National Wildlife Refuge** (6140 Hwy. 15, Monte Vista, 719/589-4021, http://alamosa.fws.gov/Monte percent-20Vista.html) is also nearby, drawing 20,000 sandhill cranes in spring and fall—plus three endangered whooping cranes who like to pop up and freak out the birders.

Completely unexpected is the **Jack Dempsey Museum** (412 Main St., Manassa, 719/843-5207, 10 A.M.–5 P.M. Tues.–Sat. Memorial Day–Labor Day, free), some 23 miles south of Alamosa, where the 1919 heavyweight champion of the world grew up. The museum website refers to Dempsey as "Manassa's most famous figure," which makes sense, but I wonder what the competition would be. The museum is in the cabin where Dempsey grew up, and some of his championship gloves hang here.

Great Sand Dunes National Park and Preserve

With pointy peaks, curvy bodies, various shades of brown, and shapes changing constantly in the wind, the Great Sand Dunes National Park and Preserve (11999 U.S. 50, Mosca, 719/378-6300 or 719/378-6399, www.nps.gov/grsa, always open, $3/week) looks like an alien landscape, or the kind of animated backdrop you'd see in a fancy computer-animated movie. North America's tallest dunes are otherworldly and fascinating, extending 750 feet high, with the bottle-cap Sangre de Cristo Mountains in the background. Within the 30-square-mile area, a national monument since 1932, are alpine lakes, wetlands, aspen and cottonwood trees, and the flowers and wildlife that go with them. The park is open all day, every day, and some 300,000 visitors a year show up for camping, hiking, cycling, and, in the fall, sand-boarding. In late 2004, U.S. officials designated the Dunes a national park, joining Rocky Mountain, Mesa Verde, and Black Canyon of the Gunnison in Colorado.

Colorado Gators

Colorado Gators (9162 County Rd. 9 N., Mosca, 719/378-2618, www.gatorfarm.com, 9 A.M.–5 P.M. daily, $6), also known as the San Luis Valley Alligator Farm, is the most unexpected attraction of south-central Colorado. The 450-gator farm advertises a "family-oriented, recreational, and educational farm making full use of natural resources with an integrated ecosystem that is practical and environment friendly"—and offers $50 alligator-wrestling classes.

SPORTS AND RECREATION

Anybody interested in the Colorado outdoors should load up the **bike** and the **hiking** boots and head to the **Rio Grande National Forest,** a 1,852-acre region encompassing the San Juan and Sangre de Cristo Mountains, the San Luis Valley, and the Rio Grande Del Norte—of the many mountain peaks, the elevations range from 7,500 to more than 14,000 feet. Trails are all over the area; for details, contact the forest supervisor's office at 719/852-5941 or the **Conejos Peak Ranger District** at 719/274-5193.

The **San Luis Lakes State Park** contains 2,054 acres of protected wetlands and is great for **wildlife viewing**—coyotes, rabbits, elk, songbirds, and snakes, among many others. The lake itself is open for boating and fishing.

ACCOMMODATIONS

Most of the Alamosa-area hotels are Best Westerns and Days Inns, along with a few affordable inns and lodges, such as the **Great Sand Dunes Lodges** (7900 Hwy. 150 N., Mosca, 719/378-2900, www.gsdlodge.com, $85–99) and the Clarion-owned **Inn of the Rio Grande** (333 Santa Fe Dr., 719/589-5833 or 800/669-1658, www.innoftherio.com, $64) downtown. A unique property in town is the **Cottonwood Inn B&B** (123 San Juan Ave., 719/589-3882 or 800/955-2623, www.cottonwoodinn.com, $70–125), a six-room-and-four-suite converted apartment building that's pristinely decorated with antiques and fluffy pillows.

FOOD

The **True Grits Steak House** (U.S. 160 just east of Alamosa, 719/589-9954, 4–9 P.M. Mon.–Fri., 11 A.M.–10 P.M. Fri.–Sat., 11 A.M.–9 P.M. Sun.) serves steaks, as you can imagine, but it's also an obsessive tribute to John Wayne, who once shot the movie *True Grit* in parts of Colorado—movie posters and photos

are all over the walls. "It's interesting what people bring in," owner Virgie Sheeley once told the local *Valley Courier* "We've even had John Wayne toilet paper."

INFORMATION

Alamosa's **Visitor Information Center** is in Cole Park (719/589-4840 or 800/258-7597, www.alamosa.org). Cuchara Valley splits a chamber of commerce with La Veta: http://lavetacucharachamber.com.

CUCHARA VALLEY

One of the most breathtaking drives in Colorado—which is saying a lot, given the Rockies to the north and the San Juans to the southwest—the Scenic Highway of Legends passes through the mountainous **San Isabel National Forest,** the 10,000-foot **Cuchara Pass,** and the 11,248-foot **Cordova Pass.** It begins in Trinidad and forms a sort of smushy "E" shape before hooking up with U.S. 160, which extends to Walsenburg to the east and Fort Garland to the west.

The towns along this route are more significant for their history than for their modern amenities. **Cokedale,** formed in 1906, is a ghost town (and a National Historic Landmark District) today, but once it was a massive coal-producing camp; **Segundo** was once popular among Spanish people coming up from Mexico, but today you're lucky if you can spot the gas station; and **Stonewall,** for more than a century, has been a popular spot for hunting and fishing.

Sights

The **Scenic Highway of Legends** (Highway 12) is just as rich with tales of fortune-seeking and war as it is with mountain scenery. In the 1800s, when Spanish explorers pushed north to the Spanish Peaks, they discovered gold, enslaved local Native Americans to help them dig, then killed their poor helpers and destroyed the mine. But on their way south down Cuchara Pass, they encountered more Native Americans, who wiped them out—and, according to legend (or at least the

COLORADO SPRINGS

© STEVE KNOPPER

The mountain-filled San Isabel National Forest is just northwest of Walsenburg.

official highway page at http://sangres.com/shol), their gold remains in a river valley somewhere near Stonewall. Much later, Union soldiers pushed through the hills and valleys, leaving their names and initials on a rock at Scofield Ridge, just southeast of Trinidad.

Sports and Recreation

Bear Lake is south of Cuchara, off Highway 12; to get there, turn at the northern base of Cuchara Pass, head west on a dirt road, and drive about five miles. At 10,500 feet, the beatific, tree-lined lake has 14 campsites, plus numerous trailheads for **hikers** and plenty of **fish** for outdoorspeople.

Another dirt road at the northern base of Cuchara Pass leads to **Blue Lake,** about four miles down a dirt road; there are 15 campgrounds here, as well, and the trailheads take hikers into the Sangre de Cristos.

For equipment, the **Bicycle Barn** (300 S. Main St., La Veta, 719/742-3050) rents snowshoes, cross-country skis, and bicycles for reasonable prices.

San Isabel National Forest

This is a sprawling, one-million-acre collection of mountains, valleys, and lakes with corresponding hiking, biking, camping, and cross-country skiing opportunities. It includes the **Sangre de Cristo Mountains,** a stumpy set of snowcaps that begin in Poncha Pass, Colorado, and extend into Glorieta Pass, New Mexico, including 10 peaks higher than 14,000 feet and more than 24 over 13,000 feet.

The **Spanish Peaks** have been a beacon for Native Americans, Spanish and French explorers, American settlers, and gold-rush fortune-seekers—they've been called many names, including *Wahatoya,* an early Indian word meaning "breasts of the Earth." Their best-known nickname is *Dos Hermanos,* Spanish for "two brothers."

Accommodations

It's hard to find civilization along the Scenic Highway of Legends. **La Veta,** near the intersection of I-25 and Walsenburg, is a small re-

© STEVE KNOPPER

COLORADO SPRINGS

The massive Sangre de Cristo range is part of the Rio Grande National Forest.

sort town with several excellent places to stay. Those include **La Veta Inn** (103 W. Ryus, 719/742-3700 or 888/806-4875, www.lavetainn.com, $50–75), a square, tan building that rents out the entire 21-room hotel for $1,200 a night, and **Echo Canyon Ranch** (12507 Echo Canyon Creek Road, 800/341-6603, www.guestecho.com, $860 per person with a three-night minimum), which provides its own horses on a scenic 1,500-acre private plot.

Food

The **Ryus Avenue Bakery** (129 W. Ryus Ave., La Veta, 719/742-3830, www.ryusavebakery.com, 8 A.M.–1:30 P.M. Tues., Thurs., and Sat.) serves healthy snacks, cinnamon rolls for breakfast, and deli sandwiches for lunch, but only three days a week. Grab a loaf of the home-cooked oatmeal cinnamon raisin bread for just $2.75.

The **La Veta Pub and Grub** (923 S. Oak, 719/742-3093, 10:30 A.M.–close daily) serves burgers, fries, and beer.

Trinidad and Walsenburg

TRINIDAD

The last Colorado town you encounter on I-25 south to New Mexico, Trinidad is a small collection of art galleries, historic Southwestern houses and museums, and a nearby recreation area with lakes and trails. But it wasn't always so peaceful: It was a key stop along the Santa Fe Trail in the late 1800s, and Old West villains such as Billy the Kid and Doc Holliday frequently stopped here to raise hell in the streets and casinos. The U.S. war against Mexico in 1847 led to tension and, occasionally, violence (such as the Christmas riot 20 years later), and the arrival of coal and railroads led to a massive strike in 1914.

Trinidad has been more or less peaceful ever since, celebrating its history downtown with the six-mile **La Corazon de Trinidad** (or "The Heart of Trinidad"). Even the unmemorable downtown buildings probably contain some kind of important history—the brick Carlisle building (203 E. Main St.) is across the street from the city's first stagecoach stop, and a hotel where Ulysses S. Grant stayed in 1880. (According to legend, the entire county came out to escort him.) With brick streets and century-old Victorian homes and churches, the downtown area is a nice pit stop before Santa Fe.

Sights

Overlooking the Santa Fe Trail, the **Trinidad History Museum** (300 E. Main St., 719/846-7217, www.coloradohistory.org, 10 A.M.–4 P.M. daily May–Sept., by appointment all other times, $5) is a complex of several historic buildings. Built in 1873, the **Baca House** is a two-story adobe house with Greek-style architectural flourishes and a small widow's walk out front—early Pueblo developer Felipe Baca and his wife, Dolores, bought it for 22,000 pounds of wood. The red-and-blue-brick, Victorian **Bloom Mansion** was the 1882 home of cattle baron Frank Bloom and his wife, Sarah, and the horn chair and porcelain figures inside recall the era. Also on the grounds is the **Pioneer Museum,** displaying covered wagons

and other artifacts from Trinidad's early days as a town.

The **A.R. Mitchell Memorial Museum and Gallery** (150 E. Main St., 719/846-4224, 10 A.M.–5 P.M. Tues.–Sat. and noon–5 P.M. Sun. May–Sept., tours by appointment otherwise, $5) may look from the outside like a small supermarket, but it has some of the best Western memorabilia this side of Denver—Spanish folk art, classic cowboy paintings, and turn-of-the-20th-century photos. The mezzanine still has its original tin ceiling and horseshoe shape, but preservationists have maintained the hardwood floors and shiny white pillars.

Dinosaurs are the stars of the **Louden-Henritze Archaeological Museum** (Trinidad State Junior College campus, Frudenthal Memorial Library entrance, 719/846-5508, www.trinidadstate.edu/museum, 10 A.M.–3 P.M. Mon.–Thurs., free), which puts the fossil-digging work of Trinidad State Junior College archaeology students on display for the public. Highlights include the remains of a mosasaur, discovered while workers built a house in Trinidad.

The **Trinidad Children's Museum** (314 N. Commercial St., 719/846-8220, noon–4 P.M. Mon.–Fri. June–Aug), in an original Victorian firehouse, re-creates an old fire truck and fire-fighting equipment for kids to jump around on and has replicas of an early schoolroom and a city jail.

Accommodations

Trinidad has a number of small motels and a few colorful, quiet bed-and-breakfasts befitting the town's arty, quiet downtown area. Wide, pink, and Victorian, the **Tarabino Inn** (310 E. 2nd St., 866/846-8808, www.tarabinoinn.com, $84–129) is a bed-and-breakfast with local artists' paintings in the lobby and cherry-wood bookshelves and stairs to offset the light hardwood floors. It's down the street from Trinidad Junior State College and within photo-shooting distance of Fisher's Peak and other pretty mountain scenes.

The **Stone Mansion Bed & Breakfast** (212

E. 2nd St., 719/845-1625 or 877/264-4279, $85–110) is in a shingle-covered 1904 Victorian with oak lobby furniture to match the staircase and ceiling beams. It has three rooms, but note that two of them share a bath.

Food

In the historic downtown area, the **Main Street Bakery and Café** (121 W. Main St., 719/846-8779, 7 A.M.–3 P.M. Mon.–Fri., 8 A.M.–2 P.M. Sat.–Sun.) serves breakfast (with, appropriately, Denver and Mexican omelets for $7 each) and lunch (where the $7 chicken fajitas are considered a "protein plate"). As with almost every other business in Trinidad, the café has an "artist's wall" that displays locals' work.

As for Italian, **Nana and Nano's Deli and Pasta House** (418 E. Main St., 719/846-2696, 10:30 A.M.–6 P.M. Tues.–Wed., 10:30 A.M.–7 P.M. Thurs.–Sat.) may have gnocchi Bolognese and gigantic deli sandwiches, but **Rino's Italian Restaurant** (400 E. Main St., 719/845-0949, 11 A.M.–2 P.M. and 5–9 P.M. Wed.–Sun.) has singing waiters.

WALSENBURG

Walsenburg, about a one-hour drive north of Trinidad on I-25, is slightly more than the view from the highway indicates. The main thing you'll notice is a large green building with the word "guns" printed in giant white letters on the side. The town is small but strategically located, just south of Highway 69, a beautiful two-hour drive with the San Isabel National Forest on one side and the Sangre de Cristo mountain range on the other.

Accommodations

La Plaza Inn B&B (118 W. 6th St., 719/738-5700, $65–90) probably wasn't this pink when the rectangular, two-story structure was built in 1907. (And many of the 11 rooms are just as pink.) It's one of the few truly unique and borderline luxurious places to stay between Pueblo and Trinidad.

Food

Consider making a highway stop at **Aly's Fireside**

Café (606 Main St., 719/738-3993, 11:30 A.M.–2:30 P.M. Tues., 11:30 A.M.–2:30 P.M. and 5–9 P.M. Wed.–Sat., plus 11:30 P.M.–2:30 P.M. Mon. in summer), known for its soups and desserts.

This being the Southwest, try the popular Mexican joints **Corine's** (822 Main St., 719/738-1231, 10 A.M.–9 P.M. Sun.–Thurs., 10 A.M.–10 P.M. Fri.–Sat.) or **Tes' Drive Inn** (520 Walsen Ave., 719/738-1710, 8 A.M.–8 P.M. daily).

WESTCLIFFE

Don't get so entranced by the mountainous scenery along Highway 69, northwest from Walsenburg, that you miss this in-and-out little town tucked away near the San Isabel National Forest. The seat of 3,500-population Custer County, Westcliffe has 700 residents and no stoplights. An old ranching town, Westcliffe is a local secret ensconced between the Sangre de Cristo and Wet mountain ranges.

It's also a great base to explore the prettier areas of south-central Colorado, with several homey restaurants and super-comfortable bed-and-breakfasts. About 10 miles south of town, the **Alpine Lodge** (6848 County Rd. 140, 719/783-2660, $65–80) offers small, wooden two-bedroom cabins, but it's better known in the region for its excellent steak-and-seafood restaurant. The 🄲 **Main Street Inn Bed & Breakfast** (501 Main St., 719/783-4000 or 877/783-4006, www.mainstreetbnb.com, $95–135, closed winters) is a beautiful little white-and-blue property at the center of town, in an 1880-era building. Stop for dinner at **A Wild Thyme Gourmet Deli & Bistro** (216 Main St., 719/783-2124, 11 A.M.–8 P.M. Mon.–Wed., Fri.–Sat.), which serves a killer shrimp cocktail ($9) along with cucumber melts ($7) and quarter-pound burgers ($6).

INFORMATION

The City of Trinidad offers information (135 N. Animas, 719/846-9843, www.historic-trinidad.com). Walsenburg is so small that it doesn't have a website or a major chamber of commerce, but **Downtown Colorado** keeps tourist information at http://downtown westcliffe.com.

THE EASTERN PLAINS

Having grown up in Detroit and lived for several years in Chicago, I've made the drive through endless Nebraska and Kansas to the eastern Colorado border (via I-76 and I-80) almost a dozen times. The Eastern Plains are flat and uneventful prairie land, compared to the vibrant Rocky Mountain regions of the state, but like Nebraska itself, they have their high points. Driving into Colorado, you'll feel the car begin to climb around Sterling (home of the Overland Trail Museum, filled with Native American artifacts) and might consider a stop in Crook (home of the 7,000-acre Tamarack Ranch State Wildlife Area) or Fort Morgan (around the massive Pawnee National Grassland, which goes on and on and on but is a great spot for bird- and animal-watching).

Unlike other parts of Colorado, the wide-open spaces, cornfields, and endless views of the horizon in eastern Colorado are just barely equipped for tourists. The few nice motels in this large chunk of the state tend to be chains, and the restaurants lean more toward "truck-stop diner" than "elegant bistro." The region's tourism industry is designed for drivers just passing through, and not much more than that.

But out-of-the-way wanderers who want to explore beyond the dramatic scenery of the ski towns, Boulder, and Telluride will appreciate this part of Colorado—tiny history museums like the pink-and-red Genoa Tower in Limon are filled with Native American artifacts and Old West kitsch, the reservoirs and tiny lakes are a big lure for pheasant-hunters and fishers, and county fairs pop up even in the tiniest of towns. Northeastern Colorado

© STEVE KNOPPER

HIGHLIGHTS

◖ Pawnee National Grassland: A huge (193,060 acres) nature-watching area northeast of Greeley, Pawnee is stocked with mountain plover, burrowing owl, mule deer, coyotes, foxes, and snakes (page 289).

◖ Greeley Independence Stampede: Perhaps the biggest country-music festival in Colorado—certainly bigger than anything in Denver or Colorado Springs—the Stampede draws some 450,000 fans every June to see such big-name acts as Reba McEntire, Tim McGraw, and Faith Hill. Oh, and there's a professional rodeo (page 289).

◖ Living Trees: Ex-nuclear-science student Bradford Rhea carves these massive sculptures out of actual trees in downtown Sterling—his best-known work includes the five 16-foot-tall giraffes of *Skygrazers* (page 294).

◖ Carson County Carousel: The rides on this unexpected and beautiful merry-go-round in the middle of nowhere (Burlington) cost only 25 cents—not much higher than they were before county fathers bought it for $1,200 and transported it from Elitch Gardens in Denver (page 297).

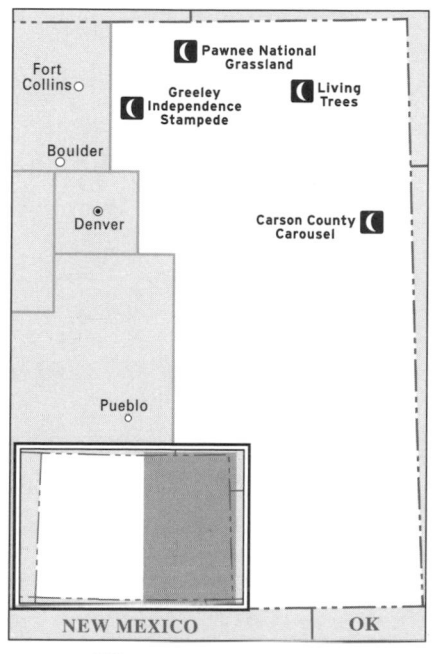

LOOK FOR ◖ TO FIND RECOMMENDED SIGHTS, ACTIVITIES, DINING, AND LODGING.

centers on Greeley and Sterling, two conservative farming-and-ranching towns along I-76 east of Denver—Greeley is particularly famous for the Greeley Independence Stampede, a country-music-and-rodeo festival that draws almost 500,000 every year. Southeastern Colorado—south of I-70 and east of Pueblo—includes Lamar (the "Goose Hunting Capital of the World"), Las Animas (whose Kit Carson Museum is a tourist monument of the kitschy persuasion, up there with the Mitchell Corn Palace and the World's Largest Badger), and, beyond that, a whole lot of nothing.

PLANNING YOUR TIME

Greeley, Sterling, and Fort Morgan are the biggest cities in the High Plains region, and the drive there from Denver is an hour or two east along a major highway (I-76). It's easy to make a day trip to either town; far more complicated is attempting to make a road trip out of the entire Eastern Plains region. Civilization is spread out, and covering Julesburg, Burlington, Lamar, Las Animas, and Limon will take a solid 10 or 12 hours.

It's best to spread out the trip—hit northeast towns like Sterling and Julesburg on one leg and Limon, Lamar, Las Animas, and, if you're really bored, the Comanche National Grassland at the bottom of the state. Of course, if you're driving west from Kansas or Nebraska to visit Denver or a ski resort, you'll encounter several of these towns automatically. Stop at a few tiny history museums for a break in the monotony.

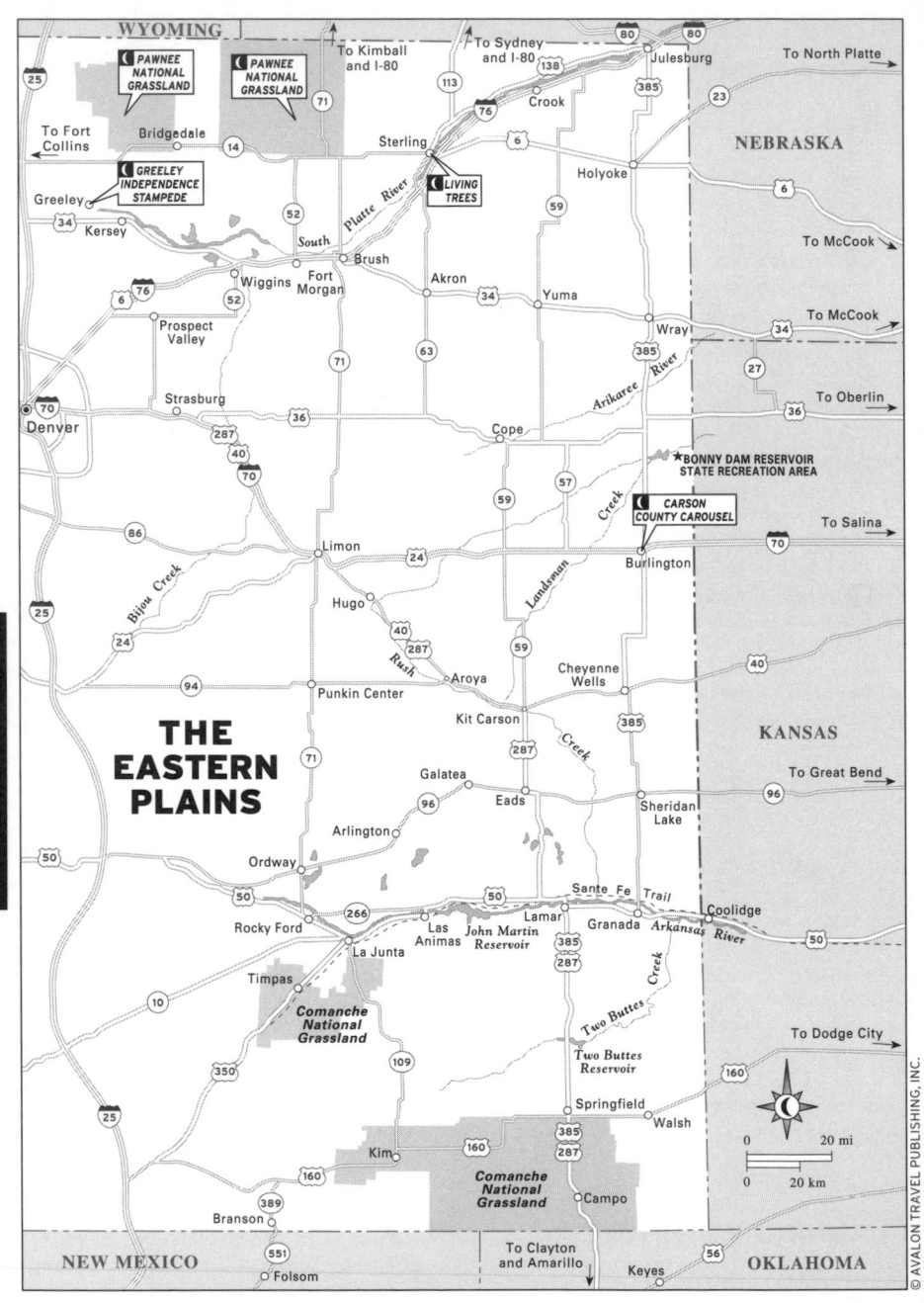

THE EASTERN PLAINS

Greeley

Here's where "Colorado turns into the Midwest," as my friend Jay Dedrick, who once lived in tiny Yuma and helped his father run the radio station there, describes the Eastern Plains. Greeley is a conservative agricultural, farming, ranching, and beef-industry region that divides metropolitan Denver (about 55 miles to the west) from the flat eastern-Colorado plains leading to Kansas and Nebraska. Country-and-western music is the standard here, particularly during the Greeley Independence Stampede, a huge early-summer festival that annually draws 450,000 fans to hear the likes of Tim McGraw, Faith Hill, George Jones, Vince Gill, and Loretta Lynn.

The city was named after Horace Greeley of the *New York Tribune,* known for declaring, "Go West, young man, go West." Greeley's underling, *Tribune* agricultural editor Nathan C. Meeker, followed his advice in 1869 and colonized the area under a strict moral code—old-school concepts like temperance and religion to go with his more progressive farming and education ideas. By the time Greeley made his first and only visit the following year, Meeker's ideas had taken hold, and the wide streets were filled with trees, along with irrigation canals and nice houses—a newspaper, schoolhouse, courthouse, and what ultimately became the University of Northern Colorado followed within a few years.

Meeker had his comeuppance a few years later in northwest Colorado—the Utes didn't take to his patronizing reformist ideas and killed the journalist and his followers in what is now Meeker, Colorado—but his impact continues to be felt in the Greeley region. The city remains agricultural, religious, and conservative, and it's growing fast—the population jumped from 70,000 in 2000 to 82,000 in 2002. Today, it's packed with historical museums, proudly American restaurants, and ranches everywhere. And it

THE EASTERN PLAINS

© STEVE KNOPPER

The Centennial Village Museum, in Greeley, is a 32-building historic area.

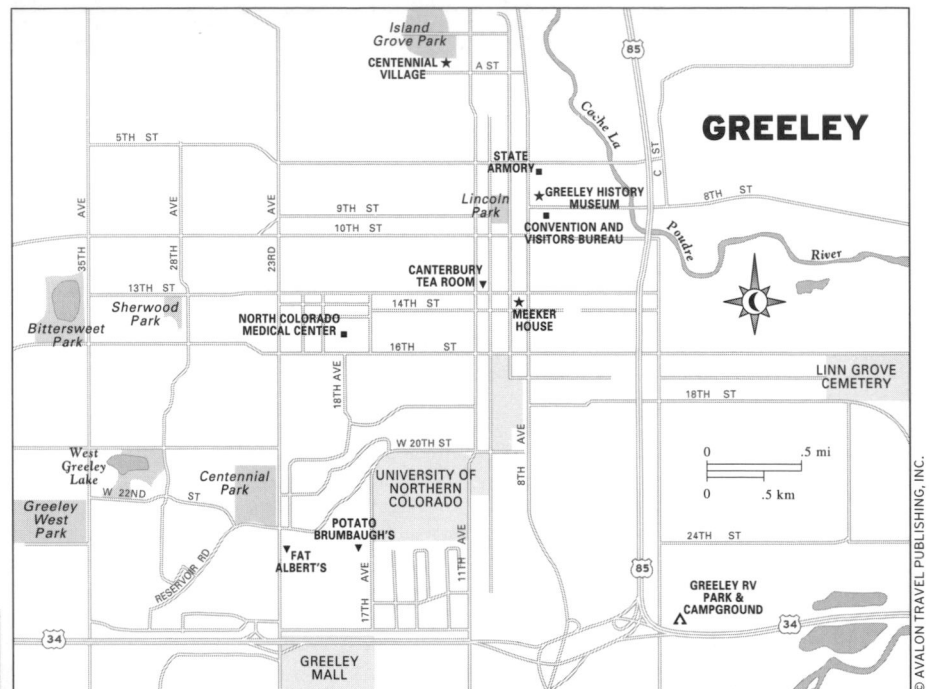

has one thing it didn't have in the 1800s—one of the largest Hispanic populations in the state, at 30 percent.

SIGHTS

Opened in 1976, **Centennial Village** (1475 A St., 970/350-9220, www.greeleymuseums.com, 10 A.M.–4 P.M. Tues.–Sat. Apr. 15–Oct. 18, $5) is a sprawling, tree-lined, 32-building historic area—including the Union Pacific Depot, which regularly shows the "From Flame to Filament" exhibit about the history of lighting. The district of restored Victorian homes (and vintage light posts and brick plazas) displays one-of-a-kind items such as a dress made of 42 rattlesnake skins (in the Shaw House) and a 1920 Federal truck. Guided tours are available—call in advance—but it's far less cumbersome to walk around the area yourself.

The **Meeker Home** (1324 9th Ave., 970/350-9220, www.greeleymuseums.com, 1–

4 P.M. Wed.–Fri. May–Sept., free, although large groups pay admission) is a modest, light-yellow, adobe-brick structure that reformer and Union Colony founder Nathan Meeker built when he arrived with his family in 1870. Many of the Meekers' original furnishings remain in the restored building. The guided tours are pretty interesting, delving into Meeker's history, his death, and his family's struggles afterward.

The **Greeley History Museum** (714 8th St., 970/350-9220, www.greeleymuseums.com, 9 A.M.–4:30 P.M. Mon.–Fri., free) opened in July 2005 with new collections of Front Range art and Weld County history. As of this writing, the hours and admission charge were in flux, but the museum should have these issues worked out by early 2006.

An Atlas E, one of the first U.S. intercontinental ballistic missiles, is the main draw at **Missile Site Park** (10611 Spur 257, 970/381-

7451), a Cold War silo that was operational from 1961 to 1965. The missiles are no longer used, so don't worry about anything blowing up in your face when you visit the museum. Surreally, this one-time product of mutually assured destruction is now a kids' park, with a playground and restrooms.

The **Plumb Farm Learning Center** (955 39th Ave., 970/350-9220, www.greeleymuseums.com, open by event) became a 160-acre farm in 1881 and is still owned by the same families on 2.5 acres—only now it's mostly known for agricultural programs, classes, and kids' events like "Pets N' Popsicles" and "Baby Animals Days."

SPORTS AND RECREATION
Hiking and Biking
The primary place for outdoor Greeley activities is **Island Grove Regional Park** (501 N. 14th Ave., 970/350-9392, 8 A.M.–11 P.M. daily, free), a 145-acre area filled with trees and grass, plus hiking-and-biking trails, various sports fields, and a pool. Beginning near Island Grove Park, along the Cache La Poudre River, the **Poudre River Trail** (11th Ave. and D St., east side of Island Grove Regional Park, 970/350-9783, www.poudretrail.org, dawn–dusk daily) is a 10-mile stretch that will ultimately extend another 9 miles to the Weld/Larimer County line. Until then, it runs between the cities of Greeley and Windsor and is a pleasant place to take a bike or a pair of in-line skates.

(Pawnee National Grassland
This 193,060-acre area (2150 Centre Ave., 25 miles northeast of Greeley, 970/295-6600) is Greeley's big nature-watching spot—**birders** go crazy over mountain plover and burrowing owl, and you can spot mule deer, coyotes, foxes, snakes, and the ever-present prairie dogs. It's a great place to hike, bike, camp, or ride a horse. Pick your spots in advance before traveling here: The Buttes, north from Colorado Highway 14 on County Road 103, are 300-foot-tall sandstone humps that make a nice backdrop for hiking (and watching falcons and

hawks). Otherwise, you'll wind up in an endless sea of green, green, and more green.

Golf
Greeley runs two municipal golf courses: the 18-hole **Boomerang Links** (7309 W. 4th St., 970/351-8934), filled with ponds and other obstacles that pop out of nowhere; and the 18-hole **Highland Hills** (2200 Clubhouse Dr., 970/330-7327), which is much older (1959) than Boomerang Links and has more trees than ponds.

ENTERTAINMENT AND EVENTS
Part of the University of Northern Colorado's jazz studies program, the early-April **UNC/ Greeley Jazz Festival** (Union Colony Civic Center, 701 10th Ave., 970/351-2492, http://usonia.unco.edu/uncjazz/festival/general.html) puts together a wide variety of jazz and pseudo-jazz artists, from middle-school big bands to the great saxophonist Benny Golson. Many of them play together.

The UNC's **Little Theatre of the Rockies** (Norton Theatre, Gray Hall, 10th Ave. and 18th St., and Langworthy Theatre, Frasier Hall, 9th Ave. and 17th St., 970/351-4849, http://usonia.unco.edu/LTR/default.html) has been putting on big comedies and musicals since the 1930s—recent shows include *My Fair Lady* and *Smokey Joe's Café*.

As for less theatrical nightlife, **Cactus Canyon** (1742 Greeley Mall, 970/351-8178, www.klmclubs.com/Greeley/) is a butt-kicking country-and-western bar with mechanical-bull-riding contests straight out of *Urban Cowboy,* line-dancing straight out of Billy Ray Cyrus's days on the pop charts, and Daisy Duke's cut-off-shorts contests straight out of *The Dukes of Hazard.*

(Greeley Independence Stampede
Although it began as a potato-farming festival in the late 1800s, this 10-day, late-June extravaganza (600 N. 14th Ave., 970/356-2855, www.greeleystampede.org) has become

so huge that many of its featured country-music performers don't even bother to play in nearby Denver the entire rest of the year. It's primarily a rodeo show—the finals have aired on ESPN and other television channels—but the musical talent draws country fans from all over the United States. The list of headliners over the years reads like some combination of the Country Music Hall of Fame and the pop charts, including Loretta Lynn, George Jones, Ricky Skaggs, Vince Gill, Faith Hill, Brooks & Dunn, and Tim McGraw.

Although **High Plains Chautauqua** (Aims Community College, 5401 W. 20th St., 970/339-6365, http://chautauqua.aims.edu/index.html) sponsors historical tours of Greeley, old movies, musical events and kids' shows, it's best known for the actors who portray famous old people—including Woody Guthrie, Franklin D. Roosevelt, and Joe Louis.

ACCOMMODATIONS

The **Greeley Guest House** (5401 W. 9th St., 970/353-9373 or 800/314-3684, www.gree-leyguesthouse.com, $109–159) kind of looks like a retirement home on the outside, but the rooms are pretty and functional—including whirlpools in the suites, high-speed Internet access, and fireplaces. Breakfast is complimentary.

Campers have a couple of viable options in Greeley: the **Greeley RV Park & Campground** (501 E. 27th St., 970/353-6476 or 800/572-2130, www.greeleyrvpark.com, $17), which has 12 tent sites on a 10-acre plot between a farm and the highway; and the small campground at **Missile Site Park** (10611 Spur 257, 970/381-7451, 7 A.M.–10 P.M. daily May–Oct., $5), where you can fantasize about retaliating against the Soviet Union in the early 1960s.

FOOD

Despite a recent Greeley-area boom in chain restaurants like Red Robin and the Olive Garden, locals such as **(｟ Potato Brumbaugh's** (2400 17th Ave., 970/356-6340, 4:30 P.M.–9 P.M. daily) are hanging in there. The 23-year-old, high-end prime rib and pasta restaurant,

The Eastern Plains are filled with ranches and farms.

named after the hard-working land owner in James Michener's *Centennial,* remains particularly crowded on Friday and Saturday nights.

Fat Albert's (1717 23rd Ave., 970/356-1999, 10:30 A.M.–9:30 P.M. Sat.–Thurs., 10:30 A.M.–10:30 P.M. Fri.), in the same brown shopping center as Potato Brumbaugh's, is a family restaurant with chicken, steak, and sandwiches. The service is friendly and kids are everywhere.

The **Canterbury Tea Room** (1229 10th Ave., 970/356-1811, www.canterburytearoom.com, 10 A.M.–5 P.M. Mon.–Sat., noon–4 P.M. Sun.) is all British, right down to the shepherd's pie ($8) and the beef Guinness stew ($8). With framed paintings and frilly curtains, it's a great place for a tea party, and the room has packages available for bridal showers and kids' parties. There's also a mystery dinner theater.

Coyote's Southwestern Grill (5250 W. 9th St., 970/336-1725, 11 A.M.–9:30 P.M. Mon.–Thurs., 11 A.M.–10:30 P.M. Fri.–Sat.) is a Southwestern fixture in the west part of the city with a big outdoor patio and contemporary art on the walls. It's mostly the typical new-and-old-Mex you'd find in these parts, but with distinctive touches like tequila shrimp scampi.

In a building that was a National Guard training center for 37 years and played host to USO dances, traveling vaudeville shows, and professional wrestling matches early last century, the **State Armory** (614 8th Ave., 970/352-7424, 11 A.M.–8 P.M. Sun., Mon., Tues., and Thurs., 11 A.M.–midnight Wed., Fri., and Sat.) is now a beloved local burger joint. Local architect Sidney Frazier designed the odd two-story building, all terra-cotta and turrets.

INFORMATION

The **Greeley Chamber of Commerce** (902 7th Ave., 970/352-3566, www.greeleychamber.com) has basic information about lodging, food, and businesses in the city. For more detailed municipal services, contact the **City of Greeley** (1000 10th St., 970/350-9770, www.ci.greeley.co.us). The daily newspaper is the *Greeley Tribune* (www.greeleytrib.com), which doesn't have the most detailed restaurant or lodging reviews in the world, but it's somewhat helpful.

GETTING THERE AND AROUND

The **Greeley Bus Service** (1200 A St., 970/350-9287) serves the entire city from roughly 5:30 A.M. to 8:30 P.M. Pilots can fly into the **Greeley-Weld County Airport** (600 Airport Rd. #A, 970/336-3000, www.gxy.net), but commercial passengers should probably fly into Denver International Airport and drive the 55 miles northeast.

Fort Morgan

A plainspoken farming town about 20 miles east of Greeley, Fort Morgan is far less interesting than it was in the old days—just after the Civil War, the U.S. government built the fort and set Confederate rebels free from prison as long as they agreed to join the Union Army and fight Indians in the West. The fort's original purpose was to protect local immigrants and the mail service from Cheyennes and Arapahos, who had revenge on their minds after massive white settlements and the Sand Creek Massacre.

The uprisings eventually disappeared, and railroads, irrigation, ranches, and a canal popped up in the late 1800s. Teddy Roosevelt showed up in 1905, on a short train stop, and inspired 1,000 locals with a short speech about how great it was that hard work turned the Great Plains into a rich farming industry.

The great big-band trombonist Glenn Miller was a high school football player here in the 1920s.

SIGHTS

The **Fort Morgan Museum** (414 Mai St., 970/542-4010, www.ftmorganmus.org,

GLENN MILLER IN COLORADO

Before he became the best-known bandleader of the swing era, tromboning his way through 1930s hits like "Chatanooga Choo-Choo" and "In the Mood," Iowa-born Glenn Miller lived in Fort Morgan and attended the University of Colorado. At Fort Morgan High School, he made the football team his senior year; the Maroons won the title in 1920 and Miller earned state honors as "the best left end in Colorado."

Although Miller scored a scholarship at the University of Northern Colorado, he had no desire to pursue a football career, thanks to his influential band director, Elmer Wells. Rather than attending his own high school graduation, he moved to Laramie, Wyoming, to join a big band. It broke up within a year, and Miller enrolled at the University of Colorado, where he stayed for two years. His college life centered on music, as he played in Holly Moyer's Jazz Band and did more arranging than studying.

The rest of Miller's story is close to legend: He quit CU to play with the Ben Pollack Orchestra in California (Benny Goodman was in the band as well), then moved with Pollack to New York City. Miller played for months in hit orchestras, arranging music for other big bands, and started the Glenn Miller Orchestra

in 1937. The most popular band in the United States, Miller's orchestra recorded 45 best-selling songs in 1940 and sold more than one million copies of "Chattanooga Choo-Choo" two years later.

World War II made big bands more popular than ever, but the war also shot the genre in the heart. Miller left his hit-making orchestra to become a U.S. Army officer, but his military career lasted just two years. While flying over the English Channel, his plane disappeared and Miller was killed. James Stewart portrayed him in the 1953 movie hit *The Glenn Miller Story* – some of which was filmed on the University of Colorado at Boulder campus – and the university christened its Glenn Miller Ballroom the same year.

Today, Miller's famous bespectacled photo – with trombone – hangs as a framed black-and-white backdrop to his namesake CU ballroom. Surreally, over the years, bands such as Radiohead, Nine Inch Nails, and Jane's Addiction have performed with Miller smiling in the background.

Fort Morgan runs a Glenn Miller swing festival every June, with bands, food, and a historic tour. Go to www.fortmorganchamber.org/glenmiller.html for more information.

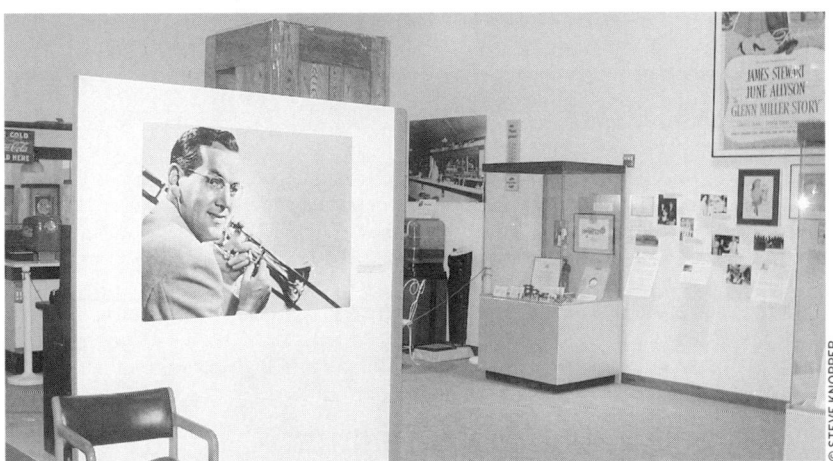

The Fort Morgan Museum has a large Glenn Miller exhibit.

10 A.M.–5 P.M. Mon., Wed., and Fri.; 10 A.M.–5 P.M. and 6–8 P.M. Tues. and Thurs.; 11 A.M.–5 P.M. Sat., donation suggested) nicely samples all the important stuff about northeastern Colorado—sugar, agriculture, railroads, Glenn Miller, the original fort from the 1860s, and the town's well-kept historic buildings downtown.

SPORTS AND RECREATION
Biking
Although cycling is far more popular in Boulder, the Rockies, and the mesas of northwestern Colorado, the Eastern Plains have one crucial advantage: They're flat. **Pedal the Prairie** (100 Ensign St., 970/867-6702 or 800/354-8660) is a 200-mile, three-day event that begins and ends in Fort Morgan and loops around the entire region.

FOOD
The **Country Steak-Out** (19592 E. 8th Ave., 970/867-7887, 11 A.M.–9 P.M. Tues.–Sat., 11 A.M.–2 P.M. Sun.) is a great old restaurant that seems like it has been here forever—actually, since the 1920s—and serves steak and chicken dishes as if the cooks know exactly what they're doing. It's also one of those roadside places where truckers (of both the rig and pickup variety) pull right up to the building from the parking lot to follow the "Eat Beef" sign.

Watch for the **Stroh's Inn** (901 W. Platte Ave., 970/867-6654, 6 A.M.–9 P.M. daily) billboard along I-76—it's American-style home cooking, just as you'd expect from the side of the road in the middle of flatland.

INFORMATION
The **Fort Morgan Chamber of Commerce** (300 Main St., 970/867-6702 or 800/354-8660) has a somewhat helpful webpage at www.fortmorganchamber.org. Or try **City Hall** (110 Main St., 970/542-3960, www.cityoffortmorgan.com) for more basic services. The *Fort Morgan Times* (www.fortmorgantimes.com) is hardly *The New York Times,* but it'll do for basic regional news and entertainment listings.

Sterling

For a city of just 1,200 people, the farming-and-ranching town Sterling has a disproportionate number of parks (12), huge trees, and stately Victorian homes whose long porches recall another era. The seat of Logan County, including tiny Atwood, Cook, Fleming, Iliff, and Merino, Sterling is the center of a booming agriculture-and-livestock area—cattle, alfalfa, corn, and sugar beets are the primary exports. (The city is particularly obsessed with the latter: The **Sugar Beet Days** (www.sugarbeetdays.com) festival is in late September, with craft booths and food, around the downtown Logan County Courthouse.)

Known as "The City of Living Trees"—a slogan derived from artist Bradford Rhea's towering downtown tree sculptures, carved straight out of the trees themselves—Sterling's modern roots are in farming. (Its true roots are with the Cheyenne and Sioux tribes, who lost the bloody Battle of Summit Springs to the U.S. Cavalry in 1869, paving the way for white settlers.) A railroad surveyor, David Leavitt, visited town in 1870 and liked it so much he started the first ranch here a year later; due to the town's geography along the South Platte River, other settlers streamed to the area, and Sterling boomed for years after its official foundation in 1881.

Each of the small towns in Logan County has a story: The county's first resident was Billy Hadfield, who settled on an island in the river just outside Atwood in 1871, and a marker on U.S. 6 reveals the spot; and Crook burned down twice before it was able to grow to a population of 300 in 1928. It's an interesting little area to visit if you're a history buff, although people experiencing Colorado for the first time might be disappointed with the lack of mountain scenery or dramatic views.

SIGHTS

The **Overland Trail Museum** (U.S. 6 and I-76, 970/522-3895, www.sterlingcolo.com/parks/pr_mus.htm, 9 A.M.–5 P.M. Mon.–Sat. and 1–5 P.M. Sun. Apr.–Oct., 10 A.M.–4 P.M. Tues.–Sat. Nov.–early Mar., $2) is a tribute to the Old West pioneers and gold miners who went west in the 1860s, turning the Overland Trail (along the South Platte River through Nebraska and northeastern Colorado) into a veritable superhighway. Opened in 1936, the museum's centerpiece is a prairie village, including a barbershop, general store, and church.

(Living Trees

Bearded sculptor Bradford Rhea earned a nuclear-science degree from the University of Colorado before his career took what you might call a sharp left turn. He moved to tiny Sterling, and, since 1983, his scripture-influenced Living

one of Bradford Rhea's Living Trees sculptures in Sterling

Trees (Columbine Park, U.S.–6, between S. 3rd Ave. and Division Ave., www.thesculptor.net) have defined the look and feel of "The City of Living Trees." The sculptures, including five 16-foot-high giraffes known as *Skygrazers* and two seven-foot rams carved out of an elm tree, weigh tens of thousands of pounds.

The Living Trees are beautiful and inspirational, but they're also a little surreal. On a recent trip to Sterling, I visited them for the first time and was surprised to learn that few people in town knew where they were—far removed from the main highways, at Ramada Inns and on the far corners of parks. They spring up out of nowhere, with Rhea's inexplicable plaques at the bottom: *Skygrazers,* at Columbine Park, is described as "a congregation of spindling appendages fused in a mass of true beliefs." I took my spindling appendages and drove out of town after seeing that.

SPORTS AND RECREATION

Fishing

The outdoor sports in Sterling mostly involve water, thanks to **North Sterling State Park** (24005 County Rd. 330, 970/522-3657) and its massive **North Sterling Reservoir,** which at 50 feet in some places is one of the state's deepest reservoirs. There's a marina and three boat ramps, and campers, fishers, boaters, and jet-skiers tend to crowd the area during summers. It's also one of the prettiest places in northeastern Colorado to view the High Plains, especially with the setting sun as a backdrop.

Other fishing opportunities in the area include **Prewitt Reservoir** (U.S. 6, near Merino, 970/842-6300) and **Jumbo Reservoir** (U.S. 138, near Crook, 970/842-6300), both of which are big with sailors and bird-watchers (check out the gulls, jaegers, terns, swans, and scoters).

ACCOMMODATIONS

Guests may initially be confused by names like the "LuLu Boone Room," but LuLu was Sterling's first librarian, and the (**Old Library Inn** (210 S. 4th St., 970/522-3800 or 866/941-3800, www.oldlibraryinn.com, $95–130) is

© STEVE KNOPPER

The Old Library Inn, in downtown Sterling, is in the city's first library, built in 1916.

in the city's first library, built in 1916 with $12,500 of Andrew Carnegie's money. It looks like a library, especially from the outside, with light-brown bricks and a triangular peak at the center; inside, the innkeepers maintain the theme, with bookshelves everywhere. The only thing missing is somebody whispering "shh!" when guests get overly rambunctious.

FOOD

Sterling's family-dining scene has been hurting ever since the spring of 2005, when a visiting entrepreneur bought the popular Shake, Rattle, & Roll diner for a reported $250,000, loaded it on a truck and transported it to Carter Lake, Iowa. But the 60-year-old **J and L Café** (423 N. 3rd St., 970/522-3625, 5:15 A.M.–8 P.M. daily) remains a classic downtown greasy spoon—try the steak-and-eggs breakfast—and locals' favorite.

INFORMATION

The **Logan County Chamber of Commerce** (109 N. Front St., 970/522-5070 or 866/522-5070, www.logancountychamber.com) has a surprisingly thorough website for such a small town. Or try Sterling city services (421 N. 4th St., 970/522-9700, www.sterlingcolo.com). Also helpful is Sterling's daily newspaper, the *Journal-Advocate* (www.journal-advocate.com), which also covers a large part of northeastern Colorado.

CROOK

A ranching town that was once a key stagecoach stop on the Overland Trail, friendly, 148-resident Crook is about 30 miles northeast of Sterling and has two primary sightseeing opportunities. The small **Crook Museum** (4th St. and 4th Ave., 970/886-2713, call for an appointment, donations suggested), in a former Presbyterian church, contains Old West artifacts like a beautiful 1800s piano that somebody once bought for 50 cents, and information about George Crook, an important U.S. general who scared the wits out of Native American tribes for decades. He accepted Geronimo's surrender in 1866.

In addition to Jumbo Reservoir, off U.S. 6,

Crook is home to **Tamarack Ranch State Wildlife Area** (half a mile north of I-76, Exit 149, 719/227-5221), a **bird-watcher's** paradise stuffed with rare species such as the red-bellied woodpecker, scarlet tanager, and black-billed cuckoo. The 7,000-acre plot along a river bottom is also a Colorado Division of Wildlife-controlled hunting area.

LIMON

Location has always been Limon's greatest asset—it's at the intersection of five major highways, including I-70, about 100 miles east of Denver, and is the midpoint between northeastern and southeastern Colorado. "Hub City" had a similar advantage in 1888, when it was a work-camp site for miners and the Chicago and Rock Island Railroad used it as a key point between Kansas and Colorado Springs.

Today, Hub City is more of a hub than a city; it's mainly known for downtown antique shops and other small businesses, a few museums, and a population of 2,400. The town became briefly famous for the wrong reasons on June 6, 1990, when the biggest of several northeastern Colorado twisters touched down in Limon, destroying numerous buildings and killing phone service and power—amazingly, nobody died.

Sights

The **Limon Heritage Museum and Railroad Park** (899 1st St., 719/775-8808, www.limonchamber.com/museum.html, 1–8 P.M. Mon.–Sat., June–Aug., free) is packed with plains-related artifacts—the big displays include a one-room schoolhouse, a restored railroad depot (with a boxcar and five train cars), a windmill, and a Native American tepee,

art, and tools. There's also a playground with picnic tables in the outdoor park, which is open all year.

On an abandoned highway next to an unused stone restaurant building, the **Genoa Tower Museum** (I-70, exit 371, in Genoa, 10 miles east of Limon, 719/763-2309, 9 A.M.–5 P.M. daily) is a six-story, red-and-pink 1920s-era tower with "six states" scrawled on the side. (On a good day, from the top of the tower, visitors can apparently see six different states.) Inside is a kitschy collection of artifacts with no discernible theme: elk and jackalope heads, Elvis Presley stuff, fossil skulls, old books, a scattered rock collection, and Native American arrowheads.

Accommodations

Limon has very few nice restaurants—unless you count the Arby's and the Rip Griffin's truck-stop diner—but its small hotels aren't bad. "Traveling with a horse?" asks the **Craig Ranch Bed and Breakfast & Horse Motel** (50452 County Rd. 23, 719/775-2658, www.craigranchbandb.com, $75). If so, corrals are available for $5 per night. The B&B has people beds, too—like the antique brass in the pretty pink Miss Molly's Room and the wooden family heirloom in Bill's Bunkhouse.

Information

The **Limon Chamber of Commerce** (205 E Ave., 719/775-9418, www.limonchamber.com) compiles online listings of restaurants, hotels, and other local businesses. For recreation and other city departments, contact the **Town of Limon** (100 Civic Center Dr., 719/775-2346, www.townoflimon.com).

Burlington

Although this town of 3,000 people was once a massive grain-shipping point, it is mostly known to drivers these days as "thank God, we're out of Kansas!" It's 13 miles from the Kansas border, and it's a huge relief to drivers who've just spanned that interminable state en route from Detroit or Chicago to Colorado. I've passed it on numerous trips, and its green highway marker is always a huge relief.

Burlington today is an agricultural town—incorporated in 1888, and still the seat of Kit Carson County—and its primary attractions for visitors are historical, including Old Town, a collection of classic buildings and a beautiful old carousel. Check out the state **Visitors Center** on I-70 nearby.

SIGHTS

Old Town (420 S. 14th St., 719/346-7382 or 800/288-1334, www.burlingtoncolo.com/oldtown.htm, 9 A.M.–5 P.M. Mon.–Sat., noon–5 P.M. Sun., $6) is a collection of 20 restored century-old buildings—a bank, blacksmith shop, train depot, law office (including an original wooden desk), schoolhouse, drugstore, and even a doll house (including one made of bread dough). To commemorate the proud era when "Burlington had six saloons and its share of female entertainment to go with it," in the words of the Old Town website, the restored Longhorn Saloon showcases women doing the cancan throughout the summer.

🄲 Carson County Carousel

Built in 1905, the Carson County Carousel (Kit Carson County Fairgrounds, north of I-70, exit 437, 719/348-5562, www.kitcarsoncountycarousel.com, 1–8 P.M. daily Memorial Day–Labor Day, 25 cents) and its 46 hand-carved horses, giraffes, and zebras were a fixture at Denver's Elitch Gardens amusement park until 1928. At that point, Elitch management sold the carousel and its elab-

orate pipe organ for $1,200 to Kit Carson County—the "extravagant expenditure" led to the political demise of certain county commissioners. It has given 25-cent rides in Burlington ever since.

SPORTS AND RECREATION
Fishing

The main reason for going to **Bonny Lake State Park** (30010 Rd. 3, Idalia, 23 miles north of Burlington on U.S. 385, 970/354-7306) is a 1,900-acre reservoir filled with walleye, northern pike, bass, and many other fish. It's surrounded by sandy beaches and, beyond the reservoir, prairie and grassland—making the area popular for campers, hunters, hikers, and picnickers.

ACCOMMODATIONS

The 🄲 **Claremont Inn** (800 Claremont Dr., Stratton, 719/348-5125 or 888/291-8910, $119–249) is a little pricey for the middle of nowhere on the High Plains, but perhaps that's because it's the *only* quaint inn in the middle of nowhere on the High Plains. Built in 1995, it has six rooms with whirlpool tubs, one with a fireplace, and at least one is cleverly named: Out of Kansas.

FOOD

Few come to Burlington for the food, unless they're really, really into Arby's and Subway. But if you happen to get stuck here at mealtime during a trip to the carousel or museum, **Shanghai City** (450 S. Lincoln St., 719/346-9365, 11 A.M.–9 P.M. Tues.–Sun.) is a good-enough Chinese restaurant with the usual egg rolls and fried rice.

INFORMATION

The **City of Burlington** (1394 Webster Ave., 719/346-8918, www.burlingtoncolo.com) has a bit of historical and tourist information on its website.

THE EASTERN PLAINS

South of Burlington

JULESBURG

An agricultural town of about 1,500 people, Julesburg is just outside Colorado's northeastern border, and hitting Julesburg off I-76 after spanning Nebraska is almost as reassuring as hitting Burlington after spanning Kansas. The town is good for a pit stop—one of the state's eight welcome centers is here, off exit 180, and the Fort Sedgwick and Depot Museums are brief diversions for Pony Express buffs. But if you've made it this far, why not drive the 188 miles west to Denver, already?

Sights

A little removed from Sterling—almost 60 miles northeast of town, on Colorado's northern border with Nebraska—Julesburg is a former Pony Express town once known for its rough and nasty ways. Today, history-buff travelers mainly know it for the **Fort Sedgwick and Depot Museums** (114 E. 1st St., Julesburg, 970/474-2061, 10 A.M.–4 P.M. Mon.–Sat. and 1–4 P.M.Sun. Memorial Day–Labor Day, 9 A.M.–1 P.M. Mon.–Fri.—Ft. Sedgwick only—Labor Day–Memorial Day, $1). The former recalls the area's general history, while the latter focuses on the Pony Express. Both museums are in one flat brown building.

Accommodations

The **Budget Host Platte Valley Inn Motel** (15225 U.S. 385, 970/474-3336, $50–60) is super-cheap and has a small restaurant, but other than that, you might want to make reservations in Sterling, Greeley, or better yet, Denver.

Information

The dinky **Julesburg Chamber of Commerce** has no website, but it's at 114 E. 1st St., 970/474-3504.

LAMAR

Lamar started with a fight: In 1866, cattleman A. R. Black owned most of the land on this uneventful Santa Fe Trail outpost along the Arkansas River, next to a key railroad depot, 30 miles from Kansas Territory and down the road from Las Animas and Denver. The U.S. government wanted to start a town on this strategic land and offered Black big money to give it up. Black refused. But the government outwitted him, buying nearby land from another rancher and hiring crews to move the railroad depot while Black was out of town.

The United States named the town after Lucius Quintius Lamar, President Grover Cleveland's secretary of the interior. It boomed for years, sometimes not so nicely, as cowboys and outlaws drove through regularly in the 1800s and early 1900s—four bank robbers even shot the president of First National Bank in 1928, wounding his son, kidnapping a worker, and getting away with almost $250,000.

Today, the heavily agricultural town is known as the "Goose Hunting Capital of the World."

Sights

The **Big Timbers Museum** (7515 U.S. 50, 719/336-2472, 10 A.M.–5 P.M. Mon.–Sat., free) is filled with relics from the late 1800s and early 1900s, when Lamar was an important trading post—a plow, thresher, hay balers, windmill, wedding dress, grand piano, washing machine, and an impressive arrowhead collection. There's also a bunch of Civil War stuff, like a sword and uniforms.

About 20 miles west of Lamar is Las Animas, a flat ranching town where the legendary western explorer Kit Carson died in 1868. Its primary attraction is the **Kit Carson Museum** (Bent Ave. and 9th St., Las Animas, 719/456-2507, 1–5 P.M. Memorial Day–Labor Day, $2), which opened in 1961 in a building that once housed German prisoners of war and, later, field-working Jamaicans. But there are no monuments to Rastafarianism or Bob Marley here, just the standard collection of

Old West memorabilia, such as farming and Native American artifacts. Outside, there are numerous building replicas—jail, blacksmith shop, house, and even a gallows.

Accommodations

Lamar's best hotels are chains—the Best Western is called a "Cow Palace"—but the **El Mar Budget Host Hotel** (1210 S. Main St., 719/336-4331, $45) is somewhat more distinctive (and cheap!).

Information

The **City of Lamar** (102 E. Parmenter St., 719/336-4376, www.ci.lamar.co.us) has all the information you need about the fire, police, and recreation departments. Not much on tourism, though.

BACKGROUND

The Land

With an area of more than 104,000 square miles, Colorado is the eighth-largest state, although, with just 371 square miles of water, it's also one of the driest. The terrain varies wildly, from the prairies and dry mesa cliffs in the northwest to the San Juan Mountains in the southwest, through the massive Rocky Mountains in the west, to the flat plains of the east. The southwest tip of Colorado is part of the Four Corners, where travelers can touch Colorado, Utah, Arizona, and New Mexico simultaneously.

Colorado's geography is an extension of its bordering states. The Continental Divide, the steep and bumpy upper edge of the Rocky Mountains, runs in a curvy, vertical, continuous path between New Mexico and Wyoming. Much of northern Colorado is as rugged and lush as Wyoming, while most of southern Colorado is as dry and desert-like as New Mexico. Similarly, Colorado's eastern plains match the flat, endless terrain Nebraska and Kansas. Utah, in many spots, is the continuation of mesa cliffs, dry wilderness, and deep valleys.

Colorado's wild swings of altitude are legendary among residents and travelers, who have to put up with shortness of breath, nosebleeds, and other ailments as they climb sharply to the state's most beautiful places. The lowest point is the Arikaree River, at 3,350 feet, on

COURTESY OF THE NATIONAL PARK SERVICE

the banks of the Arkansas River due west of Kansas near Wray; the highest is Mount Elbert, at 14,433 feet of elevation, southwest of Leadville. Elbert is just one of the 53 "fourteeners" in Colorado, including Pikes Peak, Mount Evans, and Longs Peak, all visible in large cities east of the Front Range, and there are numerous "thirteeners" as well.

Most of Colorado's population is clustered just east of the Rockies' Front Range, in metropolitan Denver, the state capital, as well as college towns Boulder, Fort Collins, and Colorado Springs.

GEOGRAPHY

The Colorado region wasn't always full of mountains. Some 240 million to 750 million years ago, in the Paleozoic era, the area was almost completely underwater. Toward the end of that era, mountains shot up, as high as 10,000 feet, but many of the ranges eroded and gave way to decades of flat land again. (You can see evidence of these early ranges in Manitou Springs' Garden of the Gods and Morrison's Red Rocks Park, both strange-looking areas with gnarled, reddish rocks and hills that seem completely out of place among the massive Rockies. Huge sand dunes arose from this period as well.)

The Mesozoic era, about 70 million to 230 million years ago, brought dinosaurs and reptiles to the state—their fossils and footprints remain in places like Dinosaur National Monument, along the Utah border, and the Dinosaur Quarry in Red Rocks Park. But the Gulf of Mexico roared back into the area, the state was submerged in water once again, and the dinosaurs became extinct. Eventually the waters pulled back and the Rocky Mountains, as we know them, rose up.

Thanks to volcanic eruptions and rising mountains throughout the Cenozoic era (about 70 million years ago), tropical rainforests, large mountain lakes, and forests emerged all over the state. By the Pleistocene epoch, a little less than 2 million years ago, glaciers began their slow motions, creating huge and breathtaking mountain peaks and deep valleys, as well as prairies, forests, and grasslands. Woolly mammoths took over from their ancestors, the dinosaurs, and camels and horses appeared as well.

After the ice age ended, between 20,000 and 25,000 years ago, humans showed up, possibly in the form of hunters and early Native Americans, who wandered the mountains and valleys searching for mammoths and antelope to kill.

Rocky Mountains

Stretching from British Columbia to the Rio Grande River in New Mexico, the Rocky Mountains formed roughly 65 million to 140 million years ago, during the Cretaceous period. Volcanoes and moving tectonic plates lifted massive chunks of rock high into the air, explaining the 10,000-foot elevations commonly seen today on the Rockies' dramatic east side (best viewed in Boulder and Rocky Mountain National Park). During the ice ages, from roughly 1.8 million to 11,000 years ago, gigantic glaciers moved south from Canada and moved huge swaths of land around, forming valleys and, with the runoff, creating lakes. A few such glaciers are still around in smaller form, including St. Mary's, outside Idaho Springs.

As a result of these prehistoric geological events, Colorado has some of the highest-elevation towns in the world, including Leadville, at 10,188 feet, and more than 1,000 peaks are above 10,000 feet. The elevation leads to great skiing, clean air, dramatic views, and, if you're not careful, shortness of breath.

The water and snowmelt coming down from Rocky Mountain peaks create one-fourth of the total U.S. water supply, and the rivers flow (indirectly) into the Atlantic, Pacific, and Arctic Oceans.

Western Slope

Once you drive west from Denver or Boulder into the Rocky Mountains, you start to see fewer of the steep, dramatic dropoffs from mountain peaks to flatlands. Rather, the high country seems to go on and on. This part of the state, from the Continental Divide through the Utah border, is the Western Slope. Here, the landscape varies wildly, from the mesas and cliffs near Grand Junction to the massive San Juan Mountain peaks to the miles and miles of flat ranching and farming land around Craig and Rifle.

The Continental Divide is the upper spine of the Rockies, which more or less follows the mountain range from British Columbia to the Rio Grande. (Adventurers can follow it by foot, on a long and challenging path known as the Continental Divide Trail.) Water flows in opposite directions on either side of the Divide— on the west side, it goes to the Pacific, while on the east, it goes to the Atlantic or the Gulf of Mexico.

Eastern Plains

Colorado's Eastern Plains are the western edge of the Great Plains states—Kansas, Nebraska, and Oklahoma. They took on their "lowlands" form during the Pleistocene epoch (otherwise known as the ice age), when Canadian glaciers moved south and, according to Donald E. Trimble's *The Geologic Story of the Great Plains,*

"smoothed the contours and gave the land a more subdued aspect than it had before they came." The resulting valleys, grassland, and forest spread through the entire interior United States, through Kansas, Nebraska, Oklahoma, and northern Texas, and stopped at the edge of the Rockies.

The geologic area known as the Colorado Piedmont—roughly the base of the Front Range foothills, including Denver, the South Platte River valley, and the Arkansas River valley near Colorado Springs—formed some 28 million years ago when tectonic plates shifted in what is now the western United States. Some parts of this area, particularly Utah, boosted their elevations to more than 5,000 feet, and the resulting erosion had a massive impact on what is now Colorado. Sandstone fell away, the South Platte shifted, mounds of sedimentary rock gathered just beneath the Rockies, and the Pawnee Buttes formed in northeastern Colorado. (This is where Pawnee National Grassland, from Greeley to Limon, stretches out today.)

© STEVE KNOPPER

The Flatiron Mountains are located on the eastern base of the Rocky Mountains.

CLIMATE

Outside Colorado, people know the state from the extreme weather reports—massive blizzards, heavy droughts, fires due to extremely dry conditions, avalanches in the mountains, and so forth. But residents know that despite these dramatic weather events, the climate is generally mild, and the legend of 300 days of sunshine per year is not exaggerated. Humidity is pleasantly low in Colorado, a huge boon (especially for those without air-conditioning) during the few weeks of near 100-degree temperatures in July and August.

One great thing about Colorado's blizzards: When they're over, the snow melts quickly and within a few days it's spring again. In the mountains, the snow remains but the sun warms everything, which explains why skiers at the big resorts are often able to glide around in light jackets and, occasionally, shorts.

Temperatures and conditions vary, often wildly, according to region and altitude. The higher up you go in the mountains, the colder it gets, which makes for nice weather in July and potentially dangerous storm-and-avalanche conditions in December. The Eastern Plains and the flatlands in northwest Colorado tend to be warmer than, say, Denver, but generally these areas are milder than average as well.

Rocky Mountains

The average mountain temperature is 43°F, with very hot Julys (82°F average) and very cold Januarys (7°F average). Whenever traveling in the mountains, prepare for extreme temperature shifts, which are most dramatic in the winters. The newspapers frequently report tragic stories of hikers leaving for a mountain excursion in mild weather, then getting stranded without proper clothing or supplies when huge clumps of snow come out of nowhere. These shifts happen even in the summer.

Whereas June is wet and humid throughout most of the United States, it's Colorado's driest month. That's a great advantage for outdoors enthusiasts, but it also creates droughts and forest-fire conditions. In 2002 and 2003, Colorado suffered through particularly dry weather, and residents had to drastically cut down on water use to bring the drought under control. (A few blizzards have helped as well.)

The most extreme wildfire in recent years was the Hayman Fire, in Pike National Forest, south of Denver, which damaged 138,000 acres, drove residents from their homes, and caused general panic for weeks. The cause was arson—park ranger Terry Lynn Barton pleaded guilty to setting the fire. The lessons: 1) Don't set forest fires; 2) Even accidental fires can spread to apocalyptic proportions in the dry season.

Western Slope

Because high mountains insulate the low valleys near Grand Junction, Palisade, and other northwestern Colorado cities, the weather is more consistent here than in the rest of state. It can get hot in these parts during the summer, of course, but the nights are cool; winters tend to be a little colder than in the rest of the state. Note that winds can get fierce in Colorado, especially during winter: In 1997, they hit 120 miles per hour in the Routt National Forest outside of Steamboat Springs, leveling millions of trees.

Eastern Plains

Eastern Colorado tends to share weather conditions with neighboring Nebraska and Kansas— low humidity, plenty of sunshine, frequent high winds, and temperatures reaching well over 100°F in the summer. Fortunately for the many farmers in the region, heavy rains tend to come during high growing season, April–September, although high winds dry the soil and lead to dust storms during winter. Chinooks, or dry and warm winds that fly off the Rockies during winter, are somewhat common here.

Elevations in the plains start out flat on Colorado's far eastern border, then gradually slant upward as travelers head west toward the Rockies. With these abrupt shifts in elevation come abrupt weather changes, so if you're traveling in this direction, be sure to pack appropriate clothing and supplies.

FLORA AND FAUNA
Flora

Because Colorado's climate and altitude vary wildly—rich soil and prime farming conditions on the Eastern Plains, drier soil in the high Rockies—some 3,000 plant species live in Colorado. These range from shrubs in the alpine zones to yucca plants, prickly pears, and colorful wildflowers in the foothills to short grass and sagebrush on the plains.

The highest growing areas in Colorado are considered the alpine zone, at roughly 11,400 feet and higher, where the extended winters are too frigid for most vegetation. Shrubs, grasses, and short trees contorted from high winds, heavy snows, and low temperatures are common at this altitude.

The subalpine zone—about 9,000 to 11,400 feet—is where mountain explorers find Colorado's best-known trees, the **alpines.** Although these white-bark trees often look skinny and twisted in the winter, like something you'd see in a Dr. Seuss book, they generate explosions of

COURTESY OF THE NATIONAL PARK SERVICE

Wildflowers are abundant in much of Colorado's open spaces.

gold, red, and orange leaves in the summer and are among the best reasons for visiting Colorado in the fall. They give way to **lodgepole pine** trees, which have darker bark, as you go higher into the mountains.

In lower mountain altitudes, commonly viewed trees include **ponderosa pine** (which can grow as high as 150 feet tall), **Douglas fir,** and occasional aspen and lodgepole pine. In the foothills, shrubs such as **skunk brush** and **wild plum,** as well as **juniper** trees, become more common as reservoirs, lakes, and streams reappear.

Gardening enthusiasts plan their entire years around spring and summer, when **wildflowers** of white, yellow, red, blue, purple, and orange appear on mountainside meadows all over the state—particularly rich areas include Rocky Mountain National Park, Loveland, and Aspen. The light-purple-and-white **columbine,** discovered by Edwin James during a Pikes Peak expedition in 1820, became the official state flower 79 years later, and it's still one of Colorado's prettiest attractions. There's nothing like hiking a steep hill, reaching the summit, and seeing a green meadow filled with purple, blue, white, and yellow columbines.

The **Colorado State University Herbarium** (970/491-0496, http://herbarium.biology.colostate.edu/index.htm) is an excellent local-flora resource.

Fauna

In many parts of Colorado, it's hard to find the line between human and wildlife dwellings—mountain residents, for example, must contend with black bears digging in their garbage, groups of hungry raccoons peering into their windows, skunks walking by their screen doors at the least convenient times, and coyotes, mountain lions, and foxes having altercations with their pet dogs and cats. But that's the charm of living in Colorado, home of 130 mammal species, 460 bird species, and 87 fish species, not to mention reptiles.

The aforementioned **black bears** live predominantly in western Colorado, but my parents, on the eastern edge of the foothills near

wildlife in Rocky Mountain National Park

Boulder, frequently report evidence of garbage violation. Some of the males can be as big as seven feet and 350 pounds, and they have sharp claws and teeth, so don't start any fights. *National Geographic* magazine's informative wildlife website, www.coloradoguide.com, has this advice for bear encounters: "Stay calm. As you move away, talk aloud to let the bear discover your presence. Back away slowly while facing the bear. Don't make eye contact. Don't run or make sudden movements. Speak softly to reassure the bear that no harm is meant to it."

Bighorn sheep, with their curly horns and changing colors, from sharp gray to dark brown, are commonly found in the Rockies, particularly at Mount Evans, near Georgetown, as well as Pikes Peak and Rocky Mountain National Park. When they fight, which is rare, they ram each other from a speed of 55 miles an hour, and you can hear the resulting crash for miles. In short, don't make them angry. Slightly cuter but just as violent—they like to push each other off cliffs—are **mountain goats,** which despite name and appearance are

actually part of the antelope family. They have black beards and horns and slumped shoulders and can be found sporadically around the Rocky Mountains—also tending to congregate at Mount Evans.

Long a source of food and clothing for Native Americans, **bison** are, at 10 feet long and weighing more than a ton, at least twice as big as a standard cow. They're also much more agile, able to run as fast as horses in some cases. Few run wild anymore in Colorado, but you can see herds of livestock along I-70, a few miles west of Denver, as well as north of Fort Collins and a few other areas.

Many Colorado landowners, particularly in Boulder County, consider **prairie dogs** more irritating than rats, as the 16- to 20-inch-long critters eat grass and crops and burrow entire cities that can be as deep as 7 feet and as long as 16 feet. After much debate, Boulder County allowed landowners to kill the dogs as long as the owners make a good-faith effort to relocate them first.

Rocky Mountain elk are also seen regularly in the foothills, especially in Rocky Mountain National Park and Evergreen, outside Denver. The male has antlers that can weigh as much as 60 pounds. More common are **mule deer,** which peer out from the side of mountain roads and occasionally cross the roads—don't blow off the yellow "deer crossing" signs, because if you hit a deer at high speed, generally speaking your car will endure at least as much damage as the deer.

Finally, if anybody invites you to hunt for **jackalope,** don't join the trip. Here's why: www.museumofhoaxes.com/tall-tales/jackalope.html.

Birds hang out everywhere in Colorado's forests, meadows, and cities—some of the more interesting ones include white-tailed ptarmigans, northern pygmy owls, greater prairie chickens, brown-capped rosy finches, three-toed woodpeckers, sharp-tailed grouses, pinyon jays, lark buntings, peregrine falcons, morning doves, ravens, wrens, robins, bluebirds, sparrows, blackbirds, orioles, mountain chickadees, turkeys, mockingbirds, titmouses, and, in some parts of the mountains, bald and golden eagles.

Although you generally have to get out of big cities like Denver, Colorado Springs, Pueblo, and Boulder to find them, Colorado's lakes provide surprisingly strong **fishing** opportunities. Some of the most common species are **brook trout,** introduced in 1872 and common in high and cold streams and lakes; **cutthroat trout,** so populous in coldwater mountain streams, lakes, and rivers that they became Colorado's official state fish in 1994; the red-bodied **kokanee salmon,** which swims in warmer, shallower water near plants and trees; and the **largemouth bass,** a well-known warm-water fish that first joined Colorado's streams, rivers, ponds, and reservoirs in the 1870s.

Rarer fish in the state are the tiger muskie, pumpkinseed, orangespotted sunfish, and the endangered arctic grayling.

Contact the **Colorado Division of Wildlife** (6060 Broadway, Denver, 303/297-1192, http://wildlife.state.co.us, 8 A.M.–5 P.M. Mon.–Fri.) for information on endangered species, hunting, fishing, permits, and directions. An excellent online reference is *National Geographic Maps Trails Illustrated* (www.colorado guide.com/index.cfm).

Environmental Issues

GAS DRILLING
With the price of natural gas rising from $2 to $7 per thousand cubic feet from 2000 to 2005, according to *The Denver Post,* the U.S. Interior Department has been pushing for more gas drilling in Colorado wildernesses under the Bush administration. Although protected from drilling under President Clinton, Colorado areas such as Bangs Canyon, South Shale Ridge, Beaver Creek, and Vermillion Basin have been open to drilling since 2003.

Environmental groups and local landowners, arguing that gas drilling will destroy the beauty of Colorado land, have aggressively filed challenges to delay the permit-granting process. Still, the Bureau of Land Management approved 6,000 oil and gas wells on public lands in 2004, compared to around 1,400 in 1996—with most of the land in question in Colorado, Wyoming, and other Rocky Mountain states. The new energy law, signed by President Bush in August 2005, is, if anything, likely to speed up the drilling.

The bill split environmentalists and Bush supporters. "For Colorado, the risk is that the energy measure would let oil companies run roughshod over our landscape, particularly by exempting oil companies from clean water laws and by pushing oil shale and tar sand development," opined the generally liberal *Denver Post,* while the conservative *Rocky Mountain News* declared, "With oil prices over $60 a barrel… oil and gas drilling is going to happen. What's the point of making it slower and more expensive? That won't help the environment." No doubt debate is still raging as you read this book.

OPEN SPACE
Coloradoans of all political persuasions love their open space—27 cities and nine counties in the state have rules protecting a certain amount of land from public or private use. Many of these local governments, as well as The Nature Conservancy, have earmarked hundreds of thousands of dollars to buy such land, mostly near the mountains, and preserve them from development.

It isn't always easy, especially in today's political climate. In summer 2005, the Bush administration took away protections for 4.4 million acres worth of Colorado roadless areas. That doesn't mean developers have rushed in to tear trees out of the forests, but the state's governor, Republican Bill Owens, then created a task force to convene public hearings and make final recommendations. (Toward the end of his term, President Clinton had banned development on 58.5 million acres in the United States, but one of President Bush's first acts in office was to overturn these rules.)

Boulder, whose 43,000-acre strip of mountain and park land is one of the biggest in the United States, has debated for years just how much access to give hikers, bikers, and dog owners. Hard-core environmentalists say the land should be completely off-limits to bone-burying dogs and boot-wearing mountain climbers, while more moderate types say the land has no purpose if people can't use it. In early 2005, Boulder's city council compromised, declaring 13,000 acres "habitat conservation areas," with strict rules for staying on trails and leashing dogs, keeping 100 miles of trails open to everybody and about 9 miles totally closed.

WATER CONSERVATION

After 20 drought-free years, Coloradoans became accustomed to using as much water as they wanted for showering, dishwashing, laundry, lawn care, and car washing. Then came the summer of 2002, when rainfall and snowpack dropped dramatically in the mountains, and suddenly the dry state's drought tradition aggressively returned. Officials begged local residents to conserve water, restricting sprinkler systems to certain days of the week, and parks went almost overnight from lush and green to crinkly and yellow.

But Colorado residents were unperturbed, and they stopped taking long showers and leaving the sink running while they tossed their glasses into the dishwasher. By early 2003, thanks in part to a statewide blizzard that replenished some of the crucial mountain snowpack and filled certain key lakes and reservoirs, the drought warnings had subsided. In July 2005, despite an unprecedented heat wave, Denver Water's customers consumed 11.4 billion gallons of water, according to *The Denver Post,* compared to 12.9 billion gallons during the much cooler July 2000. Problem solved, right?

Not necessarily. First, because Colorado residents followed the rules, water use went down, so entities such as Denver Water started to lose money—and had to raise the rates on water use. Second, although the drought isn't as imminent a threat as it was in 2003, it still looms in many parts of rain-challenged Colorado.

History

THE FIRST SETTLERS

Ancient flint points found in the South Platte River indicate that people wandered Colorado as early as 15,000 years ago. They lived in what is now Weld County and hunted small game like deer and rabbits all over the state. Perhaps 1,000 years later, mammoths appeared on the Eastern Plains, then were replaced by bison and smaller animals. For the next 4,500 years, inhabitants created villages, learned how to farm in river valleys, and marked their territory with elaborate art on rocks and valley cliffs; some of these archaeological remnants can still be seen in western Colorado and elsewhere.

The Anasazis were the first in Colorado to truly build society and culture. They lived in what is today the Four Corners region, build-

ing elaborate cliff dwellings with sophisticated square-rock architecture and large, open kivas, or ceremonial rooms. The bulk of the structures survive today in Mesa Verde National Park, and other remnants of Anasazi culture are located along streams and rivers in western Colorado.

By A.D. 1300, in large part due to extreme weather events like floods, droughts, and heavy rainfall, Anasazi culture had almost completely died out. In its place came a new Native American tribe, the Utes, who started out in Utah and Nevada and, as they grew, explored and pushed into Colorado territory. Living during the winter in western river valleys, the Utes were thought to have raided the Anasazis' food storage areas—they were aggressive and resourceful and found ways to live through extreme drought conditions. Meanwhile, tribes soon to be known as Navajos and Apaches moved into the state from the Kansas and New Mexico regions, massing near the San Juan River.

WHITE SETTLERS
The Spanish

The first nonnative settlers, from roughly 1540 to 1580, were the Spanish, coming up from Mexico to continue their search for silver. They didn't find much silver, but they did like the scenery. When reports of pretty little villages along the Rio Grande reached Spanish leaders, explorer Juan de Oñate was dispatched to colonize the area. First, the Spanish took over New Mexico, intent on spreading Christianity to the native people—but the descendants of the Anasazi fought back, killing 400 Spaniards in 1680 and recapturing their land for a dozen or so years, until the Spanish returned and quashed these natives permanently.

Their foothold thus established, Spaniards began expeditions into Colorado in 1714 and 1719, mostly to fight the Utes, who despite a friendship pledge some 55 years earlier were making regular raids on Spanish farmers and others in New Mexico. Spanish troops also traveled through the Sangre de Cristo mountain range, from Taos, New Mexico, to the western Rockies, to fight the Comanches.

The Spaniards persevered, pressuring the Utes and Comanches into treaties, but more important to Colorado history was the Spanish colonization of Colorado. The Spanish would embark on the first key exploratory trips into Colorado's intimidating mountain ranges—explorer Juan de Rivera went into the San Juan Mountains and Gunnison River in 1765, and two friars, Dominguez and Escalante, traversed and named the Sangre de Cristo Range, the San Juan Mountains, and other locations in 1777.

The Louisiana Purchase and Zebulon Pike

By 1801, although the United States had been a bona fide country for 27 years, most of the West belonged to the Spanish—although rival-ing France had battled for Colorado and other areas between the Mississippi and New Mexico for decades. That year, Spain gave up north-ern Colorado to the French. And two years later, the United States made the Louisiana Purchase, spending $15 million on southern property that virtually doubled the country's landmass. For Colorado, the purchase was especially significant because it led to nego-tiations that would define the territory's bor-ders—the United States received part of the plains and the Front Range, while the Spanish maintained their hold on the rest of the Rock-ies and the western plateaus.

Into this rivalry between the Spanish and the Americans—with a little French and Na-tive American tension on the side—hiked ex-plorer Zebulon Pike. In 1806, he became the first American to truly investigate the Colo-rado territory, wandering into the south-cen-tral Rockies and naming Pikes Peak, which he said nobody could climb. (Of course, Dr. Edwin James, part of an official exploration party, scaled it in 1820.) The next year, the Spanish captured and imprisoned Pike in Santa Fe, then released him shortly afterward.

After Mexico received its independence, in 1821, the U.S. and Mexico put aside their dif-ferences and began a lucrative economic rela-tionship. Beaver pelts and other kinds of fur were the most sought-after items for trade, and traders from Missouri to Santa Fe estab-lished the Santa Fe Trail, which cut around the Rockies in southeastern Colorado—avoid-ing treacherous terrain but often running into hostile Native Americans. Of the many trad-ing posts along the route, the most famous was the adobe Bent's Fort, established in 1833, not far from Las Animas, where explorers, soldiers, and Cheyenne and Arapaho Indians could load up on food and supplies.

In 1846, when the Mexican-American War broke out, Bent's was absorbed into the United States and transformed into a real fort, a train-ing area for soldiers. The war lasted two years, and when the gunpowder had cleared, Mexico had agreed to a treaty ceding the entirety of what is now Colorado to the United States.

The Gold Rush

Rumors about gold in Colorado's Rocky Mountains circulated around the United States beginning in 1858, and that spring, 13 prospectors set out to the South Platte River to find it. After months of searching, they succeeded in early July, finding tiny gold deposits along Little Dry Creek, a few miles north of the intersection between Cherry Creek and the South Platte. (This is where Denver sits today.)

The ensuing rush basically built Colorado. Tens of thousands of miners, farmers, ranchers, outlaws, and gamblers moved to the mountains, creating human dramas and mythologies that reverberate today. According to legend, fortune-seeker William Larimer brought 30 men from Leavenworth, Kansas, in search of gold and wound up bribing a guard in St. Charles, near Cherry Creek and the South Platte River, to sign over the entire town while its founding fathers were out of town. Larimer named this new area Denver.

Denver started to grow, and its first newspaper, the *Rocky Mountain News,* was founded in 1859. But the early gold rush, which brought some 3,000 people to the area, turned out to be a bust, and many of those settlers headed dejectedly back to Kansas and Missouri. Those who stayed behind, however, were rewarded when the most determined miners started to bring back vials of gold from mines near Idaho Springs and Clear Creek, both west of Denver in the eastern Rockies. This rush lasted several years, as an estimated 500 people a year moved to Colorado, numerous small towns sprouted up in the mountains, and Central City, Black Hawk, and Idaho Springs became havens for hard-drinking, hard-gambling, and hard-fighting miners.

Colorado officially became a U.S. territory in 1861, although the mines couldn't keep up production—gold discoveries dropped dramatically from 1860 to 1866, and with them went the population, with thousands of people moving out of the area yet again. In addition, Colorado was so isolated from other territories that many miners and their families had trouble dealing with the resulting depression. To build the state, boosters such as Larimer and first governor William Gilpin coaxed railroads to extend their lines to the area, helped modernize the mines, and encouraged farmers and ranchers to settle on the fertile Eastern Plains. Colorado would slowly boom again.

Conflicts with Native Americans

Needless to say, Native American tribes weren't totally thrilled about white settlers colonizing the land they'd been living on for centuries. The conflicts weren't pretty: In 1864, Cheyenne and Arapaho tribes murdered the Hungate family on its ranch some 30 miles from Denver, striking fear of war dances in the hearts of white settlers for decades to come. American troops, led by Col. John Chivington, responded in kind, and set out with extermination in mind—he led a massacre of 500 Cheyennes, including many women and children, in southeastern Colorado. Even more infamously, religious-minded settler John Meeker, who had founded the city of Greeley, was killed along with several other whites after attempting to "reform" Native Americans according to Christian traditions. But this "Meeker massacre," in 1879, ultimately took away the leverage of Ute leaders such as Chief Ouray, who gave up wide swaths of Colorado land, allowing white settlers to assume control of the state for good.

The Bust

From 1870 to 1893, thanks to mines such as Gilpin and Clear Creek, which produced more than $3.5 million a year worth of gold for a time, Colorado's population boomed. The first railroad landed near Black Hawk in 1870, leading to many huge new industries, with stations built in Denver, Burlington, Grand Junction, Durango, Julesburg, and even tiny mountain towns such as Silverton. From roughly 1870 to 1880, the territory's population grew from about 40,000 to more than 124,000, and Colorado became a state in 1876. Fancy hotels sprouted all over the state, from the Beaumont in Ouray to the Hotel Colorado in Glenwood Springs to the Sheridan in Telluride to the Strater in Durango, and famous (and infamous) visitors such as Teddy Roosevelt, King Leopold of Belgium, and Doc Holliday stayed in the ornate rooms.

Silver mines, too, flourished during this period, particularly those in Leadville, as well as Durango and other parts of the "Silver San Juans" in southwestern Colorado. However, beginning in 1873, the U.S. Congress started to deemphasize silver—the country discontinued silver dollars, and despite the protests of Colorado and other Western mining states, Congress stopped silver purchasing for good. Gold-mining held steady during this period, but the silver bust turned out to be foreshadowing for Colorado miners.

Gold production became wobbly in the 1900s, when mines started getting so deep they were too expensive to maintain, and World War I–era inflation knocked it out completely. While gold's value remained consistent, other commodities went up, and the economics of gold-mining became obsolete.

Mines began to close, leading to a horrific domino effect throughout the state: Miners abandoned the towns they'd inhabited since the 1860s, Denver's population swelled, mostly with unemployed and homeless people, opulent hotels and stately banks closed, and entire boom towns such as Central City downgraded to ghost towns within a few months. Despite certain healthy industry cities, like Redstone, where coal-workers thrived under magnate John Osgood, Colorado's fortunes changed from rich to poor.

Colorado was a roller coaster for the next three decades. Bloody strikes in mining towns like Cripple Creek and Telluride led to confrontations between management and labor. There were unexplained explosions, Colorado National Guard activations, labor-camp violence, and, at the peak in 1914, an altercation near Trinidad resulting in dead strikers as well as women and children. The state came back during a brief World War I–era silver boom, but it didn't last long, and by the Great Depression, farmers and ranchers lost everything, creating a gloom of poverty almost through World War II.

SCENERY, SKIING, AND TOURISM

As in the rest of the United States, Franklin D. Roosevelt's New Deal programs pulled Colorado out of its longtime funk—federal agriculture and public-works projects revived farmers and built new roads. Roosevelt's Civilian Conservation Corps planted 9 million trees, stocked lakes and streams with 2 million fish, and built Morrison's Red Rocks Amphitheatre, which remains one of the state's biggest tourism and entertainment draws to this day. World War II helped the economy, too, as the military established huge training bases, such as Fort Carson, near Colorado Springs, and Buckley Field, near Denver.

Beginning in the 1950s, with major roads such as I-70 giving travelers access to the Rocky Mountains that Native Americans and Spanish explorers could never have imagined, Colorado truly began to market its scenic riches. Camping, fishing, and hunting drew thousands to mountain towns like Telluride, Durango, and Central City, and tourism became the state's third-largest industry in the 1950s and 1960s.

What really made the state take off, though, was skiing. The sport had been around as early as 1857, according to Abbott Fay's *A History of Skiing in Colorado,* when mountain guide Jim Baker lost his way in the mountains east of Gunnison and built himself a pair of makeshift skis to climb a peak for a better view. Skiers were creative in the early days, with army vehicles hauling adventurous types to a tow rope in the pre-chairlift era at Arapahoe Basin. Mountain mail carriers were some of the earliest adopters.

Thanks to pioneers such as Norwegian immigrant Carl Howelsen, who built Colorado's first ski jump in Steamboat Springs in 1914, skiing slowly developed a reputation among extreme-sports pioneers in the early 20th century. Visionary businesspeople plotted resorts in ex-mining towns like Breckenridge or uninhabited mountain regions like Vail, and by the 1960s, Vail, Breckenridge, Steamboat Springs, and Aspen were competing aggressively for tourist dollars. The moment skiing entered the international mainstream came in the early 1970s, when President Gerald Ford declared himself a Vail aficionado.

Today, skiing is a multibillion-dollar industry, with 28 total hills, 36,300 acres of skiable terrain, and 12 miles worth of mountain drops. Every major resort manufactures its own powder, expensive condominiums and affordable ski villages sit side by side in tourist-heavy but still quaint towns from Winter Park to Crested Butte, and extreme-sports festivals and outdoors magazines focus heavily on Colorado. The events of September 11, 2001, delivered a blow to the ski industry, along with the rest of world tourism, but it has mostly recovered in the last few years. Resorts market deals and packages as heavily as ever.

MODERN COLORADO

Many unexpected factors brought a variety of businesses to Colorado beginning in the 1950s. Mining boomed again—uranium, this time—and prospectors with geiger counters flooded Grand Junction and the Four Corners region searching for ore. Aspen took off as the world's posh playground, drawing celebrities and general hoity-toity types and boosting recreational tourism. The United States opened the National Coalition of Atmospheric Research in Boulder and the National Bureau of Standards in Denver, and businesses such as the Martin Marietta Aerospace Corp. and IBM relocated to the area as well.

In the Rocky Mountains, the Eisenhower Tunnel opened in the early 1970s, offering easy driving passage from Denver to Vail, Aspen, Crested Butte, Glenwood Springs, and beyond. Denver overhauled its metropolitan area in the early 1960s, drawing numerous colleges and industries to town, and it began to emerge from its longtime reputation as a "cowtown"—although plenty of farmers and ranchers lived nearby.

The city's latest rebirth happened in the 1990s, when Mayor Federico Peña spearheaded the state-of-the-art Denver International Airport, one of the largest in the country, and Major League Baseball moved to town in the form of the purple-and-black Colorado Rockies. Around the time of these developments came LoDo, a revitalization of the downtown warehouse district areas, and within a few years, major highway projects such as T-REX and FasTracks will establish light-rail trains and other fancy new transportation.

Government and Economy

GOVERNMENT

Colorado is a "red state," in the vernacular of recent U.S. presidential elections, but its modern preference for Republican George W. Bush over Democratic candidates is somewhat misleading. The majority of the state's residents, especially farmers and ranchers in the Eastern Plains and military families in the Colorado Springs area, are conservative—Bill Owens is the latest in a long trend of Republican governors, although he'll step down after the 2006 election. "The People's Republic of Boulder," a college town filled with ex-hippies, is one of the most liberal cities in the country, and Denver isn't far behind.

As a result, Colorado elections wind up with such contradictory results as an overwhelming Bush victory in 2004 paired with Democrat Ken Salazar's ascension to the U.S. Senate the same year and state Democrats taking over the legislature for the first time in decades.

Colorado has 64 counties, each with a board of commissioners, although Denver is run by a mayor and city council. As per Colorado's constitution, written in 1876, the state lawmaking body is the General Assembly, consisting of a Senate and a House of Representatives—with veto powers from the governor.

ECONOMY

Raising cattle and sheep and producing wheat, hay, corn, and sugar beets, among other things, have been the anchor of Colorado's economy

© STEVE KNOPPER

Boulder's courthouse

since the mid-1800s. Farm market receipts are roughly $5 billion per year, according to Doug Freed's almanac *Colorado by the Numbers,* and farms are pretty much all you'll see if you spend any time in Greeley, Sterling, Limon, or the rest of the Eastern Plains.

Other top business sectors include manufacturing (computer equipment is big), federal services (there are numerous military bases around the state, the Department of Defense spends about $5 billion here annually, and the U.S. Mint is in downtown Denver, not to mention prisons and airports), food processing, transportation and electrical equipment, and, particularly in the northwest, wineries and fruit orchards.

Also huge is tourism: Thanks mostly to the ski resorts, travelers spend some $8 billion a year in the state, from renting ski boots to buy-ing T-shirts at the Greeley Independence Stampede rodeo and country-music festival.

Finally, Colorado cemented its reputation as a high-tech state during the Internet boom of the 1990s, when numerous startup companies formed in Denver, Boulder, Colorado Springs, and elsewhere, and large companies such as Sun Microsystems expanded their presence here. The resulting bust briefly damaged the economy—as with other states, Colorado officials had "irrational exuberance" and spent far too many millions on poorly thought-out projects like the Ocean Journey Aquarium in downtown Denver.

Although Colorado is lovingly remembered as a gold-mining state, most of those mines have shut down, leaving abandoned shafts all over the state. Colorado companies continue to mine gas, coal, gravel, and uranium, though.

The People

STATISTICS

About 4.3 million people live in Colorado, as of the 2000 U.S. Census, and while the state has undergone some severe busts and depressions, most notably after gold and silver rushes in the late 1800s, it has never gone 10 years straight with a population decrease. Miners built the state, particularly Denver, Colorado Springs, and the small towns from the Front Range to the Western Slope, and while many of those original regions have devolved into ghost towns or tourist-trap areas, the layouts roughly remain the same.

Colorado is the third-fastest-growing state, with a population increase of 30 percent from 1990 to 2000. Although the state has traditionally had a dismally small African-American population—just 3.8 percent, compared to 12.3 percent in the United States—it has a large and rapidly multiplying Hispanic populace. About 17 percent of the state is Hispanic, particularly in Denver County, where the number jumps to 32 percent, and many predict Hispanics will account for a quarter of the population by 2025.

Denver is easily the state's most diverse area, but some of the other large cities are almost disturbingly homogeneous. For all its other qualities, Boulder County's African-American population is 0.9 percent, while its Hispanic population is 10.5 percent, far lower than its metropolitan neighbor, Denver County. For people visiting or moving from urban areas, this can make for culture shock.

ATTITUDES

Colorado is a divided state, politically and socially, in many ways. In most of Denver and Boulder, as well as Telluride and Aspen, you're likely to encounter "Rush Is Rong" bumper stickers, while George W. Bush signs are far more common in Colorado Springs and the Eastern Plains. This makes for a bit of tension, as evidenced on radio talk shows and the letters-to-the-editor pages of the *Rocky Mountain News* and *The Denver Post*.

Some issues throw these political polar opposites into out-and-out battle. In 1992, the Colorado Springs–based Focus on the Family spearheaded Amendment 2, an effort to deny gay people anti-discrimination rights under city laws. Conservatives accused gays and lesbians of pushing for "special rights," while liberals cried homophobia—voters passed the law, but after many months of protests and boycotts, the U.S. Supreme Court struck it down a few years later.

Mostly, though, Colorado is a friendly, laid-back state, filled with individualists who've moved to the mountains to escape the stress of their more complicated lives in California or New York.

Arts and Culture

MUSIC

Some of the many thousands of people who came to Colorado in the 1960s and 1970s to ski, relax, and enjoy the laid-back Rocky Mountain atmosphere were rock stars—and several of them stayed behind. Around the time they started making hit records in the mid-1970s, members of the Eagles held court regularly at Tulagi, the late, lamented night-club near the University of Colorado campus in Boulder. Before long, rockers from Stevie Wonder to Joe Walsh were living and recording at the $1,500-a-day-per-entourage Caribou Ranch, in Nederland, and Elton John even titled an album *Caribou*.

For years afterward, Colorado had a reputation as a sort of summer home for rising rockers, especially gentle, country-leaning ones like Dan Fogelberg, Firefall, and Poco's Richie Furay, who retired from the music business to open his own ministry in Boulder County. From these seeds, as well as regular stops by the Grateful Dead through the mid-1990s, grew the local jam-band culture. Homegrown artists like Big Head Todd and the Monsters, the Samples, Leftover Salmon, and the String Cheese Incident used Red Rocks Amphitheatre as their home base and turned into solid international touring acts.

Also serving this scene are numerous summer mountain festivals, such as the Telluride Bluegrass Festival, RockyGrass in Lyons, and Jazz Aspen Snowmass. (For a thorough and lively study of pop music in Colorado, former *Denver Post* rock writer G. Brown's *Colorado Rocks!* is highly recommended.)

The rodeo culture of the Eastern Plains spawned hundreds of thousands of country-music fans, and the Greeley Independence Stampede has become one of the biggest festivals this side of Cheyenne Frontier Days in Wyoming.

Opera, by contrast, isn't quite as big as it was in the late 1800s, when the most sophisticated miners gussied themselves up on a regular basis and headed to the Wheeler Opera House in Aspen or the Sheridan Opera House in Telluride. Nonetheless, many of these historic old venues survive, sponsoring pop, rock, country, and jazz shows in addition to theatrical productions, and entities such as the **Denver Performing Arts Complex** (which recently opened a fancy new opera hall) and the **Colorado Symphony Orchestra** do an excellent job of keeping classical, chamber, and opera music alive in the state.

THEATER

With Denver and Boulder acting as a cultural center—the University of Colorado's outdoor **Colorado Shakespeare Festival** is a must for bard devotees, and Denver has a strong collection of local theaters, including the **Denver Center Theatre Company**—Colorado is a surprisingly rich and diverse place to see a play. It's no New York City or Chicago, but the options, as you drive around the state, are as var-

Boulder's Pearl Street Mall attracts its share of unicyclists and other street performers.

© STEVE KNOPPER

ied as the historical and goofy **Diamond Circle Melodrama & Vaudeville** in Durango and the colorful **Buell Children's Theatre** in Pueblo.

SHOPPING

The best shopping districts in Colorado are part of the biggest cities—the **16th Street Mall** and **Larimer Square** in Denver, the **Pearl Street Mall** in Boulder, and **Old Town Square** in Fort Collins. But every tiny mountain town, from Ouray to Crested Butte, has its own strip of tourist-oriented, mom-and-pop-style shops that sell books, sunglasses, T-shirts, western clothing, sports equipment, and organic food supplies. Most famous (and infamous) is Aspen, whose hoity-toity stores cater to the super-rich (or at least the super-rich-looking).

FOOD

Colorado restaurants are rarely listed in the glossy pages of *Esquire* and *Gourmet,* but the food here has touches of high class that rival anything in New York or Los Angeles. True gourmets should consider spending a few days in Denver, for high-end restaurants such as **Mizuna** and **Rioja,** but they should also build an itinerary around Aspen, Beaver Creek, and Telluride. These mountain towns can't exactly choose from an unlimited pool of the best chefs and waitpeople, the way New York and Los Angeles eateries do, but they manage to attract some of the top talents in the world. Also worth visiting are hidden gems such as **Alice's Restaurant,** off the Peak-to-Peak Highway outside Boulder, and **Toscanini** in Beaver Creek.

Colorado also has a number of food-oriented festivals, including Aspen's **Food & Wine Classic,** Denver's **Great American Beer Festival,** the **Olathe Sweet Corn Festival,** and the **Annual Chili Pepper and Brewfest** in Snowmass Village.

Recreation

Colorado's marquee attraction is its outdoor scenery—towering mountains that pop up unexpectedly as you're driving to the grocery store, meadows and wildernesses that rival anything in the Swiss Alps, and some of the best skiing, biking, and hiking trails in the world. So the outdoors is the heart of Colorado's tourism industry, and casual outdoor wanderers and professional ski and bike racers alike spend serious time here for training and races. The range of outdoor activities is daunting, from mountain biking in Crested Butte to fishing in Rifle to skiing in Aspen to hiking in Rocky Mountain National Park.

PUBLIC LANDS

Colorado has 41 state parks, 4,000 campsites, and 58 cabins and yurts that are open to the public—almost 219,000 acres of land and water overall. In addition, the Bureau of Land Management oversees 8.64 million acres of land, or 12.6 percent of the entire state, according to *Colorado by the Numbers.* The **Colorado State Parks** main office is in Denver (1313 Sherman St., Denver, 303/866-3437, http://parks.state.co.us); daily vehicle fees are $3–7, and campsites range $7–20 depending on the amenities. The **Bureau of Land Management** can be reached at 303/239-3600, although throughout 2005 the bureau's website (www.blm.gov) was totally inoperable; access to most lands is free, and campsites cost $3–10 per night.

The **U.S. Forest Service** manages 14 wilderness areas and national grasslands, including Routt National Forest outside Aspen. The service has three park-ranger offices in the state (100 Main St., Walden, 970/723-8204; 2103 E. Park Ave., Kremmling, 970/724-3000; and 300 Roselawn Ave., Yampa, 970/638-4516). The main webpage, which has information on Wyoming, Kansas, Nebraska, and South Dakota as well, is www.fs.fed.us/r2. Day passes run about $5–8, and campsites are about $15 per night.

Finally, the **National Park Service** (12795 Alameda Pkwy., 303/969-2500, www.nps.gov) maintains 15 parks, monuments, and historic trails in Colorado, including Rocky Mountain National Park, the Curecanti National Recreation Area, and Black Canyon of the Gunnison National Park. Day use is roughly $3–5.

OUTDOOR ACTIVITIES
Skiing

Consult individual chapters in this book for details about specific ski resorts—each one has a website with just about everything you need to know, from weather to lesson times—but suffice to say that "Ski Country USA" has some of the best skiing in the world, enough to satisfy a multibillion-dollar tourist industry. Numerous magazines—try *Ski* (www.skimag.com) and *Skiing* (www.skiingmag.com)—emphasize Colorado skiing, as do websites such as **Colorado Ski Country USA** (www.coloradoski.com) and the **Colorado Ski Resort Guide** (www.coloradoskicountry.com). Almost any sporting-goods store—and there are many scattered around the

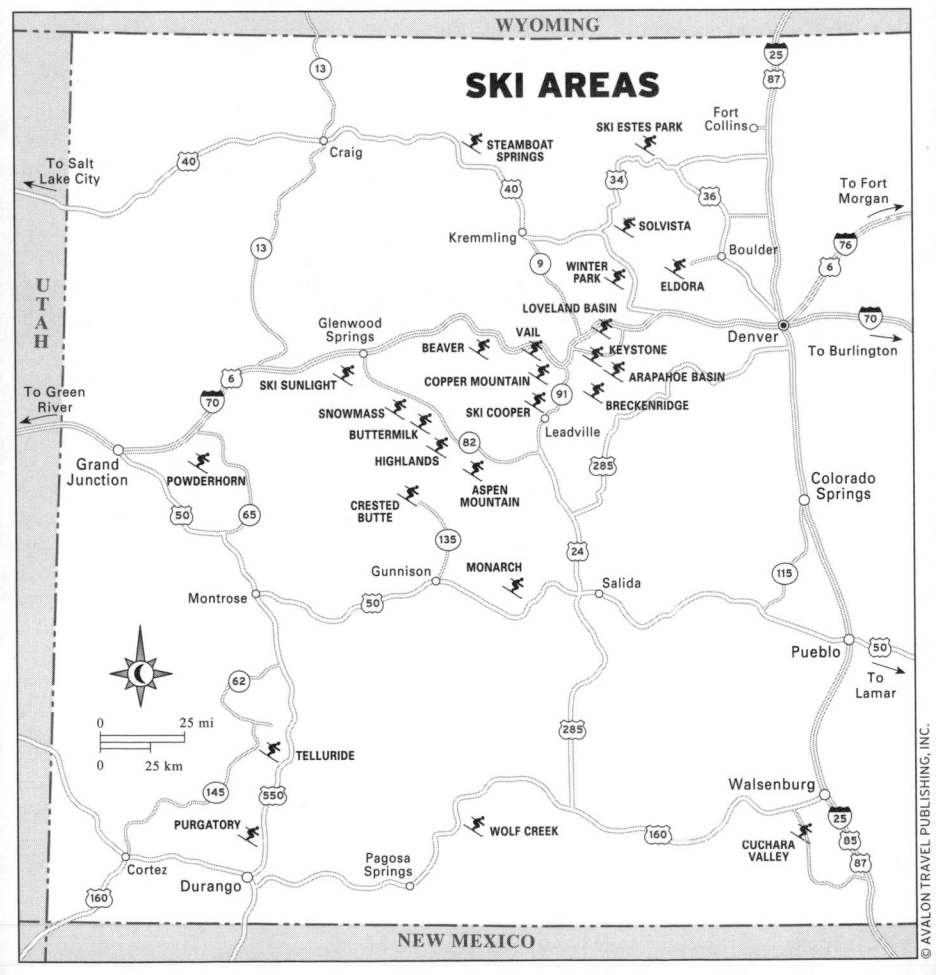

COLORADO'S FOURTEENERS

Colorado has 53 mountain peaks more than 14,000 feet high (many are part of the San Juans, in the southwest part of the state), and some hardy outdoorspeople make a sport out of climbing all of them. Here's a list, including elevation in feet and nearest (relatively) big city:

- Mount Elbert, 14,433, Leadville
- Mount Massive, 14,421, Leadville
- Mount Harvard, 14,420, Buena Vista
- Blanca Peak, 14,345, Alamosa
- La Plata Peak, 14,336, Buena Vista
- Uncompahgre Peak, 14,309, Lake City
- Crestone Peak, 14,294, Westcliffe
- Mount Lincoln, 14,286, Breckenridge
- Grays Peak, 14,270, Georgetown
- Mount Antero, 14,269, Salida
- Torreys Peak, 14,267, Georgetown
- Castle Peak, 14,265, Aspen
- Quandary Peak, 14,265, Breckenridge
- Mount Evans, 14,264, Georgetown
- Longs Peak, 14,255, Estes Park
- Mount Wilson, 14,246, Telluride
- Mount Cameron, 14,238, Breckenridge
- Mount Shavano, 14,229, Salida
- Mount Belford, 14,197, Buena Vista
- Crestone Needle, 14,197, Westcliffe
- Mount Princeton, 14,197, Buena Vista
- Mount Yale, 14,196, Buena Vista
- Mount Bross, 14,172, Breckenridge
- Kit Carson Peak, 14,165, Westcliffe
- El Diente Peak, 14,159, Telluride
- Maroon Peak, 14,156, Aspen
- Tabeguache Peak, 14,155, Salida
- Mount Oxford, 14,153, Buena Vista
- Mount Sneffels, 14,150, Ouray
- Mount Democrat, 14,148, Breckenridge
- Capitol Peak, 14,130, Snowmass Village
- Pikes Peak, 14,110, Colorado Springs
- Snowmass Mountain, 14,092, Snowmass Village
- Mount Eolus, 14,083, Silverton
- Windom Peak, 14,082, Silverton
- Challenger Point, 14,081, Alamosa
- Mount Columbia, 14,073, Buena Vista
- Missouri Mountain, 14,067, Buena Vista
- Humboldt Peak, 14,064, Westcliffe
- Mount Bierstadt, 14,060, Georgetown
- Conundrum Peak, 14,060, Aspen
- Sunlight Peak, 14,059, Silverton
- Handies Peak, 14,048, Silverton
- Culebra Peak, 14,047, Alamosa
- Ellingwood Point, 14,042, Alamosa
- Mount Lindsey, 14,042, Alamosa
- North Eolus, 14,039, Silverton
- Little Bear Peak, 14,037, Alamosa
- Mount Sherman, 14,036, Leadville
- Redcloud Peak, 14,034, Silverton
- Pyramid Peak, 14,018, Aspen
- Wilson Peak, 14,017, Telluride
- Wetterhorn Peak, 14,015, Lake City
- North Maroon Peak, 14,014, Aspen
- San Luis Peak, 14,014, Creede
- Mount of the Holy Cross, 14,005, Minturn
- Huron Peak, 14,003, Buena Vista
- Sunshine Peak, 14,001, Silverton

Source: www.14ers.com

© STEVE KNOPPER

Mount Columbia, 14,073 feet

resorts—will rent skis, boots, and poles in $24–30 one-day packages.

Backcountry and Nordic skiing—more commonly known as "cross-country"—are also popular at almost every Colorado ski resort, as well as major parks and trails around Boulder, Rocky Mountain National Park, and elsewhere. The **Cross Country Ski Areas Association** (www.xcski.org) is an excellent resource, as are the resorts and the **Boulder Outdoor Center** (2707 Spruce St., Boulder, 303/444-8420 or 800/364-9376, www.boc123.com). Most sporting-goods stores rent equipment.

Snowboarding

Snowboarding used to be a renegade answer to skiing, but in the past decade it has become established as a legitimate alternative, the way punk rockers Green Day are an alternative to the Rolling Stones. (In Crested Butte, the downtown benches are snowboards with legs attached.) Every major ski resort in Colorado offers snowboard-oriented runs and bowls, and almost every ski shop rents equipment—the board

is all you need, and you can get one for $24–30 per day. There's such a thing as "cross-country 'boarding," but most snowboarders tend to hate it. It's truly a downhill-only sport.

Snowmobiling

You'd think snowmobiling would be almost as huge as skiing in Colorado, but mountain erosion limits the available trails, so there are restrictions on where and when you can indulge. Contact the **Colorado Snowmobile Association** (http://sledcity.com) about how to get started. Many mountain towns rent snowmobiles as well.

Hiking and Cycling

Wherever you go in Colorado, you're bound to find some kind of scenic hiking trail—some of the best are in **Rocky Mountain National Park, Chautauqua Park** in Boulder, the hike up to **Bridal Veil Falls** in Telluride, **Dinosaur National Park** in the northwest corner of the state, and **Curecanti National Recreation Area** east of Montrose.

Many of the aforementioned hiking and backpacking areas are open to cyclists as well. Some cities in Colorado, particularly Crested Butte, Grand Junction (and neighboring Rifle), and Boulder, cater directly to cyclists, with police officers who actually enforce pedestrian-cyclist-motorist laws and designated lanes on the right side of the road. In addition, many of the well-known ski areas allow cyclists to pedal the slopes during late spring and summer, and if all else fails, just pick a mountain road and start riding upward. For more information on roads, conditions, renting equipment, or repairs, contact **American Cycling Association** (7781 E. Jarvis Pl., Denver, 303/458-5538, www.americancycling.org).

Fishing and Hunting
For a landlocked state far more famous for snow than water, Colorado has surprisingly rich fishing opportunities, from the narrow and dangerous **Black Canyon of the Gunnison National Park** east of Montrose

The Uncompahgre River, outside Ouray, is a great place to fish.

to the **Cache La Poudre River** outside Fort Collins. You have to be 16 years old or older to buy a license—$20.25 per year for residents or $40.25 for nonresidents, and one-day and five-day licenses are available—through the **Colorado Department of Wildlife** (6060 Broadway, Denver, 303/297-1192, http://wildlife.state.co.us/fishing).

Hunting, especially of deer, pheasant, elk, and certain kinds of birds, is legal with a license (from $10 for small game to $200 for bighorn sheep). Again, the **Colorado Department of Wildlife** (http://wildlife.state.co.us/hunt/) doles out the licenses, provides information, and enforces the various rules and restrictions.

Rock Climbing
Many adventure outfitters give rock-climbing tours, but experienced climbers like to find the rocks on their own. Beware climbing without equipment, especially if you're new to the sport. For more information, **Climbing Boulder** (www.climbingboulder.com) has reviews of locations around the state.

White-Water Rafting
White-water rafting is particularly popular along the Colorado River, and nearby towns such as Salida and Buena Vista are hot spots for the sport. Before finding an outfitter or guide and embarking on a trip, ask about the intensity level of the ride—some rafting trips are smooth and easy, others choppy and adventurous. For a fairly comprehensive list of guides, check out **Whitewater Rafting in Colorado** (www.raftinfo.com/colorado.htm).

SPECTATOR SPORTS
Denver is home base for professional teams in just about every sport—the National Football League's **Denver Broncos** (www.denverbroncos.com), Major League Baseball's **Colorado Rockies** (www.colorado.rockies.mlb.com), the National Basketball Association's **Denver Nuggets** (www.nba.com/nuggets), the National Hockey Association's **Colorado Avalanche** (www.coloradoavalanche.com), and even Major League Soccer's **Colorado**

Rapids (www.coloradorapids.com). In addition, the state's major colleges, including the University of Colorado and Colorado State University, compete on a high level in most of the Division I sports.

Rodeos are also big in Colorado, especially during the National Western Stock Show (www.nationalwestern.com) every January in Denver and throughout the Eastern Plains.

INDOOR ACTIVITIES
Limited-Stakes Gambling
Three towns in Colorado—Black Hawk, Central City, and Cripple Creek—legalized limited-stakes gambling in 1991, and all three have more or less boomed (with the occasional bust) since then. Limited-stakes basically means you can do whatever you do in Las Vegas, from video poker to blackjack, only with a maximum bet of $5 per hand. The people-watching is almost as good as it is in Vegas, with an emphasis on cowboys, and some of the rickety country music played at the casinos makes the trip especially worthwhile.

A few Native American–reservation casinos are scattered throughout the state, including the Ute Mountain Casino in Cortez and the Sky Ute Casino & Lodge outside Durango.

Accommodations

HOTELS AND MOTELS
Trying to find a standard rate for a Colorado hotel is almost impossible, especially in the ski towns, where there's not just a high season (roughly late Nov.–early April) and a low season (roughly early Sept.–early Nov. and late April–mid-May). There's also a "holiday high season" (Christmas and Thanksgiving), a "summer high season," and a huge gap between weekend and weekday rates. The ski hotels, in particular, offer numerous packages and deals, some involving breakfast and luxuries like sleigh rides and guided tours. Also, scan the local papers (such as the Boulder *Daily Camera* or its website, www.dailycamera.com) for lift-ticket-and-room packages, especially common at the big hotels.

The ritzier the ski area—like Aspen or Beaver Creek—the more expensive the room. Deals at Copper Mountain and Winter Park are usually quite affordable, and Coloradoans take advantage of them. Be sure to make reservations far in advance, especially during high season, because the best hotels fill up quickly.

In smaller towns that are less reliant on the ski season, rates tend to be more consistent. The Broadmoor, in Colorado Springs, is one of many high-end hotels that have surprisingly good deals in the middle of winter. Finally, consider staying just outside a ski resort, like Dillon, Silverthorne, or Frisco (or even Boulder or Denver) and taking one of the shuttles or buses that traipse through the mountains.

CAMPGROUNDS AND HOSTELS
Camping is huge in Colorado—most campgrounds are open from roughly Memorial Day to Labor Day—especially in prime scenery areas such as Rocky Mountain National Park and Colorado National Monument. The rates range from free to $20, and some spots offer running water, flush toilets, and electricity. Contact the U.S. Forest Service (303/275-5350, www.fs.fed.us/r2/recreation/camping) or the State of Colorado (303/866-3437 or 800/678-2267, http://parks.state.co.us/reservations/) about their respective facilities, or make reservations via a reliable camping-reservation website such as Reserve America (www.reserveamerica.com).

Hostels are rare in Colorado, but they exist, even in ritzy ski resorts like Aspen. Others include the Rocky Mountain Inn near Winter Park and YMCA of the Rockies in Estes Park. For general hostel information, check the Hostels.com (www.hostels.com) website or

© STEVE KNOPPER

Rabbit Ears Motel in Steamboat Springs

contact **Hostelling International USA** (8401 Colesville Rd., Suite 600, Silver Spring, MD, 301/495-1240, www.hiusa.org).

BED-AND-BREAKFASTS

In Colorado, every town seems to have at least one small bed-and-breakfast, usually in a Victorian-style house or a woodsy log cabin, and they're generally a little more expensive than a standard hotel. Breakfast, obviously, is included in the room rate, and, in some cases, so are distinctive touches like dogs, cats, llama boarding (it's true!), and horse stables. Numerous websites list Colorado bed-and-breakfast facilities, and **Bed and Breakfast Innkeepers**

of Colorado (Colorado Springs, 800/265-7696, www.innsofcolorado.org) is one of the most reliable.

DUDE RANCHES

Dude ranches, or cabin-style hotels on actual ranches with horse stables, corrals, and instructors who give riding lessons, have been serving cowboy-hatted guests in Colorado since the 1870s. They can be good deals, especially for large groups with children, and are available in mountain areas like Winter Park and Grand County. Contact the **Colorado Dude and Guest Ranch Association** (Granby, 970/887-3128, www.coloradoranch.com).

ESSENTIALS
Getting There and Around

BY CAR

Unless you happen to live in Wyoming, New Mexico, Utah, northeastern Arizona, or western Kansas or Nebraska, Colorado is a long drive from just about any destination. The main artery is I-70, which spans the state from east to west, cutting straight through the Rocky Mountains and providing easy access to most of the major ski resorts. I-25 also cuts through the state, south from Wyoming through Fort Collins, Denver (where it intersects with I-70), Colorado Springs, and Pueblo, to northern New Mexico.

The two interstates are wide and well-maintained, with speed limits of 65 to 75 miles per hour in most places, and accommodate plenty of traffic. During poor weather conditions and the occasional rock slide, however, I-70 can be frustratingly convoluted around the Eisenhower Memorial Tunnel and Idaho Springs. Denver and Colorado Springs, too, get extremely congested on the highways during rush hours.

The smaller highways, including I-76 from Nebraska into Julesburg and U.S. 24 from Kansas into Burlington, are narrower but usually without much traffic as they climb slowly west, into the Rockies. Smaller roads, especially in the mountains, can be twisty and dangerous during poor weather, and some, such as the rocky road over Kebler Pass, from Highway 133 to Crested

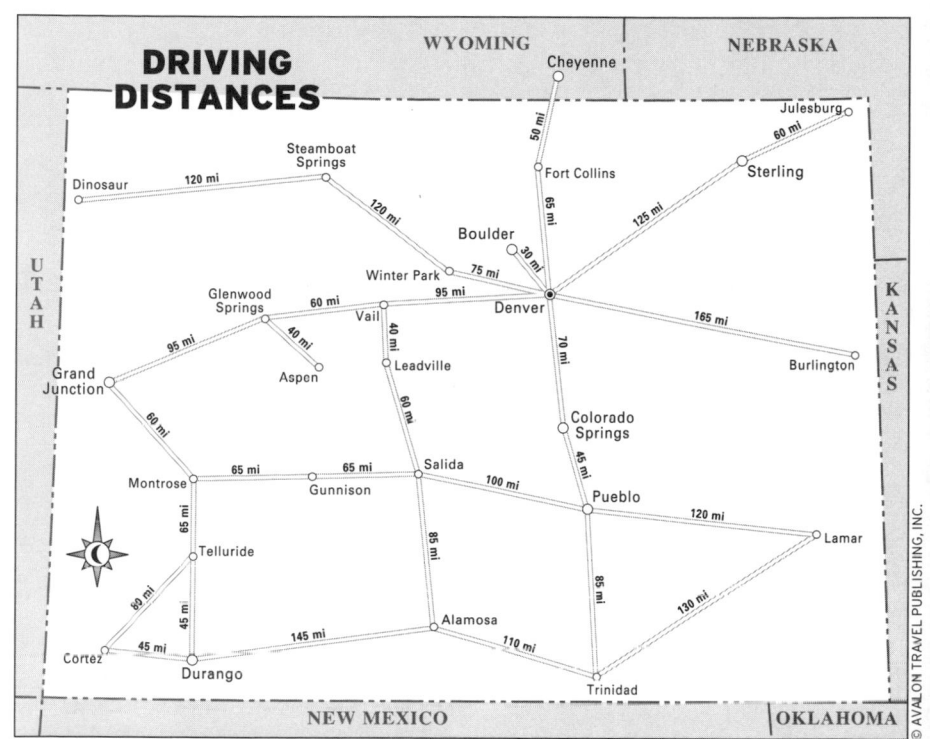

DRIVING DISTANCES

WYOMING

NEBRASKA

Cheyenne

Julesburg

Dinosaur — 120 mi — Steamboat Springs

120 mi

Fort Collins

50 mi

60 mi

Sterling

U T A H

Boulder

65 mi

30 mi

125 mi

Winter Park — 75 mi

Glenwood Springs — 60 mi

95 mi

Denver

165 mi

Vail

40 mi

Aspen

Grand Junction — 95 mi

40 mi

Leadville

70 mi

Burlington

K A N S A S

60 mi

60 mi

Colorado Springs

45 mi

Montrose — 65 mi — Gunnison — 65 mi — Salida

65 mi

100 mi

Pueblo

120 mi

Lamar

Telluride

85 mi

85 mi

130 mi

89 mi

45 mi

Alamosa

Cortez — 45 mi — Durango — 145 mi

110 mi

Trinidad

NEW MEXICO

OKLAHOMA

© AVALON TRAVEL PUBLISHING, INC.

Butte, are impassable in the winter. Some of Colorado's highways have a history and personality of their own, from the **Scenic Highway of Legends** near Alamosa to the **Peak-to-Peak Highway** outside Boulder to the **Million Dollar Highway** that connects Ouray with Silverton.

Also, all the major rental-car chains do business in Colorado, including **Hertz** (800/654-3131, www.hertz.com), **Avis** (800/331-1212, www.avis.com), **Enterprise** (800/261-7331, www.enterprise.com), and **Dollar** (800/800-3665, www.dollar.com).

BY BUS

Most of the big cities have their own bus services, particularly the reliable **RTD** (1600 Blake St., 303/628-9000, www.rtd-denver.com) of Denver and Boulder. And many of the ski resorts provide shuttle and bus transportation from condos to slopes and town to town.

To travel between select cities in Colorado, try **Greyhound Bus Line** (800/231-2222, www.greyhound.com).

BY TRAIN

A state with a rich railroad pedigree, Colorado has numerous historic locomotives and fully operational narrow-gauge railroads in several towns, notably the **Durango & Silverton Narrow Gauge Railroad.** These are fun trips, but not usually practical for getting from place to place. The more modern **Amtrak** (800/872-7245, www.amtrak.com) serves Denver, Fort Collins, Pueblo, Grand Junction, Colorado Springs, Vail, Aspen, and several other cities, and the routes are convenient.

BY AIR

The **Denver International Airport** (DIA, 8500 Pena Blvd., 303/342-2000, www.flydenver.com)

© STEVE KNOPPER

The Eisenhower Memorial Tunnel can cause gridlock in bad weather along I-70.

and **Colorado Springs Airport** (7770 Drennan Rd., 719/550-1900, www.springsgov.com/AirportIndex.asp) are the two biggest airports in the state, with service from most of the major carriers. There are also lots of smaller airports—in Gunnison, Montrose, Broomfield, and elsewhere—but these aren't as reliable, especially in bad weather. Air travelers generally should plan arrangements, around DIA, which is centrally located and rents cars, shuttles, buses, and taxis.

Tips for Travelers

TRAVELERS WITH DISABILITIES

Most of Colorado's big cities, particularly Denver, Colorado Springs, and Boulder, are well equipped with wheelchair ramps and easily accessible elevators. Many of the ski resorts have facilities for physically challenged skiers, and Winter Park's resort base area is the headquarters for the **National Sports Center for the Disabled** (970/726-4112, www.nscd.org).

TRAVELING WITH CHILDREN

The big cities have plenty of kid-oriented things to do, from the Buell Children's Museum in Pueblo to the Children's Museum in Denver.

Most ski resorts give lessons to kids ages 3–16 and provide child care for all ages; check individual chapters for the resort contact information. Touring the mountains by car can be a little tough for infants; consider bringing Dramamine or another anti-motion-sickness drug (as per your doctor's advice, of course) before hitting the twisty highways. Also, some bed-and-breakfasts don't allow kids, so ask first before making hotel reservations.

GAY AND LESBIAN TRAVELERS

Homosexuality is, sadly, a political issue at the time of this writing, and Colorado's reception

The Denver Children's Museum sits in view of Invesco Field at Mile High.

toward openly gay men and women can depend on the area you visit. Boulder, Denver, and many of the mountain towns such as Telluride and Aspen are progressive to the extreme, and several have passed laws banning discrimination against people based on sexual orientation. Colorado Springs, on the other hand, is the headquarters of the powerful Focus on the Family, which takes an unambiguous religious position that homosexuality is wrong. Another group, Colorado for Family Values, sponsored Amendment 2 in the early 1990s, which would have banned laws protecting gays and lesbians from discrimination had the U.S. Supreme Court upheld it.

Having said that, there are still those with unfavorable views toward gay men and women who live in Boulder and Denver and plenty of same-sex-marriage advocates who live in Colorado Springs. Somewhat incongruously, Boulder has few major gay clubs, while there are several in Pueblo and Colorado Springs (the scene is obviously larger in Denver). For more information, check out **Gay Colorado** (303/377-1826, www.gaycolorado.com).

Health and Safety

ALTITUDE SICKNESS

Upon climbing to thin-air elevations above 8,000 feet, you'll begin taking less and less oxygen with every breath, so it's best to take it slow. Spread your hike into two or three manageable segments, or you could wind up with nausea, dizziness, headaches, or a bloody nose—and don't just dismiss these symptoms, as they could grow into more serious problems without rest and treatment (some doctors recommend the prescription drug Diamox). One of the best ways to prepare for strenuous high-altitude activity is to get in shape at a lower altitude, although even visiting professional sports teams have been known to keep emergency oxygen on the sidelines. Once you've stayed in Colorado for a few weeks, your body tends to get used to it.

DEHYDRATION

Colorado is a dry state with extremely low humidity, and it's even drier at high elevations. Wherever you go, especially when exercise is involved, bring water. Don't ignore symptoms like thirst, dry lips (lip balm is big in Colorado), or dizziness, or they can develop into more serious problems.

SUNBURN

The higher you go in the mountains, the closer you get to the sun and the fewer barriers there are to prevent harmful ultraviolet rays from reaching your body. Sunburn can lead to skin cancer, as any modern beachcomber knows, but the snow seduces many skiers into thinking the sun isn't a problem. Apply sunscreen regularly, preferably with a sun protection factor (SPF) of 15 or higher.

GIARDIA

Longterm backpackers and hikers need to protect themselves from *giardia lamblia,* a single-celled parasitic infection of the intestine. You can contract this uncomfortable disease—leading to cramps, diarrhea, nausea, and other severe irritations—from contact with somebody else's stool, or, more commonly, drinking infected water from an untreated lake or stream. Many recommend boiling the water or purifying it with iodine tablets, but my wife, who had giardia while hiking the Pacific Crest Trail in California, says iodine isn't reliable. She suggests buying *two* water-purification filters from a reputable mountaineering store and bringing both along in case one fails. Or take a shorter hike.

HYPOTHERMIA

Your body temperature needs to stay above 95° Farenheit or, in short, you're toast. Seriously, it's a bad situation—it's caused by exposure to long stretches of cold weather, and you might feel your heart rate and breathing slow down, lethargy, and general confusion. If at all possible, get to a hospital right away; if not, abandon wet clothing and get under a warm, dry blanket immediately. Under no circumstances should anybody rub your skin, apply heat directly, or give you alcohol. The best way to prevent hypothermia is to wear warm clothing (and bring emergency reserves with you in case your gloves get wet) and drink fluids.

FROSTBITE

If it's so cold outside that your skin turns blue and feels numb, you may have frostbite, which means exposure to extreme freezing temperatures. It's usually easy to prevent this—cover yourself with wool or polypropylene clothing, and put on several layers. When it's incredibly cold outside—the kind of cold where you sniff and the sides of your nose stay frozen together—consider not venturing out at all. If you do get frostbite, put the affected areas in warm water or cover them with warm clothing.

TICKS

Scary diseases such as Lyme disease and Rocky Mountain fever can come from ticks, but don't panic—it's hardly common. More likely, when you're hiking through the wilderness, you see a small, black bug stuck to your skin and feel completely grossed out. The best way to get rid of it is simply to pull it off. If it has lodged inside the skin, pull and twist, being careful not to crush it, until it comes off. Afterward, clean the spot carefully (perhaps with hydrogen peroxide) and consider seeing a doctor. There's no fail-safe way to prevent ticks, but it helps to tuck in your clothing so there are no exposed areas. Also, in the shower after hiking, search your body to make sure you're clear of all ticks.

FIRST-AID KITS

On long hikes, bring a first-aid kit, which should include some form of identification, DEET or other insect repellent, bandages, a Mylar blanket, at least one kind of flare, aspirin, matches, a lightweight flashlight, sunscreen, motion-sickness medicine such as Dramamine, lip balm, and lots of water. It helps to take some kind of emergency rescue course before venturing out; contact **Crested Butte Outdoors** (Crested Butte, 970/596-2999, www.cboutdoors.com) to find programs in your area.

Information and Services

MAPS

The first thing I did upon researching this book was purchase the *Colorado Recreational Road Atlas* ($17) from **Mapsco** (800 Lincoln St., 303/830-2373 or 800/456-8703, www.mapsco.com), a Denver-based store that sells every kind of map you can imagine and has friendly and helpful service people. **CD Maps** (www.cd-maps.com) sells state maps on CD-ROM.

Also, the **American Automobile Association** (866/625-3601 or 800/222-4357) gives superb road maps, Triptiks, and TourBooks, as well as roadside assistance, to dues-paying AAA members. The *Colorado Atlas and Gazetteer* (DeLorme) is a strong topographical map.

TOURISM RESOURCES

If you can't find what you're looking for on its comprehensive website, the **Colorado Tourism Office** (800/265-6723, www.colorado.com) will send material via snail mail. The **State of Colorado** (303/866-5000, www.colorado.gov) is somewhat more government-focused—note the smiling photo of the governor on the website—but answers questions and provides information as well.

TIME ZONES

Colorado is in the mountain time zone—two hours earlier than the East Coast, an hour earlier than the Midwest, and an hour later than the West Coast. The state adheres to most of the U.S. standards for **daylight saving time**—set clocks an hour forward on the first Sunday in April and an hour backward on the last Sunday in October.

RESOURCES
Suggested Reading

DESCRIPTION, TRAVEL, AND PHOTOGRAPHY

Caughey, Bruce. *The Colorado Guide.* Golden, CO: Fulcrum Publishing, 1991. A well-written and thorough (628 pages!) travel companion that first came out in the early 1990s.

Collier, Grant. *Colorado: Moments in Time.* Lakewood, CO: Collier Publishing, 2004. One of the best contemporary photo books on the state, with 160 images in all.

Fielder, John. *Best of Colorado.* Engelwood, CO: Westcliffe Publishers Inc., 2002. Acclaimed nature photographer Fielder has written 30-some books and has specialized in Colorado for the past 20 years.

Fielder, John, and William H. Jackson. *Colorado: 1870–2000 II.* Englewood: Westcliffe Publishers Inc., 2005. Photographer Fielder's huge, leather-bound opus involved capturing Colorado images in exactly the same place where photographer Jackson captured them more than 135 years ago. A new edition adds another hundred photos.

Harris, Richard. *Hidden Colorado.* Berkeley, CA: Ulysses Press, 1996, 1998, 2000. Doesn't quite live up to its billing as a guide to weird and off-beat places, but gives many good suggestions.

Muench, David. *Colorado II.* Portland: Graphic Arts Center Publishing Co., 1987. Superb coffee-table book by a veteran wilderness photographer.

HISTORY

Abbott, Carl, Stephen J. Leonard, and David McComb. *Colorado: A History of the Centennial State.* Niwot: University Press of Colorado, 1982, 1994. Exhaustively researched chronology, with emphasis on union struggles and industry. A little dense in places.

Arps, Louisa Ward. *Denver in Slices: A Historical Guide to the City.* Athens, OH: Swallow Press Books, 1959. Some of the information is outdated, but the stories are good.

Bancroft, Caroline. *Colorado's Lost Mines and Buried Treasure.* Boulder, CO: Johnson Publishing, 1961, 1998. Originally written in 1961, veteran historian Bancroft's tiny book collects about 30 romantic vignettes of searching for treasure, ghosts, and similar romance in Colorado.

Bancroft, Caroline. *Silver Queen: The Fabulous Story of Baby Doe Tabor.* Boulder, CO: Johnson Publishing, 1955, 1983. A colorful retelling of the sad, mining-era tale of Leadville's Baby Doe Tabor.

Brown, G. *Colorado Rocks! A Half-Century of Music in Colorado.* Boulder, CO: Pruett Publishing Co., 2004. Exclusive interviews and colorful anecdotes about the likes of Jimi Hendrix, the Beatles, Billy Joel, the Eagles, the Fluid, and numerous others.

Byrd, Isabella. *A Lady's Life in the Rocky Mountains.* Norman, OK: University of Oklahoma Press, 1879. The Old West and gold rush days, from the perspective of an English explorer who wrote tons of letters.

Churchill, E. Richard. *Doc Holliday, Bat Masterson, and Wyatt Earp: Their Colorado Careers.* Leadville, CO: Timberline Books, 1974. A definitive history of Colorado's most infamous outlaws.

Dallas, Sandra. *Colorado Ghost Towns and Mining Camps.* Norman, OK: University of Oklahoma Press, 1984.

Danilov, Victor J. *Colorado Museums and Historic Sites: A Colorado Guide Book.* Boulder: University Press of Colorado, 2000. Comprehensive, but its prose is more like a dry list of facts than any kind of colorful narrative.

Fay, Abbott. *A History of Skiing in Colorado.* Montrose, CO: Western Reflections Inc., 2000, 2003. A slice of Colorado history that's not covered in too many other books.

Fay, Abbott. *I Never Knew That About Colorado: A Quaint Volume of Forgotten Lore.* Montrose, CO: Western Reflections Inc., 1997. Bizarre and surprising anecdotes about Colorado history, including the World War II bombing of the state.

Leonard, Stephen J., and Thomas J. Noel. *Denver: From Mining Camp to Metropolis.* Although Leonard and Noel write in a dry, fact-packed style, their books are Colorado's definitive historic resources; this Denver volume is a strong complement to *Colorado: A History of the Centennial State.*

Maclean, John N. *Fire on the Mountain: The True Story of the South Canyon Fire.* New York: William Morrow, 1999. New York: Pocket Books, 2000. A journalist's heavily detailed account of the 10-day forest fire in 1994 that killed 14 firefighters and cost the state more than $4.5 million.

Rockwell, Wilson. *The Utes: A Forgotten People.* Denver: Sage Books, 1956. Ouray, CO: Western Reflections, 1998.

Ruxton, George Frederick. *Mountain Men.* New York: Holiday House, 1966. An Old West explorer publishes his autobiography as it goes along, beginning in 1848, as a magazine series.

Ubbelohde, Carl, Maxine Benson, and Duane A. Smith. *A Colorado History.* Boulder, CO: Pruett Publishing Co., 2001.

RECREATION

Cushman, Ruth Carol, and Glenn Cushman. *Boulder Hiking Trails.* Boulder, CO: Pruett Publishing Co., 1995. One of the best and easiest-to-read guides to the many trails in this region.

Fielder, John, and Pearson, Mark. *The Complete Guide to Colorado's Wilderness Areas.* Englewood: Westcliffe Publishers Inc., undated. Covers numerous hiking and biking trails, and is a practical reference for visitors, but it's hard to search by location.

Roach, Gerry. *Colorado's Fourteeners: From Hikes to Climbs.* Golden, CO: Fulcrum Publishing, 1999. Also, *Colorado's Thirteeners: 13,800 to 13,999 Feet, from Hikes to Climbs.* Golden, CO: Fulcrum Publishing, 2001. Comprehensive and easy-to-read guide to really, really tall mountains.

Warren, Scott S. *100 Classic Hikes in Colorado.* Seattle: The Mountaineers Books, 2001. Cherry-picks the best stuff, although it's not organized in any discernible regional order.

FICTION

Dallas, Sandra. *The Diary of Mattie Spenser.* Rockland, MA: Wheeler Publishing, 1997. An 1865-era historical novel by the author of *The Persian Pickle Club.*

Dunning, John. *Denver.* New York: Times Books, 1980.

Michener, James. *Centennial.* New York: Fawcett Crest, 1987. The classic Colorado novel set in a fake town, Centennial, and spanning 136 million years over more than 1,000 pages.

Stone, Irving. *Men to Match My Mountains: The Opening of the Far West, 1840–1900.* Garden City, NY: Doubleday, 1956. Written in the mid-1950s, this collection of fictional vignettes focuses on the U.S. move westward, and includes just as much on California as Colorado.

Waters, Frank. *Pikes Peak: A Family Saga.* Athens, OH: Swallow Press/Ohio University Press, 1971. A fictional re-creation of a mining-era family and how they dealt with unions, Native Americans, and the majesty of Pikes Peak itself.

ALMANACS AND ATLASES

Freed, Doug. *Colorado by the Numbers: A Reference, Almanac, and Guide to the Highest State.* Grand Junction, CO: Virga, 2003. More numbers, with a foreword by Denver mayor John Hickenlooper.

Noel, Thomas J. *The Colorado Almanac: Facts About Colorado.* Portland: WestWinds Press, 2001. Numbers and demographics illustrating the state.

Internet Resources

State of Colorado
www.colorado.gov

The official State of Colorado website, complete with links to state parks and information on hunting and fishing licenses.

Colorado.com
www.colorado.com

The most comprehensive travel website about Colorado, with directions to historic sites, ski resorts, visitors centers, and recreation areas.

Colorado Public Radio
www.cpr.org

The Colorado Public Radio page, with links to on-air broadcasts and information about politics, music, and culture.

Colorado Music Association
www.coloradomusic.org

The state's loosely organized network of musicians of all genres, from punk to bluegrass, comes together at Colorado Music Association meetings.

University of Colorado
www.colorado.edu

Find information on enrollment, visitation, and tours at the University of Colorado's website.

Colorado in the Yahoo! Directory
http://dir.yahoo.com/Regional/U_S_States/Colorado/

The Colorado directory at Yahoo! is an easy-to-flip-through guide to the state, including directions and statistical information.

Colorado Department of Transportation
www.cotrip.org

Before traveling anywhere in the mountains, check the Colorado Department of Transportation's website for traffic and weather conditions.

Colorado Environmental Coalition
www.ourcolorado.org

The Colorado Environmental Coalition is one of the state's largest protect-the-wilderness groups, and it does good work, although conservatives may object to its policies.

National Geographic Maps
www.coloradoguide.com

National Geographic Maps runs this very handy website on all things outdoors, from wildlife to trail conditions, in Colorado.

Colorado Ski Country USA
www.coloradoski.com

Colorado Ski Country USA is an excellent first stop before you make travel, hotel, and lift-ticket arrangements.

Index

HIKING

KAYAKING/RAFTING

Acknowledgments

I'd like to thank my wife, Melissa, and daughter, Rose, who accompanied me on several whirlwind driving trips, to Vail, Montrose, Gunnison, Salida, and elsewhere, and took most of the photos in the Denver chapter. They provided insightful running commentary on the Pearl Street Mall, Denver Children's Museum, various kid-friendly restaurants and hotels, and the "bumpy cow road" outside Crested Butte.

Also extremely helpful were Stacy and Ryan Anderson, who provided a crucial overview of ski areas for this clueless non-skier; Bruce Schoenfeld, who generously shared his knowledge of Aspen and Vail restaurants, and general culture; Jay Dedrick of the *Rocky Mountain News*, who grew up on the Eastern Plains and went to school in Fort Collins; Tom Sullivan, who gave me a great late-night tour of the Minturn Inn; Tracy Ross of *Skiing* magazine; Peggy Gair of Royal Gorge Bridge & Park; Erik Wilmsen, a former Fort Collins resident who recommended bars and restaurants; my nephew Rob Knopper, a former Interlochen student, for the Aspen photo; Amy Storey, for the photo of Red Rocks during Easter services; and Jonathan Boonin, a low-stakes gambling expert who ran down the casinos.

Thanks to my magazine and newspaper editors for their understanding when I disappeared on a Friday for an impromptu drive to Trinidad or Grand Junction: Jason Fine and Jonathan Ringen at *Rolling Stone*, Genetta Adams at *Newsday*, Mark Brown and Joe Rassenfoss at the *Rocky Mountain News*, David Howard at *Backpacker*, and Greg Kot and Kevin Williams at the *Chicago Tribune*. Special thanks to Joe for giving the Avalon Travel people my name.

Finally, this book is dedicated to my father, Morton P. Knopper, who, along with my mother, Dorothy, were inspired to relocate our family from Michigan to Colorado in the 1980s.

Note: An important source for the Background and Essentials chapters, as well as the history sections throughout the book, was *Colorado: A History of the Centennial State* by Carl Abbott, Stephen J. Leonard, and David McComb (University Press of Colorado, 1994). Also helpful was Stephen Metzger's previous edition of *Moon Colorado* (Avalon Travel Publishing, 2002), with its emphasis on history and information for the Health and Safety section; he cited the American Medical Association's *Encyclopedia of Medicine*.

www.moon.com

For helpful advice on planning a trip, visit www.moon.com for the **TRAVEL PLANNER** and get access to useful travel strategies and valuable information about great places to visit. When you travel with Moon, expect an experience that is uncommon and truly unique.

HANDBOOKS • OUTDOORS • METRO • LIVING ABROAD

MAP SYMBOLS

▦▦▦	Expressway	**C**	Highlight	✗	Airfield	⚲	Golf Course
═══	Primary Road	○	City/Town	✘	Airport	**P**	Parking Area
▦▦▦	Secondary Road	◉	State Capital	▲	Mountain	▲	Archaeological Site
▫▫▫	Unpaved Road	⊛	National Capital	✛	Unique Natural Feature	⚑	Church
- - - -	Trail	★	Point of Interest			⛽	Gas Station
············	Ferry	•	Accommodation	⚑	Waterfall	⬭	Glacier
─┼─┼─	Railroad	▾	Restaurant/Bar	⚑	Park	▨	Mangrove
▦▦▦	Pedestrian Walkway	▪	Other Location	⬛	Trailhead	▨	Reef
▥▥▥	Stairs	Λ	Campground	✕	Skiing Area	▨	Swamp

CONVERSION TABLES

°C = (°F - 32) / 1.8
°F = (°C x 1.8) + 32
1 inch = 2.54 centimeters (cm)
1 foot = 0.304 meters (m)
1 yard = 0.914 meters
1 mile = 1.6093 kilometers (km)
1 km = 0.6214 miles
1 fathom = 1.8288 m
1 chain = 20.1168 m
1 furlong = 201.168 m
1 acre = 0.4047 hectares
1 sq km = 100 hectares
1 sq mile = 2.59 square km
1 ounce = 28.35 grams
1 pound = 0.4536 kilograms
1 short ton = 0.90718 metric ton
1 short ton = 2,000 pounds
1 long ton = 1.016 metric tons
1 long ton = 2,240 pounds
1 metric ton = 1,000 kilograms
1 quart = 0.94635 liters
1 US gallon = 3.7854 liters
1 Imperial gallon = 4.5459 liters
1 nautical mile = 1.852 km

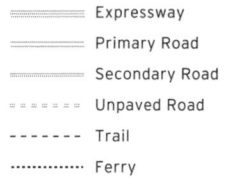

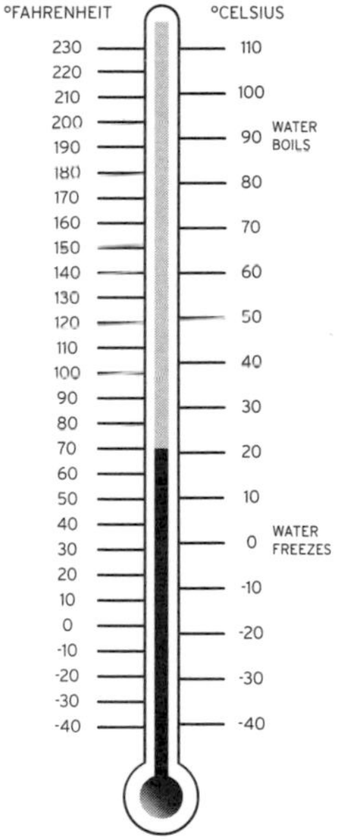

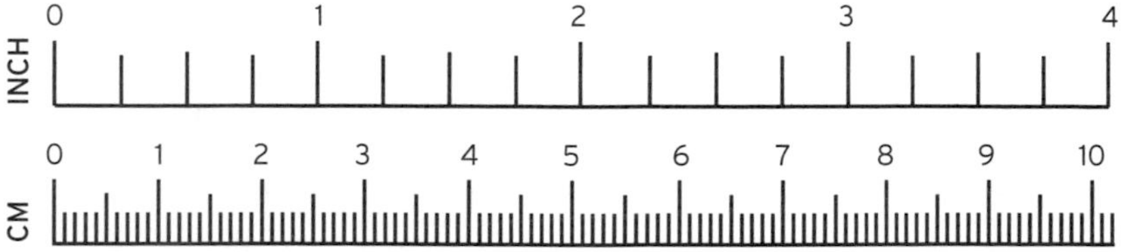

°FAHRENHEIT	°CELSIUS	
230	110	
220		
210	100	
200		
190	90	WATER BOILS
180	80	
170		
160	70	
150		
140	60	
130		
120	50	
110		
100	40	
90	30	
80		
70	20	
60		
50	10	
40		
30	0	WATER FREEZES
20		
10	-10	
0		
-10	-20	
-20	-30	
-30		
-40	-40	

INCH 0 1 2 3 4

CM 0 1 2 3 4 5 6 7 8 9 10

MOON COLORADO

Avalon Travel Publishing
An Imprint of
Avalon Publishing Group, Inc.

AVALON
publishing group incorporated

1400 65th Street, Suite 250
Emeryville, CA 94608, USA
www.moon.com

Editor: Elizabeth McCue
Series Manager: Kathryn Ettinger
Acquisitions Manager: Rebecca K. Browning
Copy Editor: Deana Shields
Graphics Coordinator: Domini Dragoone
Production Coordinator: Darren Alessi
Cover & Interior Designer: Gerilyn Attebery
Map Editor: Kevin Anglin
Cartographers: Kat Bennett, Mike Morgenfeld,
  Chris Markiewicz
Indexer: Rachel Kuhn

ISBN-10: 1-56691-701-8
ISBN-13: 978-1-56691-701-8
ISSN: 1085-2697

Printing History
1st Edition–1992
6th Edition–April 2006
5 4 3 2 1

KEEPING CURRENT

If you have a favorite gem you'd like to see included in the next edition, or see anything
that needs updating, clarification, or correction, please drop us a line. Send your
comments via email to feedback@moon.com, or use the address above.